Wittgenstein and Hegel

On Wittgenstein

Edited on behalf of the
Internationale Ludwig Wittgenstein Gesellschaft e.V.
by James Conant, Wolfgang Kienzler,
Stefan Majetschak, Volker Munz, Josef G. F. Rothhaupt,
David Stern and Wilhelm Vossenkuhl

Volume 5

Wittgenstein and Hegel

Reevaluation of Difference

Edited by Jakub Mácha and Alexander Berg

DE GRUYTER

ISBN 978-3-11-076294-5
e-ISBN (PDF) 978-3-11-057278-0
e-ISBN (EPUB) 978-3-11-057196-7
ISSN 2365-9629

Library of Congress Control Number 2019933621

Bibliographic information published by the Deutsche Nationalbibliothek
The Deutsche Nationalbibliothek lists this publication in the Deutsche Nationalbibliografie;
detailed bibliographic data are available on the Internet at http://dnb.dnb.de.

© 2021 Walter de Gruyter GmbH, Berlin/Boston
This volume is text- and page-identical with the hardback published in 2019.
Printing and binding: CPI books GmbH, Leck

www.degruyter.com

Acknowledgements

Most of the chapters in this volume were originally presented at the conference "Wittgenstein and Hegel: Reevaluation of Difference", which took place at the TU Dresden between 28 and 30 June 2017 and was co-organised by the editors of this volume. The talks at the conference were recorded and are available on the conference website: wittgensteinhegel2017.weebly.com. Jakub Mácha and I are grateful for the generous funding provided by the TU Dresden Graduate Academy, a German Federal Ministry of Education and Research's Excellence Initiative. We would like to thank the other co-organisers of the conference, namely Louisa Frintert, Marco Kleber and Alexander Romahn, as well as Thomas Rentsch and Jim Conant for their intellectual support for the conference. It goes without saying that the discussion and exchange of ideas at the conference and beyond helped to greatly enrich the articles in this volume. I am especially thankful to my son Jakob E. Berg for the video recordings of the conference presentations.

In addition to papers by the conference participants, the editors have also included six other chapters written especially for this book. We are especially grateful to the authors themselves, who have contributed their knowledge and many hours of work to make this volume a reality. Special thanks go to our reviewers (some of who were also contributors themselves), who provided valuable feedback and helped to improve the quality of this book. We note with sadness that Wilhelm Lütterfelds passed away while this volume was in preparation. We are especially glad and privileged to have been able to include his work.

We are also grateful to our proof-editor Andrew Godfrey, who edited most of the chapters by non-native speakers of English (www.agodfreytranslations.com). His valuable suggestions helped to greatly improve the clarity of these chapters. Danica Ježová helped us with the formal consistency of the volume. This publication was supported by the Faculty of Arts, Masaryk University, Brno.

Last but not least, my thanks go to everyone at De Gruyter, especially to Christoph Schirmer for his editorial advice and support, and to Stefan Majetschak and the International Ludwig Wittgenstein Society, who made it possible for the volume to appear in the series *On Wittgenstein*.

Many of the contributors to this volume, as well as other authors, have expressed a definite interest in further clarifying the relationship between Wittgenstein and Hegel and building on the results of this volume in future research. The editors would be very happy to contribute to the continuation of this work.

Alexander Berg, Prague, January 2019

Table of Contents

List of Abbreviations —— XI

Notes on Authors —— XV

Jakub Mácha
Introduction: Hegel, Wittgenstein, Identity, Difference —— 19

Part 1 General Introduction, the Analytic-Continental Split

Pirmin Stekeler-Weithofer
On Metaphysical Images in Analytic Philosophy: Overcoming Empiricism by Logical Analysis of Language —— 43

Part 2 From Identity to Difference

Thomas Rentsch
Three Key Hypotheses regarding Hegel and Wittgenstein —— 69

Tom Rockmore
Wittgenstein, Hegel and Cognition —— 77

Herbert Hrachovec
No Evaluative Authority Is beyond Evaluation: Common Ground between Hegel and Wittgenstein —— 91

David Kolb
The Diamond Net: Metaphysics, Grammar, Ontologies —— 107

Jonathan L. Shaheen
The Communitarian Wittgenstein and Brandom's Hegel on Recognition and Social Constitution —— 121

Lorenzo Cammi
Hegel and Wittgenstein on *Wirklichkeit*: Sketch of a Comparison —— 137

Kai-Uwe Hoffmann
Beauty: Hegel or Wittgenstein? —— 159

Part 3 From Difference to Identity

Paul Redding
Hegel and the Tractarian Conception of Judgement —— 179

Terry Pinkard
Forms of Thought, Forms of Life —— 199

Valentin Pluder
Rule-Following and Institutional Context —— 217

Valentina Balestracci
Hegel and Wittgenstein: Elements for a Comparison —— 231

Vojtěch Kolman
Master, Slave and Wittgenstein: The Dialectic of Rule-Following —— 245

Ingolf Max
Hegel and Wittgenstein on Identities and Contradictions —— 261

Marco Kleber
Rethinking the Limits of Language: Wittgenstein and Hegel on the Unspeakable —— 277

Part 4 Hegelian Approaches to Wittgenstein

Aloisia Moser
Hegel's Speculative Method and Wittgenstein's Projection Method —— 293

Ermylos Plevrakis
A Hegelian Reading of Wittgenstein's *Tractatus Logico-Philosophicus* —— 309

Gaetano Chiurazzi
Are There Simple Objects? Hegel's Discussion of Kant's Second Antinomy in Relation to Wittgenstein's *Tractatus* —— 329

Bruno Haas
Image, Reference, and the Level Distinction —— 343

Alexander Berg
Identity in Difference—Wittgenstein's Hegel —— 367

Part 5 Wittgensteinian Approaches to Hegel

Karl-Friedrich Kiesow
Is the System of Personal Pronouns Somewhat Mysterious? Findlay and Weiss as Critics of Hegel and Wittgenstein —— 385

Jakub Mácha
Particularity as Paradigm: A Wittgensteinian Reading of Hegel's Subjective Logic —— 397

Wilhelm Lütterfelds
„In der Sprache" (Wittgenstein) und im „Begriff" (Hegel) „wird alles ausgetragen" – Das Sprachspiel des Idealismus —— 419

Subject Index —— 431

Author Index —— 443

List of Abbreviations

Hegel's works

German works

W   *Werke in zwanzig Bänden*, Eva Moldenhauer and Karl Markus (eds.), Suhrkamp, 1969.

FS	1	Frühe Schriften
JS	2	Jenaer Schriften
PdG	3	Phänomenologie des Geistes
NS	4	Nürnberger und Heidelberger Schriften
WL I	5	Wissenschaft der Logik I
WL II	6	Wissenschaft der Logik II
GPR	7	Grundlinien der Philosophie des Rechts
E I	8	Enzyklopädie der philosophischen Wissenschaften I
E II	9	Enzyklopädie der philosophischen Wissenschaften II
E III	10	Enzyklopädie der philosophischen Wissenschaften III
BS	11	Berliner Schriften 1818–1831
PGh	12	Vorlesungen über die Philosophie der Geschichte
Ä I	13	Vorlesungen über die Ästhetik I
Ä II	14	Vorlesungen über die Ästhetik II
Ä III	15	Vorlesungen über die Ästhetik III
Rel I	16	Vorlesungen über die Philosophie der Religion I
Rel II	17	Vorlesungen über die Philosophie der Religion II
GP I	18	Vorlesungen über die Geschichte der Philosophie I
GP II	19	Vorlesungen über die Geschichte der Philosophie II
GP III	20	Vorlesungen über die Geschichte der Philosophie III

GW   *Gesammelte Werke*, Felix Meiner Verlag, 1968–.

English translations

D   *The Difference Between Fichte's and Schelling's System of Philosophy*, H. S. Harris and Walter Cerf (trans.), State University of New York Press, 1977.

E 1817   *Encyclopaedia of the Philosophical Sciences in Outline, and Critical Writings*, Ernst Behler (ed.), Arnold V. Miller, Steven A. Taubeneck, and Diana Behler (trans.), Continuum, 1990.

EL 1830 *The Encyclopaedia Logic (1830), with the Zusätze: Part I of the Encyclopaedia of Philosophical Sciences with the Zusätze*, Theodore F. Geraets, W. A. Suchting, and H. S. Harris (trans.), Hackett, 1991.

EL 1830/2010	*Encyclopaedia of the Philosophical Sciences in Basic Outline. Part 1: Logic*, Klaus Brinkmann and Daniel O. Dahlstrom (trans. and ed.), Cambridge University Press, 2010.
EPN 1830	*Philosophy of Nature: Being Part Two of the Encyclopaedia of the Philosophical Sciences, 1830*, M. J. Petry (trans.), 3 vols., George Allen & Unwin, 1970. *Philosophy of Nature: Being Part Two of the Encyclopaedia of the Philosophical Sciences, 1830*, A. V. Miller (trans.), Oxford, 1970. Cited by section (§) number.
EPR	*Elements of the Philosophy of Right*, Allen Wood (ed.), H. B. Nisbet (trans.), Cambridge University Press, 1996.
ETW	*Early Theological Writings*, T. M. Knox and Richard Kroner (trans.), University of Pennsylvania Press, 1971.
JL	*Hegel and the Human Spirit, A Translation of the Jena Lectures on the Philosophy of Spirit (1805–6) with commentary by Leo Rauch*, Wayne State University Press, 1983.
LA	*Aesthetics: Lectures on Fine Art*, T. M. Knox (trans.), 2 vols., Oxford University Press, 1998.
LHP I	*Lectures on the History of Philosophy*, E. S. Haldane and Frances H. Simson (trans.), vol. I Greek Philosophy to Plato, University of Nebraska Press, 1995 (first edition 1892).
LHP II	*Lectures on the History of Philosophy*, E. S. Haldane and Frances H. Simson (trans.), vol. II Plato and the Platonists, University of Nebraska Press, 1995 (first edition 1894).
LHP III	*Lectures on the History of Philosophy*, E. S. Haldane and Frances H. Simson (trans.), vol. III Medieval and Modern Philosophy, University of Nebraska Press, 1995 (first edition 1896).
LL 1831	*Lectures on Logic, Berlin 1831*, C. Butler (trans.), Indiana University Press, 2008.
LPH 1822–3	*Lectures on the Philosophy of World History. Volume 1: Manuscripts of the Introduction and the Lectures of 1822–3*, Robert F. Brown and Peter C. Hodgson (ed. and trans. with the assistance of William G. Geuss), Oxford University Press, 2011.
PS *year*	*The Phenomenology of Spirit* A. V. Miller (trans.), Clarendon Press, 1977. Terry Pinkard (trans.), 2012. Terry Pinkard (trans.), Cambridge University Press, 2018.
PW	*Political Writings*, Laurence Dickey and H. B. Nisbet (eds.), H. B. Nisbet (trans.), Cambridge University Press, 1999.
SL *year*	*Science of Logic* H. S. Marcan (trans.), Clarendon Press, 1912. W. H. Johnston and L. G. Struthers (trans.), George Allen & Unwin, 1929. Henry S. Macran (trans.), Clarendon Press, 1929. A.V. Miller (trans.), George Allen & Unwin, 1969. George di Giovanni (trans.), Cambridge University Press, 2010.

Wittgenstein's works

BT	*The Big Typescript. TS 213*, C. G. Luckhardt and M. A. E. Aue (eds.), Blackwell, 2005.
CC	*Ludwig Wittgenstein: Gesamtbriefwechsel/Complete Correspondence. Electronic Edition*, M. Seekircher, A. Unterkircher and B. McGuinness (eds.), InteLex, 2005.
CV	*Vermischte Bemerkungen. Eine Auswahl aus dem Nachlaß/Culture and Value. A Selection from the Posthumous Remains*, G. H. von Wright and H. Nyman (eds.), P. Winch (trans.), revised by A. Pichler, revised second edition, Blackwell, 1998.
LCA	*Lectures and Conversations on Aesthetics, Psychology and Religious Belief*, C. Barrett (ed.), Blackwell, 1966.
LO	*Letters to C. K. Ogden with Comments on the English Translation of the* Tractatus Logico-Philosophicus, G. H. von Wright (ed.), Blackwell, 1973.
LWL	*Wittgenstein's Lectures: Cambridge, 1930–1932*, D. Lee (ed.), Blackwell, 1980.
MDC	M. O'C. Drury. Conversations with Wittgenstein, in: R. Rhees (ed.), *Recollections of Wittgenstein*, Blackwell, 1981, pp.112–89.
MS	*Wittgenstein's Nachlass. The Bergen Electronic Edition*, Oxford University Press, 1998–2000, manuscript.
NB	*Notebooks 1914–16*, G. H. von Wright and G. E. M. Anscombe (eds.), G. E. M. Anscombe (trans.), Blackwell, 1961.
OC	*On Certainty*, G. E. M. Anscombe and G. H. von Wright (eds.), D. Paul and G. E. M. Anscombe (trans.), Blackwell, 1969.
PI	*Philosophical Investigations*, G. E. M. Anscombe and R. Rhees (eds.), G. E. M. Anscombe (trans.), Blackwell, 1958.
PI, 2009	*Philosophical Investigations*, the German text, with an English trans., G. E. M. Anscombe (trans.), P. M. S. Hacker and J. Schulte, revised 4th edition by P. M. S. Hacker and Joachim Schulte, Blackwell, 2009.
PR	*Philosophical Remarks*, R. Rhees (ed.), R. Hargreaves and R. White (trans.), Blackwell, 1975.
PT	*Prototractatus—An Early Version of Tractatus Logico-Philosophicus*, B. F. McGuinness, T. Nyberg, and G. H. von Wright (eds.), D. F. Pears and B. F. McGuinness (trans.), Routledge & Kegan Paul, 1971.
PU	*Philosophische Untersuchungen. Kritisch-genetische Edition*, J. Schulte, H. Nyman, E. von Savigny and G. H. von Wright (eds.), Suhrkamp, 2001.
TLP	*Tractatus Logico-Philosophicus* C. K. Ogden with F. Ramsey (trans.), Routledge & Kegan Paul, 1922. D. F. Pears and B. F. McGuinness (trans.), Routledge & Kegan Paul, 1961.
TS	*Wittgenstein's Nachlass. The Bergen Electronic Edition*, Oxford University Press, 1998–2000, typescript.
WVC	*Ludwig Wittgenstein and the Vienna Circle*. Conversations recorded by Friedrich Waismann, B. McGuinness (ed.), Blackwell, 1979.
Z	*Zettel*, G. E. M. Anscombe and G. H. von Wright (eds.), G. E. M. Anscombe (trans.), Blackwell, 1967.

Notes on Authors

Valentina Balestracci is a master's student at the University of Pisa. Her research interests are Hegel, Wittgenstein and theoretical philosophy. She is currently writing her thesis on Wittgenstein and grammar in the *Tractatus*.

Alexander Berg has studied at the TU Dresden, the Sorbonne (Paris) and the University of Florence. Following research stays at the Wittgenstein Archives (Bergen), Wren Library (Trinity College, Cambridge) and the University of Chicago, he defended his PhD thesis *Absolutes Wissen und Grundlose Gewissheit – Hegel und Wittgenstein* at the TU Dresden. He has published on Wittgenstein, Hegel, Heidegger and Charles Taylor and teaches at the Faculty of Humanities, Charles University (Prague).

Lorenzo Cammi received his PhD from Leipzig University and the University of Verona for a dissertation on Hegel's metaphysics. In 2011 and 2013/2014 he was a Visiting Scholar at the University of Pittsburgh, and in 2014/2015 he was a Visiting Fellow at Harvard University.

Gaetano Chiurazzi is Associate Professor of Theoretical Philosophy at the University of Turin. He has studied and worked as a Research Fellow at the universities of Turin, Berlin, Heidelberg and Paris. His interests centre on French and German philosophy, in particular Derrida, Kant, Hegel, Husserl, Heidegger and Gadamer. His book *Modalità ed esistenza* about Kant, Husserl and Heidegger has been translated into German as *Modalität und Existenz* (2006). With Gianni Vattimo, he is co-editor of *Trópos. Rivista di ermeneutica e critica filosofica*.

Bruno Haas is Professor for Philosophy and Art History at the TU University of Dresden and *maître de conférences* at the Sorbonne (Paris 1). Major publications include *Beiträge zu Hegels Wissenschaft der Logik, der Kunst und des Religiösen* (2003); *Die ikonischen Situationen* (2015); "Urteil" (2017).

Kai-Uwe Hoffmann is a Lecturer at the University of Auckland (New Zealand). He also acts as the representative of the German academic community in New Zealand. Prior to coming to Auckland, he held lecturer positions at the University of Jena (Germany) and Durham University (UK). Over the last four years, he worked as a representative on behalf of the German parliament. His current central research interests concern thick aesthetic concepts, theories of beauty, normativity, semantics, pragmatics and metaphysics.

Herbert Hrachovec was Professor for Philosophy at the University of Vienna until his retirement in 2013. His research covers continental and analytic philosophy and, more recently, the theory of new media. He administers a number of web services, including an Open Access repository of "electronically archived theory" (sammelpunkt.philo.at) and a collection of philosophical audio recordings (audiothek.philo.at).

Karl-Friedrich Kiesow is a researcher at the Institute for Philosophy, University of Hannover. He wrote his PhD on the philosophy of nature and epistemology of objective empiricism. He is now working on a book about Alfred North Whitehead's impact on the history of 20th-century biology.

Marco Kleber is a Research Assistant at the Department for Philosophy, TU Dresden. He researches and teaches on topics including Hegel, dialectics, political and practical philosophy, critical social philosophy and philosophy of language. He was co-organiser of the conference "Hegel and Wittgenstein: Reevaluation of Difference", and is currently working on his PhD thesis on Hegel's linguistic–analytic foundations of political philosophy.

David Kolb is Professor Emeritus of Philosophy at Bates College (Maine, USA). Inspired by classical German philosophy, especially Hegel, he has published books and articles on the tensions of modernity's new modes of unity in society, architecture and modes of writing: *The Critique of Pure Modernity: Hegel, Heidegger, and After* (1987), *Postmodern Sophistications* (1990), *Sprawling Places* (2008, and at dkolb.org) and *Socrates in the Labyrinth* (1994). He also edited *New Perspectives on Hegel's Philosophy of Religion* (1992).

Vojtěch Kolman is Associate Professor at Charles University (Prague). His main specialisations are Gottlob Frege, philosophy of mathematics, philosophy of language and philosophical logic. His recent publications include a book entitled *Zahlen* and the article "Hegel's Bad Infinity as a Logical Problem" in the *Hegel Bulletin*.

Wilhelm Lütterfelds was a Professor for Philosophy at the University of Passau (Germany) from 1985 until his retirement in 2009. From 2012 until his death in 2018 he was an Honorary Professor at KU Linz (Austria).

Jakub Mácha is Associate Professor at the Department of Philosophy, Masaryk University (Brno, Czech Republic). He has published on analytic philosophy and classical German philosophy. His most recent book is *Wittgenstein on Internal and External Relations: Tracing All the Connections* (2015).

Ingolf Max is Adjunct Professor of Analytic Philosophy and Logic at Leipzig University (Germany). His main areas of interest are multidimensional logics, logic of music, philosophy of language and Wittgenstein's philosophy. His recent articles include "The Harmony of Colour Concepts: Bridging the Early and the Late Wittgenstein" (2017) and "A Molecular Logic of Chords and Their Internal Harmony" (2018).

Aloisia Moser is Assistant Professor at KU Linz (Austria). She was awarded a PhD by the New School for Social Research (New York) and conducted her post-doc studies at UC Berkeley and in the research centre *Analytic German Idealism* at Leipzig University. Her book *Kant and Wittgenstein – A Groundwork for a Theory of the Act of Thinking* is due to be published in 2019.

Terry Pinkard is Professor at Georgetown University, known for his work on the German tradition in philosophy from Kant to the present. His books include *German Philosophy 1760–1860: The Legacy of Idealism* (2002), *Hegel's Naturalism: Mind, Nature, and the Final Ends of Life* (2012), and *Does History Make Sense? Hegel on the Historical Shapes of Justice* (2017). He also translated Hegel's *Phenomenology of Spirit* into English (2018).

Ermylos Plevrakis obtained his PhD from the University of Heidelberg (2016). Ever since, he has been lecturing on philosophy at the universities of Heidelberg, Tübingen and Jena. His research focuses on the relation between logic and metaphysics from Aristotle to Wittgenstein. He is the author of *Das Absolute und der Begriff: Zur Frage philosophischer Theologie in Hegels Wissenschaft der Logik* (2017).

Valentin Pluder received his PhD from the University of Bochum for his dissertation on the mediation of idealism and realism in classical German philosophy. Between 2014 and 2016, he was the Custodian of the Hegel Archives in Bochum. Since 2016, he has been a Lecturer at the University of Siegen (Germany).

Paul Redding is Emeritus Professor of Philosophy at the University of Sydney. He is known for his research on Kantian philosophy and the tradition of German idealism and its relation to analytic philosophy and pragmatism. He is the author of *Analytic Philosophy and the Return of Hegelian Thought* (2007) and *Continental Idealism: Leibniz to Nietzsche* (2009).

Thomas Rentsch is Professor of Practical Philosophy at TU Dresden. His research covers philosophy of language, ethics, philosophical anthropology, aesthetics, philosophy of religion, political philosophy, hermeneutics, history of metaphysics, phenomenology and gerontology. His books include *Heidegger und Wittgenstein: Existential- und Sprachanalysen zu den Grundlagen philosophischer Anthropologie* (1985), *Die Konstitution der Moralität: Transzendentale Anthropologie und praktische Philosophie* (1990) and *Philosophie des 20. Jahrhunderts: Von Husserl bis Derrida*. (2014). He is co-editor of the *Historisches Wörterbuch der Philosophie* (1971–2007).

Tom Rockmore is Distinguished Professor Emeritus at Duquesne University (Pittsburgh, USA), as well as Distinguished Humanities Chair Professor at Peking University. His main focus lies in epistemology, philosophy of German idealism, political philosophy and aesthetics. His books include *Hegel, Idealism and Analytic Philosophy* (2005) and *Marx's Dream: From Capitalism to Communism* (2018).

Jonathan Shaheen is currently a Postdoctoral Research Fellow at the University of Uppsala (Sweden) and a Postdoctoral Researcher of the FWO. He completed his PhD at the University of Michigan on the topic of "metaphysical explanation and grounding". His primary research programme combines philosophy of language, metaphysics and philosophy of science, and he has several publications on these topics.

Pirmin Stekeler-Weithofer is Professor of Theoretical Philosophy at Leipzig University. He has written widely on philosophy of language, action theory, logic and the relationship between classical and analytic philosophy (Plato, Kant, Hegel). He is the author of the seminal work *Hegels Analytische Philosophie: Die Wissenschaft der Logik als kritische Theorie der Bedeutung* (1992). His latest books are *Hegel's Analytic Pragmatism* (2016) and *Hegels Wissenschaft der Logik. Ein dialogischer Kommentar* (2019).

Jakub Mácha
Introduction: Hegel, Wittgenstein, Identity, Difference

We cannot but begin this volume with Wittgenstein's famous remark that "Hegel seems to me to be always wanting to say that things which look different are really the same. Whereas my interest is in showing that things which look the same are really different." (MDC: p.157) This is, however, a casual remark, and it seems that we should not put too much emphasis on it. (For a discussion of how the remark should properly be understood, see Chapter 20.) In compiling this collection of essays we adopted from this remark the idea that the problem of difference in identity is the common topic between Hegel and Wittgenstein.[1] The remark presents a certain interplay (or, one might say, dialectics) of identity and difference. And it is questions of identity and difference between Hegel and Wittgenstein (with respect to certain aspects of their works, under certain interpretations, etc.) that are addressed by the essays in this volume.

There are systematic reasons for investigating commonalities and differences between two philosophers: for example, that they approached the same problem or topic using the same or different methods and arrived at the same or opposed conclusions. Such an investigation might be conducted ahistorically, without taking into account possible lines of influence. This would, however, contradict Hegel's and Wittgenstein's philosophical doctrines. Before we set about looking at particular points of identity and difference discussed in this volume, let us look at the philosophical and historical context of this topic.

Analytic–continental split

One of the reasons for bringing Hegel and Wittgenstein together is to overcome or even go beyond what is known as the "analytic–continental split".[2] As is well known, at the beginning of the 20th century Russell and Moore, the founding fathers of analytic philosophy, revolted against Hegelianism. Analytic philosophy

---
[1] For the sake of brevity, throughout this introductory chapter I shall use names of thinkers, particularly Hegel and Wittgenstein, *metonymically*, with the names standing for their philosophical thought and the works where their thought is expressed.
[2] The analytic–continental split has been addressed in many different ways (cf. Bell et al. (2016) for a representative sample of recent debates).

became an explicitly anti-Hegelian philosophical movement (cf. Chapter 1 of this volume). Moreover, Hegel's writings were declared to be examples of nonsense, of nonsensical combinations of letters and words. No dialogue is possible with nonsense. On the other hand, continental philosophy (from Marxism to existentialism and structuralism) endorsed, albeit quite selectively, some Hegelian terminology, approaches, doctrines and arguments (cf. Nuzzo 2010: p.3).

All this, however, has turned out to be a myth rather than an accurate description of the philosophical landscape of the 20th century. Moore and Russell revolted against British idealism, which drew on a specific interpretation of some Hegelian doctrines but was opposed to Hegel in some respects. Continental philosophy was, in several important respects, very much opposed to Hegel or Hegelianism (we could mention, say, Heidegger or Adorno). To identify continental philosophy as Hegelian in essence is, to say the least, problematic.

To situate Wittgenstein within analytic philosophy seems to be less problematic. Wittgenstein's *Tractatus* is without doubt one of the canonical texts of analytic philosophy. Things get complicated with Wittgenstein's later philosophy. Some of the key insights brought up in the *Philosophical Investigations* (e.g., meaning as use, the private language argument, the critique of ostensive definition) were later taken up in ordinary language philosophy and by analytic philosophers such as Quine, Davidson and Sellars. There are, however, other no less important insights and aspects in Wittgenstein's later thinking that are opposed to mainstream analytic philosophy, such as his conception of philosophy as therapy, his anti-naturalism and the fragmentary style of his writing.

Hence, Hegel's philosophy does not quite belong to continental philosophy and Wittgenstein's (later) philosophy does not quite belong to analytic philosophy, although there are non-empty intersections in both cases. If any points of contact between Hegel and Wittgenstein are of relevance to the analytic–continental split, then it must be ones along these intersections. Several chapters in this volume (Stekeler-Weithofer's, Rentsch's, and Chiurazzi's) address the complicated relevance of Hegel and Wittgenstein to the analytic–continental split, as well as the possibility of overcoming it.

The story of the Hegel–Wittgenstein affinity

It is not the case that Wittgenstein has been discussed only in analytic philosophy and Hegel only in continental philosophy. Whereas Wittgenstein reception in continental philosophy is not so significant (although see Chiurazzi's and Haas's chapters in this volume, which take broadly continental perspectives), there has been an increasing interest in Hegel and Hegelian themes in analytic philosophy since the 1990s, which has brought Hegel closer to Wittgenstein. It is not difficult to find remarks in Hegel that to some extent capture the essence of analytic philosophy. He wrote in the preface to the second edition of the *Science of Logic* that: "The forms of thought are first set out and stored in human *language*" (SL 2010: p.12; written in 1831, a few days before Hegel's death). Before examining this renewed interest in Hegel in the 1990s, let us go back to two important philosophers who approached our topic in surprising depth.

John Niemeyer Findlay (1903–1987) was initially a Hegelian scholar. Later, in the 1930s, he was a student of Wittgenstein in Cambridge. Eventually, he turned back to Hegelianism and became a fierce critic of Wittgenstein's philosophy and influence. His books *Hegel: A Re-examination* (1958) and *Wittgenstein: A Critique* (1984) were written with full knowledge of both philosophers. The major parallel that Findlay identified between the conceptions of philosophy in Hegel and Wittgenstein is as follows:

> Wittgenstein says: "Philosophy is a battle against the bewitchment of our understanding through the instruments of our speech." [PI: §109] Hegel says in highly similar language: "The battle of Reason consists in this, to overcome the rigidity which the Understanding has brought in." [EL 1830: §32][3]

The crucial point of this parallel is the implicit assumption that Hegel and Wittgenstein used "understanding" (*Verstand*) in a more or less similar way ("in highly similar language"). Findlay was, of course, aware of this complex issue (cf. 1958: pp.62–3). For both Hegel and Wittgenstein, philosophical language consists of exaggerations of ordinary language. Yet philosophical exaggerations "will have 'gone back', much as the various colours vanish and annul each other in the integrity of white light" (1958: p.27). There is one major difference, however, which appertains to the final goal of this philosophical method:

> [W]hile for Wittgenstein philosophical exaggerations disappear in this final ordinariness, and need not, except for a confusion, have emerged at all, for Hegel their emergence is essential to the final result, and is in some sense "preserved" in it. (ibid.)

---

3 Findlay 1958: p.27. In his foreword to Hegel's *Logic* (1973), Findlay uses a slightly different wording: "Hegel anticipates even the ring of certain pronouncements of modern linguistic philosophy: where Wittgenstein makes it the task of the linguistic philosopher to cure the bewitchment of the understanding through the instruments of our speech (*Philosophical Investigations*, § 109), Hegel says that 'the battle of reason is the struggle to break up the rigidity to which the understanding has reduced everything', the understanding being the form of thought which continues to apply rigid rules and categories, which apply well in ordinary finite contexts, to the new, fluid, iridescent contexts and objects of Reason."

It is noteworthy that there is no consensus within contemporary Wittgenstein scholarship as to the goal of his philosophical method. There have been interpretations of Wittgenstein's philosophy stressing that the unspeakable remains preserved in the final result.[4]

Two chapters in this volume discuss Findlay's work. In Chapter 9, Paul Redding focuses on Findlay's critique of the Tractarian conception of simple objects from Hegel's point of view. Karl-Friedrich Kiesow, in Chapter 21, addresses Findlay's discussion of personal pronouns in Hegel and Wittgenstein.

David Lamb, in two book-length studies (1979, 1980) and other shorter works, made a heroic attempt to bring Hegel and Wittgenstein closer to each other. At the end of the 1970s, Wittgenstein's later philosophy was at the height of its dominance in analytic philosophy. Lamb's aim in showing similarities between Hegel and Wittgenstein was twofold: to "reveal that Wittgenstein's contribution is not such a break with the past as many of his disciples would have us think" (1980: p.xiii) and to "render Hegel intelligible to the twentieth-century perspective" (ibid.). According to Lamb, the basic parallel between Hegel and Wittgenstein is that they both move from a critical to a descriptive philosophy. The point of departure for Hegel's move is Kant's transcendental philosophy, whereas Wittgenstein moves from his early philosophy to his later thinking:

> Of particular concern will be the move from a critique of language (*Tractatus*) to a description of its use (*Blue and Brown Books*, and *Philosophical Investigations*) by Wittgenstein, which is in many ways parallel to the move from a Kantian critique of reason to Hegel's phenomenological description of the various shapes of consciousness in the *Phenomenology*. (1980: p.5)

Lamb thus interprets the *Tractatus* as a Kantian work that aims to delineate *a priori* limits of thinking and define the essence of language (the general form of propositions), which parallels Kant's attempts to locate the foundation and scope of human knowledge. Lamb finds in Wittgenstein's later philosophy "many of the old idealist arguments in a new form" (1979: p.xi).

---

4 Wittgenstein writes in the *Tractatus* that philosophy "will mean the unspeakable by clearly displaying the speakable" (4.115, Ogden/Ramsey's trans.). Furthermore, what Wittgenstein wrote about Uhland's poem "Count Eberhard's Hawthorn" seems equally true of the early Wittgenstein's ideal of philosophical writing: "This is how it is: if only you do not try to utter what is unutterable then *nothing* gets lost. But the unutterable will be—unutterably—*contained* in what has been uttered!" (Engelmann 1968: p.7 [9 April 1917])

The Sellarsian reception of Hegel through Wittgenstein

Richard Rorty (1997: p.8) once spoke in this connection of "an attempt to usher analytic philosophy from its Kantian to its Hegelian stage".[5] Paul Redding (2007) speaks of the return of "Hegelian thought" in analytic philosophy, Tom Rockmore (2001) of the "Hegelian turn" and Angelica Nuzzo (2010: p.2) of a "Hegel-Renaissance". Following Rockmore (2001: p.360), I would like to highlight that Hegelian themes relevant in analytic philosophy are, for the most part, also Wittgensteinian themes; they lie at the above-mentioned intersection.

Hegel reception in analytic philosophy goes back to Sellars' critique of the myth of the given and his quite selective interest in Hegel. A critique of what Sellars labels the myth of the given, that is, the myth of direct or unmediated epistemic access to given sensory experience, can be found in the "Sense-Certainty" chapter of Hegel's *Phenomenology* and in Wittgenstein's critique of ostensive definition at the beginning of his *Philosophical Investigations*. Despite many differences, Hegel's and Wittgenstein's arguments boil down to the fact that seemingly direct pointing at sensory experience (to "this" and "now") presupposes complex cognitive or grammatical structures.[6]

There are other Hegelian insights that Sellars introduced to analytic philosophy. Let us mention another important one: Hegel's key claim that "everything is an inference"[7] became the cornerstone of contextualism and inferentialism. "Everything" must be understood here in the context of Hegel's logic as "every judgement". The truth of a judgement is thus dependent on its place within a syllogism or, in contemporary terms, its role in an inferential structure or the normative space of reasons. This is also a Wittgensteinian insight, for the concept of inferential structure is close to the later Wittgenstein's concept of language-games (more specifically: the language of giving and asking for reasons,

---

5 One can speculate what the next "phase" of analytic philosophy will be. Perhaps a Marxist one or even a "Deleuzian turn" as suggested by Lumsden (2011).
6 This is not to say that the myth of the given can be attacked only from a Hegelian or a Wittgensteinian perspective, as Donald Davidson's critique of the myth proves.
7 "*Alles ist ein Schluß*" (E I: §181); other translations are "everything is a syllogism" (EL 1830/ 2010: p.254) and "all things are a *syllogism*" (SL 2010: p.593). To translate *Schluß* as mere "inference" is already a move towards Sellars' and Brandom's interpretation of Hegel's logic. Di Giovanni also translates *Schluß* as "syllogistic inference" (ibid.), which is probably a more accurate translation.

in Sellars' and Brandom's case).⁸ Ultimately, we can understand Hegel's slogan "Everything is an inference" as affined to Wittgenstein's "Meaning is use".

Like most previous Hegel reception, Sellars' reading of Hegel is quite selective. He incorporated some Hegelian topics into his system, while ignoring others; moreover, Sellars' system is party openly anti-Hegelian. Sellars (and Brandom) ignore Hegel's main concept of self-consciousness. His system ignores Hegel's idealism and, in the end, he endorses linguistic nominalism, epistemic empiricism and metaphysical realism, which are all anti-Hegelian doctrines. Sellars was no Hegelian, nor was he a Wittgensteinian. Rather, he took important impulses and developed themes that fall within the intersection of Hegel's and Wittgenstein's thinking.

Before moving on to the "Pittsburgh Neo-Hegelians", John McDowell and Robert Brandom,⁹ let us mention Pirmin Stekeler-Weithofer's book *Hegels Analytische Philosophie: Die Wissenschaft der Logik als kritische Theorie der Bedeutung* (1992), which anticipates many central insights of Brandom's inferentialism and his semantic interpretation of Hegel.

McDowell (1996) focuses on the Kantian roots of Sellars' philosophy and shows why it is necessary, for Sellars and for analytic philosophy in general, to go beyond Kant's transcendental idealism towards Hegel's absolute idealism. McDowell develops Sellars' critique of the (doctrine of) givenness and argues that the structure that must be presupposed in any given experience is best conceived as the Aristotelian substance. McDowell, however, insists on Sellars' empiricism, which does not contradict his minimally or non-standard empiricist interpretation of Hegel.¹⁰ The idea is that it is a mistake to interpret either Kant's or Hegel's idealism as lacking empirical constraints on knowledge: that is, mental events and perceptual experience can be justifications for beliefs. Then, however, Sellars' critique of the myth of the given rests, in McDowell's view, on a mistaken interpretation of Hegel. In this context, McDowell's Hegel can be deployed against analytic criticism of empiricism, which includes the later Wittgenstein (cf. Rockmore 2005: p.147).

---

8 On the analogy between Wittgenstein's language-games and Sellars' space of reasons, see Sellars (1954) and Rockmore (2005: p.145). Furthermore, Koreň and Kolman (2018: p.31) conceive Wittgenstein's concept of language-game as Hegelian.
9 McDowell and Brandom are not the only ones who have developed Sellars's Wittgensteinian–Hegelian legacy. Terry Pinkard's book *Hegel's Phenomenology: The Sociality of Reason* (1994) appeared in the same year as Brandom's *Make It Explicit* and McDowell's *Mind and World*. However, Pinkard's focus is primarily on Hegel with only passing references to Wittgenstein.
10 Cf. Rockmore (2005: p.146) and Redding (2007: p.24).

In contrast to Sellars' and McDowell's selective reception of Hegel, Brandom attempts to provide a genuine reading that he calls the *semantic interpretation*, which allows him to assimilate Hegel into the analytic tradition in the wake of the "linguistic turn". Brandom describes his programme as "inferentialism". He contrasts it to "representationalism", which is indebted to the myth of the given (cf. Rockmore's discussion of representationalism in Kant and the early and later

Wittgenstein in Chapter 3). Following Koreň and Kolman (2018: p.1) we can define inferentialism in a narrow and a broad sense.[11] In the narrow sense, inferentialism is a doctrine in the philosophy of language that takes linguistic meaning as being grounded in an inferential structure (and not the other way around). In the broad sense, it is an epistemological doctrine that gives the concept of inference a privileged explanatory role. In both senses, inferentialism is motivated by Hegel's above-mentioned slogan: "everything is an inference". The concept of inference is related to Hegel's concepts of "determinate negation" and "mediation", which Brandom interprets as "material incompatibility" and "material consequence" (where mediation/material consequence can be defined in terms of determinate negation/material incompatibility).[12] As already mentioned, the concept of inferential structure also has roots in Wittgenstein's concept of a language-game. But Brandom deliberately restricts Wittgenstein's plurality of language-games into a single, most fundamental game, namely the rationalistic and normative game of reason-giving (cf. Koreň and Kolman 2018: p.39). Wittgenstein, in contrast, does not give priority to any particular language-game. Brandom is also critical of Wittgenstein's negative attitude towards philosophical theories and sides instead with Hegel's constructivist approach and system-building (Brandom 2014: p.7). Consider Brandom's schematic view of Wittgenstein's philosophical development: "we can see the Wittgenstein of the *Tractatus* as a neo-Kantian, without Kant's residual empiricism, and the Wittgenstein of the *Investigations* as a neo-Hegelian, without Hegel's revived rationalism." (Brandom 2014: p.4) Brandom is, then, a neo-Hegelian with Hegel's rationalism and a Wittgensteinian without Wittgenstein's anti-rationalism. Several of the papers in this volume address and critically evaluate Brandom's Hegel; see Shaheen's, Redding's and Kolman's chapters.

---

[11] Not to be confused with Brandom's broad and narrow conception of inferentialism (1994: p.131).
[12] Cf. Brandom (2014: p.11).

Major interpretative approaches in Hegel and Wittgenstein scholarship

Both Hegel and Wittgenstein scholarship have become philosophical subdisciplines in their own right. There have been diverse and often mutually exclusive interpretations of both thinkers. It is not surprising that these interpretations follow various aims and methodologies and place emphasis on different aspects, such as exegetical accuracy, charity, the viability of a given philosophical position or compatibility with other, earlier or later philosophical views and theories. Bringing together and comparing Hegel and Wittgenstein is, then, often relativized to this or that interpretation; a certain interpretation of Hegel is compared with a certain interpretation of Wittgenstein. The authors in this volume are not only aware of these complications, but work creatively with them. In this section, I want to outline the major interpretative approaches to Hegel and Wittgenstein, and briefly discuss their possible compatibilities and irreconcilabilities. I shall only mention the interpretative approaches that are represented in this volume.

The reception of Hegel's thinking has been marked by (at times very creative and productive) misunderstandings and (at times quite deliberate) misinterpretations.[13] Many readings have focused solely on one of his works or taken one aspect of his system, one "shape of consciousness" or one particular concept (the master–servant dialectic, the unhappy consciousness or plasticity). Such interpretations are not without importance, but I will focus only on those approaches to Hegel that attempt to interpret his system as a whole. As one would expect, there is no accepted way of classifying these interpretations. I shall combine two recent overviews of Hegel scholarship by Terry Pinkard (2013) and Paul Redding (2015).

The *traditional metaphysical* or *Neoplatonic* view takes Hegel's philosophy as a kind of rational theology. The Absolute Spirit is like the Neoplatonic or Christian God. Various stages of Hegel's dialectic, notably various shapes of consciousness presented in the *Phenomenology*, are interpreted as emanations of this God. Many of Hegel's claims and formulations support this view, e.g., his invoking the concept of God in the preface to the *Phenomenology* or later claiming that "philosophy has no other object but God and so is essentially rational theology" (LA: p.101). Representative advocates of this view are Taylor (1975)

---

[13] This might also be said of Hegel himself in relation to his reception of his predecessors and contemporaries.

and Beiser (2005), as well as the German scholars Heinrich (1971), Horstmann (2006) and Siep (2014).

There are *revised* or *realist* variants of the metaphysical view, mostly Aristotelian (Stern 2002, Westphal 2003 and, in certain respects, McDowell 2009), but also Spinozist (Houlgate 2005) or Platonist. It is essential for this view that reality is inherently rational or conceptually structured. The concept is the fundamental structure of thinking as well as reality. This is true also for the traditional view, but the revised metaphysical view does not attribute to Hegel the robust teleological spirit monism attributed by the Neoplatonic interpretation.

The third group of interpretations takes Hegel to be carrying out, extending and eventually completing Kant's critique of (traditional) metaphysics. There are many varieties of this *post-Kantian* view. Some of them, notably those of Pippin (2005), Rockmore (1997), Pinkard (1994) and Gabriel and Žižek (2009), explicitly interpret Hegel in this post-Kantian fashion. Brandom's semantic interpretation and inferentialism and McDowell's interpretation are also broadly post-Kantian (although McDowell, in contrast to Brandom, is committed to Aristotelian realism). Another strand of this post-Kantian view comprises analytic–pragmatic interpretations, for instance Stekeler-Weithofer (2016).

Finally, there is the view that Hegel's philosophy does not aim to present any (first-order) metaphysical theory, but is rather a meta-critique or a *meta-metaphysical* critique of any metaphysics. The most explicit formulation of this view is in Gabriel (2016: p.185): "Hegel's absolute idealism is not a *first-order metaphysical view* about the composition of ultimate reality [...]. Rather, it is a defence of *the meta-metaphysical idea* that there are different kinds of facts [...] which share a logical structure that guarantees their overall intelligibility." We can already find an inclination towards this meta-metaphysical view in Findlay (1958), and more recently in Redding (2017), who focuses on Hegel's category of actuality (*Wirklichkeit*), which includes possibility and necessity as abstractions (cf. Cammi's realist view of *Wirklichkeit* in Chapter 7). Hegel's metaphysics is, thus, a form of modal actualism that includes first-order metaphysical theories as abstractions. This view is not necessarily in conflict with the post-Kantian interpretation (for there are meta-metaphysical aspects in Kant too). There is a milder version of this view which holds that Hegel provides meta-metaphysical arguments compatible with the realist view.[14]

---

[14] Here is an apt formulation of this view: Hegel dismisses "the question concerning whether metaphysics *tout court* is possible, and [insists] on asking the 'real' meta-metaphysical question: 'What kind of metaphysics is the right kind of metaphysics?'" (Giladi 2016: p.157) Giladi, however, concludes that Hegel's metaphysics is "a sophisticated *melange* of Aristotelianism, Spinozism, Kantianism and post-Kantian philosophy of nature" (ibid.: p.159).

Let us turn now to the labyrinthine world of Wittgenstein scholarship, which in its baroque exuberance exceeds even Hegel studies. Two major interpretative disputes will be presented here. The first is the dispute between the *traditional* (or metaphysical/irresolute/theoretical/Tolstoyan) and *therapeutic* (or New/resolute/liberatory/dialectical/Kierkegaardian/Cavellian) readings of Wittgenstein's philosophy, predominantly of the *Tractatus* (but also of later texts).[15] For obvious reasons it is useful to characterise these two groups of readings according to their attitude to the Kantian programme of delineating the limits of knowledge. On the traditional view, Wittgenstein provides in the *Tractatus* a broadly Kantian argument that aims to delineate the limits of *language*.[16] On the therapeutic view, Wittgenstein is combating our natural desire for such an argument or for metaphysics in general. The traditional view stresses the many logical, metaphysical and epistemological insights expounded in the *Tractatus*; the therapeutic view, in contrast, insists on the analogy with the ladder presented in the closing remarks of the treatise, which proclaim the sentences that make it up to be nonsensical. These sentences serve as elucidations and must eventually be discarded, just like "the ladder after he has climbed up it" (TLP: 6.54). This dispute can be extended to or transposed onto Wittgenstein's later philosophy. The difference is, however, that there is no main or central argument to be identified there, but rather several, more or less interconnected arguments which the traditional view concentrates on. The so-called private language argument is the most famous one.

This brings us to the second main dispute, namely the debate over rules, private language and scepticism between Saul Kripke (1982) and his opponents. The conclusion of the private language argument (PI: §§244–271 and elsewhere) seems to be that a language intelligible solely to its originator (i.e., a private language) is ultimately unintelligible to this very language user. In other words,

---

15 Cf. Crary and Read (2000), the manifesto for the therapeutic view, and a good exposition of recent debates in Read and Lavery (2011).
16 Cf. Floyd (2007: p.177): "The most fundamental divide among interpreters of Wittgenstein lies [...] between those who detect in Wittgenstein's writings some form of semantic or epistemic resource argument, an argument ultimately appealing to the finitude or expressive limitations of language—whether it be truth-functional, constructivist, social-constructivist, antirealist, assertion-conditionalist, formalist, conventionalist, finitist, empiricist, or what have you—and those who instead stress Wittgenstein's criticisms of the assumptions lying behind the desire for such resource arguments, criticisms that in the end turn upon stressing the open-ended evolution, the variety, and the irreducible complexity of human powers of expression. The former kind of reader sees the inexpressible as a limitation, a reflection of what is illegitimate in grammar or fails to be epistemically justifiable; the latter sees the inexpressible as a fiction, an illusion produced by an overly simplified conception of human expression."

there is no private language, or language is essentially social. Kripke argues that this argument is actually a corollary of a more general paradox concerning rule-following: "This was our paradox: no course of action could be determined by a rule, because every course of action can be brought into accord with the rule." (PI 2009: §201) This is, for Kripke, a sceptical paradox Wittgenstein was facing and attempting to overcome. Kripke's solution to this paradox rests on the requirement of community agreement (which is why his position is known as the "community view").

The opponents of the community view either deny that Wittgenstein is dealing with scepticism in these passages[17] or they accept the charge and present different solutions. There are two prominent alternatives: the *disposition view* (speakers grasp a rule due to their dispositions to apply the rule in novel situations) and *primitive non-reductionism* (a speaker's grasp of a rule is a primitive mental fact about the speaker).[18]

* * *

Where does this very brief overview of recent interpretations of Hegel and Wittgenstein leave us? Only a few connections between the two can be discussed here. The traditional metaphysical view of Hegel and the traditional view of Wittgenstein can be brought together, as in Rentsch's, Lütterfelds's and Kleber's chapters. Lamb's proposal to interpret Wittgenstein's early works in a Kantian manner and Wittgenstein's later works in a Hegelian manner is possible only on the traditional view of Wittgenstein and the post-Kantian view of Hegel. This interpretative strategy is advanced in Haas', Chiurazzi's and Pinkard's chapters (Pinkard also considers the resolute reading). Redding addresses the traditional and therapeutic readings of the *Tractatus* together with the post-Kantian reading of Hegel, but eventually turns to Findlay's modal actualism. Brandom's post-Kantian semantic interpretation of Hegel draws on the community view of Wittgenstein (cf. Kolman's and Shaheen's chapters), while McDowell's Wittgenstein is openly against the community view. The realist view of Hegel can be compared to the traditional metaphysical interpretation of the *Tractatus* (as in Cammi's chapter). Rockmore interprets Wittgenstein, in his chapter, as "either a metaphysical realist or an epistemic skeptic", that is, he invokes both the traditional and sceptical views. Pluder considers the community view of rule-following in relation to Hegel's ethics and ethical life. Balestracci draws on the thera-

---

17 Cf. Baker and Hacker (1984). Advocates of the resolute view would also deny that Wittgenstein is advancing any argument here or elsewhere.
18 For the disposition view, see for example Horwich (1984); for primitive non-reductionism, see for example McDowell (1984).

peutic reading of the *Tractatus* and compares it with the dialectics of the *Phenomenology of Spirit*. Plevrakis adopts the therapeutic view in his Hegelian interpretation of the *Tractatus*. Moser also interprets the *Tractatus* within the therapeutic perspective (albeit in a rather unorthodox way), but her account has a strong Kantian accent too. This is only an outline of the interpretative complexities. Let us next turn to the structure and content of the volume in detail.

The structure of the volume and the individual chapters

How to bring two different philosophers together? As we know from Fichte,[19] every difference presupposes a common ground, an identity (and every identity presupposes a ground of difference). Both Hegel and Wittgenstein followed Fichte in this respect. Hegel did so when he maintained that everything has a ground and everything is a judgement,[20] Wittgenstein when he proclaimed self-identity to be nonsensical (for an identity without difference would be a self-identity).[21]

Re-evaluating the differences between Hegel and Wittgenstein, then, will consist either in highlighting their differences against the background of their identity, or in highlighting their common points against the background of their differences. Let us label these approaches "From identity to difference" and "From difference to identity" respectively. The latter approach, "From difference to identity", might be sketched as follows: let us assume that the thinking of these two philosophers is very different (they might have different goals, use different methods and terminology; they might differ in what they take for granted; they might focus on different topics, etc.). And this is *prima facie* indeed so. Within these differences, however, one might try to find a point of contact and establish whether they agree on some particular issue. The former approach, "From identity to difference", in contrast, begins by establishing a common ground or rather a common background (a presupposition, a topic, a perspec-

---

[19] This is the distinction between a "ground of distinction" (*Unterscheidungsgrund*) and "ground of relation/conjunction" (*Beziehungsgrund*) from the third paragraph of Fichte's *Science of Knowledge*.
[20] Hegel claims this at many points, e.g. in his Berlin lectures of 1831 (LL 1831: p.131).
[21] Curiously enough, Carlson (2005: p.xi) thinks that the denial of self-identity in Hegel constitutes his fundamental difference from analytic philosophy. If that were so, Wittgenstein's thinking, early and late, would also fundamentally differ from analytic philosophy.

tive) against which a difference (in the form of a disagreement) between Hegel and Wittgenstein can be established. This passage from identity to difference or vice versa can be embedded in a dialectical process. Any identity (or difference) that is reached is a point of departure for a new passage towards another difference (or identity). So Hegel and Wittgenstein may initially be taken to be very different philosophers; next, a common ground (thesis, perspective, concept) between them is established (identity), but within this common ground, there may be specific differences.

Following this general consideration, we divided the first half of the volume into two main sections, "From identity to difference" and "From difference to identity". We begin our volume with two chapters that are more general in scope, exploring the relevance and sustainability of the analytic–continental split.

Pirmin Stekeler-Weithofer investigates, from a broadly Hegelian perspective, metaphysical commitments of various strains of analytic philosophy, specifically logical atomism, physical atomism, naturalism and materialism. He identifies (sometimes latent) empiricism in these movements and counters with the Hegelian claim that "[s]cience is collective work on concepts, not merely a process of gathering empirical facts". These movements do not understand the so-called "transcendental turn", which Stekeler-Weithofer traces back to Descartes. The materialist/mechanist/objectivist worldview amounts, in the end, to manifestly incoherent metaphysics.

Thomas Rentsch presents, closer to the main topic of this volume, three key hypotheses about Hegel and Wittgenstein: (1) the proposition is the fundamental unit of dialectics/meaning construction, (2) Hegel systematically anticipates the thesis of meaning as use, and (3) we can find the private language argument in Hegel.

* * *

The first major section is comprised of chapters that proceed from identity to difference, that is, they take some point of identity between Hegel and Wittgenstein as a (sometimes only implicit) presupposition and then focus on the difference between them.

Tom Rockmore opens his chapter with the observation that both Wittgenstein and Hegel challenge the view that philosophical problems can be dealt with through a theory. They do so, however, in different ways. Although they both aimed to bring the philosophical tradition to its end, for Wittgenstein, philosophy ends in scepticism, while for Hegel this end is, at the same time, the culmination of philosophy, its fulfilment.

Herbert Hrachovec begins by remarking that both philosophers often approach philosophical problems not head-on, but by discussing (and criticising) established cognitive attitudes. Hrachovec then focuses on their reflections on the ordinary understanding of measurement. He proceeds by "triangulating" Hegel and Wittgenstein vis-à-vis a non-partisan account of measurement that allows one to find an interesting shared concern, namely a shared alertness to a concealed side of standards. It is against this background affinity that some of their differences appear in sharper contrast.

David Kolb's point of departure is the observation that both Wittgenstein and Hegel see our many languages and forms of life as constituted by different diamond nets of categories or grammars. Kolb then proceeds to argue that both Wittgenstein and Hegel take a non-reductive attitude toward this plurality of local ontologies. They disagree, however, about the philosophical implications of this plurality. Their disagreements stem from divergent notions about the structure and mode of being of the diamond nets.

Jonathan Shaheen identifies an analogy or shared concern between Hegel and Wittgenstein. They both give arguments for the social constitution of philosophically central entities. Shaheen focuses on seminal interpretations of these arguments, on Brandom's reading of the self-consciousness chapter of the *Phenomenology of Spirit* and on the communitarian reading of the private language argument in the *Philosophical Investigations*. Against this background, several differences are established: first, their different conceptions of mind; second, their different accounts of the relation between time slices of a single mind and genuine social contributions. Shaheen maintains: "Whereas communitarianism buys the Wittgensteinian so little that it can be had for the cost of individual time slices, the sociality Brandom is selling costs so much that the resources it takes to buy it can equally well purchase self-consciousness with no social contribution whatsoever."

Lorenzo Cammi elaborates in great detail on Hegel's and Wittgenstein's notions of *Wirklichkeit* before attempting a comparison of them. Given Cammi's realist/metaphysical interpretations of Hegel and Wittgenstein, several common points are established, in order to point out important differences. Both Hegel and Wittgenstein were convinced that it is possible to know the world. Yet according to Wittgenstein, some aspects of the world are inexpressible. In contrast to Hegel, Wittgenstein's notion of *Wirklichkeit* is restricted to empirical facts. Both Hegel and Wittgenstein maintain that reason and the world share the same essence; moreover, reason constitutes *Wirklichkeit*. Yet in Wittgenstein the constitutive role of reason is passive compared with Hegel. Hegel's conception of the actualisation of the world is dynamic whereas Wittgenstein's is static.

Kai-Uwe Hoffmann focuses on the concept of beauty. He starts out from similarities between Hegel and Wittgenstein with regard to their critique of scientism and other minor points. Within this common ground, several differences appear: Wittgenstein would reject Hegel's metaphysical, epistemological and scientific claims concerning the concept of beauty.

* * *

The second main section groups together chapters that proceed from (sometimes tacit) differences in order to find some common point (identity) between Hegel and Wittgenstein.

Paul Redding begins by remarking that comparing Hegel and Wittgenstein can be a hazardous affair. With this consideration in mind, he attempts to find some specific points of intersection between Hegel and the Wittgenstein of the *Tractatus*. More specifically, these points of contact are found between Hegel's (positive and negative) existential judgement and Wittgenstein's atomic propositions. After this specific comparison is made, further Hegelian themes emerge in the context of the *Tractatus*. Hegel and Wittgenstein were both opposed to the practice, common among logicians, of generalising by eliminating singular terms.

Terry Pinkard states at the outset that Hegel and Wittgenstein are an odd pairing: Hegel sought unity and created a forbidding technical vocabulary; Wittgenstein, in contrast, focused on heterogeneity (of language) and aimed at clarity in philosophy. Despite these differences, however, they both shared an interest in the (Kantian) problem of the limits of thought. Furthermore, both Wittgenstein and Hegel rejected Kant's sharp distinction between things in themselves and appearances. And finally, they were both convinced that "in making sense of things, we are inevitably driven to make sense of making sense, to a kind of logic".

Valentin Pluder admits that Wittgenstein and Hegel are very different kinds of philosophers in every respect. His aim is to find a point of contact where they can be compared. This point of contact is their concern with the connection between rules and acts: a mere formal rule cannot establish or cause interpersonal action. This similarity lies in Hegel's critique of Kant's categorical imperative and Wittgenstein's critique of rule-following. Moreover, they also share similar solutions for how to make this connection between rules and acts: there must be some internal relation between a rule and an act. For Hegel, this relation is the ethical life; for Wittgenstein, it is social institutions and forms of life.

Valentina Balestracci aims to investigate whether there can be a connection between Hegel and Wittgenstein. Such connections are found in comparing tautologies and contradictions in the *Tractatus* on the one hand and speculative propositions in the *Phenomenology of Spirit* on the other. Moreover, Balestracci pursues a deeper analysis of Hegel's speculative propositions, in order to shed light on the much-discussed relation between the *Phenomenology* and the *Science of Logic*.

Vojtěch Kolman starts his chapter with the suggestion that Wittgenstein's remark that his and Hegel's philosophies are opposed to each other can be read with Adorno's eyes as a critique of Hegel's "identity philosophy". In this sense, Wittgenstein's and Hegel's. He claims that their philosophies might be easily seen as opposedare, in some important respects, identical or similar to each other. But this difference presupposes another kind of identity, namely an overall commensurability of both philosophies. According to Kolman, this identity consists in the way Hegel and Wittgenstein develop their concepts of knowledge from more primitive forms of consciousness and bring them to a cautiously optimistic closure based on the sociality of reason, particularly as mirrored in Hegel's *master–slave parable* and Wittgenstein's *private language argument*.

Ingolf Max compares the beginning of the chapter on "Being" in Hegel's *Science of Logic* (pure being without further determinations) and the first sentence of Wittgenstein's *Tractatus* ("The world is everything that is the case"). Although these accounts seem to be different or even opposed to each other, Max finds a striking analogy between Hegel's global identity of pure being and pure nothing and Wittgenstein's world as the total reality. He thus focuses on Hegel's category of contradiction and its Wittgensteinian counterpart.

Marco Kleber asserts at the beginning of his chapter that Wittgenstein and Hegel have opposed views concerning the concept of the unspeakable. For Wittgenstein, the logical form of the world is unspeakable, whereas the immediately given, the fact, can be expressed in language. For Hegel, the immediately given is precisely what is unspeakable. What is revealed in language is the concept, which, according to Kleber's metaphysical interpretation, is the logical form and structure of all reality. Kleber thus speculatively equates Wittgenstein's logical form with Hegel's concept.

* * *

The second half of the volume is made up of chapters that aim not at a comparison but at a fresh interpretation of some aspects of Hegel's or Wittgenstein's thinking. Interpretations of one of the two philosophers are inspired by or taken from the perspective of the other. More specifically, these chapters present either a Hegelian interpretation of Wittgenstein's thinking or a Wittgensteinian interpretation of Hegel's thinking (and some, notably Kiesow's chapter, focus on both approaches). These perspectival approaches must presuppose that Hegel's thinking is different from Wittgenstein's; they proceed from a difference. A successful interpretation of one of the thinkers through the lens of the other reveals, however, that they have something in common. Interpreting one of the thinkers through the lens of the other is thus a special case of the approach from the previous section, "From difference to identity". We divided this second part of the volume into two sections, "Hegelian approaches to Wittgenstein" and "Wittgensteinian approaches to Hegel". Let us begin with "Hegelian approaches to Wittgenstein".

Aloisia Moser concentrates on Wittgenstein's projection method and its privation, the so-called *zero-method*. The zero-method is an activity of the mind akin to the "I think" of Kant's transcendental apperception or Hegel's speculative method in logic in which "method is the consciousness of the form of the inner self-movement of the content of logic" (SL 2010: p.33). Drawing on these parallels, Moser concludes that Wittgenstein's philosophical method goes beyond merely pointing out misunderstandings of the logic of our language. Method, in Wittgenstein and Hegel, is something that happens within concepts.

Ermylos Plevrakis attempts to interpret the *Tractatus* by referring to the reader's thoughts, feelings and understanding, imagining that this reader is Hegel. The core of his interpretation consists in taking the Tractarian "sole logical constant" (TLP: 5.47) as being equivalent to Hegel's concept, as developed in the *Science of Logic*. Hegel's sole logical constant can be regarded as "something like the missing logical elucidation of Wittgenstein's N-operation"; it is the concept of concept from the very first chapter of the *Doctrine of the Concept*, the sequence of universality, particularity and singularity.

Gaetano Chiurazzi focuses on Hegel's discussion of Kant's second antinomy in order to show the anti-analytical presuppositions of Hegel's philosophy. He then identifies what he calls the "cosmological antinomy" of the *Tractatus*, that is, its internal tension between an analytic principle (centred on the concept of simple objects) and a synthetic one (centred on the concept of form). His Hegelian interpretation of the *Tractatus* brings the *logical form* closer to the *form of life* from Wittgenstein's later philosophy. The logical form has "life", or, in Hegelian terms, it has a "soul"; it is, in the end, a concept (as Marco Kleber and, implicitly, Bruno Haas also maintain in their chapters).

Bruno Haas aims, at the outset, to address a group of philosophical problems present in the *Tractatus* from a Hegelian point of view. He interprets the *Tractatus* as a treatise on the Being of logic, that is, a treatise aimed at making logical form explicit. Haas focuses on Wittgenstein's remarks on the nature of subjectivity in relation to reference, especially 5.5422, "there is no such thing as the soul", which is, Haas argues, a misleading translation of *"die Seele ist ein Unding"* that wrongly implies there is no such thing as an *Unding*. Haas then proceeds to provide a general characterisation of Wittgenstein's theory of reference, focusing on its lack of differentiation between logical levels (through the image paradigm). He interprets this lack against the background of Hegel's theory of reference, as developed in his theory of contradiction.

Alexander Berg investigates what Wittgenstein actually said about Hegel and critically evaluates these remarks. Berg considers (openly anachronistically) what Hegel might have replied to Wittgenstein's words about his philosophy: "Wittgenstein seems to think that I always want to say that singular things only get their meaning from the universality. Whereas he himself is interested in showing that we can say this only in particular situations."

★ ★ ★

The final group of authors aim to make contributions to Hegel scholarship from a Wittgensteinian perspective.

Karl-Friedrich Kiesow starts out from the observation that both Hegel and Wittgenstein were aware of the privileged position of pronouns in linguistic discourse. In order to make a comparison possible, he narrows down his discussion to a critical analysis of the contributions of two distinguished interpreters of Hegel and Wittgenstein, namely, J. N. Findlay and Paul Weiss. Kiesow focuses on Findlay's Wittgensteinian reading of §184 of the *Phenomenology*, where Hegel presents his theory of acknowledgement, and on Weiss's Hegelian reading of §§220–1 of the *Zettel*, where Wittgenstein examines facial expressions. Findlay adopts a standard of meaningfulness that he erroneously connects with Wittgenstein and, therefore, comes to the conclusion that Hegel fails to capture the normal linguistic usage. Findlay's demand for an existential phenomenology in which the normal usage is restored is met by Weiss, who also justifies the need to explore the system of personal pronouns by submitting them to speculative transformations.

Jakub Mácha provides a distinctively Wittgensteinian interpretation of Hegel's subjective logic, especially the parts on the concept, the judgment and the *Schluß*. He argues that Wittgenstein implicitly recognised the moments of universality, particularity and individuality. More specifically, the moment of particularity occupies in Wittgenstein the status of a paradigm sample which mediates between a universal concept and its individual instances. Given this interpretation, Mácha provides a generic account of the emergence of concrete universals through a series of negations that follows the basic structure of Hegel's judgement: the individual is the universal.

Wilhelm Lütterfelds, in the sole chapter in German, understands Wittgenstein's late philosophy (taken mostly from *On Certainty*) as a kind of linguistic idealism. From this perspective, he interprets Hegel's dialectic as an idealist language-game. The most fundamental element of this language-game lies in Hegel's identification of the substantial being with the subject. This identity makes up an instrument or paradigm of this language-game (like Wittgenstein's measuring instrument from PI §50).

* * *

I sincerely hope that both Hegel and Wittgenstein are treated with respect in this volume. None of the authors excessively privileges one over the other, though they may express a preference. Hegel is not treated as the one who knew everything all along, nor is Wittgenstein taken as the only philosopher that can make Hegel intelligible.[22] Situating Hegel in the Wittgensteinian tradition of analytic philosophy and Wittgenstein in the Hegelian tradition of German idealism may prove to be a fresh perspective in either case. In a similar way, a new perspective may consist in seeing Hegel through a Wittgensteinian lens or Wittgenstein through a Hegelian lens.

References

Baker, Gordon P. and Hacker, P. M. S.: *Scepticism, Rules and Language*, Blackwell, 1984.
Beiser, Frederick C.: *Hegel*, Routledge, 2005.
Bell, Jeffrey A., Cutrofello, Andrew and Livingston, Paul M. (eds.): *Beyond the Analytic-Continental Divide: Pluralist Philosophy in the Twenty-First Century*, Routledge, 2016.
Brandom, Robert: *Making It Explicit: Reasoning, Representing, and Discursive Commitment*, Harvard University Press, 1994.
Brandom, Robert: *Articulating Reasons: An Introduction to Inferentialism*, Harvard University Press, 2000.
Brandom, Robert: *Tales of the Mighty Dead: Historical Essays in the Metaphysics of Intentionality*, Harvard University Press, 2002.
Brandom, Robert: *Between Saying and Doing: Towards an Analytic Pragmatism*, Oxford University Press, 2008.
Brandom, Robert: *Reason in Philosophy: Animating Ideas*, Harvard University Press, 2009.
Brandom, Robert: *Perspectives on Pragmatism: Classical, Recent, and Contemporary*, Harvard University Press, 2011.
Brandom, Robert: "Some Hegelian Ideas of Note for Contemporary Analytic Philosophy", *Hegel Bulletin* 35:1, 2014, pp.1–15.
Brandom, Robert: *From Empiricism to Expressivism: Brandom Reads Sellars*, Harvard University Press, 2015.
Carlson, David Gray (ed.): *Hegel's Theory of the Subject*, Palgrave Macmillan, 2005.

---

22 Cf. deVries (2008), who finds the same value in Redding (2007).

Crary, Alice and Read, Rupert (eds.): *The New Wittgenstein*, Routledge, 2000.
deVries, Willem A.: "Review of Paul Redding, *Analytic Philosophy and the Return of Hegelian Thought*", *Notre Dame Philosophical Reviews* 2008.04.18, URL = https://ndpr.nd.edu/news/analytic-philosophy-and-the-return-of-hegelian-thought/, accessed 20 May 2018.
Engelmann, Paul: *Letters from Ludwig Wittgenstein, with a Memoir*, Blackwell, 1967.
Findlay, John N.: *Hegel: A Re-Examination*, Allen and Unwin, 1958.
Findlay, John N.: "Foreword", in: Hegel's Logic. Being Part One of *The Encyclopaedia of the Philosophical Sciences* (1830), trans. by W. Wallace, Clarendon Press, 1973.
Findlay, John N.: *Wittgenstein: A Critique*, Routledge, 1984.
Floyd, Juliet: "Wittgenstein and the Inexpressible", in: Alice Crary (ed.): *Wittgenstein and the Moral Life: Essays in Honor of Cora Diamond*, MIT Press, pp.177–234.
Gabriel, Markus and Žižek, Slavoj: *Mythology, Madness, and Laughter: Subjectivity in German Idealism*, Continuum, 2009.
Gabriel, Markus: "What Kind of an Idealist (If Any) Is Hegel?", *Hegel Bulletin* 37:2, 2016, pp.181–208.
Giladi, Paul: "Hegel's Metaphysics as Speculative Naturalism", in: Allegra de Laurentiis (ed.): *Hegel and Metaphysics: On Logic and Ontology in the System*, de Gruyter, 2016, pp.149–162.
Henrich, Dieter: *Hegel im Kontext*, Suhrkamp, 1971.
Horstmann, Rolf-Peter: "Substance, Subject and Infinity: A Case Study of the Role of Logic in Hegel's System", in: Katerina Deligiorgi (ed.): *Hegel: New Directions*, Acumen, 2006, pp.69–84.
Horwich, Paul: "Wittgenstein on Rules and Private Language. Saul Kripke", *Philosophy of Science* 51:1, 1984, pp.163–171.
Houlgate, Stephen: *An Introduction to Hegel: Freedom, Truth and History*, Blackwell, 2005.
Koreň, Ladislav and Kolman, Vojtěch: "Introduction. Inferentialism's Years of Travel and Its LogicoPhilosophical Calling", in: O. Beran, V. Kolman and L. Koreň (eds.): *From Rules to Meanings: New Essays on Inferentialism*, Routledge, 2018, pp.1–45.
Kripke, Saul: *Wittgenstein on Rules and Private Language*, Blackwell, 1982.
Lamb, David: *Language and Perception in Hegel and Wittgenstein*, St. Martin's Press, 1979.
Lamb, David: *Hegel – From Foundation to System*, Martinus Nijhoff Publishers, 1980.
Lumsden, Simon: "Hegel, Analytic Philosophy and the Return of Metaphysics", *Parrhesia* 11, 2011, pp.89–93.
McDowell, John: "Wittgenstein on Following a Rule", *Synthese* 58, 1984, pp.325–364.
McDowell, John: *Mind and World*, second ed., Harvard University Press, 1996.
McDowell, John: *Having the World in View: Essays on Kant, Hegel, and Sellars*, Harvard University Press, 2009.
Nuzzo, Angelica (ed.): *Hegel and the Analytic Tradition*, Continuum, 2010.
Pinkard, Terry: *Hegel's Phenomenology: The Sociality of Reason*, Cambridge University Press, 1994.
Pippin, Robert: *The Persistence of Subjectivity: on the Kantian Aftermath.* Cambridge University Press, 2005.
Pinkard, Terry: "Hegel and Marx: Ethics and Practice", in: Roger Crisp (ed.): *The Oxford Handbook of the History of Ethics*, 2013, pp.505–526.
Read, Rupert and Lavery, Matthew A. (eds.): *Beyond the Tractatus Wars: The New Wittgenstein Debate*, Routledge, 2011.

Redding, Paul: *Analytic Philosophy and the Return of Hegelian Thought*, Cambridge University Press, 2007.
Redding, Paul: "Georg Wilhelm Friedrich Hegel", *The Stanford Encyclopedia of Philosophy*, E. N. Zalta (ed.), 2015, URL = https://plato.stanford.edu/archives/sum2018/entries/hegel/, accessed 20 May 2018.
Redding, Paul: "Findlay's Hegel: Idealism as Modal Actualism", *Critical Horizons: A Journal of Philosophy of Social Theory* 18:4, 2017, pp.359–377.
Rockmore, Tom: "Analytic Philosophy and the Hegelian Turn", *The Review of Metaphysics* 55:2, 2001, pp.339–370.
Rockmore, Tom: "Some Recent Analytic 'Realist' Readings of Hegel", in: Nuzzo 2010: pp.158–172.
Rockmore, Tom: *Cognition: an Introduction to Hegel's Phenomenology of Spirit*, University of California Press, 1997.
Rockmore, Tom: *Hegel, Idealism and Analytic Philosophy*, Yale University Press, 2005.
Rorty, Richard: "Introduction", in: Sellars 1997: pp.1–12.
Sellars, Wilfrid: "Some Reflections of Language Games", *Philosophy of Science* 21:3, 1954, pp.204–228.
Sellars, Wilfrid: *Empiricism and the Philosophy of Mind*, Harvard University Press, 1997.
Siep, Ludwig: *Hegel's Phenomenology of Spirit*, Cambridge University Press, 2014.
Stekeler-Weithofer, Pirmin: *Hegels Analytische Philosophie: Die Wissenschaft der Logik als kritische Theorie der Bedeutung*, Schoningh, 1992.
Stekeler-Weithofer, Pirmin: *Hegel's Analytic Pragmatism*, unpublished manuscript, 2016.
Stekeler-Weithofer, Pirmin: *Hegels Wissenschaft der Logik. Ein dialogischer Kommentar. Band 1: Die objektive Logik. Die Lehre vom Sein*, Meiner, 2019.
Stern, Robert: *Routledge Philosophy Guidebook to Hegel and the Phenomenology of Spirit*, Routledge, 2002.
Taylor, Charles: *Hegel*, Cambridge University Press, 1975.
Westphal, Kenneth R.: *Hegel's Epistemology: A Philosophical Introduction to the Phenomenology of Spirit*, Hackett, 2003.

Part 1 **General Introduction,
the Analytic-Continental Split**

Pirmin Stekeler-Weithofer
On Metaphysical Images in Analytic Philosophy: Overcoming Empiricism by Logical Analysis of Language

Abstract Overcoming metaphysics by logical analysis of language had been Carnap's slogan in the spirit of Bertrand Russell and the younger Wittgenstein, directed mainly against Heidegger's philosophical phenomenology as a paradigm of what later got the label 'Continental' philosophy. After we realise that formalist conceptual analysis heavily works with counterfactual mathematical metaphors and metaphysical world images of the 17th and 18th century, developed in Hobbes's materialism, Locke's physiology of cognition and Hume's sensualism, it is about time to undo these insular moves of Logical Positivism and other forms of Empiricism and Naturalism. Any real linguistic turn in critical philosophy has at least to take up Kant's constitutional analysis and Hegel's insights into historically developed norms of differentially conditioned inferences. Such generic rules, canonized as conceptual truths, always already lie at the ground of meaningful empirical *Konstatierungen* in a synthetic a priori way.

1 The method of logical analysis vs. the movement of Analytic Philosophy

In this paper I propose to distinguish philosophy that uses all available methods of logico-linguistic analysis from Analytic Philosophy in upper case letters. This means distinguishing the philosophical *movement* with the word "Analytic" in its name from philosophy that has, since its inception, developed conceptual analysis as a basis for critical reflections on the very meaning of empirical, theoretical and reflective sentences in everyday language, scientific texts and logical commentaries. An especially important case is the "speculative" form of sentences used in philosophical "geographies" of knowledge and science, and in all kinds of figurative articulations of attitudes towards the world as a whole.

The movement of Analytic Philosophy was, so the story goes,[1] founded by Bertrand Russell and G. E. Moore, with Bernard Bolzano, Gottlob Frege and some Neo-Kantians as grandfathers. Its opposition to Hegelianism—or rather

---
[1] Cf. Passmore (1994), Glock (2014), Otte (2014).

what was held to be Hegelianism—seems to have been the main unifying bond at the beginning. The movement's real roots, however, lie in the tradition of (British) Empiricism stretching from Thomas Hobbes to John Stuart Mill and, in Vienna, to Ernst Mach. The basic ideas were taken up, in Vienna, by the Circle around Moritz Schlick and Rudolf Carnap, strongly influenced by the younger Ludwig Wittgenstein, in Berlin by the school around Hans Reichenbach and Carl Gustav ("Peter") Hempel. From the 1930s on, Analytic Philosophy turned into a self-declared *anti-continental movement*, with Edmund Husserl's post-Kantian philosophical phenomenology, Martin Heidegger's post-Hegelian philosophical hermeneutics and the post-Marxian dialectics of Leftist circles (including many French philosophers) as its main opponents. From a "continental" point of view, Analytic Philosophy seems to restore "scientific enlightenment" of 17th and 18th-century debates on the ground of a gross overestimation of logical formalism in semantical analysis. Despite its international success, it appears as an insular movement mainly because of its abandoning the Kantian task of understanding science as a special region in our life-world, thus falling back even behind Neo-Kantians such as Rudolf Cohen, Paul Natorp and Ernst Cassirer.

A first problem of Analytic Philosophy lies in the ideal image of language, developed by Frege, and the corresponding mathematical picture of ideal knowledge and perfect truth. The adherence to a prototypical ideal of a mathematical concept script and mathematical truth distinguishes the *formalist* approach in Analytic Philosophy from linguistic *phenomenology* (Gilbert Ryle, John L. Austin and many others). The formalist approach takes deductive rules defined for canonical notations in mathematical "language" directly as a model for norms of good inference in its attempt to make the inferential form of content in the use of expressions in ordinary language explicit. The problem is that ordinary language does not allow for the same merely syntactic rules of recursive definition for well-formed complex expression. It also does not fulfil the same semantic conditions of mathematical notations, for example, the bivalence principle in elementary arithmetic according to which every syntactically well-formed "sentence" already has one of two truth-values attached, namely, true or false, *tertium non datur*. A further crucial point is that the mainstream of Analytic Philosophy defends an *empiricist* world-picture.

Empiricism always comes in one of two versions. The first version suggests a logical analysis of the content of meaningful propositions (and its syntactic parts) on the ground of *presupposed sense data*. Wittgenstein's *Tractatus*, for example, talks about *elementary states of affairs* corresponding to logically basic or elementary sentences without being able to give robust examples, neither for elementary sentences nor for their counterparts in my perceptual access to the world. Sentences are viewed under the guidance of a "deep structure," a canonical notation. The projections between sentences in ordinary language and sentences in a canonical formal notation have, at best, the form of a useful analogy—such that the very method of formal logical analysis is metaphorical. I talk of metaphors here in the very general sense of figurative tropes, including analogies.

The second version of empiricism is physical atomism. Because of the instability of the first version, due to the obvious obscurity of talk about immediate sensations or qualia and elementary facts, it tends to collapse into the second. The development from Carnap's *The Logical Structure of the World* (colloquially called "*Aufbau*") to Otto Neurath's physicalism and Quine's postulates of *stimulus meanings* shows this quite nicely. The *Aufbau* appeals to a formally *solipsistic* basis. The move to Quine's *naturalized epistemology* corresponds, so to speak, to a move that leads us from the radical empiricism of David Hume, informed by George Berkeley, back to John Locke and Thomas Hobbes.

Quine's *behavioural theory* of "sense-impressions" corresponds to Locke's "ideas." It forms, as such, a "physiology of the understanding", as Kant critically labelled Locke's version. The problem is that theories about physiology and physical forces are uncritically presupposed. Neurath, Quine and their followers ignore or do not grasp the "transcendental" arguments in the continental tradition—from Descartes, Kant and Hegel to Husserl's and Heidegger's phenomenology—that warn us against presupposing a whole system of science and "explaining" human understanding and cognition by embedding it into neurophysiological theories. Neurath's famous simile, according to which the way we reconstruct a holistic system of science is like the way sailors repair a ship on the high seas, is a dangerous rhetorical device to support dogmatic scientism. Despite the problems of Humean empiricism, the turn back to Locke and Hobbes forsakes any critical impulse of radical empiricism and results in a merely dogmatic worldview.

A third problem lies in a far-too-narrow concept of logic and logical analysis. Frege's logic holds only for purely sortal domains or classes of entities. Such domains and classes presuppose sharp boundaries between different classes and between their individual members. However, such sharp borders of identity and inequality exist only in purely mathematical domains of higher arithmetic, i.e., in *pure set theory*. (I ignore here the peculiar status of the ideal points, lines and forms of pure geometry.) In other words, Frege's logic is only mathematical logic. All "application" of it in actual languages, with which we refer to the actual world of experience, is highly metaphorical. We cannot understand it "literally" at all. This fact relativizes Analytic Philosophy's *criticism of the use of metaphors* in philosophy and the humanities. Such a criticism stands in the tradition of Thomas Hobbes—who defended a purportedly precise and rigorous literal meaning against any *figurative* speech, despite the fact that the basic method of all sciences consists in finding good enough *analogies*. Literal meaning exists then, ironically, only if we do not leave the domain of a mathematical *Urbild* or model at all.

In any case, Wittgenstein's *Tractatus* ranks, alongside with Russell's *Philosophy of Logical Atomism*, as the foundational text of logical positivism and logical empiricism in the starting phase of Analytic Philosophy. In the following, I will attempt to show that the *Tractatus* contains at least as much speculative metaphysics as it contributes to critical philosophy.

Wittgenstein's first main thesis is this: only statements that can be understood as true or false *Konstatierungen* defined by truth-conditions on the ground of elementary statements are meaningful. His second thesis is that the sentences of the natural sciences are of this sort. These claims are, however, utterly wrong. The first thesis is wrong since there are no pure *Konstatierungen* at all. The second thesis is wrong because the scientific sentences codified in science textbooks do not have the logical form of *empirical propositions* or *Konstatierungen* at all. Rather, they express general, i.e., generic, rules of conditioned inferences. To the credit of Wittgenstein and his genius, however, he did ultimately recognize the problem and tried to save the critical impulse of his truly analytic philosophy from hidden metaphysical dogmatisms and, more importantly, from Russell's philosophical movement. Philosophers such as Friedrich Kambartel and John McDowell who take up these insights of the middle and later Wittgenstein in a radical way are ironically "excommunicated" by ardent followers of Analytic Philosophy.

However, the world-picture of Russell and the early Wittgenstein ultimately assumed two forms. The first form is empiricist in the sense of starting with subjective sense data or qualia, which, as I have already said, do not exist at all in the sense of well-determined states of affairs. There are no well-defined entities because there are no meaningful identities that can be defined. The second form is the picture of scientism or, what amounts to the same thing, physicalism. This naturalistic "materialism" views the world as a holistic system of relative movements of atomic substances, without reflecting enough on what it means to do so. In an ideal mathematical model, lines as extensions of functions represent movements of point-like (centres of) bodily atoms. Mathematically, the functions take (real) numbers representing time as arguments and points in space as values. This picture goes back to Descartes, the first and greatest of all theorists to reflect on the very form of modern mathematical science.

In Wittgenstein's formal empiricism, the world is a kind of four-dimensional colour movie with "space, time and colour [...] as forms of the objects" (TLP:

2.0251). Contemporary Analytic Philosophy remains limited in its views by this ambivalent metaphysical image. This diagnosis is nicely supported by a remark about David Lewis:

> Lewis makes a profound Realist assumption: the world is, fundamentally, a four-dimensional space-time mosaic of instantiations of point-size categorical properties [...]. You, me, tables, and chairs are ultimately composed of such pixels, too. (Schrenk 2016: p.136)

It is interesting that empiricism overlooks from the beginning its own crypto-religious metaphysics, as made explicit in the following remark:

> Suppose you knew everything about the past, present, or future, all facts, all events, just everything (ibid.).

It is impossible to "assume" anything like this. It is as misleading as assuming an ideal God-like perspective. In contrast to theology, which at least makes its anthropomorphic metaphors explicit, metaphysical empiricism does not know what it is doing linguistically and logically or how to understand its own reflective and speculative commentaries on "my world" and "the world". Any such mathematical model of a *metaphysics of science* produces at best an *eidolon*, as Plato would have said. Such an *eidolon* is a linguistic toy-model; it would remain only a linguistic *toy*, an artificial *Sprachspiel*, if it did not show us some features of our real use of language in world-related *language-games*—as the double meaning in the use of this term by the later Wittgenstein shows.

If one imagines the "movie" of the world as already shot—which seems to be possible in either version of empiricism, sensation-based or physicalist—then there is, for example, no place left for free will. Nevertheless, in the Humean picture of Wittgenstein's *Tractatus*, the belief in a given causal nexus is also called superstition (TLP: 5.1361). Wittgenstein seems to think it wrong to deny *contingencies* in the real world. In the empiricist version of the pixel picture, natural laws are just attempts to represent some or many facts about the past, present or future in an axiomatically and inferentially "thick" way, i.e., in such a way that we can predict some future facts or prove that some past facts "must have" occurred. There is, of course, no solution to Hume's induction problem. Steps from relative frequencies to probabilities always rest on some free decisions. There is no general logic of induction beyond some rules of thumb for relatively reliable statistical methods. Probability judgements are in the same way generic as any other concrete law of nature. Genericity means that we have to take possible exceptions to default inferences and normal expectations into account.

2 Generic material knowledge in conceptual inferences versus belief in scientism

Science is collective work on concepts, not merely a process of gathering empirical facts. In its canonization of generic truths and conceptual norms, it always operates with a great deal of pragmatic opportunism to set rules that fit general experience more or less well.

Like historical narratives, verbal information and communication make use of conceptually articulated differences and default inferences, as they are supposed to "hold *a priori*" despite resulting from our generic knowledge, which is developed, critically assessed and canonized in the joint institution of *scientia* and *mathesis*, i.e., of science, teaching and learning.

Any general content is generic. Relative to corresponding empirical statements, its logical status is *a priori*, as it determines our material, meaningful judgements and inferences as *prima facie* true, valid or allowed.

Scientific theories are systems of idealized generic truths that talk about types or forms of things and states of affairs, about genera and species, not about arbitrary sets of singular and individual entities. Generic sentences about the typical behaviour (prototype examples) of species cannot be reconstructed, as logical empiricism and Analytic Philosophy assume, in terms of quantified sentences in sortal classes of objects. This is the deepest and least-understood insight of Hegel's dialectical logic of conceptual truths and their applications.

Generic or eidetic truth is conceptual truth. As such, it expresses time- and situation-invariant, but conditioned, default norms of allowed inferences and normal expectations. We should not confuse generic statements about generic objects—standing for good paradigms of a species of things—with universally quantified sentences about all singular entities in a (semi-)sortal set of entities. Such sets presuppose clear identities and strict inequalities, defined in a relational domain fulfilling Leibniz's principle, the most crucial principle of predicate and quantificational logic in (semi-)sortal domains. The usual talk of an identity of *indiscernibles* in this context is misleading: Any identity results from a decision to limit the allowed predicates $\varphi(x)$ to a system based on a relation of equivalence between certain representations and presentations. Technically, this means the following: Representations (or presentations) t and s that are evaluated as equivalent turn into denotations of abstract or concrete objects, namely by the following substitution rule: if s is equivalent to t, we can infer $\varphi(s)$ from $\varphi(t)$ for any $\varphi(x)$ in our *limited* class of one-place predicates $\varphi(x)$. With respect to this (a priori presupposed) class, we say then that s and t *denote* the same object and we write s = t. The principle bearing Leibniz's name is thus a *logical* rule of equipollent substitution in fixed classes of predicates; it belongs to a logic of abstraction, not to ontology, despite the fact that Leibniz himself might have thought otherwise. No equation or identity statement can really say that there are no "finer" distinctions in an "absolute" way, i.e., not relativized to a certain class of predicates. All mathematicians learn the logical technique of turning an equivalence relation into an identity by limiting the predicates to a class of open sentences $\varphi(x)$ for which the substitution principle holds as outlined above.

We have fully sortal domains with exact definitions of identities for clearly defined possible representations only in mathematics, simply because any inner-worldly *thing* or *matter* exists only in a limited period. In other words, we can say only of *abstract* and *ideal* (or generic) objects or entities that they exist across all times and in a manner invariant with respect to situations.

In order to appreciate the problem that results if we look at real and concrete objects in the real world, we should remember an example proposed by Frege himself, namely, the sentence "the horse is a quadruped animal". Frege explicitly says that the sentence is logically "best understood as an expression of a universal judgement of the form 'all horses are quadrupeds' or 'all well-developed horses are quadrupeds'."[2] Frege attempts to be more precise in the second half of the sentence by excluding possible exceptions from his consideration. However, horses with only three legs remain horses, as long as they survive. Aristotle uses the label "steresis", Latin "privatio", for cases like these. Frege and his followers do not seem to concede that we have *two* readings of *general* judgements, a *generic* reading and a reading as *universal quantification*. The generic mode in which we talk about a generic horse or lion[3] is, in world-related discourse, even the default or normal mode. Only in mathematical contexts do we find universal quantification over every singular entity in a sharply defined class of entities. Pure set theory (as higher arithmetic) together with pure geometry are, indeed, the *only* domains with *purely sortal* objects or entities with wholly situation-transcendent identities—as presupposed in formal readings of quantificational and predicate logic.

---

[2] Frege (1980: p.70). On pp.59–60, Frege declares that words like "although" and "however" are just variants of the word "and". By assuming that the only additional thing they express is an element of subjective surprise, Frege misses the non-monotonic logic of the word "but" as a signal for the logical form of *privation*.

[3] Husserl tries, accordingly, to distinguish general (i.e., generic) "objects" from individual "entities", as his *Logische Untersuchungen* shows; see Husserl (1992: pp.110–126).

In fact, Frege's schematization of the formal meaning of logical particles like "and", "not" and especially "for all" presupposes idealist meanings that do not exist at all in our linguistic reference to the real world. Frege's logic is not a general logic, but only a mathematical one. It is universally valid only in mathematical models. This fact becomes especially problematic in the case of modalities. Contemporary modal logic interprets words like "possible", "necessary", "real" and "contingent" as quantifiers in a sortal, set-theoretical model of so-called possible worlds. In model theoretic semantics, such "worlds" are structured sets in systems of such sets. We define mathematical models as models in which some lists of schematic axioms for supposedly universally valid calculations with modal words are evaluated as formally true. The technical insights into the relation between a deductive system and a "semantic" interpretation in formal set theory continue to this day to overshadow the fact that we should not be satisfied with these modal theories, at least if we are interested in the more complicated actual use of the words "possible" and "necessary" and the generic constitution of possibilities, which are, as such, no sortal "worlds".

Mathematical idealism in philosophical logic results in a kind of rhetoric, in which schematic rules—like those we might need and use in computational linguistics or automatic language processing—are confused with norms of good and correct language use by human beings. As a result, the principles for good communicative and cooperative actions are wrongly attacked for being vague and obscure, and the hope for "rigorous" norms is confused with an idealist quest for schematic rules. This shows in what sense true analytical philosophy still has to overcome what Hegel aptly called the "childhood of philosophising" namely, Pythagoreanism.

Pythagoreanism comes in two versions. The first version consists in a mystification of pure mathematics and is often (erroneously) called "Platonism". The second version is physicalism, which consists in an ontological hypostatization of the mathematical structures we use in our models of physics.

Notably, Heraclitus, Parmenides, Plato and Aristotle were already aware of the flaws in the Pythagoreans' enthusiasm for the results of mathematics and mathematically formed *episteme* or *scientia*. This fact ironically contradicts a common picture of the history of philosophy. In contrast to the common picture, Socrates, who was an admirer of Heraclitus, attacked excessive love of literal meanings and tried hard to overcome early formalism. On the other hand, he also saw the naivety of early empiricism. Plato's Socrates even defines the *sophists* by reference to their incorrect attitudes towards scientific methodology and the logic of eidetic meaning: a sophist is a scientist with some serious flaw. Whereas Russell and the early Wittgenstein believed that traditional philosophy produced metaphysical problems that modern logical analysis has to dissolve, the actual problems consist in formalist and empiricist (mis)understandings of science and knowledge.

It was, as we can see now, a flawed diagnosis in early Analytic Philosophy that led from sense-data empiricism back to scientism as dogmatic belief in the "truth" of the "most advanced" natural sciences. Despite the fact that there are, in fact, no qualia or immediate propositions, as the solipsistic foundations of Wittgenstein's *Tractatus* and Carnap's logical *Aufbau* presupposes, the path back to physicalism is not a good option. The danger of dogmatism is still salient in the Sellarsian *scientia mensura* formula, according to which it is the natural, i.e., physical, sciences and not our life experience that form the ontological measure of being and truth, of what is and what is not. The physical sciences seem to detect a real reality behind the "manifest" world view of everyday talk—just as Copernicus, Kepler, Galileo and Newton did with respect to celestial phenomena. Science, with physics as its ideal prototype, thus supposedly uncovers the true nature or essence of things. In their phenomenological reflection on the very constitution of the sciences, Husserl and Heidegger uncover the metaphysical content of such an idea by showing how science is just an institution to improve our ordinary, everyday understandings.

3 Basic errors of materialism—and of its critics

If *naturalism* or *materialism* were simply the view that everything there is consists of matter, and that matter consists of atomic particles, we could grant this and deny that there are any independently existing mental or spiritual entities. Any such entity would instead be constituted by our abstract ways of talking about forms of being and forms of life. What we should not grant, however, is materialism and naturalism's *mechanism*. The functioning of machines such as clocks and steam engines is one paradigm for mechanical movements. We find a second prototype in the way billiard balls move when hit, together with the parallelogram of forces. Newton's gravitational forces form a third example. According to the basic conceptions of mechanism—or, as we call it today, physicalism—we explain movements and changes causally as if material objects were, as such or in themselves, "dead" and unmoved "things" that need some external force in order to be set in motion.

In a sense, the Aristotelian image of a prime mover already presupposes a naive conceptual framework of this kind. Cartesian dualism still views objects in the external world as "passive". Only the thinking subject or *res cogitans* can act in a spontaneous and self-determined way. Nature is not yet understood as a comprehensive system of self-determining events and processes, developments and changes. The "semantic" or "realist" picture of nature first appears with Spinoza and Leibniz.

The metaphysical debates about naturalism/materialism are, however, not at all sophisticated. They make errors of the most simplistic kind. A first group of such errors is *mathematical*. These errors are rooted in confusions about the theories' own *ideal* notions of the infinite divisibility of space and counterfactual ideas about the indefinite existence of eternal substances with the same structural properties as real things and states of affairs. In actual reality, there are no unextended points in time, infinitesimal lines, moments or forces. All these things are just internal features of *mathematical models*, constituted by *ideal abstractions*. Such abstractions have to be understood as *linguistic techniques*. We use them, for example, to talk about *forms* of real processes of cutting things or times into smaller parts, and presuppose the idealizations that lead to pure intuitions in geometry and arithmetic when we add them up again.

Leucippian atomism rests on the (correct) view that in reality the possibility of cutting matter into smaller pieces quickly hits a limit. "Mathematical infinity" refers only to some "in-principle" indefiniteness in the possibility of cutting lines, areas or volumes into smaller parts. The metaphorical prototype for physical atoms, on the other hand, is at base anthropomorphic: just as with other higher animals, human individuals cannot be cut into two halves without destroying the being (life) of at least one part.

In precisely this sense, a corpse is no longer human, and a carcass is no longer an animal. Moreover, Lucretius's principle "ex nihilo nihil fit" is entirely wrong.[4] Everything develops out of nothing, if "nothing" is properly understood as a negation of the existence of a thing of a certain type or species. In other words, any determinate thing develops from other things. A sperm and an egg are not yet human beings or animals, a spiral cloud is not yet a solar system, etc.

A second type of argumentative error results from confusing necessary and sufficient conditions. Voltaire, for one, is guilty of this mistake when he tells a story of the following form: If a certain Brahman had started a promenade with his right left leg rather than with his left, Henry IV would not have been murdered.[5] In the story, Voltaire presents only a *conditio sine qua non* for the

---

[4] Lucretius (2009: I, 205): "nil igitur fieri de nilo posse fatendumst" resp. "nil posse creari de nilo" (I, 155). See also Voltaire, *Dialogues entre Lucrece et Posidonius:* "Ex nihilo nihil, in nihilum nil posse reverti Tangere enim et tangi nisi corpus nulla potest res." (Voltaire 2010: pp.375–402).
[5] Cf. Voltaire: *Dialogue entre un brahmane et un jésuite, sur la nécessité et l'enchainement* (2006: pp.97–118, esp. p.113).

birth of the murderer, which is, as such, not yet a *sufficient* condition for the murder to occur.

Causal determinism claims that every event has *sufficient* conditions that are "causal" in the sense of a system of previous events from which the event in question necessarily follows. Unfortunately, a whole range of thinkers believe that we only need to sum up "all" necessary conditions in order to get "sufficient" causal conditions, without realizing that the word "all" is not at all well-defined here.

The real problem is that there are many notions of possibility and just as many concepts of relative necessity.

A third type of mistake results from a flawed logical understanding of abstract and ideal "entities" in our talk about forces, dispositions, faculties and forms of behaviour and action. Even Voltaire and later Kant recognized that understanding, freedom, consciousness and attention are just the abstract meanings of nominalizations. By nominalizing the attributive predicate "free", for example, we can use "freedom" as a title for texts that reflect on the use of the predicate or the adverb "freely". The same holds for the word "will" or "volition" as titles for talking about acting *voluntarily* instead of being forced by *compulsion*. There are no separate agents going by names such as *spirit*, *mind*, *reason*, *soul* or *res cogitans* inside us that "do" something as the "real" subject of *emotions*, *sensations*, *perceptions*, *desires*, *intentions* and *plans* for behaviour and action.

The inability to deal with abstractions and (mathematical) idealizations is, however, equally shared by materialists and anti-materialists or "spiritualists"/"dualists", if we read their texts with sufficient critical understanding. Materialists like to talk carelessly about *forces* and *causes*, *dispositions* and *impulses*, *stimuli* and *impressions*—from Hobbes and Locke to Francis Skinner and Quine. Anti-materialists seem to enlarge the domain of "entities." They include *mental agents* and *modules* of various sorts, ranging from some *animal soul* or *sub-consciousness* to *self-consciousness* and *reason* (as if these words were not just labels or titles for specific forms of behaviour and action), from animal life with its desires (appetites) and enactive perception to human apperception.

Heidegger's labels are often criticized for being obscure. However, they are logically more developed than the talk about entities, events or possible worlds in Analytic Philosophy. Being-at-hand is, for example, a title referring to the form of being an immediate object in our practical dealing with present things. It replaces Kant's confusing talk about forms and objects of intuition. We can happily grant that objects at hand are just medium-sized dry objects that can be geometrically formed and moved, and sometimes keep their geometrical shape for some time. Time, in turn, is always already ordered with respect to an observing and acting subject who distinguishes between what has happened, what is happening and what might or will happen or can be expected or feared.

The measurement of time goes beyond the being of time in past, present and future. Talking about past, present and future presupposes a present situation I am in right now. Measuring time presupposes much more, namely, reproducible processes as natural clocks like the apparent movement of the sun and/or technical constructions of paradigmatic movements in artificial "clocks".[6]

The riddle of time and space disappears if we understand the words as titles for the way we orient ourselves "in time and space", as we say, and how we technically produce time-numbers and count distances. The results of spatial and chronological measurements lead to a four-dimensional number space, if we abstract from the fact that we measure time-numbers always at certain places or "points". It took a long time to notice the problematic presupposition of space-invariant time in this abstraction.

Even though Kant's talk about "forms of *our* intuition" (*Anschauung*) and "our sensibility" (*Sinnlichkeit*) is highly confusing (or even confused), he is right to approach the *concept* of space and time and their pure (ideal) representations in geometry and (Cartesian) phoronomy or kinematics by starting with *present* spatial and chronological orientations, datings, comparisons and so on. In proceeding this way, he shares with Descartes (and, unknowingly, with Leibniz) the insight that *all* quantitative (arithmetical) characterizations of "points in time and space" presuppose some zero-point, which is always a real or possible *finite subject* who (or that) observes things moving about and places them in a spatiotemporal ordering relative to her (or "its") own place and time here and now, together with the corresponding dimension of orientation (up and down, in front and behind, left and right) and a corresponding time measurement. Understanding all details of the relation between "real" intuition or "actual" reference to the "external world" of movable things and "pure intuition" or our theoretical, mathematical models of space and time, with their infinite extension and infinite divisibility, is certainly difficult. It suffices to have a general understanding of the problem and to robustly refrain from mystifying *unextended points* in "real" space and time.

---

[6] Our languages still have no proper expressions for "time-beats" (in German: *Zeit-Takte*) of a natural or artificial clock that might correspond to certain "points" on a "line" through which another point moves at a certain moment: we "count" time by counting such beats. The beats correspond as "time-points" to the points on the line through which the moving "point-like" object moves at the corresponding moment.

A fourth problem goes back to the fact that "I", "self", "the I" and "the self" are by no means simple words. They do not name any "thing" or "entity", even though they are used formally as names and refer to "topics" of reflection.

A fifth, and most general, type of mistake in the modern and ancient debate about materialism concerns the recognition of *grand facts* and *basic principles* together with a refusal to give further *causal explanations* of them. The most basic of these most general facts can be expressed in the following way: every *object* in the world is physical or natural, a *res extensa*, insofar as its spatial and temporal "place" has to be specified in a *finite* region "in space and time". Standard paradigms are *bodies* as bodily *things* or medium-sized dry goods. But waves and fields are also "local" in this sense. It was Leibniz who formulated this basic principle (as well as he could), and it must be accepted by anybody who wants to know what it means to talk about the world. Descartes also realized (before Leibniz) that the notion of an object (*Gegenstand*) is, in a sense, *ambivalent* or, rather, that it *presupposes* the complementary notion of a (perceiving and knowing, thinking and acting) *subject*. By realizing this logical fact – namely, that objects are things in the "external" world, i.e., relative to *us* as *thinking* and *apperceiving subjects*, Descartes's insight into the "absolute" stance of the knowing or doubting, believing or justifying, and hence already "thinking" and "acting", subject is *the Big Bang of modern philosophy*. It is, as such, the beginning of *transcendental philosophy*.

Unfortunately, the mechanistic materialism of Hobbes (and his followers) is still pre-Cartesian metaphysics. Descartes's logical meditation on the very notions of knowing and doubting, ambivalent as it is, leads to the well-known worries of Cartesian dualism and the *placement problem* of "spiritual" ("rational") and "mental" (animal) powers and faculties with respect to the mechanical world of "mere" objects. On the other hand, it already shows why any concrete claim about objective facts in the external world of objective things presupposes the personal subjectivity of the agent and speaker.

On a charitable reading of Descartes, the contrast between *res cogitans* and *res extensa* is not an *ontic* contrast between different *things*, but a contrast between *modes* of *being*. An object is an object *for* a subject. Since the paradigm case of explaining the relative movements of material objects is "mechanical" explanation, we can at least understand why Descartes declares that for a "scientific" approach to the world even the behaviour of animals is a topic for "mechanical" explanation. Remarkably, the same biologists and naturalists who follow Descartes in this methodological approach—namely in addressing life only in terms of a "mechanical" (neuro-)physiology—accuse him of making an excessively radical categorical distinction between animal behaviour and human action. Descartes tries to make the contrast between enactive perception of animals as mechanical reaction or conduct and (self-)conscious action clear and distinct. This sounds *literally* as if he did not see continuities here at all. Continuities are everywhere. The interesting point here is the discontinuity between a true human language by which we can represent non-present possibilities in contrast to so-called signal languages used by animals to coordinate conduct. Only persons are "veraloquens", i.e., beings that, in contrast to ants and bees, not merely use signals but rather possess a *full* language.

Descartes's seemingly "metaphysical" claim that plants and animals are "merely complex machines" can and should be understood as a methodological maxim for descriptive and explanatory biology. Even though there are good reasons to criticize this approach to life, even understood as a methodological maxim, it is no different from modern methodological physicalism. In contrast to metaphysical physicalism, which claims dogmatically that everything there is could be explained in principle by an ideal and perfect physical theory, methodological physicalism holds that the "best" way to explain processes and the behaviour of things in the world is "mechanical". Default movements of things are represented by mathematical functions in a spatiotemporal model of analytic geometry. The crucial question is, however, what we can know about these functions *a priori, praeter hoc*. That is, how far do we have to recognize empirical contingencies?

In other words, the Cartesian *world-picture* of trajectories of "atomic" movement in space and time is, as such, *still neutral* with respect to predeterminism. The mistake of scientism and its belief in predeterminism consists in overlooking this absolutely crucial fact.

Predeterminism is, in substance, identical to theological *predestination*. The mistake lies in misidentifying predetermined functions for prognostic calculations *a priori* and functions that can be known only *ex post*, empirically.

4 The view from nowhere as a divine perspective

A charitable reading of Descartes's main line of thought should reconstruct his talk about God as an expression of a holistic assessment of knowledge claims about possible worlds from a counterfactual perspective *sub specie aeternitatis*, i.e., from the fictional perspective of the end of all times. The image of God *beyond space and time* just expresses the contrast to our always internal and fallible empirical knowledge claims *in* time and space. It is, in a sense, already a version of what was later reinvented as the pixel theory of the world by Wittgenstein and David Lewis.

The "rule" that God is good rather than evil, as proposed by Descartes, just expresses the grounding fact that we can *trust* and have *faith* in our clear and distinct knowledge about generic "facts" in the world, i.e., about what we can technically achieve and predict in our canonized theories, even though there might always be *contingent* errors, exceptions, cases of *steresis* and so on. All real knowledge, even in the sciences, holds only "in principle", "in general", "ceteris paribus".

Even though the talk of a *res cogitans* and the metaphor of "internal" mental processes accompanied by (self-)consciousness as "acts" of thinking (which includes intentional "feelings" and actions, but not merely physical sensations and moods) can be misleading, Descartes is obviously reflecting on what I call *performative forms* here. Heidegger's word is "Vollzug". Such forms cannot be accounted for totally in the framework of merely *object-related* explanations. In other words, Descartes is the first to see the absolutely crucial contrast between an *object of knowledge* or belief and *being a living and thinking*, knowing and acting *being*. Heidegger later explicated this distinction between being an object and *being* (i. e., being a subject) with the label "ontological difference": the difference between "to be" and "being (an object)".

Descartes also realized before Leibniz and Hegel, and in contrast to Spinoza and La Mettrie, that self-conscious being and acting *limits* the possibility of scientific explanation insofar as doing science is itself a way of performing thinking and not just an "objective" behaviour that could be "explained" causally or mechanically in the framework of physics (in the most general version of Cartesian kinematics). As such, Descartes sees that there is a *placement problem for physics and physical mechanics* rather than a placement problem of "the mind" and "consciousness", as presented in post-Quinean Analytic Philosophy.

Hegel sees, accordingly, that it is a naive metaphysical assumption that every movement and change in the world has a sufficient *mechanical* cause. The problem of materialism or physicalism does not consist in the principle that every event in space and time must somehow relate to "matter" or "things" and that material things have parts and always move relative to some other things. It consists, rather, in the belief that "mechanical" causes, as in architectonical statics, billiard-ball kinematics and gravitational ballistics, are *sufficient* for *explaining* and *predicting all possible* events in the spatial and temporal world we live in.

Leibniz's *Monadology* can now be read as a first step towards generalizing the Cartesian insight into the contrast between being an object (of knowledge) and being a performative and (ap)perceptive centre of "subjective" world relations. Monads express at the same time the contrast between "inner" forces (abilities, perfomative forms) and "outer" behaviour as it can be observed. Performing observation thus stands in contrast to being observed, just like thinking to being thought of. The "inner" of thinking is no "outer" process inside the head as we can make it visible in MRT. Talking about the "inner" is, as Hegel sees much more clearly than his predecessors, metaphorical *and* conceptual. It refers to performative forms that we can actualize at will, as we say. Such abilities, faculties, capacities and skills are said to be "inner" in contrast to observable ("empirical") changes and movements (*post hoc, ex post* or *a posteriori*).

Another mistake, which is deep and highly general, is to confuse "explanations" with "explications". The problem is that what is logically or conceptually true goes far beyond merely formal rules for defining the use of words like "not", "and" and "for all" in sortal domains.

Talk of a Big Bang as the beginning of the physical universe is, in a sense, a merely verbal regress-stopper in response to questions of where "the world" has come from, and the traditional metaphor of God as "the Creator" had just the same function. As a result, it is just a matter of taste whether we believe in a divine creation or accept a temporal beginning of the physical, cosmological universe in which we live. Both express in the end the mere recognition of the grand fact that the world exists and that we exist in it—provided we understand the difference between talking about finite things and speculative sentences about wholes like "the world" or "all sets".[7]

5 Overcoming modal formalism

It is in any case hard to accept that the regression of many "Why?" questions comes to an end at *grand* axiomatic truths and principles, such as "Everything in the world is finite". This holds for inner-worldly objects of knowledge as well as for subjects (whether persons or animals) with finite performative attitudes towards the world. In Leibniz's model, even a monadic centre of force, a physical atom, is viewed as a "subjective" point, a "monad".

The principle "ex nihilo nihil fit" is not true, at least not if we understand the word "nothing" in a logically informed manner: The word always means "not a thing or entity of a certain limited sortal kind or species". Principles like the preservation of matter or energy are only generic and local (not holistic and total) principles "in our world". Nevertheless, principles like "no one can

---

[7] Of course, the anthropomorphic metaphor of a divine Creator and the corresponding biblical myths should not be over-interpreted and certainly not taken literally. The superstition in the different religions and religious sects and churches in this world results, as Leibniz and Hegel clearly see, from an inability to deal with metaphors when reflecting on holistic and total forms of being and thinking. However, talking about a Big Bang is also a grand metaphor.

travel into the past" or "every movement needs time" are *universal* principles. It does not make sense at all to say that they are only "empirical" truths. Even though we can "consistently" think of a being like God or angels who are *not* limited to the finitude of spatial and temporal locality, our actual and always limited way of being in the world is an absolute precondition of all possible knowledge. We share it with all other finite beings, objects and subjects in the world. In a similar way, we should just accept as a truism that there is no "eternal" matter, no "eternal" world (contra ancient and modern atomism and materialism). Not only life is finite. Every thing there is came into being and everything will totally disappear at some time.

The world as a whole is, like time and space, only the referent of a title-word. We should also not use the word "God" as a name of an *entity* and "nature" as a name of a huge "object". Nevertheless, we can say that there is only one world. Talking about possible worlds is merely a metaphor for talking about possible fictional scenarios, situation types or "possibilities" in the sense of "alternative facts".[8]

The incoherence of materialism or naturalism can now be understood quite precisely as the incoherence of mechanism. It is incoherent in the sense that it presupposes in its very formulation the performative forms of meaningful discourse. Propositions and intentional content are, however, "inner", "semantic", in a sense abstract forms, not only as objects of reflection but also as performative forms of (free) action. This is what philosophical phenomenology means when it says that intentionality and normativity cannot be explained in naturalistic terms.

The *placement problem* in modern materialism looks for a "place" for "content" or "meaning", "form" and "intention" and other "inner" or "mental" entities and processes ("events"), such as awareness and attention, pain and pleasure, in the one and only "physical" ("material", "natural") world. However, the contrast between *the whole world*, including all performances of life and nature, and the mere domain of *external objects* that are observed and talked about in mechanical physics should already make it clear that there is no way of placing

---

[8] Principles expressing the most fundamental facts, such as the directedness of time, the fact that there is no *perpetuum mobile* or that there is a limited preservation of "matter-and-energy", hold "conceptually", are "logically" true. If we do not use them in a coherent way, we are only talking about verbal "possibilities", i.e., mere "impossibilities". In other words, verbal consistence to corresponding schemes of defining sortal predicates $\psi(x)$ in some presupposed (ideal) sortal domains (mathematical models) is far from sufficient to secure the meaningfulness of a theory.

performances in acting, thinking, feeling or even enactive perceiving into the external world of merely observed objects.

The "transcendental turn" of Descartes, Kant, Leibniz and Hegel brings the absoluteness of performing performative forms to the focus of our attention. Naturalism and empiricism in the vein of Hobbes and Locke do not really understand what such a "transcendental turn" is and what is going on logically, as Hume's implicit "physiology of human understanding" still shows, and so too does Quine's theoretical conception of stimulus meanings, which, just like pure sense data, do not exist.

6 Transcendental reflections

An incorrect understanding of transcendental reflections reads them as arbitrary answers to questions of the form "What is the condition of possibility of the fact that p?" We should instead read them as attempts to make presuppositions of *any form* of knowledge claims explicit, but not from scratch, and not through a genealogical story, but in a robust sense of reflecting on the semantic and pragmatic preconditions of empirical sentences ("This is/was a P"), on conceptual inferences and generic truths ("Birds fly", "Water extinguishes fire") and on the status of reflective and speculative sentences ("Every claim and doubt presupposes the form of thinking and knowing", "God is a transcendent idea of a counterfactual perspective *sub specie aeternitatis* and defines as such the 'absolute' (i.e., non-relative) notion of non-perspectival empirical truth").

As a result, the "placement question" of how there can be consciousness and other mental phenomena in a material world is *not* a transcendental question. It asks only for a narrative story *post hoc*, starting, perhaps, with some Big Bang and the *emergence* of life and leading to the world we live in today. Elements of such a story may include the emergence of human cooperation, language, special cultures, techniques, arts and religion, and later of sciences and nation-states. But any such story presupposes, as Kant pointed out contra Herder, that we *know* that we live as thinking beings in this world.

The "explanations" given are grand stories. The traditional name for a grand story is "mythos". Cosmological science is work on a canonized mythos. It is storytelling after the events, not explaining the events causally in the mode of *causa efficiens* or "mechanical" (physical) explanations.

Efficient causes are used as a kind of "cement" in good cosmological *stories* about the universe. They are the cement of the universe itself, according to John Mackie. The world in which we live allows for some efficient causes. But it is impossible to explain all events mechanically. This is a grand truth which we have to swallow together with the fact that the form of "explaining" the world "physically" is still mechanical.

If "naturalism" means investing all possible generic causal knowledge about necessary and sometimes sufficient conditions for types of events and processes in a canonized cosmological story (and leaving arbitrary poetic metaphors like anthropomorphic gods, souls, spirits and demons out of the picture), I am a self-declared naturalist, too. The only "placement problem" for this brand of naturalism is recognizing the very fact that there is life and human action, free thinking and knowing, animal sensation and human feeling in the world at large and telling a plausible genealogical story *post hoc.*

The question of how to explain subjective awareness, sensation and emotion in a "material" ("natural") world seems to be a "hard problem" of (self-)consciousness (David Chalmers). However, it is actually a grand fact and truism that no one can get out of one's skin and walk around outside in order to look upon oneself as a mere object and not as a (sensing, feeling, and ultimately thinking and knowing) subject. There is nothing as "objective" or "true" as the tautology that *every* pro-attitude, belief, appetite, desire, knowledge claim and feeling is subjective and bound to the individual being and its peculiar perspective ("mind", "*Gemüt*", "*mens*" as the "inner" of the "monad"). In other words, there is nothing to be explained here if we look at the placing problem in the right way. What we have to explain is what "objectivity" or a "shared perspective on the world" is, if we look at it in an immanent way, and how it is constituted in contrast to the triviality that any cognitive access to the world via perception, apperception or thinking runs first through "my world". If we do not proceed in this way, we fall back into the metaphysics of looking at the world sideways on, with or without a belief in a transcendent God.

From a cognitive point of view, the path from "my world" to "the world" is constituted by a practical linguistic system of perspectival changes. We have to learn to refer in different ways from changing perspectives (places, times) to the "same" objects and the same "objective", i.e., object-related events and to coordinate our approaches to the same objects with the approaches of other persons. Merely subjective feelings, sensations and emotions, including dispositions, inclinations and pro-attitudes, are tautologically "subjective." Here there is no fixed practice of perspectival change to the same. On the contrary, it is a truism that nobody can have the sensations of other persons. Logically, this means that we do not have well-defined equivalence relations and identities together with a fixed class of predicates to talk about individual sensations or objects or entities in a semi-sortal way as we can do with regard to things and some actualizations of discernible event-types. Types of feelings and sensations, however, can be shared nevertheless, sometimes as easily as we can change places in order to change our perspective or viewpoint: Perspectival change thus frequently means simply moving to other places.

Again, we do not have to explain how subjective sensations are possible in the "material" and "objective" world, but rather how objective knowledge of objective things and events is constituted on the ground of subjective cognition, i.e., differential sensation and differentially conditioned conceptual inferences. In other words, subjective experience, expression, declaration and performance are presupposed in any human cognition. "Objective" knowledge is *generic*, general. Thus it is trivial that objective (intersubjective) knowledge does not suffice for a *full* representation of subjective cognition. On the other hand, objective knowledge cannot be attained by merely subjective cognition without language-based conceptual perspectival changes.

7 Limiting notions, reflecting the finitude of being

It is thus as naive to assume that I could attain "objective" knowledge just by "subjective" experience as to assume that anybody else could have my experience or enter into the subjective position or perspective of "my world".

Of course, "the world" can also stand for how things are for themselves independently of their relations to my, your or our cognitive access to them. However, if we abstract from all cognitive access, we cannot identify any object and its properties. This thought stands behind Kant's talk of the thing-in-itself or *Ding an sich*, which is actually not a "thing" or "object" but the whole world without any differential specification of spatially and temporally limited objects *in* the world. In other words, Kant's *Ding an sich* collapses into Spinoza's substance, which is tantamount to the whole world or God "beyond" space and time. Seen in this way, it is unsurprising that we do not "know" the thing-in-itself, or know why "it" transcends all human knowledge as well as any finite being in the world.

Talking about the *Ding an sich* as such serves only to make explicit the basic fact that our access to the world is "local", "perspectival" and "limited" to our places in space and time and to the "we" of conceptual knowers and empirical cognizers. We collectively control the perspectival changes, including the reliability and correctness of predictions.

The incoherence of a "materialist" or "objectivist" worldview ultimately consists in our confusing our *limited* objective knowledge ("about appearances", as Kant says) with counterfactual "absolute" knowledge of God as a perfect physicist *beyond* all experience, i.e., beyond any limitation of cognition by time and space. For such a God, there is no "freedom" of action because there is no "contingency". The distinction between facts *ex post* and necessities *praeter hoc* disappears. In other words, it is a conceptual triviality that a God's-eye view *destroys* the relevant distinction for any *real* human knowledge and action. The same holds for a "perfect" physicist who could predict everything in the world by means of "ideal" generic laws. This is a counterfactual assumption which is, again, only formally consistent but not coherent with basic facts about the real world.

Real knowledge and real action are *finite*, just as real things and real events in the world are finite—such that God or a perfect physicist are only *fictional entities* in *counterfactual fables* which may serve some purpose, as all fairy tales and novels do. It is not formally *inconsistent* for a person to say and "believe" they are just a "living corpse" or "complex mechanism", predetermined by the Big Bang or God, mediated by billions of still unknown facts and events in the course of evolution, just as it is not inconsistent to become a radical sceptic who no longer takes part in the human practice of making claims and giving reasons. Aristotle therefore sees that one can, in such a manner, turn oneself into a plant. But both attitudes, the mechanistic picture of self and world as well as sceptical Humeanism (in which one views oneself as an animal), are *practically incoherent* and hence "irrational", i.e., in a deep sense without "good reason".

Descartes's "ontic" belief in dualism, i.e., his talk about "substances", namely, mechanical matter and non-mechanical, non-causal thinking subjects, is certainly "false" or, rather, misleading, because there are no separate "things" (*res*) involved. Each of us is only one living and thinking being. However, he is right to distinguish between a "passive and mechanical" mode of being and a "spontaneous" mode of being, and the basis of his "proof" is legitimate, namely, that we can only reasonably and coherently understand ourselves and our claims and knowledge about the external world if we *grant* that free acts of thinking and acting are presupposed in all world-related claims, and that their very content and internal truth evaluation is still the absolute ground for any *coherent* thinking and acting. Any knowledge, any doubt and any recognition of a worldview or world-picture presupposes this, together with the absoluteness of the personal *subject*, the present "I", who I *am* and not just as an *object* of self-observation and self-referential talk and belief.

In the end, any "belief" in an unknown God, in an unknowable *Ding an sich* or "world-in-itself" beyond all phenomena and appearances, any absolute truth in this sense is incoherent, even though it is not formally inconsistent, as Leibniz and Kant clearly agree.

Traditional theology and transcendent metaphysics coincide, in a way. Both are incoherent because in their absolute perspectives they deny the basic principles of meaning that accept the finitude of any access to the world. An all-knowing God, for example, contradicts the basic facts of life and being, the temporal and spatial finitude of *everything* in a world of "becoming" (Heraclitus, Hegel) and its *continuity* (or rather contiguity, which excludes "external" intervention). The same holds for the sweeping faith in some form of a causal predetermination of all events in the world.

Obviously, the real problem of coherence is, again, the recognition of all kinds of finitudes in the world and in our knowledge (science), the understanding of the difference between: (1) empirical claims (from here and now), (2) generic knowledge and conceptual inference rules, expressed by timeless scientific sentences, (3) nominalized abstractions used in reflections on capacities and on forces and dispositions ascribed to nature, (4) speculative sentences and titles which name totalities such as "the whole world" or "nature" and, finally, (5) the crucial distinction between nature, as the topic of the natural sciences, and the whole world, which includes the performative forms of our actions and practices, "objectified" and canonically described in the institutionalized disciplines

The dichotomy of *res extensa* and *res cogitans* now turns into the contrast between the sciences and the *humanities*. The "natural sciences" only develop knowledge about what happens in the world *by itself*, i.e., without human (technical) intervention. The technical sciences, including mathematics as a technique of formal modelling and developing schematic "languages", do not describe and "explain" *nature*. As a result, the idea is incoherent that a *technical* "causa efficiens" in "mechanics" can be a "natural" cause. Mechanism is the metaphorical view of non-technical nature *as if it were* a grand *machine*, either built by a God or evolved by itself. This world-picture is obviously incoherent metaphysics, as Martin Heidegger clearly recognized, but not many have understood this yet.

References

Frege, Gottlob: "Über Begriff und Gegenstand", *Vierteljahresschrift für wissenschaftliche Philosophie* 16:2, 1892, pp.192–205; also in Frege, Gottlob: *Funktion, Begriff, Bedeutung. Fünf logische Studien*, G. Patzig (ed.), Vandenhoeck & Ruprecht, 1962, ^{5}1980.

Glock, Hans-Johann: *Was ist analytische Philosophie?*, WBG, 2014.

Husserl, Edmund: *Logische Untersuchungen, Zweiter Band, I. Teil, Gesammelte Schriften 3*, Meiner, 1992.

Lucretius Carus, Titus: *Titi Lucreti Cari, De Rerum Natura, Libri Sex*, Vol. I, H. A J. Munro (ed. and trans.), Cambridge University Press, 2009.
Otte, Michael: *Analytische Philosophie. Anspruch und Wirklichkeit eines Programms*, Meiner, 2014.
Passmore, John: *One Hundred Years of Philosophy*, Penguin, 1994.
Schrenk, Markus: *Metaphysics of Science: A Systematic and Historic Introduction*, Routledge, 2016.
Voltaire: *Les oeuvres complete de Voltaire, 32 A: Ouvres des 1750–1752*, Voltaire Foundation, 2006.
Voltaire: *Les oeuvres complete de Voltaire, 45B: Ouevres de 1753–1757*, Voltaire Foundation, 2010.

Part 2 **From Identity to Difference**

Thomas Rentsch
Three Key Hypotheses regarding Hegel and Wittgenstein

Abstract In my chapter, I focus on three systematic similarities between Wittgenstein and Hegel. These similarities are due first to the fundamental role of *the elementary propositional structure* and its status as the foundation of dialectics, second to the role of *meaning as use* and its status as the foundation of the later transcendental pragmatism, and third to Wittgenstein's *private language argument* and its anticipation by Hegel. The approach sketched here is paired with a changed understanding of philosophy, which I conceive as a model for the future. All three topics not only give an insight into an often-overlooked connection between Hegel and Wittgenstein but also—through giving a Wittgensteinian reading of Hegel and vice versa—help facilitate a better understanding of both authors.

1. The key to the philosophy of Hegel, its core in the *Phenomenology* and *Science of Logic*, is first and foremost the elementary structure of the proposition, and this propositional structure also constitutes the foundation of *dialectics*. Hegel writes that language has "the divine nature" (*göttliche Natur*) to turn opinion immediately away, namely from the *per se* singular or individual to the universal (Köhler 1998: p.8).

In this context, he analyses the basic indicators or deictic acts, and this analysis in "Sense-certainty or the 'this' and meaning something" (PS 2012: §§90 f.)[1] is also the main beginning of the *Phenomenology*. The deictic logical forms are the fundamental structure of the predicative synthesis, i.e., the proposition. With reference to Wittgenstein, it should be noted that he once considered *The Proposition* (Der Satz) as a title for the *Tractatus*. And with regard to the forefather of the *linguistic turn*, we could also ask: to what extent can the influence of Hegel's fundamental insight into the structure of the predicative synthesis already be seen in the work of Frege?

In Hegel, this basic structure of the proposition as the only possible constitution of meaning (sense and reference) leads to dialectics, because the synthesis of *universality, particularity* and *singularity* reveals its fundamental structure, i.e., this triad is the basic form of all meaning, viz. the meaning of meaning.

---

[1] "Die sinnliche Gewißheit oder das Diese und das Meinen" (PdG: p.82).

https://doi.org/10.1515/9783110572780-006

It should be further pointed out that in Hegel's analysis of sense-certainty as the immediate and fundamental transition from the singular to the universal—"this is that" (*dies ist das*)—this transition is also the primordial form of time or, as Heidegger would put it, the ecstatic structure of temporality (*Zeitigung der Zeitlichkeit*).

The present singular or individual, *the now* as such is—as I try to conceptualise it in a universal predicative manner—already in a different moment of the future, and thus simultaneously has disappeared. For Heidegger, this propositional structure sets the following form: being-ahead-of-oneself-already-in-the-world-as-being-together-with-innerworldly-encountering-beings (Heidegger 1996: p.180).[2]

It is this analysis of sense-certainty that leads Hegel from the still-static transcendental philosophy to a view that the constitution of meaning is unfolding within the world and its history: in short, it leads him from being to time.

Thus, it is also the propositional structure that enables Hegel to understand the history of religion at the very summit and centre of the revelation of the Trinitarian God as the becoming-self-aware (*Sichselbstdurchsichtigwerden*) of the human spirit. Epistemic knowledge of God is true self-knowledge. Thus, ratio (*Vernunft*) and experience of God, rationality and mysticism are fundamentally connected; absoluteness, unity and wholeness—*deus sive natura*. Ratio, religion and science—really understood and conceptualised, they form an unbreakable unity. What would it mean for the present, if this were deeply understood? I also want to point out that this thesis of the propositional structure in Hegel and Wittgenstein was already noted by Charles Taylor (1975) in his groundbreaking Hegel study, where he points to underlying conceptual similarities:

> Now Hegel's démarche in face of his conception is very similar to Wittgenstein's: He challenges sensible certainty to say what it experiences. The underlying principle is the same, viz. that if it is really knowledge then one must be able to say what it is. (Taylor 1975: p.49)

2. After this first thesis on the fundamental propositional structure, I come to the second thesis. That is: Hegel systematically anticipates the later transcendental pragmatism, and thus the thesis of *meaning as use*.

In his text about "Perceiving; or the Thing and Illusion" (PS 2018: §111) Hegel makes it clear that we are the ones who decide with our own conceptual reflec-

---

[2] "Sich-vorweg-schon-sein-in-(der-Welt-) als Sein-bei (innerweltlich begegnendem Seienden)" (Heidegger 1967: p.192).

tions about our predications' truth or untruth: the human being "differentiates its grasping the true from the untruth of its perceiving" (PS 2018: §118).[3]

> The thing is therefore in fact only white as it is brought to *our* eyes, it is *also* tart on *our* tongues, and *also* cubical to *our* feel, etc. We do not take the entire diversity of these aspects from the thing but from ourselves. To us, they come undone from each other in this way because the eye is quite distinct from the tongue, and so on. We are thus the *universal medium* [and as well] within which such moments dissociate themselves from each other, and in which each is on its own. (PS 2018: §119)[4]

Perception becomes aware that "it is not a simple, pure comprehending, but rather in its *comprehending* has at the same time taken a *reflective turn into itself from out* of the true" (PS 2018: §118).[5] That means: meaning something, sense, conception, is only possible "*out* of the True", through and with universal predicates, and this (and this is crucial) is a human activity based on reflection and the concrete use of language with its claims of truth. If we analyse (for example, following Klaus Düsing 1998: p.154) the function of subjectivity in Hegel's logic, the systematic connection between meaning and use becomes obvious. In the *Jena Lectures* of 1805–6 (JL), Hegel puts this basic insight in a particularly pointed way, writing that the "copula" in the proposition—as the connecting element—is the "I" (JL: p.95, n.26). So if *I* am the copula then it is *me* who *uses* it in thinking and speaking. And equally in the *Phenomenology*, while clarifying the relation of the singular individual being to the world of science, Hegel points clearly to this insight into *meaning as use* (see Weisser-Lohmann 1998: pp.185–210). The *Phenomenology* is about the knowing knowledge and its *exemplary experiences*, which have to *appear as independent forms* (see ibid.: p.186).

---

3 "*unterscheidet sein Auffassen des Wahren von der Unwahrheit seines Wahrnehmens*" (PdG: p. 99).
4 "*Dies Ding ist also in der Tat nur weiß,* an unser *Auge gebracht, scharf* auch, *an* unsere *Zunge,* auch *kubisch, an* unser *Gefühl usf. Die gänzliche Verschiedenheit dieser Seiten nehmen wir nicht aus / dem Dinge, sondern aus uns; sie fallen uns an unserem von der Zunge ganz unterschiedenen Auge usf. so auseinander. Wir sind somit das* allgemeine Medium *[als Auch], worin solche Momente sich absondern und für sich sind.*" (PdG: p.99)
5 "*Es hat sich hiermit für das Bewußtsein bestimmt, wie sein Wahrnehmen wesentlich beschaffen ist, nämlich nicht ein einfaches reines Auffassen, sondern* in seinem Auffassen zugleich aus dem Wahren *heraus in sich reflektiert zu sein. Diese Rückkehr des Bewußtseins in sich selbst, die sich in das reine Auffassen unmittelbar – denn sie hat sich als dem Wahrnehmen wesentlich gezeigt – einmischt, verändert das Wahre.*" (PdG: p.98)

> The individual has the right to demand that science provide him at least with the ladder to reach this standpoint. The individual's right is based on his absolute self-sufficiency, which he knows he possesses in every shape of his knowing (PS 2018: §26).[6]

In other words, without my *self-sufficient* use of language, there will be no science, and no truth claims. And, of course, for Wittgenstein the image of the ladder also plays a central role.

That at the centre of all reason, reflection and science must be the mediation of the *universal*, the *particular* and the *singular*, was already essential for Hegel's, Schelling's and Hölderlin's reception of Kant as students in the Tübingen seminary. They recognised a gradual radicalisation of Kant's reflection on the status of the *synthesis a priori* from the first to the second to the third critique, the *Critique of Judgment*, in which that radicalisation culminates and this mediation becomes the centre of reason and reflection. Likewise, it should be noted that historically the foundations of transcendental pragmatics came via reception of Kant and Hegel from Peirce to Apel and so back to Habermas. It is moreover possible that Hegel's approach was also known to Wittgenstein via Russell and C. D. Broad, who both developed their approaches against the (at the time strong) background of British Hegelianism.[7] Wittgenstein's years of intensive engagement with Kierkegaard are well known, and Kierkegaard's existential dialectics cannot be understood without Hegel. We are the ones who constitute meaning and sense; nobody can take that away from us whether we like it or not. And we accomplish this, in all ordinariness, at any time, whether we are aware of it or not. It belongs to the linguistic constitution of meaning. That Hegel's claim to absoluteness of reason has nothing to do with a superficial romanticising rationalism cannot be underlined enough. For Wittgenstein's ordinary-language approach, this is clear anyway. Nevertheless, Hegel emphasises: *we are the copula*.

3. After the *elementary structure of the proposition* and *meaning as use*, I come to the third thesis: namely, that the private language argument can be found in Hegel. In central passages of the *Phenomenology*, Hegel analyses the constitutively intersubjective structure of self-consciousness, which he also

---

6 "*Umgekehrt hat das Individuum das Recht zu fordern, daß die Wissenschaft ihm die Leiter wenigstens zu diesem Standpunkte reiche, ihm in ihm selbst denselben aufzeige. Sein Recht gründet sich auf seine absolute Selbständigkeit, die es in jeder Gestalt seines Wissens zu besitzen weiß; denn in jeder – sei sie von der Wissenschaft anerkannt oder nicht, und der Inhalt sei welcher er wolle – ist es die absolute Form, d. h. es ist die* unmittelbare Gewißheit *seiner selbst und, wenn dieser Ausdruck vor/gezogen würde, damit unbedingtes* Sein." (PdG: pp.29–30; see Weisser-Lohmann 1998: p.187)

7 See Alexander Berg's chapter in the present volume.

calls—anticipating Honneth—the "movement of recognition". The notion of *self-consciousness* (PS 2012: §26) leads to the structure of the *spirit* (Geist), and this is precisely the common self-consciousness in which individual subjects ("various self-consciousnesses") can develop in "their complete freedom and self-sufficiency, namely, in the oppositions of the various self-consciousnesses" (PS 2018: §177). The unity of "The *I* that is *we* and the *we* that is *I*" (ibid.)[8] leads in later passages to the analysis of the modes of recognition [*Erkennungsmodi*] in law, religion, politics and philosophy. Hegel is thus saying: precisely the highly individuated aspect of the singular self-consciousness, including its highly individual freedom and independence, precisely this highly "private" dimension, is only understandable and graspable at all if it is constitutively intersubjective.

The intersubjective structure of the singular self-consciousness is therefore constitutive of this—I am we, and we are I. A private language argument *par excellence*. And, most importantly, this analysis of constitutive intersubjectivity, of the social nature of self-consciousness, leads precisely to central parts of Hegelian philosophy, to the *philosophy of right*, to *politics* and finally to the *world history of reason*. These analyses are paradigmatically substantiated by passages that have become classic, such as those on the struggle between master and slave. In my terminology, these are *interexistential analyses*, because in them it becomes unambiguously clear that and how linguistically and practically constituted social interaction precedes all private and subjective, even the most intimate, human possibilities. This applies as well to all forms of *ethical life* (*Sittlichkeit*) that Hegel paradigmatically introduces. The recognition of the "we" in the "I" and the "I" in the "we", in accordance with the concept of the spirit in the *Phenomenology*, is always a necessary condition (Siep 1998: pp.122f.). The analyses of recognition from his Jena period already deepen and clarify Hegel's critique of subjectivism by working out the affective, the emotive, the cognitive and finally the institutionalised modes of recognition and mutual respect. While Habermas and Honneth argue that Hegel later abandons this early intersubjectiv approach, I agree with Siep, who rightly insists that Hegel understands the notion of the spirit (*Geist*) precisely "as a 'we' within which individuals become independent" (ibid.: p.125). The motion of recognition itself then contains all the structural elements of the conception of recognition in the earlier writings (see ibid.: pp.125f.).

---

[8] "Indem ein Selbstbewußtsein der Gegenstand ist, ist er ebensowohl Ich wie Gegenstand. – Hiermit ist schon der Begriff des *Geistes* für uns vorhanden. Was für das Bewußtsein weiter wird, ist die Erfahrung, was der Geist ist, diese absolute Substanz, welche in der vollkommenen Freiheit und Selbständigkeit ihres Gegensatzes, nämlich verschiedener für sich seiender Selbstbewußtsein[e], die Einheit derselben ist; *Ich, das Wir*, und *Wir, das Ich* ist." (PdG: p.145)

Hegel's manifold analyses of language, work and family testify and confirm his fundamental insight into the primarily social, intersubjective constitution of all subjectivity, privacy and individuality.

I now come to a brief conclusion. The three systematic theses undoubtedly touch on core notions or basic insights with which Wittgenstein is closely identified—the *structure of the proposition*, the analysis of *meaning as use* and the *private language argument*—and rightly so, because it was thanks to Wittgenstein's work that the linguistic turn became *the* paradigm shift of the 20th century. Falling behind the linguistic turn has since become impossible in systematic philosophical reflection.

Nevertheless, according to my analysis, these basic insights, upon closer inspection, are constitutive of Hegel's overall system and its foundations. To show this precisely and in detail, and to make it explicit in subtle individual interpretations, is an extensive research project, and the fact that aspects of these similarities in Wittgenstein's and Hegel's approaches have already been recognised is shown, among other things, by the work of Charles Taylor, whose remarks already convincingly confirm the approach discussed in this volume.

Following my theses, it still remains to be shown that and how the three basic insights in Hegel's approach work together and enable his comprehensive overall system. This applies especially to the foundations of dialectics and their mediation of universal, particular and singular as well as to the structure of the proposition in the *Science of Logic*.

This applies to the theory of *meaning as use* and the criticism of the picture theory with regard to Hegel's reception of Kant and his analysis of pragmatic forms of the constitution of meaning at all levels, for example in regard to *work*, *struggle* and *communication* and to all forms of social interaction. And finally, it applies to the private language argument with regard to Hegel's analysis of the foundations of the constitution of the world, starting from sense-certainty before extending to family, law, state and science and eventually to religion, theology and philosophy. All of these forms of practice are from a private and subjective point of view completely incomprehensible, as Hegel explicitly states. And furthermore, these basic insights make it possible to rationally reconstruct even the main proclamations of Christian religion and theology, and in regard to world history to trace them back to authentic human practices. In this way, world history is comprehensible as a history of reason, and this, it should be emphasised, precisely in Hegel's analysis, even considering all setbacks and catastrophic aberrations, all concrete negativity, which Hegel does not deny in the slightest.

The systematic interaction of the three basic insights can also briefly be sketched in the light of Hegel's thinking. Without the use of propositions, no constitution of conceptual meaning is possible at all. However—thus the basic insight of the dialectic—isolated proposition in itself is almost nothing. Only in the context of the use of many propositions, each in turn with their own specific contexts, only in such circumstances can propositions be understood and used meaningfully. And only thus does the pragmatic constitution of meaning enable all inter- and trans-subjective forms of life and practice, all forms of community spirit and social institutions.

These three primal phenomena of human practice all reciprocally enable each other, are irreducible to, inseparable from, each other—they are equiprimordial (*gleichursprünglich*). Hegel's dialectics reconstructs and unfolds this equiprimordiality.

It should also be noted that Hegel's core theses can only be precisely understood if they are deliberately read through the eyes of Wittgenstein. Then, in my view, their meaning for Hegel's dialectics and his entire system becomes very obvious, and this can be shown and reconstructed even without reference to anything external to Hegel's work, precisely through Hegel's many important singular analyses.

Finally, the approach sketched here is paired with a changed understanding of philosophy, which I conceive as a model for the future. The change pertains in particular to our understanding of the many philosophical schools and approaches. In many philosophical histories these schools and approaches seem almost like large objectifiable blocks or chunks, like giant, solid structures. And these structures seem to be extremely helpful at first; and so, of course, philosophers call themselves Kantians, Hegelians, Marxists and so forth. And yet on closer inspection, this view is very misleading, because it underestimates the complex internal differentialism, the internal complexity of philosophical reflection, its—as Hegel would put it—*inner-infinity*, or—as Wittgenstein would say—its indeterminability (*Unabschließbarkeit*). All reductionisms, isms and simplifications at this level eventually result in ideologies. In order to avoid these simplifications from the outset, a systematic linkage to Wittgenstein's complex analysis of language-games and, in particular, family resemblance is required. As an example, just consider Kant. His theories cannot be understood without a reception of both Leibniz-Wolff's metaphysics and Hume's empiricism.

Since the beginning of my work on *Heidegger and Wittgenstein* (Rentsch 2003), my aim has been to overcome the pernicious and misleading division into analytic and continental philosophy with which I had to grow up. By contrast, Wittgenstein is concerned with a systematic elaboration of differentialism as critical hermeneutics.[9]

---

[9] Translated from the German by Alexander Berg.

References

Düsing, Klaus: "Der Begriff der Vernunft in Hegels Phänomenologie", in: Köhler and Pöggeler 1998: pp.145–164.
Heidegger, Martin: *Sein und Zeit*, Max Niemeyer, 1967.
Heidegger, Martin: *Being and Time*, Joan Stambaugh (trans.), State University of New York Press, 1996.
Köhler, Dietmar and Pöggeler, Otto (eds.): *Georg Wilhelm Friedrich Hegel, Phänomenologie des Geistes. Klassiker Auslegen*, vol. 16, Akademie Verlag, 1998.
Köhler, Dietmar and Pöggeler, Otto: "Einführung", in: Köhler and Pöggeler 1998: pp.1–34.
Rentsch, Thomas: *Heidegger und Wittgenstein: Existential- und Sprachanalysen zu den Grundlagen philosophischer Anthropologie*, Klett-Cotta, 2003.
Siep, Ludwig: "Die Bewegung des Anerkennens in Hegels *Phänomenologie des Geistes*", in: Köhler and Pöggeler 1998: pp.109–130.
Taylor, Charles: *Hegel*, Cambridge University Press, 1975.
Weisser-Lohmann, Elisabeth: "Gestalten nicht des Bewusstseins, sondern einer Welt – Überlegungen zum Geist-Kapitel der Phänomenologie des Geistes", in: Köhler and Pöggeler 1998: pp.185–210.

Tom Rockmore
Wittgenstein, Hegel and Cognition

Abstract Philosophy is often thought to deal with problems, enigmas or conundra it seeks to answer, for instance through a theory. Wittgenstein and Hegel both challenge this view in different ways. Wittgenstein can be understood as passing through two main phases. In an initial phase, he proposes a view that presupposes a conception of language he later rejects. In a later phase, he rejects his earlier theory and philosophy in all its forms. In other words, after the effective refutation of what he earlier thought was the only approach, he drew the conclusion that there was no longer any possibly valid approach. This suggests the only possible result is skepticism, not about knowledge but rather about philosophy as a source of knowledge. In this sense, Wittgenstein suggests that in his later thought he brings philosophy to a skeptical end. In comparison to Wittgenstein, Hegel has a less extreme view. He neither claims to formulate the only possible approach to knowledge, hence to bring the tradition to an end, nor that philosophy ends in skepticism. He rather vindicates the Parmenidean approach that we are justified in claiming to know that knowledge is possible within the limits of the identity of thought and being.

This paper provides some preliminary remarks on the nature and significance of the difference between Wittgenstein and Hegel. One way to depict the difference is with respect to the philosophical tradition that Hegel is sometimes thought to bring to a high point and to an end, and that for Wittgenstein is widely believed to rest on the misuse of language.

Wittgenstein and Hegel are related within the wider philosophical discussion of knowledge, which they approach from incompatible perspectives. Now the problem of knowledge can be understood in different ways that count as alternatives to a basic understanding of the problem. Parmenides, the pre-Socratic, influentially suggests that thought and being are the same. This claim, which echoes through the entire later tradition, can be interpreted in at least three main ways: as metaphysical realism, or the view that we must know the mind-independent real as a condition of knowledge; as epistemic constructivism, or the idea that we do not and cannot know the mind-independent real since we know only what we in some sense construct; and as epistemic skepticism, or some form of the Socratic thesis that we know only that we do not know.

The approach to cognition through metaphysical realism runs from pre-Socratic thought through the entire tradition right up to the present. In the modern

https://doi.org/10.1515/9783110572780-007

tradition, the emergence of epistemic constructivism creates an ongoing debate between metaphysical realism, or the claim to know mind-independent reality, and epistemic constructivism, or the rival claim to know only human reality. This debate, which is contained within the single position of Kant, who at different periods defends both claims, continues in Wittgenstein and Hegel.

On "idealism"

Since Hegel is an idealist and Wittgenstein is an analytic thinker, it will be helpful to begin with remarks on "idealism" and "analytic philosophy". These terms refer to broad philosophical movements that, perhaps unlike political movements, rarely if ever exhibit more than general cohesion. Both are misunderstood but in different ways. So-called idealism is misunderstood at least since Kant. The latter, who was annoyed by the description of the critical philosophy as a higher form of Berkeleyanism, objected strongly to the supposedly idealist views of Descartes and above all Berkeley.

"Idealism" is neither often studied nor well understood. Few observers are now willing to lay claim to idealism whose rejection is one of the founding acts of analytic philosophy. Ancient idealism, for instance Platonism, differs from modern idealism that, depending on how it is understood, includes perhaps Descartes and certainly Berkeley, then the German idealists (Kant, Fichte, Schelling and Hegel), perhaps Marx, more recently Rescher and others. Modern idealists apparently share two characteristics: a turn away from metaphysical realism, hence a rejection of a claim to grasp what is variously designated as the mind-independent real, reality, or the world, as well as the turn toward a constructivist approach to cognition. I come back to that point below.

Kant, who claims to be an idealist, is routinely understood as a pre-idealist thinker who intervenes in the debate before the rise of German idealism, which is post-Kantian. In the *Prolegomena*, he responds to the supposed conflation between his view and Berkeley's. According to Kant, idealism concerns the "sensuous representation of things" (Kant 1950: p.41). He distances himself from the problem of the existence of things, or in effect a form of solipsism, which he identifies as ordinary idealism. More than a century later, G. E. Moore (1903: pp.433–453), without reference to a single position, takes the denial of the existence of the external world, which no thinker who is identified as an idealist suggests, as the criterion of idealism.

Further according to Kant, Berkeley holds that knowledge through the senses and experience is sheer illusion (Kant 1950: p.123). Kant, on the contrary, holds that knowledge based either on the pure understanding or on pure reason is illusory, since truth is limited to experience (ibid.).

The point at issue is important. Berkeley, who is a skeptic, thinks we cannot reach knowledge through the senses, that is, empirically. Kant, who rejects skepticism, denies we can reach knowledge through either the understanding or reason, but rather can and do reach knowledge through experience. "All knowledge of things merely from pure understanding or pure reason is nothing but sheer illusion, and only in experience is there truth" (ibid.). According to Kant, knowledge is not a posteriori but a priori. He suggests that critical idealism, which he favors, differs from other forms in grasping "the possibility of our a priori knowledge of objects of experience" (ibid.: p.124, n.3).

On "analytic philosophy"

So-called Anglo-American analytic philosophy is also supposedly misunderstood. In a recent book, a series of authors react against a so-called narrow-minded, but still popular, conception of analytic philosophy based on a simplistic interpretation of the revolt against idealism, then the linguistic turn, and finally the neo-positivist rejection of metaphysics. According to this book, this view of the origin and nature of analytic philosophy does not withstand closer historical scrutiny. This is the central message that the present collection wants to get across (see Preston 2017).

This three-fold approach to analytic philosophy requires further qualification. If Kant is an idealist, then he espouses a form of idealism and the revolt against idealism in general could not have been begun by him. At most he rejects specific kinds of idealism associated, for instance, with Descartes and Berkeley. After Hegel passed from the scene in 1831, the return to Kant mediated through the writings of Liebmann and others, and the rise of neo-Kantian schools in Germany was not the beginning of an attack on idealism in general. It was rather an attack on the idealist views of Fichte and Hegel, especially the latter, in the course of a generalized return to Kant.

At least some analytic thinkers are open to idealism in whole or in part. Frege, who according to Dummett is the founding father of analytic philosophy, admired Kant and, according to Sluga, should perhaps be understood as an idealist (see Sluga 1980). The full-fledged analytic revolt against idealism that began around the turning of the twentieth century was at least as much, and perhaps more, a revolt against then widespread British idealism as against idealism.

Metaphysics is not the whole of philosophy. The rejection of metaphysics through the Vienna Circle positivists is linked to their resolute emphasis on empiricism as the only legitimate source of knowledge. This rejection is not, however, characteristic of analytic philosophy. It is absent, for instance, in Wittgenstein. The term "metaphysics" only appears in passing three times in the *Tractatus Logico-Philosophicus*. Many observers think the *Tractatus* shows how to apply logic through language to metaphysics. In *Philosophical Investigations* the later Wittgenstein is not concerned with rejecting metaphysics but rather with rejecting, or at least criticizing, traditional philosophy.

The most likely candidate for the central thrust of analytic philosophy lies in the linguistic turn. The mature Russell takes this view as a defining characteristic of philosophy. In remarks on Parmenides in *A History of Western Philosophy*, he describes the latter's poem, *On Nature*, in writing: "This is the first example in philosophy of an argument from thought and language to the world at large." (Russell 1945: p.140) For a certain period, analytic philosophy was understood by both its practitioners and critics as based on linguistic analysis. Gellner (1959), an early, staunch critic of analytic philosophy, understood it in this way. Rorty apparently coined the phrase "linguistic turn" and put together an influential anthology with that title. Yet at roughly the same time that some were celebrating what Quine described as "semantic ascent" (1980: p.249), others, such as Rorty's former Princeton colleague, Gilbert Harman (1977: pp.vii–ix), were denying that philosophy consists in the analysis of language. Rorty himself rapidly abandoned analytic philosophy in turning toward pragmatism.

Kant, metaphysical realism and epistemic constructivism

The difficulty in formulating a general definition of either "idealism" or "analytic philosophy" suggests both terms are better understood not in isolation but rather within the context of Western philosophy.

Kant, whose position evolves, features representationalism in the form of metaphysical realism, at least into the beginning of the critical period, and anti-representational constructivism later on. Representationalism, which presupposes metaphysical realism, is any form of the view that knowledge requires correct representation or knowing things in themselves whose possibility Kant later denies. There are different kinds of realism. Metaphysical realism is the view that there is a way the world is and that under the right conditions we know it as it is. From the dawn of the Western tradition until the present a long succession of thinkers has argued in favour of knowledge of the world, reality, or the mind-independent real.

Though a promising argument for representationalism has never been formulated, this approach continues to attract attention. If representationalism is the best epistemic theory, then constructivism is the second-best epistemic theory. Epistemic constructivism presupposes the failure of epistemic representationalism.

Constructivism arises in ancient Greek geometry and comes into modern philosophy through Francis Bacon, Hobbes, Vico, and others leading up to and then away from Kant. Constructivists, who are sceptical about knowledge of the world, think we only know what we in some sense construct, while differing about what that means.

Kant (1998: B xxvi-xxvii; p.115) distinguishes between a cause and its effect. He holds that, on causal grounds, if there is an appearance, then something appears. Like Plato, Kant denies the backward inference from effect to cause. Further like Plato, Kant holds that it does not follow that if something appears, we know the cause. Since, according to Kant, we cannot infer backward from the appearance, or the effect, to the cause, we do not and cannot know the thing in itself or noumenon.

Representationalism and constructivism are incompatible. In different phases of his development Kant is a representationalist or a constructivist. Representationalism is arguably the main modern approach to knowledge. At the dawn of modern philosophy Descartes claims we can infer backward from clear and distinct ideas, which correctly represent the world, to the world. According to Locke complex ideas, which can be false, are composed of simple ideas that cannot be false and must be true. Locke believes that the ideas in the mind match up one to one with world.

Kant initially favors a representationalist approach to cognition before later changing his mind. It is only later during his critical period that he comes to realize that we cannot correctly infer from the appearance to what it represents and representation cannot be defined. Kant's so-called Copernican Revolution is an effort to avoid epistemic scepticism since he cannot know the world in claiming to know the human world. Since this view is well known, we can go quickly here.

Suffice it to say that the Copernican Revolution, which is often mentioned but rarely studied, consists in two main claims. First, we cannot and do not know the world. According to Kant, on the assumption that the subject depends on the object there has been no progress in knowing at all. In other words, we do not and cannot know independent objects. Though Kant is in principle an a priori thinker, his claim that we cannot correctly represent the world is not a priori but rather a posteriori, hence based on experience. Second, he suggests that, instead of assuming that the subject depends on the object, we should assume that the object depends on the subject.

Hegel and historical constructivism

Wittgenstein, who only occasionally mentions others, is akin to a planet whirling in its own orbit. Unlike Wittgenstein, who refuses the customary distinction between philosophy and the history of philosophy, Hegel works out his theories against the background of the entire philosophical tradition.

For present purposes, it will be sufficient to reconstruct Hegel's view in terms of two crucial texts: the *Differenzschrift* in which in considering the contemporary debate he for the first time sketches the outlines of a position with respect to Kant and the philosophical tradition, and the *Phenomenology of Spirit* in which he describes an original approach to cognition.

The young Hegel is, like the young Wittgenstein, committed to a strongly systematic approach. According to Hegel, philosophy originates in difference (*Differenz*). His position originates in the aptly named *The Difference Between Fichte's and Schelling's System of Philosophy*, or so-called *Differenzschrift*. This text has a two-fold role in Hegel's writings as an opportunity for the first time to react to the main thinkers of the day as well as an occasion to state a certain number of ideas he later develops into his distinctive position. Here, at the turning of the nineteenth century he surveys the immediate post-Kantian reaction to the critical philosophy through remarks on various forms of contemporary philosophy. He is especially interested in Fichte, Schelling and Reinhold. In Kant's wake, Fichte was the leading contemporary thinker. Schelling was at the time Hegel's patron as well as a Fichtean prior to the break between them. Reinhold was in Hegel's view the leading contemporary non-philosopher. The pretext for this text is Reinhold's conflation of the views of Fichte and Schelling.

Here as elsewhere Hegel typically reacts to other thinkers while simultaneously pointing to ideas he will later develop. In the short preface, Hegel immediately turns to the difference between what he depicts as the speculative spirit and the dogmatic letter of the critical philosophy. According to Hegel, Kant relies on things in themselves that have no content and categories that are mere "static, dead pigeonholes of the intellect" (D: p.80). They are incapable of expressing the Absolute itself, or Spinoza's substance. Unlike Reinhold, who makes a return to the conception of philosophy as logic, Kant, Fichte, Schelling and Hegel are at least in principle if not in reality to be understood as speculative thinkers. "The principle of speculation is the identity of subject and object" (ibid.). Though a speculative thinker, Kant, who merely inverts the relation of reason and the understanding, does not reach the level of genuine speculation. In the deduction of the categories the critical philosophy is true idealism that is only accomplished for the first time by Fichte.

Hegel immediately turns from Kant to his contemporaries Fichte, Schelling and Reinhold. He treats Fichte and Schelling as further milestones on the road to philosophy worthy of the name that is simply absent in the Reinhold's view. Hegel's remarks on Fichte and Schelling characterize them as respectively subjective and objective idealists and his own view as absolute idealism. Fichte's principle is Ego = Ego (D: p.81). But, since he "surrenders" reason to the understanding, his principle of the subject-object turns out to be subjective. Schelling improves on Fichte in two ways: he invents an objective subject-object, or objective idealism, and he unites both of them in something higher than either.

If we reflect now on Hegel's intention, we see that he is concerned with the ancient problem of the unity of thought and being in its Kantian and post-Kantian forms. This problem, which originates in ancient Greece, more specifically in Parmenides' claim for the unity of thought and being, reaches a new level in Kant's Copernican turn. Modern philosophy exhibits a renewed speculative series of efforts to demonstrate the unity of subject and object, or thought and being. According to Hegel, Kant points toward but fails to reach genuine speculation. It is also not reached by such post-Kantians as Fichte and Schelling. Though original thinkers, Fichte's and Schelling's views belong to the Kantian system, on which Hegel further builds in his approach to cognition.

Hegel on speculative constructivism

In the *Differenzschrift* where he studies a series of recent reactions to the critical philosophy, Hegel is mainly concerned with post-Kantian figures, above all Fichte. The latter is the crucial mediating figure between Kant, whose position he claims to understand better than its author, and Schelling, who at the time understood himself as Fichte's disciple. In the Introduction to the *Phenomenology*, Hegel returns to Kant in describing a general approach to knowledge he then works out in a series of chapters. In the *Differenzschrift*, Hegel claims that Kant should be understood as interested in, but failing to formulate, a speculative theory of knowledge. In the Introduction to Hegel comes back to Kant in formulating a speculative approach to cognition presumably intended to correct the shortcomings of the critical philosophy. In his remarks, Kant's position a priori, asocial, ahistorical approach to cognition is transformed into an a posteriori, social, and historical approach to cognition.

Hegel begins the Introduction in revising and restating his view of Kant in the *Differenzschrift*. After describing Kant's theory of cognition, Hegel turns to describing his own rival conception of knowledge. Since this passage is extremely dense, and the translation is at the limit of being acceptable, it will be useful to paraphrase.

Hegel's account of the critical philosophy is intended to show that it is in principle impossible in calling for its replacement by a successor theory. Everyone knows that Kant is an a priori thinker concerned to identify the conditions of knowledge in general and to avoid skepticism. According to Hegel, it is natural to assume that cognition is either an instrument or medium to get hold of the absolute, or what is, also known as the real, reality, or the world. Hegel confronts the Kantian approach in the first sentence in writing: "It is a natural assumption that in philosophy, before we start to deal with its proper subject-matter, viz. the actual cognition of what truly is, one must first of all come to an understanding about cognition, which is regarded either as the instrument to get hold of the Absolute, or as the medium through one discovers it." (PS 1977: §73; p.46)

According to Hegel, the very project is suspect for various reasons he quickly reviews. We might, for instance, select the wrong form of cognition. Second, if cognition is an instrument, it might "reshape" and "alter" the Absolute it seeks to know. If it is a medium, it is possible that truth comes to us only as it exists in the medium. Nor would an acquaintance with the instrument do more than bringing us back to the starting point. And finally, it would not help us if we knew and subtracted from the result "the of its refraction" since it is what we do not subtract that is cognition.

This line of argument has two crucial results. Though it is theoretically plausible to isolate the conditions of knowledge from knowledge, this turns out to be impossible in practice. Yet although Kant takes the critical philosophy to be the only path to knowledge, its failure of the critical philosophy need not lead to skepticism about which we should be skeptical.

Hegel's positive argument for knowledge, which is only rarely examined, can now be stated in outline form as follows. Like Kant, Hegel thinks knowledge requires experience. Unlike Kant, he holds that knowledge is not all or nothing but rather an ongoing process of historical approximation. Later theories improve on earlier theories. According to Hegel, knowledge is stated in the form of a relation between thought and being, concept and object. A concept [Begriff] is a theory about knowledge formulated on the basis of experience and then tested against further experience.

Now there are only two possible results of the evaluation of a theory. Either the concept survives the test of experience and the process ends temporarily, [though. If] or, on the contrary, it fails the test of experience, [it] and needs to be reformulated in a stronger theory that explains everything the early theory explained but at least one thing it ought to explain.

Consider, as an example, the oddly shaped orbit of Mercury that results in what is called the precession of the perihelion. Newtonian mechanics that is intended to describe the planetary orbits is unable to do so for Mercury, whose orbit is explained by general relativity theory. It follows that relativity theory is comparatively stronger than Newtonian mechanics.

The cognitive process is not ahistorical but intrinsically historical. There is no way to know how our cognitive views relate to world, no way to know if as is sometimes said we are justified in dreaming of a final theory. Our views that are formulated on the basis of available experience are in principle never beyond the possibility of later change. In other words, we think out of and never go beyond the present historical moment.

The early Wittgenstein and cognitive representationalism

After these remarks on Hegel, we come now to Wittgenstein, a very different thinker. Hegel is an historical epistemic constructivist. Wittgenstein is on the contrary not a constructivist but either a metaphysical realist or an epistemic skeptic.

Wittgenstein sketches a version of Parmenides' effort to overcome the cognitive problem through metaphysical realism, or knowledge of the world, in his early view. In his introduction to the *Tractatus Logico-Philosophicus* Russell describes Wittgenstein as showing what is in common between the fact and the picture providing an extra-linguistic account of knowledge of the world. As described by Russell, Wittgenstein's early theory is a highly original form of the traditional philosophical effort to cognize reality.

According to Russell, Wittgenstein is concerned with ignorance of symbolism and misuse of language, especially the way in which one fact, e.g., a sentence, is a symbol for another. He claims Wittgenstein is concerned with conditions for a perfect language, including meaning and reference based on something they have in common between the structure of the sentence and of the fact. What they have in common cannot be said but only be shown to have the same structure.

In the TLP, Wittgenstein begins with the view that we make to ourselves pictures of facts, which share with facts the form of representation. A logical picture of a fact has an identity of logical form (or *Gedanke*) that corresponds or fails to correspond, hence is true or false. Facts make the propositions true or false. Wittgenstein, like Kant, believes, or at least believed in his early phase, that there are final answers to philosophical questions. According to Wittgenstein, who believes that the problems of philosophy derive from misunderstanding the logic of language, his early view described in the TLP is the final, supposedly unrevisable solution of the problems discussed.

The later Wittgenstein and cognitive representationalism

In *Philosophical Investigations* the later Wittgenstein rejects the view of the early Wittgenstein in the TLP about the definitive status of his earlier view in the course of rejecting philosophy in all its many forms. The early view was based on a particular conception of language. In his later work, specifically in PI, he puts forth the view that conceptual confusions surrounding the use of language are at the root of most philosophical problems, contradicting or discarding much of what he argued in his earlier work. In the Preface to PI, Wittgenstein states that, as it is sometimes put, his new view is best understood against the background of his old thoughts in the TLP. Wittgenstein now gives up his hyper-systematic, quasi-deductive earlier approach for a new approach traversing the conceptual domain in all directions.

He is especially interested in working out a new view of language. It is as if Wittgenstein came to realize that his philosophical approach in the early work depended on an unexamined, mistaken conception of language that he subjects to deep criticism in his later work. The correct relation between the early and the later view is unclear and controversial. One way to regard the relation between the early and the later works is that in the latter Wittgenstein gives up the idealized picture of a perfect language that Russell thought was central in for that reason abandoning the claims to show the relation between words and fact that now simply vanishes. In moving from the logical use of language to an account of ordinary language, he now turns to new ideas such as family resemblance and language games.

PI begins with a passage from Augustine's *Confessions* that provides a particular, but, according to the later Wittgenstein, mistaken view of language as a vehicle for representation. According to Wittgenstein, the traditional view of language described by Augustine is based on the idea that the words in language name objects and sentences are combinations of such names. Wittgenstein believes that the mistaken view of language as representation that underlies his early work is assumed throughout philosophy.

According to Wittgenstein, Augustine's *Confessions* "give[s] us a particular picture of the essence of human language," based on the idea that "the words in language name objects," and that "sentences are combinations of such names" (PI: §1). Despite its plausibility, this reduction of language to representation cannot do justice to the whole of human language; and even if it is to be considered a picture of only the representative function of human language, it is, as such, a poor picture.

Wittgenstein now proceeds to sketch a new view of language based on meaning in use and language games. According to Wittgenstein, the meaning of a word is its use in a language (PI: §43) that basically differs from the traditional essentialist approach. Wittgenstein is supposed to have had this insight while watching a football game. In football and other games, the meaning of the various actions resembles a so-called language-game, since language has meaning in context and not otherwise. Language games belong to what Wittgenstein now calls a form of life. Wittgenstein's anti-systematic view in PI takes an anti-philosophical form arising because 'I don't know my way about.'" (PI: §123), and enigmatically suggesting that the aim of philosophy is "to show the fly the way out of the fly-bottle" (PI: §309). Wittgenstein thinks that philosophy leaves everything, including language, in the world as it is (PI: §124).

Now philosophical problems are stated in order to be solved, resolved or otherwise overcome. One consequence of this new view is that what earlier seemed to be a philosophical problem no longer is one. The proper attitude to problems is no longer the same, since, as he puts it, "philosophical problems should *completely* disappear" (PI: §133).

The early view of language relies on definite reference to overcome philosophical problems. According to this view, which Wittgenstein now restates, every word has a meaning. This meaning is correlated with the word, which is the object for which the word stands. After sketching this early view, Wittgenstein sets out throughout the rest of the book to demonstrate the limitations of this conception in identifying many traditional philosophical puzzles and confusions to which it leads.

In PI §23, he points out that the practice of human language is more complex than the simplified views of language held by those who seek to explain or simulate human language by means of a so-called formal system. In criticizing his formal view, Wittgenstein now thinks it would be a disastrous mistake to see language as being in any way analogous to formal logic.

Conclusion: Hegel, Wittgenstein, and cognition

Philosophy is often thought to deal with problems, enigmas or conundra it seeks to answer, for instance through a theory. Wittgenstein and Hegel both challenge this view in different ways. Wittgenstein can be understood as passing through two main phases. In an initial phase, he proposes a view that presupposes a conception of language he later rejects. In a later phase, he rejects his earlier theory and philosophy in all its forms. In other words, after the effective refutation of what he earlier thought was the only approach, he drew the conclusion that there was no longer any possibly valid approach. This suggests the only possible result is skepticism, not about knowledge but rather about philosophy as a source of knowledge. In this sense, Wittgenstein suggests that in his later thought he brings philosophy to a skeptical end.

In comparison to Wittgenstein, Hegel has a less extreme view. He neither claims to formulate the only possible approach to knowledge, hence to bring the tradition to an end, nor that philosophy ends in skepticism. He rather vindicates the Parmenidean approach that we are justified in claiming to know that knowledge is possible within the limits of the identity of thought and being.

It is sometimes thought that we have finally overcome the difference between idealism and analytic philosophy. This view seems to be a mistake since the differences are not minor but major. In simplifying, we can say that Wittgenstein initially agrees that philosophy teaches us that we name reality through language, but later comes to think, in turning to a new view of language, that philosophy cannot grasp the world. From his perspective, since we cannot grasp reality through language, philosophy understood as the exploration of that possibility comes to an end. Hegel, on the contrary, denies that we either can grasp, or again correctly represent the real, or that we cannot know, in suggesting we do not know the world but do know the human world.

The relation of Wittgenstein and Hegel to Parmenides is obvious. Wittgenstein initially accepts but later rejects the metaphysical view that we can or again cannot know reality. He begins in thinking that through words we can name the real before changing his view of language to abandon any hope of progress in philosophy. Hegel follows the later Kantian turn away from metaphysical realism as a criterion of knowledge and toward epistemic constructivism. In conclusion, unlike Wittgenstein and Kant, Hegel understands that knowledge, hence philosophy that is a form of knowledge, is not an a priori but rather, like knowledge itself, intrinsically historical.

References

Gellner, Ernest: *Words and Things, A Critical Account of Linguistic Philosophy and a Study in Ideology*, Gollancz and Beacon, 1959.
Harman, Gilbert: *The Nature of Morality*, Oxford University Press, 1977.
Kant: Immanuel: *Prolegomena to Any Future Metaphysics*, LLA, 1950.
Kant, Immanuel: *Critique of Pure Reason*, P. Guyer and A. W. Wood (trans.), Cambridge University Press, 1998.
Moore, George Edward: "The Refutation of Idealism", in: *Mind, New Series* 12:48, 1903, pp.433–453.
Preston, Aaron (Ed.): *Analytic Philosophy: An Interpretive History*, Routledge, 2017.
Quine, Willard V. O.: *Word and Object*, MIT Press, 1980.
Russell, Bertrand: *A History of Western Philosophy*, Simon and Schuster, 1945.
Sluga, Hans: *Gottlob Frege*, Routledge, 1980.

Herbert Hrachovec
No Evaluative Authority Is beyond Evaluation: Common Ground between Hegel and Wittgenstein

Abstract Correlations between Hegel and Wittgenstein are not easily established. This chapter starts with an attempt to define some common ground. Both Hegel and Wittgenstein often approach philosophical problems not head on, but by discussing (and criticising) established cognitive attitudes. I take their responses to the popular understanding of measurement as a case in point. Hegel's treatment of "a measure" is shown to deviate from an ordinary understanding of the term insofar as it provides a criterion which is itself sensitive to the object of measurement. A similar point can be observed in Wittgenstein's work: for example, his memorable remark that one might use a table in order to check the measuring rod rather than the other way around. Triangulating Hegel and Wittgenstein vis-à-vis a non-partisan account of measurement reveals an interesting common concern, namely a shared alertness to a concealed side of standards. It is against this background affinity that some of the differences between them appear in sharper contrast.

Question: "Why does Henry call his mother long-distance?" Answer: "Because that is her name." This joke draws on the occasionally surprising ambivalence of words or phrases. Relating philosophical issues by means of decontextualised terms ("Freedom", "Logic", "Hegel", "Wittgenstein", etc.) is at times prone to similar equivocations. An initial concern when discussing Hegel and Wittgenstein is, therefore, to provide a framework which ensures a basic methodological and semantic similarity between these philosophers. Once such a framework is in place, the next step is to delineate their contributions to a given subject matter and, subsequently, to relate them to each other in terms of the common matrix introduced in the first step. Intersections and discrepancies can then be identified determined within this common frame of reference.

Triangulation

In view of the pervasive stylistic and systematic differences between them, a comparison of Hegel and Wittgenstein seems to lack a sound methodological

https://doi.org/10.1515/9783110572780-008

basis. One, admittedly highly abstract point should be noted all the same. Philosophy, for Hegel and the early Wittgenstein, is systematically closed. The concluding vista of Hegel's *Phenomenology of Spirit* is clear on this. "Absolute Knowing, or Spirit that knows itself as Spirit" (PS 1977: §808) has been established as "the actuality, truth, and certainty of his throne" (ibid.). The boat is full, to put it disrespectfully.[1] This sounds somewhat like Wittgenstein's apodictic pronouncement: "the truth of the thoughts that are here communicated seems to me unassailable and definitive. I therefore believe myself to have found, on all essential points, the final solution of the problems." (TLP: p.4) One could, in a Hegelian vein, regard this claim as a comprehensive mediation between open questions and their appropriate solutions.

There is little overlap between the matters explicitly discussed by Hegel and Wittgenstein, and even less common ground between their methodological approaches, but one structural similarity can be observed: they do not address items from the philosophical canon in a piecemeal way. Their strategy is, rather, to draw up a holistic panorama of interlocking arguments. Both construe their stage in a *confrontation between forms of knowledge.* The point of Hegel's PS is to incrementally trace increasingly sophisticated stages in the development of "how knowledge makes its appearance" (*des erscheinenden Wissens*) (PS 1977: §76). This procedure takes its cue from the Socratic *elenchos* (GP I: pp.456 ff.), presupposing that the philosopher's interlocutors will find their way to truth on their own, with minimal outside prompting. "Since our object is phenomenal knowledge, its determinations too will at first be taken directly as they present themselves" (PS 1977: §82) and, as we will discuss in a later section, a philosopher's task is to "simply look on" as this presentation unfolds (cf. PS 1977: §85). The later Wittgenstein's approach to philosophy is, on the face of it, reminiscent of Hegel's (supposed) theoretical non-invasiveness.

The initial setting of Wittgenstein's *Philosophical Investigations* places a philosopher vis-à-vis *another* philosopher's view of an *everyday* phenomenon. Wittgenstein considers Augustine's understanding of a child's initial acquisition of language. His criticism of Augustine's view is in accordance with Hegel's guidelines. He points out that Augustine does not "simply look on" and implies that philosophy should refrain from narrowing down the multiplicity of the phenomenal world. "Augustine does not mention any difference between kinds of word."

---

1 However, a note of discord occurs in this synthesis, namely Hegel's mention of "the Calvary of absolute Spirit" (*Schädelstätte des absoluten Geistes*), referring to the cemetery of its previous manifestations, albeit merely recollected (*erinnert*). There is, one could argue, a certain awareness that philosophy's triumphant apex comes at a price: the utter appropriation of its entire history.

(PI 2009: §1) Later in the PI, Wittgenstein remarks that the person who finds the phenomenon of a proposition "very remarkable" "is unable simply to look and see how propositions work" (PI 2009: §93). This is an intriguing correspondence which, I submit, can reveal a significant similarity between Hegel's and Wittgenstein's approaches towards philosophy. The insights they strive for must, according to Hegel, be gleaned from "how knowledge makes its appearance" (PS 1977: §76). Employing a Hegelian twist, one could describe the later Wittgenstein's recourse to ordinary language as philosophical attentiveness to forms of knowledge uncoerced by a (Kantian) critical apparatus of methodological asceticism.

Within this general outline, the present chapter will focus on the topic of *measurement standards*, which can be discussed in isolation from the rest of the respective systems with relative ease but nonetheless proves to be of considerable theoretical weight. Two kinds of pertinent discussions can be found in Hegel and Wittgenstein: logico-semantic remarks on the one hand and observations of a more general, pragmatic nature on the other. The claim that I am defending here is that both philosophers share a characteristic concern with the analysis of measures. It might be labelled "alertness to a concealed side of standards". *Prima facie*, a benchmark or rule prescribes a certain matrix applied to a medium or recipient. This is how the phenomenon initially presents itself. Hegel and Wittgenstein, in spite of their "phenomenological" pronouncements, both find this account incomplete and undertake a more thoroughgoing investigation into the character of measurement processes, and both arrive at insights that are seemingly counterintuitive from the point of view of "what is ordinarily understood by experience" (PS 1977: §87). They concur in demonstrating that the prescriptive outward appearance of standards conceals important features of their operation.

Flexible criteria

Hegel's systematic account of measurement standards can be found in section 3 of his *Science of Logic*, vol. I: *The Objective Logic*.[2] His remarks are embedded within a dialectical argument that makes use of concepts introduced earlier in the work: Being, Something, Quantity, Quality. Hegel's extraordinarily dense argument has been carefully reconstructed by Stephen Houlgate[3] and will not be

---

[2] SL 2010: pp.282ff. For general introductions to Hegel's arguments see Tabak (2017), Rosen (2014), Burbidge (2006), Hibben (2012), Harris (1983).
[3] Houlgate (2014). See also Arndt and Kruck (2016), Kruck (2014), Stekeler-Weithofer (2002).

repeated here. I will just give an outline of the main ideas. The tone is set by a motto: "Whatever is, has a measure." (SL 2010: p.288) Rather than starting with observations about the common use of measuring devices, Hegel flatly affirms this time-honoured ethico-metaphysical principle.[4] His claim is not that everything can be subjected to a metric procedure, but rather that exhibiting a specific balance between a qualitative core and quantitative parameters belongs to the essence of an entity. One of his examples is the proportions of the human body. Something can, presumably, not *be* a human body unless it conforms to a set of quantitatively defined ratios (SL 2010: p.287). A straightforward illustration (not to be found in Hegel) would be the colour blue, which *has to have* a frequency range of 450–482 nm.

It is against this background that Hegel discusses the more pedestrian phenomenon of a ruler. Starting from a "measure", which he defines as "the simple self-reference of quantum, its own determinateness in itself" (SL 2010: p.288), he proceeds to explore the application of this kind of self-sustained entity to another entity. "*First*, this measure is a rule, a measure external to the mere quantum." (SL 2010: p.291) This "rule, or the standard" (ibid.) is used to determine a certain quantity (manifestly exhibited by the measure) of a "mere quantum", i.e. to quantify some object of measurement according to the standard's synthesis of quality and quantity (its measure).[5] It is at this point that Hegel draws on common usage, namely the use of a measuring rod, which clearly offers "a specific quantity determining the external quantum" (ibid.). Measurement, in everyday use, is commonly conceived as the employment of some standardised device to quantify the amount of a measurement. According to Hegel this falls short of a philosopher's requirements. "This comparison is an *external* act" (ibid.). There is no profound connection between systems of measurement units and ontological specifications of something captured by quantitative measurement.

The crucial expression is "external". I have indicated that "the measure" everything has is not an accidental feature. Hegel elaborates on his motto: "Every existence has a magnitude, and this magnitude belongs to the very nature of a something." (SL 2010: p.288) External measurements do not suffice to fulfil this ambitious dictum, so Hegel triggers one of his usual tripartite dialectical arguments to demonstrate the *internal* relationship between a standard and the "quantum" it is applied to. The details are convoluted, but the general idea

---

4 Cf. Tengelyi (2003), Marx (1983).
5 The German original has "Maßstab" (W 5: p.399) for "standard", a term associated with measurement by scale, reminiscent of a prominent Latin meaning of *regula*, in the sense of "linear ruler".

can be illustrated by an example offered by Hegel himself, namely the impact of environmental change upon an object.

> Inasmuch as a something has an internal measure, an alteration of the magnitude of its quality comes to it from outside, and the something does not take on the arithmetical aggregate of the alteration. Its measure reacts against it, behaves towards the aggregate as an intensive measure and assimilates it in a way typically its own; it alters the externally imposed alteration, makes something else out of this quantum and demonstrates through this specifying function that in this externality it is for-itself. (SL 2010: p.292)

In plain English: an object's inherent temperature does not generally correspond to its ambient temperature due to its specific material composition. This is, of course, the parlance of contemporary popular science, whereas Hegel uses the scenario to conjure up an anthropomorphic drama, pitting an inanimate entity against extraneous alterations ("does not take", "assimilate", "demonstrate").[6] The idiom of reflexivity, omnipresent in Hegel's *Logic*, is introduced to enrich the discussion of standards. Subjecting an object to measurement establishes a conceptual interdependency. Hegel's attempts to flesh this out in speculative dialectics is a testament to the proficiency of German idealism, but probably not the best starting point to show its lasting importance. Taking a look at the introduction to his PS is a better choice in this respect.

The passages quoted from the SL show Hegel reconstructing developing the conceptual minutiae of the measuring process. The introduction to the PS offers a broad outline of the general impact of his intuition.[7] Within the framework of one form of knowledge (philosophy) exploring another ("ordinary" knowledge), the issue of appropriate judgements arises. How do we (the interrogating party to this arrangement) *know* what to make of self-proclaimed "common knowledge"? We seem to need a standard to ascertain its validity. But, Hegel argues, this is to disregard a basic feature of philosophers' involvement in forms of knowledge. Their "discoveries" must not surprise them, since their engagement in ordinary forms of *knowledge* is, in principle, matched to their own understanding. There cannot occur an elemental cognitive disconnect within this correlation, because that would amount to an incommensurability between the inquiring and the revealing party. In other words, since both sides share consciousness, their forms of knowledge are a common disposition that does not need outside scrutiny.

---

6 But notice that locutions like "its own measure" might be inconspicuous in contexts that do not also stipulate that such objects are "for-itself".
7 For an overall discussion of the PS, see Siep (2014).

Philosophy cannot, in an attempt to start from an entirely clean slate, bracket its cognitive capacity in order to be properly receptive to cognitive capacities as they emerge. The formal structure of this reflexive move is validated by interconscious exchange. "The essence or criterion" (PS 1977: §83) determining Consciousness[8] can therefore not lie solely within the investigative part.

> Consciousness provides its own criterion from within itself, so that the investigation becomes a comparison of consciousness with itself; for the distinction made above falls within it. [...] Consequently, we do not need to import criteria, or to make use of our own bright ideas and thoughts during the course of the inquiry. (PS 1977: §84)

The right way to think of a standard, according to this passage, is to regard it as an interactive measure which adapts to its target object. This adaptation is, as Hegel points out, nothing other than *experience* (cf. PS 1977: §86), inasmuch as it amounts to an auto-correction of preconceptions in the light of information made accessible by these very preconceptions.[9] This view of standards runs counter to objectivism conceived as rigid determination of some matter of interest, according to an external scale or matrix. Such an account, Hegel maintains, fails to capture the deep grammar of standards.

Intentional directedness

The early Wittgenstein's ontological imagery makes prominent use of terms drawn from measurement practices. "A proposition is a standard to which facts behave." (NB: p.95) "Proposition and situation are related to one another like a yardstick and the length to be measured." (NB: p.32) On a superficial reading this could be taken as an external relation, like garments that are related to a clothed body without determining its natural shape. But Wittgenstein's metaphor is more sophisticated. Proceeding from a basic stipulation—"We picture facts to ourselves." (TLP: 2.1)—he regards pictures as models of reality (TLP: 2.12) insofar as their internal structure enables them to represent its ontological composition. This isomorphism has been widely noted (though see Proops 2000), yet its use within the TLP's picture theory depends on a crucial, less prominent, feature: the role played by measurement. Notice that a picture may *fail to represent anything* and that isomorphism does not account for this eventuality. It is introduced as correspondence between two predefined domains of

---
[8] I use a capital "C" throughout to refer to Hegel's specific notion of consciousness.
[9] On the notion of experience in the PS cf. Emundts (2012), Stern (2002), Imhoff (1973).

discourse. (The photocopy of one page does not represent another such copy.) What's missing for Wittgenstein's purposes is the role of a standard imposing its normative claim onto its relatum. "*That* is how a picture is attached to reality; it reaches right out to it. It is laid against reality like a measure." (TLP: 2.1511f) The implication is that reality either does or does not *conform* to this standard. Measurement introduces logical truth and falsity into Wittgenstein's picture theory.

There is a cognitive tension between the use of the picture and measure metaphors here. While pictures do not have to conform to real life, a measure does not tell us anything about the specific composition of its target object. Wittgenstein tries to bridge the gap by introducing an additional metaphor. The "end points of the graduating lines" of a measure "*touch* the object that is to be measured" (TLP: 2.15121). This touching is, however, an external contact. It cannot *represent* a state of affairs, so Wittgenstein supplements his metaphor with an extra feature: "These correlations are, as it were, the feelers of the picture's elements, with which the picture touches reality." (TLP: 2.1515) The pictorial relationship thus conceived is a hybrid between corresponding structures and the application of standards.[10] It fulfils the double function of subjecting sentences to judgements (in propositional logic) *and* endowing them with an internal structure (in predicate logic). Wittgenstein does not accord equal status to these components, though. The term "*Maßstab*" occurs but once in the TLP, whereas the pictorial relationship is extensively discussed. "A picture can depict any reality whose form it has." (TLP: 2.171) This explanation suggests that the representational capacity of pictures is entirely a matter of form. The complementary requirement is much less conspicuous:

> A picture represents its subject from a position outside it. (Its standpoint is its representational form.) That is why a picture *represents its subject correctly or incorrectly*. (TLP: 2.173; emphasis mine)

Correctness is not simply a matter of pictorial form, which can only show *possible* configurations of objects (TLP: 2.151). In spite of being indispensable, the role of standards is only hinted at in Wittgenstein's book.

Wittgenstein's dictum, quoted above, has a distinctive syntactical feature. "*We* picture facts to ourselves." (TLP: 2.1; emphasis mine) The active role of an epistemological subject is not usually highlighted in the TLP, which largely presents his picture theory as an apersonal affair between sentences and situations.

---

[10] For Tractarian semantics, see Morris (2008), Frascolla (2007), Friedlander (2001), Carruthers (1989).

It is, however, obvious that a measuring rod, insofar as it serves to ensure the correctness of a picture, is not just another machine-like tool. A standard is *applied* by a cognisant being in order to achieve conformity with certain aims, an issue that exceeds the scope of the TLP. Wittgenstein takes up this point in a 1930 manuscript. His slightly awkward metaphor of correlation as "feelers of the picture's elements" (TLP: 2.1515) is replaced by an analysis of prospective rules guiding the employment of a *Maßstab*. "This is how this machine ought to work" (MS 109: p.263, translation mine[11]) is a prescriptive expression *directed towards* a desired fit between a standard and a standardised process. The operative rules are no longer feelers but intentions. "The intention sets a standard which enables one to judge the fact." (ibid.) Our picturing-of-facts is thus construed as a normative activity relating a *Maßstab* to a situation via intentions. "The intention is nothing but a yardstick applied by us to events and used by us to describe them." (MS 109: p.268.) By introducing intentions into his account of our interactions with the world, Wittgenstein prepares the ground for one of the most consequential discussions to be found in his later work, namely his discussion of rule-following.

Pictures cannot automatically describe reality correctly. Introducing intentions to mediate the epistemological rapport adds a new twist to Wittgenstein's account. The "feelers" have been replaced by a propositional attitude, i.e. a person's conscious approach towards a state of affairs via some symbolic representation. This change of view raises a problem largely suppressed in the TLP. "Only the intentional picture reaches reality like a measure. Regarded from the outside it just stands there, dead and isolated." (MS 114: p.207) Wittgenstein has hit here on the perennial difficulty of reconciling a material substratum and an operative meaning within a signifying practice. Remember that according to the TLP the end point of a measure touches the object to be measured (TLP: 2.15121). This literal sense of touching obviously does not aid our understanding of the intentional character of measurements. Intentions are supposed to somehow *reach* reality in their own right, so it is questionable how helpful bridging metaphors are here. The problem is, of course, that intentional meaning is to be distinguished from physical prompts ("dead and isolated") while, at the same time, the tangible presence of material signifiers is presupposed. Such is the semiotic conundrum, which (we might say) is analogous to someone recognising an elephant on the basis of sense-data reports describing its trunk, legs and tail by three blind people.

---

[11] All translations of quotations from Wittgenstein's manuscripts are my own.

The phenomenon of a measure serves as a comparatively simple model for a discussion of rule-governed behaviour within the conceptual framework that I have outlined. A closer look at this topic is beyond the scope of the present chapter, which also has to omit a discussion of Wittgenstein's most famous measuring device, the Paris standard metre.[12] Given these restrictions, one basic feature of rule-following is, however, thrown into sharp relief. The purpose of a rule in ordinary use is closely related to the application of a measure. The rule is regarded as a particular, predetermined specification guiding a domain of human conduct, appropriately specified. The wording of a rule is, under these assumptions, regarded as a functional equivalent to a measure's physical implementation. There are two points to note here: (1) Measures and rules are, in one sense, crucially different, and (2) familiar rule-following concerns result directly from disregarding this difference. Notice, on the one hand, that a measuring rod is by definition a thing with a purpose. It is characterised by its prospective use in measurement. As it happens, the rod, regarded as a "bare object", shares the quality of possessing a particular length with the objects measured.[13] The measurement standard, because of its embodiment, fulfils the desired condition of its target objects. On the other hand, however, this does not hold for words. Even though both a yardstick and a concatenation of letters are "dead and isolated", these are different kinds of separation.

The point of blurring the distinction becomes apparent now. Regarding a rule as a kind of measure suggests that one merely has to look at how it is articulated/expressed to know how to use it. Wittgenstein touches on this point in a remark on the seductive simile of railway tracks.

> Whence the idea that the beginning of a series is a visible section of rails invisibly laid to infinity? Well, we might imagine rails instead of a rule. And infinitely long rails correspond to the unlimited application of a rule. (PI 2009: §218)

It makes no sense to even imagine a measuring rod of infinite length, whereas a rule, being a conceptual entity, lacks spatial coordinates.[14] In order to demystify the idea of an unerring, perpetual command, Wittgenstein conjures up limitless rails as ostensibly unswerving support for correct rule-following. His point is that one should not, in this case, put one's trust in a yardstick-like procedure. Rules are immaterial constructs and do not afford direct, tangible guidance as rulers

---

12 For further discussion of measures, see Jacquette (2010).
13 Loosely expressed, we could say that the paradigm rod can also be regarded as a token of the length it determines.
14 See Crispin Wright (2001) for an extensive discussion.

do. This is, however, not the whole story. The shortcomings of the TLP's treatment of measures, as discussed above, led Wittgenstein to realise the essential role played by intentions in the measuring process. A number of his *Nachlass* remarks address this issue. They also contain ideas strongly reminiscent of Hegel's views on measures.

Common ground

Standard contemporary theories of measurement systems describe a structural interdependence between manifest events and observers. The system takes an input from given processes and delivers an output for the monitor. "The purpose of the measurement system is to link the observer to the process".[15] In operational terms this can be done by an "information variable". "The input to the measurement system is the *true value* of the variable, the system output is the measured value of the variable." (Bentley 1995: p.5) The values are identical in a perfect measurement device.[16] Both Hegel and Wittgenstein emphasised, against this formalisation, the inseparable interdependence of a "measurement system's" physical implementation and its quantitative output. The rule, according to Hegel, is "a magnitude which is determinate in itself" and serves to measure "a quantum with a concrete existence which is other than the something of the rule" (SL 2010: p.291). A crucial point in Hegel's ensuing dialectical treatment is that the two quanta involved are interacting with one another. There is no unilateral "true variable" to be gleaned from the target object of a measurement. The very notion of truth has to be reallocated with regard to the entire process, including effects exerted by the chosen instruments.

Hegel's treatment of "measures" is an inconspicuous part of his SL, but the underlying motivation is forcefully expressed in the introduction to the earlier PS, in which he broadens the outlook to cover his entire philosophical enterprise. In view of the more deductive considerations found in the later book, Hegel's programmatic claims gain additional weight. Returning to the passage discussed in the second section of this chapter, this is how Hegel describes *his* version of a measurement system, that is to say the methodological super-construct of Consciousness:

---

15 Bentley (1995: p.5). Cf. Allen and Yen (2002).
16 For more on this point see Hrachovec (2013).

> For consciousness is, on the one hand, consciousness of the object, and on the other, consciousness of itself; consciousness of what for it is the True, and consciousness of its knowledge of the truth. (PS 1977: §85)

The intuition, generalised from the simple activity of measuring with a ruler, is that it is impossible to extract some "objective truth" from the pervasive process of the ongoing personal experience typical of a self-conscious being. This intuition might strike one as excessively speculative, and none of this grandstanding is found in Wittgenstein. Yet the latter's remarks on measurement standards share Hegel's concern with the peculiarity of reflexive systems.

Hegelian reflexivity is a universal moving force throughout his comprehensive system. Wittgenstein, on the other hand, is led to some of its features in the course of investigating selected phenomena. One incisive remark on the issue is built around the notion of rulers. Wittgenstein starts with an observation on temporality and verification. "The stream of life, or the stream of the world, flows on and our propositions are so to speak verified only at instants." (PR: V, §48) This outlook is comparable to Hegel's epistemological setting in the PS insofar as it pits the contingency of individual truth claims against the aspiration of objective, matter-of-fact truth. "If the world of data is timeless, how can we speak of it at all?" (ibid.) Wittgenstein's answer is a reflective move. To put it in Kantian terms: if sentences *are* thus verified it is because they *can* be used for this purpose. In Wittgenstein's unassuming phrasing: "So they must be so constructed that they *can be verified* by it." (ibid.; emphasis mine) And here Wittgenstein's recourse to enabling conditions takes a decidedly non-idealist turn.

Wittgenstein compares the spatiotemporal character of sentences to a ruler. We have seen that a ruler's particular nature consists in its being a hybrid device, its physical presence being inseparable from its normative employment. One cannot claim that length, an immaterial concept, can be determined *in spite* of a ruler's physicality.

> No, if a body has length, there can be no length without a body and although I realize that in a certain sense only the ruler's length measures, what I put in my pocket still remains the ruler, the body, and isn't the length. (ibid.)

Measuring systems are of necessity put into practice, and one has to take into account ("reflect upon") features of this implementation to get a comprehensive view of their nature. Even though words and sentences are, as I have argued, categorically distinct from rulers, Wittgenstein's simile makes an important point. Propositions, like yardsticks, operate on the basis of (in a manner of speaking) a body-mind synthesis. The finitude of spatiotemporal life has to be squared with concerns of a non-physical nature. Hegel and Wittgenstein, as it turns out, both pointed to examples of measuring practices to illustrate this insight.

For Hegel, consciousness is, as we have seen, directed towards objects and—simultaneously—towards itself. It is because of this peculiar structure that it can switch roles between examination of an external object and of its own examining status. Dialectical knowledge consists in mediating between the way things present themselves and how they are comprehended. Compare the following notable deliberation by Wittgenstein: "How does it express itself in measurement whether I measure the measure or the table? I also sometimes check whether the measure is correct by using it to measure the table." (MS 118: p.90) Occasionally one checks the sun's position to determine whether a watch is working. This is, admittedly, not standard usage, but it cannot be dismissed as an irrelevant anomaly either. We have, on the contrary, hit upon a crucial feature of measures, the "concealed side of standards" I alluded to at the beginning. It is by virtue of the very nature of the devices discussed that this option is available. Wittgenstein is to the point: one cannot claim that measurement by a ruler functions *in spite* of its "corporality". A constitutive asymmetry has to be conceded. Not every stick is a measure; yardsticks are picked out by the abstract notion of a length. Yet length is, in this usage, itself an embodied concept. No evaluative authority is beyond evaluation.

Wittgenstein's remark about using the table to check the measure is a paradigmatic example of a more general structure. Hegel puts the point in terms of the development of Consciousness. Objects as they are in-themselves are not what they are for Consciousness, which has to adapt to its objects. But, Hegel argues, the object does not remain unaffected, since its nature is only accessible via conscious apprehension. The object is initially supposed to be the measure of correct recognition but, in a striking passage, Hegel argues that this measure itself is altered by corrections on the apprehensive end:

> Since consciousness thus finds that its knowledge does not correspond to its object, the object itself does not stand the test; in other words, the criterion for testing is altered when that for which it was to have been the criterion fails to pass the test [...]. (PS: §85)

This runs entirely counter to the conventional way of looking at things. The object of measurement should ordinarily not have a say in determining the correctness of the ruler's application.[17] According to this objection, Hegel is advocating shifting the goalposts in the middle of the game. Wittgenstein's role reversal between measure and table looks harmless compared with Hegel's general propo-

---

17 Favouritism is, after all, a matter of bending rules for a select clientele.

sition that seems to willfully subvert the very concept of a measure. But the systematic impact of these considerations is equally important. Hegel continues the passage quoted above: "and the testing is not only a testing of what we know, but also a testing of the criterion of what knowing is." (ibid.) Subtract the story about Consciousness and you get the Wittgensteinian idea of a role reversal in testing procedures.

Wittgenstein does in fact discuss a hypothetical everyday case that precisely exemplifies what Hegel generalises as auto-correction of Consciousness on the basis of feedback. Imagine the scenario of an elastic ruler:

> How would we come into conflict with truth if our rulers [Zollstäbe] consisted of soft rubber instead of wood or steel? Well, we would not get to know the correct measure of the table. (MS 117: pp.9f.)

Wittgenstein's answer to this obvious reply is, in a nutshell, that the underlying correctness is *defined* by using the rigid measure. If someone employs a non-standard procedure she is thereby entitled to her own type of measurement. Her interlocutor protests: "But then, this is no measurement at all." Wittgenstein's reply: "Certainly, it is not what we call 'to measure', but it may, depending on circumstances, also fulfil practical purposes." (ibid.) The term is used in a different, albeit related, sense. It is, in fact, not difficult to imagine circumstances that call for a change of established techniques of measurement, when we are faced with unforeseen situations.[18] Hegel and Wittgenstein have both been accused, on the basis of such considerations, of disregard for objective truth. This complaint, voiced by practitioners of common measuring techniques, brings us back to the matter of interference between forms of knowledge that I raised at the beginning of this paper.

Substantive comparisons, as distinct from associative impressions, demand a *tertium comparationis*. The present case calls for Hegel's and Wittgenstein's ideas about measures to be triangulated with their reader's understanding of the subject matter of their remarks. In the initial section, I indicated a discursive setting shared by both philosophers, namely their exploration of forms of knowledge. Taking up this thread, the question then becomes what concept of measure their addressees assume when they attempt to compare the given statements. At this point it becomes clear that the implied reader for these philosophers is the self-assured user of a particular evaluative regime. I hope to have shown that

---

[18] A variation on the idea of rubber rules is rules that expand under heat (MS 117: p.10). And it is well known that modern physics has – in its domain – vindicated Hegel's and Wittgenstein's "reflective" approach.

both Hegel and Wittgenstein took up the task of challenging one-sided views on standards by analysing the logical infrastructure underlying their application. This finding should, however, be qualified with an important caveat stemming from a decisive difference between the discursive settings that the two authors chose. In Hegel, a philosopher meets ordinary opinions head on, whereas Wittgenstein shifts the roles involved. His philosophy confronts *traditional philosophy* (cf. Augustine) *on behalf of* ordinary language.[19] The ensuing differences are just as striking as the point of contact we have been exploring.

Hegel's PG rests on the confident assumption that philosophy, in dealing with our common notions of cognition, psychology, history and culture, is able to transform these inputs into a consistent system, resolving contentious issues along the way. The price to pay is a heavy deployment of dialectics, which is not only an all-pervasive methodology, but also, in the end, an instrument for achieving universal cognitive closure. While Wittgenstein is basically silent on Hegel, it is obvious that his recourse to ordinary language is directed against the very attempts at system-building of which his earlier self represents a prime example. I have downplayed this manifest discrepancy in order to emphasise a common concern, yet throughout this chapter I have made clear my scepticism towards Hegelian dialectics. It is, therefore, ironic that Wittgenstein's remarks on measures fall on the side of the Hegelian attempt to—*sit venia verbo*—deconstruct unwarranted assumptions about the working of standards. He is (along with Hegel, who at best pays lip service to common sense) no ordinary "ordinary language philosopher" after all.

References

Allen, Marry J. and Yen, Wendy M.: *Introduction to Measurement Theory*, Waveland Press, 2002.
Arndt, Andreas and Kruck, Günter (eds.): *Hegels "Lehre vom Wesen"*, De Gruyter, 2016.
Bentley, John P.: *Principles of Measurement Systems*, Wiley, 1995.
Burbidge, John.: *The Logic of Hegel's Logic: An Introduction*, Broadview Press, 2006.
Carlson, David Gray: "Hegel's Theory of Measure", *SSRN Electronic Journal*, 2003, http://dx.doi.org/10.2139/ssrn.413602.
Carruthers, Peter: *Tractarian Semantics: Finding Sense in Wittgenstein's Tractatus (Philosophy Theory)*, Blackwell, 1989.
Emundts, Dina: *Erfahren und Erkennen. Hegels Theorie der Wirklichkeit*, Vittorio Klostermann, 2012.
Frascolla, Pasquale: *Understanding Wittgenstein's Tractatus*, Routledge, 2007.

---

19 This relationship is discussed in more detail in Hrachovec (2011).

Friedlander, Eli: *Signs of Sense: Reading Wittgenstein's* Tractatus, Harvard University Press, 2001.
Guzmán, Luis: *Relating Hegel's "Science of Logic" to Contemporary Philosophy*, Palgrave Macmillan, 2015.
Harris, Errol: *An Interpretation of the Logic of Hegel*, University Press of America, 1983.
Hibben, John Grier: *Hegel's Logic an Essay in Interpretation*, Prism Key Press, 2012.
Houlgate, Stephen: *The Opening of Hegel's Logic: from Being to Infinity*, Purdue University Press, 2006.
Houlgate, Stephen: "Hegel on the Category of Quantity", *Hegel Bulletin* 35:1, 2014, pp.16–32.
Hrachovec, Herbert: "What Wittgenstein forgot to mention about Socrates", in: E. Ramharter (ed.), *Ungesellige Geselligkeiten/Unsocial Sociabilities. Wittgensteins Umgang mit anderen Denkern*, Parerga, 2011, pp.29–37.
Hrachovec, Herbert: "Identität ist Spurensuche", in: Arbeitsgruppe Informatik in Bildung und Gesellschaft (eds.), *Biometrische Identitäten und ihre Rolle in den Diskursen um Sicherheit und Grenzen*, Humboldt-Universität, 2013, pp.3–17.
Imhoff, Hans: *Der Hegelsche Erfahrungsbegriff*, Euphorion, 1973.
Jacquette, Dale.: "Measure for Measure? Wittgenstein on Language-Game Criteria and the Paris Standard Metre Bar", in: A. Ahmed (ed.): *Wittgenstein's Philosophical Investigations*, Cambridge University Press, 2010, pp.49–65.
Koch, Anton F. and Schick, Friedrike (eds.): *G.W.F. Hegel, Wissenschaft der Logik*, Akademie Verlag, 2002.
Koch, Anton F. et al. (eds.): *Hegel – 200 Jahre Wissenschaft der Logik: Beiträge zur internationalen Tagung "200 Jahre Hegels Wissenschaft der Logik"*, Felix Meiner, 2014.
Kruck, Günter: "Von quantitativ-qualitativen Verhältnissen zum entwickelten Fürsichsein als Begriff des Maße", in: Koch et al. 2014: pp.123–138.
Marx, Werner: *Gibt es auf Erden ein Maß? Grundbestimmungen einer nichtmetaphysischen Ethik*, Felix Meiner, 1983.
McGinn, Marie: *Wittgenstein and the Philosophical Investigations*, Routledge, 2002.
Morris, Michael: *Routledge Philosophy Guidebook to Wittgenstein and the* Tractatus Logico-Philosophicus, Routledge, 2008.
Nuzzo, Angelica (ed.): *Hegel and the Analytic Tradition*, Continuum, 2010.
Proops, Ian: *Logic and Language in Wittgenstein's Tractatus*, Garland, 2000.
Roberts, Fred S.: *Measurement Theory: With Applications to Decisionmaking, Utility, and the Social Sciences*, Cambridge University Press, 1984.
Rosen, Stanley: *The Idea of Hegel's Science of Logic*, University of Chicago Press, 2014.
Siep, Ludwig: *Hegel's Phenomenology of Spirit*, Cambridge University Press, 2014.
Stekeler-Weithofer, Pirmin: "Die Kategorie der Quantität", in: Koch 2002: pp.51–64.
Stern, David G.: *Wittgenstein's* Philosophical Investigations: *An Introduction*, Cambridge University Press, 2006.
Stern, Robert: *Routledge Philosophy Guidebook to Hegel and the* Phenomenology of Spirit, Routledge, 2002.
Tabak, Mehmet: *The Doctrine of Being in Hegel's* Science of Logic, Palgrave Macmillan, 2017.
Tengelyi, László: "Ordnung, Maß, Mitte bei Platon und Aristoteles", in: Karl-Heinz Lembeck and Ernst Wolfgang Orth (eds.): *Phänomenologische Forschungen 2003*. Felix Meiner, 2003, pp.39–53.

Wright, Crispin: *Rails to Infinity: Essays on Themes from Wittgenstein's* Philosophical Investigations, Harvard University Press, 2001.

David Kolb
The Diamond Net: Metaphysics, Grammar, Ontologies

Abstract In the introduction to his *Philosophy of Nature*, Hegel speaks of metaphysics as "the entire range of the universal determinations of thought, as it were the diamond net into which everything is brought and thereby first made intelligible. Every educated consciousness has its metaphysics, an instinctive way of thinking". Both Wittgenstein and Hegel see our many languages and forms of life as constituted by different diamond nets of categories/grammars. I argue that both Wittgenstein and Hegel take a non-reductive attitude toward this plurality of local ontologies, but that they disagree about what that plurality implies for history and philosophy. Their disagreements come in part from their differing choice of examples, influenced by atomism and holism. Even more, their disagreements stem from divergent notions about the structure and mode of being of those diamond nets. During the discussion, I distinguish three uses of the word "ontology", and I ask each thinker about what might improve the other's philosophical project.

Invitation

I have invited Wittgenstein and Hegel to walk with me for a while. We go to a hilltop overlooking the disputed land of ontology and metaphysics, with its famous baroque castles in the air and its scenic historic ruins visited by busloads of students every year, as well as the land's sleek modern factories and austere monuments.

This may seem an unlikely place to bring Hegel and Wittgenstein together. Hegel feels at home with the fantastic architectures and bizarre constructions in the land of ontology. After all, he wrote one of the earliest guide books for those visiting the area, as well as a handbook for those seeking citizenship there. But Wittgenstein finds the area distasteful, a land of traps and illusions. He would prefer a simplified house in Vienna, or an ordinary flat in England, or a friend's house in America. There, in October 1949, conversing with Oets Kolk Bouwsma, Wittgenstein praised the logical work of Bertrand Russell and Alfred North Whitehead, but he scorned Whitehead's later move into ontology and metaphysics. Bouwsma recounts that "Wittgenstein said Whitehead was good once, before he became a high priest [and] a charlatan" (Bouwsma 1986: p.49).

We know that Wittgenstein could wield contempt like a sword, often wounding himself. Hegel's grand schemes should also earn that contempt. Yet on this walk together I will try to persuade the two thinkers that they share certain projects, even though their paths do diverge.

Our diamond nets

I have structured our discussion using an excerpt from Hegel's introduction to his *Philosophy of Nature:*

> Metaphysics is nothing else but the entire range of the universal determinations of thought, as it were the diamond net into which everything is brought and thereby first made intelligible. Every educated consciousness has its metaphysics, an instinctive way of thinking, the absolute power within us of which we become master only when we make it in turn the object of our knowledge. Philosophy in general has, as philosophy, other categories than those of the ordinary consciousness: all education reduces to the distinction of categories. All revolutions, in the sciences no less than in world history, originate solely from the fact that spirit, in order to understand and comprehend itself with a view to possessing itself, has changed its categories, comprehending itself more truly, more deeply, more intimately, and more in unity with itself. (EPN 1830: §246 A)

Both Wittgenstein and Hegel observe the nets of categories that we use to structure our experience of the world. Diamond-like, transparent: are these Kant's categories? Or are they those of Hegel's *Logic?* Yes, Hegel is aiming in that direction, but no, in this paragraph he has other categories in mind. In the text surrounding the excerpt above Hegel draws a contrast between the categories used in the physics of his day and the categories used in the philosophy of nature. He is talking about the nets used to organise experience, even when those categories lack the pure diamond character of his logic.

Wittgenstein would not speak of diamond nets, but he does speak of grammars and their nets of internally related concepts. He distinguishes between statements showing internal relations and statements expressing empirical relations and causal connections.[1]

Furthermore, if "every educated consciousness has its metaphysics", then there are *many* diamond nets. Both Hegel and Wittgenstein describe the nets

---

1 On this point, see Mácha (2015).

of concepts and practices they find in the world. These nets can be, as Hegel says, "instinctive", that is, not constructed self-consciously.

In his philosophy of nature and spirit, Hegel describes organisms' growing abilities to discriminate, and their many stages of developing self-awareness. He finds many diamond nets in history, politics and art, and tries to understand and master them.

Wittgenstein for his part finds multiple language-games, many grammatical nets in our forms of life, most not consciously planned. We must learn not to be mastered by them or by the pictures they suggest.

Local ontologies

These diamond nets are often referred to these days as local ontologies. We can ask about the ontology of a database, or of a computer game, or of a bureaucratic procedure. What types of entities are taken as significant, and what are their relationships, connections and the rules for moves allowed with them? What is the repertory of objects to be discussed? How are they to be connected or used or played with?

Such diamond nets allow us to classify objects, or make moves in a game, or study a social phenomenon. For instance:

> *Slab, brick, carry, put on the pile.*
> *The rook moves along the board in straight lines forward or sideways.*
> *Temperature, humidity and barometric readings are recorded hourly in the database, correlated with the velocity and direction of the wind.*
> *The 19th-century novels on this list will be analysed in terms of the connections between their characters' actions and the locations where those actions occur.*

Ontologies, in this sense, develop naturally, but also by planning and regimentation. There are many ontologies. They do not need to compete with one another, although they can be rivals, as when we choose among different databases for analysing economic history, or among rival conventions for playing a game of bridge, or different constitutions for a new city charter. These ontologies are pragmatic in the sense that they are tried and tested in our interactions with the world. They are not philosophically self-aware or certified. Nor do they need to be.

Universal ontology

To help clarify the different ways Hegel and Wittgenstein deal with the nets of categories and rules that structure language in action, I want to link the older usage of the word *ontology* in philosophy with its newer usage in information sciences.

In philosophy, *ontology* names a very old investigation, though the word itself was not applied to that investigation until later on. In the 300s BCE, Aristotle's students collected his essays into groups. The first essay in the group on logic and argument was called *Categories*. There Aristotle offered a list of the basic kinds of entities we can speak about.[2]

In another set of essays, Aristotle took the list from the *Categories* and studied the basic features that any existing being must possess in order to be real. Aristotle called this investigation *first philosophy*, but his students named these essays *Metaphysics*. The usual explanation is that they placed those essays *after* a group of essays on changes and processes in the material world, a group they called *Physics* (from *physika*, natural things). But besides meaning *after*, the Greek *meta* can also mean *beyond*. So, whether or not it was intended, *metaphysics* soon took on the meaning *beyond physics*, because first philosophy studied the basic properties of any being, material or immaterial, concrete or abstract. Recently given a New Age twist, this meaning has resulted in the many exotic books found on the Metaphysics shelves in bookstores, which is one reason why philosophers today often use the word *ontology* as a safer term for Aristotle's *first philosophy* in its modern guises.

The word *ontology* appeared in late medieval times and first came into English in the 1500s. It combines the Greek words for being (*onto*) and study (*logos*) to name the study of being as such, the study of the basic qualities of any entity.

Ontology then came to designate not only the investigation but also the doctrines developed in that investigation. For instance, Descartes, Newton and Leibniz argued about the laws of motion, and historians noticed how each thinker

---

[2] Scholars disagree about the exact method Aristotle employed, and about its results. See the article "Aristotle's Categories" in the Stanford Encyclopedia of Philosophy. The word *category* comes from the Greek *kategoriai*, from the verb *kategoreuein*. This verb's original meaning was *to accuse* or *to make a charge in public* (*kata* against, *agora* public square). It came to mean *to make a statement, to assert a fact about something*. So, a list of *categories* would contain the general kinds of facts which could be asserted, and/or the kinds of entities that could have facts asserted about them.

was relying on a different notion of what it meant to count something as real. They had different *ontologies*.

Through the years, philosophers tried many different methods in their search for the basic properties shared by all entities. They generalised from everyday observation and the grammar of their languages. They searched their minds for what seemed to them intuitively "first" or most basic concepts. They studied the sciences of their day.

Then in 1774 Immanuel Kant reformulated the old question "What are the properties any being must have in order to be real?" into the question "What are the categories any language must use in order to successfully designate and describe an entity?" What necessary basic categories of thought and actions of synthesis are required for a mind to assert a statement about an object? Kant argued for a particular list of basic categories and mental actions. Throughout the 19th century his successors worked on his lists and his theory of mental activity. Some sought to bolster his arguments for one universal set of categories while others argued for historically varying lists of categories.

Meanwhile, logicians were developing new formalised tools and notations that allowed them to systematise the sprawling patterns of logical argument. They then realised that their search for the most basic and economical logical concepts and operations paralleled Kant's search for the necessary structures of all thought.

For Information Science's current use of the word *ontology*, the decisive turn came in the 1930s when Stanislaw Leśniewski and other Polish logicians were constructing systems of axioms, definitions and rules that they hoped would provide the foundation for clarifying and analysing any language. They named their set of highest-level categories and rules *ontology*. These rules prescribed what objects were and how they could be spoken about.

So, *ontology* came to designate systems of rules that enable classification and communication. With computer programming based on logical tools, information scientists began using *ontology* to describe systems for analysing and recording information. New ranges of words began to be used with *ontology*. Using Google's Ngram tool, you can track the growth of phrases such as "ontology mapping", "ontology and the semantic web" and "ontological reduction".

Reducing local ontologies

The dispute among Kant's successors about whether there is one universal category or historically diverse sets of categories then reappeared in disputes over universal versus local ontologies. Due to their ability to construct many different logical systems, logicians often accepted a multiplicity of ontologies. But many philosophers were not so sure. Once the scientific revolution challenged the ultimacy of the objects of ordinary perception, local vocabularies began to be questioned. It became important for philosophers to figure out "what was real". This mode of doing *ontology* was enriched with 20th-century tools of linguistic and logical analysis, theories of reference, model theory and the like. Nowadays, when pursuing materialist or naturalistic goals the basic set of entities is usually supposed to be provided by the latest and best science, as both Quine and Sellars argue in their different ways. There are whole libraries filled with books and articles disputing about how to perform these reductions. Wittgenstein, however, refuses to play that game.

Perhaps surprisingly, Hegel too refuses the game of reductionism. "But wait a minute!" you may object, "Isn't Hegel the Complete Reductionist? Doesn't he claim that there is only one truly real entity: *Geist*, spirit?" Yes, at times he does say things like that, but he does not mean this as a theory of reductionist reference. You cannot understand what he is saying until you understand spirit's mode of existence.

For Hegel does not think spirit exists as an immediate present object, a simple factual presence. He argues that any simple factual presence, on any level, results from complex internal mediations and ongoing interactions. Spirit is not a block entity, a Big Fact; not a Bradleyan absolute. It is an ongoing self-reflective process.

A process *in what*, we might ask, but Hegel argues strenuously that that is precisely the wrong question. One of the goals of his *Phenomenology* and *Logic* is to eliminate any possibility of an external view of spirit, as if it were an object we study rather than the act and structure of studying itself. Is that so different from Wittgenstein's refusal to let philosophy make absolute ontological claims? Let us see. To do so, we need to return to that first and oldest use of *ontology*.

Reality as such

The study Aristotle called *first philosophy* examines being qua being (*to on he on*). It seeks categories that can be used to study the entities revealed in any local language or form of life. Aristotle has a set of conceptual tools. These include his list of the basic categories of entities (substance, quantity, quality, and relation), plus his concepts of the four causes, matter and form, and above all his notions of actuality and potentiality. Using these he can analyse historical change, biological reproduction, the writing of poetry, the growth of cities and political structures.

He describes the being of entities on many different levels; he does not reduce everything to one single level. So, for instance, when attacking Plato, he does not reduce Plato's universal Forms to nominalist collections of individuals; instead, he argues that the mode of being of Plato's Forms, the way they are supposed to exist, renders them powerless to achieve the functions that Plato thought demanded their existence. When he discusses pre-Socratic theories of the nature of matter, he argues that the modes of being for their proposed basic entities are not capable of accounting for the orderly regular actualisation of natural processes.

Hegel too does ontology in this Aristotelian mode. He is not trying to produce the Ultimate List of the Truly Basic Entities. Hegel's *Logic* does not produce an ontology in the reductionist sense, but rather a set of categories that can be used to analyse and clarify any local ontology.

Hegel's toolbox includes the categories developed in the third section of his *Logic*, the *Doctrine of the Concept*. These involve multiple permutations and involuted combinations of the universal/particular/individual aspects of things, keyed to the traditional logical terms of judgements and syllogisms. He uses these categories to analyse space and time, the solar system, the types of rocks, biological processes, the levels of subjectivity, the different branches of government, and on and on, including a self-reflective account of the genesis of these tools themselves.

This crystalline sequence of categories does not precipitate into a final reductive list; it culminates in a self-aware motion of categories which can be used to criticise, or to locate at an appropriate level, any local categories. None are denied, but they are put in their place.

Local ontologies get swept up into the motion but then are left where they are. Different local ontologies continue to function but within an awareness of their ... limitations? ... locations? Neither of those terms is quite correct because they suggest some kind of static whole where each local ontology is a piece in a jigsaw puzzle. Hegel's proclaimed Absolute Knowledge and the Absolute Idea provide no list of the Final Objects; instead, they bring a self-comprehension of the process of developing local ontologies within the activity of spirit, while revealing the form of that activity.

Hegel usually lets local ontologies be, noting their inadequacies. However, if he sees someone trying to draw from inadequate categories practical conclusions concerning ethics, art, politics or education, then he applies corrections. To criticise, say, a proposal about the legislature of a city, he will do what Aristotle did, namely, present the concepts from the rival theory, show their inadequacies and inner tensions, and then provide a better recommendation based on his own account of how the universal/particular/individual aspects of things mutually constitute each other. And if he thinks a practical issue is serious enough, he will criticise the rival theory in a contemptuous tone that Wittgenstein would recognise.

Mastering the nets

Both Hegel and Wittgenstein want us to become aware of our diamond nets, our instinctive ways of thinking, and "become master [...] when we make [them] in turn the object of our knowledge" (EPN 1830, §246 A). They both want us to find a new freedom with our ways of thinking and speaking, even as we realise how we are constituted by them. Diamond nets are not infinitely pliable. They have their own constraints. We become their masters only when we realise that they are not our arbitrary creations. The master potter knows his or her clay and kiln, and the sculptor knows what marble can and cannot do.

Wittgenstein wants us to become master craftsmen understanding what our language can and cannot do, what changes we can and cannot make. Hegel too hopes for such sensitive awareness of our situation and concepts, though he pictures this awareness arising through unique, purer experiences of thought.

Hegel conducts exercises in studying and manipulating ontological concepts, feeling out their connections and movements, their flexibilities and their resistances, coming to understand the pattern of movement that is their mode of being.

So, when Hegel looks out over the fabled land of metaphysics, he sees antique constructions that were believed by their architects to be solid but whose structures are riven with inner tensions. But he also perceives how the architects' tools are being refined.

If Hegel can plan the right path among those castles and ruins, and properly reveal the architectural changes in each design, a traveller on that path can come to see how the diamond nets grew subtler and, upon reaching the final palace, the traveller will find in its corridors and rooms the self-comprehension of the traveller's own path and the principles behind its design.

We could perhaps speak of these tortuous explorations as a kind of philosophical *therapy*. Hegel sets us exercises in working through negativity, accepting change, reconciling us with our situation, freeing us from constricting modes of thought and action. One-sided questions get pushed aside, dualities are transcended, just as therapy is supposed to do. Hegel's desired effect resembles Wittgenstein's linguistic therapy insofar as it dispels illusion, turning us away from fruitless quests that we think we must follow because we are under the spell of inadequate categories.

Objections!

At this point in our walk together, Wittgenstein can hold silent no longer. He erupts: "Kolb, no! I protest! I don't accept your parallels. Hegel and I see the history of ontology and metaphysics very differently. He may see an optimistic progress, but I see a wasteland littered with wrecked projects and delusive monuments, with mazes of confusion amid the ruins.

And then, you see him trying to offer some total vision of spirit that can encompass all that diverse wreckage! But that total vision of spirit is just another trap, trying to domesticate my ideas and lock my philosophical practice in a systematic cage!

And even worse, to continue the insults, you have the nerve to try to make my philosophical therapy and Hegel's dialectical manipulations sound like they have the same goal. No! You miss the crucial difference: I lead the fly out of the fly-bottle. Hegel constructs a more intricate bottle to more deeply imprison the fly. True therapy is to let the fly go free."

Before I can reply to this outburst, Hegel grumbles: "Wittgenstein, what kind of freedom are you offering the fly? The open space outside any bottle still has its own geometry and curvature. Our logical space is finite and closes in upon itself; true freedom consists in moving with the natural curves of that space, not in some illusory infinite openness where all directions of flight are arbitrary and meaningless."

Basic disagreements

Wittgenstein begins a heated reply about geometry, but I interject, "Gentlemen, calm down, be patient. I suggest that your disagreements have two deep roots: first, you choose very different sorts of examples, and second, you have different notions about the weave of the diamond nets on which your examples are strung."

They turn on me for explanation, and I say: "Wittgenstein, your examples tend to be simple language-games: Slab, Promise and so on. I know that these are deliberately simplified and meant to show how to approach more complex modes of living and speaking. But they set the tone. Your simple language-games echo the atomic simple objects of your *Tractatus*, each independent and self-sufficient. You suggest a picture of simple language-games, each more or less complete, that get assembled into more complex social roles and forms of life."

To clarify my point, I recall how when I taught at the University of Chicago, Paul Ricoeur and I led a number of courses together on Hegel and on Nietzsche. Once, when we were discussing the then-current analytic philosophy of action by Donald Davidson and others, Paul argued that those philosophers had chosen the wrong kind of examples. They sought to understand the nature of intentional actions by focusing on so-called *basic actions* such as raising one's arm. Paul argued that such examples were impoverished. Philosophers of action should have taken as their examples full-bodied episodes of action such as starting the French Revolution or living in the feudal system.

Those examples are movements within what Hegel called shapes of spirit. These are not wholes assembled out of already individualised components. They are complex unities inside of which their component sub-actions achieve their individuality. For Hegel a *small* example might be the operations of a national legislature or a city court system.

"So," I tell Hegel and Wittgenstein, "you speak at cross purposes when you cite concrete examples of diamond nets."

"Furthermore," I add, "Your deepest disagreement is that Hegel affirms and Wittgenstein denies that the weaving of those diamond nets produces, and depends on, internal tensions and contradictions."

Hegel claims that these inner tensions have two sources. The first is that the individual diamonds in the net are not independent units. They depend on their net of connections. This Wittgenstein could agree with, given his notion of internal relations. But for Hegel there is more; the diamond net is not a static framework of fixed relationships. Apparently simple categories, such as form versus content, individual versus universal, thing versus qualities, contain twists and mediations.

Even and especially the most abstract ontological categories, such as *being*, *unity* or *thing*, achieve their apparent simplicity only within ongoing mediations through other categories. In the first part of Hegel's *Logic*, categories that are supposed to be rigidly separated keep slipping over into something else. In the second part, categories that are supposed to be locked in clear dualities cannot maintain their separations. In the third part, categories come in triads that refuse to settle into a clear hierarchy or primacy: there is no "first", each member is both primary and mediated. These shifts and mediations are not a run-up to an eventual static net; rather, they are the way in which the categories dynamically exist.

Hegel's second source of a diamond net's internal tensions is a fold or doubling *within* a shape of spirit, bringing change and revolutions. In the introduction to his *Phenomenology*, Hegel claims that any form of conscious awareness directed at an object includes an implicit self-comprehension of that intended object and what consciousness must do to reach that object. Later he argues that forms of consciousness concretely exist only within social shapes of spirit. And those shapes depend on the same inner doubling, a self-comprehension of the shape's inner project of a social world and its mode of attaining mutual recognition. This twists an inner fold along which a shape of spirit can fracture when it fails to find itself at home in the world it projects.

Changes and revolutions

Hegel and Wittgenstein might agree that "all education (*Bildung*) reduces to the distinction of categories", as long as the associated practices are counted as well. Wittgenstein would add, though, that for him, our grammars (for instance, the grammar of the get me a slab game, or of our talk about colours, or the rules of chess) have *as diamond nets* no contradictions, no *internal* pressure for change. But equally, he insists that they *can* produce contradictions and confusions if we misunderstand what grammar is, or confuse reports on grammar with empirical reports.

Furthermore, Wittgenstein insists that *in use* a given diamond net may prove unsatisfactory. Our colour talk could prove inadequate for discussing a painting by Caravaggio. Or, while the rules of chess contain no inner tension, playing actual games of chess might not go as we would like. If that happens, we can change the game. The move called *castling*, allowing king and rook to be moved at the same time, was perhaps introduced to speed up the game or provide more excitement. Yet Wittgenstein asserts that there is no built-in self-understanding that would direct the changes in the game's rules. Quite other rules could have been introduced, and the game could have been altered in many different creative ways.

Hegel insists that the problem goes deeper. The diamond nets within shapes of spirit make distinctions that cannot be maintained, and define unions that cannot be achieved, not just because the world is recalcitrant, but because at heart the net's concepts secretly depend upon and move into one another.

The owl of Minerva does not suddenly wake up and show us the inadequacies of our concepts. Structural changes do not start from armchair reflection. Change comes when internal tensions reveal the inadequacies of a structure of lived experience. In the dialectic of master and slave it is the productive labour of the slave that provides in practice a new kind of self that then can be philosophically conceptualised.

For instance, later in his *Phenomenology* Hegel analyses the structure of a post-feudal absolute monarch's royal court, such as France's *ancien régime*.

The courtier's life brings dependence, struggle for recognition and constant demands for elegance and wit, yet no substantive social goals. This creates in practice a new kind of unrooted, active but pointless ironic self. Combined with its cousin, an earnest enlightened self-fighting superstition, a new social role is created, one committed to the revolutionary demand for absolute freedom.[3]

It is not that the *ancien régime* for some contingent reason could not manage to deliver the identities and self-affirmations it promised. It had a social grammar that defined what is to count as being a recognised and affirmed individual in that particular community. But that grammar's diamond net was woven out of particular versions of more abstract categories: form and content, individual and society, freedom and duty. Taken in themselves these categories are not static abstract structures contemplated by a pure eye. They are schemes for active thinking grasping together other active graspings. They exist in the act of bringing together opposed subsidiary categories.

Their internal tensions are revealed when individuals are unable to verify themselves in the community. The old shape of spirit fails to produce its proposed type of mutually recognised individuals at home in their world. The outline of that failure prefigures a new shape of spirit. In the process, a social grammar that defined certain key oppositions mutates into a new social grammar with new oppositions, each side of which includes in tension elements of both sides of the older oppositions. Hegel calls this *determinate negation*. It is crucial to the necessity of his dialectic and is one of the more valuable (and more vulnerable) parts of his philosophy.

Wittgenstein's examples, on the other hand, have less historical depth and provide no intermediate-sized social or historical concepts to guide changes. So, Jean-François Lyotard can read Wittgenstein as claiming that the creation of new language-games and forms of life happens through discontinuous creative leaps with no guidance except a sense of value that cannot be put into words.[4]

At this point in our discussion Hegel wants to return to his comment about the natural geometry and curvature of logical space, with its implications for history and liberation.

But I break off our discussion. For we are here up against another fundamental issue, the status of ontological and categorial/grammatical analysis:

---

[3] The section of the *Phenomenology* referred to here, *Der sich entfremdete Geist: die Bildung*, contains many more layered transitions than this short summary (PS: §§484–581).

[4] Lyotard (1985). Lyotard's is an inadequate reading of Wittgenstein; the essays in Grève and Mácha (2016) make important strides toward clarifying how for Wittgenstein the creation of new language-games can be free yet non-arbitrary.

how do the contours and movements of thought and language relate to those of things in the world? That discussion could get very noisy, but I have been implying that Hegel and Wittgenstein may not be as far apart on this issue as so many of their feuding descendants think they must be.

Parting words

As they part, neither philosopher is happy with my attempts to force them together. But each now understands better what the other was trying to do, although each still disapproves of the other's project. Before they go their separate ways, I ask them to offer a suggestion each thinks might improve *the other's* philosophical project.

Hegel urges Wittgenstein to look more closely at his examples, at how they live within larger cultural units that bring their supposed independence into question, and at how they contain inner tensions. He suggests Wittgenstein look carefully at what we do when we combine and coordinate language-games, and how that combining is not a matter of assembling atomic units.

Wittgenstein in his turn asks Hegel to consider that he might be being led astray by a picture. A picture of a pure self-developing totality of diamond nets. A picture of the transparency of pure thought to itself. A picture of a single great narrative or action being accomplished. He urges the great proponent of history to face up to the historicity of his own philosophy's language and self-understanding.[5]

When they leave, Hegel returns to his post on the bridge between the land of ontology and the world of politics. Wittgenstein returns to his ordinary life. And we ourselves, here and now, go on with our ordinary philosophic lives, trying to find trustworthy paths and adequate shelters amid the mazes of philosophy today, whose paths owe many of their twists to our two recent companions.

References

Bouwsma, Oets Kolk: *Wittgenstein Conversations 1949–1951*, Hackett, 1986.
Grève, Sebastian and Mácha, Jakub (Eds.): *Wittgenstein and the Creativity of Language*, Palgrave Macmillan, 2016.
Kolb, David: *The Critique of Pure Modernity: Hegel, Heidegger, and After*, University of Chicago Press, 1987.

---

5 For explorations of this line of critique, see Kolb (1987: ch.11) and Kolb (2009).

Kolb, David: "The Necessities of Hegel's Logics", in: Angelica Nuzzo (ed.): *Hegel and the Analytic Tradition*, Continuum, 2009, pp.40–60.

Lyotard, Jean-François: *Just Gaming,* translated from *Au Juste* (1979) by Wlad Godzich, University of Minnesota Press, 1985.

Mácha, Jakub: *Wittgenstein on Internal and External Relations: Tracing all the Connections,* Bloomsbury Academic, 2015.

Jonathan L. Shaheen
The Communitarian Wittgenstein and Brandom's Hegel on Recognition and Social Constitution

Abstract This paper critically pushes back against social constitution arguments that scholars have found in Wittgenstein and Hegel. Where the communitarian Wittgenstein holds that the normativity of meaning depends on intersubjective agreement within a language community, and where Brandom's Hegel holds that the emergence of self-consciousness depends on intersubjective recognition, I argue that the intersubjective element *per se* is inessential to the solutions provided. Against the communitarian Wittgenstein, I argue that the social element contributes too little to be necessary. Diachronic, intrasubjective agreement provides everything intersubjective agreement does. Against Brandom's Hegel, I argue that the social element requires so much to be able to contribute anything that it, too, turns out to be unnecessary. The substantial powers that have to be built in for symmetric and transitive relations of recognition to be possible themselves allow for the possibility of the emergence of self-consciousness without social interaction.

Hegel and Wittgenstein have both been read as giving powerful arguments for the social constitution of philosophically central entities that are in a certain sense analogous. Taking Hegel first, on Robert Brandom's reading of the self-consciousness chapter of the *Phenomenology of Spirit*, Hegel argues that reflexive self-consciousness can only arise through a transitive and symmetric relation of recognition. That is, one can only become self-conscious, on Brandom's reading of Hegel, by being recognized as a recognizer by another recognizer whose recognitions one recognizes as such. This recognition-based requirement means that self-consciousness as such is socially constituted, at least according to Brandom's Hegel.

Turning now to Wittgenstein, on a communitarian reading of the private language argument in *Philosophical Investigations*, Wittgenstein argues that the standards of correctness implicated by the normativity of meaning can only consist in the intersubjective agreement of a community of language users. That is, one can only become a language user, on the communitarian reading of Wittgenstein, by being recognized as competent by the members of a linguistic community. This recognition-based requirement means that the normativity of meaning

https://doi.org/10.1515/9783110572780-010

as such is socially constituted, at least according to the communitarian Wittgenstein.

Though I wrote the preceding paragraphs so as to emphasize the analogy between Brandom's Hegel and the communitarian Wittgenstein on recognition and social constitution, here I want to probe the arguments for differences. A first difference concerns the anti-Hegelian (or, at least, anti-Brandomian) theory of mind entertained at points of Wittgenstein's private language argument. As I read §258 of *Philosophical Investigations*, the text around which my discussion of Wittgenstein will revolve, Wittgenstein does not go nearly as far as Brandom's Hegel. The problem Wittgenstein discerns with private language is supposed to arise for a diarist with an intention to use a sign in a certain way, that is, for an already constituted and (mental-, if not linguistic-) rule-following mind. The central question is whether the diarist can establish a meaning for a sign for a private sensation that leaves open the possibility that the diarist will make mistakes in its application. But nothing here requires understanding the diarist's mind itself as socially constituted, and in that respect Brandom's Hegel goes farther than the private language argument on its communitarian reading.

A second difference concerns the success of a certain individualist response to the social constitution arguments of Brandom's Hegel and the communitarian Wittgenstein. In particular, I explore whether relations between different time slices of a single mind can stand-in for genuine social contributions. It is unclear, in Wittgenstein's case, what is gained by positing intersubjective agreement (in a broad sense of "agreement", encompassing a form of life, going on in the same way, etc.) over and above diachronic intrasubjective agreement (again in the broad sense of "agreement"), that is, over and above agreement (in the broad sense) between different time slices of an individual. But in the case of Brandom's Hegel, as already mentioned, it is not just agreement with what a putative language user does that intersubjectivity brings to the table, but the constitution of the recognitional subject itself. If this is right, then the answer to the question of the private language argument may turn on the question that Brandom's Hegel answers in the master-slave dialectic. That is, insofar as using a private language requires self-consciousness, Brandom's Hegel is in the position of supplying a more fundamental argument against the possibility of a private language. My criticism of the argument Brandom finds in Hegel here will be in some measure the inverse of my criticism of the communitarian Wittgenstein. Whereas communitarianism buys the Wittgensteinian so little that it can be had for the cost of individual time slices, the sociality Brandom is selling costs so much that the resources it takes to buy it can equally well purchase self-consciousness with no social contribution whatsoever. That is, an entity that has the particular powers of recognition required to get socially constituted self-consciousness off the ground in the way Brandom suggests can just as well become self-conscious by interacting individualistically with the world, using only those powers of recognition admitted by Brandom himself.

1 Intersubjective and Diachronic Agreement

First Wittgenstein. Consider the following gloss of the private language argument and its supposed communitarian upshot. What is missing for the private linguist is a standard in comparison with which our Robinson Crusoe or solipsistic neurasthenic can be found wanting. There is only the long-suffering hermit's own unrivaled and therefore unimpeachable use of signs.

> One would like to say: whatever is going to seem correct to me [that is, the private language user] is correct. And that only means that here we can't talk about "correct". (PI 2009: §258, p.99e)

A community of language users, however, might agree or disagree with the linguistic usage of one of its (would-be) members. The social component here is simply the possibility of agreement or disagreement, which allows us to "talk about 'correct'," as it were.[1] As Meredith Williams put the idea:

> The origin of normativity, then, lies in the agreement that creates the place for standards and in the possibility of deviation from the actions of the community that hold the standard in place. (Williams 1999: p.177)

To be clear, by "agreement" here, something more than just making an explicit positive judgement is meant. The community participates in a social practice, sharing a form of life in which the individual language user can participate. It is the practice, the form of life, that the community brings to the table.

Nevertheless, if the solution to the private language argument requires only the possibility of agreement or disagreement, even in this expansive sense of "agreement"—that is, if the solution requires only a form of life to serve as a standard of correctness—then the social element is inessential to the solution (cf. Goldfarb 1985: pp.482–484). For a single individual, participating alone in a standard-giving form of life, can agree or disagree with past time slices of her-

---

[1] See, e.g., Malcolm (1954); Rhees (1954: pp.78–79); and Kripke (1982: e.g., p.91, p.95, and pp.109–110).

self as regards her usage of a sign for a private sensation.² The suggestion that time slices of an individual might suffice to compose a linguistic community is not new.³ The basic idea is that, whatever conditions are thought to be required of a plurality of individuals in order for them to constitute a linguistic community whose agreement and disagreement can contribute to the establishment of linguistic meaning, those very conditions are plausibly fulfilled by time slices of an individual.⁴ Here those conditions are taken to be participation in a standard-giving form of life. The crucial claim is that time slices of an individual can share in the same form of life, even when there is diachronic, intrapersonal disagreement over a particular deployment of a sign (cf. Kusch 2006: p.39).

Changes in form of life are unnecessary, in particular, for coming to judge that one's past deployments were due to perceptual distortions, slips of the tongue, or even mistakes about the meaning of the sign.⁵ This claim should be uncontroversial in the first two cases.⁶ But in the last case, it is controversial: Bar-On (1992: p.35) suggests that mistakes about meaning require a social element, viz., the "behavior, environment and history of a community". Bar-On (1992) thinks that these community features mediate the transformation of a teleological norm, which is concerned with the accomplishment of some end, into a linguistic norm, which is concerned with meaning. While Bar-On (1992) is arguing against the possibility of a solitary language, I want to argue that mistakes about meaning can be recognized even for a private language, and so a fortiori for a solitary language.⁷

Consider the following scenario. A subject experiences a series of three feelings, separated in time. The subject initially takes the second feeling to be the

---

2 As noted by an anonymous referee, there could be another sense of "agreement" for which a social element is explicitly written into the semantics. If the relevant sense of "agreement" were like that, the argument made here wouldn't work. I take agreement, on a non-question-begging version of the communitarian picture, to be a matter of those substantive factors that plausibly contribute to the establishment of linguistic meaning. These are describable, even in Wittgensteinian terms, without explicit talk literally requiring sociality. That's because, as I argue in the main text, sociality is not required for their fulfillment.
3 Haukioja (2005) discusses three examples of this move in the literature.
4 Cf. Baker and Hacker (2009: p.162), whence: There is little use for the assertoric form of the sentence "I think this is correct, but it is actually incorrect" (by contrast with the utterances "I thought that this was correct, but it is actually incorrect" or "This seems to him to be correct, but is actually incorrect").
5 Cf. the tripartite distinction between recognitional, performance, and meaning errors at Bar-On (1992: pp.33–34).
6 See, e.g., the discussion of a mistake in counting at Canfield (1996: pp.487–488).
7 Solitary languages are unshared, while private languages are in principle unsharable. See, e.g., Baker and Hacker (2009: ch.V, §5).

same as the first, and so to fall within the extension of the sign she has introduced to pick out feelings that are the same as the first. But then the subject experiences the third feeling, which is particularly striking in one respect. This third feeling is striking in the respect that it is vividly experienced as being more like the first feeling than the second, in retrospect, was. The similarity between the first two feelings then pales in comparison with the similarity between the first and third feelings. The subject thus gains reason to think that the second feeling, previously taken to be the same as the first feeling, was actually different in some relevant respect. Such an individual can then disagree with the past time slices of herself that took the second feeling to be the same as the first. She should thus abandon her earlier view that the second feeling falls in the extension of the relevant sign, not because of some perceptual distortion or slip of the tongue, but because she judges herself to have been wrong about the sign's meaning.

Notice that an individual, who has the epistemic advantages provided by her own memory, is better positioned than her community to decide whether she made a mistake about meaning or instead changed the underlying practice. But even in the midst of her conviction that her earlier use of the sign was mistaken and her newfound identification of similarity between the first and third feelings, a circumspect diarist might well come to doubt her certainty about the third feeling being like the first: maybe she is rewriting history, misremembering the first feeling and conflating it with the more recent and striking third one. (For readers to whom this seems far-fetched, just consider the variance over time in the claims of your nearest melodramatic friend about whether or not he was in love with a given person at a given time. For readers with only more stoic friends or who demand somewhat greater precision in examples, just consider the discussion of the coffee-tasters Chase and Sanborn in the seventh intuition pump of Dennett (1988).)

I take it that the possibility of doubt can arise even for the diarist tracking the reoccurrences of his own pains. But Wittgenstein says, in the passage of §258 already quoted above, that *one would like to say* that there is no difference between the diarist's seeming correct and his being correct. As McNally (2017) notes, §258 presents at most a fragment of an argument, because it does not tell us why one should want to say this. Some scholars have read Wittgenstein as here applying a previously established conclusion to the effect that linguistic normativity is essentially social, but McNally (2017) points out that such a procedure would be at odds with Wittgenstein's own metaphilosophical aversion to constructing arguments and theorizing (see ibid.: ch.4, esp. p.110). The argument is also just uninteresting to the extent that it depends on some verificationist principle or other, as some have thought.[8] I want to suggest that in fact Wittgenstein is not importing a conclusion drawn elsewhere, but just reporting an intuition about the case, namely, the intuition that there seems to be no room to consider someone to be wrong about her own sensations.[9]

This intuition seems very plausible if Wittgenstein is read as having taken on board something of a Russellian assumption, though one that we would do well to reject. This is the assumption that we can perfectly re-identify our own sense data, and it is not a far cry from the kind of infallibilism about sense-data present in Russell's early epistemology, e.g., in Russell (1912) and Russell (1913).[10] For Russell held that sense-data are perfectly known, through that most secure of epistemic relations: acquaintance. Taking Wittgenstein to have a notion of sense-data as perfectly known in mind helps to make sense of the otherwise puzzling feature of §258 of *Philosophical Investigations* that Wittgenstein reports that *one would like to say* there is no difference between seeming right and being right. That feature is otherwise puzzling because, absent such a notion of sense-data, there is very little temptation to want to deny that there is such a difference.[11]

---

[8] See Thomson (1964: §IX). (To correct an error in the scholarly record, note that the otherwise very useful discussion of communitarian readings of the private language argument in ch.4 of McNally (2017: p.100) mistakenly attributes to Judith Jarvis Thomson the view that "Wittgenstein relies on the principle of verification" when in fact on the last page of her article, Thomson distinguishes between Wittgenstein's views and the private language argument as described by Malcolm (1954: p.31), asserting that "Wittgenstein himself would never for a moment have subscribed to" the verificationist principle she uncovers in Malcolm's reconstruction.)

[9] An anonymous referee objects here that Wittgenstein explicitly rejects references to intuitions at, e.g., PI: §213. If that is how §213 is to be read, so much the worse for Wittgenstein. What it is to appeal to an intuition is to appeal to what we want to say about some case, and that is precisely what Wittgenstein does at the end of §258. Fortunately, there are more limited readings of §213. For instance, it's possible to read §213 as a rejection of the idea that some intuition or other can definitively resolve whatever uncertainty faces someone instructed to continue a series based on its initial segment, but not as a general rejection of appealing to what we want to say about various cases, that is, not as a general rejection of references to intuitions.

[10] Russell (1959) claimed that his views on sense-data would later change, though the historical facts remain a matter of scholarly debate, some discussion of which can be found in Savage (1989).

[11] Here is another way to put the point, with thanks due to Elinor Hållén for a helpful discussion of Wittgenstein's views on sense-data: Wittgenstein is here trying to show that sense-data theories cannot be sustained. But his accomplishment is limited by his having argued against a sense-data theory that comes together with an implausible Russellian epistemology, rather than having argued against a less committed sense-data theory. The limitation of his accomplishment then leaves room for a private language to get off the ground insofar as the private linguist countenances the possibility of incorrect judgements about her own experiences.

Indeed, insofar as we should believe in sense-data or qualia, we should not take ourselves to be able to reidentify them perfectly.[12] This was, in part, the point of the scenario considered above, but it is also easy to experience directly. Look at some patch of color near you, look away, then look at it again. Any initial confidence you might have that the color appears exactly the same to you ebbs upon repetition of this experiment. I submit that you have no idea whatsoever if the color experience is the same across viewings. (A flickering light or moving shadow might secure assent to this claim. But even in perfect laboratory conditions, as it were, confidence ebbs.) If there are qualia, this need not mean that there is no fact of the matter as to whether the color experience really was the same. Insofar as you attempt to deploy a sign to pick out one quale or another, as the diarist of §258 intends to do, there may well be a fact of the matter about whether you deploy the sign correctly on subsequent occasions. So, one ought not want to say that whatever seems to the private language user to be correct is correct. The private language user can make mistakes, even about the meaning of her own signs.

To give the barest indication of how correctness can arise for an individual more generally, let me briefly describe the Platonist theory of the constitution of meaning that I actually prefer. On that theory, the language user helps to determine which deployments of a sign are paradigmatic, and the sign then gets its meaning on the basis of which referents out in the world best fit the usage. I prefer, that is, a projectivist account of the selection of paradigmatic deployments, and a Lewisian account of eligibility for reference.[13] Here one commonly meets the metaphor of reference magnetism. That metaphor is nevertheless inadequate, on my view, to the extent that sometimes it is use itself that determines that a referent should be maximally eligible. That is, sometimes we use words with a semantic intention to pick out a natural kind, as in the cases of "fish" and "mammal".[14] It is thus the existence of semantic intentions (and not something

---

12 In fact, Russell (1913: p.78) clearly distinguishes between (allegedly infallible) presentations of sense-data and (admittedly fallible) judgements about sense data. (In distinguishing as he does between presentation and judgement, Russell seems to have had in mind something like the Brentano School's taxonomy of mental acts. See, e.g., Brentano (1995: Book II, ch.7).)
13 See Blackburn (1984) for the relevant notion of projectivism and Lewis (1983) for the relevant notion of eligibility and its connection to (Platonic) universals. But note that my invocation of projectivism is limited to the selection of deployments that count as paradigmatic: the language user or interpreter has to determine which uses settle the meaning of the sign, and only then can eligibility take over to settle the meaning facts.
14 I owe this observation to David Manley.

like magnetism) that explains how the meaning of "fish" could remain unchanged by the discovery that whales are mammals. To be clear, my positive view involves an out-and-out denial of one of the purported "lessons" of *Philosophical Investigations*. David Pears counts the following as (in Barry Stroud's phrase) a "recurrent theme" of that work: "'we do not, and cannot, rely on any instant talisman', and 'the meanings of our words are not guaranteed by any independent pattern already existing in the world and waiting for language to be attached to it'."[15] If I might pluck a contrary slogan from a different Germanophone philosopher of roughly the same period, I would reply with this encapsulation of my view:

Den Bedeutungen wachsen Worte zu. (Heidegger 1926: p.161)[16]

But the details of my positive theory are beside the immediate point about the communitarian response to Wittgenstein.

The immediate point is just that whatever is gained by the appeal to community is just as well provided by diachronic reflection among time slices of an individual. Maybe agreement alone, in the expansive sense of having the same form of life, isn't enough. If so, the communitarian is wrong. Or rather, maybe what has to be presupposed to get agreement off the ground is an existing rule-following practice. On the communitarian picture, a community of rule-followers agrees or disagrees with the usage of a putative individual rule-follower. According to the diachronic response, an individual agrees or disagrees with her past usage. But does she have to be a rule-follower to do this? According to my positive theory, she is. After all, she projects paradigmatic rule-constraining status onto certain privileged uses, and then eligibility facts (that is, facts about the world) fix what rule is being followed on the basis of these privileged uses. The positive theory even mentions semantic intentions to pick out, for example, natural kinds. But an adequate response to Wittgenstein might be thought to require more than the grounding of meaning in the interaction between an individually constituted, rule-following (even: semantic-intention-having) mind and the world.

The extent to which this adequacy condition—that a successful individualist response to the private language argument would have to get linguistic rule-following off the ground without presupposing other, non-linguistic rule-following

---

15 Stroud 2001: p.153. One place that this theme appears is in Wittgenstein's discussion of appeals to memory in *Philosophical Investigations*, §265, a passage raised by Hans-Johann Glock in the question period following the reading of a previous draft of this paper.
16 To meanings, words accrue. (Author's translation.)

behavior—is present in Wittgenstein's texts is unclear. The opening of PI 2009, §258 reads as follows:

> Let's imagine the following case. I want to keep a diary about the recurrence of a certain sensation. To this end I associate it with the sign "S" and write this sign in a calendar for every day on which I have the sensation.

Here already we have a mind with a certain semantic intention, private though its subject matter may be. Wittgenstein denies the possibility of a distinction between seeming right and being right even in this case, so the private language argument cannot rest entirely on the claim that mental rule-following is required in order to get linguistic rule-following off the ground. Even mental rule-following is supposed to be insufficient.

There is a parallel worth noting here between what Wittgenstein's texts suggest and the picture of the emergence of language present in the 1928 lecture of Brouwer's that brought Wittgenstein back to philosophy.[17] Language, for Brouwer, is in general no more than a means of "will transmission," a "function of the social activity of man" (Brouwer 1929: p.48). The invention of language by the mathematician is preceded by languageless mathematical activity of the mind. It is only when the mathematician, who is already possessed of a rule-following mind, wants to remind himself or compel others to perform the constructions that he has already performed that he introduces language. The use of language fundamentally to compel appears prominently in the builders' language game of *Philosophical Investigations*. The introduction of a linguistic symbol to serve the purpose of some pre-existing, rule-following mind, with its echoes of the Brouwerian conception of language, is present even at the heart of the private language argument in §258.[18] But contra Brouwer, I take it, Wittgenstein doesn't think language can get off the ground in this way.

Candlish (1980: p.91) argues that the problem is that the initial ostensive definition of a sign in §258 is bound to fail. Does the possibility of coming to recognize mistakes about the meaning of a sign—and I suppose that really is possible, in the kind of scenario mentioned above—undermine the ability of an individual to establish meanings in the first place, even for a diarist with some definite pur-

---

17 *Pace* Marion's (2003) rather strident denial of influence, it is worth noting these parallels in the present context if only for clarification of the dialectic at §258.
18 I note these parallels between Brouwer (1929) and *Philosophical Investigations* without prejudice to Kevin Mulligan's idea that Wittgenstein gets much of his philosophy of language from Austrian sources: see, e.g., Mulligan (1997).

pose in mind? Candlish and Wrisley identify the conclusion of the private language argument as follows:

> The conclusion is that a language in principle unintelligible to anyone but its originating user is impossible. The reason for this is that such a so-called language would, necessarily, be unintelligible to its supposed originator too, for he would be unable to establish meanings for its putative signs. (Candlish and Wrisley 2014: §1)[19]

I have been arguing that the possibility of doubt is rather what makes meaningful, intrasubjective, diachronic agreement and disagreement possible. It is the reason that we really can "talk about 'correct'" in the individual's deployment of signs. But this doubt cannot be too great, as Wittgenstein himself emphasized in *On Certainty*:

> Certain events would put me into a position in which I could not go on with the old language-game any further. In which I was torn away from the *sureness* of the game.
> Indeed, doesn't it seem obvious that the possibility of a language-game is conditioned by certain facts? (OC: §617)[20]

A Goldilocks principle applies to the relationship between doubt and rule-following. Too much doubt and the ambition to follow a rule is abandoned. Too little doubt and any pretense of following a rule is exposed. (The melodramatic friend who retrospectively revises his opinions about when he was truly in love still meaningfully deploys his terminology, though another who despairs of any confidence at all about what he has experienced forbears from the attempt.) But there is an amount of doubt that's just right for generating correctness, and it is available even on desert islands, and even about sensations.

To take stock, in §258, Wittgenstein tries to establish the impossibility of a private language even for a rule-following mind. The plausibility of the ultimate claim of the passage—that here one would like to say there is no difference between what seems right to the diarist and what is right—derives, on my reading, from a quasi-Russellian assumption about our ability to perfectly re-identify qualia. That assumption gets Wittgenstein his conclusion because there is no doubting what is certain, but the diarist can and should doubt re-identifications of sensations: the quasi-Russellian assumption is to be rejected. Nevertheless, there is much more to say about social constitution, because the dialectic thus

---

[19] The impossibility of an individual's establishing meanings for the putative signs of a private language is also cited by Luntley (2003: p.134) as the "central claim" of the private language argument.
[20] See Hertzberg (1976) for discussion.

far has presupposed that we can make sense of an individualistically constituted, mental-rule-following mind. It is just that presupposition that Brandom's Hegel calls into question.

2 The Constitution of the Mind

Brandom and his version of Hegel hold that in order to be "the subjects of experience, knowers, and agents," we must be "the subjects of determinately contentful commitments and responsibilities, concept users" (Brandom 1999: p.173). The emphasis here is on determinacy, because Brandom takes Hegel to be responding to a perceived deficiency in Kant's notion of concepts, wherein subjects are supposed to fully determine or institute concepts before deploying or applying them.[21] The Hegelian response to Kant is supposed to understand the determinacy of concepts on the basis of an analogy with selves, with the possibility of both turning out to be dependent on the presence of other selves. Brandom's idea, as he puts it, is that "the idealist thesis" that "the structure and unity of the concept is the same as the structure and unity of the self" is Hegel's way of making "the semantic pragmatist thesis" that "the use of concepts determines their content" work (Brandom 1999: p.164; italics purged). But here I will be concerned only with the social constitution of the self that Brandom finds in Hegel.

Selfhood for Brandom's Hegel is thoroughly social:

> The core idea structuring Hegel's social understanding of selves is that they are synthesized by mutual recognition. That is, to be a self—a locus of conceptual commitment and responsibility—is to be taken or treated as one by those one takes or treats as one: to be recognized by those one recognizes. (ibid.: p.169)

Brandom takes this social-constitution account to be put forward by Hegel in the self-consciousness chapter of the *Phenomenology of Spirit*. Early in that chapter, Hegel rather mysteriously claims that "self-consciousness is *desire* [*Begierde*] in general" (PS 1977: §167). He then goes on to describe a struggle to the death for recognition (PS 1977: §§178–196).

Hegel's transition from desire to recognition can be puzzling (PS 1977: §178). To closely follow the text, Hegel identifies self-consciousness with desire, describes the satisfaction of that desire as "the reflection of self-consciousness in itself," which we should understand as the conceptualization of itself as a

---

21 Brandom 1999: pp.165–167. N.B.: McDowell (1999: pp.190–191) denies that this is a fair description of Kant's view of concepts.

self-consciousness, and then requires that this reflection, and thereby self-consciousness itself, is "doubled."[22] Whether or not Hegel thought of this doubling as involving two self-consciousnesses actually distinct from one another is a substantive interpretive question. The doubling might instead just be that a single self-consciousness must be conscious of itself as a self-consciousness. In that case, the doubling consists in the self-consciousness appearing as both object and agent of the conscious act. But according to Brandom's interpretation, at any rate, the doubling in question requires two self-consciousnesses.[23] Interpretive disputes aside, it is clear from the text that a consequence of this doubling is that "[a self-consciousness] is a self-consciousness for a self-consciousness" (PS 1977: §177). And from that it is supposed to follow that self-consciousness "exists only as something recognized" (PS 1977: §178). So Hegel makes the move from desire to recognition because the satisfaction of the desire that self-consciousness is requires recognition.

Brandom explains this shift in Hegel's argument by taking recognition as what is characteristically desired by self-conscious beings. But he argues that this desire can only be satisfied socially. In particular, Brandom (1999) suggests the Wittgensteinian inference that in the case of a lone recognizer recognizing itself, whatever would seem right to it would be right, which would undermine the possibility of error and therefore (apparently) prevent a desire-fulfilling individualistic recognition of the self (see ibid.: p.171).

To see how social constitution comes into the picture, we have to survey Brandom's interpretation of Hegel's accounts of desire and recognition. Brandom reads Hegel's invocation of desire as a reference back to his earlier discussion of animal reactions to food in the practical sphere.[24] Desire is to be understood fairly common-sensically.[25] But to flesh it out a bit, according to Brandom's rendering of this familiar notion, desire is an element in "erotic awareness," which has a "tripartite structure" made up of three elements – the desire or some other at-

---

[22] PS 1977: §§176–177. Reflection is bound up with recognizing or conceptualizing something as falling under some concept.
[23] McDowell (2006) takes the opposite position, and provides a reading that I prefer if only because I think it gives Hegel a better chance of being right.
[24] PS 1977: §109. The term "*Begierde*" does not appear there, but see Jenkins (2009: pp.109–110), which also defends reading Hegel as making this reference.
[25] Jenkins (2009: p.122) also argues in favor of understanding desire in this way, since "animal desire is a notion familiar to natural consciousness that can enter the dialectic at any point." But note that understanding Hegel's introduction of desire in this way is badly at odds with his usual claims about the necessity of the progression of his works; at ibid.: p.104, Jenkins suggests that Hegel's claims about necessity are too fraught to have any claim on our interpretations of him.

titude (for example, hunger), a responsive activity (for example, eating), and a significance (for example, food) – and the relations between them.[26]

According to Brandom (2007), recognition happens socially, via the recognition of another as a recognizer.[27] Recognition of a recognizer involves applying the tripartite structure of erotic awareness to itself, so the elements here—the attitude, responsive activity, and significance—are, not surprisingly, quite complicated. The significance attributed to an object when it is recognized as an erotically aware organism is, of course, that it is erotically aware, i.e., that it is the sort of thing that things can be something for (Brandom 2007: p.139). In the case of recognizing a recognizer, then, the significance attributed to an object is that it is a recognizer, and in the case of recognizing a recognizer of selves, the significance attributed is that it is the sort of thing that can recognize selves. The relevant attitude, which is clear enough from the aforementioned requirement in Hegel's text that its satisfaction should result in recognition, is the desire to be recognized (ibid.: p.146). Given this significance and that desire, Brandom is able to reconstruct what the responsive activity that fills out the tripartite structure of erotic awareness in the case of recognizing a recognizer of selves must be. It must be whatever activity counts as taking or treating an object as a recognizer of selves, which could also be motivated by a desire for recognition.[28] The further details of the activity are tortuous, and torturous, and confined to a footnote here to memorialize their omission from the conference

---

26 Brandom (2007: p.138). Those relations are as follows:
1. The attitude must motivate the activity, in the sense of activating a (more or less reliable) disposition to respond differentially to objects.
2. Responding to an object by engaging in the activity is taking or treating it in practice as having a significance defined by the attitude that motivates the activity. This is the subjective significance of the object.
3. The desiring attitude assesses the object, implicitly attributing to it an objective significance, accordingly as responding to it by engaging in the activity the attitude motivates does or does not satisfy the desire. If it does not, if what the object was subjectively or for the animal does not coincide with what it was objectively, or in itself, that is, if the activity was not successful in satisfying the motivating desire, then an error has been committed. In that case, the desire motivates changing the reliable differential responsive disposition to engage in the associated activity when activated by the desire and stimulated by a range of objects. (ibid.: pp.138–139, with changes to enumeration, italicization (as usual), and a slight shortening of the parenthetical remark in 1.)

27 See also Brandom (2014: pp.8–9).
28 See Brandom (2007: p.138) on the relation of activity to significance in the tripartite structure of erotic awareness.

text for reasons of time and basic humanity.[29] What is crucial is that recognizing another as an authoritative recognizer has normative implications for one's own activity (ibid.: p.143). To recognize you as a recognizer is in part to commit to the authority of your recognizings, to take them seriously. These normative implications serve to make recognition of recognizers a transitive matter: if I recognize you as a recognizer of recognizers, I am to recognize as a recognizer anything that you recognize as such (ibid.: p.144). So if you then recognize me as a recognizer, I am to recognize myself as such as well. It is therefore possible for me to recognize myself as a recognizer, i. e., as a self, as long as someone I recognize as a recognizer of recognizers does so. Symmetry yields reflexivity via transitivity.

The issues here are complex, but the individualist solution towards which I want to gesture here is relatively simple. Given the normative powers of recognition and commitment Brandom's Hegel attributes to the creature that desires recognition, that creature too is already a rule follower, though one that needs to, as Habermas put it in a discussion of George Herbert Mead's social constitution theory of the self, "catch sight of itself."[30] One way to catch sight of ourselves is via others, sure. Brandom's Hegel tells us that story. But another way might well be to run into things, feel hunger, get sick from bad berries, and so on, that is, to interact with the world, taking seriously one's past judgements while also subjecting them to the tribunal of experience.[31] This looks just like the individualist response to Wittgenstein, and to a certain extent it is. In the case of the private language argument, I claimed that Wittgenstein's texts don't direct us to account for linguistic rule-following in the absence of mental rule following, and in effect that what little is bought by social constitution—that is, mere intersubjective agreement—can be purchased without it—that is, with diachronic intrasubjective agreement. Here I just claim that the substantial meta-

---

29 To take or treat an object as a recognizer of anything is to attribute to it (1) an activity whereby it recognizes objects as such things; (2) an attitude that licenses or authorizes its recognizing things as such things by engaging in the activity in (1); and (3) a distinction between correct and incorrect such recognitions, where correctness is assessed relative to the attitude in (2) (Brandom 2007: p.141). Thus, when one recognizer recognizes another as a K-recognizer, for any value of K, the first recognizer commits itself to the authority of the K-recognizings of the second, regarding it as (1) attributing K-hood to objects, acting with respect to those objects as if they were K's, and having an attitude that (2) licenses the activity and (3) assesses whether or not the objects actually are K's, by either being satisfied or motivating a change in the disposition to attribute K-hood (ibid.: p.143).
30 Habermas (1992: p.174), discussing Mead (1903).
31 Cf. the discussion at Boghossian (1989: p.520) of the gap between providing a social account of assertability conditions and providing an argument that assertability conditions are necessarily social.

physical powers of recognition and commitment that Brandom's Hegel attributes to the slave desirous of recognition suffice for the individual constitution of the thing in question: social constitution is so expensive that individual constitution costs nothing more.[32]

References

Baker, Gordon P. and Hacker, Peter M. S.: *Wittgenstein: Rules, Grammar and Necessity*, volume 2 of *An Analytical Commentary on the Philosophical Investigations: Essays and Exegesis, §§185–242*, Second edition, extensively revised by P. M. S. Hacker, Wiley-Blackwell, 2009.
Bar-On, Dorit: "On the Possibility of a Solitary Language", *Noûs* 26:1, 1992, pp.27–45.
Blackburn, Simon: "The Individual Strikes Back", *Synthese* 58:3, 1984, pp.281–301.
Boghossian, Paul: "The Rule-Following Considerations", *Mind* 98:392, 1989, pp.507–549.
Brandom, Robert B.: "Some Pragmatist Themes in Hegel's Idealism: Negotiation and Administration in Hegel's Account of the Structure and Content of Conceptual Norms", *European Journal of Philosophy* 7:2, 1999, pp.164–189.
Brandom, Robert B.: "The structure of desire and recognition: Self-consciousness and self-constitution", *Philosophy & Social Criticism* 33:1, 2007, pp.127–150.
Brandom, Robert B.: "Some Hegelian Ideas of Note for Contemporary Analytic Philosophy", *Hegel Bulletin* 35:1, 2014, pp.1–15.
Brentano, Franz: *Psychology from an Empirical Standpoint*, International Library of Philosophy, Routledge, 1995.
Brouwer, Luitzen E. J.: "Mathematics, Science, Language", 1929, in: Paolo Mancosu (Ed.): *From Brouwer to Hilbert: The Debate on the Foundations of Mathematics in the 1920s*, Oxford University Press, 1998, pp.45–53.
Candlish, Stewart: "The Real Private Language Argument", *Philosophy* 55, 1980, pp.85–94.
Candlish, Stewart and Wrisley, George: "Private language", *The Stanford Encyclopedia of Philosophy (Fall 2014 Edition)*, 2014.
Canfield, John V.: "The Community View", *The Philosophical Review* 105:4, 1996, pp.469–488.
Dennett, Daniel: "Quining Qualia", 1988, reprinted in: William G. Lycan (Ed.): *Mind and Cognition: A Reader*, MIT Press, 1990.

---

32 This paper begins to develop views that I first came to almost a decade ago, as an MSc Logic student at the University of Amsterdam, by grappling with Martin Stokhof's account of Wittgenstein on radical interpretation and Robert Pippin's Spinoza seminar on the self-consciousness chapter of PS. Each of them had a formative influence on the paper, though it ought to be said that the views developed in the paper are in large part reactions against the positions they found most plausible, and so they can't be expected to agree, in any measure, with the claims I advance. Thanks are also due to the audience in Dresden at the *Wittgenstein and Hegel – Reevaluation of Difference* conference, to my Uppsala colleague Elinor Hållén, and to an anonymous referee for this volume.

Goldfarb, Warren: "Kripke on Wittgenstein on Rules", *The Journal of Philosophy* 82:9, 1985, pp.471–488.
Habermas, Jürgen: *Postmetaphysical Thinking*, Polity Press, 1992.
Haukioja, Jussi: "Is Solitary Rule-Following Possible?", *Philosophia* 32, 2005, pp.131–154.
Heidegger, Martin: *Sein und Zeit*, Niemeyer, 1926.
Hertzberg, Lars: "On the Factual Dependence of the Language-Game", *Acta Philosophica Fennica* 28:1–3, 1976, pp.126–153.
Jenkins, Scott: "Hegel's Concept of Desire", *Journal of the History of Philosophy* 47:1, 2009, pp.103–130.
Kripke, Saul: *Wittgenstein on Rules and Private Language*. Harvard University Press, 1982.
Kusch, Martin: *A Sceptical Guide to Meaning and Rules: Defending Kripke's Wittgenstein*, McGill-Queen's University Press, 2006.
Lewis, David: "New Work for a Theory of Universals", 1983, in: Lewis, David: *Papers in Metaphysics and Epistemology*, Cambridge University Press, 1999, pp.8–55.
Luntley, Michael: *Wittgenstein: Meaning and Judgement*. Blackwell Publishing, 2003.
Malcolm, Norman: "Wittgenstein's Philosophical Investigations," *The Philosophical Review* 63:4, 1954, pp.530–559.
Marion, Mathieu: "Wittgenstein and Brouwer", *Synthese* 137:1/2, 2003, pp.103–127.
McDowell, John: "Comment on Robert Brandom's 'Some Pragmatist Themes in Hegel's Idealism'", *European Journal of Philosophy*, 7:2, 1999, pp.190–193.
McDowell, John: "The Apperceptive I and the Empirical Self: Towards a Heterodox Reading of 'Lordship and Bondage' in Hegel's *Phenomenology*", in: Katerina Deligiorgi (Ed.): *Hegel: New Directions*, McGill-Queen's University Press, 2006, ch.2, pp.33–48.
McNally, Thomas: *Wittgenstein and the Philosophy of Language: The Legacy of the Philosophical Investigations*, Cambridge University Press, 2017.
Mead, George Herbert: "The Definition of the Psychical", *Decenniel Publications of the University of Chicago* III, 1903, pp.77–112.
Mulligan, Kevin "The Essence of Language: Wittgenstein's Builders and Bühler's Bricks", *Revue de Métaphysique et de Morale* 2, 1997, pp.193–215.
Rhees, Rush: "Can There Be a Private Language?", *Proceedings of the Aristotelian Society, Supplementary Volumes* 28, 1954, pp.77–94.
Russell, Bertrand: *The Problems of Philosophy*, Oxford University Press, 1912.
Russell, Bertrand: "The Nature of Sense-Data. – A Reply to Dr. Dawes Hicks", *Mind* 22:85, 1913, pp.76–81.
Russell, Bertrand: *My Philosophical Development*, Allen and Unwin, 1959.
Savage, C. Wade: "Sense-Data in Russell's Theories of Knowledge", in: C. Wade Savage and C. Anthony Anderson (Eds.): *Rereading Russell: Essays on Bertrand Russell's Metaphysics and Epistemology*, Minnesota Studies in the Philosophy of Science, vol.12, University of Minnesota Press, 1989, pp.138–168.
Stroud, Barry: "Private Objects, Physical Objects, and Ostension", in: David Charles and William Child (Eds.): *Wittgensteinian Themes: Essays in Honour of David Pears*, Oxford University Press, 2001, pp.143–162.
Thomson, Judith Jarvis: "Private Languages," *American Philosophical Quarterly* 1:1, 1964, pp.20–31.
Williams, Meredith: *Wittgenstein, Mind and Meaning: Toward a Social Conception of Mind*, Routledge, 1999.

Lorenzo Cammi
Hegel and Wittgenstein on *Wirklichkeit*: Sketch of a Comparison

Abstract In my paper, I aim to present Hegel's and Wittgenstein's notions of *Wirklichkeit*. As a first step, I offer my view on Hegel's treatment of actuality, which consists in the following stages: firstly, the consideration of the knowledge of actuality as the fundamental purpose of philosophy; secondly, the distinction between *Wirklichkeit* and *Realität*, that is, between actuality and reality; and thirdly, the distinction between actuality and actualization, which traces back to Aristotle's concepts of *entelecheia* and *energeia*. On this line, I offer a dynamic interpretation of Hegel's understanding of the constitution of actuality. As a second step, after addressing the possibility of knowing actuality from Wittgenstein's standpoint, I outline the issue concerning the relation among language, logic, and world, as well as the view regarding the way the actual world comes to be constituted as such, springing from what Wittgenstein calls substance of the world. By way of conclusion, I sketch a comparison of Hegel's and Wittgenstein's conceptions of *Wirklichkeit*.

1 The Hegelian way to the manifestation of the actual world

1.1 Disclosing the essence of the world: *Wirklichkeit* as the content of philosophy

Hegel's perspective on what is the fundamental tendency of human beings insofar as they are rational beings is straightforward: "What human beings strive for in general is cognition of the world; we strive to appropriate it and to conquer it" (EL 1830: §42 A1). Moreover, he is convinced that this endeavor is accessible, thanks to "the greatness and power of the spirit; the closed essence of the universe *contains no force* which could withstand the courage of cognition" (PW: p.185; "Inaugural Address, Delivered at the University of Berlin" [1818]). Thus, understanding the essence of the universe—the essence of the world—can be considered as the main target of philosophy. Indeed, the content of philosophy "is nothing other than the basic import that is originally produced and produces itself in the domain of the living spirit, the content that is made into the *world* [...]; in other words, the content of philosophy is *actuality* [*Wirklichkeit*]" (EL 1830: §6).

https://doi.org/10.1515/9783110572780-011

The meaning of Hegel's notion of actuality includes everything that is produced by the power of spirit, which by means of the concept determines the world as the actual world it is. However, for my purpose I will focus on the notion of *Wirklichkeit* as it is described in the chapter of the same name in the Doctrine of Essence. Specifically, Hegel defines *real actuality*—as opposed to *formal actuality*— as follows: "Real actuality *as such* is at first the thing of many properties [*das Ding von vielen Eigenschaften*], the concretely existing world" (SL 2010: p.482).

If the power of spirit aims to disclose the essence of the universe, it is logic that has to take the responsibility of the knowledge of actuality: "*logic* coincides with *metaphysics*, with the science of *things* [*Dinge*] grasped in *thoughts* [*Gedanken*] that used to be taken to express the *essentialities of the things* [*die Wesenheiten der Dinge*]" (EL 1830: §24). In other words, Hegel's logic takes the place of the old metaphysical thought, systematized by Wolff. The aim of logic is more precisely elucidated in the *Fragment of a System*, where we read that philosophy "has to disclose the finiteness in all finite things and require their integration by means of reason" (ETW: p.313). This "integration" is what Hegel defines as "idealization": "the *reality of the world* [*Realität der Welt*; my italics] must be crushed as it were; i.e., it must be made ideal" (EL 1830: §42 A1). Put another way, the world acquires its truth inasmuch as it is spiritualized—that is, rationalized. This means, in turn, that the world truly exists in its actual and full determinateness only if made concrete by way of reason. Therefore, Hegel's philosophy can be understood as follows: in order to make the rationality of the universe explicit by grasping the essential features of spirit, the philosophical system has to embody the path that spirit goes through in depicting the rational essence of the world.

1.2 *Wirklichkeit* and *Realität*

Hegel clearly distinguishes between the *reality* (*Realität*) and the *actuality* of the world. What is the difference between the world as *Wirklichkeit* and the *Realität der Welt*? The former conception does not rule out the latter; rather, *Wirklichkeit* represents the ground for giving reason for *Realität*. *Realität* coincides with the empirical world, that is the world we encounter in our everyday life as well as the world which is examined by the sciences. These perspectives on the world are usually based on an *atomistic* conception of reality, which is understood as made up of discrete, independent and autonomous entities. These entities might be particles (from the point of view of physics) as well as chairs and tables (from the point of view of common sense). To conceive the world in terms of *Wirklichkeit* does not mean to deny the plurality of the world, which manifests itself also in the form of the existence of particles or tables; instead, it means to find a truer and more fundamental way of understanding how these entities make up the world itself. Therefore, the distinction between *Wirklichkeit* and *Realität* does not want to deny the reality of these entities; rather, it means to deny that they are in their truth when considered in their immediate existence; and it means, accordingly, to ground their existence by showing how they emerge from a process of mediation. This process consists in the determination of the world, which is the condition of possibility of the appearance of the world itself, at first, in its empirical form. As said, the upshot of the process of determination is indeed the "concretely existing world", made up of particular things. Here is how Hegel extensively defines it in the form of *reale Wirklichkeit:*

> Real actuality is *as such* at first the thing of many properties, the concretely existing world; but it is not the concrete existence that dissolves into appearance but, as actuality, it is at the same time an in itself and immanent reflection; it preserves itself in the manifoldness of mere concrete existence; its externality is an inner relating only to *itself*. What is actual *can act*; something announces its actuality *by what it produces*. (SL 2010: p.482)

The process of determination of the world in terms of *Wirklichkeit* makes us able to ground "the manifoldness of mere concrete existence", that is, of our physical world, which "can act" and is announced "by what it [physically] produces"[1].

Now, if this process of determination is necessary in order to make the world true, then in addition we have to distinguish between *Realität* before and after the process of determination. Indeed, we have said that, to be determined in its truth, the world in terms of *Realität* needs to be grounded by the process of actualization deployed by reason. Hence, we might wonder: what about the concretely existing world before being apprehended in its "concrete determinacy" (EL 1830: §124 A)? Put another way, what is the status of the world before being determined by reason? The answer is: nothing. Or better, it is *pure being* which is at the same time *pure nothing*. Indeed, the consideration of the world in its pure immediacy means the consideration of it by prescinding from any determination, since determination is necessarily a result of mediation. But the world without any determination, in its "indeterminate immediacy", is nothing but *pure being*, nothing but *nothing*, "pure indeterminateness and emptiness" (SL 2010: p.59). Moreover, there is another way of describing the total absence of determinateness on the part of the world: by using the Kantian notion of *in itself*. According to Hegel, the way Kant treats it necessarily leads one to conceive

---

[1] In my view, this is how the *Logic* is to be understood, that is, in terms of how the process of determination of things by concepts happens.

what is in itself as "nothing but the completely abstract and indeterminate thing in general" (EL 1830: §124 A). A thing-in itself is actually a *"thing without properties [Ding ohne Eigenschaften]"*, namely "an empty indeterminate ground" (SL 2010: p.554), a thing in its "abstract immediacy", that is, apart from its "development and inner determinacy" (EL 1830: §124 A). Hence, we might say that the world-in itself, that is, apart from its process of determination and actualization, is just "the empty abstraction of all determinateness" (SL 2010: p.428). In consequence, this process of determination of the world can be further summarized by using Hegel's words as follows: "Everything is initially 'in itself,' but this is not the end of the matter", because "the thing generally [...] progresses beyond its mere in itself (understood as abstract reflection-into-itself) to reveal itself to be also reflection-into-another, and *as a result it has properties*" (EL 1830: §124 A), namely, it has determinations. In parallel, the world is initially in itself, but it also has to progress towards its actualization, which ends up in a plurality of things.

In fact, according to Hegel, the right way of conceiving the in itself is not apart from reason: the in itself is "what something is in its concept; but this concept is in itself concrete: as concept, in principle conceptually graspable; and, as determined and as the connected whole of its determinations, inherently cognizable" (SL 2010: p.94). In light of this, to be in itself means to be implicit, to be *potential:* this is the feature of *pure being*, in virtue of its being equal to *pure nothing*; in turn, by means of the concept, reason triggers the in itself and makes it actual. Therefore, the actual world is shaped by reason, whose activity consists in the power of the concept; this is to say that the concept structures the world insofar as the latter is actual.[2] However, to be precise, it is important to clarify what kind of relationship is present between the world before being ac-

---

2 This view is endorsed in different ways by:
 a.) M. Rosen (1988: p.262): "concepts are part of the structure of [actual] reality";
 b.) Westphal (1989: p.140): "Hegel holds that the world has a fundamentally conceptual structure, not because we constitute the world by thinking about it, but because concepts are structures in the world; only upon that basis can they become conceptions in our language and in our heads".
 c.) Brandom (2014 unpublished: I, p.24): "the way the world objectively is is conceptually articulated".
 Pinkard (2013: p.506) calls these kinds of positions on Hegel "conceptual realist interpretations", according to which Hegel's system traces out or mirrors "the conceptual structure already there in reality". He attributes such perspective to Horstmann (1991), Siep ([2000] 2014), Stern (2009), Westphal (2003), Henrich (2003), Kreines (2004, 2006), and McDowell (2009). Also, Fleischmann (1968: ch.X; "The Conceptual Structure of the World") is to be considered, in my view, as a conceptualist realist.

tualized and the concept: the latter is neither external nor alien to the former; rather, the concept is the internal principle of activation of the process of actualization. More precisely, the concept and the world as pure being are two aspects of the essence of reason. What Hegel categorically rejects here is the idea that things are determinable and determinate on their own: things are not concrete when considered apart from their concept; rather, it is the concept itself that makes them determinate. This aspect is clarified by the relationship between pure determinations of thought and pure determinations of objects, namely, between categories of thought and categories of objects. As Hegel underscores, "although the categories (e.g., unity, cause and effect, etc.) pertain to thinking as such, it does not at all follow from this that they must therefore be merely something of ours, and not also *determinations of objects themselves* [*Bestimmungen der Gegenstände selbst*; my italics]" (EL 1830: §42 A3). Logic, in other words, shows the content of objects according to the necessary relationships and determinations which characterize the content itself. This endeavor can be guided only by the concept, which "is the ground and the source of all finite determinateness and manifoldness" (SL 2010: p.520).

In sum, then, outside rationalization, nothing is determinate. And, since reason operates by means of the concept, Hegel's *Wirklichkeit* is to be conceived as "conceptually formed reality" (Stekeler-Weithofer 2015: p.569). For this reason, we might say that the activity of spirit does not consist in introducing unity into the multiplicity of the world, but in showing how the world comes to be differentiated and determined, starting from its original identity with spirit itself. Thus, Hegel's logic aims to show the work of reason in determining and actualizing the world. We find a description of this process of determination in a passage from the *Difference between Fichte's and Schelling's Systems:*

> Reason constructs itself in [... the] emanation [of its appearance] [*Emanation ihrer Erscheinung*] as an identity that is conditioned by this very duplicate; it opposes this relative identity to itself once more, and in this way the system advances until the objective totality is completed. Reason then unites this objective totality with the opposite subjective totality to form the infinite world-intuition, whose expansion has at the same time contracted into the richest and simplest identity. (D: p.114)

The emanation of reason is the process of determining the world. The pay-off of this process is "the infinite world-intuition", or better, the *"rational image of the universe"* [*vernünftiges Bild des Universums*] (GW 11: p.9). Key here is to point out that this image is nothing different from the universe itself understood in terms of the actual world. Not that the world is just an image, but this rational image is the actual world itself, once the latter has been determined as such in virtue of conceptual thought.

1.3 *Actuality* and *actualization*

The clarification concerning the relationship between the world before being actualized and the concept directly leads us to speak of actuality, since it is the notion itself of actuality which demands an elucidation. To this end, we have to look at Hegel's definition of *das Wirkliche*. As Hegel writes,

> The actual [*Das Wirkliche*] is therefore *manifestation*. It is not drawn into the sphere of *alteration* [*Veränderung*] by its externality [*Äußerlichkeit*], nor is it the *reflective shining* of itself in *an other*. It just manifests itself, and this means that in its externality, and only in *it*, it is *itself*, that is to say, only as a self-differentiating and self-determining movement. (SL 2010: p.478)[3]

Actuality is to be understood in terms of a process of manifestation. It is nothing other than its own process of determination, and what is manifested by actuality is nothing but actuality itself. Also, the self-actualizing process which leads actuality to be manifested is a *necessary* process, since actuality *is* its manifestation and would be nothing if not manifested. First and foremost, actuality is *actualization*. It is the actualizing process which, starting from the world as pure being, gives rise to the emergence of the actual world. Actuality is not only the pay-off of a process: it is at the same time that same process leading to its own achievement. In Aristotelian terms, actuality is both *energeia* and *entelecheia*. Concerning Aristotle, in the *Encyclopedia Logic*[4] Hegel comments on the notion of *energeia* as follows:

> Actuality certainly does form the principle of Aristotle's philosophy, but his actuality is that of the idea itself, and not the ordinary actuality of what is immediately present [*die gemeine Wirklichkeit des unmittelbar Vorhandenen*]. More precisely, therefore, Aristotle's polemic against Plato consists in his designation of the Platonic idea as mere *dynamis*, and in urging, on the contrary, that the idea, which is recognised by both of them equally to be what is alone true, should be regarded essentially as *energeia*, i.e., as the inwardness [*das Innere*] that is totally to the fore; so that it is the unity of inward and outward. In other words, the idea should be regarded as actuality in the emphatic sense that we have given to it here. (EL 1830: §142 A)[5]

---

[3] On the section "Actuality" in Hegel's *Logic*, see in particular Longuenesse ([1981] 2007: pp.110–159) and Ng (2009, 2017).
[4] For an analysis of the section "Actuality" in the *Encyclopedia Logic*, see Stekeler-Weithofer (1992: pp.282–336).
[5] See also Hegel's (LHP II: pp.137–153) analysis of the Aristotelian metaphysics, which focuses in particular on Aristotle's *energeia* and *dynamis*. See Hartmann (1923) and Ferrarin (2001) on the relationship between Hegel and Aristotle. More specifically, on Hegel's interpretation of *dynamis* and *energeia* see Ferrarin (2001: pp.15–27 and pp.107–148).

Actuality is the activity of reason (here described in terms of the idea), namely, the activity by means of which the world as pure being is triggered and actualized. This is a pivotal point. When Hegel writes that the actuality we are dealing with is "not the ordinary actuality of what is immediately present", he does not mean to say that actuality has nothing to do with the process of actualization of the world. Rather, he means exactly the opposite. More precisely, "what is immediately present" is the physical world. Understanding actuality as a process concerning the immediate empirical reality would mean considering the process of manifestation of the world in physical terms. This is what Hegel decisively denies, since otherwise we would be treating the activity of reason as something like a physical process. Obviously, this is not acceptable at all from the Hegelian standpoint. In parallel, Hegel's notion of actuality is not meant to describe the physical process of actualization on the part of potential features of the world, where the latter are taken as physical possibilities; instead, actuality is meant to explain the metaphysical process of actualization on the part of the world as something in itself, as something potential pointing to its own actualization. While the former is a *temporal* process, the latter is an *atemporal* one, that is, the self-determining and self-differentiating process which gives life to the actual world.

Now, it is necessary to elucidate Hegel's employment of the Aristotelian terminology. When Aristotle talks about the actual world, he clearly understands *energeia* as a sensible principle: it is the physical process of actualization which affects particular substances.[6] For this reason, I take Hegel as translating Aristotle's *energeia* from the language of the Aristotelian (meta-)physics to the language of speculative philosophy—the language of the Hegelian logic. In this regard, actuality is *energeia* insofar as it is the process of the manifestation of the world in terms of the potential pure being. The upshot of such process is not itself *energeia* in the first place: it is *entelecheia*, that is, the world once it has been actualized.

Regarding Hegel's treatment of Aristotle, another point is of great importance. He praises Aristotle in virtue of his comprehension of the idea in terms of *energeia*. On the contrary, he blames Plato, due to his consideration of it as mere *dynamis*. Does it mean that the category of possibility is discarded from Hegel's metaphysics? Does it mean that we are not allowed to make reference to the world as something *potential*? Both answers are negative. Rather, we should say that *dynamis* is subsumed into and sublated by actuality. The sublation of *dyna-*

---

[6] Longuenesse ([1981] 2007: p.112): "For Aristotle, existence in act (*energeia*) is the full realization of the form in the *sensible object* [my italics]".

mis is its eternal passing over into *entelecheia*. The *Lectures on the Philosophy of History* might help us to shed light on this subject matter. From the point of view of the historical development, Hegel describes the movement of spirit—that is, the manifestation of the activity of reason—as follows:

> Spirit *begins* with its infinite possibility [*Möglichkeit*], which however is *only* a possibility. This possibility contains spirit's absolute content as something *implicit* [*seinen absoluten Gehalt als Ansich*], as the purpose and goal that it attains only as a result—a result that is only then its actuality [*Wirklichkeit*]. Thus in existence [*Existenz*] the progression appears as one from incompleteness to completion, although the former is to be understood not merely in the abstraction of incompleteness but rather as something that contains within itself its opposite, the would-be completion, as a germ or drive; just as possibility, at least for a reflective way of thinking, indicates something that ought to be actual, and, more precisely, just as the Aristotelian *dynamis* is also *potentia*, energy [*Kraft*] and power [*Macht*]. (LPH 1822–23: pp.110–111; trans. amended)

For our purpose, let us translate this content into the language of metaphysics. First and foremost, Hegel underscores how, at the very beginning, spirit is *only* possibility. At the level of metaphysics, this is the world before being actualized, which is the "absolute content as something *implicit*". What is extremely interesting in the passage is the explanation concerning the way in which the infinite possibility of spirit has to be understood. In Aristotelian terms, we are dealing with a kind of possibility which is not just *dynamis*, but also *potentia*. The point is that *potentia* is not inert possibility but has in itself the principle of its own activation. To put it otherwise, *dynamis* is not to be conceived as *formal possibility*, but as *real possibility*. To clarify the distinction, let us read Hegel's words. In the *Logic*, he defines real possibility as follows: "[t]he real possibility of a fact [*Sache*] is [...] the immediately existent manifoldness of circumstances that refer to it" (SL 2010: p.482). It is the "in itself *full of content*" (ibid.). To put it otherwise, real possibilities have gathered in themselves—implicitly—the entire spectrum of connections and relations with *real* circumstances (but not *actual* circumstances, in this case, since there is nothing actual yet) which would permit them to pass from potentiality to actuality. In contrast, formal possibility is mere abstract possibility, that is, possibility as completely devoid of content. It is the concept that permits formal possibility to be translated into real possibility.

Accordingly, whereas the world as pure being would be merely formal possibility if taken outside reason, when it is taken as embodied by reason itself, then it comes to be real possibility. What is implicit in spirit is not mere inert possibility; on the contrary, the world before being actualized has in itself, at the same time, the principle of its own activation. This principle is nothing but the concept. Thus, since the concept is the trigger of the potential pure being—and since they are one and the same principle, understood in terms of content on one side, conceived as form on the other side—the possibilities of the world as pure being are never mere possibilities. On the contrary, they are always already actualizing real possibilities. This is what I mean by saying that *dynamis* is subsumed into and sublated by actuality. Hence, the power of the concept consists in the continuous process of actualization, which coincides with the Hegelian *energeia*. In this way, the concept is the trigger of *dynamis* and leads it to be actualized, that is, to become *entelecheia*.

1.4 The actuosity of the substance of the world

Since the world before being actualized is something purely indeterminate, it is a unique undifferentiated whole; nevertheless, it manifests itself as a plurality of things. Therefore, we might say that Hegel's conception of *Wirklichkeit* is based on a metaphysical holistic perspective, which however does not rule out that physical reality can be manifested in terms of a plurality of things.[7] Now, by way of conclusion, we can employ Hegel's characterization of substance at the end of the Doctrine of Essence in order to better describe how the process of actualization of the world happens. He writes that substance is *"the flux of accidents"*, where accidents are to be understood as the things full of properties. In my view, we are dealing with the flux in virtue of which things emerge from the world conceived in terms of a potential substance. Indeed, this flux is described by Hegel as the self-manifestation of substance:

> Substance manifests itself through the *actuality* [my italics], with the content of the latter into which it translates the possible, as *creative power*, and, through the *possibility* [my italics] to which it reduces the actual, as *destructive power*. (SL 2010: p.491)

As Hegel writes, the flux of accidents, that is, "[t]his movement of accidentality[,] is the *actuosity* [*Aktuosität*] of substance *as the tranquil coming forth of itself*" (SL 2010: p.490) and "[t]he ceasing-to-be of the accident is its return as actuality into itself, as into its in itself or into its possibility" (SL 2010: p.491). Now, what does *actuosity* mean? It is not to be interpreted as the movement of physical actuality

---

7 Here, I have in mind the distinction drawn by Jonathan Schaffer (2010: p.66) between *priority monism*, which does not deny pluralism at the physical level, and *existence monism*, that is "the doctrine that there is one and only one actual concrete object". Schaffer correctly attributes *priority monism* to Hegel.

understood as *Wirklichkeit*, that is, what produces physical effects; rather, it is the *atemporal* process of realization of *actu*ality itself. The actualization of substance is not first and foremost a physical manifestation, and the power of substance is not basically a physical possibility. Correctly understood, the power of the potential substance of the world has in the first place the meaning of a *metaphysical power*. We are not dealing with the possibility of physically acting on the part of an already actualized substance; on the contrary, what is at hand is the metaphysical power of *coming to be* actual by a substance in itself—specifically, by the potential substance of the world. Hegel's substance of the world can be interpreted as the power from which things are generated. This potential substance metaphysically manifests itself making itself actual through the actual world, which in turn consists in things with their properties.[8] Prescinding from the actualization of things in the empirical world, the substance of the world is nothing but a mere potentiality. It is not *actual* yet; it is *dynamis*. When things are not metaphysically actualized, the one substance is in itself—just a possibility, which is still to be actualized as well. However, as we have said, this *dynamis* is at the same time *potentia*, since it has in itself the determining power of the concept. Therefore, the potential substance of the world is destined to be always already actualizing itself.

2 Wittgenstein's *Tractatus:* from the substance of the world to empirical reality

2.1 Showing the essence of the world. How the world is and that the world is

Concerning the objective of his philosophy, Wittgenstein maintains that his "work has extended from the foundations of logic to the nature of the world" (NB: p.79e). Thus, the knowledge of the essence of the world appears to be the fundamental aim of Wittgenstein's intellectual endeavor. Yet, despite this straightforward declaration of intent, it is not so obvious either *if* or *how* it is possible to get knowledge of the world. For this reason, it is necessary to wonder whether philosophy can really address this issue. From Wittgenstein's point of view, the answer cannot be plainly positive, since in the *Philosophical Remarks* we read that

---

[8] As S. Rosen (2014: p.386) maintains, substance as power is "*self-manifestation* [my italics] through the production of accidents".

what belongs to the essence of the world simply *cannot* be said. And philosophy, if it were to say anything, would have to describe the essence of the world. But the essence of language is a picture of the essence of the world; and philosophy as custodian of grammar can in fact grasp the essence of the world. (PR: p.85)

The fact that philosophy cannot simply say anything about the essence of the world means that, if it wants to accomplish the only task it can be able to pursue, it has to use a stratagem. To this end, the distinction between the possibility of *saying* something about the essence of the world and the possibility of *grasping* it—which refers to the pivotal distinction between *saying* and *showing*—helps us to understand the extent to which it is possible to address and answer the question concerning the knowledge of the world. *Showing* and *saying* are mutually exclusive: "What *can* be shown, *cannot* be said" (TLP: 4.1212) and, vice versa, we can maintain that, if we cannot *say* anything about something, the latter can perhaps be *shown*. So, if the essence of the world cannot directly be said by means of language, this does not mean that we cannot indirectly show *how* the world is. This strategy of understanding the world consists in analyzing language—which is supposed to mirror the world—and is based on the fact that "[t]he proposition *shows* how things stand" (TLP: 4.022). In particular, what the proposition shows is "the logical form of reality [*die logische Form der Wirklichkeit*]" (TLP: 4.121).[9]

Before going further, it is pivotal to understand the way Wittgenstein conceives the notion of reality in the sense of *Wirklichkeit*. The latter coincides with the world: "The total reality [*die gesamte Wirklichkeit*] is the world" (TLP: 2.063). This world is nothing but the world of empirical reality, which can be surely and clearly described by the propositions of natural sciences.[10] For instance, physics can describe without doubt the features of the objects of the world it aspires to represent; more precisely, "[m]echanics is an attempt to construct according to a single plan all *true* propositions which we need for the description of the world" (TLP: 6.343). In other words, physics can say "how things stand". This means that, if we want to say something true about the world, we should let science speak about it, because "[t]he totality of true propositions is the total natural science (or the totality of the natural sciences)" (TLP: 4.11). Hence, we might say that Wittgenstein's notion of *Wirklichkeit* is clearly restricted

---

9 See Cook (1994: pp.45–54) for an analysis concerning the possibility of *showing* the essence of the world.
10 Nonetheless, *Wirklichkeit* and *empirische Realität* do not mean the very same thing; rather, they represent two ways of understanding the very same world. More on that later.

to its empirical meaning; Wittgenstein's *atomistic* world is the world of sciences.[11]

Thus, to *say* something true about the world pertains to science, not to philosophy. In contrast, the philosophical work has to aim to clarify the form of the proposition: "The object of philosophy is the logical clarification of thoughts. [...] A philosophical work consists essentially of elucidations" (TLP: 4.112). Therefore, philosophy is not able to directly say anything about the world, yet the attempt of grasping the world should remain its main objective. In sum, the fact that the (deceptive) language of philosophy cannot say anything about the world does not mean that language itself cannot be used as a Trojan horse to penetrate into the configuration of the world itself.

Eventually, at the end of the *Tractatus*, Wittgenstein draws a further distinction: the one between *the way* the world is—or might be—and *that* the world is: "Not *how* the world is, is the mystical, but *that* it is." (TLP: 6.44) So, in Wittgenstein's eyes, while we are able to deal with the issue concerning *how* the world is, we can say nothing about the fact *that* the world is. Indeed, searching for the profoundest reason for the existence of the world is philosophically impracticable. Actually, we might be puzzled by how the distinction between *saying* and *showing* recurs here. While above we have seen that philosophy can somehow point to the essence of the world, now we read that philosophy should "say nothing except what can be said, *i.e.* the propositions of natural science" (TLP: 6.53). Philosophy must not aspire to any kind of metaphysical thought, if this means to try saying what "the inexpressible" is; the latter "*shows* itself" (TLP: 6.522), but nothing can be *said* about it. Hence, we wonder whether or not there is the possibility that philosophy *shows* how things stand. Wittgenstein seems to distinguish between *showing itself* and *showing something other than itself:* while the inexpressible—which is nothing but *that* that world is, that is, the mystical—shows itself as such, and philosophy cannot grasp it, *how* the world is can be *shown* by philosophy itself by means of the form of the proposition.

2.2 Language, thought, and world. The logical form

What makes it possible that the proposition *shows* the essence of the world is the identity between the form of the proposition and the form of the world. In turn, this identity is based on a more fundamental one, which might be called *thought-*

---

[11] In the last paragraph of the Wittgenstein section, I will clarify the crucial role played by physics in the determination of the world.

world identity, since thought and world share the same logical form as well. In his analysis, Wittgenstein starts with language and shifts towards the world by passing through the notions of picture, proposition, and thought, which are reciprocally bound by *mirroring relations*. More precisely, the thread connecting language, thought, and world can be summarized as follows:

I. Language is the totality of propositions (TLP: 4.001);

II. "The proposition is a measure of the world" (NB: p.41e);

III. Moreover, "[t]o give the essence of [the] proposition means to give the essence of all description, therefore the essence of the world" (TLP: 5.4711);

IV. But, the significant proposition is the thought (TLP: 4);

V. Then, in turn, the thought is "[t]he logical picture of the facts" (TLP: 3).

And, since "[t]he logical picture can depict the world" (TLP: 2.19), this is what the thought essentially does as well. This happens since the essence of thought is the same as the essence of the world, but this is not the end of the matter. What we have said raises the issue concerning the eventual priority of one of the elements here at play. This issue is clarified by Wittgenstein in his *Notebooks*: "The great problem round which everything that I write turns is: Is there an order in the world *a priori*, and if so what does it consist in?" (NB: p.53e) To make it explicit: is there a priority of the form of proposition and of thought over the world, or vice versa? Or, rather, does the issue of priority demand that thought is taken to be on the side of the world? [12]

On the one hand, Wittgenstein's metaphysics is certainly parasitic on his analysis of language, so that the essence of the world—the way it comes to be discovered—would seem to depend on the structure of the proposition. In other words, we notice that, by analyzing the structure of language, the latter

---

[12] Carruthers (1990: p.26) summarizes the issue as follows: "Should we say that the essences revealed to us through our study of language really belong to the essential nature of an independently existing reality? Or should we say that, since any apprehension of reality is language-mediated, the essential structure of language merely imposes an essential structure upon reality *in so far as it can be apprehended in thought by us?*"

Mácha (2015: pp.57–65) describes the two contrasting intepretations on the matter: the metaphysical or *de re* view, according to which the logical form is language independent, and the semantic or *de dicto* view, which tends to consider the logical form as parasitic on language itself. In particular, Mácha aims to illustrate that Wittgenstein's perspective does not necessarily need to be committed to the *de re* view. In this paper, I want to outline a third view, close to the metaphysical view, but not underestimating the eventual role of language in the constitution of reality.

has a certain form that consequently we attribute to the essence of the world. On the other hand, the relation between language and world might perhaps be overturned. In the first place, the proposition pictures the world and creates an image of an existent atomic fact. The picture is a representation of what is the case, because it shares the same logical form with the fragment of the world it depicts. The link between pictures provided by language and correspondent facts is such that language is certainly able to reach up to the world (TLP: 2.1511), yet, since pictorial representations are compared with a "scale applied to reality [*Wirklichkeit*]" (TLP: 2.1512), it would seem straightforward that language itself arrives when the existence of facts has already been determined—at least to some extent. Indeed, something has to exist in order to be represented by the elements of a picture. But now the question is this: to what extent does the determination of facts obtain before language comes into play? What is existent independently of the application of language to reality? With regard to this, in the *Tractatus* we read that "[t]he picture can represent every reality [*Wirklichkeit*] whose form it has. The spatial picture, everything spatial, the coloured, everything coloured, etc." (TLP: 2.171). Put another way, for the picture to represent a fact of the world, the latter and the picture itself need to share the same form, as said. Accordingly, propositional representations certainly need *forms* of a certain kind already to exist in the world: we are dealing with forms of space, forms of colours, forms of geometrical shapes, and so on. As Wittgenstein maintains: "What every picture, of whatever form, must have in common with reality [*Wirklichkeit*] in order to be able to represent it at all—rightly or falsely—is the logical form, that is, the form of reality [*Wirklichkeit*]" (TLP: 2.18). Language and world share the very same logical form; if they did not, the world could not be represented by the pictures of language. For this reason, the logical form—the essence—of the world is necessarily prior to the structure of the proposition, which shows this essence.[13]

Now that we have shed light on this aspect of the priority issue, let us consider the relation between logic and world. For sure, the priority of the form of the world over the structure of language does not mean that the former is also prior over the logical form of thought. However, at first glance, the link between logic and world would seem to replicate the one between language and world; indeed, just as language represents the world, logic too is "a reflexion of the world" (TLP: 6.13). In brief, "the all-embracing logic [...] mirrors the world" (TLP: 5.511). Now, since we have said that Wittgenstein is committed to the priority of the essence of the world over language—to some extent—should we in turn

---

13 In the next paragraph, I will go deeper into the nature of the logical form of the world.

take him to be committed to the priority of the world over logic? No, we should not. Indeed, language presupposes the logical space: "Although a proposition may only determine one place in logical space, the whole logical space must already be given by it." (TLP: 3.42) Accordingly, logic is to be taken on the side of the world, so that language is preceded by them both. World and logic are simultaneously given.[14] This is due to the consubstantiality of world and logic, according to which the logical space coincides with the substantiality of the world, as we will see in a while.

Hence, the answer to the priority issue is the following: the "essence [of thought], logic, presents an order, in fact the a priori order of the world: that is, the order of *possibilities*, which must be common to both world and thought" (PI: §97). The logical essence of the world—embodied by its substance—establishes the form of all possible worlds. But, what about the actualization of our world, starting from all possible states of affairs? Has language something to say with regard to this actualization or does it come when everything is already done by logic?

2.3 Substance of the world

Thus, there is a certain priority of the essence of the world over language. Yet, what we have said does not sufficiently clarify the issue. In addition, we should ask: what kind of world is presupposed by language? In my view, we are not dealing with the world conceived in terms of the actual *empirical reality*. Rather, we are dealing with what Wittgenstein calls the *substance of the world*, which "exists independently of what is the case" (TLP: 2.024). It is "form and content" (TLP: 2.025); while "form is the possibility of the structure" (TLP: 2.033)—and the structure of the world is the "totality of existent atomic facts" (TLP: 2.04)—we should understand substance in terms of content as the possibility of being filled by material properties. The substance of the world is what exists before language —and before all experience in general as well[15]—and is the condition of possibility of the existence of facts, which indeed need a logical space to exist.[16] (As said,

---

14 If logic preceded the world, "how could we apply logic? We could say: if there were a logic, even if there were no world, how then could there be a logic, since there is a world?" (TLP: 5.5521).
15 The form of the world is *"prior* to all experience, must run through all experience; no empirical cloudiness or uncertainty can be allowed to affect it. – It must rather be of the purest crystal" (PI: §97).
16 The logical space means "the possibility of an existence [*Existenz*]" (TLP: 3.411).

the latter is presupposed by language, whose structure mirrors the logical relations at play.) A definitive clarification about the relation between substance and language is given by the proposition 2.0211: "If the world had no substance, then whether a proposition had sense would depend on whether another proposition was true".[17]

In Wittgenstein's eyes, the substance of the world has some specific features: it is made up of simple *objects* (TLP: 2.02–2.021) and has a fixed form (TLP: 2.023). "Roughly speaking: objects [*Gegenstände*] are colourless" (TLP: 2.0232), but, we should add, they are always already configured to become coloured. Objects do not belong to the physical world; objects as such are not part of the empirical reality. It is for this reason that they are colorless, soundless, or shapeless, for instance; in other words, they do not have any property which pertains to the empirical world. Put another way, we are dealing with something *atemporal*. In addition, we can conclude that the substance of the world is something indeterminate. However, its indeterminateness is not *pure*, exactly because, as mentioned, it is made up of objects which are configured to acquire the properties they do not possess yet. This is what Wittgenstein means by saying that "[t]he substance of the world *can* only determine a form and not any material properties" (TLP: 2.0231). The substance of the world is certainly indeterminate to some extent; nonetheless, we are not dealing with the world as something absolutely indeterminate. The world as substance, that is the world considered as being made up of objects, is indeterminate from the point of view of empirical content, but determinate from the point of view of form. In turn, objects are indeterminate insofar as there are no properties which have been attributed to them yet. But there is something more: substance is disposed to acquire determinateness, objects are disposed to be subjects of properties.[18]

Even though Wittgenstein does not ever clarify what objects *are*,[19] they can be described as follows. Objects are configured in such a way that they are dis-

---

[17] On the relation between propositions and substance of the world, see Proops (2004).
[18] Here is how Anscombe (1959: p.111) clarifies the emergence of material properties like colours: "Red is a material property, and therefore formed by a configuration of objects and, as I have said, by the *same configuration* of *different* objects in the different facts that exist when different things are red. These different objects, having the capacity to enter into configurations forming the material property red, will be of the same logical form: that of objects whose configurations yield colours. (Hence colour is a 'form of objects': 2.0251)."
[19] As Kenny underscores: "We are given no information in the *Tractatus* as to what kind of thing simple objects are—specks in the visual field and the material points are no longer put forward as candidates. It is not even clear whether the simples would be particular individuals or universal types. Among the examples listed in the recantation in the *Investigations* both categories appear: individuals such as bits of wood, molecules, atoms, colour-patches, segments of

posed to be actualized in certain ways rather than others. We might think of objects as things in their potential status, where things are in turn objects eventually actualized and making up the empirical world. We might think of objects as spatial points having no properties, but being disposed to acquire properties by occurring in atomic facts, that is by being caught in relations with other objects. Indeed, a combination of objects is an atomic fact [*Sachverhalt*] (see TLP: 2.01) and "[t]he possibility of its occurrence in atomic facts is the form of the object [*Gegenstand*]" (TLP: 2.0141). All told, objects represent the potential layer of the world and contain all the possible ways the world might be, since they "contain the possibility of all states of affairs [*Sachlagen*]" (TLP: 2.014). If a state of affairs is the possibility of the existence of an atomic fact—which represents a fragment of the actual world—atomic facts themselves might exist or not, depending on the configuration of objects. Thus, "if a thing [*Ding*] *can* occur in an atomic fact [*Sachverhalt*] the possibility of that atomic fact [*Sachverhalt*] must already be prejudged in the thing [*Ding*]" (TLP: 2.012). For instance, let us consider *something* which is a red cube. We say: "This is a cube and it is red". From Wittgenstein's perspective, a proposition like that pictures an atomic fact whose relation to the thing is a necessary one from the point of view of the thing itself. Obviously, it is not a logical necessity either that it is a cube or that it is red; however, inscribed in this *something* are the possibilities of being cubical as well as that of being red.

Objects are ways things are when not yet actualized; objects become the things they might be only if considered as constituent parts of atomic facts. This is how things come to be constituted and actualized. Whereas the potential and partially indeterminate stage of the world is described by substance, *Wirklichkeit* and *empirische Realität* are terms employed by Wittgenstein to refer to the actual world. For sure, *Wirklichkeit* and *empirische Realität* are two sides of the same coin—the world—but, whereas the former coincides with both "the existence and non-existence of atomic facts" (TLP: 2.06), the latter is restricted to what actually exists.[20] Strictly speaking, the actual world is some-

---

curves; universals such as colours, type-letters (PI: §§47–8, 58). But this lack of clarity accords with Wittgenstein's insistence that it is only a priori that he knows of the existence of simples, not that he can give any examples." (Kenny [1973] 2006: p.68)

Redding's chapter in this volume takes into consideration Wittgenstein's simple objects with regard to Hegel's singulars, by analyzing them from the point of view of their conception of judgement.

20 While the term *Wirklichkeit* constantly appears throughout the *Tractatus*, it might seem interesting that Wittgenstein uses the term *empirische Realität* on just two occasions. However, thing different from *Wirklichkeit*, since the latter also includes the non-existent, while actuality itself strictly coincides with *empirical reality*. Therefore, substance, *Wirklichkeit*, and *empirische Realität* are three different ways of describing the world: substance is the world at its potential stage, where everything is still possible—at this stage, everthing is still materially indeterminate; *Wirklichkeit* obtains when simple objects hang together in atomic facts and determine the existence and non-existence of atomic facts themselves—the world is here both formally and materially determined; eventually, *empirische Realität* is a restricted view on *Wirklichkeit:* it is the set of everything actually existent.

Now, is there anything which functions as a trigger for the passage from the substance of the world to actuality? How does it happen that objects come to be actualized and turn into things?[21] Unexpectedly, language—as a part of experience—might play a significant role here. As seen, the proposition shows "the logical form of reality [*die logische Form der Wirklichkeit*]" (TLP: 4.121); yet, language itself merely mirrors the form of *Wirklichkeit*, so that it would not seem to possess any capacity of making the configuration of objects actual. (And logic, in turn, does not say anything about the reason why a thing occurs in a particular atomic fact.) Nevertheless, we might suppose that language and all experience have the task of materially filling the logical space of objects, giving content to the form of the world. According to this line of interpretation, the metaphor of language as a "scale applied to reality [*Wirklichkeit*]" (TLP: 2.1512) might mean that language itself contributes to discerning what exists. In consequence, although Wittgenstein does not offer any solution to this conundrum, we might guess that the scientific language of empirical laws guides the instantiation of particular properties rather than others. To this end, two things are to be born in mind: first of all, propositions *determine* reality by filling a fragment of the logical space (see TLP: 4.463); secondly, "[t]he truth or falsehood of *every* proposition alters something in the general structure of the world" (TLP: 5.5262). That said, propositions of physics *alter* the structure of the world by describing it:

---

this follows quite obviously from the fact that *Wirklichkeit* is dealt with by philosophy, while *empirische Realität* by natural science: "Logic is interested only in reality [*Wirklichkeit*]" (NB: p.9e).
21 In other words, how does the passage from being to existence happen? Wittgenstein draws the latter distinction in the *Notebooks* (NB: p.39e), where he points out that his task has to do with being, not with existence. Indeed, as Pinkard's chapter in this volume underscores, Wittgenstein's logic is a logic of being. (More precisely, it is "the logic of 'being' to the extent that 'being' is intelligible" (p. 189 in this volume). And this is, Pinkard says, something that Wittgenstein's *Tractatus* shares, in spite of crucial differences, with Hegel's *Logic*.) Notwithstanding, here I want to show what resources the *Tractatus* might offer to go beyond being, towards existence.

physics "determine[s] a form of description" by applying a network of propositions. In this manner, physics "provides the bricks for building the edifice of science" (TLP: 6.341). Now, although "the physical laws still speak of the objects of the world" (TLP: 6.3431)—and although the description offered by physics is "always quite general"[22] (TLP: 6.3432)—we might say that the "axioms" (TLP: 6.341) of physics represent a first step towards the actualization of the world.

To sum up, then, objects make up the substance of the world, that is potential *Wirklichkeit*. Objects are potentially the things we encounter in the actual world. However, they are not yet any particular thing, since they have no properties yet. Rather, objects are characterized by configurations of properties, and the specific properties they acquire at the actual level of the empirical world depend on their occurrence in a specific atomic fact rather than others. This is the logical form of objects, which determines the ways in which an object can acquire determinateness. By occurring in a particular atomic fact, objects acquire determinateness, starting from a previous stage of material indeterminateness. This is the process of actualization that objects pass through by their being bound to other objects, which in turn acquire determinateness by their being bound to the former. Although it seems that nothing can play the role of a trigger for this process, we might say that, following Wittgenstein's perspective, the fundamental propositions of natural science function as the first stage of the process of actualization of the world.

3 Conclusion: sketch of a comparison

3.1 On the possibility of knowing the essence of the world

Both Hegel and Wittgenstein bolster the conviction that the possibility of knowing the world is within our range. Yet, whereas Hegel does not restrict at all this possibility in virtue of the boundlessness of the power of spirit, Wittgenstein maintains that there are some aspects of the world which pertain to the inexpressible. According to Wittgenstein, the world has something mystical, which cannot be grasped. Interestingly, in the *Encyclopedia Logic*, Hegel writes that "everything rational can equally be called 'mystical'; but this only amounts to saying that it transcends the understanding. It does not at all imply that what is so spoken of must be considered inaccessible to thinking and incomprehensible" (EL

---

[22] In mechanics, "[t]here is, for example, never any mention of *particular* material points in it, but always only of *some points or other*" (TLP: 6.3432).

1830: §82 Z). In Hegel's eyes, if something is considered to be mystical, that is, mysterious, it is just because the power of spirit has not been invoked and one has been trapped into the hooks of the understanding.

3.2 The meaning of *Wirklichkeit*

Even though for my purpose I restricted Hegel's conception of *Wirklichkeit* to its empirical manifestation, it includes every aspect of the world that has been determined and actualized by the power of the concept, from empirical reality to every spiritual—that is cultural—manifestation of the world. Hegel's *Wirklichkeit* is not just the physical world as it is spiritualized by reason, but includes every aspect of human spirit. Put another way, the range of *Wirklichkeit* clearly emerges from the issues addressed by the *Encyclopedia of Philosophical Sciences*, which aims to deal with every aspect of actuality. In contrast, Wittgenstein deliberately restricts the notion of *Wirklichkeit* to empirical facts, and includes, in addition, both existent and non-existent facts. Thus, whereas according to Hegel the true understanding and foundation of *Wirklichkeit* depends on philosophy —logic in particular—Wittgenstein thinks that philosophy just has to elucidate the propositions of natural science. The latter are the only propositions which can say something true about the world.

3.3 Identity between reason—or thought—and world

Both Hegel and Wittgenstein maintain that reason—or thought—and world share the same essence. Moreover, both think that reason—or thought—precedes and constitutes *Wirklichkeit*. However, whereas Hegel maintains that the world has the same essence of reason because it is the latter that makes the world the actual world it is, in Wittgenstein's *Tractatus* thought seems to have a less dynamic role in the process of the constitution of actuality.

3.4 *Wirklichkeit:* before and after actualization

According to my account, both Hegel and Wittgenstein distinguish between the world before being actualized and the actual world. Moreover, if Hegel takes the world to be *nothing* apart from the concept, Wittgenstein thinks that the being of thought and of the world entail each other. Thus, if what I called Hegel's *substance of the world* is purely indeterminate—and actually it is *nothing* apart from the concept—what Wittgenstein calls "substance of the world" could not exist independently of the essence of thought. Yet, whereas the Hegelian concept fully determines the substance of the world, the Wittgensteinian thought contributes to determine it only partially, that is, only formally.

3.5 Actualizing the world

Whereas Hegel's philosophy presents a dynamic conception of the actualization of the world, grounded in the activity of the concept, Wittgenstein risks to be trapped into a fixed and static conception of the substance of the world. For sure, Wittgenstein's perspective would need a more active role of language and experience to be capable of giving reason for the emergence of actuality. But this is not the task of his philosophy. So, we might conclude that, whereas Hegel is able to clarify the way actuality comes to be determined, Wittgenstein needs to appeal to natural science.

References

Anscombe, Gertrude E. M.: *An Introduction to Wittgenstein's* Tractatus, Hutchinson University Library, 1959.
Brandom, Robert: *A Spirit of Trust. A Semantic Reading of Hegel's Phenomenology*, unpublished, http://www.pitt.edu/~brandom/spirit_of_trust_2014.html, 2014.
Carruthers, Peter: *The Metaphysics of the* Tractatus, Cambridge University Press, 1990.
Cook, John W.: *Wittgenstein's Metaphysics*, Cambridge University Press, 1994.
Ferrarin, Alfredo: *Hegel and Aristotle*, Cambridge University Press, 2001.
Fleischmann, Eugène: *La Science Universelle ou la Logique de Hegel*, Plon, 1968.
Hartmann, Nicolai: "Aristoteles und Hegel", *Beitrage zur Philosophie des Deutschen Idealismus* 3, 1923, pp.1–36.
Henrich, Dieter: *Between Kant and Hegel. Lectures on German Idealism*, David S. Pacini (ed.), Harvard University Press, 2003.
Horstmann, Rolf-Peter: *Die Grenzen der Vernunft. Eine Unteruschung zu Zielen und Motiven des Deutsches Idealismus*, Anton Hain, 1991.
Kenny, Anthony: *Wittgenstein* [1973], Blackwell, 2006.
Kreines, James: "Hegel's Critique of Pure Mechanism and the Philosophical Appeal of the Logic Project", *European Journal of Philosophy* 12:1, 2004, pp.38–74.
Kreines, James: "Hegel's Metaphysics: Changing the Debate", *Philosophy Compass* 1:5, 2006, pp.466–480.
Longuenesse, Bèatrice: *Hegel's Critique of Metaphysics* [1981], Cambridge University Press, 2007.
Mácha, Jakub: *Wittgenstein on Internal and External Relations: Tracing All the Connections*, Bloomsbury, 2015.

McDowell, John: *Having the World in View. Essays on Kant, Hegel, and Sellars*, Harvard University Press, 2009.
Ng, Karen: "Hegel's Logic of Actuality", *Review of Metaphysics* 63:1, 2009, pp.139–172.
Ng, Karen: "From Actuality to Concept in Hegel's *Logic*", in: Dean Moyar (ed.): *The Oxford Handbook of Hegel*, Oxford University Press, 2017, pp.269–290.
Pinkard, Terry: "Hegel and Marx: Ethics and Practice", in: Roger Crisp (ed.): *The Oxford Handbook of the History of Ethics*, 2013, pp.505–526.
Pippin, Robert: *Hegel's Idealism. The Satisfaction of Self-Consciousness*, Cambridge University Press, 1989.
Proops, Ian: "Wittgenstein and the Substance of the World", *European Journal of Philosophy* 12:1, 2004, pp.106–126.
Rosen, Michael: "From *Vorstellung* to Thought: Is a 'Non-Metaphysical' View of Hegel Possible?", in: Dieter Henrich (ed.): *Metaphysik nach Kant?: Stuttgarter Hegel-Kongress 1987*, Klett-Cotta, 1988, pp.248–262.
Rosen, Stanley: *The Idea of Hegel's Science of Logic*, University of Chicago Press, 2014.
Schaffer, Jonathan: "Monism: The Priority of the Whole", *Philosophical Review* 119:1, 2010: pp.31–76.
Siep, Ludwig: *Hegel's Phenomenology of Spirit* [2000], Cambridge University Press, 2014.
Stekeler-Weithofer, Pirmin: *Hegels Analytische Philosophie. Die Wissenschaft der Logik als kritische Theorie der Bedeutung*, Ferdinand Schöningh, 1992.
Stekeler-Weithofer, Pirmin: "Metaphysics and Critique of Metaphysics", in: Michael Forster and Kristen Gjesdal (eds.): *The Oxford Handbook of German Philosophy in the Nineteenth Century*, Oxford University Press, 2015, pp.569–590.
Stern, Robert: *Routledge Philosophy Guidebook to Hegel and the* Phenomenology of Spirit, Routledge, 2002.
Westphal, Kenneth R.: *Hegel's Epistemological Realism: A Study of the Aim and Method of Hegel's* Phenomenology of Spirit, Kluwer, 1989.
Westphal, Kenneth R.: *Hegel's Epistemology: A Philosophical Introduction to the* Phenomenology of Spirit, Hackett, 2003.

Kai-Uwe Hoffmann
Beauty: Hegel or Wittgenstein?

Abstract In this article, I argue that Hegel takes a centralist view of the concept of beauty whereas Wittgenstein rejects the centralist view outright. Hegel's and Wittgenstein's approaches to beauty are very different. There are some commonalities with respect to the critique of causal explanations in aesthetics. However, despite such minor similarities, it is undeniable that their respective approaches lead to very different theories of aesthetics. Should one be obliged on that basis to choose between Hegel and Wittgenstein on beauty? I argue that such a decision is neither necessary nor useful.

The debates surrounding the concept of beauty are as old as philosophy itself. In many of the investigations which we might term "aesthetic" the term takes on a central role. Kant's, Schiller's and Hegel's thoughts on the subject of aesthetics could not be articulated without recourse to it. Hegel's aesthetics in particular can be understood as an attempt to deduce the scientific nature of art on the basis of the concept of beauty. It can thus be said that Hegel takes a centralist view of the concept of beauty. A number of more recent philosophers, such as G. E. Moore, Mary Mothersill and Jerrold Levinson, to name but a few, ascribe to beauty a similarly central position. In terms of its metaphysical, epistemological and scientific claims and their formidable complexity, however, Hegel's centralism goes far beyond these modern thinkers, thus making it a project that cannot simply be ignored.

Although Wittgenstein may not have been the first to question such a centralism, his anti-centralist objections to the concept of beauty influenced generations of philosophers, particularly in the tradition of analytic aesthetics. One would think that, in knocking centralism off its pedestal, Wittgenstein would have tackled the same lofty questions of metaphysics, epistemology and scientificity as Hegel did. Although Wittgenstein never explicitly comments on Hegel's project, the textual evidence strongly suggests that he would have vigorously rejected Hegel's claims in these areas. If this turns out to be the case and it is possible to present a clear picture in which Hegel and Wittgenstein represent two antipodes on the field of aesthetics, then it would be reasonable to demand any aestheticist to champion the one or the other. But are things really as clear-cut as this? Are we forced to choose either Hegel or Wittgenstein? I think not. In what follows I will defend the thesis that, at least in the field of aesthetics, the decision is neither necessary nor helpful. I will attempt to justify this thesis by exploring these two philosophers' motives and arguments in the four areas of metaphysics, epistemology, scientism and centralism.

1 Hegel's metaphysical and epistemic strategies as a basis for aesthetics

At several points in his lectures on aesthetics, compiled and edited by Hotho,[1] Hegel makes it clear that the idea, as it is presented in aesthetics, has nothing to do with the so-called absolute, as it appears in the *Science of Logic*. The *Logic* does, however, establish the essential conditions for aesthetics by providing a scientific proof of that which is presupposed by it. That is, the elevation (*Erhebung*) to the standpoint of the absolute. It would go beyond the scope of this paper to elaborate too much on how such an elevation can be understood. Nonetheless, I wish to outline two strategies which arise out of these considerations and which form the basis of Hegel's aesthetics. Namely one epistemological and one ontological strategy, whose foundations were laid during Hegel's time in Jena. It is Hegel's goal to eliminate the chasm between the "I" and the world which, in his opinion, Kant posited, and Fichte deepened. The absolute must not be located entirely on the side of the object—as in Kant's things-in-themselves—nor entirely on the side of the subject, in the form of Fichte's absolute I. Roughly speaking the absolute is that which connects the two sides. As Hegel writes in the *Science of Logic*:

> But since the result now is that the idea is the unity of the concept and objectivity, the true, we must not regard it as just a *goal* which is to be approximated but itself remains always a kind of *beyond*; we must rather regard everything *as being* actual only to the extent that it has the idea in it and expresses it. (SL 2010: p.671)

Hegel's move, in effect, is quite straightforward even if the terminology impedes its immediate understanding. According to Hegel, we must cease the attempt to reach the absolute through an infinite approach, as Fichte endeavoured to do, but rather consider whether it might not present itself in some other place. Hegel does indeed find such a place, namely the idea. According to Kant ideas are the spheres of soul, world and god, as they appear in classical meta-

---

[1] The question of whether the lectures contain more Hotho than Hegel is one of which I am certainly conscious. I do, however, think that the topics discussed here can, without question, be ascribed to Hegel. The edition of T. M. Knox (1988) will serve as the textual basis in the following.

physics. They are, however, epistemologically problematic, which is why they are investigated in the *Dialectic* of the *Critique of Pure Reason*. Hegel intends to establish an adequate approach to them. But what ontological means are available to that end? Either we attempt to use the understanding to cognise reality, or we appeal to reason. The understanding is, for Hegel, a faculty that structures reality as an additive composition of moments. One act of cognition is systematically joined to another act of cognition so that they form an infinite and yet non-coherent series of cognitions. This is his main charge against Fichte. Rational cognition would, in contrast, understand reality as a unity that is entirely without dualism and is organised organically. Hegel does not reject the cognition of reality by means of the understanding outright, understanding it rather as a preliminary form of rational cognition. We must critically reflect and sublate the failings of the faculty of understanding. What does this mean in concrete terms? A cognition by means of the understanding would determine a concrete object to be an object that is independent of cognition. On one side we find the rationally cognising subject, on the other the object that is cognised. Hegel considers this approach to be highly problematic, since our cognition always makes certain presuppositions with regard to the process of cognition. We have concepts for objects, assimilate these concepts into judgements, and judgements into inferences. We could say that which we perceive always already has the structure of a concept, is dependent on our logical capacities in a certain way, though not in the way of a transcendental grounding. An object of perception is thus not an additive composition, like, say, a table, which is defined through its properties, but rather the concept is a complex organic entity that connects elements of the cognising subject and the cognised object. Hegel mirrors this development on a theoretical-categorical level. The *Doctrine of Being* is concerned with immediately given but not yet conceptually or categorically determined Being, whereas the *Doctrine of Essence* pursues the question of the ground of Being. In the process, principles such as those of sufficient reason and of noncontradiction are investigated, although not, as he accuses Kant of doing, in a disjointed manner, but rather in their systematic connection. Here the concept of appearance is of central importance: "Appearance is what the thing is in itself, or the truth of it." (SL 2010: p.418) The intelligible world, or the world as it is in itself, must appear, i.e., come into existence, and it must do so not in the Kantian form of something that is impossible to cognise, a mere construct of thought, but as a form of self-reflection of the conditions of possibility of cognition. The ontological constitution of reality remains, at least in the *Doctrine of Essence*, a question of necessary relations—of those originally Kantian categories of substance, causality and reciprocity. Finally, the *Doctrine of the Notion* further continues the process of uncovering the conditions of possibility and attempts to develop the connection between these categorical forms and the logical relations, which are differentiated into concepts, judgements and inferences. The idea turns out to be a type of result, but one that, in contrast to other philosophical projects of the time, can actually be reached. The idea is the process of uncovering the conditions of possibility of the unity of subject and object, or of cognition and cognised, which runs through the entire *Science of Logic*. This process is only possible if the cognitive faculty of reason is brought to bear and does so in each of the categories explored. This is illustrated by the oft quoted passage:

> The *understanding determines*, and holds the determination fixed. *Reason* is negative and *dialectical*, since it dissolves the determinations of the understanding into nothing; it is *positive*, since it generates the *universal*, and comprehends the particular therein. Just as the understanding is usually taken as something separate from reason in general, so also dialectical reason is taken as something separate from positive reason. In its truth reason is however *spirit*, which is higher than both reason bound to the understanding and understanding bound to reason. It is the negative, that which constitutes the quality of both the dialectical reason and the understanding: it negates the simple, thereby posits the determinate difference of the understanding; but it equally dissolves this difference, and so it is dialectical. (SL 2010: p.10)

What does it mean that "we must rather regard everything *as being* actual only to the extent that it has the idea in it and expresses it" (SL 2010: p.671)? The idea is the process of going from the simplest, most immediate logical determination of thought to the most complex one. Reality can only be grasped if the entire process is comprehended and, further, is comprehended by means of reason, which unites the additive thought of the understanding with negative rational thought.

2 Aesthetic metaphysics and epistemology and the question of their scientificity

I wish to open this section with two theses:
(1) Aesthetic-metaphysical thesis: Art is a necessary element of the self-development of the spirit, and
(2) Aesthetic-epistemological thesis: Within art, cognition of the true and absolute is possible.

Both of these theses can only be understood if Hegel's claim of scientificity of aesthetics is taken seriously. In the introduction to the *Lectures on Aesthetics*, Hegel proposes a dilemma: Everything seems to point towards the conclusion that art is not a scientific discipline and does not meet the required standards to be one. The following arguments are brought to bear in favour of this proposal:

(1) Fine art tempers the "seriousness of our circumstance" (LA: p.3). It would thus be unfitting to treat the unserious in a serious manner;
(2) Art was, however, also given a serious purpose, for example by Schiller, as a mediator between reason and sensuousness. Art then becomes a means to an end, the more so as it can serve as a means to other ends, such as the encouragement of frivolity;
(3) The means of art itself is deception, is appearance. These means do not, however, fit its end, which is truth. Truth, says Hegel, can only be advanced through truth;
(4) The scope of science is thought. The beauty of art, however, falls within the gamut of experience, sensation, intuition and imagination;
(5) Art is free in its production and resists any normative restrictions on it. Rules and laws do not, as such, appear to be compatible with art;
(6) Fantasy is a source of art and cannot very well be employed as a scientific criterion; and
(7) Necessity is one of the central criteria for scientificity, but one which does not appear to be applicable to art.

Hegel nonetheless comes to the conclusion that art must be treated scientifically, since all these arguments are plain false. In order to enable such a scientific treatment of art, he first differentiates between serving art, which serves the ends mentioned above, and free art, which is dedicated solely to its own ends and is thus the only true art. "Expressing the *Divine*, the deepest interests of mankind, and the most comprehensive truths of the spirit" (LA: p.7) is the function of true art. Hegel's solution can be summarised in three steps:
(a) Art is a sensuous representation of the absolute;
(b) In order to be capable of being this, free thought must first rid itself of the immediately given and attend to supersensory objects in the imagination; and
(c) The break between immediate, everyday reality and the pure activity of thought that is thus produced must, finally, be overcome. Works of art, as they are created by the artist, bridge this chasm.

Hegel then goes on to expand on the arguments against a scientific treatment of art listed above. These, in turn, are connected to Hegel's epistemological and ontological claims as developed in the previous paragraph. Appearance as described in argument (3) above is, as he had shown, an element of essence. Without appearance, essence, the absolute and truth cannot appear or be realised.

Appearance, however, pertains to aesthetics in two different ways. Besides the first form already mentioned, Hegel develops a second, epistemically inferior, form of the understanding that makes a significant distinction between inner reality, i.e., subjectivity, and outer reality, i.e., the objective world.[2] This distinction represents a deficient metaphysical position insofar as it is impossible to develop a unified conception of reality on its basis, but rather such a conception remains non-uniform and there remains a break between the inner and the outer:

> For this reason, after all, it is impossible for the Understanding to comprehend beauty because, instead of penetrating to this unity, the Understanding clings fast to the differences exclusively in their independent separation by regarding reality as something quite different from ideality, the sensuous as quite different from the Concept, the objective as quite different from the subjective, and thinks that such oppositions cannot be [reconciled and] unified. (LA: p.111)

Hegel seeks to understand this break from the standpoint of art, insofar as it is a deception, an appearance that does not correspond with the so-called true reality, which does not accept any breaks. Through art the absolute, the adequate metaphysical conception of reality, appears and thus exposes these difficulties. Although the concept of appearance thus makes sense in a Hegelian context, it remains to be seen how art can be reconciled with the seriousness, rules and necessity of science if its essential elements are fantasy and freedom. Hegel's argumentation begins from an approach that must be criticised in two distinct ways. Art and thought, as the object of philosophy as science, thus stand in irreconcilable opposition to one another. In its process of perceiving reality, thought furthermore destroys art because art can be characterised as an activity and concepts fix the active and living elements of reality. This approach also represents an epistemologically deficient stage of the understanding which, according to Hegel, cannot do justice to reality. He proposes the following solution: Thought is conscious of itself—this is a criterion of the absolute spirit. In being conscious of itself, thought reflects on itself—as is demonstrated in the *Science of Logic*—as well as its products, such as art, that originate from the spirit. These products must therefore be of the same kind as the spirit. Hegel understands the production of a work of art as a divestiture to feeling and sense. The trick

---

[2] In the *Lectures on Aesthetics* two relevant forms are explicitly considered in the chapter "The Idea of Beauty". On the one hand there is the theoretical, in which objects are presumed to be independent and isolated, and on the other the practical, in which objects are viewed as means to external ends. Only in overcoming and uniting these two forms is a solution to the problem possible (cf. LA: pp.111 ff).

is now that the spirit must be able to recognise itself as divested in the work of art. This takes place when the spirit thinks about it, reflects on it, when it treats it in its own terms, in thought. Thought, for Hegel, is conceptual thought, based not on the deficient means of the understanding. Rather it is rational thought, which distinguishes itself through an active and living element contained within it, insofar as it is dialectically exploring the forms of thought. Thought and reality are also in structural agreement since both can be shown to be active and living. But what space remains for necessity, rules and seriousness? Philosophy is the science of thought, a necessary, serious and rule-based observation as a self-reflection of its object. If the work of art can be conceptualised as a divestment of thought to sensation, and one that is systematically returned to the scope of thought through reflection, then art must attain scientific status:

> Thus the work of art too, in which thought expresses itself, belongs to the sphere of conceptual thinking, and the spirit, by subjecting it to philosophic treatment, is thereby merely satisfying the need of the spirit's inmost nature. For since thinking is the essence and Concept of spirit, the spirit in the last resort is only satisfied when it has permeated all products of its activity with thought too and so only then has made them genuinely its own. (LA: p.13)

Furthermore, if the highest purpose of art is to "bring the highest interests of spirit to our minds" (ibid.), then Hegel must conclude that the imagination does not produce art in an unregulated manner. The interests of the spirit determine its content and give direction to unbridled fantasy. From this argument it follows for Hegel that fine art is worthy of scientific consideration.

3 Beauty and centralism

At the very beginning of the lectures, the author restricts the scope of the inquiry. He is concerned only with a very specific concept of beauty, the concept of the beauty of art. The beauty of nature is explicitly excluded from his discussion. He goes on to illustrate what does not fall within his scope through a series of examples: beautiful colours, a beautiful sky, a beautiful stream, beautiful animals and beautiful people. These are all examples from everyday life. Aesthetics thus does not deal with statements that are made in everyday life.

A scientific treatment of the beauty of art must, first of all, deal with the decisive question of what the concept of the beauty of art is. This question includes two perspectives. The sceptical perspective seeks to resolve whether such a concept actually exists, i.e., "that there is such an object" (LA: p.23). In the context of the lectures this means that it must be demonstrated that the concept necessarily exists and is not merely contingent. This is motivated by a cogent example. If we are so frequently deceived by our perception of external objects, how can we know that we are not also deceived by our inner representations? The only way out of such a sceptical scenario is the demonstration of necessity. The concept of beauty is initially included as a lemma, in order for its scientific conditions subsequently to be elucidated. If we are capable of this demonstration, i.e., of developing the concept of the beauty of art, we are immediately confronted by the second perspective, which consists in determining what the object of beauty is. The investigation then runs through a number of stages: a restriction of the scope of the object, a resolution of the question of whether a scientific examination of the object is possible, the determination of the concept, and the structure in which the plan is presented. The first part thus develops the idea of the beauty of art, while the second part considers the development of this ideal into the various forms of artistic beauty.

What is beauty? If we consider this question in relation to the function of the concept in the overall theory, there can only be one answer: From the perspective of the lectures here discussed, beauty is the central element of aesthetics. Hegel, in my understanding of him, therefore argues for a centralism with respect to beauty. The entire conception of beauty depends on the derivation and the proof of the beauty. Beauty, understood as an idea and as a totality, is the yardstick by which all other theories must be measured. Theories that understand beauty to be something that gives pleasure, that describe properties of objects that stimulate the senses or the mind, and that understand the object of perception to be independent of the observer or as a means to a particular end, must all be rejected when measured against this yardstick. As the core of Hegel's aesthetics, beauty is contemplated in a liberal way:

> Thus the contemplation of beauty is of a liberal kind; it leaves objects alone as being inherently free and infinite; there is no wish to possess them or take advantage of them as useful for fulfilling finite needs and intentions. So the object, as beautiful, appears neither as forced and compelled by us, nor fought and overcome by other external things. (LA: p.114)

Furthermore, Hegel's approach ties the theory of beauty to an entirely novel theory of truth that aims to sublate the contradictions between freedom and necessity, mind and nature, knowledge and object, and law and appetite. The conception of philosophy as a form of therapy of philosophical misunderstandings penetrates all the way into this conception of aesthetics. Hegel seeks to heal the misunderstandings that arise out of the concept of beauty with the same methodological remedies as he applied in the *Logic*, merely altering the level on which they are applied. Concretely, this therapy consists, on the one hand, of identifying the points at which the deficient understanding, which is incapable of cognising beauty (cf. LA: p.111), is at work and is applying its limited faculties to the field of aesthetics and, on the other hand, raising these limited faculties systematically into the scope of reason, demonstrating that they are necessary elements of the whole and thus overcoming their tendency to isolation and abstraction.

4 Wittgenstein, beauty and Hegel

If one now considers Wittgenstein's discussion of aesthetics in general and of the concept of beauty in particular, as it can be found scattered throughout his various notes and publications, one would be inclined to draw a sharp distinction between Wittgenstein and Hegel. They nigh-on call for a study of the significant differences between the two. They do so for the following reasons:

(1) Wittgenstein represents a strongly anti-metaphysical position. Since Hegel's project is so profoundly metaphysical, such an approach would appear to be entirely obsolete for Wittgenstein;

(2) Closely tied to this is Hegel's thesis of epistemological access to the so-called absolute in the field of aesthetics. This too appears to be untenable from Wittgenstein's point of view;

(3) Wittgenstein is sceptical of scientism. For Hegel, however, the link between aesthetics and science is of central importance; and

(4) Particularly in *Lectures and Conversations on Aesthetics, Psychology, and Religious Belief*, Wittgenstein is critical of approaches that grant beauty a central role in their theory. Although in doing so Wittgenstein appears to be addressing his contemporaries, his criticism should be readily applicable to Hegel.

4.1

Wittgenstein's *Tractatus* famously claims that metaphysical, aesthetic, and ethical statements do not fall into the scope of things about which we can make statements with a sense. They are assigned to the realm of the mystical. This argument is expanded upon in 6.53 with reference to metaphysical statements:

> The correct method in philosophy would really be the following: to say nothing except what can be said, i.e. propositions of natural science—i.e. something that has nothing to do with philosophy—and then, whenever someone else wanted to say something metaphysical, to demonstrate to him that he had failed to give a meaning to certain signs in his propositions.

It follows that everything that cannot be expressed in the propositions of natural science, as well as sentences whose signs are not fully designative, are nonsensical. Although they make no sense, insofar as they are not propositions of natural science, Wittgenstein does not seem to want to abandon them entirely. Those acquainted with Wittgenstein will know that only silence can follow. In the early *Notebooks* Wittgenstein seems to develop a point of view that is echoed in the *TLP:* "The work of art is the object seen *sub specie aeternitatis*; and the good life is the world seen *sub specie aeternitatis*" (NB: p.83, 7 October 1916). In the *TLP* this slogan is put to use in a slightly different way. There the work of art has been replaced by the world: "The contemplation of the world sub specie aeterni is its contemplation as a limited whole" (TLP: 6.45). The important question seems, however, to be what *a work of art* and the world have in common. In one case we are dealing with a spatially and temporally delimited object, in the other with the entire world as a limited object. The similarity can only consist in the perspective from which the object is viewed, which is from the point of view of eternity. If eternity is conceived of not as an "infinite temporal duration" but as "timelessness", "then eternal life belongs to those who live in the present" (TLP: 6.4311). We could understand Wittgenstein to be saying that in contemplating an aesthetic object, the observer is absorbed in the presence of the moment. In such a moment of contemplation there is neither past nor future —time is of no concern, nor are causal relations or spatial boundaries. At the same time, Wittgenstein emphasises that this is not a propositional statement, but an intuition that considers the aesthetic object in its totality. It is crucial that the perspective is an external one: "The view *sub specie aeternitatis* from outside" (NB: p.83, 7 October 1916). The wording of 6.45 seems to point in a similar direction. The perception of the world as a limited whole is further described as a feeling. It seems as if the observer inhabits an external perspective of the world of facts, states of affairs and substances, as if the observer were beyond a boundary, outside a realm of scattered facts. This interpretation is strengthened by the fact that the statements on the concept of world are embedded in statements on the mystical, on that which cannot fall within the scope of natural science. Wittgenstein, however, never ceases to remind us that when we move beyond the limits of what can be said, we are in the realm of the nonsensical. In his introduction to the *TLP* he clearly states that we cannot think both sides of this boundary. Our thought always remains on the side of that which can be said. In the talk of a boundary, however, there always lurks the danger that there is something beyond it and Wittgenstein seems to be deliberately rousing this thought by speaking of the mystical and the aesthetic. Wittgenstein remains expressly paradoxical and acknowledges his own inconsistency when, in 6.54, he points out that the propositions of the *TLP* are themselves nonsensical. Hegel must reject such a paradoxical solution, for paradoxes must be sensibly resolved. What he is attempting to show is that there is a line that can be considered, viz. thought, from both sides and which must be systematically integrated and overcome. It is only in this way that we can *think* beauty. The early Wittgenstein does not permit such a point of view, and in doing so is entirely consistent with his own systematic presuppositions. In contrast to the late Wittgenstein, however, the concept of beauty does seem to play a role: "there is certainly something in the conception that the end of art is the beautiful" (NB: p.86, 21 October 1916). In (4) it will be shown that this approach, if we can call it that, is later abandoned by Wittgenstein.

4.2

According to Hegel's aesthetic-epistemological thesis, a cognition of the absolute is possible through art. One would be on very insecure footing if one were to defend the thesis that Wittgenstein claimed anything of the sort. We must not, however, lose sight of the fact that, in his early philosophy, Wittgenstein conceives of the aesthetic as contemplating something like a totality, to which we have no epistemological access, since no valid propositions of natural science can be made about it. The early notebooks and the *TLP*, however, appear to offer the possibility that a position *sub specie aeternitatis* can be assumed. It is in this context that Wittgenstein speaks of intuition and of feeling.

4.3

It is a central presupposition for Hegel that art is a scientific discipline. Wittgenstein would reject such an assumption outright. I want to argue, however, that it is worthwhile to examine his position more closely. He would, of course, not couch his position in such stark terms, but there may be some overlap in approach between Wittgenstein and Hegel that can be found with regard to these ideas.

First I want to explore Wittgenstein's scepticism with regard to science. Although he states in the *TLP* that the propositions of natural science are the only meaningful ones, he also sounds a note of caution by noting that this touches nothing that is truly important in human life: "We feel that even if all possible scientific questions be answered, the problems of life have still not been touched at all." (TLP: 6.52) Later, in his *Philosophical Investigations*, he insists that his investigation is not a scientific one (PI: §109). Rather, he is con-

cerned with showing that philosophy and science must be strictly distinguished from one another with regard to their purpose and mindset (cf. CV: p.7). Finally, in *Culture and Value* we find two scathing assessments:
(1) We cannot speak in science of a *great*, essential problem (CV: p.10); and
(2) I may find scientific questions interesting, but they never really grip me. Only conceptual and aesthetic questions do that (CV: p.79).

Although in the second quotation Wittgenstein displays his interest in conceptual and aesthetic questions, how does he treat aesthetics as such? Are his scathing critiques applicable to it as well? Yes, certainly. And this is where things get interesting, as Wittgenstein makes it clear who his opponent is. But before we introduce this opponent properly, let us turn to one final scathing pronouncement from the *Lectures on Aesthetics:* "You might think Aesthetics is a *science* telling us what's beautiful—almost too ridiculous for words. I suppose it ought to include also what sort of coffee tastes well." (LCA: p.11) At this point it ought to be clear that a comparison to Hegel is not worth the effort. But, as I have said, matters are not as straightforward as that. Wittgenstein's critical argument, that is later to be analysed with respect to his concept of beauty, contains attacks on three important elements of science. These include psychology, the empirical method, and causal explanations. It is indubitable that Wittgenstein had a great interest in psychology, a fact that surely contributed to his understanding of philosophy as therapeutic. In aesthetics, however, his doubts about it are particularly pronounced. Specifically, with regard to an experimentally grounded psychology that works empirically and offers mechanically-causal explanations. What is his problem with all these scientific assumptions that do, after all, represent the essential elements of modern research methods. In the *Philosophical Investigations,* Wittgenstein points out that these methods are inadequate at solving the problems in question: "The existence of the experimental method makes us think we have the means of solving the problems which trouble us; though problem and method pass one another by" (PI: II XIV, p.232). Aesthetic problems in particular require a different methodological inventory. The slogan underlying this critique is *reduction*. An experiment restricts the population to be investigated. If we think back to the early conception of a perspective *sub specie aeternitatis*, in the sense of an external perspective, one that contemplates the whole, then an experiment that has as its method a form of statistical analysis is doomed to fail. It restricts the field of view and leads up the wrong path. Wittgenstein concludes that:

> People often say that aesthetics is a branch of psychology. The idea is that once we are more advanced, everything—all the mysteries of Art—will be understood by psychological experiments. Exceedingly stupid as the idea is, this is roughly it. (LCA: p.17)

If we turn to the argument regarding the empirical method we find Wittgenstein's alternative. Instead of an empirical investigation that is guided by the model of a classical experimental situation, in which, for example, 12 people are confronted by a particular question and the results are statistically analysed, Wittgenstein calls for a method of conceptual clarification. With respect to causal explanations Wittgenstein vehemently opposes the co-optation of this subject matter by (mechanically-causal) strategies of explanation:

> The sort of explanation one is looking for when one is puzzled by an aesthetic impression is not a causal explanation, not one corroborated by experience or by statistics as to how people react. (LCA: p.21)

Why the vehemence against this co-optation? We can find an answer in the discussion of aesthetic reactions, a topic Wittgenstein views as essential in this context. What appears at first glance to cut across the common debates on causality, on closer inspection turns out to be a Wittgensteinian argument without equal. I will attempt to offer a brief outline of it. The famous example of an incorrectly installed door led Wittgenstein to develop the notion of discontent, which is to be distinguished from discomfort. His initial question is, of course: "Is what I call an expression of discontent something like an expression of discomfort plus knowing the cause of the discomfort and asking for it to be removed?" (LCA: p.13) In order to demonstrate that aesthetic reactions cannot have anything to do with mechanically-causal explanations, because they are, simply put, too cumbersome and are at odds with the immediacy of the aesthetic reaction, the underlying problem is illustrated by a variety of examples. If, for example, one touches a hot plate we do not think about the causes, but just pull back our hand. If the way in which the door was installed causes discontent, it is more probable that we will say "too high!" than that we will express discomfort and note that its causes are known. According to Wittgenstein, noting that the causes are known leads in completely the wrong direction. This is precisely because it makes it seem as if in an aesthetic reaction two processes are taking place simultaneously: the statement of discomfort and the reflection on its causes. If I understand Wittgenstein correctly, then aesthetic reactions are to be understood as immediate reactions. These reactions do not contain a reflexive process of analysing causes on the basis of mechanically-causal explanations. This is why the recourse to psychological experiments makes no sense, since they do not grasp the actual problem.

The various motifs discussed in the previous paragraph, if we consider them in general and not in their specific presentation, would not be unfamiliar to Hegel. I mean that certain slogans such as empiricism and causality are also treated very critically in his work. Hegel too, would emphasise the turn towards the concept, even if not in the form Wittgenstein proposes. Hegel's conceptual analysis is in no way Wittgensteinian and to claim that it is would be absurd. Hegel would also probably question Wittgenstein's analysis of aesthetic reactions, possibly with reference to his critique of immediacy. Both, however, are united in their scathingly sceptical opposition to the possibility of isolating and abstracting from the state of affairs, which are the objects of the investigation. As Wittgenstein suggests removing one's glasses (PI: §103) in order to gain the right perspective, so does Hegel advocate abandoning the perspective of understanding in favour of that of reason. One could say that both are at pains to get the whole picture into view, an endeavour that is currently discussed under the heading of complexity, which is to be made visible through adequate methodological means.

4.4

It is now time to let go of possible connections to Hegel. When it comes to the concept of beauty itself, all possible bridges seem to be out. Wittgenstein advances a whole string of arguments in order to criticise conventional approaches to the concept of beauty. I will briefly discuss the most salient of them.

Wittgenstein's *argument of use*, with which we are acquainted from the *Philosophical Investigations*, has a critical function in the field of aesthetics because it calls attention to the fact that Wittgenstein's contemporaries were concerned only with the form of words and not with their use. One of the central figures whom Wittgenstein criticises is, of course, Moore. We should not be focused on particular concepts such as good or beauty, as is the case in the statement "This is beautiful" (LCA: p.2). This is an example of a constellation of subject and predicate that expresses nothing. This begs the question why such a constellation of subject and predicate is "entirely uncharacteristic" (LCA: p.2). In order to explain this, a further argument, the *argument of context*, is introduced. It states that it makes no sense to consider forms outside of their context of use. The particular context of use must be taken into account:

> We are concentrating, not on the words "good" or "beautiful", which are entirely uncharacteristic, generally just subject and predicate ("This is beautiful"), but on the occasions on

which they are said—on the enormously complicated situation in which the aesthetic expression has a place, in which the expression itself has almost a negligible place. (LCA: p.2)

The use of aesthetic concepts must occur against the background of the use of concepts in context and in doing so it must be remembered that the context consists of extremely complicated situations in which there is no generalisable relation between subject and predicate. This argument leads to the rejection of the *argument of qualities following predicates:* Just because beauty is used as a predicate, it does not follow that it expresses an aesthetic quality. Wherein lies the problem? Wittgenstein clearly wants to emphasise that there is no necessary connection between the predicate beauty and any particular subject. We can use an aesthetic concept in a variety of contexts, but in doing so the meaning will vary. Moreover, a concept can have multiple meanings, which is established in the *argument of family resemblance* (cf. PI: §77). In the wake of the argument of context there follows the *argument of cultural context:*

> The words we call expressions of aesthetic judgement play a very complicated role, but a very definite role, in what we call a culture of a period. To describe their use or to describe what you mean by a cultured taste, you have to describe a culture. (LCA: p.8)

Wittgenstein thus considers not only the particular context of use to be essential, but also the time and the cultural period in which the concept is used. In doing so he falls back on conceptions he developed in *On Certainty* in order to resolve the problem of scepticism. Context alone, however, is not sufficient to understand the use of aesthetic concepts. It is also necessary to understand which specific language game is being played, thus introducing the *language game argument.* Only if we know what language game is being played, are we, for example, able to understand what makes a particular concept an expression of approval.

If we look at all of these closely interwoven arguments, it is important to note that they all run together to a clear conclusion regarding the concept of beauty: The conclusion that this concept is almost never used in the way philosophy had, up to then, suggested it was used. Wittgenstein states that "'beautiful' is an odd word to talk about because it's hardly ever used" (LCA: p.2). The counter-strategy is to ask how a concept is learned and it turns out, according to Wittgenstein, that we learn approval more through gestures and facial expressions, than through concepts. It is for this reason that the lectures seek to do away with common errors:

> We think we have to talk about aesthetic judgements like "This is beautiful", but we find that if we have to talk about aesthetic judgements we don't find these words at all, but a word used something like a gesture, accompanying a complicated activity. (LCA: p.11)

If we ask what it is that we do when we use concepts that express aesthetic approval, then we must not forget that rules play a certain role in it. The *argument of rule-following* is also familiar from the *Philosophical Investigations*. In the *Lectures and Conversations on Aesthetics, Psychology and Religious Belief* rules again have a central role to play, insofar as the learning of rules is essential to the expression of aesthetic judgements. It would be tempting to explore the consequences of the rule-following paradox, as articulated by Kripke, for aesthetics. That, however, is a topic for another investigation and here I will briefly return to Hegel.

There are undoubtedly numerous parallels, none of which are, however, particularly promising in the present context. Although Hegel discusses the relation between subject and predicate, context, rules, relations of necessity and so forth, his investigation remains metaphysical and is not concerned with the use and acquisition of concepts. The concept of beauty plays a central role and his scientific conception of artistic beauty is inconceivable without it. He is not concerned with how we learn such a concept, but rather how the science of artistic beauty can be derived from the concept of beauty. Hegel's and Wittgenstein's approaches thus diverge considerably with regard to the concept of beauty.

5 Conclusion

As has been shown, there are certainly similarities between Hegel and Wittgenstein with regard to their critique of scientism, as well as several other minor points, but there is no denying that Wittgenstein would reject Hegel's metaphysical, epistemological and scientific claims. The difference in their approach to the concept of beauty is also obvious. Whereas Hegel is solely concerned with the concept of beauty within the framework of art and in doing so assigns it a central role, Wittgenstein covers much more ground and focuses on other issues. He is primarily concerned with that, which Hegel would call the ordinary use of the concept. He, for example, is concerned with a visit to the tailor. At the same time, he discusses cases which certainly would fall within the scope of Hegel's aesthetics, such as our artistic judgement. Wittgenstein's goal, however, is entirely different to Hegel's. He seeks to draw our attention to a problem with our use of aesthetic concepts. According to him it is wrong to assume a standard for the concept of beauty. It is impossible to normatively prescribe what is beautiful and what is not. Rather, we should examine the many and varied occasions and activities in which the concept is used. The object of Wittgenstein's investigation is the plurality of life, which cannot be captured in psychological tests that rely on causal explanations.

What then can be said in answer to the question, posed in the introduction, of whether it is necessary to choose between the two strategies? I am of the opinion that we are not confronted by an either-or choice. From a purely historical perspective it is possible to claim that each approach must be understood in the context of its time and can be interpreted as reactions to the problems posed by their predecessors. Hegel is reacting, not exclusively but significantly, to the problems posed by Kant, thus giving rise to his three strategies. Wittgenstein is reacting to contemporaries such as Moore and seeks to offer alternative solutions.

But what of the systematic arguments? Is one of the approaches superior to the other? I think not. The two projects operate on completely different levels. They are not competing with one another, but rather offer different perspectives on the same problem. It is not useful to demand a decision for Hegel and against Wittgenstein or vice versa. To do so would be naïve and unphilosophic. On the scale of particular arguments, however, evaluations are certainly possible. For example, I would argue that Wittgenstein underestimates the role of the concept of beauty. Hegel, on the other hand, is somewhat extreme in his assertion of a scientific ideal, which might be off-putting to a modern audience. Perhaps Hegel and Wittgenstein do ultimately meet in the thought that an isolating perspective on aesthetic states of affairs is not particularly conductive to understanding the topic at issue.

Part 3 **From Difference to Identity**

Paul Redding
Hegel and the Tractarian Conception of Judgement

Abstract Parallels are often drawn between Hegel and the later Wittgenstein, but an examination of Hegel's conception of judgement from the *Science of Logic* reveals curious parallels with central doctrines of Wittgenstein's *Tractatus*. There Hegel appeals to a type of primitive linguistic structure or *Satz* consisting of the concatenation of two singular terms or names, and like Wittgenstein's "*Elementarsäzte*", these have the properties of being mutually independent, essentially positive, and with only one way of being true (or for Hegel, "correct"). For Hegel, to play a role in reasoning, such a *Satz* must have one of its terms re-determined as general such that it can now enter into inferential relations with other judgements. The immediate product of this type of transformation was a form of judgement, the judgement of existence (*Dasein*) that he exemplified by colour judgements, and such judgements had a logical form *different to* that of the *Tractatus*' compound *Sätze* that *Elementarsäzte* were meant to constitute. When in the late 1920s Wittgenstein moved away from the doctrines of the *Tractatus*, considerations of the logic of colour judgements with similar features to those of Hegel's judgements of *Dasein* played a role.

Comparisons of the views of philosophers across the boundaries of time and culture are hazardous, and surely this applies especially in the case of Hegel and Wittgenstein. Hegel had been effectively eliminated from serious consideration early within the analytic movement during first half of the twentieth century, and *part* of this effect can be traced back to the influence of Wittgenstein. While Bertrand Russell had been keen to dissociate the new style of philosophy from Hegel, this antipathy had been consolidated by the positivist direction taken by analytic thought in the 1920s and 30s, a movement significantly influenced by Wittgenstein's early great work, *Tractatus Logico-Philosophicus*. Exactly *how* to read the *Tractatus* has, of course, always been contested: the positivists seem to have understood it as providing a metaphysics-free *semantic* theory for the new logic introduced by Frege and Russell, while for Russell and others it was more a type of exercise in realist metaphysics.[1] However, from the 1950s,

---

[1] Carnap attested to the influence of the *Tractatus* on his work (Carnap 1963: p.25). Concerning the more general influence of the *Tractatus* on what would become the modern discipline of se-

signs of a thaw in analytic attitudes to Hegel were starting to show, with the influence of Wittgenstein recognized *here* as well. In this case, it was *via* his later work, the influence of which spread after the publication of *Philosophical Investigations* in 1953.

One of the first signs of such a thaw was the publication in 1958 of John N. Findlay's *Hegel: A Re-Examination*, in which the author described Hegel as having anticipated "many of the views that we now associate with the name of Wittgenstein" (Findlay 1958: p.80). The views in question concerned the relation of thought to language, and in particular, to socially grounded and historically variable patterns of language *use*. A little over a decade and a half later, such issues were familiar via the influence of Charles Taylor's *Hegel*, in which he directed attention to elements in Hegel's work on the relation of mind and language, seen as emanating from the pre-romantic thinker, J. G. Herder (Taylor 1975: ch.1).[2]

Four decades after Taylor, changes within the general landscape of analytic philosophical debate have tended to counter motivations for such comparisons. For its part, work in analytic philosophy has witnessed a *reassertion* of the *style* of philosophy closer to the earlier than later Wittgenstein,[3] rendering such comparisons less attractive for contemporary defenders of Hegel. Added to this, there now seems less *need* for such comparisons. In the case of Taylor, the comparison of Hegel and Wittgenstein had been used to emphasise *particular* ideas within Hegel, who was otherwise understood in a quite traditional manner. In the intervening decades, however, the traditional interpretation of Hegel accepted by Taylor has been criticized on a number of fronts, lessening the need for any such indirect and partial defences. Nevertheless, I suggest that there is still much to be learnt from such a comparison, but here want to refocus it away from such general issues to more specific and "formal" ones. In particular, I will compare views on the nature of *judgement* found in Hegel's *Science of Logic* with the central doctrines of Wittgenstein's *Tractatus Logico-Philosophicus*. Some preliminary

---

mantics, see, for example, Lokhorst (1988) and Stokhof (2008). On the limitations of the "semantics" of the earlier work of Frege and Russell see Goldfarb (1979).

2 Taylor and Findlay interpreted the differences *differently*, however. While Taylor saw Hegel as ultimately *lapsing* into the sort of traditional metaphysical views of which Herder and late Wittgenstein were, correctly, critical (Taylor 1975: pp.567–571), Findlay, regarded Hegel as having "gone beyond" the sorts of views associated with Wittgenstein (Findlay 1958: p.80).

3 Partly this would seem to have been associated with the extension of formal semantics from logic to linguistic theory, thus bringing natural languages within its scope. From a Hegelian perspective, conceived as an empirical discipline semantics would be relevant to, but could not replace, philosophy of spirit (*Geist*).

justification for what might be understood as a misdirected effort, however, might be required.

A critic might point out that even were some particular similarities to be found, surely these would be eclipsed by the radical differences separating their background assumptions about the natures of logic and philosophy more generally. The standard view is that in his logic Hegel was indebted to a traditional framework coming from Aristotle, in which the logical structure of a judgement was naively assumed to mirror the subject–predicate structure of grammar, resulting in an Aristotelian metaphysics of finite substances. Wittgenstein, on the other hand, had been attracted to the attempts of Russell and Frege to ground mathematics in logic—a project continuing a modern and deeply *anti*-Aristotelian revolution in logic and philosophy. However, the chasm here, I want to suggest, may not be as great as commonly assumed.

For its part, interpretations of Wittgenstein's *Tractatus* have not been limited to either the "realist" metaphysical account of the world or proto-semantic theory as seen by the positivists. In particular, the realist reading of the *Tractatus* is now commonly challenged by interpretations couched in broadly *Kantian* terms.[4] Moreover, on such non-realist readings, there is far more scope for continuity between the earlier and later philosophies of Wittgenstein than conventionally acknowledged. On the other hand, for his part Hegel is now commonly understood as *some* kind of "post-Kantian" thinker, rather than the traditional theo-centric metaphysician as presupposed by Taylor.[5] Here, a quick glance at Hegel's account of formal syllogisms in *Science of Logic* might indicate something of Hegel's "modern" critical distance from Aristotle's logic and metaphysics.

While traditionally a syllogism had been conceived as holding between two types of judgements—"particular judgements" predicating some characteristic of *some* As and "universal judgements" predicating some characteristic of *all* As—Hegel's conception of the syllogism involves *three* term types—singular, particu-

---

[4] Metaphysically *realist* interpreters of the *Tractatus* have included Max Black (1966) and David Pears (1987), while critics of such a view have included Anscombe (1959), Ishiguro (1969) and McGuinness (1981). Non-realist interpreters have commonly offered interpretations closer to the transcendental idealism of Kant, this being especially true of the "resolute" reading developed by Cora Diamond (1991) and James Conant (Conant and Diamond 2006). Non-realist readers of the *Tractatus* find much greater continuity between the early and late Wittgenstein than is common with other readers.

[5] From the late 1980s the strongly post-Kantian reading of Hegel was pressed by Robert Pippin (1989) and Terry Pinkard (1994). While this produced reactions from those wanting to stress Hegel's differences to Kant, many of the critics nevertheless acknowledged enough of a Kantian influence to be similarly critical of the traditional reading.

lar, universal—with the consequence that a much greater number of judgement types will be found within his syllogisms. The crucial addition here of the singular judgement form that had been precluded from the traditional syllogistic reflects its reintroduction by *nominalist* logicians in the medieval period.[6] Later, Leibniz had attempted to integrate this nominalist dimension within the overall framework of the syllogistic, in many ways transforming the latter from within in such a way that it could be treated mathematically, specifically with the use of algebra (Lenzen 2004). This direction, as noted early in the analytic period (e.g., Yost 1950), has affinities with the conception of logic as found in Frege and Russell. Here, however, Leibniz is almost always treated as an historical exception, whose logical innovations had gone unappreciated until late in the 19th century.

This conventional story ignores the fact that Leibniz's logic, and especially, his project of a "universal characteristic", had been discussed in the 18th century, albeit, more amongst mathematicians than philosophers. Among the philosophical exceptions, however, was the logic authority at the Tübingen Stift when Hegel had been a student there: Gottfried Ploucquet. Ploucquet had been a strong advocate of Leibniz's universal characteristic and the algebraic logic on which it was based. His logic textbook (Ploucquet 2006) had been used in classes Hegel attended at Tübingen, and the doctrine of the universal characteristic, attributed to both Leibniz and Ploucquet, is discussed in Book III of *Science of Logic* (SL 2010: pp.602–608; GW 12: pp.104–110). It is clear that Hegel was well aware of the structural antagonisms that this distinctly modern mathematical approach had introduced within both traditional metaphysics and logic, as reflected in the role attributed to "singularity" as a determination of "the concept". Hegel is explicit as to the logical moves involved in Leibniz's and Ploucquet's mathematization of the syllogism: the essentially extensionalist treatment of both subject and predicate terms of a judgement as *predicates*, giving expression to abstract "universals" conceived as "subsuming" some range of singular, but *otherwise indeterminate* elements (SL 2010: p.602; GW 12: p.104). The resulting analysis of judgement structure, of which Hegel is critical, is what anticipates the later approach of Frege.

While clearly antagonistic to any project of *reducing* logic to its mathematical modeling, it is nevertheless clear that Hegel had appreciated, here as elsewhere, the role played by "negation" within the history of philosophical doctrines. In logic, this concerned the negating role played by the new

---

6 The Aristotelian syllogism had no place for "singular" judgements made about individuals *as such*. In this system, were one to reason about some particular individual, *Socrates*, say, one could consider that individual *as* a "particular" instance of the human species, and consider Socrates as *a man* or *some man*.

mathematical logic within the structure of traditional logic. In light of this, the intent of the *Science of Logic* was clearly that of *reconstructing* something of the traditional syllogistic and the "speculative" metaphysics it supported, in such a way as to *accommodate* the negative role played by Leibniz and his Tübingen follower (Redding 2014). With such general considerations in mind we might now move to some specific points of intersection between Hegel and the doctrines of Wittgenstein's *Tractatus*.

1 Wittgenstein's Elementarsätze and Hegel's "positive existential judgements"

It is clear that Wittgenstein's motivations in writing the *Tractatus* were very different to those of the positivists influenced by him. The specifically *logical* doctrines for which it is mostly known seem part of a conception of the realm of ethics, pursued "*ex negativo*" (TLP: 6.42), by way of an exhaustive conception of a realm *from which* the ethical was excluded: the realm of science. It is the more "positive" logical doctrines that will be our focus here, however. These are centered on the idea of all meaningful statements being truth-functional constructions of atomic "elementary statements" (*Elementarsätze*), in turn understood as expressed in articulated *statement-signs* (*Satz-Zeichen*) able to "picture" homologous atomic facts, "*Sachverhälte*". Such *Sachverhälte* are in turn considered to be the elements to which can be reduced all the facts, "*Tatsachen*" that, existing in "logical space", make up "the world".[7]

Following Anscombe (1961: pp.31–40), we might summarize this doctrine of *Elementarsätze* as including the following central claims. The contents of these elementary statements are to be understood as: (1) mutually independent, the truth or falsity of any one depending on that of no other; (2) essentially *positive*, there being no *negative Elementarsätze*; (3) being such that there is only one way of an *Elementarsatz*'s being true or false, one way of its *picturing* a *Sachverhalt*; (4) being such that there is no distinction between internal and external negation with regard to *Elementarsätze*; and (5) consisting of concatenations of

---

7 For the idea of *Sätze* as sentence-involving statements, I here follow Goldstein (1999: p.501, n.13). Anscombe uses "proposition" to translate "*Satz*" which, while according with an older meaning of "proposition" *qua* act of proposing or stating, can be misleading in the more general philosophical context where "proposition" is likely to be taken as an abstract content *expressed* in a sentence-using statement.

names.[8] These elements will appear in one way or another in Hegel's consideration of structure of judgement in the *Science of Logic*.

In the introductory passages to his discussion of judgement structure in the *Science of Logic*'s "Subjective Logic", Hegel distinguishes an *Urteil* or *judgement* from what he calls a *Satz*. While Hegel's use of the latter term is often translated as "proposition", it is clear that here the meaning is better captured by "statement", *qua* particular use of a concrete linguistic entity, a grammatical sentence, for conveying some information about empirical states of affairs. Thus Hegel considers as a mere *Satz*, the statement "Aristotle died at the age of 73 in the fourth year of 115th Olympiad", and in this context takes the sentence employed as having a structure in which *both* subject and predicate are considered as name-like singular terms: "what is said of a singular (*einzelnen*) subject" says Hegel, "is itself only something singular (*nur etwas Einzelnes*)" (SL 2010: p.553, GW 12: p.55). Considered in this way as something like a concatenation of two *names*, Hegel's "*Satz*" looks close to Wittgenstein's "*Elementarzatz*",[9] involving a *Satz*-sign [*Satzzeichen*] which, *as itself a Sachverhalt*, can be considered "in its projective relation" to the world, thus "picturing" other *Sachverhälte* (TLP: 3.12 and 3.2).[10]

Conventionally conceived, Wittgenstein's logical project in the *Tractatus* is concerned with how to think of the "grounding" relations between such elementary statements and those compound *Sätze* that are *not* constrained by conditions 1 to 5 and which are to be thought of as built truth functionally from the latter. Tractarian "elementary" statements are employed by Hegel within the context of a very different project, one meant to *counter* any atomistic, "frozen" picture like Wittgenstein's. Nevertheless, Hegel's progress through a series of purported judgement forms will *start* with his version of an *Elementarsatz*, and something even closer to Wittgenstein's notion will return in the context of his later critical discussion of the "mathematical syllogism" of Leibniz and Ploucquet.

---

8 There has always been disagreement over whether the "objects" named in a basic proposition included properties and relations. The dominant, and most literal line of interpretation (Copi 1958; Anscombe 1959) limits the objects named to so-called "bare particulars", or what Hegel would call "singulars".

9 Again, like Wittgenstein's "*Satz*", Hegel's use of this term is often translated as "proposition". See Hegel's comments (SL 2010: pp.552–3; GW 12: p.55) concerning how a *Satz* may have the grammatical structure of subject and predicate but fail to be a judgement. The *context* in which such a sentence is used will determine whether or not it constitutes a judgement.

10 This is not to say that "Aristotle", as in Hegel's example, would count as the type of *name* found in a tractarian "*Elementarsatz*", as its object is far from simple.

With respect to the relation between the configurations of *elementary statements* and the *facts* pictured, Wittgenstein says that linguistic configuration "*entspricht*", corresponds to, the other, while Hegel talks of "the agreement [*Übereinstimmung*] of representation with the subject matter" (SL 2010: p.562; GW 12: p.65). However, for Hegel the *Satz* considered in such a *projective* way is itself *neither* true nor false, but *correct* (*richtig*) or *incorrect* (*unrichtig*), and as the capacity for being *true or false* is the mark of a judgement, a mere *Satz*, considered in this way, is *not a judgement*.[11] Understood as concatenations of *names* or singular terms, *Sätze* cannot be proper judgements because paradigmatically judgements have at least one non-singular (particular or universal) term. These concatenations can become the *vehicles* of judgements, however, as singular terms can become redetermined *as* universals in Hegel's logic. Thus a basic "*Satz-sign*" involving *only* names can be redetermned as the expression of a judgement.

In order for a *Satz* to count as a judgement (*Urteil*), it must be used in more than in a simple reporting sense: specifically, it must form part of a larger piece of *inferential reasoning* (SL 2010: 553; GW 12: pp.55–6),[12] and it is in relation to *this* function that the judgement must contain universals.[13] The clear suggestion here is that we must be able to think of the predicate "happening in the fourth year of the 115th Olympiad", considered first as simply *naming* a period of time, now as an *abstract* universal capable of being true of (Hegel will say, "subsuming") *diverse* events, thus allowing it to mediate evidentiary relations among judgements.

It is this link of logical structure to inferential functioning that has been underlined in recent years by Robert Brandom in his "inferentialist" approach to semantics that he attributes to Hegel and finds also in the early Frege (Brandom 1994, 2002). This inferentialist dimension is later made explicit in Hegel when he shows a complex form of judgement—the "judgement of the concept"—to be an implicit "syllogism" (SL 2010: pp.585–587; GW 12: pp.87–9). Elsewhere I have ar-

---

11 Even here, however, as *richtig* or *unrichtig* the act of producing a *Satz* is to be conceived as an evaluatively judgeable event (an *act*) rather than a simply natural one.

12 "There would be in it an element of judgement", writes Hegel, "only if one of the circumstances, say, the date of death or the age of the philosopher, came into doubt [...]. In that case, the figures would be taken as something universal, as a time that, even without the determinate content [*bestimmten Inhalt*] of Aristotle's death, would still stand on its own filled with some other content or simply empty." (SL 2010: p.553; GW 12: pp.55–56)

13 Cf. "It can also be mentioned in this context that a *statement* [*Satz*] can indeed have a subject and predicate in a grammatical sense without however being a *judgement* [*Urteil*] for that. The latter requires that the predicate behave with respect to the subject in a relation of conceptual determination, hence as a universal with respect to a particular or singular." (SL 2010: pp.552–553; GW 12: p.55)

gued that Brandom's attribution of "inferentialism" to Hegel is too strong and that for Hegel, having the capacity to function in an inference is a *necessary* but not *sufficient* condition for being a judgement (Redding 2015). While Hegel suggests that the mind's representational capacities are somehow consequential upon the human being's capacity for language use, there must still be *some* kind of representational contribution coming from the side of an individual's perceptual experience. It is just *this*, I suggest, that is reflected in the role played by those name-containing quasi-Tractarian *Elementarsätze* with which he starts. Rather than simply *denying* a role for such elementary singular judgements, by a process involving the redetermination of their terms, they become *integrated* (*aufgehoben*) within higher level judgements. But these preserve the original naming function of the subject terms: in judgements of necessity, the subject term is now conceived as naming the *kind itself*, rather than an individual instance of the kind (SL 2010: pp.575–581; GW 12: pp.77–83).

The idea that for a *Satz* to function as a judgement *one* of its terms must express an inference-articulating universal is developed in Hegel's dynamic inventory of judgement *types* within his "Subjective Logic". Here Hegel presents a series of judgement types in terms of their capacity to instantiate the very concept of what a judgement is, each new type correcting some failure of its antecedent. Progress through this series will cycle between versions of two basic forms distinguished by the type of predication involved. In one form, a property expressed in the predicate will be understood as *inhering* in the thing designated by the subject term; in the other, the predicate will express an "abstract universal" that *subsumes* that referred to by the subject term. The first major example of an *inherence* judgement will be the *judgement of existence* (*Dasein*) (SL 2010: pp.557–68; GW 12: pp.59–71),[14] while the predicative relation of *subsumption* will first be exemplified in the judgement of *reflection* (SL 2010: pp.568–81; GW 12: pp.71–84). It is clear that this distinction is between judgements dependent upon the perceptual experience of actual, observable things and those not so dependent, as in *inferentially* elicited judgements, and that each judgement type exhibits a quite different logical form.

Significantly, the *first* form of the qualitative judgement, the *positive judgement*, is such that subject and predicate terms are, like Wittgenstein's *Elementarsätze*, both "*names at first*" (SL 2010: p.557; GW 12: p.60). However, in contrast to Wittgenstein's *Elementarsätze*, the objects of which are "colourless" (TLP: 2.0232), Hegel's positive judgements are *qualitative*. This is a difference to

---

14 Or the "judgement of being-there [Dasein]", as it is also called in *Science of Logic* (SL 2010: pp.557–568; GW 12: pp.59–71).

which we will return. For the moment, however, let us concentrate on the obvious parallel in that Hegel's judgement is one whose content is (by definition) necessarily positive, meeting Anscombe's rejection of *negative Elementarsätze* —criterion 2. Hegel's positive judgement, however, is at most a type of proto-*Urteil*; to become a true judgement, *one* of the terms of course must become universal. The story of this transition will centre on the role of *negation*.

The positive judgement might *start* as a concatenation of names, but to function *as a judgement* one of these names must be understood as expressing a universal. Here, however, Hegel's account takes a surprising turn. We typically think of positive judgements about individuals, such as "Gaius is learned" or "the rose is red" on the model of the predicate expressing something general, *being learned* or *being red*, about that individual, and yet Hegel treats the positive judgement as equally able to be read as construing *the subject* as determined as universal and *the predicate* as singular.[15] In short, in the very act of *judging* the logical roles of subject and predicate terms are able to be *reversed*.

In treating the *predicate* term as expressing the conceptual determination of *singularity,* Hegel's intention is clear enough: the singular predicate of the positive judgement, such as "red" in "the rose is red",[16] is to be thought as acting in a name-like way so as to pick out the *particular* redness *inhering* in *some specific rose*—we might say, pointing to a rose before us—*this rose's* particular *shade* of red, or its way of being or *looking* red, *now*.[17] With the predicate *as a singular*, we might be tempted to think of it as capturing something like the content of a Kantian *intuition*, or some *concrete property instance*, while the universality of the subject allowing Hegel's criterion for *being* a judgement to be satisfied. Ignoring for a moment the universality of the subject, the positive qualitative judgement aligns with a feature of Wittgenstein's *Elementarsatz* corresponding

---

15 Medieval logic had treated singular terms *as* universals, and Leibniz had also rendered them as "particulars". Moreover, this reversibility seems a consequence that flows from the very concept of what it is *to be a judgement:* it is the very identification of the terms by the copula in the judgement, Hegel suggests, that signals their "reciprocal determination". Thus the *subject* is "determined as universal by the predicate" and so *becomes* universal, while the predicate is "determined in the [singular] subject" and "is therefore *a singular.*" (SL 2010: p.560; GW 12: p.62)
16 Hegel switches between the examples "the rose is red" and "the rose is fragrant". For simplicity sake, I will keep to the former. No logical point hangs on the difference between examples.
17 Cf. "'The rose is fragrant.' This fragrance is not some indeterminate fragrance or other, but the fragrance of the rose. The predicate is therefore *a singular.*" (SL 2010: p.560; GW 12: p.62) It is important that the subject term here counts *as* involving a universal in the way that the subject term of a judgement within an Aristotelian syllogism must. It is in this sense that the subject *is* a (particular determinate of a) universal, and *not* a singular.

to Anscombe's criterion 3—the idea that there is only *one way* of the sentences being "true"—as becomes apparent when we contrast *this* conception of predication with the *conventional* understanding of a predicate as a "subsuming" universal. In the latter form, typical of Hegel's *reflective* judgement, there will be a variety of ways in which a sentence attributing the property of *redness* to a thing can be true. If I am told that Alice's new car is red, then this statement can be true regardless of which *shade* of red the car instantiates. Hegel will link negation to the logic of "subsuming" predicates, but crucially we encounter *two* stages of negation in his account.

2 Hegel's First Negative Judgement: Negating Predicates of Inherence

Hegel's positive judgement, with its universal subject and singular predicate might *be* a judgement, but it is not an adequate instantiation of the concept of a judgement. With its proximity to its starting point as a mere *Satz*, the positive judgement "is *not true* but has its truth in the negative judgement" (SL 2010: p.562; GW 12: p.64). With this, Hegel's opposition to the empiricist idea of *grounding* all judgements in simple positive judgements is obvious.

Hegel's account of the passage from the qualitative judgement to the more developed judgement of reflection will reveal the complexity of the two different ways in which negation is involved with predication, a difference aligning with that between predication as inherence and as subsumption. First, when one says, for example, "the rose is *not* red", negation here *can* be taken as applying only to the *determinateness* of the predicate, such that saying that the rose is *not* red does not imply that it is not *coloured*;[18] rather it being assumed "that it has a color, though another color" (SL 2010: p.565; GW 12: p.68). Such judgements cannot be conceived as meeting the demands of logical independence as in Anscombe's condition 1. With the predicate understood in this way, a rose that *is* red is thereby *not* yellow, *not* pink, *not* blue and so on, and one that is *not* red, will be either yellow *or* pink *or* blue, and so on.[19] Along with this, "This

---

[18] "From the side of this universal sphere, the judgement is still positive." (SL 2010: p.565; GW 12: p.68)
[19] Moreover, what counts as a determinable of any entity depends up what *sort* of entity it is. While numbers can be characterized as either odd or even, but *not* as either red, or blue, or yellow, or …, roses can be characterised as either red, or blue, or yellow, or …, but not as either odd

rose is not red" or "this rose is *non*-red" would be ruled out as an *Elementarsatz* on Anscombe's criterion 3, as there clearly is a plurality of ways in which a rose might *not* be red, by being yellow, pink, or blue, for example.

This judgement type, in which some *contrary* one-placed predicate is said of the same subject (some *non*-F of a subject *a*), seems to have no equivalent in the modern Frege–Russell system, nor in the *Tractatus*. The idea of negation as contrariety, however, was central to the Aristotelian *term* logic that modern "classical" logic replaced, and a more modern version is found in the logic of the Cambridge logician, W. E. Johnson, who in the early 1920s, described colour predicates such as red, green, blue, etc., as the particular "determinates" of a general "determinable", and distinguished the determinate–determinable relation to the more conventionally conceived genus–species relation (Johnson 1921: ch.11).[20]

For Hegel the type of negative judgement employing such a predicate structure is just an initial and *limited* form of negative judgement, the first "*positive* expression of the negative judgement" with the structure "the singular is *a particular*" (SL 2010: p.563; GW 12: p.65; my emphasis). In this intermediate form of negation the predicate is thus neither a singular nor an abstract universal, but a *particular* instance *of* a universal (a particular *determinate* of the determinable *colour*).[21] This capacity for a *particular* to mediate the relation of singular to universal will become explicit in Hegel's account of the syllogism, and it will depend upon the idea of a type of translatability between judgements that *construe* some object or property *as* singular on the one hand and as a particular instance of a universal on the other. Moreover, such qualitative judgements of inherence with their peculiar negation would play a role in the unravelling of the *Tractatus* in the late 1920s.

---

or even. This is why the subject term of such judgements must express a *particular* instance of a universal.

20 Johnson argued that this determinable–determinate relation differed from that produced when a genus divided into its species. In the former, there is no specific differentiating property separating determinates of a determinable in the way that, say, the feature *rational* divides the genus "animal" into rational and irrational species. One cannot invoke some specific differentiating property possessed by "red", say, but lacking in "blue", for example, other than its *being* red.

21 Thus it still fits the criterion of having a universal as one term of the judgement.

3 Hegel's Second Negative Judgement: Negating Predicates of Subsumption.

In Hegel's series, this still *positive* first expression of the negative judgement will itself be negated such that the "second negation" negates "the determinateness [*Bestimmtheit*] of the predicate of the positive judgement, its abstract universality, or, considered as content, the singular quality that it possesses of the subject" (SL 2010: p.655; GW 12: p.69). In Johnson's terms, we can say that the first negation is restricted to the predicate *qua* particular *determinate* of its determinable, while the second negates the general *determinable* itself. With this, the type of "external" or "propositional" conception of negation standard since Frege (1997), but dating back to the Stoics, comes into play. This negation, which is conceived as applying to the entire propositional content of the judgement rather than to any part of it, will characterize Hegel's following judgement form—the *judgement of reflection*—as well as "subsumptive" judgements more generally. The transition from the qualitative judgement to the judgement of reflection, however, is prefaced by Hegel's treatment of the "infinite judgement", an anomalous judgement form that signals problems for any judgement which regards negation in *exclusively* external form.

Examples of the *infinite judgement*—"the rose is not an elephant" and "the understanding is not a table" (SL 2010: p.567; GW 12: p.70)—seem like responses to *category mistakes*, statements that could be meaningfully made *only* in response to someone who had radically misunderstood what *sorts of thing* a rose or the understanding might be. There is a *sense* in which such judgements can be considered "true" (roses are *indeed* not elephants) but Hegel describes them as offering a type of truth that is "nonsensical and fatuous" (SL 2010: p.567; GW 12: p.70). Moreover, unlike the first "*positive*" negative judgement, for example, the infinite judgement does not support inferences. That the rose is not an elephant *does not* imply that it is some *other* animal, and fails to convey any real information about roses. The infinite judgement, one might say, has *vacated* "logical space" entirely.

The judgement of reflection, into which the infinite judgement transitions, will include universally and particularly quantified judgements understood in a broadly modern way, and has a logical form closer to that familiar in the modern classical logic of Frege and Russell. Here the predicate is an *abstract* universal that *subsumes* singular subjects, such that that universal can be understood as truly or falsely attributed to some subject that is considered in abstraction from any consideration of the *kind* of thing it is. The subject of the reflective judgement comes with no *sortal* or kind-term, so there seems no way of indicating as malformed, judgements such as "this is an elephant", said *of* a rose. Clearly, the infinite judgement signals a problem for the reflective judgement, which will partially explain why it needs to be superseded by a judgement type, the judgement of necessity, whose subject term *is* a kind term.[22] Read superficially, Hegel's treatment of the judgement of necessity can seem an easy target for the charge that Hegel is in the grip of Aristotelian logic and metaphysics, but a careful consideration of this section here shows Hegel's distance from any such Aristotelianism.

The judgement of necessity first transitions into the overtly *evaluative* analogue of the judgement of necessity—the judgement of the concept—which in turn is shown to have *its* "truth" in inferentially articulated set of judgements, the *syllogism*. Like the earlier qualitative judgement, and *unlike* the earlier judgement of necessity, the judgement of the concept is crucially about *some specific observable thing*, in Hegel's example "*this* house" judged to be *good or bad* on the basis of a qualitative and evaluative perceptual experience (SL 2010: p.656; GW 12: p.85). It is clear here that the example presupposes the context of argumentative contestation. The house is declared to be good *for having such and such properties*. *Qua* sentence structure, the relation of singular subject to universal predicate is thus mediated by a determination of the house described in a certain way, as a *particular* instance of certain universally normative properties.

Spelt out in traditional syllogistic form, we would have something like: "all *houses* having such and such properties are good" (major premise or rule), "this house has such and such properties" (minor premise), therefore "this house is good" (conclusion). However, we shouldn't understand Hegel's inference here as a deduction from those premises to that conclusion. Hegel is clear that here reasoning *starts* from the perceptual judgement that this house is good—that is, it starts from the formal *conclusion*, and the judge then invokes a description of this house as *a house having certain properties* to justify the original assertion. Judging in this manner involves *finding* some complex predicate (a description) under which one subsumes *this* house, in the way that Kant had, in the *Critique of Judgement*, characterized *aesthetic* judgements. Considered as an *inference*, Hegel's moves from the formal "conclusion" *to* "minor premise" in the way C. S. Peirce had characterized "abductive" inference.[23]

---

[22] That is, a universal judgement such as "All humans are mortal" will eventually be replaced by judgements about "The human being as such", that is, the human essence.
[23] I have explored further these parallels to Kant and Peirce in Redding (2003 and 2007: chs 5 and 6).

Hegel's replacement of the traditional Aristotelian categorial judgement (the judgement of necessity) by this internally inferentially articulated judgement signals his resolutely *anti-Platonist* stance: *merely* conceptually formed ideals (think of Plato's "the good", for example) are indeterminate *unless* they are able to be instantiated in specific concrete experienceable *things*.[24] And while Hegel lauded Aristotle's attempts to bring Platonic "ideas" into the actual world, the consequences of this for logic had been greater than Aristotle had appreciated, as Aristotle had stopped at treating individual things simply *as* instances of Platonic universals. It had only been in the medieval period that the status of individuals as counting *as* individuals, and so as *more* than just instances of a kind, had come to be recognized in logic—a type of individualism that became widespread in the early modern period. Nevertheless, the integration of *singularity* with the other determinations of the concept, *particularity* and *universality*, as carried out by Leibniz and Ploucquet, remained incomplete. Thus this category became isolated and tied to *subjectivity* itself, as is typified by the Cartesian ego. In relation to this phenomenon, I suggest, there are in Hegel both parallels and conflicts with the way in which Wittgenstein was to insist on the presence of names of objects in the *Tractatus*. Moreover, when Wittgenstein became aware of problems in the *Tractatus*, it was in the context of considering judgements like those Hegel had dealt with as expressing the *first* stage of negation!

I take part of Wittgenstein's motivation for having given a *fundamental* role to names and to the elementary sentences formed from them to have been a broadly *semantic* concern that the type of quantificational apparatus developed by Frege and Russell was insufficient for logic to connect *to the world*.[25] Moreover, were logical connectives, quantifiers, negation and so forth allowed into the fundamental sentences of the language there would be the problem of confusing *genuine* objects with what were simply logical constructions. Anscombe makes this type of point in relation to the word "someone" when she criticises the claim that, while it is not part of the "logic" of the word "nobody" to refer to somebody, it *is* part of the logic of "somebody" to do so (Anscombe 1961: p.85). But, as she points out, the claim that "everybody hates somebody" does not imply that there is some person who is universally hated. The connection between language, thought and world must be *deeper* than this.

Thinking of *names* as able to be replaced by definite descriptions, as in Russell's "theory of descriptions", replaces an immediate direct cognitive connection

---

24 We might think of this as *his* interpretation of Kant's dictum that concepts without "intuitions" are "empty".

25 Thus Wittgenstein was critical of the idea that this function could be simply specified within language itself, as if we could be *informed* as to how our thought was actually about the world.

with some specific worldly object with an *indirect* one in which the intentional connection is with *whatever* object satisfies that description. For his part, Russell had thought of "logical proper names", akin in some ways to Wittgenstein's basic names or Hegel's "singular" determinations, as designating phenomenal sense-data knowable directly in "acquaintance", the *epistemological* ambitions of this move later coming to be widely criticised in broadly Hegelian ways.[26] But Wittgenstein seems to have grasped that the cost of allowing *qualities* to so characterise the fundamental simples of the *Tractatus* would be that such things would thereby be able to be *specified* in terms of those qualities: the *distinction* between names and descriptions being thereby lost (TLP: 2.0232–2.02331). Rather, Wittgenstein's names seem intended to be more like "rigid-designators" such that the objects they pick out are unable to be specified entirely in terms of "repeatable properties" (Bradley 1992: pp.86–87). Thus Wittgenstein's approach was meant to work at a deeper level than the approach of Russell or the positivists—a purely *logical level*, bypassing any such epistemological and "psychological" issues. But from an *Hegelian* point of view this creates a problem for the "determinacy" of the thought involved. As is often pointed out, Wittgenstein seems not to have been able to offer *examples* of his fundamental objects. Later, Wittgenstein would seem to come to the view that logic cannot be so simply detached from epistemological concerns.

Anscombe, in summing up the "powerful and beautiful theory" at the heart of the *Tractatus*, would write that there is "surely something right about it—if one could dispense with 'simples' and draw the limits of its applicability" (Anscombe 1959: p.77). Hegel, I suggest, was searching for a way to *maintain* Wittgenstein's distinction between names and logical constructions, but *without* such categorially isolated and untranslatable "indeterminate" simples.

4 The Unraveling of the Tractatus with the Logic of Qualities

Hegelian themes directly emerge in the context in which the central doctrines of the *Tractatus* had started to come into question for Wittgenstein in the late 1920s. In a talk to members of the Vienna Circle in late 1929, Wittgenstein is reported as modifying the *Tractarian* metaphor of likening a statement to a ruler laid against the world:

---

[26] It is the problems surrounding such epistemological grounding where the "Pittsburgh School" of Sellars, Brandom and McDowell draw parallels with Hegel's critique.

> The statements describing for me the length of an object form a system, a system of propositions. Now it is such an entire system of propositions that is compared with reality, not a single proposition. If I say, for example, that this or that point in the visual field is *blue*, then I know not merely that, but also that this point is not green, nor red, nor yellow, etc. I have laid the entire colour-scale against it in at one go." (WVC: p.64)

In the *Tractatus* Wittgenstein had described the assertion attributing two *different* colours to one point in the visual field at the same time as a contradiction (TLP: 6.3751), and here he distances himself from that view: "All this I did not yet know when I was writing my work: at that time I thought that all inference was based on tautological form" (WVC: p.64).[27]

In his book on Wittgenstein, the *Hegelian* dimension of J. N. Findlay's criticisms becomes apparent when he comments on the significance of Wittgenstein's changing views on the application of colour judgements. He notes that some paragraphs concerning colour in the *Tractatus* appear to anticipate his later move. Thus Wittgenstein's comments on colour and tone at 2.0131 seem to suggest that such ultimate objects "might *differ* in type or form, and so be surrounded by a distinctive logical space of their own" (Findlay 1984: pp.81–82). But any such move would be "ruinous to the principles of the *Tractatus*, which holds to the unlimited combinatory capacities of every ultimate object with every other" (Findlay 1984: p.82).[28] Such "distinctive logical spaces" are what Hegel had explored in the peculiar logic governing judgements of perceptual qualities. Problems posed by such irreducibly opposed logical spaces might have been

---

27 In fact, there has been speculation that Wittgenstein had, around this time, become influenced by W. E. Johnson, whose determinable/determinate analysis of colour judgements mirrors Hegel's treatment. See Gandon (2016).

28 Findlay had been in a good position to appreciate the proximity of Wittgenstein's philosophy to such issues in Hegel. He had been attracted to the work of Russell, Moore and Wittgenstein while a student at Oxford in the 1920s, had then spent some time in Cambridge in the company of Wittgenstein in 1930 (Findlay 1985: p.56), and had considerably more contact with him in 1939. Prior to all this Findlay had started out attracted to Hegelian idealism, then passing through a period of "de-idealization" in the 1920s, partly due to his dislike of Oxford idealism. His deflection from Hegel however was transitory, describing Wittgenstein's influence on him as that of pushing him "in directions that he would not have sanctioned, but which coincided in part with my original Hegelianism" (Findlay 1985: p.32). Those directions included further exploration of the idea of local, non-generalizable logical spaces present in Hegel and discovered by Wittgenstein in the late 1920s, and in particular, the logical space of *temporal* determinacy (Findlay 1941), which had a striking effect on one of his former students, Arthur Prior. Prior was the inventor of "tense logic" and an early contributor to the resurgence of interest in the late 1950s and 60s in *modal logics*, which came to be treated as logics of contextually specific propositions such as tensed ones. On some of this history see Redding (2017).

avoided had Wittgenstein stuck to his claim concerning the general "colourlessness"—that is, *lack* of any qualitative features—of his ultimate objects, but leaving such ultimate objects *in principle* unobservable had come at a cost. Detached from any sorts of epistemological considerations, Wittgenstein's "objects" would remain mysterious and our capacity to know them perplexing.[29]

Like Wittgenstein in the *Tractatus*, Hegel had opposed the way that logicians pursued the path of generalization by eliminating genuinely singular terms. This elimination had been explicit in the traditional syllogistic in which singular terms had no proper place, but it was also *implicit* in the ways later employed to get around this limitation. One of these was that of redetermining a name (Socrates, for example) as a "particular term" ("some philosopher") or a definite description ("the inspirer of Plato"). The second, less obvious, solution favoured by medieval logicians was to treat singular terms as *universals*. Both forms of substitution had in fact been used by Leibniz and Ploucquet.[30]

Leibniz had nominally kept a place for singular terms *qua* singular concepts as the ultimate units arrived at in the complete analysis of any concept, but this was at the expense that only *God* was able to cognize the world in this way. From the human point of view, Leibniz's ultimate monads were, like Wittgenstein's objects, "nothings nugatorily related" (Findlay 1984: p.81). That is, from the human point of view these ultimates are simply the indeterminate *whatevers* securing relations between predicates in the mathematisable syllogism—merely logical devices. Hegel's critical relation to this doctrine was complex. Like Leibniz he allowed terms instantiating the categories of singularity, particularity and universality to be interchanged within judgements, as is clear from his "judgement of the concept". *This house*, that stands before me and that I *perceive* as good (the house determined as *singular*), must be able to count also as a *mere* instantiation of some *type of house*, a house characterisable as having such and such properties (the house determined as *particular*) (SL 2010: p.585, GW 12: p.87). It is this second determination of the house that allows the rational application of *another* universal, to it—its being "good". *Without* this link, the original "judge-

---

[29] Another influence on Wittgenstein around this time contributing to such a turn may have been that of the intuitionist mathematician, L. E. W. Brouwer, who criticised the Platonism of modern logic from a type of subjectivistic epistemological point of view. It was attendance of a lecture by Brouwer in 1929 that was supposed to have rejuvinated Wittgenstein's urge to do philosophy. Brouwer's influence on the middle period Wittgenstein has been urged by Mathieu Marion (2008).

[30] More recently the same move was repeated by Quine as an extension to proper names of Russell's way of replacing *common names* (Greeks, unicorns) by *descriptions*—*Socrates* becoming something that *socratizes*.

ment" would remain nothing but a type of visceral reaction. Kant had argued that these types of substitutions—in his terms, substitutions between intuitions and concepts—would generate contradictions or "antinomies", but Hegel held that rational thought demanded them, making it the task of reason to *take on* and *think through* these contradictions, thus producing his strangely "dialectical" logic.

Conclusion

During the early decades of analytic philosophy, J. N. Findlay had opposed the abstractly negative attitude of the Oxford Hegelians to the new philosophy emanating from Cambridge (Findlay 1985: pp.16–18). To simply oppose Hegel and analytic philosophy in this way was, he thought, not *Hegelian*. Rather, he came to think of the dynamically evolving history of the logical doctrines within analytic philosophy as *itself* expressing features that could be understood in Hegelian terms (Findlay 1963: pp.221–222).

This general perspective, I suggest, might be brought to the more specific terrain of the relation of Hegelian philosophy to that of Wittgenstein. Thus, to better understand the obvious parallels between the *later* thought of Wittgenstein and the approach of Hegel, we might first locate the doctrines of Hegel's logic in relation to the strengths and weaknesses of Wittgenstein's *early* thought. The account above is meant as a contribution to such a project.[31]

References

Anscombe, G. E. M.: *Introduction to Wittgenstein's Tractatus*, Hutchison, 1959.
Black, Max: *A Companion to Wittgenstein's Tractatus*, Cornell University Press, 1966.
Bradley, Raymond: *The Nature of All Being: A Study of Wittgenstein's Modal Atomism*, Oxford University Press, 1992.
Brandom, Robert B.: *Making It Explicit: Reasoning, Representing, and Discursive Commitment*, Harvard University Press, 1994.
Brandom, Robert B.: *Tales of the Mighty Dead: Historical Essays in the Metaphysics of Intentionality*, Harvard University Press, 2002.
Conant, James and Diamond, Cora: "On Reading the *Tractatus* Resolutely", in: Max Kölbel and Bernhard Weiss (eds.): *Wittgenstein's Lasting Significance*, Routledge, 2004.

---

[31] This research was carried out with the help of a Discovery Grant from the Australian Research Council, DP130102346. I wish to thank Jakub Mácha, as well as Mike Beaney, Peter Hylton and Tom Raysmith for helpful comments in relation to earlier drafts of this paper.

Diamond, Cora: *The Realistic Spirit: Wittgenstein, Philosophy and the Mind*, MIT Press, 1991.
Findlay, John N.: *Hegel: A Re-examination*, Allen and Unwin, 1958.
Findlay, John N.: "The Contemporary Relevance of Hegel", in: *Language, Mind and Value*, Allen and Unwin, 1963, pp.217–231.
Findlay, John N.: *Wittgenstein: A Critique*, Routledge, 1984.
Findlay, John N.: "My Life: 1903–1973," and "My Encounters with Wittgenstein", both in Robert S. Cohen, Richard M. Martin and Merold Westphal (eds.): *Studies in the Philosophy of J. N. Findlay*, State University of New York Press, 1985, pp.1–51 and 52–69.
Frege, Gottlob: "Negation", in: M. Beaney (ed.): *The Frege Reader*, Blackwell, 1997, pp.346–61.
Gandon, Sebastian: "Wittgenstein's Color Exclusion and Johnson's Determinable" in S. Costreie (ed.): *Early Analytic Philosophy—New Perspectives on the Tradition*, Springer 2016, pp.257–282.
Goldstein, Laurence: *Clear and Queer Thinking: Wittgenstein's Development and His Relevance to Modern Thought*, Duckworth, 1999.
Ishiguro, Hidé: "Use and Reference of Names", in: P. Winch (ed.): *Studies in the Philosophy of Wittgenstein*, Routledge and Kegan Paul, 1969, pp.20–50.
Johnson, William E.: *Logic. Part 1*, Cambridge University Press, 1921.
Lenzen, Wolfgang: "Leibniz's Logic", in: Dov M. Gabbay, John Woods & Akihiro Kanamori (eds.): *Handbook of the History of Logic*, Elsevier, 2004, pp.5–92.
Lokhorst, Gert-Jan: "Ontology, Semantics and Philosophy of Mind in Wittgenstein's *Tractatus*: A Formal Reconstruction", *Erkenntnis* 29:1, 1988, pp.35–75.
Marion, Mathieu: "Brouwer on 'Hypotheses' and the Middle Wittgenstein", in: Mark van Atten, Pascal Boldini, Michel Bourdeau, Gerhard Heinzmann (Eds): *One Hundred Years of Intuitionism (1907–2007)*, Birkhäuser, 2008, pp.96–114.
McGuinness, Brian: "The So-called Realism of Wittgenstein's *Tractatus*", in: Irving Block (ed.): *Perspectives in the Philosophy of Wittgenstein*, Blackwell, 1981, pp.60–73.
Pears, David: *The False Prison: A Study of the Development of Wittgenstein's Philosophy. Volume 1*, Clarendon Press, 1987.
Pinkard, Terry: *Hegel's Phenomenology: The Sociality of Reason*, Cambridge University Press, 1994.
Pippin, Robert B.: *Hegel's Idealism: The Satisfactions of Self-Consciousness*, Cambridge University Press, 1989.
Ploucquet, Gottfried: *Logik*, ed. and trans. by Michael Franz, Olms, 2006.
Redding, Paul: "Hegel and Peircean Abduction", *European Journal of Philosophy* 11:3, 2003, pp.295–313.
Redding, Paul: *Analytic Philosophy and the Return of Hegelian Thought*, Cambridge University Press, 2007.
Redding, Paul: "The Role of Logic "Commonly So Called" in Hegel's *Science of Logic*", *British Journal for the History of Philosophy* 22:2, 2014, pp.281–301.
Redding, Paul: "An Hegelian Solution to a Tangle of Problems Facing Brandom's Analytic Pragmatism", *British Journal for the History of Philosophy* 23:4, 2015, pp.657–680.
Redding, Paul: "Findlay's Hegel: Idealism as Modal Actualism", *Critical Horizons: A Journal of Philosophy of Social Theory* 18:4, 2017, pp.359–377.

Stokhof, Martin: "The Architecture of Meaning: Wittgenstein's *Tractatus* and formal semantics", in: David Levy and Eduardo Zamuner (Eds): *Wittgenstein's Enduring Arguments*, Routledge, 2008.
Taylor, Charles: *Hegel*, Cambridge University Press, 1975.
Yost, Robert M.: *Leibniz and Philosophical Analysis*, University of California Press, 1954.

Terry Pinkard
Forms of Thought, Forms of Life

Abstract Hegel and Wittgenstein at first seem like an odd pairing: Hegel, the system builder who sought unity and who created a corresponding and forbidding technical vocabulary; and Wittgenstein, whose model was clarity and who focused on the heterogeneity of language. I argue that there is a shared problem at the core of their philosophies. Both are concerned with the limits of thought. This leads Wittgenstein in the *Tractatus* to a conception of the subject of thinking that dovetails in crucial ways with Hegel's conception of subjectivity; perhaps surprisingly, the *Tractatus* and the *Science of Logic* turn out to be in many basic ways, as it were, the same book, except for the latter's more detailed account of self-conscious subjectivity. Likewise, in Wittgenstein's *Philosophical Investigations* and in Hegel's *Phenomenology*, the very idea of an objective world is bound up with the idea of that world showing itself to thinking, self-conscious creatures.

At least on the surface, Wittgenstein and Hegel seem like an unlikely pairing, lining up on opposite sides of the philosophical spectrum. On the one side, there is Hegel, the great system builder, adept at non-ordinary terminology, and on the other side, Wittgenstein, the elegant philosopher insisting on clarity, ordinary language and the non-systematisable heterogeneity of the use of language.

What I wish to show here is that there is a deeper affinity at work in both that is very likely not a matter of any historical influence of Hegel on Wittgenstein. I also do not intend simply to compare and contrast two philosophers to see where they might overlap or contradict each other. Rather, it is to look at how each reacted to and took up a Kantian idea that still resonates with us. Each, that is, was grappling with the same (or very similar) set of problems but which led them to go down the different roads they took. The problem, put most generally, is that of the limits of thought. Are there metaphysical or logical features of thinking that show that there are limits to thinking beyond which it cannot go? Kant of course argued that there were, and that, furthermore, things in themselves went beyond the bounds of consistent thinking.

Both Wittgenstein and Hegel rejected Kant's sharp distinction between things in themselves and appearance. In his *Tractatus*, Wittgenstein remarked that "to set a limit to thought, we should have to find both sides of the limit thinkable (i.e., we should have to be able to think what cannot be thought). It will therefore only be in language that the limit can be set, and what lies on the other side of the limit will simply be nonsense" (TLP: p.3). Hegel more economically noted: "Where there is a *limit*, it is a negation only *for a third* [perspective], for an external comparison." (E III: §359)

All told, both Hegel and Wittgenstein begin with a central worry about how, to use A. W. Moore's helpful characterization, in making sense of things, we are inevitably driven to make sense of making sense, to a kind of logic (Moore 2012). However, overall, the question is whether it even makes sense to set any such limits. A corollary issue is whether what goes beyond the bounds of making sense should be classified as some form of nonsense, and if so, whether it is a special kind of nonsense. Hegel and Wittgenstein each responded to this with doctrines that have raised any number of interpretive issues—Wittgenstein's distinction between saying and showing and his sibylline advice to be silent about that of which one cannot speak; and Hegel's notorious idea of the absolute as including contraries within itself. Ultimately, of course, understanding either position cannot be done outside of the history to which each thinker was responding and, to the extent that any overall single view emerges from this investigation, it will almost certainly end up in a position that cannot be labeled purely Wittgensteinian or Hegelian in any non-question-begging sense.

1 Forms of thought

1.1 Wittgenstein, logic and limits

Just as Kant's *Critique of Pure Reason* was the founding text of European philosophy for the next couple of hundred years, Wittgenstein's *Tractatus* was the founding text for developments in (largely Anglophone) philosophy for the twentieth century and beyond. Both were concerned with establishing the limits of thought and for circumscribing if not entirely eliminating traditional metaphysics. In both cases, what exactly they even meant by their key terms became one of the more contentious issues among those who wished to continue their program or to take it in new directions.

In the *Tractatus*, Wittgenstein was clearly interested in the relations between linguistically formulated propositions and the world. When things went right, those propositions were true. They told us the way the world was. Propositions are true when they picture—or we could just say "represent"—the world as it really is. The sense of a proposition is the possible state of affairs it represents, and thus if there is no possible state of affairs it could represent, the proposition is quite literally senseless. What the proposition cannot picture is how it pictures. It cannot give a picture of itself picturing since picturing is not itself a fact in the world. Since no picture can violate the laws of logic and still be a picture—if it could, its sense would not be that of any possible object—logic itself is the form of the world.

The limits of sense-making are thereby given by logic itself. Whatever transgresses that is not just a failure to make sense, it is literally nonsense, and thus any and all efforts to represent the world as a whole are also nonsense since to represent the world as a whole we would have to step outside of the world as a whole, and there is and can be no such vantage point. Logic does not tell us what there is in the world—how the world of facts contingently turns out to be—but it is the form of that world. If so, then logic prescribes the bounds of sense such that even the attempt to think illogically reveals itself not so much as failed thought but as non-thought. Logic just is what thinking is. Everything else is a statement of (possible) fact, and the facts could always be (logically speaking) otherwise.

Now, as is well known, at the end of the book Wittgenstein revealed that, strictly speaking, all of those assertions about representing the world as a whole had to be quite literally nonsense. If the only meaningful propositions are those that purport to speak about facts, then attempts to speak about the form of those facts (or about the "substance of the world") are already using the form, and statements about the form are not statements about facts. If the only sensible propositions are about facts, and statements about the logical form of the world are not propositions about the facts, then propositions about such form are not sensible. They too are nonsense. To ask about the form of the world would be in effect as if one asked how it is that logic makes sense possible, and the person who answered the question simply showed the questioner more logic.

If logic is the form of the world, then it is also the limit. One can express individual limits (the way one thing is not another, and so on), but the world as a whole has no limit in that sense. There is nothing beyond it with which to contrast it. The world as a whole simply "shows itself" (*zeigt sich*) (TLP: 5.62). In picturing the world, the activity of picturing cannot itself picture how it is that it pictures what it does picture.

But "shows itself" to what, or to whom? It is important to note that Wittgenstein thinks that this question too is ultimately nonsense. Why? It might seem that if the world were to "show itself" to something, it would show itself to the thinking subject. However, as Wittgenstein says, if he were to write a book called "the world as I found it," one of the things he would not find in the world is himself as a thinking, willing subject. He would never find the subject to whom the world "shows itself," and thus there could be no representation of it and thus no statement about it. The thinking and willing subject could never be an item in the world but would itself belong to the form of the world.[1] Thus, *in the world itself*, "there is no thinking, representing subject" (TLP: 5.631). Nor could there be any such subject.

If the thinking subject cannot be another fact in the world, then it is more like the point of view on the world which is not itself an element in that world. Yet in its most abstract form, this point of view on the world and the world itself are identical. They are both "the form of the world". They are the formal limits of the world, but beyond this limit is nothing, and that is where one must be standing if one wishes to describe the world as a whole.

Wittgenstein claims that this establishes what is true in solipsism—not that solipsism *is* true but that there is some truth in it: "For what the solipsist *means* is quite correct; only it cannot be *said*, but rather shows itself." (TLP: 5.62) If the world shows itself to a subject, and the subject is not in the world, and there is nothing beyond or outside of the world, then the statement that the world shows itself to the subject leads to nonsense, since it leads to a fundamental contradiction. The world shows itself to a subject, but in principle there is no subject to which it shows itself. What truth there is in solipsism is captured in part of that contradiction, namely, that the world shows itself to an "I" that itself cannot be represented and cannot be either beyond the world not in it. The "I" cannot be either outside nor inside what makes sense.

The world thus shows itself to a subject that understands it is picturing the world but cannot picture how it is that it pictures and which understands that the very question of how it pictures what it pictures is itself, when pressed, a nonsensical question since it cannot have a non-nonsensical answer. Thus, we can only say that the world shows itself to me, except that "me" ("I") here has a sense that defies the limits of what makes sense. In his preparatory sketches for the *Tractatus*, Wittgenstein said of this: "There really is only one world soul, which I for preference call *my* soul and as which alone I conceive what I call the souls of others." (NB: p.49e) As we might take that, he is expressing the idea that the very concept of an objective world of facts, states of affairs

---

[1] TLP: 5.631–5.633: "There is no such thing as the subject that thinks or entertains ideas. / If I wrote a book 'The world as I found it,' I should also have therein to report on my body and say which members obey my will and which do not, etc. This then would be a method of isolating the subject or rather of showing that in an important sense there is no subject: that is to say, of it alone in this book mention could *not* be made."/ "The subject does not belong to the world: rather, it is a limit of the world." / "Where *in* the world is a metaphysical subject to be found?"

TLP 5.641: "The philosophical self is not the human being, not the human body, or the human soul, with which psychology deals, but rather the metaphysical subject, the limit of the world—not a part of it."

and objects is not a world beyond all viewpoints but one which the idea of a viewpoint is already included in the conception of what the limits of the world are. It is not the view that the world is constituted by our representations of it (either in subjective idealism or in most versions of orthodox Kantianism), nor is it the view, as the younger Schelling once had it, of a "world soul" that is generating the physical directions of the world and of our consciousness in participating in the world soul's activities (see Schelling 2000). Nor is it the thesis that there can be no universe without thinking subjects (or people) in it. It is rather that the world as intelligible to "pure reason" is logical form, and that logical form is the shape of the (pure) thinking subject. Outside of logic, there is no intelligible world, simply a world of contingency. Had the "objects" of the world been rearranged into different states of affairs (which logic alone cannot rule out), everything would be different—except logical form itself and therefore the structure of thinking subjectivity. Without the concept of the subject, there would not be an intelligible world. There would just be "objects" arranged in various ways.[2]

That suggests at least that there could be many possible worlds but that "logic" would be the same in all of those worlds. Yet Wittgenstein also seems to rule out that rather "positivist" way of taking that. He speaks in many places of how "I" make judgments and so forth, but he also says things such as "We picture facts to ourselves." The truth contained in solipsism is that the "I" of the solipsist actually includes a "we" within itself. "My" point of view linked internally to the point of view of others as "we" (and "our" use of signs, etc.).

In his preliminary sketches in the *Notebooks*, he also noted: "My *whole* task consists in explaining the nature of the proposition. That is to say, in giving the nature of all facts, whose picture the proposition *is*," to which Wittgenstein immediately added: "In giving the essence of all being. / (And here Being does not mean existing—in that case it would be nonsensical)." (NB: p.39) This suggests, but only suggests, that although reality is purely contingent from the logical

---

[2] Wittgenstein also spoke of the "internal" properties of things, but his conclusion has to be that these two can only be formal in character. In a broad sense, Schelling's early philosophy takes up this point in a related way, especially as found in Schelling (1988, 1978). For Schelling, to put it anachronistically, such Wittgensteinian "objects" can be grasped but not discursively. At best, they could be named. Schelling in effect then argues that such internal properties can therefore only be apprehended through some form of "intellectual intuition" which both grasps them and how they relate to the other such "objects", in particular as objects develop out of themselves and their "indifference points" in combination with each other new kinds of objects. For an alternative argument to the effect that the internal properties of Wittgensteinian objects can be seen to divide themselves in particulars and universals, see Mácha (2015).

point of view—or from the point of view of "being" and not "existence"—the actual world is the one that the subject actually has as "his" world.³ We cannot say a priori what the "objects" of the world will be (and thus we cannot do anything even approaching the traditional task of metaphysics, which is to do just that). But he also says that "the world of the happy man is a different one from that of the unhappy man" which he seems to infer from: "If the good or bad exercise of the will does alter the world, it can alter only limits of the world, not the facts —not what can be expressed by means of language. In short the effect must be that it becomes an altogether different world. It must, so to speak, wax and wane as a whole." (TLP: 6.43)

The limits of the world are thus the limits of the *actual* world for the thinking subject. Within those limits, non-philosophical thinking—natural science, common sense, and so on—can carry on just fine and exhibit an ongoing self-criticism so that they can get better at what they are doing. Metaphysics, however, wants to know if there is more to things, wants to know what the world as a whole really is. Wittgenstein's metaphysics in the *Tractatus* says that the world as a whole is a contingent affair and "pure thought" cannot determine anything much more about the ultimate makeup of the world other than that it not contradict itself. It can also determine that its determination of this makes no sense since it results itself in a series of contradictions having to do with the subject to which the world shows itself. Since there is no way out of the paradox, one has to live with it.

Interpreters of the *Tractatus* have more or less divided recently into two camps to respond to this. We can call them the Tolstoyians and the Kierkegaardians. The Tolstoyians⁴ claim that since on Wittgenstein's own terms, what he has said in his book is literally nonsense, he is thus pointing beyond to something that cannot be put into words but which is of ultimate importance in living one's life. It is the "mystical" which cannot be put into words but which nonetheless has meaning (TLP: 6.522).

The Kierkegaardians, on the other hand, see Wittgenstein as self-consciously producing nonsense in order to lure the reader into a comprehension of how easy it is when one is doing metaphysical philosophy to think one is in fact pro-

---

3 This is obviously suggestive that Wittgenstein might be given a somewhat Heideggerian interpretation. That has in fact been carried out, although without much mention of Heidegger, by Friedlander (2001, 2014).

4 See Lovibond (2016). Another, older reading which resembles the Tolstoyian is positivist, which sees Wittgenstein as recommending (non-nonsensically) a sharp distinction between the logical and the factual and thus dismissing all non-factual propositions (metaphysics, religion, aesthetics, etc.) not as false but as nonsensical.

ducing sense when in fact one is actually producing nonsense. (One version of this interpretation takes it that it is not each statement in the *Tractatus* that shows itself to be nonsense but the project as a whole turns out to be nonsense. It is in trying to comprehend how the propositions even could coherently hang together in the book as a whole that one finds the sense of the book evaporating, and that it is in retrospect that one understands that the entire project—comprehending the world as a limited whole—is necessarily bound to failure, i.e., to the utterance of nonsense.[5])

Wittgenstein correctly draws the conclusion that all talk of the subject is nonsensical if the rest of the book's premises are accepted and that therefore the book itself is nonsensical. The Tolstoyian Wittgenstein thinks that he has shown that the real point of living cannot be put into words, and that any attempt to do so results in nonsense, not just in falsifying the point. The Kierkegaardian Wittgenstein thinks that there is a constant danger—existential and intellectual—in trying to grasp the world as a whole in pure reason, all of which ultimately shows simply the folly of trying to do just that. Which one is Wittgenstein, or is he none of the above?

---

5 There are several versions of this Kierkegaardian reading in terms of the critique of all philosophy, especially that which tends to "apriorism." Among them are Cora Diamond and Juliet Floyd, who each created early versions of it without calling it that, and James Conant gave it its truly Kierkegaardian polish, while others (such as Peter Sullivan) have argued for something like this too, and recently A. W. Moore has offered his "combined reading" of the two approaches:

> The *Tractatus* helps us to make sense of propositional sense. But the sense that it helps us to make of propositional sense is not itself propositional. The understanding that Wittgenstein imparts has to be expressed, not in words, but in good philosophy, where good philosophy, recall, is an activity, not a body of doctrine. (2012: p.242)

On the difference between good and bad philosophy, Moore notes:

> Wittgenstein distinguishes between good philosophy and bad philosophy. And he holds that the mark of bad philosophy is just such confusion (3.324–3.325 and 4.003). The aim of good philosophy, then, is to combat bad philosophy. (And this is its sole aim. If there were no bad philosophy, there would be no need for good philosophy.) (Moore 2012: p.226)

That qualifies as a kind of modified Kierkegaardian since it is always on the lookout for the "paradox" that is lying behind what poses as good philosophy but is in fact confused. As far as I can tell, none of the Kierkegaardian-readers go so far as to recommend the real Kierkegaard's claims for the leap of faith in light of the paradox.

What Wittgenstein (at least in the *Tractatus*) does not have is any conception of the subject as a self-conscious subject. He in fact rules out the possibility of thought thinking about what it is to be a thought of a limited whole.

1.2 Hegel, logic and limits

Hegel too was concerned with the so-called limits of the world and the limits of knowledge as he came to terms with metaphysics in the wake of Kant's philosophy. (Indeed, he started his philosophical life more or less as a Kantian of sorts.[6]) Kant, unlike Wittgenstein, thought that the limits of thought were the limits of possible experience, but the limits of the latter did not exhaust the limits of the world. Like Wittgenstein, Hegel thought that Kant's way of drawing the limits did not make sense. The limits of thought were the limits of reality itself, or, as both Hegel and Wittgenstein noted, "of being" itself. Hegel notes that the pure knowing that constitutes logic (and which traditional metaphysics wishes to extend into what Wittgenstein called "objects") is itself at first empty, or so it seems. This pure knowing takes itself not as representing objects ("... has sublated all relation to an other and to mediation ...") but, taken as such, a pure knowing is really not a knowing at all.[7] It does not, cannot, distinguish its "pure" thought from reality, and is thus equivalent to "pure being", to the thought that there is anything at all and not the thought of what things there are.[8]

From the beginning, Hegel thus subscribes to the same idea that Wittgenstein puts as the thought that "logic pervades (*erfüllt*) the world: the limits of the world are also its limits" (TLP: 5.61). What he does not do is draw the same conclusion that Wittgenstein immediately draws: "so we cannot say in logic, 'The world has this in it, and this, but not that'" (TLP: 5.61). Why?

Both Hegel and Wittgenstein make their moves, perhaps surprisingly, around the same idea. There is a thinking subject who thinks about there being anything at all, and this thought is itself empty. As Wittgenstein puts it:

---

6 See Pinkard (2000). See also Bondeli (1997).
7 WL I: p.68: "Das reine Wissen, als in diese *Einheit zusammengegangen*, hat alle Beziehung auf ein Anderes und auf Vermittlung aufgehoben; es ist das Unterschiedslose; dieses Unterschiedslose hört somit selbst auf, Wissen zu sein; es ist nur *einfache Unmittelbarkeit* vorhanden." (SL 2010: p.45)
8 WL I: p.68: "In ihrem wahren Ausdrucke ist daher diese einfache Unmittelbarkeit das *reine Sein*. Wie das *reine* Wissen nichts heißen soll als das Wissen als solches, ganz abstrakt, so soll auch reines Sein nichts heißen als das *Sein* überhaupt; Sein, sonst nichts, ohne alle weitere Bestimmung und Erfüllung."

"The 'experience' that we need in order to understand logic is not that something or other is the state of things, but that something *is:* that, however, is not an experience." (TLP: 5.552) The thought is of the being of the world and outside of that is… nothing. One cannot think of the nothing; that is just nonsense upon stilts, *Unsinn* parading as sense. The world is all that is the case, and there is nothing beyond that. Or, to shift to Hegelian prose, at the outset are the two thoughts of being and nothing, and that thought itself is not really a logical thought. It looks like a thought, but it is in fact itself a contradiction. It is a thought of the world as a whole in terms of the empty concepts of being and nothing which is a thought from a standpoint that cannot be, since it would be a thought occupying a conceptual place outside of being and nothing.[9] Mystics may indeed claim to have such a thought, but they cannot make it intelligible, and an unintelligible thought is a thought that cannot be thought.

For Wittgenstein, the thought of "being" cannot really be a thought since it requires a distinction between being and non-being, which cannot itself be said. Beyond that is the world of "objects" that have no logical relation to each other and whose concatenations are therefore purely contingent. Hegel's proposal runs counter to this. His *Logic*, like Wittgenstein's logic, is a logic of the form of thought, which is itself the logic of "being" to the extent that "being" is intelligible. As a logic, Hegel's logic is concerned with the form of thought, not with what things in particular there are (which is a matter of fact, not of form).[10] However, the form of thought itself seems to be fractured at the outset, not able to make sense of itself about how it is to be the form of the (actual) world, since it seems to have to say that the world as a whole, identified simply as "being," is linked to the concept of nothing, but not of the negation of any particular object. It is rather the idea of there being anything at all (a Wittgensteinian thought) that is a statement that fails to make sense. Outside of the world itself is… nothing. However, the difference between nothing and being, drawn at this level of abstraction, of "pure form," can only show itself since it cannot be stated. Stating it strikes all the notes of nonsense: "Being is nothing." Instead, what we have is a whole, grasped in thought, of coming to be and passing away, of some being going into nothing and nothing coming to be something, or just "becoming" in general. The world as a whole is that of things coming to

---

9 WL I: p.75: "Was den Anfang macht, der Anfang selbst, ist daher als ein Nichtanalysierbares, in seiner einfachen unerfüllten Unmittelbarkeit, also *als Sein*, als das ganz Leere zu nehmen."
10 WL II: p.550: "Die absolute Idee selbst hat näher nur dies zu ihrem Inhalt, daß die Formbestimmung ihre eigene vollendete Totalität, der reine Begriff ist."

be and vanishing.[11] That this is a conception of existing objects with qualitative and quantitative features follows from the attempt to state the very idea of the world as a whole, which seems to require a standpoint outside of the whole, which is itself nonsensical on its own terms.

The rest of Hegel's *Logic* is in some ways simply a development of that basic idea which he shares, by and large, with Wittgenstein. It is the development of the form-determinations (*Formbestimmungen*, Hegel's term) of the world in "pure thought," that is, in logic, broadly construed. Hegel, so we might very anachronistically put it, thinks that he can show that the "form-determinations" of Wittgenstein's objects lead to the introduction of pure content, which runs completely against Wittgenstein's original idea that there could be no a priori determination of such things.

On Hegel's own terms, all the attempts to linguistically express the world as a whole are bound to fail at making sense in any full way, even though the judgments generated by using those forms may indeed make sense. Taken formally, logically, they generate conundrums and contradictions in fulfilling their claim to grasp the world as a whole. So Hegel argued—the details of which of course have to be omitted here—that his *Logic* thus falls into three basic divisions, each of which can be seen as what is required in terms of *form* to answer certain types of questions. In matters of "being," we have judgments about what there is, identifying things ("that one over there"), generalizing about them ("Usually they are only so big") and counting them ("there are five of them"). Together, they lead to the concept of the world as an infinite whole, and the paradoxes of infinity drive the process forward. In "Essence," the judgments have to do with why the appearing world of the individual things of "being" take on the shape they do. It can lead to judgments such as, "The tie looks green in the shop but blue in the sunlight" to "A mouse chewing the electric cord caused the short which caused the fire." This leads to conundrums about the explanatory dependence and independence of the terms of explanation.

Another sphere of judgments altogether is those that which involve thinking-willing-judging subjects moving self-consciously within a logical space (such as when one says that another's conclusions do not follow from his premises or when one judges that a statement about nature is not coherent with the current state of physics). These types of judgments and inferences (or syllogisms) involve

---

11 WL I: p.113: "Dies Resultat ist das Verschwundensein, aber nicht als *Nichts;* so wäre es nur ein Rückfall in die eine der schon aufgehobenen Bestimmungen, nicht Resultat des Nichts *und des Seins.* Es ist die zur ruhigen Einfachheit gewordene Einheit des Seins und Nichts. Die ruhige Einfachheit aber ist *Sein,* jedoch ebenso nicht mehr für sich, sondern als Bestimmung des Ganzen."

judgments very generally of good and bad (most generally in the case of valid versus invalid arguments). Hegel classifies such judgments under the rubric of "the concept." Like the rest of the *Logic*, it turns on the conception of a self-conscious subject who is part of the world and conscious of the *things* in the world but is also conscious of his or her access to the things of the world.[12] It involves the unity of the subject's consciousness in the activity of judging being the same as the consciousness of its unity, that is, to be self-consciousness.

This kind of self-consciousness requires the statement of itself that requires a more dialectical expression than does the simple awareness of things in the world or the forming of representations of facts. It is, as the "absolute Idea" (the unity, Hegel says, of concept and reality, that is, a kind of fact-stating evaluation of embodied human subjects in a historically shaped conceptual environment[13]), the whole making a statement about itself in full consciousness of the kinds of difficulties that it necessarily generates in doing so; or, as Hegel puts it in his own terms: "For the sake of freedom, the Idea also has [...] the *hardest opposition* within itself; its being at rest consists in the security and certainty with which it eternally creates and eternally overcomes that being at rest and therein brings itself together with itself." (WL II: p.468; SL 2010: p.759; my translation)

In this way, we see that what fundamentally, most basically divides Hegel and Wittgenstein on logic and the limits of thought has to do with how they understand the point of view of the subject to be part of the account. For Wittgenstein, the subject is necessary for "being" to "show itself" whereas for Hegel, the same is true, but he thought that required us to fashion a very different sense of how form and content function in logic as it expresses the limits of thought.

All in all, though, and perhaps surprisingly, the *Tractatus* and the *Science of Logic* turn out to be in many basic ways, as it were, the same book, except for the latter's more detailed account of self-conscious subjectivity. But that more detailed account of "the concept" as self-conscious subjectivity makes a huge difference.

---

[12] WL II: p.254: "Es gehört zu den tiefsten und richtigsten Einsichten, die sich in der Kritik der Vernunft finden, daß die *Einheit*, die das *Wesen des Begriffs* ausmacht, als die *ursprünglich-synthetische* Einheit der *Apperzeption*, als Einheit des "*Ich denke*" oder des Selbstbewußtseins erkannt wird."

[13] This conception of a "fact-stating" evaluation draws on Philippa Foot's (2001) employment of the term.

2 Forms of life

Wittgenstein's *Philosophical Investigations* was, at least on the surface, a very different book from the *Tractatus*. But before Hegel had written his *Logic*, he too had written a very different book, at least on the surface: the *Phenomenology of Spirit*. That book begins with some themes that have, to use a Wittgensteinian phrase, a family resemblance to those of the *Tractatus:* Hegel tries out some representations of the world as a whole in terms of sensuous certainty, perception and the intellect (the understanding, der *Verstand*), only to find that at the end of each presentation, the position taken by each of these stages as it tries to present itself as self-contained finds itself, as it were, babbling. The position had tried to say such and such, but it found that as it did so and refined its statements, it made less and less sense until it was finally pressured to move on to the next stage, at which point what had seemed in isolation like babbling in fact seemed to have an appropriate place in a larger setting. However, none of the stages of "consciousness"—a stance organizing its self-understanding around the idea that it represented individual facts to itself—was self-sufficient. Each collapsed as a conception that was consistent with itself, and the whole scheme ended with a conception of the world as "infinity," that is, as something that cannot be represented or perceived but can only be conceived, that is, thought. The boundlessness of the infinite—for "boundlessness" here is merely another word for "the infinite"—is available only to a subject that is not bound to the statements of facts but who can think of a whole—a limited whole—that is not enumerated in any actual statement of the facts. The true is the whole, Hegel famously said, which also meant that anything less than the whole was going to land itself in a nest of seemingly intractable contradictions.[14]

In his later work, Wittgenstein turns to a "therapeutic" conception of philosophy in which he tries to show that philosophical problems are not so much motivated by a misunderstanding of the logic of our language, as he thought in the *Tractatus*, but rather that such problems are motivated by more or less natural pictures we form when we exercise our reflective capacities on what might be otherwise ordinary activities. Once those pictures are formed, on reflection we then see that there are various problems and contradictions (or paradoxes) when one follows out the implications of that picture. His working principle of philosophical therapy was therefore to go through a series of reflections and arguments to show either that the picture itself was thoroughly misleading

---

14 In this way, "being" can only show itself to a self-conscious subject. To other intelligent animals, what shows up are only beings, entities, not the infinite (although limited) whole itself.

or that the picture was not itself required but was just one way among many of looking at things, and it should be asked of it how helpful it was in getting us to see things that way. It was not, as many have argued, simply to gain clarity (which was the point of the *Tractatus*) but to lead us out of the problems we had generated for ourselves by adopting a picture of what it was we were doing and then finding it inexplicable how what we were actually doing could even be possible.[15] There was therefore no master principle at work in the *Investigations* as there was in the *Tractatus*. Instead, there was an ongoing series of remarks and reflections on (mostly) the concepts of understanding, meaning, and thinking (See PI: §81). Common to both books, however, was the conception of philosophy as activity, not as a body of doctrine, a view Wittgenstein shared with Kant.[16] There is no general view of how attempting to state a view of the world as a whole is doomed to nonsense. Instead, there is a picture of various ways in which language can be used for which there is no master-story or big picture of how all those uses logically tie together. There is no general reason to think they do.

Wittgenstein tries to undo the grip that various conceptions or "pictures" of understanding, meaning, and thinking have had on us. In particular, he tried to show how the initially plausible idea that understanding the meaning of a proposition as involving some kind of determinate mental state in one's mind (or in the brain) itself engendered a whole set of philosophical stances trying to come to terms with all the problems reflection would discover in such a position, problems that one need not have if one did not begin with that picture of understanding, meaning, and thinking to be all encompassing. In particular, and especially in the passages on rule-following, Wittgenstein brings out how in performing an action, first, one knows what one is doing even if one has not plotted out all the commitments involved, and second, how this kind of knowing is based in a shared set of judgments about what the terms mean, which includes not merely how they are applied but also a whole host of other things that simply cannot be laid out as if there were an explicit program delimiting the use of the term.[17] As Wittgenstein puts it in his well-known summation: "It is what human beings say that is true and false; and they agree in the language they use. That is not agreement in opinions but in form of life. If language is to be a means of communi-

---

15 A very good case and summary of the "clarity" view is given by Moore (2012).
16 Kant (1929): "philosophy can never be learned, save only in historical fashion; as regards what concerns reason, we can at most learn to philosophize" (A837/B865).
17 For example, PI: §69: "Someone says to me: 'Shew the children a game.' I teach them gaming with dice, and the other says 'I didn't mean that sort of game.' Must the exclusion of the game with dice have come before his mind when he gave me the order?"

cation there must be agreement not only in definitions but also (queer as this may sound) in judgments." (PI: §§241–242)

This of course sounds close to Hegel's own conception of the involvement of self-consciousness in sociality. The conclusion of the "consciousness" chapter of the *Phenomenology* showed that the problems arising with "consciousness" have to do with its opening onto a world that cannot be grasped all at once in perception or in making judgments that involve positing non-observable explanatory forces and entities. Rather, it opens on to infinity, which can never be fully traversed. This infinity is also self-consciousness, in that in being conscious not merely of the world but also our access to that world, we find ourselves always and already in a world of meaning and practices.

Hegel used the term, *Geist* (spirit), to characterize that species of animal who is self-conscious in that way. Self-consciousness is not merely an additional property of such primates; it transforms them into a new species altogether that has its own species-specific needs. This self-consciousness proves itself to be irremediably social. At first, it is simply the self-consciousness of a living being confronted with all the demands that life makes. The unity, however, of a self-conscious agent is just that: an empty identity. In his treatment of the "Paralogisms" of pure reason, Kant used this to show how it was illegitimate to infer from the identity of a subject over time to any kind of substantial basis (such as an immaterial soul) of that identity. The content of self-conscious engagement thus must come, as Hegel says, either from nature or from spirit itself.[18] In seeking self-consciousness through the recognition of another as oneself having a certain status, one acquires a more determinate sense of the "I" engaged with the world. Without any further way to mediate the reception of content, such a relation between self-conscious beings transforms itself into life and death struggles that eventuate in relations of master and slave, in which one person or group extracts a recognition of status from others through force, fraud or both.

For there to be a consciousness of the world (as stretching out to infinity), we must therefore be in a place where the individual "I" who has his or her own world shares a common ground with other "I's." This common ground is not merely that of the different subjects sharing beliefs about things—such as, e.g., whether certain plants are edible or, e.g., who has the authority to compel others to do things—but each having the meta-belief that the others also have

---

18 EPR: §6: "In the same way, 'I' is the transition from undifferentiated indeterminacy to *differentiation, determination* [...] This content may further be given by nature or generated by the concept of spirit."

those beliefs.[19] Such a system of organized I-subjects opening up to their world as a shared world is historically mediated through various relations of power, authority and natural contingency. The shared world—a "shape of spirit" as a whole—rests on this sharing of judgments, of knowing how to "carry on" in that way of doing things. Its unity fractures when the shared judgments come under pressure from themselves because of internal contradictions elicited within the reflections on what that assemblage of judgments requires of people. The content of self-consciousness that the members of a form of life give each other begins to unravel as its internal contradictions become more apparent, and when what had seemed like legitimate authority becomes seen merely as the expression of individual power. At that point, the form of life begins to fall apart.

Hegel thought that there was a larger whole within which the story of such breakdowns in forms of life played out, and this had to do with the way in which certain forms of life take the shape they do in a self-conscious manner of picking up the pieces from such a breakdown and crafting something new out of them. The sequence of such forms of life thus takes on a kind of logic as the agents moving within them work out the consequences of the shared forms of authority they have and always at first within the limits of their natural and social worlds and then beyond those social worlds as this development works itself out.

Wittgenstein, at least on the surface, did not seem to pay much attention to such things. Yet he did acknowledge that historical forms of life could put limits on what one could accomplish or appreciate in a specific period not just in knowing but in the arts as well.[20] He also speculated about the way in such breakdowns in a form of life are breakdowns of what had been conceived as limits of thought but in the breakdowns came to be seen instead as limitations, as something to be transcended or replaced.[21]

Hegel described his *Logic* metaphorically as a "realm of shadows." In part, he was gesturing to the difficult nature of getting at the basic forms of thought

---

19 This is a point amply brought out by Paul Redding (forthcoming). Redding draws our attention to the way Hegel's discussions of recognition play out along similar lines in the writings of Robert Stalnaker on subject-centered worlds.

20 For example, in PI: p.230, he noted: "Compare a concept with a style of painting. For is even our style of painting arbitrary? Can we choose one at pleasure? (The Egyptian, for instance.) Is it a mere question of pleasing and ugly?"

21 For example, in CV: p.48e (1947 remark): "There are problems I never tackle, which do not lie in my path or belong to my world. Problems of the intellectual world of the West which Beethoven (& perhaps Goethe to a certain extent) tackled & wrestled with but which no philosopher has ever confronted [...]. If you want to see the epic of a whole culture written, you will have to seek it [...] at a time when the end of this culture can only be foreseen, for later there is no one there any more to describe it."

about the world which were identical to the world itself, just as Wittgenstein originally thought that the form of the world was logic and thus not logically accessible. It makes sense to ask therefore what Hegel thought was the metaphorical light source of those shadows, and the answer has to be, of course, the absolute.[22] That would be the very end of the third volume of his *Encyclopedia*, where absolute spirit gathers up its account of itself. On Hegel's view, and, so I have suggested, on Wittgenstein's view too, the very idea of an objective world is bound up with the idea of that world showing itself to thinking, self-conscious creatures. The limits of thought are the limits of the world, not because thought creates the world but because genuine thought—true thought—is identical in content with the world.

In his later work, Wittgenstein thought that there was simply too much heterogeneity in the uses of language to see them all as emanating from or reducible to one single use. The unity that existed in his later work was, as it was in the former, formal: It is what "we" do with our words, with what form of life in which "we" move when we conduct ourselves or when we ask ourselves skeptical questions. That too is Hegel's final word: It is in thought thinking thought, as he quotes Aristotle, that he concludes his *Encyclopedia*. The form of subjectivity generating its content as it makes itself into a moving target in history is the proper object of philosophy, and the way it does so is surely heterogeneous. "Absolute knowing, or spirit knowing itself as spirit," (PS 2018: §808) and Wittgenstein's focus on the heterogeneous language games such subjects play are perhaps not as far from each other on the spectrum as we might have thought.

References

Bondeli, Martin: *Der Kantianismus des jungen Hegel: die Kant-Aneignung und Kant-Überwindung Hegels auf seinem Weg zum philosophischen System*, Felix Meiner, 1997.
Foot, Philippa: *Natural Goodness*, Clarendon, 2001.
Friedlander, Eli: *Signs of Sense: Reading Wittgenstein's Tractatus*, Harvard University Press, 2001.
Friedlander, Eli: "Missing a Step Up the Ladder", *Philosophical Topics* 42:2, 2014, pp. 45–73.
Kant, Immanuel: *Immanuel Kant's Critique of Pure Reason*, Macmillan, 1929.
Lovibond, Sabina: "Wittgenstein, Tolstoy, and the 'Apocalyptic View'", *Philosophy of the Social Sciences* 46:6, 2016: pp.565–583.

---

[22] See the contrasting discussions of the "realm of shadows" in Nuzzo (2012), and Pippin (2018). See my own discussion of Hegel's "shadows" metaphor in Pinkard (2017).

Mácha, Jakub: *Wittgenstein on Internal and External Relations: Tracing All the Connections*, Bloomsbury, 2015.
Moore, Adrian W.: *The Evolution of Modern Metaphysics: Making Sense of Things*. New York, Cambridge University Press, 2012.
Nuzzo, Angelica: *Memory, History, Justice in Hegel*, Palgrave Macmillan, 2012.
Pinkard, Terry P.: *Hegel: a Biography*, Cambridge University Press, 2000
Pinkard, Terry P.: *Does History Make Sense?: Hegel on the Historical Shapes of Justice*, Harvard University Press, 2017.
Pippin, Robert: *Realm of Shadows: Logic as Metaphysics in* The Science of Logic, University of Chicago Press, 2018.
Redding, Paul: "Hegel, Modal Logic, and the Social Nature of Mind", https://www.academia.edu/32035037/Hegel_Modal_Logic_and_the_Social_Nature_of_Mind (accessed March 1, 2018).
Schelling, Friedrich Wilhelm Joseph: *System of Transcendental Idealism*, 1800, trans. by Peter L. Heath, University Press of Virginia, 1978.
Schelling, Friedrich Wilhelm Joseph: *Ideas for a Philosophy of Nature: As Introduction to the Study of This Science*, 1797, Cambridge University Press, 1988.
Schelling, Friedrich Wilhelm Joseph: *Von der Weltseele—eine Hypothese der höhern Physik zur Erklärung des allgemeinen Organismus (1798)*, Historisch-kritische Ausgabe, Reihe I: Werke, Band 6, J. Jantzen et al. (eds.), Frommann-Holzboog, 2000.

Valentin Pluder
Rule-Following and Institutional Context

Abstract In his *Elements of the Philosophy of Right* Hegel points out that the reference to an abstract ethical rule like the categorical imperative is not enough to establish consistent interpersonal actions. In his *Philosophical Investigations* Wittgenstein points out that a mere rule cannot be the cause of regular actions. But Hegel and Wittgenstein do not only share similar and therefore comparable concerns in connecting rules and acts. They also share similar solutions how to provide this connection. This similarity will be shown by comparing simple interpretations of Hegel's critique of Kant's categorical imperative and Wittgenstein's critique of rule-following. The comparison will proceed in two stages. In the first stage, it will be shown that both philosophers share the opinion that general rules, in the form of theoretical propositions, can be related to an unlimited range of actions and that individual actions can be related to an unlimited range of rules. Both believe that this problem cannot be solved by bringing in more theoretical propositions that interpret the original rule. So rule and act are left disconnected and the whole concept of rule-following is challenged, which both philosophers regard as a problem. The second stage of the comparison focuses on the suggestion that the solutions both philosophers provide can be situated within the same framework. The thought that rule and act can ever be adequately understood apart from each other is rejected. Instead, some kind of internal relation, if not identity, has to be assumed. This relation that binds rule and act together is ultimately located within some kind of social institution. For Hegel the necessary institutional context is the *Sitte* or *Sittlichkeit* (ethical life), while for Wittgenstein it is customs, uses, institutions or forms of life.

Wittgenstein and Hegel are, in every respect, very different kinds of philosophers. Due to this fact, simply finding any point at all where they can be compared is—in my eyes—an achievement. By this I do not mean points where they share the same opinion, but merely ones where the differences between them can be related to one another. In such cases, it is, of course, the differences that render the comparison fruitful. Among the passages that could be compared are, on the one hand, Hegel's critique of the categorical imperative and conscience in his *Elements of the Philosophy of Right* (EPR: §§129–141) and, on the other, Wittgenstein's critique of rule-following and private language in the *Philosophical Investigations* (PI: §§185–242).

https://doi.org/10.1515/9783110572780-015

These passages are, of course, well-trodden ground; they have already been interpreted in many and varied ways over the course of time. So it would perhaps be helpful to explain my motivation for comparing them. The answer is that I would like to know under what conditions institutions, understood as social mechanisms, function. By "institution" I mean, roughly, a valid rule or a valid set of rules that draws its validity from its actual usage in shaping performance and not from another rule. Given that it is its performance that makes a rule valid, the theory and practice of valid rules must clearly be interdependent and—to make matters even more complicated—this interdependency needs to be located within the realm of relations between more or less autonomous persons who know or at least could know what they are doing. In short: institutions have something to do with the practice of freely, or at least consciously, shared rule-following.

At first glance, the above-mentioned passages seem to be quite unsuitable for this purpose. They present good reasons for questioning whether there are: (a) objective criteria to decide whether a rule has actually been followed or not, and (b) whether there is an unmediated and non-arbitrary appeal to an act of spontaneous autonomy by the subject.

Although, in my view, Wittgenstein's and Hegel's critique of the categorical imperative, rule-following, conscience and private language is justified, I would like to argue that these four phenomena do nonetheless exist and that they deliver what they promise: the categorical imperative is useful for judging actions, rules can usually be followed, referring to one's conscience can be reasonable, and anybody could invent their own private language. To affirm the critique and nonetheless assert that the phenomena exist might seem inconsistent. But the critique is not directed against the phenomena. It is directed against a certain interpretation of them, namely one holding that they can be understood independently of any context. This would mean that the categorical imperative or any rule could explain by itself which actions are required, or that conscience could judge without being bound by its moral environment, or that there could be a private language that is unconnected to a common language. Since the context in these cases is always established by rule-governed interpersonal actions, the argument returns to institutions as social mechanisms. For Hegel the institutional context is the *Sitte* or *Sittlichkeit* (ethical life), while for Wittgenstein it is "customs (uses, institutions)" (PI: §199) or forms of life (PI: §23).[1] In other words: the only way to understand all four phenomena adequately is to

---

[1] The standpoint of this chapter is therefore one of communitarianism or collectivism (Bloor 1997: ix).

view them in the light of their realization within an institutional context. Wittgenstein and Hegel aim their critique at abstract and context-free conceptions of the four entities, and in this respect they are comparable.

This chapter will confine itself to comparing very simple interpretations of Hegel's critique of Kant's categorical imperative and Wittgenstein's critique of rule-following. The comparison will proceed in two stages. In the first stage, I will attempt to show that both philosophers share the opinion that general rules, in the form of theoretical propositions, can be related to an unlimited range of actions and that individual actions can be related to an unlimited range of rules. Both believe that this problem cannot be solved by bringing in more theoretical propositions that interpret the original rule. So rule and act are left disconnected and the whole concept of rule-following is challenged, which both philosophers regard as a problem. The second stage of the comparison focuses on the suggestion that the solutions both philosophers provide can be situated within the same framework. The thought that rule and act can ever be adequately understood apart from each other is rejected. Instead, some kind of internal relation, if not identity, has to be assumed. For Hegel and Wittgenstein this relation that binds rule and act together is ultimately located within some kind of social institution.

1 Similar difficulties in connecting rule and act

1.1 Hegel

In its first formulation, the categorical imperative reads: "Act only according to that maxim whereby you can, at the same time, will that it should become a universal law." *(Kant 1785: p.30)* The categorical imperative is claimed to be a general and unconditionally valid norm or duty which it is obligatory to follow under all circumstances. Its general validity is grounded founded in its purely formal conception. By having no content on its own, it is open to any possible content and therefore universally applicable. At the base of this formalism lies the postulate of consistency: one cannot will that the maxims of one's action cannot be generalized, and the criterion for the possibility of generalization is the absence of contradiction. It is quite safe to say that under everyday circumstances the categorical imperative seems to work quite well as an instrument for judging actions.

The problems with the categorical imperative reveal themselves when it is asked what exactly is not supposed to be in contradiction with what. I could ask myself, for example, whether I could possibly will that the maxim I act on when planning an extramarital affair become a general law. Then I realize that I cannot will it to be my maxim, because it is unsuitable for this task since it contradicts the institution of matrimony. I therefore change my maxim, and consequently also my plans for the evening.

But these considerations are based on at least two assumptions. The first is that matrimony ought to exist. The second assumption is that the specific kind of matrimony that would be contradicted by the maxim my planned actions are based on ought to exist. These assumptions both have a specific content and must therefore be located outside the categorical imperative, which is supposed to be purely formal. That means that in order to make the categorical imperative work, additional premises have to be stated. The real problem becomes apparent when we realize that the categorical imperative can be combined with any additional premises without contradiction, no matter the content of these premises. This is, again, due to its formal nature. Obviously, there is no problem in sharing the idea of the categorical imperative while not sharing the idea of the necessity of matrimony. There is simply nothing to contradict: it is not contradictory to deem matrimony unnecessary. Hegel makes the same point with his own examples:

> The fact that *no property* is present is in itself [*für sich*] no more contradictory than is the non-existence of this or that individual people, family, etc., or the complete *absence of human life*. But if it is already established and presupposed that property and human life should exist and be respected, then it is a contradiction to commit theft or murder; a contradiction must be a contradiction with something, that is, with a content which is already fundamentally present as an established principle. (EPR: §135)

The consequence of this view is that there is no relation between the single concrete act and the categorical imperative unless one has been established by some additional assumption of specific content. Hegel describes this lack of a determined relation between the general rule and the specific, concrete action:

> it is impossible to make the transition to the determination of particular duties from the above determination of duty as *absence of contradiction*, as *formal correspondence with itself* [i.e., the categorical imperative], and even if such a particular content for action is taken into consideration, there is no criterion within that principle for deciding whether or not this content is a duty. (EPR: §135)

Neither the step from the general to the concrete nor the step from the concrete to the general can be determined by recourse to an abstract rule as such or a concrete action as such.

Of course, the objection can be raised that even if this were true, it only shows that some mediating instance has to be established to bridge the gap between the categorical imperative and the specific action. This could be the following imperative: act only according to that maxim whereby you can, at the same time, will that it should become a law of matrimony. But this would not help at all: on the one hand, the transition from the categorical imperative to this specific imperative remains entirely arbitrary and, on the other, even the more specific imperative allows a vast number of possible actions depending on how matrimony is defined, which, when and to what degree actions are assumed to be threatening, and so on. Regardless of how specific an imperative is, the need remains for mediation between the imperative and the individual concrete action; and even if the mediation is specified by a general rule, this rule must be mediated too, etc.: "The infinite progress of mediation is thereby set in motion" (SL 2010: p.665; GW 12: p.168),[2] and this is a "bad infinite" (SL 2010: p.113; GW 21: p.129). No matter how detailed a rule is, it is still a general formula and, being general, it cannot bridge the gap to the concrete individual action on its own. Considered in this way, it is not only the formal nature of the categorical imperative that makes it seem useless, but also its very nature as a general rule. This step from the purely formal rule to any rule might be inadmissible: in the *Elements*, Hegel reflects on his interpretation of a very specific and strictly formal ethical principle. It is possible that this critique cannot be generalized. But Hegel himself does not seem to be reluctant about making a generalization:

> In toto this [the lack of mediation between the categorical imperative and the specific individual action] is the same defect as in the other sciences. One has the conception of space, this is the general; the specific comprises the figurations. How do they get their specificity? One says there are triangles et cetera, but this is not the transition from the general to the specific. From where do the determinations of the particular types derive?[3]

This passage shows that even Hegel believed there is a general problem. As a consequence, it does not seem unjustified at this point to interpret Hegel in a manner that brings him closer to Wittgenstein and his critique of rule-following, if only in order to start a fruitful debate between the two philosophers.

---

[2] This quote is taken from the *Teleologie*, where Hegel analyses the relation between ends and means more closely.
[3] My translation. The original reads: "*Im Ganzen ist dieß derselbe Mangel, wie in den anderen Wissenschaften. Man hat die Vorstellung von Raum, dieß ist das Allgemeine, das Besondere sind die Figurationen, wie erhalten diese ihre Bestimmung? Man sagt es giebt Dreiecke pp aber dieß ist nicht der Uebergang vom Allgemeinen zum Besonderen. Woher kommen nun die Bestimmungen für die besonderen Arten?*" (GW 26,3: p.1234)

Since the general and the concrete are entirely disconnected, the application of the general formula is totally unrestricted. That means the general formula can be combined with any specific action without contradiction: depending on which "already established principle is fundamentally present [...] it is possible to justify any wrong or immoral mode of action by this means [i.e., the categorical imperative]" (EPR: §135). The range of possible interpretations therefore allows actions which are considered to be diametrically opposed (without implying any dialectical relation between the extremes). But if the categorical imperative can be brought into accord with any action, it is of no help in deciding which actions should be performed and which should not.

1.2 Wittgenstein

The *Philosophical Investigations* explores rule-following *inter alia* as the relation between rule and rule application, as in the example of the pupil who is asked to continue a sequence of numbers. In this case, a concrete sequence of numbers is confronted with a general demand: always do the same! The demand "to do the same" is not arbitrary in this context because, according to Wittgenstein, the notions of "rule" and "doing the same" are strongly connected: "The use of the word 'rule' and the use of the word 'same' are interwoven. (As are the use of 'proposition' and the use of 'true')." (PI: §225)

Advocates of the view that the rule and the sequence of numbers stand in an unambiguous relation would say that they "perceive something drawn very fine in a segment of a series, a characteristic design, which only needs the addition of 'and so on' in order to reach to infinity" (PI: §229). Or, looked at from the side of the rule: "All the steps are really already taken." (PI: §219) That might mean something like the rule "traces the lines along which it is to be followed through the whole of space" (PI: §219). This idea corresponds to the thought that a rule determines its own application, which seems only natural at first glance because otherwise the question arises of how we can distinguish between a correct and an incorrect application of the rule (Ebbs 2017: p.399). Before discussing the problems with this conception of rules, I would like to bring Hegel into the picture. If we include Hegel, the following schema becomes apparent: on the one hand, there is a general instruction like "Don't do anything that leads to contradictions" in the case of Hegel or "Always do the same" in the case of Wittgenstein. On the other hand, there is something concrete and specific, like a specific action in the case of Hegel or a specific series of numbers in the case of Wittgenstein.

The problems are comparable in both cases, if not the same. The mediation between the general instruction and its supposed specific realization does not work out, or at least does not work out under the assumption that an abstract and isolated general rule can link itself with a concrete occurrence. Wittgenstein famously illustrates this problem with the example of the pupil who is asked to continue a sequence of numbers that is established by constantly adding two. Having reached 1,000, the pupil starts adding not two but four, without being able to understand why in doing so he is no longer following the original instruction (PI: §184).

A closer look reveals two problems that have already been mentioned. The first emerges when we look at the concrete, specific side, since there is an infinite quantity of possible formulas that would match this specific sequence of numbers. The second problem originates on the general side. It is revealed when Wittgenstein asks "What is 'the same'?":

> We seem to have an infallible paradigm of identity in the identity of a thing with itself. I feel like saying: "Here at any rate there can't be a variety of interpretations. If you are seeing a thing you are seeing identity too." Then are two things the same when they are what one thing is? And how am I to apply what the *one* thing shews me to the case of two things? (PI: §215)

Hegel would certainly agree if this statement were paraphrased as: no (nonempty) identification without difference. But if the instances that are supposed to be identified have to be different, the necessity for interpretation arises. To identify apples and oranges as fruit, one has to distinguish between the aspects that are to be highlighted because they can be seen as "the same" and the aspects that have to be obscured because they cannot be seen as "the same."

So interpretation it is. The pupil has to be brought to interpret the rule in the right way. But if the rule has to be interpreted before it can be applied, it does not determine its own application. For the interpretation exceeds the rule in a way that is not governed by the rule itself, and hence is undetermined and arbitrary. Attempting to control the interpretation by means of another rule cannot prevent the loss of unambiguity because every rule for how to apply another rule itself needs to be interpreted, and so forth. Here Hegel's "bad infinite" appears again. By giving "one interpretation after another" (PI: §201) or one rule after another, the gap between the universal and the concrete cannot be bridged. Wittgenstein makes this clear when he explains what interpretation means: we "ought to restrict the term 'interpretation' to the substitution of one expression of the rule for another" (ibid.). So no interpretation will ever be able to break through to the actual individual act that claims to be an application of the rule.

Again, this result leaves the general and the concrete entirely disconnected. Thus, no matter how rigid an abstract rule might seem, its application is boundlessly flexible: "But how can a rule shew me what I have to do at *this* point? Whatever I do is, on some interpretation, in accord with the rule." (PI: §198) That means "every course of action can be made out to accord with the rule" (PI: §201). This is, of course, the paradox from which Kripke's reflections on a sceptical-solution derive (Kripke 1982: p.7).

2 Similar solutions to connecting rule and act

2.1 Wittgenstein

But according to Wittgenstein, all this is a misunderstanding.[4] In reality, rule-following is not based on a universal rule that governs its own application or an interpretation that mediates between rule and concrete act. There is, rather, an alternative conception of "rule" "which is *not* an *interpretation*, but which is exhibited in what we call 'obeying the rule' and 'going against it' in actual cases" (PI: §201). According to this conception, the rule expresses itself not, or at least not primarily, by means of interpretation but directly through its specific application in every actual case. From the outset, the general and the specific are thought of as undivided, so that there is no gap to bridge. Of course, if one cannot specify how exactly the general and the specific are supposed to be conceived as undivided, this is at most a gesture towards a solution. Since the general and the specific are obviously not simply the same, there seem to be essentially two options to describe their connectedness: firstly, looked at in terms of unity, the general and the specific can be seen as aspects of a whole that has internal distinctions; and secondly, looked at in terms of the different aspects, the general and the specific can be seen as internally related. These two ways of looking at matters are, of course, intertwined, and the relations between them—or, rather, the different standpoints from which the relations between them can be viewed—are one of the central objects to which Hegel applies his method in his *Science of Logic*.

If the general rule and its concrete application are in fact undivided, asking how the general rule determines the concrete application is already a mistake

---

[4] And hence the interpretation presented by Kripke (1982) is also a misunderstanding, at least in the eyes of Baker and Hacker (1984: pp.1–55), though this view is not universally shared (Kusch 2006: pp.237–263).

because it implies that there is a relation between two separate entities: something that determines and something that is determined. Nonetheless, expressions like "The steps are determined by the formula" work very well for, say, algebraic formulas. To address the question of how this is possible, Wittgenstein asks how the expression is used. He answers himself as follows:

> We may perhaps refer to the fact that people are brought by their education (training) so to use the formula $y = x^2$, that they all work out the same value for y when they substitute the same number for x. Or we may say "These people are so trained that they all take the same step at the same point when they receive the order 'add 3'". We might express this by saying: for these people the order "add 3" completely determines every step from one number to the next. (In contrast with other people who do not know what they are to do on receiving this order, or who react to it with perfect certainty, but each one in a different way.) (PI: §189)

According to this passage, the application of a formula or rule is, in certain cases, determined. That is quite the opposite of saying that the application is boundlessly flexible. This discrepancy can be cleared up by looking at the assumed source of determination. While the assumption that the rule or the formula determines its own application by itself leads to arbitrary outcomes, the assumption that the determination does not come from something abstract but originates from specific training leads to the successful description of definite behaviour by a rule or a formula. But in the latter case the concession has to be made that different training leads to different actions no matter whether the abstract description by means of a rule changes or not. Conversely, the rule in itself is unconnected to the training. The connection derives entirely from the side of the training as a specific practice that has to be performed in front of the pupil so that they can imitate it.

The introduction of an entity that is neutral towards the rule as an abstract formula is similar to the conclusions Hegel draws from his analysis of the categorical imperative. For Hegel, the connection between the categorical imperative and a specific action could only be made through "something, that is, with a content which is already fundamentally present as an established principle" (EPR: §135), such as a special form of monogamous matrimonial practice. Based on this principle, the categorical imperative can be used to prevent promiscuous actions, for example. For Wittgenstein, the connection between the abstract formula, like $y = x^2$, and the specific action, like saying "4" after having heard "2," can only be made on the basis of practical training. In both cases, the mediating instances, on the one hand the "established principle" and on the other hand the "training," cannot be deduced from the universal abstract instances, that is the categorical imperative and the formula. On the contrary: the mediating instances clearly have primacy.

But there is obviously a difference. Hegel talks about a principle, which is something that is supposed to be only abstract, whereas Wittgenstein talks about training, which is something that is supposed to be only specific and concrete. However, both instances unfortunately have in common that they are unsuited for their purpose: a principle can be easily linked or mediated with the categorical imperative because they are both general, but principles as such cannot link themselves with concrete actions. This is the premise of the whole argument. Training can be easily linked with concrete actions because it is, in itself, a sequence of concrete actions, but as such it cannot link itself with a general instance in a definite way. There is always an infinite number of possible generalizations based on even one specific action. It seems the problem is not solved at all.

One might get the impression that Wittgenstein reacts to this by dropping altogether the concept of a general rule that can be followed by reflecting on it: "When I obey a rule, I do not choose. I obey the rule *blindly*" (PI: §219), or "'obeying a rule' is a practice" (PI: §202), and at the base of all justification is not an ultimate justification but only a reference to the actual practice: "This is simply what I do." (PI: §217)

But at the same time—in my eyes—there seems to be a need for the general part of the rule that cannot be met by reducing rule-following to blind practice. And in fact, Wittgenstein does not state that there is only unreflective practice. The agent is aware of the rule that is obeyed; it is the *way* that the rule is obeyed which they do not reflect on, because asking how rule and act are related implies a difference that does not exist. In fact, the general part cannot be reduced even if rule-following is ultimately due to training, because if someone is supposed to be trained by showing them a specific practice, this practice has to be more than just one specific, concrete incident. It has to be linked to an invitation to understand the individual instance of the practice as a model, or an exhortation to do "the same." That means the practice that is shown can only train someone if it is understood not only as something concrete and specific but also as something general.

This aspect of generality that is inherent to any form of training cannot be shown directly, by pointing at something concrete. It is, for example, not true that if "you are seeing a thing you are seeing identity too" (PI: §215). The general as such is essentially non-deictic. It becomes apparent only through the negation of something specific as specific. The general shows itself, as it were contradictorily, through the identification of several different concrete incidents. That is one of the reasons why it "is not possible that there should have been only one occasion on which someone obeyed a rule" and why to "obey a rule ..., to give an order, are *customs* (uses, institutions)" (PI: §199, cf. PI: §198).[5] The practice that trains has to be concrete and general at the same time, so to speak.

2.2 Hegel

Just as Hegel was earlier interpreted in a way that brings him closer to Wittgenstein by generalizing his critique of the categorical imperative to a critique of all rules, here I am interpreting Wittgenstein in a way that brings him closer to Hegel, because the "concrete general" or the "concrete universal" is of course a Hegelian concept—the solution, or the label of the solution, that Hegel offers to solve the problem of the mediation between the general and the concrete. But it would be a misunderstanding to think of the concrete general as a third, discrete instance that stands between an independent and isolated general instance and an independent and isolated concrete instance. The concrete general is, rather, the underlying unity from which the concrete and the general derive. They both have to be taken as an abstraction from it. (Since Hegel's notion has three aspects—universal, particular and singular—this is of course a simplification.) The concrete general is: "The true, infinite universal, the one which, immediately in itself, is just as much particularity as singularity [...]" (SL 2010: p.533; GW 12: p.36). This means that the universal [i.e., the concrete general] is thus the totality of the concept; it is what is concrete, is not empty but, on the contrary, has content by virtue of its concept—a content in which the universal does not just preserve itself but is rather the universal's own, immanent to it. It is of course possible to abstract from this content, but what we have then is not the universal element of the concept but the abstract universal, which is an isolated and imperfect moment of the concept, void of truth. (SL 2010: p.532; GW 12: p.35)

As abstractions, the concrete and the general are not "in themselves." Rather, as partial descriptions they express aspects of a whole that is composed of internal distinctions. Looked at in this light, it becomes clear that one fragmentary description cannot directly determine another fragmentary description, since the rule on its own cannot directly determine the individual act and vice

---

5 Unfortunately, "Wittgenstein at no point explained or defined the words 'custom', 'convention', or 'institution'. He treated them as he treated the other basic terms of his analysis (such as 'game') as well-understood words of ordinary language." (Bloor 1997: p.27) It is therefore merely an assumption that it has something to do with the practice of freely shared rule-following mentioned above.

versa. Every determination depends on or is mediated by the entity which is described in different ways from the two sides.

Understood in this way, the general and the concrete seem to be only negative or maybe even useless. Their positive aspect is that the whole can only be represented by them because there is no determination that would grasp the whole as a whole without omitting its internal distinctions, apart from inconsistent descriptions like "concrete general": the "whole" or the "underlying unity" cannot be properly addressed in a direct way. Precisely this point justifies the general and the concrete in their own right. Applied to the problem of rule-following, this would mean that, on the one hand, the abstract and general rule is necessary but not sufficient for following a rule because the general rule is only the expression or description of a "concrete general" instance. In fact, the possibility of relating a general rule to a concrete general instance, like a custom, through either a process of abstraction or a process of concretization, might make the difference between following a rule and acting in accordance with it (Glock 2003: p.247). On the other hand, the same goes for the concrete practice. The practice must necessarily be shown, but this alone is not sufficient. It has to be shown as the expression of a "concrete general" instance that also includes the general rule.

The only way for the rule to be understood sufficiently is to point out that to be determining and determined the rule on its own is not enough, and that for this purpose the rule has to be connected to a concrete practice. This means the rule has to become more than an abstract proposition. And the only way for the individual act to become sufficient to determine other acts, within the context of training for example, is to point out that the individual act on its own is not enough, that it has to be connected to a general rule like "Do the same" in the simplest case. This means the act has to become more than an individual, concrete piece of behaviour. Both sides are brought together in institutions, i.e., a commonly performed practice of conscious rule-following.

While it is possible neither for the concrete practice to be deduced from the general rule on its own nor for a general rule to be derived unambiguously from a concrete practice, both sides are clearly determined within the context of concrete general practices such as customs, institutions or forms of life. This leads to "a sort of *context principle for rules:* don't ask what rules, correctness, agreement, or disagreement are in isolation, but only in the context of our rule-following practices" (Ebbs 2017: p.400).

If that is right, Hegel's "established principle" cannot in the final analysis be a mere principle, an abstract rule; it has to be based upon a concrete general practice as well. Matrimony, for example, would not just be a specific set of rules but also an interpersonal practice within an ethical institution that is expressed adequately only through general norms that are always connected to their concrete realization and vice versa. Only within such an institutional context of reciprocal determination can the relation between general rule and concrete implementation be unambiguously clear and therefore binding. The same is true at a broader level. Laws as abstract general rules lose the contingency they might have for the abstract individual who judges only based on their own private morality when they and the interpersonal shared practice of customs are embedded together in the institution of the Hegelian state: "Through the public nature of the laws and the universality of customs, the state takes away from the right of insight its formal aspect and that contingency which this right still has for the subject within the prevailing viewpoint [of morality]." (EPR: §132)

References

Baker, Gordon P., and Hacker, Peter M. S.: *Scepticism, Rules and Language*, Blackwell, 1984.
Bloor, David: *Wittgenstein, Rules and Institutions*, Routledge, 1997.
Ebbs, Gary: "*Rules and Rule-Following*", in: Hans-Johann Glock and John Hyman (eds.): *A Companion to Wittgenstein*, Blackwell, 2017, pp.390–406.
Glock, Hans-Johann: *Quine and Davidson on Language, Thought and Reality*, Cambridge University Press, 2003.
Kant, Immanuel: *Grounding for the Metaphysics of Morals*, trans. by James W. Ellington, Hackett, 1993.
Kripke, Saul A.: *Wittgenstein on Rules and Private Language*, Harvard University Press, 1982.
Kusch, Martin: *A Sceptical Guide to Meaning and Rules*, Acumen, 2006.

Valentina Balestracci
Hegel and Wittgenstein: Elements for a Comparison

Abstract The aim of this essay is to investigate whether there can be a connection between Hegel's and Wittgenstein's philosophies. The comparison immediately presents some difficulties since Wittgenstein never declared to be a Hegelian and the only brief remark confessed to M. Drury about Hegel's thought is not comforting in this respect. This seems not to have discouraged D. Lamb who attempted the comparison at issue, taking into consideration language and perception in both authors. His aim was not to show that Wittgenstein was in any way influenced by Hegel, rather to what extent the linguistic revolution was bound up with the Hegelian or neo-Hegelian tradition, against which it originally defined itself. Assuming Lamb's investigation as a starting point, I will overlook the aspect concerning perception in order to focus on the roles of language and logic in both authors. As a consequence, this comparison is not intended to be exhaustive. Firstly, this paper will be comparing tautologies and contradictions in the *Tractatus* on the one hand and the speculative proposition in the *Phenomenology of Spirit* on the other, focusing on their function as limits. Secondly, through the analysis of the speculative proposition, which turns out to be different from absolute knowing, the relation between the *Phenomenology* and the *Science of Logic* will be investigated.

1 Introduction

Even though no evidence of influence can be given, authors have not been discouraged from establishing a connection between Hegel and Wittgenstein. David Lamb, for example, showed the possibility of a comparison between the two authors in his 1979 book *Language and Perception in Hegel and Wittgenstein*. Lamb states his general thesis as follows:

> [R]eacting against Logical Atomism, the later Wittgenstein came up with many of the old idealist arguments in a new form. Hence the doubts cast upon the analytic—synthetic dichotomy, the corner stone of positivist thought. (Lamb 1979: p.xi)

Using Wittgenstein's thought as an instrument for the above conclusion, Lamb's aim consists in re-opening the discussion about the two tendencies in order to show that the gulf between analytical and continental philosophies is not so profound. For this reason, a few lines later, Lamb states that, "despite the fact that Wittgenstein was never a Hegelian, his thought confirms the old Hegelian tradition" (ibid.: p.xii).

My contribution takes its bearings from the above-quoted work with regard to the possibility of such a comparison, but with the difference that I will make no reference to perception and I will focus on the so called early Wittgenstein, that is, the period of the *Tractatus Logico-Philosophicus*. Furthermore, my interest will not be in identifying Wittgenstein as the heir of Hegelian philosophy, but in showing how some characteristics of language and logic emerge in Hegel and Wittgenstein's perspectives. Most importantly, I will show how the comparison between the logical propositions in the *Tractatus* and the speculative proposition in the *Phenomenology of Spirit* can illustrate why the speculative proposition cannot be identified with absolute knowing; this being paramount to understanding the connection between the *Phenomenology* and the *Science of Logic*.

Having said that, it must be noticed that this contribution is not exhaustive. I will be taking into consideration the *Tractatus* on the one hand and the connection between the *Phenomenology* with the *Science of Logic* on the other, focusing on a few aspects only.

The first section will take into consideration tautology and contradiction in the *Tractatus* in order to explain their function and their characteristics. Then, in the third section, I will focus on the speculative proposition in the *Phenomenology* in order to draw its affinity with the logical propositions of the *Tractatus*. In the fourth section I will illustrate the consequences of this comparison.

2 Tautology and contradiction as *Grenzfälle* of language

Tautology and contradiction are introduced in the fourth section of the *Tractatus* as follows:

> Among the possible groups of truth-conditions there are two extreme cases. In the one case the proposition is true for all the truth-possibilities of the elementary propositions. We say that the truth-conditions are *tautological*.
>
> In the second case the proposition is false for all the truth-possibilities. The truth-conditions are *self-contradictory*.

In the first case, we call the proposition a tautology, in the second case a contradiction. (TLP: 4.46, Ogden/Ramsey's translation)[1]

Truth-conditions of a proposition are what makes it possible for a proposition to be judged as true or false in comparison to what happens in reality. If the proposition says something that does not correspond to reality, the proposition is called false, otherwise it is true. Tautology and contradiction maintain their truth-conditions, albeit not in the same sense of an ordinary proposition. In fact, they do not require a comparison with the facts in order for their truth or falsehood to be known, since they are the extreme cases of language, respectively, which are always true or always false. Since the position they occupy is—in reference to ordinary propositions—special, they are defined as "extreme cases."

I will now deepen some specific aspects about these cases. In 1913, Wittgenstein wrote that "[e]very proposition is essentially true-false [...]. Thus a proposition has two *poles*, corresponding to case of its truth and the case of its falsehood. We call this the *sense* of a proposition" (NB: p.98).

This is what will be defined—below—as the "bipolarity" of the proposition. In physics, the term "bipolarity" indicates the north and south poles of a magnet being inseparable from each other.[2] Analogously, truth and falsehood are conceived as two opposite poles which stay together in the proposition since they have not yet been determined through a comparison with reality. Such a bipolarity constitutes the sense of the proposition which is, therefore, independent of being true or of being false.

Returning to tautology and contradiction, these lack any such bipolarity or sense. Therefore, they are defined as senseless [*sinnlos*]:

> The proposition shows what it says, the tautology and the contradiction that they say nothing. The tautology has no truth-conditions, for it is unconditionally true; and the contradiction is on no condition true.
> Tautology and contradiction are without sense. (TLP: 4.461)

A comparison with reality in order to know whether the proposition is true or false is no longer required in the case of tautology or contradiction. They make no sense and "unhook" themselves from their truth-conditions. The above proposition, which attributes no truth-conditions to tautology and contra-

---

[1] I use Ogden/Ramsey's translation of the *Tractatus* throughout this chapter.
[2] Even if it were possible to separate a magnet, one would not obtain a north pole on the one hand and the south pole on the other; with the division of a magnet two parts will be obtained, each of them characterised by two opposite poles together.

diction, would seem to be contradictory with the proposition 4.46 where Wittgenstein defined the truth-conditions as tautological and contradictory with regard to the two propositions. This can be explained starting from the fact that "tautology and contradiction are the limiting cases [*Grenzfälle*] of the combination of symbols, namely their dissolution" (TLP: 4.466).

In this passage, Wittgenstein gives the definitions of the limiting cases as opposed to ordinary propositions. In fact, if the term "dissolution" indicates, in the most general sense of the term, the disappearance of something, in this case, what Wittgenstein calls "articulation of the proposition" has disappeared, i.e. the multiplicity and the combination of the elements of the proposition, without which a proposition is incapable of expressing anything (TLP: 3.251).

This means that the definitions of tautology and contradiction cannot be given independently from that of an ordinary proposition. In fact, it is impossible to understand what the term "dissolution" refers to, if it is not known what the articulation of an ordinary proposition is. Therefore, tautology and contradiction are not simply the cause of the disintegration, but they are the dissolution or the limits of the articulation of ordinary propositions.

Consider the following passage:

> Tautology and contradiction are, however, not nonsensical; they are part of the symbolism, in the same way that "0" is part of the symbolism of Arithmetic. (TLP: 4.4611)

Although it has just been said that tautology and contradiction are the dissolution of ordinary propositions, the first part of this passage claims that tautology and contradiction still belong to language. If this were not the case, according to the definition of "nonsense" given in the preface to the *Tractatus*, tautology and contradiction would be placed outside language and, therefore, characterised as "nonsensical" [*unsinnig*] instead of "senseless" [*sinnlos*].

The second part of the quote clarifies this apparent contradiction, showing the particular way in which tautology and contradiction still belong to language. With the above comparison, Wittgenstein introduces the quarrel concerning "0", whether it can be considered a positive integer or not. The matter remains unsolved since "0" is what divides negative from positive numbers and is usually considered neither positive nor negative. Analogously to "0", tautology and contradiction are limits, therefore they can be neither placed outside language (as nonsenses) nor considered ordinary sentences (as sensible propositions). This is why Wittgenstein needs the distinction between the adjectives "senseless" [*sinnlos*] and "nonsensical" [*unsinnig*].

In fact, although they differ from ordinary propositions inasmuch as they say nothing, tautology and contradiction cannot be completely excluded from language since they are still well-formed sentences, grammatically in order (Nordmann 2005: p.148; Floyd 2000: p.253).

Wittgenstein says that ordinary propositions are "[t]he expression of the agreement or disagreement with the facts which constitute reality" (TLP: 4.431).

Their truth expresses agreement, their falsehood disagreement with the facts. Tautology always expresses agreement with reality since its truth-values are always true. On the contrary, contradiction always expresses disagreement since its truth-values are always false. This means that where the highest level of agreement or disagreement between propositions and facts is satisfied, truth-conditions renege. For example, if the truth-values satisfy every truth-condition and, therefore, result always true, this means that the conditions are tautological. The analogue occurs in the case of the contradiction for which the truth-conditions are contradictory. So, on this very point the truth-conditions of the tautology or of the contradiction are lost in comparison to ordinary propositions. This means that truth-conditions for tautology or contradiction are not absent, but they disappear in the point where ordinary propositions reach their extremes. For this reason, Wittgenstein says that tautology and contradiction are the dissolution of the connection of signs, this meaning the destruction of the articulation of ordinary sentences. This also explains the reasons why Wittgenstein refers to the truth-conditions of these extreme cases saying, immediately after, that they have no truth-conditions. Where language reaches its peaks, it disappears.

In this sense, I follow G. H. von Wright who claims that tautology and contradiction are "degenerate propositions" (von Wright 2005: p.100). Firstly, this definition is important because it summarises the fact that tautology and contradiction still refer to the propositions of ordinary kind, since they do not violate any rule of grammar and since they cannot be placed on the other side of language, as nonsenses.

Secondly, they are "degenerate" compared to ordinary propositions since they say nothing, they are the limits of ordinary propositions and, above all, because they can be compared to an ordinary proposition that has lost its truth-conditions or sense.

As a consequence, the adjective "senseless" [*sinnlos*] indicates the loss of sense (or truth-conditions) by tautology and contradiction, with reference to an ordinary proposition. The fact that they are the dissolution of the combination of symbols which constitute the structure (or articulation) of an ordinary proposition can also be seen as the limit of sensible propositions which degenerate in tautologies and contradictions.

The fact that a "loss" is concerned suggests the tight relation between ordinary propositions on the one hand and tautology and contradiction on the other.

This is well expressed by Ostrow who claims that "sense and senselessness spring from the same root and so care must be taken in tease them apart" (2001: p.98). In fact, since tautology and contradiction cannot be placed outside language, this means that they are on the same side of the propositions, from which they cannot be fully separated. This means that tautology and contradiction are placed, as well as ordinary propositions, on the inner side of the limit which is defined in the preface to the *Tractatus*.

This allows me to introduce the next topic regarding the matter of the internal limit. In fact, it needs to be underlined that the limits reached by language should be regarded differently than obstacles externally imposed. In the following passage, Wittgenstein says:

> Man possesses the capacity of constructing languages, in which every sense can be expressed, without having an idea how and what each word means—just as one speaks without knowing how the single sounds are produced.
>
> Colloquial language is a part of the human organism and is not less complicated than it.
>
> From it it is humanly impossible to gather immediately the logic of language.
>
> Language disguises the thought; so that from the external form of the clothes one cannot infer the form of the thought they clothe, because the external form of the clothes is constructed with quite another object than to let the form of the body be recognized. (TLP: 4.002)

First of all, language is able to communicate every possible sense so that, in Wittgenstein's view, it cannot be defined as inadequate with regard to its function. Second, the passage claims that language works as a kind of mask for thought, this being exactly the function which language is apt to because it has "quite another object than to let the form of the body be recognised." (ibid.)

This means that language does not have any deceiving purpose regarding thought, but carries out its specific function, the limits of which are signed by tautology and contradiction. Therefore, the limits of propositions do not express an inadequacy; rather, they express the completeness of language which fulfils its function.

Therefore, the limits reached in the extreme cases of tautology and contradiction are naturally reached by language. In fact, language reaches these limits in the peaks of maximum agreement or disagreement between propositions and reality, i.e., if the truth-conditions are maximally satisfied or dissatisfied by the truth-values of propositions. Having expressed every possible sense, language has complied with its function and reneges since it has nothing more to express. This identifies with its limits which are reached in language, at the point of the dissolution of the articulation of ordinary propositions. To put it another way, language is complete as the following passage from *The Big Typescript*, that Wittgenstein writes several years after the publication of the *Tractatus*, confirms:

> When I say: Here we are at the limits of language, that always sounds as if resignation were necessary at this point, whereas on the contrary complete satisfaction comes about, since *no* question remains. (BT: p.310)

3 Hegel's speculative proposition as a limit of the *Phenomenology of Spirit*

The speculative proposition is introduced at the end of the path of consciousness and it is defined in the preface to the *Phenomenology*, where Hegel talks about the speculative proposition as the destruction of the general form of judgement which is understood as the distinction between subject and predicate, considered also as the general structure of an ordinary sentence (PS 1977: p.22). True or false judgements are the form through which consciousness expresses itself (Chiereghin 2008: pp.56 and 69).

Since it is the destruction of judgements, even though the term "proposition" keeps it in a linguistic context, the speculative proposition cannot be regarded as an ordinary sentence. Notwithstanding, since consciousness can also be considered "the spirit as concrete knowing, that is immersed in externality" (Chiereghin 2008: p.24), this demolition can also be seen as the content of judgement which has been completely externalised. Therefore, this means that, in the speculative proposition, the content has been completely expressed, the proposition having nothing more to say, as though consciousness was pulled to its extreme possibility of expression.

Furthermore, the above proposition has in common with logic the word *speculative*, a fact which has important consequences since "their movement, [of the moments] which organizes itself in this element into a whole, is *Logic* or *speculative philosophy*" (PS 1977: §37).

Since *speculative*—as can be noted in the passage mentioned—is linked with the movement and the organization of the moments into a unity, the speculative proposition can be similarly considered as what gathers into a unity the totality of the previous moments, demolishing the distinction between subject and predicate at the same time.

Now, the fact that logic is defined as *speculative*, like the proposition, shows not only that there is a connection between the two, but that logic has the same function of destroying the structure subject-predicate as well, having as a consequence the fact that every difference among the elements of the judgement vanishes into the whole. Therefore, since it is not made of judgements, logic cannot be regarded as a language.

At this point some similarities with the tautologies of the *Tractatus* can be drawn. Both tautologies and the speculative proposition can be considered the extreme points that language has reached in expression and, at the same time, as the destruction of the structure of an ordinary proposition.

It needs to be recalled that Wittgenstein claims a destructive role for both tautologies and contradictions in the *Tractatus* since they are not just the propositions which are always true or always false, but they are defined, first of all, as the dissolution of the articulation of an ordinary sentence. Besides, since tautologies are also defined, for Wittgenstein, as "logical propositions" (TLP: 6.1), they contain a reference to logic as what is beyond language and, therefore, what is not language. Similarly it happens, as the above quoted paragraph 37 of the PS shows, for the adjective "speculative" for the proposition of the PS.

This comparison with the logical propositions shows its importance in that it allows one to see the speculative proposition as a limit in the same sense as the tautologies.

On the one hand, tautologies cannot be considered limits in the sense of a mathematical asymptote because they do not show a tendency towards anything. In fact, remaining on the internal side of language, they are still well-formed sentences which cannot be placed outside language. The fact that they contain a reference to logic does not mean that they are hints pointing to logic: tautologies stay inside language, since they are on the inner side of the limit. If tautologies showed a tendency towards anything, this would mean that the completeness of language (in contrast to its inadequacy) could not be explained. Therefore, a limit is drawn in language and nothing is left with the dissolution of the proposition.

On the other hand, the speculative proposition is collocated at the end of the path of consciousness, having the double function to gather all the previous moments and to destroy the structure of judgement. Therefore, the speculative proposition is the highest point reached by language and also the internal limit of consciousness and of the *Phenomenology*. Since it is a limit, it indicates the end of the path of consciousness, drawing the separation between the *Phenomenology* and the *Science of Logic*. Therefore, both the speculative proposition and the tautologies have the function of separating language from logic. For this reason, it can be said that the *Phenomenology* is concluded with the speculative proposition.

4 A=A, the transition between the *Phenomenology* and the *Science of Logic*

Absolute knowing is introduced in the last chapter of the work from 1807 as the last shape of consciousness. Consciousness recognises the object before it *as itself* because it frees itself from any opposition with it (Chiereghin 2008: pp.15–16).

Since the difference between consciousness and object, which is found at the beginning of the work, vanishes, this means that the former difference reveals itself as the identity between consciousness and object. Now, the moment in which consciousness recognises the most profound difference (the object) as itself corresponds to the shape of absolute knowing (ibid.: p.34).

With the act of consciousness freeing itself, the *Phenomenology* opens to the *Science of Logic* which can begin. In fact, it is well known that the absolute can be regarded as the transition between Hegel's two works, in that it is the topic of the last chapter of the *Phenomenology* and what begins the *Science of Logic*, as can be seen from the following passage:

> A beginning is logical in that it is to be made in the element of a free, self-contained thought, in pure knowledge; it is thereby mediated, for pure knowledge is the ultimate and absolute truth of consciousness. (SL 2010: p.46)

Here Hegel is referring to the last chapter of the *Phenomenology* in which consciousness frees itself from any opposition, reaching pure or absolute knowing. Free of these oppositions, as a result of the path of consciousness in the *Phenomenology*, the *Science of Logic* finds its beginning. Since the absolute is the transition mentioned, whereas the speculative proposition is a limit, this means that the absolute and the speculative proposition cannot be identified.

It has been said that the two works are connected by the absolute which is defined in the preface to the *Phenomenology* as the identity A=A (PS 1977: §16).

Furthermore, the quoted passage from the *Science of Logic* also shows that the absolute is what connects the two works. This very absolute is what can be found in the last chapter of the *Phenomenology* as what presents no difference between consciousness and object, as seen before. This means that there is an identity between the "absolutes" of the two works and that a transition between the *Phenomenology* and the *Science of Logic* occurs through the equals sign. Therefore, the connection between the two works can be pictured as if the first A of the equivalence finds itself on the other side of it, as if it were projected through the equals sign. If the transition can be found in the equals sign, this means that we are talking about the absolute of the *Phenomenology* or the absolute of the *Science of Logic*, depending on which side of the equals sign one switches. The relation between Hegel's works is explained as follows:

> The moment does not appear as this movement of passing back and forth, from consciousness or picture-thinking into self-consciousness and conversely: on the contrary, its pure shape, freed from its appearance in consciousness, the pure Notion and its onward movement, depends solely on its pure *determinateness*. Conversely, to each abstract moment of Science corresponds a shape of manifest Spirit as such (PS 1977: §807).

Therefore, the transition which occurs through the equals sign connecting the "absolutes" gives rise to a correspondence between the two works.

The topic of the absolute introduces the much-debated question about the relation between the *Phenomenology* and the *Science of Logic*, this due to the consequences of some ambiguous remarks from Hegel:

> Hegel first speaks of the *Phenomenology* as follows: "This becoming of science in general or of knowledge is that which this *Phenomenology of Spirit* presents as the first part of the system of this science." Shortly before his death in 1831, Hegel was engaged in the preparation of a new edition of the *Phenomenology*. He then struck out the phrase "as the first part of the system of this science." At the same time however he left unaltered (in the course of revising for a new edition of his works) a passage in the *Science of Logic*, dating originally from 1812, in which he refers to the *Phenomenology* as "the science of appearing Spirit," the "presupposition" of the Logic. (Rosen 2000: p.124)

Some pages later, Rosen claims that the majority of commentators prefer to take into consideration Hegel's mature view according to which the *Phenomenology* works as an introduction to the whole system, assuming that "presupposition" and "introduction" are synonyms. For example, Chiereghin states that the *Phenomenology* works as an introduction to the concept of science which is found in the *Science of Logic* and, according to Hegel himself, the Concept does not need any justification since it was received from the *Phenomenology* (Chiereghin 2011: p.14). Similarly, Lamb claims:

> The *Phenomenology* was originally intended as a ladder to the standpoint of philosophy which, in the course of writing became a major work of philosophy capable of existing alongside the *Logic*—his second attempt at a system—and his other works. For this reason there were no major revisions of the *Phenomenology*. The *Logic* is not the second part of the system, it is the second attempt to produce one. (Lamb 1979: p.94)

In sum, the problem regards Hegel's change of mind about the status of the *Phenomenology*, the condition of which is ambiguous because of the term "presupposition," which divides the commentators concerning the question of whether the *Phenomenology* is to be considered an introduction to the *Science of Logic* or an autonomous work.

Nevertheless, the fact that the speculative proposition has been identified as a limit of the *Phenomenology* means that Hegel's 1807 work is complete. Therefore, it has to be considered an autonomous work; this meaning that the *Phenomenology* cannot be regarded as a simple introduction to Hegel's system of science.

If the *Phenomenology* is equated with the *Science of Logic*, it means on the one hand that the 1807 work cannot be regarded as subordinated or depending on the *Science of Logic* and that, on the other hand, the *Science of Logic* is not simply a sequel to the *Phenomenology*. Therefore, since the *Phenomenology* is not an introduction, the term "presupposition" cannot be a synonym of the term "introduction." The term "presupposition" directly connects with the characteristics of logic being mediated.

According to Rosen logic is mediated for Hegel (although in a particular sense). The meaning of this regards, for Rosen, the much-debated question about the relation between the *Phenomenology* and the *Science of Logic* in such a way:

> We can now continue with Hegel's own exposition of the problem of a beginning. The beginning must be either immediate or mediated, and yet it is easy to show that neither of these is possible. Hegel means that each is self-contradictory. A mediated beginning is one that arises out of antecedent terms; it is therefore not a beginning. But an immediate beginning is impossible, because everything in heaven or on earth or in spirit contains *both* immediacy and mediation. What we call "immediate" is always the result of a previous mediation. (Rosen 2013: p.82)

First of all, the *Science of Logic* can be said to have a beginning, despite the fact that the *Phenomenology* works as its presupposition, because the term does not mean "introduction," but the necessary path of consciousness which finds a limit to its experience and which logic is beyond, which consciousness cannot access. Logic is mediated because, without the path of consciousness through its shapes and its limit, it would be impossible to come to the absolute, this determining the impossibility of the *Science of Logic*. Logic, therefore, is mediated in one sense because it needs the experience of consciousness in the *Phenomenology*, but it is not mediated because this experience is annulled so that it can be spoken of as a beginning of logic. Rosen's explanation solves the apparent oddity that Hegel generates, claiming that logic is without presupposition: logic can annul the experience of consciousness, since it stands in its autonomy as well as the *Phenomenology* which has, therefore, the same dignity of the *Science of Logic*. Consider proposition 5.552 from the *Tractatus*:

> The "experience" that we need in order to understand logic is not that something or other is the state of things, but that something *is:* that however is not an experience.
> Logic is *prior* to every experience—that something *is so.*
> It is prior to the question "How?", not prior to the question "What?" (TLP: 5.552)

In the *Tractatus*, Wittgenstein does not say much about experience. Still, with reference to the case of tautologies, it is said that experience cannot contradict or confirm their truth (TLP: 6.1222). Therefore, experience is what the proposition is compared to and what confirms the truth or falsehood of the proposition. If this is so, it means that the limits of language coincide with the limits of experience, which logic is beyond, as opposed to experience, like the above passage shows. Nevertheless, this quote seems paradoxical because we would need an experience of something that is not determinate (we just know that something is), which, in the end, reveals itself as not an experience. The problem is solved if we bear in mind that logic does not have to be understood because the process of understanding is a criterion related to the proposition and to its sense (TLP: 4.02). So, the passage is intended to explain not only that logic is neither an experience nor a descriptive process (which would answer to the question "How?"), but also that logic annuls the range of language circumscribed by tautologies and contradictions, which coincides with that of experience. In fact, it needs to be recalled that logic establishes a close connection with the tautologies which are defined as "logical propositions." This, together with the fact that logic is not a language, shows that the dissolution of the articulation of an ordinary proposition is a characteristic that tautologies share with the logic of the *Tractatus*. For this reason, it can be said that logic annuls language in the same way tautology and contradiction destroy the structure of an ordinary proposition. In fact, experience tells that something "is so," i.e., that something is determinate, but this determination is what is lost with the destruction of the structure of the proposition in tautologies and contradictions. Therefore, what remains is that "something is", i.e., no determination, no proposition, no experience. The range of language or experience has come to an end and logic begins beyond the realm of propositions. Logic, therefore, is not immediate, something which we access directly, but requires the necessary step of the limits of language reached in tautology and contradiction. From the passage, a further reference to logic can be noted, as what is mediated through the limit of language. Therefore, the function of tautology and contradiction consists of limiting the language coming to the "destruction" of the proposition and of separating it from logic, which is not a language for Wittgenstein, since it does not coincide with the realm of propositions and is beyond it.

Eventually, the *Phenomenology of Spirit* and the *Tractatus* have the same function—as we might call it—of "liberation." As Chiereghin says, in the *Phenomenology* consciousness frees itself from all its oppositions with the object, whereas in the *Tractatus* it is language "freeing from itself". This can be seen in propositions 6 and 6.54. Proposition 6 is the general form of the proposition, and it shows the composition of language (from elementary propositions to their totality) and the self-negation of it. Negating itself, language negates its limits found in tautology and contradiction. Therefore, language frees itself. Consider proposition 6.54:

> My propositions are elucidatory in this way: he who understands me finally recognizes them as senseless [*unsinnig*], when he has climbed out through them, on them, over them. (He must so to speak throw away the ladder, after he has climbed up on it.)
>
> He must surmount these propositions; then he sees the world rightly. (TLP: 6.54)

This proposition does not mean that the *Tractatus* is useless or self-defeating. Nonsense [*Unsinn*] is something that cannot be judged (TLP: 5.5422), something, therefore, that is not a proposition since, like logic, it is beyond language. So, the above proposition means that language reneges, having complied with its function in the points where it reaches its limits. Beyond these limits language cannot be.

Now, the metaphor is explicative of the matter. The fundamental point about the ladder representing language is that the ladder must be not only climbed but overcome. Therefore, those who climb the ladder go through it as well as through language and, being able to overcome it, access nonsense where no proposition or language can be found. This means that the propositions of language stop being themselves, once the ladder has been overcome. This can be elicited by the fact that the propositions of the *Tractatus* are *recognised* as nonsenses (*erkennen* is the German verb used by Wittgenstein), this meaning that they undertake this process, overcoming their dimension. In fact, the recognition indicates not that the propositions are to be considered absurdities, but that they *become* nonsenses if they overcome their linguistic dimension.

This is paramount because it shows that the *Tractatus* is not to be considered a plain nonsense being constituted of nonsenses. The point lies in overcoming the ladder made of propositions: they find their limits in tautology and contradiction, going beyond their own dimension and becoming nonsenses much like how consciousness reaches its limit in the speculative proposition beyond which occurs the transition through absolute knowing of the *Phenomenology* and absolute knowing of the beginning of the *Science of Logic*.

References

Black, Max: *A Companion to Wittgenstein's Tractatus*, Cambridge University Press, 1964.
Chiereghin, Franco: *La Fenomenologia dello Spirito di Hegel. Introduzione alla lettura*, Carocci, 2004.
Chiereghin, Franco: *Rileggere la Scienza della logica di Hegel*, Carocci, 2011.
Floyd, Juliet: "Wittgenstein, Mathematics and Philosophy", in: Alice Crary and Rupert Read (eds.): *The New Wittgenstein*, Routledge, 2000, pp.232–261.
Lamb, David: *Language and Perception in Hegel and Wittgenstein*, Avebury, 1979.
Nordmann, Alfred: *Wittgenstein's Tractatus. An Introduction*, Cambridge University Press, 2005.
Ostrow, Matthew: *Wittgenstein's Tractatus. A Dialectical Interpretation*, Cambridge University Press, 2001.
Rosen, Stanley: *G.W.F. Hegel. An Introduction to the Science of Wisdom*, St. Augustine's Press, 2000.
Rosen, Stanley: *The Idea of Hegel's Science of Logic*, Chicago University Press, 2013.
Von Wright, Georg: "Pictures, Logic, and the Limits of Sense", in: Alois Pichler and Simo Säätelä (eds.): *Wittgenstein: The Philosopher and his Works*, Ontos Verlag, 2006, pp.98–106.

Vojtěch Kolman
Master, Slave and Wittgenstein: The Dialectic of Rule-Following

Abstract *Pace* Wittgenstein's saying that he sees differences where Hegel sees identities, I start this chapter by claiming that Hegel's and Wittgenstein's philosophies are, in some important sense, identical or similar to each other. And I suggest that this identity consists in the way Hegel and Wittgenstein develop their concepts of knowledge from more primitive forms of consciousness and bring them to a cautiously optimistic closure based on the sociality of reason, particularly as mirrored in Hegel's *master–slave parable* and Wittgenstein's *private language argument*. The basic idea behind my line of thought is to read Hegel's master–slave parable not as a loose reference to the problem of *mastering* a rule but as a complex epistemological argument concerning the *struggle* between mere "private" opinions, resulting in the emergence of intersubjective knowledge. According to Wittgenstein's examples, the mastering of a rule arises from the mutual conditioning of the *pupil and his teacher* in the process of following a rule. What is risked here, I claim, is the certainty of one's private opinion, which, in its aiming at objective knowledge, necessarily becomes fallible.

Besides some minor remarks concerning Schopenhauer and Kant, one of the most explicit links connecting Wittgenstein to the tradition of German idealism is the seemingly inconsequential remark reported by Drury:

> Hegel seems to me to be always wanting to say that things which look different are really the same. Whereas my interest is in showing that things which look the same are really different. (MDC: p.157)

This remark is of particular interest for many reasons, one of them being that it seems to anticipate Adorno's (1966) critique of Hegel's absolute idealism as being an *identity philosophy* which tries to sweep all the differences and dissonances of life under the carpet of some unified whole, thus making it sterile or even unhuman.

It would be interesting to investigate whether and to what extent Wittgenstein's philosophy (with its concepts of language-game, forms of life and family resemblances) qualifies as a *non-identity* or *difference philosophy* in Adorno's terms. But taking into account the dependency of Adorno's thinking on Hegel's philosophical system, before such a task might even be considered—and applied

https://doi.org/10.1515/9783110572780-017

to Wittgenstein as, for example, Bowie (2013) did with respect to Brandom and his unifying concept of sapience—I believe that another work has to be written; a work that presents Hegel and Wittgenstein, if not as working on the same project then as being at least roughly commensurable as far as their general principles, methods and goals are concerned.

I aim to do this by focusing on the rule-following episode of the *Philosophical Investigations* and the arguments that Wittgenstein gives there in favour of his new concept of knowledge based on game-related metaphors as opposed to the picturing metaphors of the *Tractatus*. I will read these arguments as carrying out what Hegel considered one of the main goals of his philosophy: to overcome *the subject–object distinction* that arises within so-called *natural* consciousness—and leads subsequently to various forms of epistemic scepticism—and, by way of continuous transformation, replace it with the *subject–subject distinction* known under the heading of self-consciousness or, in the end, *Absolute Spirit* (see, for example, JS: p.22). In my reading, Wittgenstein, with his concept of the language-game, not only associates himself with Hegel's goal, but also adopts Hegel's own remedy, namely a socially rooted concept of knowledge. This thesis of mine will be supported by a parallel reading—or rather reconceptualization—of the first paragraphs of Wittgenstein's *Philosophical Investigations* and the first chapters of Hegel's *Phenomenology of Spirit*, particularly in relation to their respective endpoints: the private language argument on the one hand and the master–slave parable on the other.

1 Idea and Concept

Before I turn to the rule-following enterprise, which will constitute the backbone of my argument, let me quickly sketch a broader idealist framework into which Wittgenstein's philosophy can be embedded. The largest arc—known also as the transformation of the early Wittgenstein into the late Wittgenstein—stretches between two points: the *Tractatus* and the *Philosophical Investigations*. In a sense, this arc repeats the transformation of Kant's transcendental idealism into its Hegelian version within the work of a single author. This time, the role of the *a priori* structures of the mind is played by the structure of *language*, according to a transcendental reading of language as a condition of the possibility of any experience.

As is known, the first point of this large Wittgensteinian arc, *Tractatus Logico-Philosophicus*, is based on the *difference* between two holistic structures: the totality of all meaningful propositions, or *language*, and the corresponding *world* of elementary facts, in their projective relation based on the *identity* of the representational form. Now, it is not difficult to interpret Hegel in his *Science of Logic* as drawing the same picture under the heading of *Idea*, or *Concept*, which is analogous to Wittgenstein's totality of language in its projective relation to the world. This is how I read the following passage from his *Encyclopaedia*:

> The idea is the *truth*; for the truth is this, that objectivity corresponds to the concept [...]. (E 1817/E I: §213)

For Hegel, of course, the Idea of the *Tractatus* is an undeveloped one, suffering heavily from antinomies such as those of Kant or Russell. It is because this Idea has not yet reached the status of dialectical reason but only the level of mere Understanding which "makes easy work of pointing out that everything said of the idea is self-contradictory" (EL 1830/2010: §214). Not being able to solve the antinomies, but only to avoid them by preaching the "oath of silence" (see Section 3 for further details), the Wittgenstein of the *Tractatus* treats the whole subject–object (language–world) difference in a detached and static way. But: "the idea is essentially a process" (E 1817/E I: §215).

It is the insight that language is not a mere picture of something different from it but a living substance that develops itself from its own resources and by its own measures with which Wittgenstein enters the second phase of his philosophy, this time under the heading of *language-games*. As a self-subsistent whole which cannot have any external other, for the late Wittgenstein language represents an analogue of the *Absolute Idea* in which "every sentence [...] is in order as it is" and for which "there must be a perfect order even in the vaguest sentence" (PI: §8). Put another way, language is not a mere tool for achieving the goals given independently of it, e. g., to describe the external prelinguistic world, but a *form of life*, justified by its own means and having itself as its own goal.

2 Sense certainty

Let me now focus on the finer structure of the point at the other end of Wittgenstein's arc, the *Philosophical Investigations*. Here, Hegel's *Phenomenology of Spirit* presents itself as a natural comparative standard, containing a corresponding arc that stretches from an initial critique of attempts to provide significance by pointing to the world, that is by *ostensive definition*, to knowledge primarily conceived as a *social institution*. The peculiar structural feature of this arc is its overall negative quality, in which no part of the argument is an outspokenly positive standpoint but instead a refutation of some previous, seemingly natural concept of knowledge.

Both Wittgenstein and Hegel believe that *scepticism* arising from this negative journey might be brought to a cautiously optimistic conclusion connected to the essential sociality of reason. This conclusion is, in fact, what Kripke (1982) in his famous reading of Wittgenstein calls a *sceptical solution* to the *sceptical paradox*. It corresponds to Hegel's transformation of knowledge from a *path of despair* to the *path of progress*. Hence, the general congruence of Hegel's and Wittgenstein's endeavours, as I intend to show, is guaranteed by:
(1) the similar structure of the first parts of the *Philosophical Investigations* and *Phenomenology of Spirit*, and
(2) the consequences that this isomorphism has for the resulting concept of knowledge.

Let me start with (1). This first and rather obvious similarity is reflected in the opening sections of the respective books, which deny the idea (on which "natural consciousness" is based) that there is a direct link between our knowledge and its object. In the analytic tradition of Russell and Wittgenstein, this link goes back to the idea of words functioning as names for objects external to them, with their relation being based on ostensive definition. Hegel's chapter on sense certainty deals with this very problem (to the extent that one can say, following Solomon (1983: p.326), that "whether or not Russell ever read his Hegel [...], Hegel knew his Russell") by deconstructing the presupposition that ostensive definition works in this way. The seemingly rich and direct meaning assignments by proclamations and gestures such as "here" and "now", which according to Russell are the only true names, are shown to be the most empty and indirect ones.

As Lamb (1980: pp.77–78)—*mutatis mutandis*—put it: if it is in the immediacy of the "here" and "now" that you find knowledge, then tell me what it is that you know. And if your reply is, "I know that there is a table in front of me", you are bringing in other matters. You are making a classification, thus mediating the alleged immediacy. And finally:

> If I say that this stapling machine is eight inches from my nose at 10 p.m. on the 18th March 1978, I have brought in a reference to the whole history of mankind. (ibid.)

And this is also exactly what Wittgenstein was aiming at. He does not deny the importance of ostensive definition, but stresses that the act of pointing out or naming something requires the *whole stage* on which it can be played (PI: §257). Thus, ostension is never a matter of a singular gesture totally isolated from its environment and thus determinate, but a complex holistic affair with what might be called an *infinite* dimension. In a kind of Hegelian short cut, this point brings us to the concept of infinity.

3 Infinity

One of the main benefits of Kripke's famous reading of Wittgenstein's *Philosophical Investigations* consists in its focus on mathematics, where meanings are quite typically of an *infinite nature*. To master, for example, what the expression 7 + 5 = 12 means, one must quite obviously know what 2 + 2 = 4 or 1345 + 2344 = 3689, and so on, mean; that is, one must be able to follow the infinite rule associated with the operation of addition. In light of this, it seems rather obvious that such a mastering cannot be reduced only to pointing to some worldly object, as Augustine suggested, because the given addition is never completely realised. In other words, one is never able to perform all the individual additions at once.

And this observation is quite general: to learn something—for example, what the word "cat" means—is to master some rule allowing me to apply this word to instances of a cat that I have never seen before. As such, these instances, or their *re*-presentations, are obviously unlimited or *infinite* in their number as opposed to the *finite* number of instances of cats on which my mastering was based. Now, it seems that this *infinity of meaning* works in the same way as the *indeterminacy of ostension*, namely overthrowing the notion of "natural consciousness" with its simplistic picture of knowledge as based on the direct correspondence of subject and object. But there is more to it than this.

In the Kantian and early Wittgensteinian picture, every part of the world of which one can speak is, by definition, *finite*. Infinity, on the other hand, pertains exclusively to the whole, be it language, the world or the mysterious God who does not reveal himself in this world. This explains why talk about these totalities necessarily leads to the paradoxes of reason: by talking about the whole one makes—by the very form of the talk—the infinite finite. As for the indeterminacy of ostension, it does not change this overall picture, but only forces us to compare the whole of language with the whole of the world instead of only comparing their elements. Wittgenstein in his "middle" period phrased it like this:

> I once wrote "A proposition is like a ruler laid against reality. Only the outermost graduating marks touch the object to be measured." I would now rather say: a *system* of propositions is laid against reality like a ruler. What I mean is this: when I lay ruler against a spatial object, I lay all the graduating lines against it at the same time. It is not individual graduating lines that are laid beside it, but the whole scale. If I know that the object reaches up to the mark 10, I know also immediately that it does not reach to the mark 11, 12, and so on. (WVC: p.63)

With the infinity of meaning, however, the situation becomes untenable because the infinity permeates every single element of the picture. In Wittgenstein's parable, there are no fixed graduating lines on the ruler. This makes the antinomies of reason not only unavoidable—as Kant admitted in the transcendental dialectics—but also, as Hegel argued, constitutive of the development of knowledge, which becomes infinite simply by definition.

4 Life

With the rule-following phenomenon at hand, it is now easy to see how both Hegel and Wittgenstein use the concept of infinity in a complex dialectical way. If understanding what something (for example, a particular cat) is amounts to mastering the (potentially) infinite progression of instances and counter-instances of cats in a finite way, as a rule of some game, then this rule cannot exist only abstractly on some piece of paper or in the mind, as Kant still seemed to suggest, but must be lived and as such freely developed according to somebody's needs. In this sense, every object is at the same time both finite and infinite, something for which Hegel reserved the term *true infinity*, as opposed to the mere possibility of extending the given progression of cats and non-cats in an indefinite way, in the manner of *bad infinity* (SL 2010: p.109). (See also Kolman (2016) and Stekeler-Weithofer (2005: ch.7) for further details concerning the difference between "bad" and "true" infinity.)

It is no coincidence that in the *Phenomenology of Spirit* the topic of infinity is raised at the very verge of the transition from natural consciousness to self-consciousness, connected to the reflective ascent in which knowledge becomes its own object, and thus self-knowledge. This is where the subject–subject model of knowledge first appears. It comes, incidentally, quite naturally after the section devoted to the *inverted world*, where the subject–object difference is revealed to be reversible, and as such inadequate to its purported goal (see particularly PS 2018: §160). In the *Tractatus*, a similar proto-step towards the reflective turn is taken when Wittgenstein (TLP: 3.14) relativises the difference between the picture (such as a sentence) and the depicted fact by observing that the picture in its projective relation to the world is also a fact and might be, as such, inversely depicted by the given piece of reality.

In a surprising and radical explanatory twist, Hegel calls the resulting reflective turn "the simple essence of life" (PS 2018: §162), life now being the very object of knowledge as well as knowledge itself (PS 2018: §168). In the *Science of Logic* (SL 2010: p.676), life is determined as the first stage in the development of the Absolute Idea. The stress on this animate, "self-sufficient" and "restless" quality of knowledge (PS 2018: §§168 ff.) corresponds, in my reading, quite naturally to Wittgenstein's general insight that all words have their meanings only if *used* in linguistic practices. Accordingly, language is self-sufficient because it does not have any external goal and always subsists off its own resources. And it is restless because *it is not* simply *there* but lives as a part of human practices that must be maintained.

5 Sceptical paradox

When dealing with knowledge that is based on the subject–object distinction, scepticism arises regarding the possibility that we can know anything at all. Its basic form looks like this: if knowledge's role is to enable a pregiven object to be described by a cognising subject distinct from it, the possibility will always be open that the meaning has not been correctly captured. Similarly, the history of knowledge as an unending story of one theory being succeeded by another, and then by another, etc., evokes in us the picture of what Hegel (PS 2018: §78) called a path of despair, where no stable point can be found or guaranteed. Both the indeterminacy and the infinity of meaning only seem to support these sceptical conclusions.

In Kripke's (1982) reading, Wittgenstein depicts this very situation in the form of a *sceptical paradox*. How can I know, the Wittgensteinian sceptic asks, that somebody to whom I am teaching some rule—for example, what a cat is— has acquired this rule as I meant it? The only testimony that I can have will be based on the finite number of examples she or he will give me if asked, and these do not suffice to justify the conclusion, which relates to the potential infinity of instances constituting the rule. According to Kripke, this "sceptical paradox" corresponds to what is known as Hume's *problem of induction* in its original application to the justification of the laws of nature. Historically, there are two basic approaches to this phenomenon, which can be interpreted respectively as a negative and a positive solution to the paradox:
1. The *negative* solution is that of Hume, who concludes that the inferential transfer from finitely many instances to some general law is unjustified and unjustifiable by rational, logical means. As such, it is quite "irrationally" based on our *habit* of expecting that which happens more frequently rather than that which happens less frequently.
2. Kant's solution is a rather specific example of the *positive* approach, which finds a way to justify the rationality of the general law without justifying the validity of the inductive inference. According to Kant, laws and rules are

valid because they stem from the apriority of our reason, which prescribes them to the world as it appears to us.

The overall positivity of the Kantian solution, of course, depends on the positive nature of the *a priori* structures of reason and the corresponding transcendental I that guarantees them. And this holds equally for the position adopted by Wittgenstein in his *Tractatus* (5.6331) and its idea of the unseeable Big Eye. But the question arises: are these positions not merely replacing the untenable subject–object model with the subject–subject model, which, because it leads to epistemic *solipsism*, is also untenable? In such a case, the path of despair turns itself into the conceited path of self-congratulation and is thus another reason for scepticism. The positivity of the given solution would only be a virtual one.

6 We are the world

Placing the sceptical paradox along with its two solutions—the negative one of Hume's empiricism and the positive one of Kant's idealism—into the historical context of modern philosophy enables us to foresee where Wittgenstein's own solution is going. In the given context, it quite straightforwardly corresponds to a Hegelian synthesis of both. Here, the unexplained status of the transcendental I as something that unifies the subject–object difference and as such—being neither subject nor object—cannot be talked about, is dissolved into the structure of the transcendental We. This We (or Hegel's *Spirit*) is society as a dialectical middle point between the radical objectivity of the external and thus unreachable world and the radical subjectivity of the private and thus utterly solipsistic mind.

In Kripke's reading of Wittgenstein, this synthesis corresponds to what Kripke calls the sceptical solution to the sceptical paradox. The question "How do I know that somebody has already mastered some rule?" cannot have a positive answer in the sense of pointing to some directly accessible evidence such as an external object. Its apparent unsolvability disappears, though, if one asks inversely "How can the given subject *himself* know that he has mastered what he was supposed to?" From this, the promised sceptical solution easily follows because the sought-after answer obviously can be found *neither* in the external world of objects *nor* in the privacy of the given subject's mind, but, so to speak, between them, in the very "fact" that both the teacher and the student understand each other sufficiently. This is the point Wittgenstein (PI: §199) arrives at when he says that rule-following is an institution.

The resulting solution is not positive, simply because one can never eliminate the prospective discord of society's members. But it is not negative either, because knowledge is not only possible, but real, stemming from the existing consensus already presupposed, for example, in formulating the sceptical paradox as something others can understand. As such, it might be compared either to the naturalisation of Kant or the idealisation of Hume. Both are anticipated by Hegel who, on the one hand, places the apriority of reason into the structures of society, and, on the other, stresses the active and prescriptive property of habit which does not arise passively, but always in a mutual interaction with the environment.

7 Desire

The point of the preceding exposition is not only to depict the transition from the subject–object model of knowledge to the subject–subject model, as is in my reading entertained by both Hegel and Wittgenstein, but also to point out their joint emphasis on the non-trivial, non-solipsistic nature of the latter concept of knowledge. This emphasis corresponds to the moment where the initial fragments of the respective books coincide and, moreover, at which the sketched exegetical arc is closed. In the rest of my paper, I want to identify this closure with the private language argument in Wittgenstein's part of the arc and the master–slave parable in Hegel's part.

As for the private language argument, Kripke (1982) suggested its core can be found in the paragraphs preceding §243, namely in the very formulation of the sceptical paradox. The key passage is the following:

> And hence also "obeying a rule" is a practice. And to think one is obeying a rule is not to obey a rule. Hence it is not possible to obey a rule "privately": otherwise thinking one was obeying a rule would be the same thing as obeying it. (PI: §202)

One can read this passage quite straightforwardly as follows: if one leaves matters of rule-following so that they only depend on the decision of the cognising subject, then obeying some rule—and thus deciding what things *are*—will become identical with thinking that one is obeying some rule or what things only *seem* to be. And this will qualify the whole enterprise of rule-following as useless, because to master this or that rule will be as good as mastering any other rule and as such is good for nothing.

Hegel's master–slave parable is the segment of the *Phenomenology* that begins the part concerning self-consciousness. Though the parable does not seem, at first, to have a lot in common with Wittgenstein's private language argument, I claim that it actually offers us a finer and richer version of it. To see this, let us first keep in mind the already-described explanatory arc that starts by casting doubt upon the subject–object difference and the direct representational relation that obtains between its poles. In the transitional paragraphs of the *Phenomenology*, where the inadequacy of natural consciousness is made transparent, Hegel replaces this relation with what he calls "desire", thus stressing its basically subjective, human-oriented drift, which is connected essentially to the previously established concept of "life". In the second step, the continuous transition from primitive desires such as hunger or sex to complex ones—including the desire to know—comes into focus. This transition, of course, needs some time and space, as Brandom demonstrated in his paper (2007) and in the manuscript of his forthcoming *The Spirit of Trust* (2014).

Brandom's basic idea is that human desire, as described by Hegel, has a *tripartite* structure. He means by this that, unlike the *dyadic* relation of some stimulus to the reaction it directly causes (for example, of the wet environment to the rusting iron bar), phenomena such as being hungry include:
(1) the object of the given desire, as well as
(2) the subjective pole of desire in which one treats an object as food by trying to eat it (which makes the object food *for* consciousness), and
(3) the desire's objective pole in which the thing taken for food satisfies the given need (it is food *in* itself).

These poles are, of course, only relative to each other, both depending in some sense on the desiring subject. As such, they are in principle affected by Wittgenstein's private language argument, and the question arises of whether this is not, in fact, the last word in the whole story. Is there some *a priori* reason why one could not treat desire as having the private structure in which to desire something and to think that I desire something is the same thing? And the straightforward answer—supposing that one takes Wittgenstein's argument to be valid—is "No". But the point of Wittgenstein's, as well as Hegel's, exposition is that one needs to keep the desire's subjective and objective poles (their "in itself" and "for itself") apart if one wants to achieve the more complex desires which are not defined just by their direct satisfaction, as in the dyadic case of the rusting iron, but also by a concurrent intention. In the case of knowledge—as opposed, for example, to the desire for an itch to stop—this differentiation creates the possibility of error. The resulting fallibility of knowledge is an epiphenomenon connected to the general sociality of human experience, which both Hegel and Wittgenstein promote and justify in their subject–subject model of knowledge.

8 Master and pupil

This is where the master–slave parable comes in, within the context of what Hegel calls the desire for *recognition*. The basic situation looks like this: the subject wants to see his desire as having objective validity and, to achieve that, he makes his desire explicit, as being something that he is prepared to die for. The death, in the end, does not have to be the physical death of the desiring subject, but the metaphorical death or falsification of his public claim by another subject (see Brandom (2014) and Stekeler-Weithofer (2008; 2014) for further elaboration on this reading). It is in this very act of abandoning the privacy and safety of one's own mind that the difference between what is and what only seems to be is established, by making the objective pole of the original desire guaranteed by recognition by another subject. In this way, the social version of the subject–subject difference gradually arises from the subject–object difference not as its rejection, but as its sublation or *Aufhebung* in Hegel's sense of the word.

In his *Phenomenology*, Hegel devotes substantial space to the continuous advance of the sociality of reason from its "deficient modes", as Heidegger would say, starting with the asymmetric relations of master and slave. In the master–slave parable, this relation arises from the struggle for recognition in which one of the struggling subjects is—as a result of his unconditional surrender—*objectified*, and the other assumes the role of the primeval all-dominating *subject*. In the turn known as the dialectic of master and slave, this again leads to the instability of the subject–object model, though in a different, more refined sense.

Though he does not do it explicitly, nor in Hegel's systematic fashion, in his *Philosophical Investigations* Wittgenstein also allows for this stage of spirit's development by introducing the topic of rule-following in a fictive dialogue between a teacher (of mathematics) and his pupil. This recapitulates Hegel's parable in the following sense: first, it is the teacher who, by definition, stipulates what there *is*, or what there is to *know*, making the pupil totally dependent on what the teacher means to be followed: that is, what is right and wrong. At the same time, it is obvious that this situation is not by its own measure stable, because somebody is a teacher only if he is able to teach somebody something, the success of which is not completely dependent on the teacher. (Notice that we have here Brandom's tripartite structure of desire, this time with respect to the desire to teach somebody something.) Confronted with a teacher who thinks of himself as the absolute authority, to the extent of being able to jeopardise the student's every attempt at giving the correct answer, the student—like the slave in Hegel's parable—becomes at least derivatively autonomous by willingly recognising the teacher as an authority from which he might learn something and/or by being forced to find the answer on his own. Hence, it is in the very act of learning, not only in its results, that the student overcomes the subjectivity of knowledge to which the dogmatic teacher falls prey.

Arguably, it is the aim of every sound educational practice to avoid this as a final stage and to develop a curriculum that purposefully ends up with teacher and student being more or less equal partners in their dialogue. In proclaiming the rule and the activity of rule-following to be a social institution, Wittgenstein, contrary to Hegel, omits the intermittent stages and jumps almost directly to the fully developed, symmetric concept of knowledge so as to primarily deal with the refutation of its purely solipsistic reading. This is the content of the paragraphs devoted explicitly to the private language argument from §243 on, which deal with problems such as the criteria for my referring to sensations, claiming that I have pain, that I intend to do something, etc.

This anti-solipsistic emphasis is more than justified in the light of the prevailing tendency to hold social concepts of knowledge as being purely conventional, in the sense that it is society, as opposed to the "objective world", that decides on what there is by simple fiat. What one forgets here is that the social consensus is not something that is easy to comprehend; it certainly cannot be revealed by a simple proclamation or by voting. The fully developed society in Hegel's or Wittgenstein's sense is not a new master with the society's members as its subordinates, but the totality of free agents maintaining symmetric relations with each other. As a result, the difference between the acting subject and the "hard to get" object is still preserved, but this time mediated by another subject.

9 Fallibility of knowledge

In the previous sections, the similarity of the structures of the first parts of the *Philosophical Investigations* and *Phenomenology of Spirit* was discussed. Describing this similarity was the first part of the task formulated above in Section 2, namely to show that there is a congruence between Hegel's and Wittgenstein's philosophies. Now I will move on to the second part of my task: evaluating the consequences that this similarity has for the resulting concept of knowledge.

The main benefit of comparing the master–slave parable with the private language argument consists in making the *fallibility* of knowledge explicit as one of its defining and positive features. At first, of course, it looks instead to be the other way around, because knowledge is traditionally held to be endowed with certainty, particularly in its delimitation from mere opinion. But after the subject–object model and its solipsistic subject–subject counterpart (as corresponding, e.g., to the dogmatic teacher–student relation) are shown to be unsustainable, it is the fallibility that makes the social concept of knowledge a cautiously optimistic way out of the resulting scepticism. To get this "optimistic" quality right, I recommend considering the following points of interest.

(1) In the course of its refutation or, rather, sublation, the subject–object difference is made symmetrical by treating the object as subject and object at once. It is an *object* in the sense that it serves as an independent standard for measuring the objectivity of truth. It is a *subject* because such a measure is always relative to society's needs and the development of these needs. Knowledge is thus, as Brandom (1994) said, the *hybrid deontic status* pertaining to the whole of society and not only to some of its individual members. These members, of course, can be wrong in their individual opinions, but they cannot be wrong *in toto*, in the same sense in which not *all* money can be counterfeited, because—given the interdependency of the concepts of right and wrong—in such a case there would be no money or knowledge at all.

(2) This fallibility or mediacy of knowledge, as Hegel would say, has some related properties which we have already encountered on our way here. One of them is the overall *negativity* of cognition in the sense that it cannot be positively identified with any of the epistemic contents or stages achieved so far, if only because these might soon, like every other content or stage before them, be refuted and/or "sublated" into some of its later stages. The general insight behind this point is, of course, the idea of knowledge as a process rather than as a simple state of mind. But the master–slave parable deepens this insight, showing that the cognitive significance of some claim or body of knowledge consists in the long path and the strenuous work that led to it rather than in the short-lived feelings of victory that accompany scientific discoveries and "breakthroughs". Such self-proclaimed triumphs only foreshadow the fate of the master who forgets that it is not this or that battle which made him who he is but the preparedness to fight again and again for his cause; in other words, it is not some contingent state of mind but the mind sufficiently aware of its social nature.

(3) Again, this negative quality of knowledge can be remoulded in a cautiously optimistic way into a positive quality of a higher order, if identified with the *self-reflective* and *self-correcting* nature of the whole enterprise. This is what the main modern proponents of fallibilism, Peirce (1868) and Sellars (1997), did in following Hegel's example:

> [K]nowledge, like its sophisticated extension, science, is rational not because it has foundation but because it is a self-correcting enterprise which can put *any* claim in jeopardy though not *all* at once (Sellars 1997: §38).

The resulting cautious optimism might be formulated like this: knowledge is fallible, but one can, if discord occurs, arrive at some socially accepted equilibrium as a new basis for further progress.

(4) The last collateral quality of fallible knowledge to be mentioned is its *infinity*, by which I refer not only to knowledge's always-unfinished nature (responsible for the above-mentioned scepticism and the delimitation of knowledge as a path of despair), but also to the moments of its relative stability and the self-correcting means which stabilise the existing discord. As Hegel noticed, the general self-reflexivity of knowledge, that is, the necessity of measuring what is there by knowledge's own standards, leads to the fact that even the most stable and fixed parts of our universe, such as tables and cats, are the result of the opposing tendencies of our reason to, on the one hand, make the difference between what things are for us and what they are in itself more determinate by developing it *ad infinitum* and, on the other, make this prospective infinity determinate or finite.

This is explicitly known from mathematical phenomena such as the development of real numbers, which are, by no coincidence, dealt with by both Hegel and Wittgenstein as examples of logical significance *sui generis*. In the end, one gets an overall picture of knowledge which is socially mediated; that is, the structure of the Concept is somehow identical with the structure of the Self, but also with the structure of Concept's proper parts.

10 Conclusion

Pace Wittgenstein's saying that he sees differences where Hegel sees identities—which seems to anticipate Adorno's critique of Hegel as an identity philosopher—I started this chapter by claiming that Hegel's and Wittgenstein's philosophies are, in some important sense, identical or similar to each other. And I suggested that this identity consists in the way Hegel and Wittgenstein develop their concepts of knowledge from more primitive forms of consciousness and bring them to a cautiously optimistic closure based on the sociality of reason, particularly as mirrored in Hegel's master–slave parable and Wittgenstein's private language argument.

The basic idea behind my line of thought (which can also be found in Stekeler-Weithofer (2008; 2014) and Brandom (2014)) is to read Hegel's master–slave parable not as a loose reference to the problem of *mastering* the rule but as a complex epistemological argument concerning the *struggle* between mere "private" opinions, resulting in the emergence of intersubjective knowledge. According to Wittgenstein's examples, the mastering of a rule arises from the mutual conditioning of the *pupil and his teacher* in the process of following a rule. What is risked here, I claimed, is the certainty of one's private opinion which, in its aiming at objective knowledge, necessarily becomes recognised as *fallible*.

But there is a complementary side to this story, closer to Wittgenstein's self-proclaimed difference between him and Hegel and their final conceptions of human knowledge: *Geist*—known for its ultimate unity—and *Sprachspiel*—known for its plurality. The origin of this side lies in the fact that the transformation of the transcendental I into the transcendental We, connected to the intersubjective stabilisation of the subject–subject difference, has the consequence of specifying who to count as "one of us", who to count as another subject and who not to. Now, it is exactly this necessity of drawing lines between Us and the Others that makes the corresponding social concepts of knowledge suspicious to those who, like Adorno, claim that every attempt at totality in the end only pretends to have achieved such a totality while, in virtue of its restrictive nature, suppressing or even causing discord and suffering to those who are excluded. Bowie recently applied this Adornian complaint to Brandom's neo-Hegelianism with its delimitative concept of sapience, which separates brutes from men, claiming that:

> The neo-Hegelian account of the sociality of reason is often presented in a way which takes too little account of how social relations specific to modernity produce disaster. (Bowie 2013: p.59)

I am mentioning this critique not because I think it is somehow self-explanatory or obvious, but because I believe that at this particular point—now that the analysis of the similarities between Hegel and Wittgenstein have been completed—it can shed more light on their differences, particularly with respect to the anti-systematic features of Wittgenstein's philosophy. This includes his restless life in which, like in Adorno's work, epistemic questions were inseparable from the matters of ethics and art.

Acknowledgments

Work on this chapter was supported by the European Regional Development Fund project "Creativity and Adaptability as Conditions of the Success of Europe in an Interrelated World" (No. CZ.02.1.01/0.0/0.0/16_019/0000734). I would like to thank Dr. Tereza Matějčková and the anonymous referee for valuable comments.

References

Adorno, Theodor W.: *Negative Dialektik*, Suhrkamp, 1966.
Bowie, Andrew: *Adorno and the Ends of Philosophy*, Polity Press, 2013.
Brandom, Robert: "The Structure of Desire and Recognition. Self-Consciousness and Self-Constitution", *Philosophy & Social Criticism* 33:1, 2007, pp.12–150.
Brandom, Robert: *A Spirit of Trust: A Semantic Reading of Hegel's Phenomenology*, unpublished manuscripts (http://www.pitt.edu/~brandom/spirit_of_trust.html), version 2014.
Kolman, Vojtěch: "Hegel's Bad Infinity as a Logical Problem", *Hegel-Bulletin* 37:2, 2016, pp.257–80.
Kripke, Saul: *Wittgenstein on Rules and Private Language*, Harvard University Press, 1982.
Lamb, David: *Hegel – From Foundation to System*, Martinus Nijhoff Publishers, 1980.
Peirce, Charles Sanders: "Questions Concerning Certain Faculties Claimed for Man", *Journal of Speculative Philosophy* 2:3, 1868, pp.103–14.
Rhees, Rush (ed.): *Recollections of Wittgenstein*, Oxford University Press, 1984.
Sellars, Wilfrid: *Empiricism and the Philosophy of Mind*, Harvard University Press, 1997.
Solomon, Robert C.: *In the Spirit of Hegel: A Study of G. W. F. Hegel's* Phenomenology of Spirit, Oxford University Press, 1983.
Stekeler-Weithofer, Pirmin: *Philosophie des Selbstbewußtseins. Hegels System als Formanalyse von Wissen und Autonomie*, Surkamp, 2005.
Stekeler-Weithofer, Pirmin: "Wer ist der Herr, wer ist der Knecht?", in: K. Vieweg and W. Welsch (eds.): *Hegels Phänomenologie des Geistes*, Suhrkamp, 2008, pp.205–37.
Stekeler-Weithofer, Pirmin: *Hegels Phänomenologie des Geistes. Ein dialogischer Kommentar*, Meiner, 2014.

Ingolf Max
Hegel and Wittgenstein on Identities and Contradictions

Abstract Take the beginning of the chapter *Being* of Hegel's *Science of Logic* "*Being, pure being* – without further determination" (SL 1929: p.94) and the first sentence of Wittgenstein's *Tractatus Logico-Philosophicus* "The world is everything that is the case" (TLP: 1). What could be more different? But a closer look shows that there are more resemblances than can be expected at a first glance. I show the striking analogy between Hegel's global identity "Pure being and pure nothing are therefore the same" (SL 2010: p.59), and Wittgenstein's version "The total reality is the world" (TLP: 2.063). The specific uses and the categorical positions of *contradiction* are emphasized. Finally, I display similarities of detail by a Wittgensteinian illustration of Hegel's category *contradiction*. Contrasting Hegel's and Wittgenstein's ways of philosophizing with respect to *overall similarities* and *similarities of detail* shed some new light on two inventive thinkers.

1 Introduction

Take the beginning of the chapter *Being* of Hegel's *Science of Logic* "*Being, pure being* – without further determination" (SL 1929: p.94), and the first sentence of Wittgenstein's *Tractatus Logico-Philosophicus* "The world is everything that is the case" (TLP: 1).[1] What could be more different? But a closer look shows that there are more resemblances than can be expected at a first glance. Of course, there are important differences. We will follow a methodological hint given by the late Wittgenstein for the first time in 1936 when he tells us: "we see a complicated network of similarities overlapping and criss-crossing: sometimes overall similarities, sometimes similarities of detail" (PI: §66). Using selected fragments of Hegel's SL and Wittgenstein's TLP some *overall similarities* and some *similarities of detail* will be shown. That gives us at least a first impression of the complicated Hegel-Wittgenstein-network. Contrasting both ways of philosophizing in such a way shed some new light on two inventive thinkers.

---

[1] Ogden/Ramsey's translation of the *Tractatus* is used throughout this chapter.

https://doi.org/10.1515/9783110572780-018

2 Holism and internal logic

One basic assumption of our analysis is that Hegel and Wittgenstein understand philosophy as an investigation of *everything—the totality—*in its most extreme form: not only at the beginning but throughout their whole works up to their ends. Hegel uses "pure", "without any further", "only to itself" (SL 2010: p.94) at the beginning, later more and more "totality" and finally "its own completed totality" ("the absolute idea"): "More exactly, the absolute idea itself has only this for its content, namely that the form determination is its own completed totality, the pure content." (SL 2010: p.736) We observe the line regarding "pure" from "pure being" (SL 2010: p.94) to "pure content" (SL 2010: p.736). Wittgenstein has a lot of formulations at hand to indicate his holistic position from the very beginning: "The world" (TLP: 1, 1.1, 1.11, 1.13, 1.2), "everything that is the case" (TLP: 1), "the totality of" (TLP: 1.1 and 1.12) and "being *all* the facts" (TLP: 1.11). Throughout his work he combines two lines: The explicitly logical line leads to "the general form of proposition" (TLP: 6). The ethical/aesthetical line leads to the last sentence: "Whereof one cannot speak, thereof one must be silent." (TLP: 6)

Another basic assumption is that logic has to be *internal:* For each concept, each category of logic there is a context-free position of this concept/category. Any concept/category can become a moment of a sub-totality. Hegel indicates that by "for its", "its own", "in(to) itself", "self-", "itself into itself". With respect to the absolute idea this holds without any restriction: everything is internal. If we say that *B* follows from *A* it seems to be that "... follows from ..." is something external relative to *A* as well as to *B*. But from a pure logical, holistic point of view inference is an *internal* relation:

> If the truth of one proposition follows from the truth of others, this expresses itself in relations in which the forms of these propositions stand to one another, and we do not need to put them in these relations first by connecting them with one another in a proposition; for these relations are internal, and exist as soon as, and by the very fact that, the propositions exist. (TLP: 5.131)

A remarkable difference between Hegel and Wittgenstein is of course, that Hegel allows external occurrences of categories and the *movement* of a category into another context (as moment) where this category is used internally: "It is, first, Positing Reflection. Secondly, it begins from the presupposed immediacy and thus is External Reflection. Thirdly, however, it transcends this presupposition, and, since in this act of transcendence it itself presupposes, it is Determining Reflection." (SL 1929: p.26) Determining Reflection is the *unity* of Positing Reflection and External Reflection. I assume that it would be very difficult to find a (local) similarity to "this act of transcendence" in Wittgenstein. In Wittgenstein's *Tractatus* there is no room for (temporarily) external moments of logic. Logic is completely internal with respect to *the* world: "The limit can, therefore, only be drawn in language and what lies on the other side of the limit will be simply nonsense." (TLP: Preface)

3 Global identity of being and nothing vs. identity of the world and the total reality

"1. Unity of being and nothing" of "C. Becoming" of "Chapter 1 Being" of "Section I Determinateness (Quality)" of Hegel's *Science of Logic* starts with the cryptic sentence "Pure being and pure nothing are therefore the same" (SL 2010: p.59). It sounds like the identity between everything (pure being) and its absolute negation "pure nothing". How could that be? If we would—mistakenly—interpret *pure being* as the universal set $\top$ and pure nothing as the empty set $\emptyset$, then $\top = \emptyset$, $\top = \sim\top$, $\sim\emptyset = \emptyset$ ("$\sim$" as negation sign) look like contradictions.

In Wittgenstein's *Tractatus* we find a similar astonishing argument: *The world* is the totality of (existent) facts (cf. TLP: 1.1, 1.11). But *the total reality* is the totality of existent and non-existent facts (cf. TLP: 2.06, 2.063). The supposed analogies are: (a) The world $\simeq$ Being, (b) the counterworld (the total reality without the world) $\simeq$ Nothing and (c) the total reality $\simeq$ Being together with Nothing. The total reality seems to be much greater than the world. But Wittgenstein says: "The total reality is the world." (TLP: 2.063)[2] Corresponding to Hegel's case *the total-reality without the world* should be identical with *the world*. How could that be?

The answer is: We have to consider *everything* (the totality) *including* its *internal* logic. No use of local logical laws (law of identity, law of contradiction), no use of a negation sign or any other connective (truth function) which belongs to the logical formalism itself is appropriate here. Wittgenstein says: "For the totality of facts determines what is the case, and also whatever is not the case." (TLP: 1.2) What does "the totality ... determines" mean?

---

[2] It is remarkable that Wittgenstein indicates a kind of argumentation loops by using the constructions "The world is ..." (TLP: 1, 1.1., 1.11) and "... is the world" (TLP: 2.04, 2.063). The structures seem to be closed by using the apparent equations "the world = the total reality = the world".

Let us begin with a very small "Tractarian" world: {*Fa, Fc, aRb, bRb*}. This world *shows* exactly four facts: *Fa, Fc, aRb* and *bRb*. It *shows* that its *substance* consists of a set of *things* (here: *names* represented by individual constants) {*a, b, c*}. It *shows* that it contains exactly one unary configuration (logical form) indicated by "*F*..." and exactly one binary configuration indicated by "... *R* ...". *As a whole* (closed world) it *shows* that there are no such things like "*d, e, f,* ..." and there is no *n*-ary "C^n" which is different from "*F*" and "*R*". In our case we simply *see* that.

It would be a *philosophical* mistake to assume for this world a syntax which would give us more syntax than our small world shows. The unrestricted syntax for atomic (elementary) formulas is: If $i_1, ..., i_n$ are individual constants (objects or names)—not necessarily different—and C^n is any *n*-ary configuration symbol without any restriction regarding its concrete kind and arity, then $C^n i_1...i_n$ ($1 \leq n$) is an elementary formula (a state of affairs, an elementary sentence):

$$\frac{i_1, ..., i_n \in \{a, b, c, d, ...\}, C^n \text{ for any } C \text{ with } 1 \leq n}{C^n i_1 ... i_n}._3$$

It seems that we get more information from our world than shown by it. Alternatively, we have access to more logic than given: *Fd, Fe, Racf* could be part of our world. Many logicians belief that there is an infinite number of individual expressions independently of the formation rules (syntax of well-formed expressions). But that is not true of our world. Our world shows only the following rules:

$$\frac{i \in \{a, b, c\}, F}{Fi} \text{ and } \frac{i_1, i_2 \in \{a, b, c\}, R}{i_1 R i_2}.$$

This is exactly what our world shows. It shows not only its facts *Fa, Fc, aRb* and *bRb*. The facts internally show a logic explicitly given by the two rules above. And this shows that *Fb, aRa, aRc, bRa, bRc, cRa, cRb, cRc* are possible facts (state of affairs) of this world and that there are no more of them. We get the following correspondences:

This world ≃ this Being: {*Fa, Fc, aRb, bRb*} together with its internal logic.

This total reality without this world (counterworld) ≃ this Nothing {*Fb, aRa, aRc, bRa, bRc, cRa, cRb, cRc*} together with its logic.

---

3 "C^n" is the meta-variable of any *n*-ary configuration symbol. "*F*" is a special case of "C^n" with $n = 1$ and "*R*" is a special case of "C^n" with $n = 2$ and "$R i_1 i_2$" is then used instead of our "$i_1 R i_2$".

This total reality ≃ this Being and this Nothing:
{Fa, Fc, aRb, bRb, Fb, aRa, aRc, bRa, bRc, cRa, cRb, cRc}[4]

We observe the following: (a) all of these three cases are logically identical, (b) all determinations are positive, (c) no negation is needed to describe the situation,[5] and (d) there are other worlds (counterworlds) which show the same internal logic. Examples are {Fa, cRb}, {Fc, aRb} and others.

The facts that our world is small and finite cannot be an argument against this consideration. We can assume that our world shows an unrestricted formation rule which produces an infinite number of states of affairs (elementary propositions). But *we* are not able to decide from outside the world how many facts our world consists of. Therefore, the question concerning the logic of our world remains open: "What *can* be shown *cannot* be said." (TLP: 4.1212)

This argument illustrates how the seemingly strange sentences "Pure being and pure nothing are therefore the same" (Hegel) and "The total reality is the world" (Wittgenstein) make perfect sense. *Nothing* is not the result of an application of a logical operator (negation) to *Being*, but contained in it. There is no logical preorder between Being and Nothing. "*Being, pure being*—without further determination. In its indeterminate immediacy, it is equal only to itself and also not unequal with respect to another; it has no difference within it, nor any outwardly." (SL 2010: p.59) Our demonstration in a Wittgenstein-style yields a possible interpretation of "is equal only to itself and also not unequal with respect to another": There cannot be another Being which is completely equal

---

[4] "(Nothing in the province of logic can be merely possible. Logic deals with every possibility and all possibilities are its facts.)" (TLP: 2.0121).

[5] That is an interesting difference between Wittgenstein's holistic strategy in philosophy and Carnap's model-theoretic program of using *state-descriptions* as a new undefined semantic concept. "We shall introduce the L-concepts with the help of the concepts of state-descriptions and range. Some ideas of Wittgenstein were the starting-point for the development of this method. / A class of sentences in S_1 which contains for every atomic sentence either this sentence or its negation, but not both, and no other sentences, is called a *state-description* in S_1, because it obviously gives a complete description of a possible state of the universe of individuals with respect to all properties and relations expressed by predicates of the system. Thus the state-descriptions represent Leibniz's possible worlds or Wittgenstein's possible states of affairs." (Carnap 1967: p.9) Carnap would say that {Fa, Fc, aRb, bRb} yields only a consistent but incomplete state description. A complete version would be {Fa, ~Fb, Fc, ~aRa, aRb, ~aRc, ~bRa, bRb, ~bRc, ~cRa, ~cRb, ~cRc}. "Wittgenstein intends to show that there is no room for ethics within logic. Using negation internally for characterizing worlds would be an *ethical decision* for him because he is not interested in a semantic *theory*. Carnap makes a *theoretical decision* to get a new semantic framework for modal logic and a general meaning theory." (Max 2009: p.261)

with respect to its facts. But it is impossible that Being is unequal to (its) Nothing with respect to their states of affairs. Otherwise, if we interpret "has no difference within it" as "not having any internal logical form" then we run into trouble. Our assumption is that Being (the world) and Nothing (the counterworld) coincide in their logical form. "*Nothing, pure nothingness*; it is simple equality with itself, complete emptiness, complete absence of determination and content; lack of all distinction within." (SL 2010: p.59) We see that Hegel tells us similar things with respect to "pure" and "equality" (Being: "equal only to itself" vs. Nothing: "simple equality with itself"). He plays with words if he says "without further determination" with respect to Being and "complete absence of determination" with respect to Nothing. Maybe he intends to realize two steps at once: The *logical* step is simply *Nothing = Being:* "Nothing is therefore the same determination or rather absence of determination, and thus altogether the same as what pure *being* is." (SL 2010: p.59) From this point of view there is no preorder. The *dialectical* step says that Being is the *first* moment and Nothing the *second* moment in the movement to their unity *Becoming*. For Wittgenstein, there is no internal reason for such a direction of moments and such a movement.

> The truth is neither being nor nothing, but rather that being has passed over into nothing and nothing into being – "has passed over," not passes over. But the truth is just as much that they are not without distinction; it is rather that *they are not the same*, that they are absolutely distinct yet equally unseparated and inseparable, and that *each* immediately *vanishes in its opposite*. Their truth is therefore this *movement* of the immediate vanishing of the one into the other: *becoming*, a movement in which the two are distinguished, but by a distinction which has just as immediately dissolved itself. (SL 2010: pp.59–60)

Again, some points are in accordance with our demonstration: The world and the counterworld are "absolutely distinct" in the sense that there is no common fact to both of them. They are "unseparated and inseparable" in the sense that both share their logical syntax, and they are opposed to each other. But this opposition is not expressible by a negation operator "~" with some proposition as its argument. In addition our demonstration cannot show an anologon with respect to "this *movement* of the immediate vanishing of the one into the other" except we read this in the sense of metaphorical speaking with respect to the relation between the world and its counterworld.

4 Ways of using *contradiction* in Hegel's *Science of Logic* and Wittgenstein's *Tractatus*

With respect to new terms formal logicians prefer the strategy to introduce these terms as undefined, well-motivated basic terms or as defined terms first, and then they continue to use them. Hegel uses the term *contradiction(H)* (*Widerspruch* in the sense of Hegel) not only in the *Preface to the Second Edition* and the *Introduction* of his *Science of Logic*, but also in *Book One* very often. This is a typical feature of Hegel's method of representing and using a lot of categories: He uses several expressions frequently in different contexts before he introduces them categorically. I call this method *pre-mentioning categories*. As a category *contradiction(H)* is introduced in Book Two *The Doctrine of Essence*, Section I: *Essence as the Reflection Within*, Chapter Two *The essentialities or the determination of reflection*, C *Contradiction*. Contradiction(H) is the unity of *identity* and *difference*.

This method of pre-mentioning expressions (normally in longer decimal numbers) is also used by Wittgenstein in the *Tractatus*. But with respect to contradiction there is a remarkable difference: Wittgenstein uses two German words which usually get—unfortunately—the same English translation: *contradiction*. He uses *widersprechende[s]* (TLP: 3.032), *widersprechen* (TLP: 4.1211) and *Widerspruch* (TLP: 4.211) before he introduces the technical term *Kontradiktion*—here contradiction(C):

> Among the possible groups of truth conditions there are two extreme cases.
> In one of these cases the proposition is true for all the truth-possibilities of the elementary propositions. We say that the truth-conditions are *tautological*.
> In the second case the proposition is false for all the truth-possibilities: the truth-conditions are *contradictory*(C).[6]
> In the first case we call the proposition a tautology; in the second, a contradiction(C). (TLP: 4.46)

But there are two cases of pre-mentioning versions of contradiction(C) using the German expressions "einander widersprechen" and "im Widerspruch stehen": "If two propositions contradict(C) one another, then their structure shows it [...]." (TLP: 4.1211) "It is a sign of a proposition's being elementary that there can be no elementary proposition contradicting(C) it." (TLP: 4.211)

---

[6] Here and in several following quotations I use expressions of the form "contradiction(...)" to indicate the specific uses by Wittgenstein and Hegel.

Contradictions(C) are an internal part of any logic with an unrestricted syntax. If our syntax allows $p \land q$ and q can be replaced by any well-formed expression of our language, then we have to allow not only $p \land \sim q$ (a significant proposition) but also the contradiction(C) $p \land \sim p$. "Tautologies and contradictions(C) lack sense." (TLP: 4.461) But: "Tautologies and contradictions are not, however, nonsensical. They are part of the symbolism" (TLP: 4.4611).

But there can be uses of *Widerspruch* which are nonsensical or lack sense—indicated by contradiction(N): "It is as impossible to represent in language anything that 'contradicts(N) logic' as it is in geometry to represent by its coordinates a figure that contradicts(N) the laws of space, or to give the co-ordinates of a point that does not exist." (TLP: 3.032) Here "contradicts(N)" occurs in the context of "impossible" as a kind of impossibility that lacks sense in contrast to impossibility to be represented as contradiction(C): "The certainty, possibility, or impossibility of a situation is not expressed by a proposition, but by an expression's being a tautology, a proposition with a sense, or a contradiction(C)." (TLP: 5.525)

5 Categorical positions of contradiction(H) and contradiction(C)

Both Hegel in *Science of Logic* and Wittgenstein in *Tractatus Logico-Philosophicus* use a hierarchic number system. It is like a many-dimensional coordinate system which can be used to create a very complex network. We can localize the precise positions of occurrences of concrete concepts or categories within this network. We can determine co-occurrences of and cross-connections between distinct categories. And we can look for occurrences of different categories at the same level or at other types of corresponding positions within the network. Wittgenstein's own comment to his numbering system is:

> The decimal numbers assigned to the individual propositions indicate the logical importance of the propositions, the stress laid on them in my exposition. The propositions $n.1$, $n.2$, $n.3$, etc. are comments on proposition no. n; the propositions $n.m1$, $n.m2$, etc. are comments on proposition no. $n.m$; and so on. (TLP: footnote to 1)

Of course, "the logical importance" is only a metaphor and it is known that Wittgenstein put a lot of his attention to find a perfect form for his *Tractatus*.[7] Each

---

[7] I think it should be possible to show that selected forms of representation in Wittgenstein's

number has one of the following forms: i with $1 \leq i \leq 7$, $i.j$ with $0 \leq j \leq 6$, $i.jk$ with $0 \leq k \leq 9$, $i.jkl$ with $0 \leq l \leq 8$, $i.jklm$ with $1 \leq m \leq 5$ and $i.jklmn$ with $n = 1$.

The following picture shows the seven main numbers, the number immediately following each main number, the last number in the section of the main number and the position of the introduction of the category contradiction(C) (TLP: 4.46). The different arrows from left to right indicate the different distances between the respective main number to its directly subsequent number. The different arrows from right to left indicate the different distances between the respective last number of a main section to the immediately following main number. We observe that contradiction(C) has a three-digit number in the midfield. We see that there is no number of the form $i.0$ and that the numbers 1.01., 3.01, 4.01, 6.01 do not exist.

Table 1

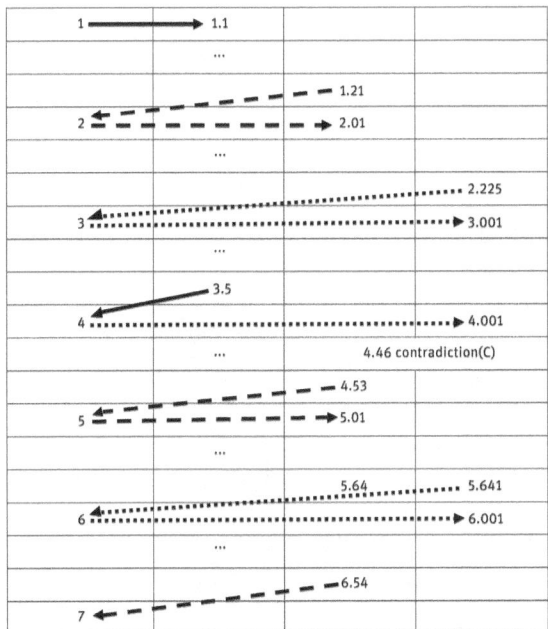

Tractatus Logico-Philosophicus resemble known patterns of classical music compositions in several respects.

Hegel uses in his *Science of Logic* a similar number system which can be translated into the numbering system of the *Tractatus*. If we neglect the main division into two volumes (Volume I: Objective Logic and Volume II: Subjective Logic) we have the following hierarchy:

Table 2

I					Book
	J				Section
		K			chapter
			L		German capitals: A, B, C
				M	German lowercases: a, b, c or digits: 1, 2, 3
				N	Greek lowercases: α, ß, γ

Mostly, but not continuously, it holds: $1 \leq I, J, K, L, M, N \leq 3$. It is interesting to observe which categories can be located at the same level. Some examples with respect to *identity, difference* and *contradiction* are:

Table 3

1	1	2	1		Determinate Being
2	1	2	1		*Identity* Observation 1. Abstract Identity Observation 2. First Original Law of Thought: The Law of Identity
3	1	2	1		The Judgment of Inherence

Table 4

1	1	2	2		Finitude
2	1	2	2		*Difference*
3	1	2	2		The Judgment of Subsumption

1	1	2	2	1	Something and an Other
2	1	2	2	1	*Absolute Difference*

Table 4 (continued)

1	1	2	2	2	Determination, Modification, and Limit
2	1	2	2	2	*Variety* Observation. The Law of Variety

1	1	2	2	3	Finitude
2	1	2	2	3	*Opposition* Observation. Contrary Magnitudes of Arithmetic

Table 5

1	1	2	3		Infinity
2	1	2	3		*Contradiction* Observation 1. Unity of Positive and Negative Observation 2. The Law of Excluded Middle Observation 3. The Law of Contradiction
3	1	2	3		The Judgment of Necessity

We observe that Hegel places all the famous laws of thought in the *observations* and not in the main text: *the Law of Identity* in observation 2 of 2121, *the Law of Variety* in the observation of 22222, the Law of Excluded Middle in observation 2 of 2123 and the Law of Contradiction in observation 3 of 2123. They are secondary with respect to a philosophical understanding of logic. This is in accordance with Wittgenstein's position that each tautology is on the same level. "'Laws of inference', which are supposed to justify inferences, as in the works of Frege and Russell, have no sense, and would be superfluous." (TLP: 5.132) Laws only show what is already internal to logic. This is in accordance with: "There cannot be a hierarchy of the forms of elementary propositions." (TLP: 5.556)

Both Hegel and Wittgenstein put the category *contradiction* in the midfield. We will show that this is due to the fact that *contradiction* depends on several logical preconditions.

6 Similarities of detail: A Wittgensteinian illustration of Hegel's category *contradiction*

Table 6

		examples p q ~ ∧	examples a b R
Determinate Being [1121]. We take atomic signs. Any Determinate Being is initially *finite* [1122]. With other words: We have discrete signs.			
In isolation they are *Something* [11221].		p	a
If we have *Something* [11221] we can have an *Other* too [11221].		q	b s
If logic is universal including the possibility to have finite lists of unconnected symbols than any *Something* can be an *Other* [11221] as well.		p as Something and p as an (its) Other	a (R) as Something and a (R) as an (its) Other

So far, we do not have any direct connection, any relation between discrete signs. But we can speak of a *repetition* of signs if we list an Other which is the same Something. This makes signs to *symbols*. In a modern way of speaking: Symbols have to be *types*. Each occurrence of a type counts as an occurrence of the same type. Before it comes to *Reflection* we already have *identity* and *difference* in the form of an Other as the Something again. In a list like *p, q, q, r, s* it has to be clear that the second occurrence of "*q*" is a repetition of the first occurrence of "*q*" and vice versa. We have *different* occurrences of the *same* symbol. Without such a symbolic use of signs it would be impossible to formulate tautologies as well as contradictions. It would be a nonsensical task to formulate tautologies or contradictions without using symbols.[8]

---

[8] Hegel allows constructions like $A = A$ in observations: "Thus identity, as an essential determination, is enunciated in the proposition, 'Everything is equal to itself; $A = A$,' or, negatively, 'A cannot be A and not-A at the same time.'" (SL 2010: p.353) "In its positive formulation, $A = A$, this proposition is at first no more than the expression of empty tautology. It is rightly said, therefore, that this law of thought is without content and that it leads nowhere." (SL 2010: p.358) Wittgenstein would say: Whether $A = A$ is a tautology or not depends on the logical status of A. If A is an atomic expression like an individual constant "*a*" "$a = a$" tries to *say* what can only be *shown:* "'*a*' is a symbol": "And now we see that in a correct conceptual notation pseudo-propositions like '$a = a$' [...] cannot even be written down." (TLP: 5.534) Additionally, "$a = a$" as a tautology would be an a priori true elementary proposition. But each elementary proposition has to be a picture and cannot be a tautology: "There are no pictures that are true a priori." (TLP: 2.225) Against this: "$p \equiv p$" is a perfect tautology if "*p*" represents an elementary or arbitrary complex proposition.

With respect to these considerations it becomes clear that Hegel does it well in putting *Finitude* [1122] and *Difference* [2122] at the same level in his coordinate system. The same holds for *Something* and an *Other* [11221] and *Absolute Difference* [21221].

Up to now it is not known that pure repetition can be thought as a relation between *Something* and itself. But we can move to *The Essentialities or Determinations of Reflection* [212]. Now we consider relations between Something and an Other. The simplest form of relation is the relation between Something and itself. *Identity* as the first Determination of Reflection is a logical precondition of the Law of Identity, but not expressed by this law itself.

Table 7

Identity as pure Determination of Reflection with respect to arguments:	p ∧ p	aRa
Identity as pure Determination of Reflection with respect to connectives / functions:	p ∧ (q ∧ r)	f(f(x))
We need relational determinations of reflection to get logical (tautological) identities:	e.g., p = p q = q	e.g., a = a b = b[9]

In order to get a formal contradiction(C) we have to go through the following steps:

Table 8

Absolute Difference [21221] between Something and an Other	"p" and "q" ("a" and "b") are absolutely distinct.	
Variety [21222] in relation	p ∧ q	aRb
Opposition [21223]: The strongest form of opposition is the (absolute) negation represented by classical negation "~":	p as opposed to ~p	aRb as opposed to ~aRb
Special kinds of relation of Opposition (Opposition in concrete Reflection) leads to formal Contradiction:	p ∧ ~p p ≡ ~p	aRb ∧ ~aRb aRb ≡ ~aRb

Hegel criticizes rightly the position that A and not-A (A ∧ ~A) could characterize *Contradiction* out of the blue. "Difference as such is already *implicitly* contradic-

---

9 Cf. the previous footnote.

tion; for it is the *unity* of beings which are, only in so far as they are *not one* – and it is the *separation* of beings which are, only in so far as they are separated *in the same reference connecting them.*" (SL 2010: pp.374–5) Like in the global case of Being = Nothing the critical point is, that "*A*" and "*~A*" seem to have different logical complexity. In Wittgenstein's terminology: "*A*" can be an elementary proposition. But "*~A*" is never an elementary proposition. To put it in another way: The length of "*~A*" is one greater than the length of "*A*". But Hegel says: "Positive and Negative are the same." (SL 2010: p.63) It would be nice to have formal representations of two elementary propositions which have the same logical complexity (which contain the same number of symbols), is free of use of negation and show already that there is the possibility to combine them in such a way that we get a contradiction(C). Wittgenstein has some interesting proposals for that: "We can represent truth-possibilities by schemata [...] ('T' means 'true', 'F' means 'false' [...])." (TLP: 4.31)

The schema of an elementary proposition is: $\begin{array}{c} p \\ T \\ F \end{array}$. There is exactly one distinct alternative significant schema: $\begin{array}{c} p \\ F \\ T \end{array}$. It does not matter which of both schemas represents "*p*" or "*~p*". $\begin{array}{c} p \\ T \\ F \end{array}$ and $\begin{array}{c} p \\ F \\ T \end{array}$ have the same logical complexity. Both schemas contain exactly three symbols. Each of them—"*p*", "T", and "F"—occurs exactly once in each expression. In this respect both expressions are *identical*. With respect to the order of "T", and "F" their *inner* logical forms are *different*. With respect to the position of "*p*" there is *no difference*. Combining both forms in an appropriate way yields a contradiction(C): $\begin{array}{cccc} p & \wedge & \sim & p \\ T & F & F & T \\ F & F & F & F \end{array}$. But using the conjunction "∧" is only one possibility which is already *internally* given by the *inner* logical forms of the two expressions alone. Wittgenstein offers another possibility without doubling "*p*" (a possible instance of the variable ξ): "In our notation the form '~ξ' is written as 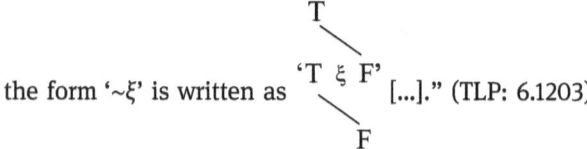 [...]." (TLP: 6.1203)

There are some remarks by Hegel which can be interpreted using these patterns: "Difference as such is already *implicitly* contradiction; for it is the *unity* of beings which are, only in so far as they are *not one* – and it is the *separation* of beings which are, only in so far as they are separated *in the same reference connecting them*." (SL 2010: p.374–5) But Hegel mentions a lot of examples of contradictions(H) for which we do not have an explication as contradiction(C) at hand. Again, the limit of our analogy is reached if it comes to Hegel's process-driven, dynamic way of speaking with respect to contradiction(H) as *unity* as well as the step to the next category *Ground* (p.213): "For this self-subsistence consists in that it contains the determination which is other than it in itself and does not refer to anything external for just this reason; but no less immediately in that it is *itself* and excludes from itself the determination that negates it. And so it is *contradiction*." (SL 2010: p.374) "According to this positive side, since self-subsistence in opposition, as excluding reflection, makes itself into a positedness and equally sublates this positedness, not only has opposition *foundered* but in foundering it has gone back *to its foundation, to its ground*." (SL 2010: p.377) It would be an interesting task to find adequate logical forms for "excludes from itself", "makes itself into", "sublates" and "has gone back to".

References

Carnap, Rudolf: *Meaning and Necessity. A Study in Semantics and Modal Logic*, 5th ed., University of Chicago Press, 1967.

Max, Ingolf: "Ways of 'Creating' Worlds", in: Volker Munz, Klaus Puhl and Joseph Wang (eds.): *Language and World. Papers of the 32nd International Wittgenstein Symposium* Vol. XVII., Austrian Ludwig Wittgenstein Society, 2009, pp.259–262.

Marco Kleber
Rethinking the Limits of Language: Wittgenstein and Hegel on the Unspeakable

Abstract When interpreting Wittgenstein's and Hegel's major works, the concept of the "unspeakable" and conflicting philosophical views concerning it can be understood as the major point of difference between these philosophies. For Wittgenstein, the "logical form" *of* the world is unspeakable and the facts and things *in* the world may be represented by the propositions of language. As opposed to this view, Hegel argues that the immediate and finite beings and situations *referred to* by language are the unspeakable, whereas "logical form" *totally reveals* itself *within* thinking and language, which has the nature of the "concept". Hegel does not identify the unspeakable with the "limits of language", which are essential both to Wittgenstein's earlier and later philosophical writings, but rather understands language as limitless and infinite. Thus, Wittgenstein's and Hegel's philosophies may be related to each other in a philosophically productive way: the Wittgensteinian "limits", interpreted in Hegelian fashion, are not limits *of language itself*, but do *manifest* themselves within the *usage* of language, when human finitude *relates* the universal meanings of language to *immediate* situations of life. This is also where Hegel's *dialectical* concept of the *contradiction* can be located. In this respect, both Wittgenstein and Hegel are of substantial importance to the philosophy of language in general, and to the development of a dialectical view of language in particular.

1 Introduction

Despite the various similarities between the philosophies of Wittgenstein and Hegel, we can nevertheless consider a fundamental *difference* and *contradiction* between two understandings of the essence of what may be *thought* within philosophy or, in other words, what a *meaningful proposition* might be—and what, by contrast, is supposed to be *the unspeakable.*

According to Wittgenstein's *Tractatus Logico-Philosophicus*, only propositions that can refer to facts in the world are *meaningful* propositions, whereas "logical form", the *limit* of language and world, is considered to be "the unspeakable" and is, therefore, ascribed to a higher, transcendent sphere, which can only be made a subject of discussion in an indirect way. In continuity with this earlier philosophy, Wittgenstein's later writings, such as the *Philosophical Investigations*, develop an ordinary language philosophy which distinguishes between, on the one hand, what can be said and done *within* the usage of language—what he terms "language-games"—and what, on the other hand, are the "limits of language", which manifest themselves in every language-game situation. Hence, Wittgensteinian philosophy as a whole is defined by the difference between what can be expressed via language, and what cannot be said at all.

By contrast, Hegel demonstrates that the concept or proposition, insofar as it refers to an *immediate and finite being* in the world, is indeed *meaningless* and that—contra Wittgenstein—the world of facts should be considered the "unspeakable" because every *determination* of a singular entity in the world by general categories entails a (dialectical) contradiction insofar as it cannot be defined by language abilities in an *absolute* way. Quite the contrary: "absolute determinateness" is a capacity of the *logical form and structure of all reality*, which Hegel calls "the concept".

Obviously, Hegel's and Wittgenstein's philosophical assumptions concerning the question of what is "unspeakable" could not be more contradictory: according to Wittgenstein, the facts *in* the world can be meaningfully articulated, whereas for Hegel it is the logical form *of* the world that can be. And for Wittgenstein the unspeakable is the logical form of the world itself (as opposed to the facts *in* the world), whereas Hegel demonstrates that the unspeakable can be found within the sphere of immediate beings (as opposed to logical form, which can be thought).

Hence, the question arises of whether immediate beings in the world are unspeakable and logical form can be articulated, even defined absolutely (Hegel), or whether the facts in the world can be expressed by the usage of language, and it is logical form that is unspeakable (Wittgenstein). This chapter attempts to show what philosophical questions turn on by this difference between Wittgenstein and Hegel and, furthermore, that Wittgenstein's philosophy—both in his earlier and his later work—may be characterised as an overdetermined *negativism* with a *dualistic* structure, whereas Hegel's *dialectics* follow the concept of *sublation* ("Aufhebung") of negativity, which means both the *negation* of the negative and its *affirmation*.

2 The unspeakable as the logical form of the world

The *Tractatus Logico-Philosophicus* tries to demonstrate that we need to consider a fundamental paradox concerning the relationship between *language* and *world*, or between the *proposition* and its corresponding *reality*. Wittgenstein's most important argument for this might be theorem 4.12 of the *Tractatus:*

> Propositions can represent the whole of reality, but they cannot represent what they must have in common with reality in order to be able to represent it—logical form. In order to be able to represent logical form, we should have to be able to station ourselves with propositions somewhere outside logic, that is to say outside the world. (TLP: 4.12)

Logical form, the "internal relation of depicting" which "holds between language and the world" (TLP: 4.014), cannot be represented by language because of the impossibility of a proposition capable of referring to what language (as the totality of propositions) and the world (as the totality of reality) must have in common. The propositions of language can refer to the world as the totality of all matters of fact, but they *cannot refer to this reference*, to the logical form that makes the language-world relation possible at all, because this would lead to an infinite regress (which means that we would have to make reference to the reference to the reference, and so on). Only a particular proposition that refers to the objectivity of facts can be "true" or "false" and is, thus, a *meaningful* proposition. Every proposition that cannot refer to existing or non-existing states of affairs, or that cannot be deduced from these so-called "elementary propositions" ("names in immediate combination" (TLP: 4.221)), cannot be true or false, is meaningless and points towards the mysterious sphere of the "unspeakable" (see also TLP: 4.114, Ogden/Ramsey's translation).

The unspeakable is the logical form itself, the internal relation between language and world, which cannot be represented within language because there is no external standpoint that transcends language and world. The logical form that world and language must have in common so that the one can be a representation of the other cannot be another representation of the same kind; there is, according to Wittgenstein, no representation of the representation. The *logical form* cannot be *objectivised* by representing thoughts: "There are no 'logical objects'." (TLP: 4.441)

This argument ultimately leads to the paradoxical self-negation of the *Tractatus Logico-Philosophicus*, which claims that there is an identity of the *unspeakable* and the *mystical* which cannot be *expressed* by words but *which makes itself manifest* (TLP: 6.522); the *pure existence* of the world, *that* it exists, in contrast to *how* things are in the world (TLP: 6.44). Because of human beings not being able to have a thought which *transcends language* and stands *outside the world*, the totality of the world, its logical form, cannot be represented by propositions. In conclusion, the "limits of *language*" mean "the limits of *my* world" (TLP: 5.62). These limits of language and world, which define the unspeakable as the mystical, only indirectly *manifest* themselves within the finitude that characterises human existence in all its aspects.

Even though there are important differences between Wittgenstein's *Tractatus* and his later work, his philosophical interest in the mystical unspeakable— the approach of demonstrating that the limits of language manifest themselves in every aspect of human existence and life, which is essentially characterised by this finitude—is a constant characteristic of his *entire* philosophical thinking (Rentsch 2003: pp.340–373). In his *Philosophical Investigations*, Wittgenstein writes that the "results of philosophy" are the "bumps that the understanding has got by running its head up against the limits of language" (PI: §119). The *limits of language*, which define the unspeakable, no longer refer to the language-world relationship *in general*; rather, Wittgenstein's *Philosophical Investigations* relates to the question of how and with what meanings we can use language (symbols, words and sentences) in our *everyday life*; in situations of language usage which Wittgenstein calls "language-games" (PI: §7). Wittgenstein intends to demonstrate that the limits of language, which reveal the fundamental finitude of the human condition, manifest themselves in *all* of these language-usage situations again and again (Rentsch 2003: p.373). The meaning of *every single word* which is used in situations of everyday life is limited. For example, the unspeakable manifests itself as soon as we ask what the word "game" means. According to section 66 of the *Philosophical Investigations*, we may say that there are board games, card games, ball games, Olympic games, etc. But it is impossible to define in an absolute way what all the things that are called "games" essentially refer to; there is no absolutely determinate concept of games. "For if you look at them you will not see something that is common to all, but similarities, relationships, and a whole series of them at that." (PI: §66) However, it is only possible to refer to certain kinds of games, which are characterised by certain qualities, and then say: "This *and similar things* are called 'games'." (PI: §69) "What does it mean to know what a game is? What does it mean, to know it and not be able to say it?" (PI: §75) According to Wittgenstein, it means that the unspeakable manifests itself in every single word of our everyday language, because every concept, like that of "game", is related to an infinite and complex set of other notions, but we are nevertheless able to use language meaningfully. The limits of language, which according to the *Tractatus* mean the "logical form" of the mysteriously existing world, are present in every word, sentence and phrase. In the next section, I shall attempt to reinterpret this result in a Hegelian way.

3 The unspeakable as reference to immediate beings

A very different view of the unspeakable is to be found in the first chapter of Hegel's *Phenomenology of Spirit*, entitled "Sense-Certainty: Or the 'This' and the 'Meaning' [*Meinen*]" (PS 1977: p.58). By interpreting *deixis* (the indexicality of phrases such as "this", "here", "now" and "I") on the basis of a linguistic analysis, Hegel for the first time articulates a philosophical insight which is fundamental to his philosophical system in its entirety: the *immediately given being* of sense-certainty—which means "nothing but the sheer being of the thing [*Sache*]" (PS 1977: p.58), the Wittgensteinian world made up of all states of affairs—is negativity and contradiction, and is unspeakable. But this *negativity* is *sublated* ("aufgehoben") in a higher sphere, namely language, which, according to Hegel, has the nature of the "concept". This is a very different philosophical interpretation of the essence of language than Wittgenstein's.

Hegel's famous example regarding the logical behaviour of *deixis* goes as follows: we write down the true sentence of "Now is Night" and then we *preserve* ("*aufheben*", the central Hegelian notion which is also translated as "to sublate") the sheet of paper until the next day:

> The Now that is Night is *preserved*, i.e. it is treated as what it professes to be, as something that *is*; but it proves itself to be, on the contrary, something that is *not*. The Now does indeed preserve itself, but as something that is *not* Night; equally, it preserves itself in face of the Day that it now is, as something that also is not Day, in other words, as a *negative* in general. (PS 1977: p.60)

The indexicality of the word "now" functions such that it refers to *immediate* beings only if it *does not* only refer to the immediate, but is mediated and relational:

> This self-preserving Now is, therefore, not immediate but mediated; for it is determined as a permanent and self-preserving Now *through* the fact that something else, viz. Day and Night, is *not*. (PS 1977: p.60)

This is where Hegel makes the important distinction between *to mean* and *to say*. We may interpret *to mean* ("meinen") as the *reference* of a term, or as the content of a *representation*. And Hegel's *to say* may be understood as the *universal sense* or *general meaning* of words—though it is very important in the following that the German word for meaning, *Bedeutung*, is completely different to the word *meinen*, which is also translated as "to mean" or "meaning". Hegel's main thesis is that there is a remarkable difference and contradiction between what we *mean* to say and what we actually *say*; between the matters of fact *referred* to by deixis, and the universal *sense* or *meaning* (Bedeutung) of these terms:

> What we say is: "This", i.e. the *universal* This; or, "it is", i.e. *Being in general*. Of course, we do not *envisage* the universal This or Being in general, but we *utter* the universal; in other words, we do not strictly say what in this sense-certainty we *mean* to say. (PS 1977: p.60)

If words such as "this", "here", "now" and "I" are used within language, they do not *have the universal sense* of what they represent (*this* single night or day which *I* recognise *here* and *now*). The *sense* or *meaning* ("Bedeutung") of these terms is quite different and opposed to the immediate situations to which they *refer*, because the former is *universal* and the latter are *singular*. Sense (or meaning) and reference (or representation) relate to one another in a *contradictory* way.

> When I say "this Here", "this Now", or a "single item", I am saying all Thises, Heres, Nows, all single items. Similarly, when I say "I", this singular "I", I say in general all "Is"; everyone is what I say, everyone is "I", this singular "I". (PS 1977: p.62)

Here, the *unspeakable* is considered to be the sphere of *immediate beings* in their entirety, referred to by deixis, as "it is just not possible for us ever to say, or express in words, a sensuous being that we mean" (PS 1977: p.60). Wittgenstein's understanding of what can be expressed by words, and of what the unspeakable might be, could not be more opposed to this understanding of the unspeakable in Hegel. Whereas Wittgenstein wants to show us that the words and sentences of language can only express *facts* in the world, Hegel says that language *cannot* express facts about the world—for it is obvious that the sphere of facts is immediate and representational—but that, if we intend ("meinen") to talk about matters of fact (like "Now is Night"), our language always expresses a *universality* which is *contradictory* to what we mean to say, to what we actually *refer* to. For example, the concept of "I" refers to all human individuals, not only to the one who I am—here and now—meant to be.

"It is as a universal too that we *utter* what the sensuous [content] is." (PS 1977: p.60) The sensuous content is *singular* (the singular "this" or "I" which is "now" "here"), and language expresses all immediate singularities as *universalities* (like the universal "I"). We can now ask about the deeper reason why Wittgenstein's and Hegel's concepts of the unspeakable are different. Unlike

Wittgenstein, Hegel can identify the unspeakable with the sphere of immediate beings *because* he can attribute to language the ability to express the universal. Because of the *deixis* expressing universality, the sensuous content can be interpreted as *opposed* to this sense of language, and appears now to be *contradictory* to what language may express. And this contradiction *sublates* within the universal meaning of language (because—as we will see—the concept of the "concept" is inherent to language). This is exactly where Wittgenstein and Hegel come apart. According to Wittgenstein, language cannot express the absolute, like religion or ethics:

> Propositions can express nothing that is higher. It is clear that ethics cannot be put into words. Ethics is transcendental. (TLP: 6.42–6.421)
>
> How things are in the world is a matter of complete indifference for what is higher. God does not reveal himself in the world. (TLP: 6.432)

If only a proposition that can refer to immediate beings, to states of affairs in the world, is regarded as a meaningful proposition, then there is no revelation of a higher sense *in* the world, neither in ethics nor in religion. These topics can only be made a subject of discussion in an indirect way, i. e., by explaining the "limits" of language and world. This negativism, which is essential to Wittgenstein's earlier (and probably even to his later) philosophical thought, has been interpreted in recent research as being related to the Christian mystical tradition and to its negative theology (Tyler 2011) and even to the religion of Gnosticism (Rentsch 2011: pp.131–147). These are dualistic concepts of the God-world relationship, which deny, like Wittgenstein does, the possibility of a higher meaning that is revealed *within* the world, and support the idea that the absolute (and this is precisely why it is called *the absolute*) cannot be represented by any human thought. The early writings of Hegel, the works of his youth, argue that the absolute can by no means be *objectivised* within philosophy (Simon 1966: p.17). Later on, Hegel changed his position and, as Josef Simon points out, interpreted language as the phenomenon which makes the absolute manifest and objective (Simon 1966: pp.14–19). Wittgenstein remarks in the preface to the *Tractatus:* "I do not wish to judge how far my efforts coincide with those of other philosophers." Because it originates from the tradition of negative theology, the *early* theological standpoint of the young Hegel would be precisely such an effort. The *Phenomenology of Spirit* develops a new understanding of language. The unspeakable is no longer ascribed to a higher, theologically interpreted sphere, and is no longer identified with the absolute as in negative theology, but is related to the *finitude of beings* within the world. According to this new position, "what is called the unutterable is nothing else than the untrue, the irrational, what is merely meant" (PS 1977: §110). By contrast, language can *express* the truth by *reversing* the negativity of pure being: it is "language—which has the divine nature of directly reversing the meaning of what is said" (PS 1977: §110). (This "meaning" is *meinen*, not the *universal* meaning, which is *Bedeutung* in German.) Combining this statement with Wittgenstein's talk of the "limits of language" would entail that the divine nature is limited, which must be wrong. This shows how incommensurable the two philosophies apparently are.

However, it is possible to say *why* Wittgenstein can notice *limitations* and *finitude* with respect to our language usage, as he does in the overall approach of his philosophical investigations.

The *limits* that Wittgenstein considers to be the limits *of language as a whole* become manifest in the sphere of that which (as Hegel puts it) we *mean* but do not *say*; they are related to *Meinen*, not to (universal, general or "higher") meaning. The Wittgensteinian limits are the negativity and contradiction that become manifest, if humans *relate* the universality of linguistic sense to *immediate* situations and matters of fact. Whereas Wittgenstein interprets the unspeakable by *identifying* this philosophical subject with the "limits of language", Hegel makes an important distinction between language *itself*—its universality, "higher" meaning and "divine nature" (which, as will be shown in the next section, is infinity rather than finitude or limitedness)—and the *reference* to immediate and finite situations *by the use of* language, which is a *human* action. One of the most emphasised doctrines of Wittgenstein's philosophical investigations concerning the concept of *Bedeutung* is that for "a large class of cases – though not for all – in which we employ the word 'meaning' it can be defined thus: the meaning of a word is its use in the language" (PI: §43). By contrast with this tendency to use *language* synonymously with language *usage*—i.e., to treat *Bedeutung* as synonymous with *Meinen*, to equate *universal* meaning with *referring* to immediate situations *by* the universalities of language—Hegel's dialectical view of language insists on the *non-identity* of these two aspects of the constitution of *Bedeutung:* what we *mean* to say (the things and facts that are referred to within our language usage) may be opposed and contradictory to what language *actually expresses* (the universal).

Hence, Hegelian philosophy insists on a sphere in which the sublation (both the negation and the affirmation) of the negative is conceivable. This additional sphere marks an important difference between Wittgenstein and Hegel. It is the *concept* or the *idea*, which Hegel describes in his major work *Science of Logic*. As we know from the *Phenomenology of Spirit*, the nature of the concept must be inherent to language, and thus language is meant to have the ability to overcome negativity and finitude.

4 The absolute determinateness of logical form

The argument of the *Phenomenology*'s first chapter, namely that *immediate* beings can only be uttered as *universal* and that, therefore, singular and distinct beings are in opposition and contradiction to their general words/concepts, has its analogy in the *Science of Logic*. This major work is divided into three books: *The Doctrine of Being*, *The Doctrine of Essence* and *The Doctrine of the Concept*. The logical objects of *immediacy* and *finitude* belong, among many others, to the logic of being. The logical objects of *opposition* and *contradiction* are (together with notions such as identity, difference, diversity and grounds) analysed in the logic of essence, and contradiction is *sublated* within the logic of the concept. "Essence stands between being and concept; it makes up their middle, its movement constituting the transition of being into the concept." (SL 2010: p.339) The logic of essence, which focuses on analysing the structure of contradiction (SL 2010: p.374), stands between being and the concept. Immediate and finite *beings*, referred to by general *concepts*, are *contradictory* because of the relationship (which Hegel makes a subject of discussion under the heading of *essence* or *reflection*) between immediacy/finitude and the universal concept. Hegel's *dialectical* view of *contradiction* (see also Wandschneider 2013 and Wolff 2017) is thus related to the very possibility of *determinateness* and *predication* (Haas 2003: p.60). The *dialectically* interpreted contradiction is the contradiction of every *thing*, insofar as it is *reflected*, determined as *some* thing, that is, insofar as it is *referred to* by language (see also Haas 2003: p.61).

"Finite things, in their indifferent variety, are therefore just this: to be contradictory, internally fractured and bound to return to their ground." (SL 2010: p.385) In every finite being, in every thing, there is a manifestation of a contradiction, because no finite thing or entity can be defined in an absolute way, or subsumed to general categories so that the entity is described in all of its aspects and relations, and absolutely distinguished from all other singular entities of the same category. If I wish to distinguish one entity from another entity of the same category, I could use a list of ten qualities that definitely separate the one from the other. But there could be one additional entity in the world that fulfils all these ten criteria. So, I could expand the list so that there are, for example, 20 or 30 qualities to define the singularity. But there could always be another example of the general category and the list with the criteria must be *infinite*. Between every *concept* of a general category, and every particular *example* of this category, there must always be a difference and a contradiction, because the immediate and finite thing or entity can never be expressed by concepts in an absolute way, and there is no concept which totally complies with its examples. For Hegel, there is no "*absolute determinateness*" of immediate entities, but only "finite determinateness and manifoldness" (SL 2010: p.520).

This is another way to show why we cannot refer to the (Wittgensteinian) world of facts without contradiction. There are objects that exhibit a completely different logical behaviour to entities, things or states of affairs and their corresponding concepts or propositions. These are the *logical* objects which are not *opposed* to thinking, but which are in fact *produced* by thinking because they are the *forms* of thinking itself. The object of the *Science of Logic* is "thinking or more specifically *conceptual* thinking", and "its concept is generated in the course of this elaboration and cannot therefore be given in advance" (SL 2010: p.23). Because the *Logic's* only object is thinking—*thinking* which, thus, is intended *to be thought*—the object of logic is not *distinguished* from its scientific method. Moreover, this object is *generated* within the process of logical thinking itself —which Hegel actually *carries out* in the *Science of Logic*—because it absolutely *identifies* with this thinking. The *Science of Logic* is about how thinking is able to think itself, about the absolute self-reference of thinking. Furthermore, by producing its logical objects during this process, the *Logic* generates the *absolute* as an object which is totally *detached* (which is the original meaning of the Latin *absolutus*) from reference to *certain* kinds of beings, such as matters of fact in the world. If Hegel's views on thinking about thinking are right, the absolute can be objectivised, and "logical form" (SL 2010: pp.523 f.) is not to be identified with the unspeakable but can rather be expressed by words. All the concepts of the *Science of Logic*, such as "being", "immediacy", "finitude", "opposition", "contradiction" and "concept", are logical objects in which thinking refers to itself. In *this* sense, it is wrong to say that there "are no 'logical objects'" (TLP: 4.441).

As demonstrated, propositions cannot refer to immediacy or finitude without contradiction. However, this is only true if this immediacy is understood as the immediacy of things or states of affairs. In Hegel's *Logic*, there is a new kind of immediacy to which propositions can refer in an absolute way. This is the "concept of the concept" (SL 2010: p.514). Hegel distinguishes between the way *particular* concepts refer to *particular* states of affairs (as the concept of "Night" refers to all nights and may be related to *this* special night), and the way the concept of "concept" refers to all concepts.

Every *certain* concept is a *general/universal* term which subsumes a *manifoldness* of *particular* other determinations. These other determinations are subcategories or potential quantities of the concept and of its specific content. This entails that this content, insofar as it is immediate and finite, must be opposed and contradictory to its concept. But what does the concept of "concept" mean? The word "concept" expresses *that* every concept is a *negative unity*—and, hence, a *singularity*—of a *manifoldness* of *particular* determinations (Haas 2003: p.113). Thus, the logical form of every concept is determined in an absolute way. The *logical form* of the concept is totally defined by its three aspects, which Hegel names in the *Doctrine of the Concept:* universality, particularity and singularity (SL 2010: p.529). Hegel says:

> The *universal* is, on the contrary, a *simple* that is at the same time *all the richer in itself*, for it is the concept. First, therefore, it is simple self-reference; it is only in itself. But, second, this identity is in itself absolute mediation but not anything mediated. Of the universal which is mediated, that is to say, the abstract universal, the one opposed to the particular and the singular, of that we shall have to speak only in connection with the determinate concept. (SL 2010: pp.530f.)

Unlike every determinate concept of an immediate being, the concept of "concept" is absolute self-reference. Due to this, the *universal* concept is *not opposed* to the particular and the singular, like concepts that refer to the finitude of situations. Hence, the concept of "concept" expresses that the *universal* concept is determined by its three *particular* aspects—which are again universality, particularity and singularity—and, hence, the concept itself is a *simple* and *singular* object. Universality, particularity and singularity are *united* within the concept of the concept, and achieve what is denied to the immediate beings: the absolute determinateness of the object of a referential proposition, such that words can express that this, and nothing else, is the concept. The possibility of an absolute determination of logical form depends precisely on the fact that logical objects, insofar as they are produced by the thinking of thinking (for example, the concept of "concept", which is totally defined by its three particular aspects universality, particularity and singularity), exhibit a remarkably different logical behaviour to concepts of sensuous content, such as immediate beings, entities, things or matters of fact, which are to be analysed in the *Doctrine of Being*. The unspeakability of immediate and finite beings is sublated (negated and affirmed) in the determination of the concept of the concept. This is why the concept of "concept" can *express* that *all* determinate concepts are *negative* units of manifoldness, and this *reference* to the entirety of the concept is an *affirmation*, a *positive* proposition.

Consequently, the word "concept" belongs to a different logical sphere than the "game" about which Wittgenstein says that there is no absolute determination, such that we are only able to say: "This *and similar things* are called 'games'." (PI: §69) The concept of the "game", which Hegel would allocate to his logic of being, manifests "finite determinateness and manifoldness" (SL 2010: p.520) since it is defined by an indifferent variety of subcategories (such as board games, card games, ball games, Olympic games and so on) which have in common nothing but particular similarities. Hegel distinguishes the *absolute* determinateness of logical form from the *finite* determinateness of immediate beings. Wittgenstein, by contrast, does not distinguish between these two logical patterns and also relates this finite and limited determinateness to concepts such as proposition, word, language and world. Otherwise, he would not criticise the philosophy of "super-concepts" in this way:

> That is, the order existing between the concepts of proposition, word, proof, truth, experience and so on. This order is a super-order between – so to speak – super-concepts. Whereas, of course, if the words "language", "experience", "world", have a use, it must be as humble a one as that of the words "table", "lamp", "door". (PI: §97)

Wittgenstein's basic intention that there are no "super-concepts", such as Hegel's concept of the concept, necessarily takes into account that the use of particular concepts such as "table" is just as *humble* as the use of self-referential concepts such as "language", "proposition" or "word". This is analogous to the *Tractatus*'s approach to demonstrating that logical form is unspeakable on the basis that there is no reference to the reference, or representation of the representation, because there is no logical standpoint outside language and world. Instead, there are concepts such as "representation" and "reference" *within* language. Among all concepts, there is indeed the concept of "concept"; there is the concept of "language" within language and there is the word "word" among the totality of all words. These concepts refer to language or to thinking as a whole. Otherwise, the negativity within language usage (Wittgenstein) or within thinking (Hegel) could not be articulated, for every articulation is an affirmation. To take account of absolute negativity, limitation and finitude, these concepts— "negativity", "limitation" and "finitude"—must be taken as logical objects which have their own definition within the system of logical science. "Negativity", "limitation", "finitude" and "contradiction" are logical objects, and their *definition* must be *absolute* (*detached* from the finite determinateness of all things). Otherwise, there would not be a *limitation* that must be taken into consideration in *every* immediate situation of language usage (Wittgenstein) or, which amounts to the same, a *contradiction* in *every* immediate determination (Hegel).

Wittgenstein's basic intention of making the "limits of language" manifest by philosophical investigation parallels Hegel's insight from the first chapter of the *Phenomenology of Spirit* that there is always unspeakability if immediate and finite situations are referred to by the universalities of language. Furthermore, from a Hegelian point of view it does not seem to be accidental that Wittgenstein can notice *limitations* and *finitude* concerning the usage of language in "language-games". These are *situations* of everyday life which comply with Hegel's understanding of the *immediate*. And in *this* sphere, Hegel may also consider a fundamental negativity, which he analyses with the dialectical category of contradiction, and which is without a doubt essential to the human condition. At this point, Wittgenstein's language-game philosophy and Hegel's dialectics may be related to each other in a philosophically productive way.

On the other hand, this might be important because there is still a problem of language in Hegel's philosophy (see also Simon 1966). The *Phenomenology*'s first chapter explains that language, which has a "divine nature", has the ability to *utter* universality *against* the immediate being or situation which we *mean* by speaking the language, by *referring* with linguistic sense to particular situations ("language-games"). The *Science of Logic* tries to make the absolute thinkable and objective, by generating logical objects which do not refer to certain kinds of beings from everyday life, but that are *detached* from the immediate reference and that belong to the sphere of pure logical objects because they only refer to themselves. The question arises of how the logical objects appear *within* everyday language usage. Hegel's preface to the second edition of the *Science of Logic*, which was written almost 20 years after the first publication and only one week before Hegel's death in November 1831, points out that the logical "forms of thought are first set out and stored in human language" (SL 2010: p.12). The *Logic* certainly does not answer the question of *how* logic and language coincide, or how language should be philosophically conceived according to the *Science of Logic*. For there is an "outside" of language only *within* language insofar as language can only refer to itself by *presupposing* its own existence; there are actually *no limitations of language* at all—such as limitations *between* things or facts that are distinguished *by* the use of language—and hence language is considered to have the same nature as Hegel's concept of "concept", which is strict universality and infinity (Ungler 2014: p.138). If this proves to be true, there are no "limits of language" (Wittgenstein), but such limits do exist between the *finite* things that may be referred to *by* language, but that *sublate* within the logical forms of language itself (Hegel). The questions concerning a *dialectical view of language* of this kind may be inspired again by a new reading of both Wittgenstein and Hegel.

References

Haas, Bruno: *Die freie Kunst. Beiträge zu Hegels Wissenschaft der Logik, der Kunst und des Religiösen*, Duncker & Humblot, 2003.

Rentsch, Thomas: *Heidegger und Wittgenstein. Existential- und Sprachanalysen zu den Grundlagen philosophischer Anthropologie*, Klett-Cotta, 2003.
Rentsch, Thomas: *Transzendenz und Negativität. Religionsphilosophische und ästhetische Studien*, De Gruyter, 2011.
Simon, Josef: *Das Problem der Sprache bei Hegel*, Kohlhammer, 1966.
Tyler, Peter: *The Return to the Mystical: Ludwig Wittgenstein, Teresa of Avila and the Christian Mystical Tradition*, Continuum, 2011.
Ungler, Franz: *Bruno Liebrucks "Sprache und Bewusstsein"*, Karl Alber, 2014.
Wandschneider, Dieter: *Grundzüge einer Theorie der Dialektik. Rekonstruktion und Revision dialektischer Kategorienentwicklung in Hegels "Wissenschaft der Logik"*, Königshausen & Neumann, 2013.
Wolff, Michael: *Der Begriff des Widerspruchs: Eine Studie zur Dialektik Kants und Hegels*, Eule der Minerva, 2017.

Part 4 **Hegelian Approaches to Wittgenstein**

Aloisia Moser
Hegel's Speculative Method and Wittgenstein's Projection Method

Abstract Against the widely held but contradictory ideas that (a) there is no method in Wittgenstein and that (b) the picture theory is at the heart of the *Tractatus*, I argue that the center of the *Tractatus* is Wittgenstein's projection method, a method which shows us how propositions can have sense when they are used or, to put it another way are projected onto reality. I argue that we do not find in the *Tractatus* a static picture theory, as the common reading of the *Tractatus* has us believe, but a projection method. Although Wittgenstein presents an additional zero-method, a state of the projection method that would be transcendental, he rejects this as a limiting case. I make a connection to the later Wittgenstein and his theory of meaning based on the use of language. By means of a perspicuous representation, I compare Wittgenstein's method to Hegel's the speculative method as Hegel develops it in the *Science of Logic*. While Hegel's method is transcendental, Wittgenstein's is not.

Introduction

Method has been neglected in Wittgenstein scholarship, appearing if at all only in the guise of the therapeutic method described by the resolute reading.[1] Witt-

---

[1] In the *Tractatus* the first mention of method is in 3.11, where Wittgenstein talks about the projection method as the thinking of the sense of the proposition. I will elaborate on this. Further down, in 4.1121, Wittgenstein speaks about the problems of studying a sign language and the study of processes of thinking, as philosophers do in logic. He says that most logicians get entangled in inessential psychological investigations and sees a danger for his own "method" too. In 5.631, we find his contention that there is no thinking subject that has representations. If he wrote a book about the world as he found it, Wittgenstein contends, he would need to report about the body and which parts of it obey the will. Then he says that this would be a method of isolating the subject, or to say that there is in an important sense no subject. Wittgenstein mentions method again in 6.0123, when he gives an intuitive method for how to recognise a tautology as a tautology. The next mention is the zero-method, which I will also discuss in detail. In 6.2341, mathematics is described as a method of logic: the method that inheres in working with equations. Each proposition of mathematics must be self-evident. To arrive at its equations, mathematics uses the method of substitution. And then in 6.53 Wittgenstein speaks of the correct method of philosophy, which is to say nothing but what can be said, i.e., the propositions of natural science. He contends that this method would be unsatisfying, since the student would

genstein is said to have at best a method in the sense of a skill at dealing with philosophical problems. Another widely held conviction is that methods require theories, and because there is no theory in Wittgenstein's philosophy this shows that there is no method (cf. Wyss 2015). I argue that Wittgenstein develops a method in the *Tractatus* right before our eyes and that this method, which he calls the "projection method", is comparable to Hegel's "speculative method". While for Hegel the movement or activity of the concept is also its content, Wittgenstein gives us the thing and the concept of the thing at the same time in the projection or picturing. We do not find in Wittgenstein a static picture theory, as the common reading of the *Tractatus* has us believe, but a projection method. Although he presents an additional zero-method, a transcendental version of the projection method, Wittgenstein rejects this as a limiting case. Hegel's speculative method is transcendental, Wittgenstein's projection method is not. Hegel's speculative method is understood as the development of all natural and spiritual life out of the content of logic. He thought of it as the immanent development of the concept through which philosophy constitutes itself.

I will present Hegel's speculative method by looking at the passages on method in Hegel's *Science of Logic*. In the *Subjective Logic*, volume two of the *Science of Logic*, we find the following passage:

> There already exists for the logic of the *concept* a fully ready and well entrenched, one may even say ossified, material, and the task is to make it fluid again, to revive the concept in such a dead matter. To build a new city in a devastated land has its difficulties, even if there is no lack of material at hand; but even greater are the obstacles, of a different kind, when the task is to give a new layout to an ancient and solidly constructed city, with established rights of ownership and domicile; one must also decide, among other things, not to make use of much otherwise valued stock. (SL 2010: p.507)

The passage describes the logic of concepts as petrified, written in stone and dead. Hegel sets out to revive this logic and make it fluid. He chooses the picture of an old, solidly constructed city which he must give a new layout. We are immediately reminded of a similar yet different passage in the *Philosophical Investigations*. In section 18, for example, Wittgenstein speaks of language

> as an ancient city; a maze of little streets and squares, of old and new houses, and of houses with additions from various periods; and this surrounded by a multitude of new boroughs with straight regular streets and uniform houses. (PI: §18)

---

not feel that they had been taught philosophy; nevertheless, he concludes that this would be the only strict method.

Although similar, these two descriptions of language/logic work differently. While Hegel describes a city that is set in stone but which he wants to redesign, even at the cost of leaving out materials, Wittgenstein merely describes a city that has an old downtown with streets like a maze and is surrounded by a newer part with a more regular layout.

My overall aim is to show a similarity between two conceptions or methods that nevertheless cannot be reduced to just one. I create a perspicuous representation (*übersichtliche Darstellung*) of Wittgenstein's method of projection, or what he later calls the symbolic method or method of representation in the *Tractatus*. I discuss the projection method in a way that reveals an aspect of the Hegelian approach to method, which could be called the activation of the concept. Once we can see method under this kind of aspect switch, my claim that Wittgenstein and Hegel are not altogether different will seem less outrageous. The aspect switch will reveal that Wittgenstein's ideas about language and logic—i.e., about concepts and their internal and external relations—can be read in a Hegelian framework. The sole reason why we have not been doing this hitherto is that Wittgenstein's philosophy seemed to have been coming from the exact opposite corner.

I proceed in the following way. In part 1, I start with some of Hegel's remarks on method from the *Science of Logic*. In part 2, I trace Hegel's attempts back to Kant and show how Hegel thought he had improved on Kant. This paves the way to part 3, in which I develop Wittgenstein's projection method that he sets out in the *Tractatus* as an attempt to specify the conditions of the possibility of representation, similar to the Kantian project of specifying the conditions of the possibility of experience. Furthermore, I discuss Wittgenstein's limiting case of the projection method, the zero-method, which comes close to being a transcendental move. The discussion of the zero-method, which does not involve the work of projection, reveals how the work that happens within thought—in the projection—is often neglected.

In conclusion, I claim that we ought to understand Wittgenstein's philosophy in the *Tractatus* as developing a conception of language or thought as a logic that is already thought in application and then in the later work as an expansion of itself into grammar, language-games or forms of life. From this vantage point, the development of Wittgenstein's logic or grammar can be seen to have a lot in common with Hegel's logic.

1 Hegel on method in the *Science of Logic*

In the introduction to the translation of the *Science of Logic* from 2010, George di Giovanni introduces "method" as the category which brings logic to an end. He shows that this is akin to Kant's *Critique of Pure Reason*, which also concluded with a chapter on the methodology of pure reason. For Kant, reason seeks method and tries to discover it in experience out of a need that is its own, but that remains external to the content of experience. But (according to di Giovanni) for Hegel, on the contrary, "method" is the rhythm (*Lebenspuls*) of experience itself. It is an ordering which is internal to it and the consequence of the fact that experience is an idealising process from beginning to end (SL 2010: p.liii). Right at the beginning of the preface to the *Science of Logic*, Hegel says:

> inasmuch as philosophy is to be science, it cannot borrow its method from a subordinate science, such as mathematics, [...] on the contrary, it can only be *the nature of content* which is responsible for *movement* in scientific knowledge, for it is the content's *own reflection* that first posits and *generates what that content is*. [...] This spiritual movement, which in its simplicity gives itself its determinateness, and in this determinateness gives itself its self-equality – this movement, which is thus the immanent development of the concept, is the absolute method of the concept, the absolute method of cognition and at the same time the immanent should of the content. (SL 2010: pp.9f.)[2]

In the introduction to the *Science of Logic* Hegel takes up the issue of scientific method again: the problem that every other science has to distinguish between the matter that it treats and the scientific method it uses. In logic, by contrast, the forms of reflection, rules and laws of thinking are part of its content. Both the scientific method and the concept of science itself belong to its content (cf. SL 2010: p.23). Hegel says that for "the dead bones of logic to be quickened by spirit and become substance and content, its method must be the one which alone can make it fit to be pure science" (SL 2010: p.32). He criticises contemporary logic for not having a scientific method in this sense. Hegel says furthermore that "method is the consciousness of the form of the inner self-movement of the content of logic" SL 2010: p.33). He explains that in the *Phenomenology of Spirit*

---

[2] We first encounter this idea of self-reflection in the Neoplatonic thought of Plotinus and Porphyry, who were trying to reconcile Plato and Aristotle. In the course of this attempt, they made the following move: the highest principle, the one or *hen*, cannot itself be determined; it is not delineated from other things, as it is one and all. How then can we explicate it, if it is unspeakable in this way? Porphyry contends that the one, or *hen*, is delineated not from anything else, but from itself as its content, in a first move that he calls reflection. Plotinus thinks the *nous* turns its thought upon itself.

he presents an example of this method with respect to the concrete object consciousness. We see the shapes of consciousness, which dissolve in being realised and result in their own negation, thereby assuming a higher form. Hegel keeps repeating that the method is not distinct from its subject matter and content, for it is the content in itself, the dialectic which it possesses within itself, which moves the subject matter forward.

> It is clear that no expositions can be accepted as scientifically valid that do not follow the progression of this method and are not in tune with its simple rhythm, for it is the course of the fact itself. (SL 2010: p.33)

It is only at the end of the *Science of Logic*, when Hegel gets to the absolute idea, that he brings back method. He says that what is left to be considered is not some particular content, but the universal character of its form—that is, method.

> *Method* may appear at first to be just the *manner* in which cognition proceeds, and this is in fact its nature. [...] If the content is again assumed as given to the method and of a nature of its own, then method, so understood, is just like the logical realm in general a merely *external* form. (SL 2010: p.736)

Finally, Hegel tells us that method is only

> the movement of the *concept* itself. [...] It is the method proper to each and every fact because its activity is the concept. (SL 2010: p.737)

The last pages of the *Science of Logic* elaborate on what constitutes the method, namely the determinations of the concept itself and their connections. He says one must begin doing this right from the start. With respect to content, the beginning has to be wholly indeterminate for the method at first. Then, as the method runs its course, since method is the absolute form, the concept that knows itself and everything as concept, there is no content that would stand out against it and determine it as a one-sided external form. The content of cognition enters into the circle of consideration quite late because, as deduced, it now belongs to the method. That is how the method itself expands into a system.

I conclude this part on method with the passages from the very end of the *Science of Logic* in which it becomes clear that Hegel thought of method as something more than just a picture for representation. He aims for the "*circle* that winds around itself" (SL 2010: p.751). The *Science of Logic* returns to the conception of the absolute idea as simple units with which it began. "The method is the pure concept that only relates to itself" (SL 2010: p.752). In its own idea, the *Science of Logic* has now comprehended its own concept.³

2 Kant

I shall now turn to Kant, though I shall mainly continue to use Hegelian language. In the third part of the *Logic*, the *Doctrine of the Concept*, Hegel tries to revive the idea of the concept. If the concept comes third after Being and Essence, the immediate and reflection, and if Being and Essence are moments of its becoming, then the concept as the foundation and truth of Being and Essence is the identity into which they have sunk and in which they are contained (cf. SL 2010: p.508). The *Objective Logic*—parts one and two of which respectively concern Being and Essence—is, as it were, the genetic exposition of the concept. Hegel thinks that he can augment the understanding of the concept that he develops by adding that it is none other than the "I" or pure self-consciousness. Even though we have determinate concepts, the "I" is the pure concept itself, the concept that has to come into determinate existence. The "I" is a purely self-reflexive unity that abstracts from all determinateness and content and withdraws into the freedom of identity with itself. But the "I" is also immediately self-reflexive negativity, singularity or absolute determinateness. Neither the one nor the other can be comprehended unless these two moments are grasped at the same time, both in their abstraction and in their perfect unity (cf. SL 2010: p.515). Hegel goes on to explain what he thinks Kant achieved in the *Critique of Pure Reason*. When we say that we have the understanding as a faculty, we have concepts in that way too, which is the same way in which we have, e.g., a coat or an external property. Hegel points out that Kant sees that this is not enough. The concepts we have because we have understanding are not just external things that can be ascribed to us. The "I think" is not something externally ascribed to us, but is the very thought of itself, the "I". Let us see how Hegel presents this. He says Kant went beyond this external relation of the understanding to the "I think" and that it is

---

3 In the *Phenomenology of Spirit* this point is put differently. Hegel writes that

> Comprehending thought conducts itself in quite a different way. Since the concept is the object's own self, that is, the self which exhibits itself as the *object's coming-to-be* [*als sein Werden*], it is not a motionless subject passively supporting the accidents; rather, it is the self-moving concept which takes its determinations back into itself. (PS 2012: §60)

> one of the profoundest and truest insights to be found in the Critique of Pure Reason that the *unity* which constitutes the *essence of the concept* is recognized as the *original synthetic unity of apperception*, the unity of the "*I think*" or of self-consciousness. (SL 2010: p.515)

The transcendental deduction of the categories goes beyond the mere representation of the relation of the "I" and the understanding, and advances to the very thinking of itself in the "I think" (SL 2010). What does it mean that the "I" thinks itself in the "I think?" I have elsewhere interpreted the "I think" that accompanies all of our representations as the fact that a thought needs to be actively thought (cf. Moser forthcoming). By advancing to the thinking or the thought of the "I think", Hegel means that it is the actual thinking that happens in the transcendental apperception which is the unification of the manifold of a given intuition in the concept. In this unification as synthesis, however, we need a unity of consciousness. This objective unity of consciousness is distinguished by Kant from the subjective unity of consciousness. The "I" becomes conscious of a manifold, and the principles of the objective determination of representations are derived from the principle of the transcendental unity of apperception. By virtue of the categories, these objective determinations—the manifold of given representations—are so determined as to be brought to the unity of consciousness (B144). What unites consciousness—what makes the synthesis work—is what Kant explicates in "The Clue to the Discovery of All Pure Concepts of the Understanding". For Kant, the answer is that there already seems to be the same order in the intuitions that we find in the concepts.

Hegel holds that Kantian philosophy gives us the justification for turning to the nature of the "I" in order to learn what a concept is. It cannot be the mere representation of the "I", but needs to comprehend both the "I" and the concept. To make this a bit clearer: for Hegel, specific determinateness and differentiation are equally essential moments of the concept. The original synthesis of apperception is, Hegel states, "one of the most profound principles for speculative development" (SL 2010: p.520) as it contains the beginning of a true apprehension of the nature of the concept. But Hegel criticised Kant for not having moved past the idea of a synthesis that is a picture of an external unity, a mere combination of terms that are intrinsically separate.

What Hegel adds to Kant is that it is "precisely in the concept that the manifold is sublated inasmuch as it pertains to intuition as opposed to the concept" (SL 2010: p.521). Hegel wonders how Kant could get so far in his philosophy as to acknowledge that the relation of thought to sensuous existence is only a relation of mere appearance but then stop short at that relative relation. He also wonders why Kant asserts that truth is finite cognition and that what he had recognised as truth and had defined as such was illegitimate and extravagant, namely the cognition of the thing in itself (SL 2010: p.522). What Kant treated as a figment of truth *is* truth for Hegel. He points to the agreement of cognition with its subject matter as a trivial nominal definition. However, he thinks that Kant should have used that definition of truth, because then he would have had to treat *the idea* which expresses the required agreement as truth (SL 2010: p.523).

So far, this sums up Hegel's discussion of Kant at the beginning of the *Doctrine of the Concept*. I made this intermediate step in order to clarify in what sense the projection method can be understood as providing the condition of the possibility of representation in Wittgenstein.[4] In what sense can Wittgenstein be said to develop a theory that sets out the conditions of the possibility of representation in the *Tractatus* in a way similar to Kant's setting out the conditions of the possibility of experience in the *First Critique?* In Hegel's reading of Kant, the manifold is sublated in the concept, although it pertains to intuition rather than the concept, and thus the relation of thought to sensuous experience is only a relative one and we cannot have knowledge of things in themselves. For Hegel, the agreement of the cognition with its subject matter is not a trivial thing but truth itself. To make the transition to Wittgenstein, I will suggest that just as the meaning or content of the proposition is in the projection itself and not derived from something else, e.g., its parts, so too in the same way the manifold of sense perception is only thought in the unification/synthesis of thought. In the next section, I show that Wittgenstein's projection method in the *Tractatus* is therefore similar to Kant in that it is a movement of the mind (*Handlung/Bewegung des Gemüts*), and that what Wittgenstein is doing with the projection method is quite similar to what Hegel is doing with his notion of a concept. Unfortunately, the notion of a concept is not developed by Wittgenstein in the early work. What is developed in the *Tractatus* is the zero-method, a metaphysical theory that Wittgenstein rejects.

Wittgenstein's projection method

In a famous interview with Bryan Magee, John Searle said that the key to the *Tractatus* is the picture theory.[5] This is an established view which I think is wrong. I argue that in the process of looking for the right kind of method to teach philosophy, Wittgenstein wants to resolve the misunderstandings of the

---

4 I have traced the connection step by step in my book on *Kant and Wittgenstein* (Moser forthcoming).
5 Interview with John Searle: https://www.youtube.com/watch?v=qrmPq8pzG9Q (4.04).

logic of our language. The projection method in the *Tractatus* is intended to do away with a static logical theory of the kind represented by the picture theory. Like in the *Philosophical Investigations*, where one interlocutor is followed by another and we never know who is speaking, I argue that in the propositions of the *Tractatus* Wittgenstein presents theoretical elements that he then rejects or a theory that he does not espouse, namely the picture theory.

What he develops is an account of how propositions hang together with what they are about. He alternately calls that which propositions are about "reality", "facts" or "the existence and nonexistence of states of affairs". What Wittgenstein is concerned with are neither abstract objects nor the most general features of reality; rather, we could say that (like Kant) he is interested in specifying the essential preconditions for representation.

The work focuses on the way in which propositions as pictures of reality are able to represent possible situations or describe states of affairs. The picture theory holds that we make pictures of facts, which according to Wittgenstein is possible because each picture comes with a picturing relation that connects it to what the picture is about. This picturing relation represents the sense of the picture as true or false in comparison with reality. To be able to make pictures of facts, Wittgenstein holds, we need to look at the picture as a form of representation that operates solely as a connection between the logical picture and a situation. If the sentence represents the existence and non-existence of states of affairs, it can do so only because of the logical form or logical picture. But the logical form or picture cannot itself be represented. The logical form shows, or as Wittgenstein puts it: "this mirrors itself in the proposition". The difficulty with Wittgenstein's theory is therefore the question of the logical underpinnings of the working of the picture: how does the basic kind of proposition, the elementary proposition, assert the existence of a state of affairs in the first place? And this is where we realise that initially we are not dealing with a picture theory, but with something that should be called a picturing theory. Wittgenstein actually calls it a projection method. He sets out to make an equation: on the left-hand side we have the proposition, which is a picture or an image of something, and on the right-hand side we have the reality of what is represented. At least, that seems to be how the picture and pictured are set up. But then the meaning of the copula *is* in the equation becomes more complicated. Let us look at the text: in 2.1513 Wittgenstein says that "the representing relation which makes [a picture] a picture"[6] belongs to that picture, and then in 2.17 he continues:

---

6 Except where stated otherwise, I have used Ogden's translation of the *Tractatus*.

> What the picture must have in common with reality in order to be able to represent it at all —rightly or falsely—is its form of representation.

Now it is not the picture on the one side and the pictured reality on the other; rather, two links—the representing relation and the form of representation— must be there beforehand. This representing relation is elucidated in 2.1514 in the following way: "The representing relation consists of the co-ordinations of the elements of the picture and the things." The form of representation is described in 2.151 as "the possibility that the things are combined with one another as are the elements of the picture". The representing relation and the form of representation are pulled together in the method of projection as two aspects of the same thing: the representing relation is the actual structure of the picturing or projecting, while the form of representation is the possibility of such representation.[7] Reality, as we saw earlier, is the existence or non-existence of states of affairs. What the picture as a fact—as an existing state of affairs—has to have in common with the existence of a state of affairs is its form of representation. Proposition 3.11 allows us to move back and forth between form of representation and representing relation, in order to see the importance of the aspect of projection:

> We use the sensibly perceptible sign (sound or written sign, etc.) of the proposition as a projection of the possible state of affairs.
>
> The method of projection is the thinking of the sense of the proposition.

This means that when we picture states of affairs we use the sentence, or more precisely the perceptible sign of the sentence, as a projection of the possible state of affairs. In this proposition Wittgenstein equates the left-hand side with the right-hand side. The propositional sign is (used as) the projection of the situation, which is itself the thinking of the sense. We see this in proposition 4.01:

> The proposition is a picture of reality.
>
> The proposition is a model of reality as we think it is.

The proposition as the sensibly perceptible sign is the model of reality as we think it. Furthermore, proposition 4.2 elucidates that the sense of the proposition lies in the agreement and disagreement with possibilities of existence and non-

---

7 This interpretation is owed to Eli Friedlander's (2001) reading of the *Tractatus*. A more detailed version can be found in my forthcoming *Kant and Wittgenstein*.

existence of states of affairs. The sense of a proposition is its agreement and disagreement with possibilities of existence and non-existence of states of affairs. There is on the one hand the isomorphism between the picture and what is pictured that makes the picture possible, the form of representation, and on the other the active comparison of the sensible perceptible propositional sign as the projection onto states of affairs, the representing relation. A correct reading of the *Tractatus* has to focus on the representing or picturing or projecting that brings about the form of representation in the first place. Wittgenstein says in 4.01, "The proposition *is* a model of reality as we think it *is*." I have emphasised both occurrences of *is* in proposition 4.01, because the equation of the sensibly perceptible part of the proposition with the projection of possible states of affairs (see 3.11) means that the proposition *is* the projection of states of affairs. This means we are not dealing with a pre-existing relation between the picture and what is pictured, but with a projection that creates itself in the projection similar to how the "I" creates itself in the "I think" that has to accompany all of our representations and is at the same time the unification of the sensible manifold in a concept as well as the product of this unification, the "I" that thinks itself in the synthesis.

3 The zero-method

It is possible to show in more detail the sense in which Wittgenstein's projection method is akin to Kant's transcendental apperception as a metaphysical theory by focusing on what Wittgenstein calls the *zero-method*, a special form of the projection method.[8] To introduce this zero-method we have to look at propositions in the *Tractatus* that get a lot of attention due to their peculiar status concerning truth: namely, the ones that are tautologies or contradictions. Tautologies are always true, and contradictions are always false. With tautologies, we know at a glance that what is on the left-hand side is the same as what is on the right (a=a). With contradictions, we know that the left and right-hand sides are never the same, because they are contradictory (a=~a). Tautologies, contradictions and all other logical propositions are presented in the *Tractatus* as being such that they do not have to be projected onto reality to find out whether they are true or false. Since they are either always true or always false they do

---

[8] The only mention of the zero-method is in *Tractatus* 6.121. I discuss it in my book *Kant and Wittgenstein* (forthcoming).

not have sense in the sense that other propositions do.[9] This creates a special case of the projection method outlined above, according to which the projection onto reality is the thinking of a thought. No projection onto reality is necessary, therefore there is no thinking, no unification in a concept and in that sense no sense. I will gradually build up the method as it appears in the *Tractatus* by working my way through the propositions leading to it. In proposition 3.13, Wittgenstein asserts the pivotal importance of the projection: "To the proposition belongs everything which belongs to the projection; but not what is projected." He says in 3.327 that the (propositional) sign determines a logical form only together with its logico-syntactical application. In propositions 3.5 and 4 he makes this even clearer by equating the applied or thought propositional sign with the thought itself.

> 3.5 The applied, thought, propositional sign is the thought.
>
> 4 The thought is the significant proposition.

Therefore, the application must be part and parcel of the relation of thought and what thought is about, not as a relation of thought and reality, but as *thought reality*. This, however, creates a real problem for the kinds of proposition that do not need a projection. Logical propositions or tautologies and contradictions are lacking the constituent that makes a proposition a proposition in the first place.

Wittgenstein explains this in the course of the *Tractatus* by determining that there are propositions that are part of the symbolism just as much as zero is part of the number system. He says that these propositions do not have any projection onto reality. In tautologies, contradictions and all other logical propositions we can read their truth or falsity off the perceptible part alone. In 6.113 Wittgenstein writes that

> It is the peculiar mark of logical propositions that one can recognize that they are true from the symbol alone, and this fact contains in itself the whole philosophy of logic. (Pears/McGuiness's translation)

As we have seen above in the example for tautology a=a, one can recognise the truth of these propositions from the symbol alone, which means that no projection onto reality is necessary. Wittgenstein explains in 4.462 that this is why

---

[9] But they are also not nonsensical like propositions with parts that have not been given any meaning or that are not well constructed.

> Tautology and contradiction are not pictures of reality. They present no possible state of affairs. For the one allows *every* possible state of affairs, the other *none*.

Furthermore, Wittgenstein says in 4.466 that "tautology and contradiction are the limiting cases of the combinations of symbols, namely their dissolution" and in proposition 6.11 that "the propositions of logic therefore say nothing". Wittgenstein then goes a step further. He gives a role to the propositions of logic that should give us pause. In proposition 6.12 he writes:

> The fact that the propositions of logic are tautologies *shows* the formal—logical—properties of language and the world.

This special role that Wittgenstein bestows to logical propositions is that their being tautologies "shows" the form or logical properties of language and world. We know that "showing" is a difficult term in the *Tractatus*. What are the formal–logical properties of language and the world?

Let us now look at proposition 6.121, the only passage in which we encounter the zero-method. This passage is about propositions or language. Wittgenstein says that the propositions of logic demonstrate the logical properties of propositions by combining them so as to form propositions that say nothing.

> This method could also be called a *zero-method*. In a logical proposition, propositions are brought into equilibrium with one another, and the state of equilibrium then indicates what the logical constitution of these propositions must be. (Pears/McGuiness's translation; my emphasis)

Wittgenstein calls this a zero-method, because within the logical propositions we have equilibrium, and the state of that equilibrium shows how the propositions are constituted logically. But Wittgenstein also called logic a mirror-image of the world and described it as transcendental (6.13). In logic, everything can be read off propositions. Since mathematics is a logical method, this is true of mathematical propositions, and they are probably the best example. Mathematical propositions are equations, albeit such that you cannot always clearly see whether what is on the right-hand side equals what is on the left-hand side or not. In the case of $8+4=12$ this is easy: $12=12$. Because nothing new comes to the fore, Wittgenstein calls mathematical and all logical propositions "merely pseudo propositions" (6.2). This is similarly true for Kant's analytic propositions.

What is the role of the zero-method and of logical and mathematical propositions? I argue that it completes a twofold theory of thought and language in the *Tractatus*. On the one hand, there is a metaphysical part that holds that propositions have meaning because a number of elementary propositions put together constitute the whole of meaning. This is shown in the zero-method. Logical propositions, tautologies and contradictions are special instances of propositions. They have meaning, true or false, beyond being projected onto reality. They are as it were the connection between language and reality in the first place, without having to make that connection in thought. While Wittgenstein might be thought to have been tempted here by a metaphysical theory into explaining how propositions are, as it were, about facts or the world without anyone thinking them, in fact he merely uses these propositions to "climb up the ladder". In the end, he sees that all the propositions of the *Tractatus* are logical propositions and have to be discarded as pseudo-propositions. What is left are propositions with sense that are not static pictures, but the projection method itself in which thinking is the application of the sensible perceptible sign to that which it is about in thought.

4 Conclusion

What I have shown by elucidating the projection method and zero-method in the *Tractatus* is that Wittgenstein was already developing a conception of language or thought as applied logic in the *Tractatus*, and not only later in the *Philosophical Investigations* where we see the expansion of logic into grammar and thus into language-games and forms of life. From this point of view the development of Wittgenstein's logic and grammar has a lot in common with Hegel's logic. Hegel says philosophy cannot have a method that is different from its content. In the same way, Wittgenstein holds that the meaning or content of a proposition is only brought about in the projection itself and is not different from it. It is not derived from "this part means this" and "this part means this" put together. From the projection of the whole sentence sign we can derive the meaning of its parts. From the projection of the sentence sign "This is a table" one can derive the meaning of the names in the sentence: "this", "is", "table". It is a decomposition of meaning, not a composition. The analysis is not going to yield determinate distinctive or atomic parts that we could use later to determine meaning. It is already composed in a sort of transcendental composition.

The projection method as the privation of the zero-method is an active movement of the mind (the very movement of projection that is absent in the latter). And that is what Hegel's concept of method is too: it is an activity. For Hegel, it is the activity of spirit, not of an individual mind. Wittgenstein's zero-method would be something like a thinking point, a thought without extension. This cannot be, since thinking or projecting are done in time and space. The zero-method is only developed in order to set it aside; it is put in the conjunctive. "This method could be called a zero-method", Wittgenstein says in 6.121. If one needed to refer to it one could call it that. However, one does not refer to it, because it does not do any work. This method is what has been called the picture theory, which is a wrong reading of the *Tractatus*.

Wittgenstein starts from elementary propositions and thinks about how they connect. The result that both Wittgenstein and Hegel arrive at is that there is no gap between the language of the world and the world. It is all one. There is no gap between the world and language or thought that then needs to be bridged by a transcendental method that involves a transcendental apperception, an "I think" that would guarantee that there is a valid connection. While Wittgenstein does use a logic of language that he learned from Frege and Russell, and tries to build up language from there, he still thinks the whole of the proposition or the picture of reality as not static. He thinks of the connection in the proposition as a picturing or a projection, and this is very different from operations in analytic philosophy. We could still say that in the *Tractatus* Wittgenstein is coming from the opposite direction to Hegel. Hegel's starting point is the concept encompassing the whole movement. Any state of the concept would be an individual instantiation within history. Wittgenstein starting point is the whole of the projection. In the later Wittgenstein, we get the notion of a form of life: culture, habit, custom, similar to Hegel's meaning of *Geist*. However, we find a transcendental method in Hegel, but we do not get one in Wittgenstein. The logic of the *Tractatus* is not a transcendental logic—which my elucidation of the zero-method aims to show. However, because of Wittgenstein's reference to the zero-method we can count Wittgenstein among the transcendental idealists (in a Kantian sense), even though he does not have a transcendental method.

Wittgenstein's philosophical method consists not just in pointing out misunderstandings of the logic of our language. I have shown that both Wittgenstein and Hegel think of method as that which happens within concepts. By showing how such an understanding of method is brought forth in the *Tractatus* and *Science of Logic*, I hope to have thrown new light on a rarely acknowledged connection between Wittgenstein and Hegel.

References

Friedlander, Eli: *Signs of Sense. Reading Wittgenstein's Tractatus*. Harvard University Press, 2001.
Moser, Aloisia: *Wittgenstein and Kant. Thinking Acts*, forthcoming.
Wyss, Sebastian: "Does Wittgenstein have a Method? The Challenges of Conant and Schulte", *Nordic Wittgenstein Review* 4:1, 2015, pp.167–193.

Ermylos Plevrakis
A Hegelian Reading of Wittgenstein's *Tractatus Logico-Philosophicus*

Abstract Wittgenstein opens his preface to the TLP with the following words: "Perhaps this book will be understood only by someone who has himself already had the thoughts that are expressed in it—or at least similar thoughts. [...] Its purpose would be achieved if it gave pleasure to one person who read and understood it." In this chapter, I shall take this invitation literally and try to interpret the TLP by reference to the reader's thoughts, feelings and understanding, imagining this reader to be Hegel. To this end, I give an anachronistic "Hegelian reading of the TLP" in which I, firstly, focus on the thoughts—and not mere propositions, as Wittgenstein puts it in his preface—expressed in the *Tractatus* and, secondly, examine how Hegel's SL could be seen as a response to the TLP. To cut a long story short, the most important Tractarian thought from a Hegelian point of view would be "the sole logical constant" (TLP: 5.47), which the SL refers to as *the Concept*.[1]

1 The Tractarian course towards the sole logical constant

At the very beginning of his TLP, Wittgenstein introduces a kind of ontology of facts, which is meant to define the primary presupposition of all Tractarian investigations. Instead of going into detail about familiar Wittgensteinian conceptions such as "world", "state of affairs", "combination of objects" etc., I would like to point out the first thought that is of great interest from a Hegelian point of view: namely, that the world has a *substance*, which, *prima facie*, seems to constitute an epistemological postulate. For, "[i]f the world had no substance, then whether a proposition had sense would depend on whether another proposition was true" (TLP: 2.0211). Although the substance serves as the main condition for the truth of every proposition, Wittgenstein prefers not to define it any further in this part of the TLP and notes that "[s]ubstance is what subsists independently of

---

[1] Anton Friedrich Koch has drawn attention to the Tractarian sole logical constant from a Hegelian point of view by focusing on the beginning of Hegel's SL (Koch 2014: pp.64f., 237f.). In this chapter, I take his conclusions as given, and try to develop them further by showing parallels with other parts of the SL as well.

https://doi.org/10.1515/9783110572780-021

what is the case" (2.024), which happens to be merely "simple" (2.02) and inconceivable (2.0121). Hegel would probably think this is a kind of *dualism:* on the one hand the world, the totality of states of affairs, and on the other an insistent substance; on the one hand a field truly described by language, on the other something like the Aristotelian *prima materia*, i.e., a completely unformed material with no determinations at all which has to be there or else all language-determined affairs would be impossible.

Furthermore, after reading the Tractarian picture theory of meaning, Hegel would perhaps add a third element to that dualistic model, namely our pictures of the world. These pictures may square or not with the reality they represent, but they are surely not the same as the substance of the world. Hegel would therefore develop that dualism into a *triangle* conception (substance, world, (linguistic) pictures of the world), where the postulated substance is supposed to guarantee the truth-potential of our propositions. Nevertheless, one should not forget that it is the use of language that postulates this substance and not the substance that articulates itself through propositions (see Ule 2001: pp.237f.). We can hence call this conception the Tractarian *epistemological* triangle.

In the subsequent propositions from the TLP, Hegel would be confronted with Wittgenstein's theory of logic, which enquires into the relation between propositions and the way they can be derived from each other. Although this logic is quite different from the Hegelian one, Hegel would surely be enchanted by Wittgenstein's idea that there is a *general propositional form*, i.e., not only a form which constitutes "the common characteristic mark of a class of propositions" (TLP: 3.311), which is a central issue in the picture theory, but "the most general propositional form: that is, [the] description of the propositions of *any* sign-language" (TLP: 4.5). Hegel would also be content with Wittgenstein's generic definition of the general form of proposition, which in the English translation ("This is how things stand", TLP: 4.5) sounds more trivial than it really is, since in German it indicates a relation of something to itself ("Es verhält sich so und so"). But most of all, Hegel would be wildly enthusiastic about Wittgenstein's elaborate idea (to be found in TLP: 5.502–5.51 and 6–6.01) that with the general propositional form, "the general form according to which one proposition can be generated out of another by means of an operation" (6.002) is also given. Wittgenstein emphasises this general form by calling it "the sole logical constant", i.e., "what all propositions, by their very nature, ha[ve] in common with one another" (5.47). To Hegel's ears this would sound like a crucial declaration that the Tractarian Wittgenstein is indeed aiming at a logico-philosophical enterprise very similar to his own in the SL, in which he is also looking for the principle of all propositions, thoughts and logical constants and where, nevertheless, he deals with notions such as "substance" and "world". (For more on this point see sections 4 and 5 below.)

With respect to the picture theory, Hegel might raise a similar objection to the one he raised against Kantian epistemology. If we read TLP: 4.01, for instance, ("A proposition is a model of reality as we imagine it") we may assume that the general propositional form too is something that *we* imagine—something that is only *our* thought, *our* operation and *our* way of deriving propositions from each other, which may radically differ from the way the world "in itself" is. That would suggest a kind of subjectivism or human inter-subjectivism in opposition to objectivity. Contrary to this, Wittgenstein states in his theory of logic that the general propositional form is "the essence of the proposition" (5.471, translation amended) *and* "the essence of all description, and thus the essence of the world" (5.4711, 2.18). Such an assumption could surely provide enough motivation for someone to read the TLP from a post-Kantian idealist perspective. Hegel himself, whose systematic work aimed to refute the Kantian assumption of an obscure "thing in itself" which remains hidden behind the (phenomenal) world, would perhaps celebrate this approach towards the relation between (the essence of) our everyday language and (the essence of) the world. He might see in the Tractarian reflections the attempt to establish a new monism: a unity and homogeneity of language and world in terms of logic, i.e., in terms of "the sole logical constant". This might sound overly crude to those Wittgenstein scholars who are more interested in the late than the early Wittgenstein. And I will come back to that thesis in my third section, where I discuss some open issues regarding the sole logical constant and especially its relation to "substance". But I shall first mention briefly some more key features of the TLP which will help us better understand the role of the sole logical constant and which would arouse Hegel's interest in a positive way.

The first such feature is the Tractarian understanding of philosophy. Wittgenstein stresses the profound difference between philosophy and philosophical propositions on the one hand and the natural sciences and everyday propositions on the other. While everyday propositions "represent" something, which means they have "sense", "[m]ost of the propositions and questions to be found in philosophical works are [...] nonsensical" (4.003). Philosophy itself "is not one of the natural sciences" but rather something "above or below the natural sciences, not beside them" (4.111). Hegel would probably not approve of the rather pejorative expression "nonsensical", but he would fully agree with the sharp distinction between propositions that refer to particular facts in the empirical world and those that do not involve sense, do not merely "represent", but are nonetheless essential for the others and for all natural sciences.² In addition, it is obvious that Hegel's speculative dialectics "aims at the logical clarification of thoughts" and approaches philosophy as an "activity" (4.112) or even as "therapy", as Michael Quante puts it (2011: pp.64–90).

Furthermore, one can observe the same coherence with respect to logic. Hegel would immediately agree with Wittgenstein's so-called "fundamental idea", namely that "the 'logical constants' are not representatives; that there can be no representatives of the *logic* of facts" (4.0312), which means that "[t]here are no 'logical objects'" (4.441). For not even the most vulgar interpretation of the SL would ever argue that any of the things it describes, such as "quality", "quantity" or even "existence" and "objectivity", are ordinary objects that exist alongside things with which we interact empirically. Wittgenstein also mentions that logic is "transcendental" (6.13, 5.552), by which he means that it is unconditioned with respect to experience and instead constitutes the condition of experience (see Ule 2001: pp.246 ff.). Additionally, he insists that logic is (or at least should be) autonomous and faultless (5.473) and that its propositions must be "simple" and form "a completed, well-proportioned creation", some kind of "realm" ("ein[] abgeschlossene[s], regelmäßige[s] Gebilde", "ein Gebiet", 5.4541, translation amended). Hegel would indeed be far from criticising such illustrations. For he conceived his own *Logic* as the first and systematically most important part of his philosophical system, distinct from (the philosophy of) nature and spirit. And as one can read in the opening of the SL (pp.45–55), Hegel was extremely interested in articulating logic as the strictest science, with no preconditions at all but no less autonomous than Kantian pure reason (see also Houlgate 2006: pp.12 ff., 29 ff.).

Thus far, we have witnessed a great deal of affinity (rather than contradiction) between Hegel and the Tractarian Wittgenstein with respect to their fundamental intuitions and intentions. If we want to address the differences, we must dig deeper and consider how Wittgenstein and Hegel act on these intuitions and intentions, i.e., how radically each of them proceeds with the philosophical "activity", how far they go and why they stop where they do. The main question

---

2 Hegel elaborates on this distinction *in extenso* in the last two chapters of the SL, which also reflect precisely the vertical hierarchy between the natural sciences and (speculative) philosophy. The "Idea of Cognition" corresponds to empirical cognition and the propositions of everyday life and the natural sciences (Hegel terms it "finite cognition"), whereas the "Absolute Idea" provides the method for (speculative) philosophical inquiry, which does not necessarily involve sense but, according to Hegel, represents a highly specific perfection of (all) cognition, knowledge, propositions and truth.

posed by a Hegelian reading of the TLP would, thus, be: does the TLP *satisfactorily* elucidate the thoughts it says it is supposed to elucidate?

2 The Tractarian elucidation of the sole logical constant

The question raised above primarily concerns the role of logic in general and the sole logical constant in particular within the epistemological triangle of the TLP, and has great metaphysical significance. In what sense does the Tractarian theory of logic add anything new to the propositions about substance, world and language from the first half of the book? As I mentioned above, Wittgenstein refers to the general propositional form, i.e., the sole logical constant, as the "essence of the proposition" and the "essence of the world". Accordingly, we can refine the question as follows: what is the relation between the "substance" and "essence" of the world (TLP: 2.0231 and 5.4711)? I do not know whether Wittgenstein was interested at the time of the TLP in a fine terminological distinction between the strongly metaphysical terms "substance" and "essence". But I do not think that there is enough systematic space in the TLP for both "substance" of the world and the sole logical constant competing against it. The relationship between the "substance" and "essence" of the world is crucial, however, not only from a Hegelian point of view but also for the understanding of the whole course of the Tractarian inquiry, the depth and character of philosophy based on it and of course the Tractarian concept of language, world and logic.

There are two possible reconstructions of the way the "substance" and "essence" of the world could relate to each other within the bounds of the TLP: either they are the same in a certain sense or they stand for different fields indicated by the TLP. To begin with the second option, "essence" replaces "substance" only within the epistemological triangle, not throughout the whole Tractarian inquiry. The "substance" is moved "underneath" the "essence", while still playing the role of *prima materia* awaiting determination through language. The "essence", i.e., the sole logical constant, must therefore be conceived as something similar to the Aristotelian *causa formalis* or as an epistemological *causa efficiens* which gives concrete names to "substance" (i.e., objects) and constitutes facts and propositions, that is, the world and language. But there is a lot of old-fashioned metaphysics in these assumptions—which seems to be a problem at least from Wittgenstein's own point of view. So I shall instead argue for the first option, that is, for a certain identity between "essence" and "substance", which, in my opinion, is also the option that brings the TLP closer to Hegel's own logico-philosophical inquiry.

To this end, I am going to expand on my proposed Hegelian reading of the TLP by adopting a more "therapeutic" view of the Tractarian "substance", according to which "substance" is, as James Conant puts it (2002: p.422), just an *apparent premise* that has to be elucidated or even banished from the philosophical and everyday language. More precisely, I argue that in the course of the TLP Wittgenstein performatively replaces the "substance" of the world, which is only a postulate of our everyday language (that is, our everyday epistemology and metaphysics), with the sole logical constant, understood as the main result of the Tractarian investigation. "Substance" was introduced at the start of the TLP as an epistemological postulate in order to secure the truth or falsity of propositions, and it is not further elucidated other than being said to be simple and inconceivable and hence completely ineffable. But although the Tractarian theory of logic does not literally deal with "substance", it does elaborate on the concept of the ineffable.

TLP: 5.502–5.51 and 6–6.01 introduce the N-operation – $N(\bar{\xi})$ –, which means the joint negation "of all the values of the propositional variable ξ" (5.502), and hence all propositions or everything that can be said. Thus, the N-operation is the precise Tractarian clarification of what everyday language cannot express with its common propositions, and must, therefore, be called ineffable, unspeakable and inexpressible. In other worlds, the N-operation is the literal negation of everything that is speakable and expressible. At the same time, the N-operation must be understood as the very essence of all propositions of the "all-embracing logic, which mirrors the world" (5.511), that is, the form "according to which propositions are constructed [... and] can be generated out of another by means of an operation" (6.002), which produces "an infinitely fine network, the great mirror" of the world (5.511).[3] As a result, the N-operation is also the precise Tractarian clarification of what everyday epistemology and metaphysics consider to be a certain substance beneath the world that ensures the truth or falsity of their propositions.

This "therapeutic" transformation of "substance" into a sole logical constant succeeds in effectively defending the consistency of Tractarian philosophy

---

3 There have been some serious objections to the Tractarian concept of the N-operation and doubts about whether it can provide such a logical homogeneity (Glock 1996: pp.143f.; Sullivan 2004). I do not aim to solve these problems in this chapter. Hegel might in any case also have serious doubts about the consistency of a logic based on $N(\bar{\xi})$. For a Hegelian reading of the TLP, though, it is very important that the TLP formulates the vision of a sole logical constant which can produce all other (logical) propositions.

against the "mystical" attacks that claim that there is something lying *outside* the limits of language and world. The sole logical constant is not a substance in the terms of Aristotle's *Categories*, i.e., a concrete thing, or in terms of a completely unformed material. It is also not a fact, but a *logical operation*, a logical activity— just like philosophy is an activity and not a mere body of doctrine (4.112). In addition, this operation provides the most important insight into the way we should proceed with the activity of philosophy, that is, an insight into the *method* of philosophy and of clarification of the limits of language *from the inside* (see also Diamond 2011: pp.240–257). At the end of the TLP we no longer need to assume the existence of a substance, meaning that we can throw away the ladder of everyday metaphysics and focus on the activity of formulating the propositions that can be meaningfully formulated; we know that language negates itself and it is hence limited by its own negation. *This* is the mystical, the "unspeakable" and "inexpressible" (TLP: 4.115; 6.522, Ogden/Ramsey's translation): the self-negation of language, which *shows* itself performatively in every proposition. The assumption of a substance, in contrast, lying underneath logic like an unknowable *prima materia* is simply irrelevant: it neither adds something essential to the world and language nor can it be verified or falsified. On this account, philosophical activity is the very specific clarification of thoughts by means of the N-operation (rather than an obscure "substance"). And it is the same reference to the N-operation that transforms our understanding of the world and enables us to "view the world sub specie aeterni", i.e., as "a limited whole" (6.45). This view of the world differs from our everyday perspective, inasmuch as it presupposes the insight that the world is in itself limited (see also Diamond 2011: pp.257–264).

Hegel would certainly agree with that. Everyday propositions—in Hegelian terms: thoughts expressed in everyday propositions—are structured and limited from the inside by virtue of a single logical constant, and if there is something lying beyond thought, it is only accidental, a mere resemblance, void or, to use a more Wittgensteinian term, nonsense. Still, Hegel would pose a different question, which goes beyond the ambitions of a therapeutic reading of the TLP: the main concern of the final propositions of the TLP should not be whether there is something *outside* the limits of the language but rather whether there is something left *inside* it *which has not been fully clarified*. From a Hegelian point of view, it is a crucial observation that, as a result of a logico-philosophical investigation, the "substance" of the world appears to be a logical constant which limits our language from the inside. But does this revelation exhaust *ipso facto* the logico-philosophical *potential* of that logical constant? Hegel would argue that this revelation just signals the beginning of a deeper inquiry, of the logico-philosophical inquiry proper. Wittgenstein has laid the foundation but there is still much left to be *said* about the world *sub specie aeternitatis*. Without this inquiry, philosophy unfortunately still has some blind spots, so that the Tractarian clarifications cannot be considered complete. Hegel would therefore try to draw attention to the problems that, in contrast to TLP: 6.52, have not been eliminated, and which he attempted to eliminate in his *Science of Logic*.

3 Logico-philosophical desiderata regarding the sole logical constant

In TLP: 6.52 and 6.521, Wittgenstein provocatively claims that the "solution of the problem of life is seen in the vanishing of that problem" (translation amended) as a result of scientific investigation. An even more provocative thesis for the understanding of the TLP itself, though, follows in the very next proposition: "There is indeed the inexpressible. This *shows* itself; it is the mystical." (6.522, Ogden/Ramsey's translation) Obviously, the mystical cannot be found in the natural sciences, where all questions are or can be answered. And since we are not willing to accept the existence of something that limits language "from the outside", we must recognise that this mystical is somehow to be found within the bounds of language and Tractarian philosophy—which is not odd at all. For, as I argued above, the mystical, i.e., the inexpressible, is the N-operation and the sole logical constant which limits language from the inside. Otherwise, one would consider the appearance of the mystical in the TLP as completely unreasonable, as a last-minute philosophical trick to save a philosophically unclarified presupposition. But, as far as I can see, there are no obvious arguments for that reading. Instead, there are many propositions in the TLP dealing (explicitly or implicitly) with the mystical, the ineffable or whatever is manifested in terms of showing itself rather than speaking about it.

However, from a Hegelian point of view, this is exactly the core of the problem: the assumption that the mystical is something that *only* shows itself without allowing itself to be spoken of. Hegel would utterly disagree with that, and would point out that Wittgenstein does speak about the mystical and unspeakable: he does have a well-expressed theory of the sole logical constant, he does claim that this constant forms the essence of the proposition, of all description and the world, and he does also develop a notation that gives a lucid logical articulation of the N-operation. The sole logical constant is something that shows itself in every proposition and by generating every proposition out of another; and it *also* has a concretely expressible form, namely the general propositional form: $N(\bar{\xi})$. If making such remarks does not mean speaking about the "unspeakable", then we need to ask how exactly we are defining the verb "to speak".

However, if there must be a difference between mystical and non-mystical, it is not to be found in linguistic terms but rather in terms of involving the other proposition in the action of expressing itself. Both the non-mystical and the mystical are expressed by particular propositions (in the latter case, for example, as just mentioned, through propositions about the general propositional form), but the mystical also shows itself through *all other* propositions which express the non-mystical, i.e., common states of affairs. The mystical is, so to speak, *more* than propositional language, not just *other* than it. It is to be found in the form of the mystical as such, i.e., as the sole logical constant, and at the same time it shows itself in every representation of the world.

Wittgenstein, though, does not explicitly take this Hegelian option. He seems to have the feeling that either the unspeakable, i.e., N(ξ), remains mystical for him insofar as it is not sufficiently elucidated despite all the Tractarian inquiry or that the TLP has pointed towards some issues, other than the N(ξ) itself, which are unspeakable and could not find an adequate exposition in the TLP.[4] Both points seem to contradict the Tractarian intention of radical clarification. Moreover, I think both points are correct.

Let me begin with the second reservation. Wittgenstein does not hesitate to talk about the "subject" or the "self", for instance, which explicitly "does not belong to the world: rather, it is a limit of the world" (5.632, 5.631, 5.641). Since they are not part of the world, "subject" or "self" are not supposed to be expressed through common referential language and should be characterised as unspeakable and inexpressible. Nonetheless, Wittgenstein does speak about them and in the line just quoted even uses the indefinite article (*a* limit of the world), which indicates that there might be more "limits of the world" and, hence, more "unspeakables" besides the "self" and the "subject". Indeed, an example of this can be found in TLP: 6.41: it is the "sense of the world" and its "value" which also "must lie outside the world". Furthermore, TLP: 6.4312 discusses "[t]he solution of the riddle of life in space and time". And in the same proposition Wittgenstein not only rejects such a solution, but states that it can be found in some kind of field that "lies outside space and time". In TLP: 6.432, he even speaks of something "higher" and of "God".

Such statements are not intended to clarify what is meant to be unclarifiable *per definitionem*. They just indicate a variety of issues that constitute the un-

---

4 A typical example of this is TLP: 5.47 timidly introducing something as important as the sole logical constant by using the impersonal form and subjunctive ("One could say ...").

speakable and should not be discussed in terms of common language. Consequently, at this point Wittgenstein does not provide an inquiry but a list of topics that cannot be further elucidated (philosophically).

And yet, Hegel would object, if "subject", "sense of the world" "God", etc. are truly unspeakable, why does Wittgenstein use these *different* terms to express the unspeakable? Different terms are (mostly) defined differently and have (mostly) different meanings, so that by using them in different propositions Wittgenstein determines the unspeakable in obviously different ways. Why would he do that if he did not somehow already know something about the unspeakable, which is not yet logically-philosophically elucidated in the TLP? Even if he were to argue that they are all equally nonsensical (in the pejorative sense), he would still be confronted with the problem of why he uses *them* rather than simply talking about the unspeakable in general. The Hegelian point to be made here is that "unspeakable" is a generic label for different but not further clarified notions; it is itself a *thought* or a *complex of thoughts* that have not yet found their concrete and adequate expression.[5] Accordingly, Hegel would just follow the invitation of the preface ("May others come and do it better") and suggest some better expressions for the notion "unspeakable" as well as "subject", "sense of the world", etc.

More radically, Hegel would try to identify the way in which the TLP itself indicates that these thoughts must be better expressed or elucidated. For instance, TLP: 5.641 states clearly: "Thus there really is a sense in which philosophy can talk about the self in a non-psychological way. [...] The philosophical self is [...] the metaphysical subject". Hence, philosophy *can* talk about the metaphysical subject, although it is "not a part of [the world]" (TLP: 5.641) and, hence, somehow "unspeakable". This philosophical way of talking about the subject (and not just denying it) is surely worth further elaboration (see also Niedermair 1987). Such elaboration may even be found in the very next proposition (TLP: 6), which discusses the N-operation as Hegel might have proposed. I shall discuss it briefly in the fifth section of this chapter.

At this point, I would like to make another remark about how philosophy can deal with these different thoughts. According to TLP: 6.421, ethics (traditionally concerned with the sense of our world and in a way also with the self and God) is "transcendental". The same applies, as already mentioned, to logic as well (6.13). Thus, the Tractarian theory of logic, which culminates in the N-oper-

---

[5] I use the term "thought" here not in the referential sense of TLP 3 and 4 but rather in the more general and traditional sense of the preface to the TLP, where "thought" is distinguished from the mere "expression of thoughts".

ation, and ethics, which is not meant to be a genuine topic of Tractarian inquiry, share the same essential feature: they are both transcendental. As far as this is concerned, Hegel would ask why Wittgenstein does not expand his "transcendental" logical investigations in the direction of ethics as, for instance, Kant did.[6] Moreover, according to TLP: 6.421 aesthetics is also transcendental, and so too is mathematics, which "is a logical method" (6.2). Wittgenstein, therefore, indicates that there is a significant systemic connection between various philosophical issues. From a Hegelian point of view, however, it is unjustifiable that he does not elaborate equally on all these issues and prefers instead to exclude some of them from his logico-philosophical investigation.

Before moving to the primarily Hegelian part of this chapter, I shall take a closer look at the other reservation mentioned above, according to which Wittgenstein seems to consider the mystical as something merely *different from*, instead of *more than*, the non-mystical. Wittgenstein appears to be unsatisfied with his own concept of the unspeakable, while the Tractarian remarks on topics such as the self and God demonstrate that the N-operation must play a more significant role in philosophy more widely than it plays in the TLP. A sufficient elucidation of the one and only logical constant should also elucidate the concrete relation of this constant to the other topics mentioned in the TLP. The essence of the world cannot be irrelevant, for instance, to the sense of the world—it *is*, rather, the sense of the world. On that account, we should equate the $N(\bar{\xi})$ with the sense of the world, the metaphysical subject or even God instead of not talking further about them.

The reason why Wittgenstein does not do that is because he introduces $N(\bar{\xi})$ into his logico-philosophical inquiry as some ultimate *result*, which cannot be developed any further through thought. $N(\bar{\xi})$ figures as a *final*, joint negation, not to be modified or further clarified, something like Wittgenstein's last systemic word before "pass[ing] over in silence" (TLP: 7). And that would be the main point of the Hegelian immanent criticism: Wittgenstein is actually not allowed to have a single last word. For it obviously contradicts TLP: 4.112, which states that "Philosophy is not a body of doctrine but an activity", which "consists essentially of elucidations" and "does not result in 'philosophical propositions', but rather in the clarification of propositions". The N-operation could indeed clarify a lot of thoughts, so that the philosophy of the TLP is indeed an activity—until the point where the N-operation is stated. For the N-operation is itself a philosophical

---

[6] How fruitful the examination of the "transcendentality" of the Tractarian logic could be for philosophy is shown, for instance, in the debate between Peter Sullivan and Adrian Moore (Sullivan and Potter 2013).

proposition and, as soon as it is stated, the mission of Tractarian philosophy seems to have been accomplished, and there is seemingly no reason for further philosophical activity. In the end, it is a single proposition, the joint negation of all propositions, which dictates the whole philosophical attitude and evens out all philosophical activity. In this radical negation of philosophy we can even find significant similarities to Neoplatonism: just as the Neoplatonic transcendent negation of all determination leads to the absolutely transcendent *hen*, the Tractarian N($\bar{\xi}$) is not to be clarified or defined, but just points to a particular experience without being able to clarify it further. However, this should not be considered as an argument that Wittgenstein was planning a Neoplatonic philosophical project.

Hegel would propose a different reading of this Tractarian result. N($\bar{\xi}$) might be the last systemic word of the Tractarian theory of logic but not of any logic. In contrast to the TLP, Hegel would stress that N($\bar{\xi}$) is literally an *operation*, that is, a *logical activity*. It cannot be taken as a common result, i.e., as the static end of the line, but rather as the *potential* for further philosophical activity. Whereas a common result is *externally* limited by anything that is excluded from it, Hegel would insist on the *internal* limitation of thought, which is expressed through N($\bar{\xi}$). The N-operation indicates that there are some blind spots in logic such as "subject", "sense of the world" and "God", but it does not deny its own clarifying force. Accordingly, Hegel would see in those blind spots the potential for further genuinely philosophical activity, which could even have constituted the very interesting second part of the TLP—"the important one", as Wittgenstein puts it in his widely quoted letter to Ludwig von Ficker (PT: p.15). But Wittgenstein never wrote that second part. That being so, in order to bring this Hegelian reading of the TLP to an end, I shall now take a closer look at Hegel's *Science of Logic* and briefly reconstruct what Hegel means by his own sole logical constant and how he overcomes the desiderata of the TLP.

4 Hegel's course towards the sole logical constant: the *Objective Logic*

Before introducing Hegel's notion of the sole logical constant, it is important to outline in what sense Hegel's *Objective Logic*, i.e., the two first books of the SL (the *Doctrine of Being* and the *Doctrine of Essence*), struggles with the same problems as the TLP. In this section, I shall show that the *Objective Logic* also has the "therapeutic mission" to help us abandon many metaphysical conceptions, above all the conception of substance.

Hegel does not hide his "therapeutic" intention and states clearly at the end of the *Introduction* to the SL that the *Objective Logic* is meant to "replace" "former *metaphysics*" and more precisely "*ontology*" (SL 2010: p.42). The *Objective Logic* is not itself ontology—at least not in Christian Wolff's sense—but it does "investigate the nature of *ens* in general" (SL 2010: p.42). Perhaps the difference between former ontology and Hegel's ontological investigations is to be found in the method and the result of each inquiry. I will come back to the Hegelian method of philosophy later. At this point, I shall only note that both Hegel and Wittgenstein chose to begin their logico-philosophical inquiries with ontological questions. However, while Wittgenstein sketches out a specific ontology of facts and is very soon confronted with ontological difficulties when he formulates the epistemological postulate of the substance of the world, Hegel proceeds much more slowly, investigating ontological concepts *in general*—of which there are very many—and, at the beginning of the work, without even explicitly considering the problem's epistemological dimension.

The first part of the *Objective Logic*, the *Doctrine of Being*, is concerned with the concept of Being, i.e., the pure logical content and structure of thought about Being. References to empirical facts and the procedure of picturing are irrelevant at this stage of the logico-philosophical inquiry. Accordingly, Hegel can begin his investigation of the concept of Being by describing it as "the indeterminate immediate" (SL 2010: p.58), meaning simply Being without any other determinations regarding, for example, Essence or even itself. This is a very similar thought to Wittgenstein's "substance" or "object", which in TLP: 2.0121, 2.02 and 2.024 are simple, somehow subsistent and actually inconceivable. In the next chapters of the *Doctrine of Being*, one can find many similar thoughts to this Wittgensteinian conception. The Hegelian "something", "other", "one", "magnitude" and "measureless" do not represent (in the Tractarian sense). They are neither pictures of something nor facts. They are rather thoughts, clarifications about what it means to be, without being empirically conceived and essentially determinate.

Unlike Wittgenstein, Hegel presents a variety of thoughts about that which is supposed to be simple and subsistent at the same time. This may raise the objection that Hegel determines and hence contradicts the simplicity of "substance". However, Hegel argues that the *Doctrine of Being* explores the mere becoming or passing-over of one thought into another, so that all determinations to be found in the *Doctrine of Being* are not essential but void. This insight is verified by every dialectical transition in the book, while at the end of the *Doctrine of Being* Hegel states clearly that all these determinations are in fact just "an empty differentiation", their logical result being the "absolute indifference" (SL 2010: p.326). In consequence, the "therapeutic" gain of the *Doctrine of Being* is the assertion that all thoughts expressing the substance of the world, without taking the epistemological act into account, articulate nothing but the thought of a non-conceivable absolute indifference. In other words: the dualistic concept of world and substance, which does not consider any subjects that have knowledge of the world, is nonsense.

This is an interim result compatible with Wittgenstein's TLP. But there is not yet a parallel to the Tractarian epistemological element. The second part of the *Objective Logic*, the *Doctrine of Essence*, is concerned with all that about which we can articulate meaningful propositions ("world", "states of affairs") as well as with the most basic logical operations we use to make pictures of the world. The topic of this part is, in Hegelian terms, thoughts of "*reflexion and mediation*" (EL 1830: §83), that is, not just the concepts of immediacy but of the immediate Being to the extent that it relates to thought, and of thought to the extent that it relates to the immediate Being. It is here that Hegel explores what it means to use the concepts of "identity", "difference" and "contradiction" with regard to something, what it means to distinguish between the world as it is "in itself" from its "appearance" or to assert that all our propositions about the world as well as the world itself require a common "substance".

However, similar to the *Doctrine of Being*, the "therapeutic" gain of the *Doctrine of Essence* consists in the insight that all thoughts expressed in this book are void in terms of just shining-into-another. Like in the *Doctrine of Being*, every dialectical transition verifies that the thoughts of Essence are not true and subsistent by themselves. The last section of the *Doctrine of Essence* in particular elucidates impressively that all these thoughts just postulate something they cannot consistently articulate. Both the essence of the world and the essence of the proposition may be seen, according to that last section, as "the absolute", the "absolute necessity" or the "substance". But such concepts are mere logico-metaphysical assumptions about an ominous principle of the world and the logic of all thoughts, and do not provide true knowledge of and insight into such a principle. In other words: the epistemological triangle (substance, world, (linguistic) pictures of the world) cannot guarantee or even clarify its own principle. As long as we investigate thought (or language) *in relation to* the world—and not as such, i.e., for its own sake—we must either accept that there is something mystical hiding behind thought and the world, which guarantees truth and untruth, or that our thought is constructed to postulate something mystical that cannot be known. In both cases, one might think, there is nothing left to say from a logico-philosophical standpoint; we can "throw away the ladder", stop philosophising and go back to everyday life.

At the end of the *Objective Logic*, Hegel has not yet revealed his genuine sole logical constant. He has proposed the notion of "absolute indifference", which is actually the logical opposite of a constant, and then the "absolute" or "substance", which seems to be an admission that something like the sole logical constant is not (yet) conceived, i.e., the negation ("N") of everything that can be conceived or named ("$\bar{\xi}$"). The end of the *Objective Logic*, though, is not the end of Hegel's SL as a whole. To use Wittgenstein's ladder metaphor once again: *Objective Logic* is a logical ladder, which we can somehow throw away, but the point which we reach with its help is *also* a logico-philosophical one, namely the most important part of this inquiry, the *Doctrine of the Concept*. And it is precisely here that we can find the elements that would comprise the unwritten second part of the TLP according to its Hegelian reading.

5 The sole logical constant of the *Science of Logic*

In his preface to the *Doctrine of the Concept*, Hegel proclaims that this part of his logico-philosophical inquiry constitutes the "*foundation* and *truth*" of the preceding *Objective Logic* (SL 2010: p.508). That means that Hegel's notion of Concept is not only an indispensable condition of all elucidations of Being and Essence, of all their passing-over and shining-into-another, that is, of all speculative-dialectical movement and deduction of thoughts; the Concept is at the same time the completion and perfection of these elucidations. Therefore, it is here that Hegel's sole logical constant, Hegel's genuine concept of the essence of the world and thought, is to be found.

At this same point, Hegel states clearly that his sole logical constant is, unlike Wittgenstein's, not something ineffable or mystical, a joint negation of everything, but rather "the *unveiling* of substance", that is, the logical inquiry into "the *truth*" and "the *consummation of substance*" (SL 2010: pp.512, 509, 511). Accordingly, Hegel claims to provide something like the missing logical elucidation of Wittgenstein's N-operation.

In fact, Hegel elucidates his sole logical constant in the very first chapter of the *Doctrine of the Concept:* it is the concept of Concept (a singular only noun). Hegel's Concept is not a mere concept among others, but rather the particular way of conceptual thinking which infiltrates every other concept (a singular and plural noun). For Hegel, conceptual thinking means performing a determinate logical operation that differs from the usual acts of judgement and inference. Conceptual thinking means not simply to understand something, to formulate a proposition, a judgement or a syllogism. It rather means to grasp a thought as such, i.e., as it is in itself—not as a sign which represents something else or bears a (logical) relation to other signs. Hegel describes this way of thinking as the sequence of *universality, particularity* and *singularity* and argues that every concept can be analysed with regard to these three moments. It is this sequence which constitutes the famous Hegelian speculative-dialectical movement of thoughts, which guides all passing-over and shining-into-another in the *Objective Logic*, and the development of the whole of speculative philosophy in general (see Plevrakis 2017: pp.277–362). Conceptual thinking is hence precisely the logical operation of this analysis of concepts by which they are presented as internal relations, i.e., as the relations between their own three moments. Here, I think, Hegel would not hesitate to argue that such internal relations could be seen as concrete specifications of the vague relation that Wittgenstein seems to outline in TLP: 4.5. To put it in a nutshell: the internal relation in terms of universality, particularity and singularity is Hegel's clarification of the *limitation of thought* (not just language) *from the inside*.

In addition, analysis of concepts can also be construed as *generation* of concepts out of other concepts. In that sense, Hegel's Concept can be regarded not just as a mere counterproposal to Wittgenstein's "successive applications to elementary propositions of the operation $N(\bar{\xi})$" (TLP: 6.001, 5.5, 5.503, 5.2521) but rather as a concrete explanation of how this application and this operation works in terms of logic. While the Tractarian operation aims to generate oppositions in the most general sense, Hegel's conceptual thinking is an elaborated method for generating concepts, which relate to one another in a very specific, logico-philosophical way. Wittgenstein assures us that "[i]t is obvious that we can easily express how propositions may be constructed with this operation, and how they may not be constructed with it" (5.503). But it is Hegel who carries out this project and provides us with a voluminous analysis of what an "all-embracing logic" which sets up "an infinitely fine network" (5.511) and a "[h]ierarch[y]" that is "independent of reality" (5.5561) is supposed to look like. For the SL as a whole is the autonomous development of thoughts in terms of universals, which lead to particulars and these in turn to Singulars. To point out the parallel to the TLP even more clearly: insofar as this development is truly autonomous and does not presuppose reality or the way concepts appear in it, one may describe Hegel's SL—just like Wittgenstein described the Tractarian logic—as transcendental. Pirmin Stekeler-Weithofer, for instance, examines this parallel by referring to the ladder metaphor and arguing that the Tractarian philosophy preserves the Hegelian tradition of a "speculative" logical analysis (Stekeler-Weithofer 2012: p.18). It seems unlikely that Wittgenstein had something like Hegel's three steps of conceptual development in mind when he was formulating the $N(\bar{\xi})$ operation, but still: since he does not provide an inquiry into the concrete form of such negation, we cannot but accept that Hegel's Concept could be at least a legitimate candidate for it.

The most impressive thing, though, is that Hegel's *Doctrine of the Concept* conducts (or claims to conduct) a logical inquiry into all the philosophical issues that constitute the "mystical" and "unspeakable" in the TLP. For instance, by understanding the logical sequence of universal, particular and singular as the logical structure of the relation of something to itself, Hegel claims to have found the logical structure of subjectivity, since it is the relation to itself that differentiates a subject from an object. Hence, Hegel does enquire into the subject in a logico-philosophical context, although he also holds that the subject is the limit of all Being and Essence. In addition, as mentioned above, Hegel argues that the Concept is not a mere limit but also the foundation of Being and Essence. Accordingly, the *Doctrine of the Concept* also deals with what seems to be something "higher" or "God" from the perspective of the Tractarian theory of logic. Moreover, the Concept presents the truth of Being and Essence, that is the reason they are or—to put it in terms of TLP: 6.41—the "value" and the "sense of the world". Hegel agrees that such sense "lie[s] outside the world", i.e., it is not itself a being or an essence.[7] But from this he does not infer that the sense of the world must also lie outside the bounds of logic. On the contrary, the *Doctrine of the Concept* secures the Concept as the foundation of all ethics and articulates some of the most basic ethical insights. Significant in this instance is Hegel's advice to perceive the *Doctrine of the Concept* as "the kingdom of *freedom*" (SL 2010: p.513).

The question of what a logico-philosophical inquiry that addresses all these issues collectively would look like cannot be discussed in this chapter, which aims only to outline certain aspects of the preface and first chapter of the *Doctrine of the Concept* (SL 2010: pp.508 ff., 529 ff.). But it is not difficult to guess how Hegel would try to undertake such an inquiry. He would continue to think conceptually and arrange the above-mentioned thoughts in sequences of universals, particulars and singulars. It is of great importance that the SL remains an activity even after having found the one logical constant in which the logico-philosophical inquiry culminates. Hegel's SL is definitely a (monistic) philosophical doctrine which, in contrast to TLP: 4.112, is intended to result in "philosophical propositions". Nevertheless, it does clarify thoughts too. Accordingly, the

---

[7] Of course, this does not commit Hegel to the existence of something transcendent. He agrees with the expression "outside the world" only in his own very precise sense of the term "world", which he elucidates in the chapter *The world of appearance and the world-in-itself* in the *Doctrine of Essence* (SL 2010: 443 ff.). The idea of transcendence may be more applicable to Wittgenstein, who refuses further propositions to elucidate the expression "outside the world". Hegel, on the other hand, indicates clearly that there is a *logical* "beyond the world" in the sense of logically justified concepts of subjectivity, objectivity itself, life, sense of life, etc.

attractiveness of Hegelian logic in comparison with Tractarian logic is, in my eyes, that by clarifying the operation of logical clarification it does not dissolve itself but rather provides philosophy and everyday life with a clear and solid logical foundation.

6 Epilogue

I began this chapter by quoting the preface to the TLP in order to overcome the perplexity that my proclamation of a "Hegelian reading of the TLP" might provoke; for the preface shows that Wittgenstein himself, in contrast to some Wittgenstein scholars, would not deny the feasibility of such a reading. In the above sections I hope to have shown convincingly that there are indeed some significant parallels between Wittgenstein's TLP and Hegel's SL, although the SL aims at consistency on points where the TLP appears radical. The reason I think such a reading is worth attempting is not just the potential benefit for Wittgensteinian and Hegelian scholarship. Rather, it is in the interest of philosophy as a whole and also of everyday life to rid ourselves of poorly thought-through philosophical stereotypes and bad metaphysics. And this is a common aim of both Wittgenstein's and Hegel's philosophy.

References

Conant, James: "The Method of the *Tractatus*", in: E. Rech (ed.): *From Frege to Wittgenstein: Perspectives on Early Analytic Philosophy*, Oxford University Press, 2002, pp.374–462.
Diamond, Cora: "The *Tractatus* and the Limits of Sense", in: O. Kuusela and M. McGinn (eds.): *The Oxford Handbook of Wittgenstein*, Oxford University Press, 2011, pp.240–275.
Glock, Hans-Johann: *A Wittgenstein Dictionary*, Blackwell, 1996.
Houlgate, Stephen: *The Opening of Hegel's Logic: From Being to Infinity*, Purdue University Press, 2006.
Koch, Anton Friedrich: *Die Evolution des logischen Raumes: Aufsätze zu Hegels Nichtstandard-Metaphysik*, Mohr Siebeck, 2014.
Niedermair, Klaus: *Wittgensteins Tractatus und die Selbstbezüglichkeit der Sprache*, Peter Lang, 1987.
Plevrakis, Ermylos: *Das Absolute und der Begriff: Zur Frage philosophischer Theologie in Hegels Wissenschaft der Logik*, Mohr Siebeck, 2017.
Stekeler-Weithofer, Pirmin: "Einleitung: Wittgenstein zu Logik, Metaphysik und Wissenschaft", in: P. Stekeler-Weithofer (ed.): *Wittgenstein: Zu Philosophie und Wissenschaft*, Felix Meiner, 2012, pp.8–34.
Sullivan, Peter: "'The General Propositional Form is a Variable' (*Tractatus* 4.53)", *Mind* 113:449, 2004, pp.43–56.

Sullivan, Peter and Potter, Michael (eds.): *Wittgenstein's Tractatus: History and Interpretation*, Oxford University Press, 2013.
Quante, Michael: *Die Wirklichkeit des Geistes: Studien zu Hegel*, Suhrkamp, 2011.
Ule, Andrej: "Operationen im *Tractatus*", in: W. Vossenkuhl (ed.): *Ludwig Wittgenstein: Tractatus logico-philosophicus*, Akademie Verlag, 2001.

Gaetano Chiurazzi
Are There Simple Objects? Hegel's Discussion of Kant's Second Antinomy in Relation to Wittgenstein's *Tractatus*

Abstract Wittgenstein's *Tractatus* is marked by an internal tension between an analytic principle (centred on the concept of simple object) and a synthetic one (centred on the concept of form). I call this tension "the Cosmological Antinomy" of the *Tractatus*. I try then to deal with this issue on the basis of Hegel's discussion of Kant's second antinomy in the *Science of Logic*, where the general, anti-analytical presuppositions of Hegel's philosophy clearly emerge. Hegel's philosophy, as a philosophy of movement, of becoming and of life, is a philosophy of continuum, which contrasts with every atomistic conception of the world.

1

Wittgenstein's *Tractatus* is marked by a theoretical tension which, not accidentally, recalls the *Critique of Pure Reason*, to whose project it has often been compared; but, whereas Kant's question was about the limits of knowledge, Wittgenstein's is about the limits of language. Its theoretical tension polarises around two concepts: that of "simple object" on the one hand, and that of "form" on the other. The former concerns what I call the "analytic" facet of the *Tractatus*; the latter instead configures its "synthetic" facet. Both are indispensable for the definition of the world: "the world divides into facts" (TLP: 1.2), and these into simple objects. The facts (*Tatsachen*) are the existence of atomic facts (*Sachverhalten*) (TLP: 2), a combination (*Verbindung*) of objects, entities or things (TLP: 2.01). On a linguistic level, this divide corresponds to that between names and connectors or logical constants: names are the linguistic correlates of simples, while logical constants act as links among these objects (TLP: 3.14). The opposition analytic/synthetic is further reflected in the opposition between "to represent" and "to show": propositions represent (*vorstellen*) facts, and names represent (*vertreten*) (TLP: 3.22) objects; the connectors, however, show (*darstellen*) a form and thus also a sense (TLP: 2.174, 2.221).[1] Two sentences that, in light of their decimal figure, seem to be of very marginal importance in the *Tractatus*[2] sum up these distinctions clearly:

> One name stands for one thing, and another for another thing, and they are connected [*verbunden*] together. And so the whole, like a living picture [*ein lebendes Bild:* a locution to which I shall return later], presents [*stellt vor*] the atomic fact. (TLP: 4.0311)

> The possibility of propositions is based upon the principle [*Prinzip*] of the representation [*Vertretung*] of objects by signs.

> My fundamental thought [*Grundgedanke*] is that the "logical constants" do not represent [*nicht vertreten*]. That the logic of the facts cannot be represented [*Daß sich die Logik der Tatsachen nicht vertreten lässt*]. (TLP: 4.0312)

In the second of these propositions (4.0312), Wittgenstein simultaneously expresses the principle that governs the constitution of the proposition and its fundamental thought. We could call the former its "analytic principle", and the latter its "synthetic principle". The analytic principle states the existence of simple objects and atomic facts as independent constituents and as "correlates in the world for the names and elementary propositions of a fully analysed language" (Kenny 1973: p.60). The synthetic principle, on the contrary, states that, even when the analysis of the proposition is brought to completion, something remains that has no representation in the world but is responsible for the connections of the objects in states of affairs. What I call the "cosmological antinomy" of the *Tractatus* unfolds in the contrast between these two cornerstones, between its *Prinzip* and its *Grundgedanke*. The contrast consists in the fact that, on one hand, the analysis should lead to ultimate, simple, no longer divisible objects,[3] components of the proposition, which are represented by names; and yet, on the other, it cannot but leave a residue, a remainder, something that is not of the same nature as the simple objects, since it expresses a mere connection, a *Ver-*

---

1 The German term "*darstellen*", which occurs in many of the propositions concerning pictures, is normally translated into English as "to represent", but also as "to present", "to show" and even "to mean" (TLP: 4.115), a confusion that can give rise to misunderstandings.
2 This is the remark Wittgenstein makes at the beginning of the *Tractatus:* "The decimal figures as numbers of the separate propositions indicate the logical importance of the propositions, the emphasis laid upon them in my exposition. The propositions n.1, n.2, n.3, etc., are comments on proposition No. n; the propositions n.m1, n.m2, etc., are comments on the proposition No. n.m; and so on."
3 This idea is very frequent in the *Prototractatus* and in the *Notebooks 1914–1916*. See for instance PT: 3.20102 and 3.20103; NB: p.62e, 17 June 1915. The existence of simple objects is generally justified by saying that our propositions would otherwise not have a definite sense.

bindung, shaping the ineffable *form* of the world. This cosmological antinomy thus states, on the one hand, that the world is made of simple objects, and can be analysed down into these ultimate components; and, on the other, that their composition requires further elements, connectors, without which it would not be possible to express any proposition and thus to represent any fact—without which there would be no sense at all. These residual elements of the analysis are the "logical constants" which, using an obsolete locution, we could also call "syncategorems". The syncategorems are the properly grammatical, syntactical elements of language (connectors, conjunctions, adverbs, prepositions) which, unlike the categorems (that is, the nominal elements, such as the subject and the predicate, which are supposed to have a definite meaning), are responsible for the link among these elements: they are like the "glue" that holds them together.[4] The representation of language which arises from the Tractarian theory (assuming that there is such a theory) suggests that the world fundamentally consists of simple, unalterable elements—atoms—which are subsequently combined or composed together using connector terms into specific forms or more or less complex facts. "Objects are what is unalterable and subsistent; their configuration is what is changing and unstable" (TLP: 2.0271). The cosmological antinomy of the *Tractatus* therefore confronts us with the following question: in the composition of these atomic elements, is the connection a mere "addition" and thus something external to them? Or is it something more radical and fundamental, which affects, so to speak, the very nature of the supposed simple objects, making them therefore something intrinsically "indefinite"? What is, then, the nature of that synthesis: is it a mere combination of simple elements, which are given before every syncategorematic function, or is it something which precedes and intimately structures such simple elements? Put in Kantian terms: does the synthesis precede the analysis? Or even: is an "*a priori* synthesis" possible?

2

I propose to address this issue on the basis of Hegel's discussion of Kant's second antinomy of the cosmological idea. This antinomy pivots on whether or not there are simple elements, and whether the analysis reaches a final stopping point—atoms as fundamental blocks of reality, which compose more complex objects or facts—or whether some kind of synthesis precedes the analysis,

---

4 See MacFarlane 2015: sect.1.

which can therefore never reach ultimate, non-synthesised, no longer divisible elements. Such an opposition is expressible as an opposition between the discrete and the continuous.

Hegel discusses Kant's second antinomy in Note II of the chapter on quantity in the *Science of Logic*. This collocation is not accidental: quantity (*Quantität*) is for Hegel the moment of continuity, which no longer has a qualitative limit and does not yet have a quantitative limit, that is, is not yet a quantum (*Quantum*), a determinate number. Kant's thesis in the second antinomy reads: "Every composite substance in the world consists of simple parts, and nothing exists anywhere except the simple or what is composed of simples." (Kant 1998: A 434/B462) And the antithesis reads: "No composite thing in the world consists of simple parts, and nowhere in it does there exist anything simple." (Kant 1998: A435/B463)

Hegel's very first remark on the thesis is that "here the composite is contrasted with the simple, the atom, and, as determination, takes second place to the unbroken or continuous [*eine sehr zurückstehende Bestimmung ist*; literally: is a determination which lags far behind" (SL 2010: p.159). Hegel immediately detects that the contrast Kant makes between the existence or non-existence of simple elements depends from the beginning on a conceptual framework which is completely misleading—enough to make the exposition of these antinomies "awkward and eccentric" (SL 2010: p.157). The antinomy is in fact completely focused on the opposition simple/composite, a way of thinking that is far removed from the concept of the continuum (the concept of a divisibility *in infinitum*). The thesis, in particular, moves in a *petitio principii:* it asks whether simple objects exist, but the argument starts from the presupposition of the composite, which, by definition, is made of simple objects. Thus, Hegel remarks: "Now since the thesis speaks only of *composition* instead of *continuity*, by that fact it is really an analytical or *tautological* proposition." (SL 2010: p.159)

Wittgenstein argues for the claim that there are simple objects in almost the same terms as Kant does in the thesis of his second antinomy. In the *Notebooks 1914–16*, he writes:

> It seems that the idea of the SIMPLE is already to be found contained in that of the complex and in the idea of analysis, and in such a way that we come to this idea quite apart from any examples of simple objects, or of propositions which mention them, and we realize the existence of the simple object—*a priori*—as a logical necessity. (NB: p.60e, 14 June 1915)

Wittgenstein is less shrewd than Kant when he states that such a logical necessity—which, as it is posed, would be a tautology and thus, technically, a nonsense—could give rise to knowledge and worse, a claim entailing the existence of simple objects. The pretence of deriving existence from the definition, on the basis of a mere logical necessity, is from Kant's point of view the fundamental shortcoming of the old metaphysics, paradigmatically represented in the ontological proof of the existence of God and in all the theses of the cosmological antinomy, which express the viewpoint of dogmatic and theological rationalism. Such a rationalism, as we know, can never reach real knowledge precisely because existence can never be derived from logical necessity.

Despite their defective argumentation, Hegel appreciates Kant's antinomies due to their attack on the old metaphysics: in them lies the essence of the critical philosophy, which "caused the downfall of previous metaphysics and can be regarded as a main transition to more recent philosophy" (SL 2010: p.157). This downfall consists in the abandoning of the analytic form that such metaphysics gave to its reasoning—in the abandoning of their logical formality in favour of their dialectical nature. The criticism levelled against the thesis of the second antinomy therefore points the finger at the analytic or tautological relation subsisting between simple and composite, that is, at the accidental relation, which constitutes the composite. Kant writes that "with substances composition is only a contingent relation, apart from which, as beings persisting by themselves, they must subsist" (Kant 1998: A435–436/B463–464). Every composite of the world, then, would be made of simple, atomic, independent parts, which stay with each other in an extrinsic relation. For Hegel, however, as an analytic concept the composition can never give rise to a genuine antinomy:

> it is self-evident that composition has the determination of accidentality and externality; but if we are to deal here with only an accidental aggregate instead of continuity, then it was not worth the effort to construct an antinomy over it, or, more to the point, none could be constructed; so the assertion that the parts are simple is then, as said, only a tautology. (SL 2010: p.160)

Hegel's criticism therefore concerns precisely the exteriority of such a relation, which characterizes the atomistic representation of the world: a way of conceiving of the world as trivial as it is popular, which guarantees it success in every time.

> It is no wonder, therefore, that the atomistic principle has at all times held its own; the equally trivial and external relation of composition that must be added to it to attain the semblance of concreteness and multiplicity, is just as popular as the atoms themselves and the void. (SL 2010: p.134)

According to the atomistic principle, things are mere aggregates, a result of mere addition, which Hobbes claims is the case even for concepts. Reason, Hobbes writes, "is nothing but Reckoning (that is, Adding and Subtracting)", operations to which multiplication and division can also be reduced (Hobbes 2010: Part I, ch.V). Even physics, according to Hegel, "with its molecules and particles, suffers from its use of the atom, the principle of extreme externality, and therefore from an extreme lack of the concept, as does also the theory of state that starts from the singular will of individuals" (SL 2010: p.135). The representation of society, which characterises bourgeois individualism, is a representation of political life as external as that of atomistic physics and logic.

It is, then, only a different conception of logic, of physics and even of politics that allows an alternative—a *conceptual* alternative, in the Hegelian meaning of the word, which is far from a formal abstraction—to the atomistic representation of the world and its analytic principle. This different logic arises from a different understanding of what, in ancient atomism, is implicitly meant by the representation of the void: for Hegel, the void is the representation of negation, which anyway is, according to Hegel, a form of relation to other. Thanks to negation, the being-for-itself—that is, the independent being of substantial, atomic entities—passes over into attraction (SL 2010: p.141), because

> that which is excluded still stands in *connection* [*Verbindung*] with what is excluded from it. But this moment of *connection* is attraction, which is thus within repulsion itself; it is the negating of that abstract repulsion by which the ones would each be an existent referring only to itself without mutual exclusion. (SL 2010: p.142)

So conceived, the void is, just as the ancient atomists claimed, the principle of movement. But such a statement "does not have the trivial meaning that something can only move into an empty space and not into an already occupied one", but

> the more profound thought that the ground of becoming, of unrest and self-movement, lies in the negative in general, which, in this sense, is however to be taken as the true negativity of the infinite. (SL 2010: p.135)[5]

The void represents a *dynamis*, which is a kind of not-being, and which Aristotle defined literally as *arché kineseos he metabolés*, the principle of movement or change (*Met.* V 12, 1019a 15–19). In this dynamic interpretation of the void, that is, of negation, lies the reason why no formal logic can ever explain Hegel's meaning of negation: because negation is for Hegel a dynamic principle, an at-

---

[5] The same concept is repeated in the preface to the *Phenomenology of Spirit:* "That is why some of the ancients conceived the void as the principle of motion, for they rightly saw the moving principles to be negative, though they did not as yet grasp that the negative is the self." (PS 1977: p.21)

tractive and repulsive force. Hegel's logic is in its very ground not a logic but a physics, in the Aristotelian sense of the word: that is, an ontology of becoming, whose fundamental concept is continuity. The void is namely nothing but the genetic source of continuity:

> The absolute obduracy of the *one* has melted away into this *unity* which, however, as containing the one, is at the same time determined by the repulsion residing in it; as *unity of the self-externality, it is unity with itself*. Attraction is in this way the moment of *continuity* in quantity. (SL 2010: p.154)

As a result of attractive and repulsive forces, continuity is thus originally a physical–dynamical concept, completely different from the concept of composition, which is an analytic, that is, mathematical concept (unlike Kant, mathematics is for Hegel analytic) (SL 2010: pp.174 ff.). Aristotle, who deals with the concept of continuity in Book VI of the *Physics*, conceived it in this way.

Continuity, as a non-analytic principle, is for Hegel the very form of what Kant called "*a priori* synthesis": an alternative principle to analysis, of which it is even the presupposition, as well as an alternative to composition, to that form of synthesis that recomposes, extrinsically, the products of the analysis. The true synthesis for Hegel is reality itself, as becoming and movement—namely, continuity. It is the form of the true infinite, which is neither an infinite by addition (composite) nor by division (analytic), but a differential infinite, as Hegel conceives of in his discussion of differential calculus, specifically in the form it assumed under Newton:

> But from a philosophical point of view the mathematical infinite is important because underlying it, in fact, is the concept of the true infinite, and this infinite stands much higher than the usual so-called metaphysical infinite from which the objections against the other infinite, the mathematical, are made. (SL 2010: p.204)

Differential calculus is a non-arithmetical, that is, non-analytical way of understanding the continuum, a concept that Aristotle already considered essential for the concept of movement. In differential calculus, it is not a question of simple parts, of minimal elements or monads, as in the Leibnizian example (which also occurs in Wolff) where the infinitesimal is compared to a speck of sand that the wind blows off the top of the mountain, but that does not prejudice its measurement. There are no quanta, even infinitesimal ones. As disappearing magnitudes, the differentials show only the essentiality of the relation. The fact that they have a meaning only in a ratio, and that they are nil outside a ratio (so that when they occur as separate can be removed like many zeros from calculus), makes them the more appropriate expression of the true infinite, which in its essence is not a quantum, is not something that can be added or subtracted to a given quantum, increasing or decreasing it, but is instead a *relation*.

> [Q]uantum is a determination which should possess a perfectly indifferent existence outside the relation it is in and be indifferent to its difference from another quantum; the qualitative, on the contrary, is what it is only in its distinction from another. The infinite magnitudes of calculus are, therefore, not only comparable, but exist only as terms of comparison, in relation. (SL 2010: p.216)

What is shown in differential calculus is the original, constitutive, *a priori* nature of the relation, against any atomistic and compositional, merely analytic hypothesis. In this differential—that is: comparative or qualitative—nature of the infinitesimal, the true meaning of the "*a priori* synthesis" must be found.

3

The Hegelian interpretation of differential calculus has struck many mathematicians as strange. Against the "intuitive" continuum of Hegel and Bergson (though the word "intuitive" is in my opinion very problematic here, as Hegel remarks in reference to Kant) (SL 2010: p.162), Russell—the most prominent proponent of the logical atomism that he claimed to find in Wittgenstein's *Tractatus*[6]— therefore defended the arithmetisation of the analysis conducted by Weierstrass,[7] in his opinion the true inheritor of Zeno. Such a conception of the continuum, as Poincaré had earlier remarked,

> is not the ordinary conception in which it is supposed that between the elements of the continuum exists an intimate connection making of it one whole, in which the point has no existence previous to the line, but the line does exist previous to the point. Multiplicity alone subsists, unity has disappeared. (Poincaré 1913: p.23)

The continuum—the line—does not precede the point, but is made of points. So atomised, it paradoxically becomes the condition not for explaining the movement, as Aristotle did, but for negating it, as Zeno did. Recalling the paradox of the arrow, Russell writes that "[m]otion consists *merely* in the occupation of

---

[6] Wittgenstein seems to share Russell's interpretation of his own theory in the RLF. But, as Kenny reports, he disowned it by the time it was due to be delivered (1973: p.82).
[7] It has been said that Russell abandoned his previous Hegelian approach to mathematics as a result of reading Morley and Harkness's *An Introduction to the Theory of Analytic Functions*, inspired by Weierstrass's method of ε and δ instead of dy/dx (Gillies 1999: pp.171–72).

different spaces at different times. [...] There is no transition from place to place, no consecutive moment or consecutive position," which entails "the rejection of velocity and acceleration as physical facts" (Russell 2010: §447, p.480). In reality, movement does not exist and the arrow does not move—that is, a "state of motion" does not exist.

The arithmetisation of the continuum has the advantage, or at least so Russell believes, of saving the *actual* existence of things—which means their static or, as we could also say, *categorematic* nature. This is the outcome of the complete arithmetisation, or *logicisation*, of physics, where atomism turns into the negation of elementary physical phenomena such as movement, velocity and acceleration. Hegel's interpretation of differential calculus moves, on the contrary, in an entirely opposite direction: that of a physicisation of mathematics, especially since such a calculus was after all invented precisely in order to explain physical phenomena. More accurately: the *physical* meaning of mathematical formulas, and notably of the functions with which differential calculus deals— the functions of curved lines, the quadratic or higher-level functions—is for Hegel the change, as the effect of a power. A change is for instance a velocity variation (acceleration, deceleration), represented by the infinite variation of the values. This physical interpretation of the quadratic functions is evident in Hegel's polemic against a merely mathematical consideration of the powers, according to which they express only numbers: "It immediately occurs against this usage that power, as so used [i.e., as power of a number], is a category that essentially belongs to quantum and has no conceptual connection to the *potentia*, *dynamis*, of Aristotle" (SL 2010: p.280). If there is something that distinguishes the arithmetical, atomised continuum, from the differential, dynamical continuum, it is *dynamis*. We can therefore say that *dynamis* is the true connecting element of physical reality, the "glue" of the facts of the world. The logical connectors express—indeed, cannot fail to express—this possibility alone, which is a dispositional capacity. The medieval logicians defined the *syncategorems* as dispositions (William of Sherwood calls them *dispositiones alterius*, cf. 1995: ch.32, pp.16 ff.), since they are the modes of possible grammatical combinations of the categorematic terms.

The idea expressed in Hegel's conception of the true infinite—that relation precedes relata—is nothing but the expression of the priority of the syncategorems over categorems, and therefore of the power over the act. *Dynamis* is in fact intrinsically differential: a power or possibility has no meaning except in relation to another power or another possibility, whereas the act is completely self-sufficient and does not need to be defined in relation to another. This Parmenidean principle of sufficiency is what Russell sees restored in the arithmetised continuum. The way that negation functions in Hegel's system, as we saw in reference to its criticism of ancient atomism, expresses on the contrary the idea that every relation of a thing to itself implies the relation to another, and this primordial relation is the principle of the transformation and of the passage into another, that is, of a genesis of a new and different figure. Negation is not for Hegel a mere compositional connector of self-subsistent and unalterable substances; it implies a real, qualitative transformation of these substances. It is in this that the very concept of the continuum consists, which derives from the attractive and repulsive nature of negation, and which Aristotle defined as follows: "that which is continuous has distinct parts [tò d'állo tò d' állo méros], and these parts into which it is divisible [diaîreitai] are different [hétera] in this way, i.e. spatially separate" (Aristotle 1991: VI 1, 231b 5–6). The continuum involves at the same time a quantitative multiplicity, in the sense that its parts are "others" to each other, and a qualitative multiplicity: these parts are not only multiple but also different from one another. This definition not accidentally recalls Hegel's definition of the "*a priori* synthesis": "the concept of *terms that are distinct* and yet equally *inseparable*; of an *identity* which is within it an *inseparable difference*" (SL 2010: pp.174 f.).[8] If this were not the case, the continuum would be mere identity, that is, substance. So conceived, it is, by contrast, the true alternative to Eleaticism, that a priori synthesis which underlies every atomistic, discontinuous (or, for Hegel, intellectual) representation of reality.

4

We can now come back to what I called the "cosmological antinomy" of the *Tractatus*. Its analytic principle would suggest that its ontology is rigidly atomistic and that the composition of the simple elements is merely accidental, so that they could exist even independently of their relation to others. However, an object cannot be given, according to Wittgenstein, except in an atomic fact (*Sachverhalt*), namely, in a connection.

We must therefore question the relevance of this syncategorematic aspect. Wittgenstein writes that "[i]t would, so to speak, appear as an accident, when to a thing that could exist alone on its own account, subsequently a state of affairs could be made to fit. If things can occur in atomic facts, this possibility

---

[8] This remark echoes Jean Petitot's defence of the fundamentality of the concept of continuum (Petitot 1992). Petitot argues for a link between the continuum and *a priori* synthesis, on the basis that "c'est une physique fondamentale *non mécaniste* et *non atomiste* qui devrait en dernière instance permettre d'élaborer une *genèse physique* des intuitions pures elles-mêmes et du synthétique *a priori*" (p.261).

must already lie in them" (TLP: 2.0121). The simplicity of the object must be understood as independence from any relation. However, it is here clear that an object cannot occur outside a *possible* situation. It involves from the beginning the connection in states of things, and therefore, as Wittgenstein writes, a dependence: "It is impossible for words [and then for objects] to occur in two different ways, alone and in the proposition." (TLP: 2.0122; my addition) It follows that: "If I know an object, then I also know all the possibilities of its occurrence in atomic facts [*Sachverhalten*]." (TLP: 2.0123)

This argument, which sets the objects in the web of their reciprocal relations, is more similar to the antithesis of Kant's second antinomy, where the fact that a thing cannot be given but in space and time is the reason for its divisibility *in infinitum*, of its being systematically in relation with other things. Indeed, Wittgenstein writes in the *Tractatus*:

> Just as we cannot think of spatial objects at all apart from space, or temporal objects apart from time, so we cannot think of any object apart from the possibility of its connection with other things. (TLP: 2.0121)

Every possibility of connection lies thus in the very nature of the object (TLP: 2.0123). When an object is given, the possible form of the states of affairs in which it can occur is also given, as a "system of propositions" (Kenny 1973: p.129). However, if the connection is potentially given together with the object, this means that in every object there is an unavoidable syncategorematic aspect, a dispositional power of entering into a determinate state of affairs. This power enacts the real *continuity* of the world by generating a form and not a mere composite. We could even guess at this point that this unavoidable interconnection of the objects, which leads to an "embryonal" holistic conception of the world, is the reason for Wittgenstein's rejection, in the *Philosophical Investigations*, of the logical atomism of the *Tractatus*.

But the complete connections—that is the form of the world—cannot be definitively expressed: it is in fact such that no linguistic element, inasmuch as it is a discrete—that is: arithmetisable (computable)—component, can express it. Although the analysis could be carried on to the point of "objectifying" even the connectors (an operation which gives rise to our metaphysical illusions, according to Kant), what links one name to another, one term to another, can never be completely stated. This link is ultimately—as in Hegel's interpretation of ancient atomism—the void space itself; or, to put it in more Wittgensteinian terms, the silence which seems to separate the elements of the language, but which eventually enables the passage from one to another, a *dynamis* that no actual entity can ever represent.[9]

5

I am aware that such a dynamic, physical interpretation of logical connections will no doubt arouse some disagreement. Its major consequence is to bring into question the merely extensional description, supposedly offered by the *Tractatus*, of the world as made up of unrelated atoms, without the intervention of modal concepts. As Hans Poser has previously remarked, such a representation of the world is simply impossible and useless even for science, which cannot avoid referring to concepts such as law or the capacity for foresight (Poser 1988). Wittgenstein's strongly extensional thesis, which claims to make logic, ontology and thought coincide, does not therefore succeed, according to Poser, in reducing truth to truth-functions and extensions, precisely because the composition of the sentence is not reducible to a mere *addition* of predicates and arguments.[10] This means that the complex proposition is not a mere composition: it is something "continuous", which means that the reality to which we refer is a process, as Hegel says when he speaks of truth as a result together with its becoming, and not as a simple state of affairs.[11] In this perspective, no compositional conception of truth, no truth-functional conception of logic, can reasonably be defended.

---

9 In "What the Tortoise Said to Achilles", Lewis Carroll expresses this impossibility by reference to Zeno's arguments: in a syllogistic deduction every passage would require every intermediate step being made serially explicit, which produces a regress *in infinitum* (Carroll 1985). That this does not happen is due to the fact that the empty space between one step and another is the place in which the *real* operation of intelligence is achieved, which, as Dedekind would say, *creates* the continuum between them, without this connection having any explicit representative in language except the void itself.

10 Such a question concerns the role of the syncategorems in the production of truth, an issue of which Leibniz was already fully aware. The reduction of truth to a calculus implies a computability of language, that is, the elimination of the syncategorems, which Leibniz, not by chance, compared to the irrational numbers, that is, to the numbers that constitute the continuum. Only God, however, could complete such an operation, which means that only for God can factual reality be completely absorbed into formal logic (see Matteuzzi 1996).

11 "Only this self-*restoring* sameness, or this reflection in otherness within itself—not an *original* or *immediate* unity as such—is the True. It is the process of its own becoming" (PS 1977: p.10).

Hegelian logic, as I have tried to show, is an ontology of physics, or, rather, a bio-logic, a logic of life, of movement and of becoming.[12] Many of its concepts are comprehensible only by reference to life, from the impossibility of conceiving of an organism as a monad, to the increasing nature of its development, to its being genetically and essentially—we could say also: conceptually—a relation. It supposes a very different ontology (an ontology of modes[13]) to that of atomism. A proximity between Hegel's and Wittgenstein's philosophy might therefore appear more plausible in relation to the concept of "form of life", which is dealt with in the *Philosophical Investigations*. The logical form that the propositions must have in common with reality in order to represent it, turns out to be at the very end a form of life, a context of use. The addition of the word "life" thus seems to be a real innovation. Yet we can unexpectedly already find traces of it in the *Tractatus*. In the first of the two propositions quoted above, Wittgenstein writes: "One name stands for one thing, and another for another thing, and they are connected together. And so the whole, like a *living picture*, presents the atomic fact" (TLP: 4.0311, my emphasis). Wittgenstein says that when the simples are connected together, they acquire a form that makes the whole something "living": not literally, of course, but *like* a "living picture". Only insofar as they are connected together, then, do names and things give rise to a "living picture", which reflects, so to speak, the living form of life; it is then the connection as such that imprints this dynamic form on the objects. The form is always and immediately a *form of life*. Wittgenstein's subsequent investigations only add, or make explicit, the idea that a form of life—like the living picture of the *Tractatus*—is not a result, but the very *a priori* of language.

Is this not also the sense of Hegel's reformulation of Kantian transcendental philosophy? Far from being the correlate of the nominal elements of language, what Kant calls "pure concepts" are, as already noted by Ryle (1961: p.73), transcendental syncategorematic elements that structure the judgement, that is, the experience: principles of knowledge that are at the same time grammatical and logical, syntactical and semantical. Their *a priori* nature means that they do not derive from experience, and therefore, just as the *Grundgedanke* of the *Tractatus* states, have no objectual correlate in experience. Hegel injects a dynamic lymph into these syncategorematic structures: the determinations of the concept, such as the being-in-itself and the being-for-itself—their concrete articulations, as

---

12 For more about this idea I direct the reader to Chiurazzi (2017: notably pp.127–142).
13 See David Kolb's chapter in the present volume. I attempted to develop such a "modal ontology" (in which the word "mode" is not limited to the traditional "categories of modalities" but is closer to the medieval use, where it structured the syncategorematic terms as "modes of connections") in Chiurazzi (2006).

Hegel writes in the Preface to the *Phenomenology*—are in fact "souls", that is, living principles (PS 1977: p.35). The logical form which arises from the syncategorematic articulations of the concept—that is, from the I—is already for Hegel a "form of life": because, as Plato asks in the *Sophist*, when he addresses the "friends of forms" and their static representation of being,

> are we going to be convinced that it's true that change, life, soul, and intelligence are not present in that which wholly is, and that it neither lives nor thinks, but stays changeless, solemn, and holy, without any understanding? (Plato 1997: *Soph.* 248e–249a)

References

Aristotle: *Physics*, J. Barnes (trans.), in: *The Complete Works of Aristotle*, Princeton University Press, 1991.
Carroll, Lewis: "What the Tortoise said to Achilles", *Mind* 4:14, 1895, pp.278–280.
Chiurazzi, Gaetano: *Modalität und Existenz*, Königshausen und Neumann, 2006.
Chiurazzi, Gaetano: *Dynamis. Ontologia dell'incommensurabile*, Guerini & Associati, 2017.
Gillies, Donald: "German Philosophy of Mathematics from Gauss to Hilbert", *Royal Institute of Philosophy Supplements* 44, 1999, pp.167–192.
Hobbes, Thomas: *Leviathan*, A. P. Martinich and B. Battiste (eds.), Broadview Press, 2010.
Kant, Immanuel: *Critique of Pure Reason*, P. Guyer and A. W. Wood (trans.), Cambridge University Press, 1998.
Kenny, Anthony: *Wittgenstein*, Blackwell Publishing, 2006.
MacFarlane, John: "Logical Constants", *The Stanford Encyclopedia of Philosophy*, Edward N. Zalta (ed.), URL = <https://plato.stanford.edu/archives/win2017/entries/logical-constants/>, 2015.
Matteuzzi, Maurizio: "Leibniz e i sincategoremi", in: Klaus Dutz and Stefano Gensini (eds.): *Im Spiegel des Verstandes. Studien zu Leibniz*, Nodus Publikationen, 1996, pp.123–135.
Petitot, Jean: "Continu et Objectivité. La Bimodalité Objective du Continu et le Platonisme Transcendantale", in: Jean-Michel Salanskis and Hourya Sinaceur (eds.): *La Labyrinthe du Continu*, Springer Verlag, 1992, pp.239–263.
Plato: *Complete Works*, J. M. Cooper with D. S. Hutchinson (eds.), Hackett Publishing Company, 1997.
Poincaré, Henri: *The Science and the Hypothesis*, W. J. Greenstreet (trans.), Walter Scott Publishing, 1913.
Poser, Hans: "The Failure of Logical Positivism to Cope with Problems of Modal Theory", in: Simo Knuuttila (ed.): *Modern Modalities: Studies of the History of Modal Theories from Medieval Nominalism to Logical Positivism*, Kluwer, 1988.
Ryle, Gilbert: "Categories", in: Antony Flew (ed.): *Logic and Language (second series)*, Basic Blackwell, 1961.
Russell, Bertrand: *The Principles of Mathematics*, Routledge, 2010.
William of Sherwood: *Introductiones in logicam. Einführung in die Logik*, H. Brands and Ch. Kann (eds.), Meiner, 1995.

Bruno Haas
Image, Reference, and the Level Distinction

Abstract As the problem of reference touches on some of the most characteristic concerns of human endeavour, any discussion of it will necessarily encounter considerable problems of mutual understanding. Although there is a vast gulf between Hegel and Wittgenstein and the traditions in which they work, a comparison of the two thinkers reveals some important parallels, such as a shared interest in the production of logical symptoms, i.e. the effects produced by logical acts. This chapter considers the production of such effects in the TLP in relation to reference: "*A* thinks that *p*", the use of the image paradigm in the description of the proposition and its effects on level shifts. The withdrawal of level shifts seems to induce a certain form of reference. All these topics are compared and described in relation to Hegel and his philosophical programme. The chapter ends with a short account of TLP: 6 and its relation to the Kantian conception of reference set out in his theory of categories, which served as an important reference point for both Hegel's and Wittgenstein's approach to the problem.

In this chapter, I address a group of philosophical problems present in Wittgenstein's *Tractatus* from a Hegelian point of view. Before I begin the discussion, I would like to point out some structural problems with this kind of confrontation between the two thinkers. It is well known, and does not require much commentary, that attempts to combine Hegelian philosophy, and especially his works on logic, with the tradition of analytic philosophy have proved largely unfruitful until quite recently. The very important work done by Pirmin Stekeler-Weithofer, Robert Brandom and some others has shown that there is nothing inevitable about this; nonetheless, there remain huge difficulties in the dialogue between the two traditions of thought. The very existence of a volume concerned with Hegel and Wittgenstein shows the growing interest in this problem and encourages a more experimental approach.

Before I address some more detailed questions, I would like to mention three major obstacles that we must keep in mind throughout this chapter.

(a) First, when we compare Hegelian logics with traditional logics, we must always be aware that they are, in a certain sense, not dealing with the same topic, even though there is sometimes a substantial relation between the two. Hegel's *Science of Logic* is not just a new treatise on logic, but a book about the Being of logic. It is clear from the outset that the problem of reference will be treated differently in a treatise on the Being of logic than in a treatise on logic. This difference was noted by Kant when he introduced the idea of a transcendental logic pertaining to the nature of what he called *der Gegenstand überhaupt*, i.e. that to which a judgement can possibly refer. The comparison between Hegelian and Wittgensteinian thinking is encouraged by the fact that the *Tractatus* can also be regarded as a book on the Being of logics. This may explain why it holds a peculiar and somewhat peripheral position in the history of logics.

(b) Second, there are vast differences in the structure of the terminologies of Hegelian dialectics and analytic philosophy. The difference lies not just in some terminological choices which could easily be translated one into the other. It lies in the way the terminology is developed in the different conceptions of definition and reference. This becomes a particular issue if we try to articulate a comparison between the two with respect to this very topic. The terminology with which we attempt to describe the logical structure of reference may itself imply specific forms of reference. As the two philosophical traditions diverge substantially here, the dialogue risks being frustrated from the outset. In short, the analytic tradition is based on the univocity of its terms. One term refers to one idea and this reference remains stable from beginning to end. This presupposes a certain structure of reference, namely that the *referent* is not affected by the act of referring to it. If we imagine for a moment that the act of referring changes the very nature of the *thing referred to*, then in fact there cannot be univocity in this sense. The act of referring to something can have performative effects. We can largely interpret Hegel's philosophy of the Being of logic as a theory of the performative effects of logical acts. This theory goes far beyond the theory of performative speech acts as formulated by Austin. Hegel's theory is particularly efficient when applied in the field of anthropology and sociology (theory of justice, religion, art, history, psychology and so on). In fact, there are very good reasons to think that many if not all human institutions are largely structured by the performative effects of the simple fact that we can refer to something by way of speech and other types of semiosis. Given this difficulty, Hegelian terminology cannot share the same kind of univocity and simplicity as the analytic tradition. This very clearly is a disadvantage. It means that in the beginning, and for quite a long time thereafter, it has to work with the provisional terminology provided by natural language, which strongly resists formalisation.[1] This disadvantage is

---

[1] The seemingly more trivial problems of translation between the natural languages should not be underestimated. The ideal of univocity in the analytic tradition minimises these problems, whereas in other contexts scholars are well aware of them. There is a long and venerable tradition of "traductology" dating back to antiquity (e.g. to thinkers such as Augustine). Some of its major contemporary representatives are Friedrich Schleiermacher, Walter Benjamin, José Ortega

counterbalanced by the fact that it is not forced to adopt a naive conception of reference like that presupposed in the analytic tradition. It may even be able to describe the performative effects of the analytic conception that are otherwise impossible to grasp. The difference of topic thus implies a difference of methodology. As Wittgenstein's terminology is based largely on the work of Russell/Whitehead and Frege, it seems to share their mode of univocity. However, I would like to argue that, as Wittgenstein does not address the logical questions head-on but is mainly concerned with the Being of logic, the very point of his *Tractatus* is to provoke some performative effects in order to *show* what the logical form under examination actually *is*. In Wittgenstein's conception, this can only be shown, and Hegel is wrong to believe he can give a logical expression of it. Still, Wittgenstein himself actually gives an account of certain aspects of logic's Being, before retiring from doing so in the famous ladder metaphor. We may interpret this gesture as a symptom of the intrinsically dialectical nature of Wittgenstein's investigation into the Being of logic, specifically with respect to the nature of reference.

(c) The third and final obstacle to a fruitful dialogue between the schools is psychic resistance. It is a remarkable feature of philosophy's scholarly culture that the different traditions very often show little or no interest in or respect towards one another, which makes it all the more necessary to compare them in a manner that is fundamentally sympathetic to all of them. This does not mean we should conflate the different traditions, but we should always presuppose that they make sense and then enquire into why such a multiplicity of meanings and questions exists. But if we want to understand the real ground of bad polemics, I believe we cannot simply attribute them to trivial motives such as jealousy, personal hostility and attempts to gain influence, although these are obviously very successful at producing their effect. From the time of Freud, we have had more powerful instruments at our disposal for understanding intellectual reactions to knowledge. If Freudian psychoanalysis has itself encountered and continues to encounter massive resistance, this can be powerfully explained by one of the major discoveries of that self-same discipline, namely psychic resistance itself. Freud showed that psychic resistance can be extremely powerful because it is essentially unconscious and for that reason inaccessible to direct reflection. It is clear from the outset that a theory of this kind will meet significant psychic resistance.[2] Whatever we may think about the controversies around psychoanal-

---

y Gasset, Antoine Berman, Henri Meschonnic and Umberto Eco. For a good recent account, see Chiurazzi (2013).

2 On Wittgenstein's interest in and relation to Freud, see Majetschak (2008).

ysis, it does not seem very rational to believe that it is merely unscientific and that it can be definitively refuted after a century of intensive research and influence in nearly every area of knowledge (at least within the humanities). It is true that psychoanalysis has been most influential in areas of a controversial nature; but this seems to be necessarily linked to the fact that it gives access to a peculiar kind of knowledge: a dangerous, socially explosive knowledge. Such knowledge may be very well established; the very fact that it encounters powerful psychic (and other forms of) resistance makes it something intrinsically controversial, a target of unfair blame and uninformed critique. Although Freudian psychoanalysis must provoke this kind of resistance to an extreme extent, because it attacks the very core of the problem, it is far from the only discipline to have been disregarded due more to psychic resistance than rational reasons. A similar, and politically even more heated, controversy has divided Marxist and traditional economics ever since the former's inception, since it questions many of the fundamentals of bourgeois society, especially the many privileges enjoyed by the ruling classes. Here again, it is not my task to settle the question, but only to be aware that we have here a kind of knowledge that is structurally controversial and unsympathetic, and with which no final settlement can be expected.

Much of the fascination and difficulty of Hegelian philosophy lies in the fact that it is sometimes closely linked to this sort of knowledge.[3] Hegel actually inspired Marx as well as the most radical version of Freudian psychoanalysis, namely the Lacanian school.[4] However, a large part of Hegelian philology tends to cover up this particularly uncomfortable aspect of Hegel's own thinking, making his philosophy an object of exclusively historical interest on the grounds of its (supposedly) now being patently absurd. I believe that a great part of the history of Hegelianism and all its controversies could be reconstructed from this point of view. This, however, is not the point here. I would like to suggest that the theory of reference in the sense indicated here contains much of the most controversial material, and it is therefore not easy to have free discussions about it from symptomatic hostilities. It would be a difficult task to explain here why this topic has been so deeply mined, but a look at Lacan's work on the *object relation* (Lacan [1957] 1994) shows that it is because this relation is necessarily mediated by some mode of logical reference. From a psychoanalytical perspective, Lacan establishes a correlation between reference on the one hand and subjectivation on the other. The referential dimension of this correlation concerns the link be-

---

3 See Adorno (1963: pp.84–133), especially "Skoteinos oder wie zu lesen sei".
4 A well-informed cross-reading of Hegel and Lacan is given in Žižek (2012).

tween Word (*la Parole*) and the object of desire (*la Chose*). Subjectivity forms itself by working through this referential dimension. This correlation has first been articulated in Hegel's *Phenomenology of Spirit*, in the chapters on desire, fighting and work. These chapters follow Hegel's exposition of transcendental subjectivity, i.e. the kind of subjectivity defined by the fact that it underlies the very possibility of reference to the object in general (*Gegenstand überhaupt*). Hegel shows later on that subjectivity is a function of intersubjectivity, i.e. that intersubjectivity precedes the formation of the individual subject. It is clear that this thesis throws a very peculiar light on the problem of reference and communication. The paradoxical character of the relation between the individual and intersubjectivity demands more commentary than can be given here. Yet we have to keep it in mind if we want to seriously compare Hegel and Wittgenstein on the topic of reference.

The theory of reference thus seems to have some radical implications about the nature of what our tradition calls a subject or self-consciousness. This is the very heart of Hegel's speculative psychology in the *Encyclopaedia* (E III, especially §441; see also §§473 ff.). Wittgenstein, meanwhile, addresses the problem in a group of remarks in the *Tractatus* (TLP: 5.4–5.5423).

1. If the TLP is a treatise on the Being of logic, then it seems to do something the author himself considers impossible: it makes logical form explicit, i.e. it makes it an object of reference, and the correlate of explicit speech. Yet one of the main difficulties of this treatise lies in the fact that it does not so much explicitly articulate the Being of logical form as implicitly make it appear. It *shows* the Being of logical form.

One of the foremost characteristics of this discourse is its ultimate self-abolishment. This self-abolishment is a necessary consequence of the kind of reference that is at work in this discourse on form. It does not imply that the whole *Tractatus* is just an error. The general movement of this treatise consists in constructing differences and distinctions and then abolishing them, passing by-products of great interest along the way. In this, it closely resembles a Hegelian paradigm whereby we make a distinction only to then withdraw it again. Hegel seems to believe that this apparently absurd, or at least useless, process constitutes an important and very general feature of thought. This similarity between the two authors merits further investigation.

The *Tractatus* itself does not refer to its objects in the same way as, say, elementary propositions and complex propositions built from elementary ones. It is not clear whether the *Tractatus* refers to anything at all; still, it does not seem to be entirely devoid of any sense whatsoever. So if we allow a provisional use of the word "reference", then we cannot help but recognise that there must be different types of reference at work in the *Tractatus*.[5]

The *Tractatus* does not deal with the Being of every kind of logic, but exclusively with the logics developed by Frege and Russell/Whitehead. That Fregean and Russellian logics are a legitimate branch of scholarly inquiry can be inferred from their efficiency. Wittgenstein's *Tractatus* did not contribute very much to the successive process of improving this kind of logic, but it did contribute something to understanding of its Being. It did so through a sort of experiment that makes the *Tractatus* a very peculiar book in the history of philosophy. It does not so much state what logic is, but rather makes logic happen. In this sense, it is an event. This event is especially symptomatic of the Being of Fregean and Russellian logics, a reference which limits the scope of Wittgenstein's argument.

The event in fact reaches near to nothingness, given that the *Tractatus* abolishes itself in the end; yet, as noted above, this return to nothingness produces some very interesting insights into the Being of logic along the way. Wittgenstein's *Tractatus* shares this peculiarity with two major contributions to the arts, namely the poetic reductionism of Stéphane Mallarmé and the artistic "less than little" (*infra-mince*) of Marcel Duchamp. Both these artists cherished the idea of an art reduced to some form of casual event.[6]

2. Let us now look at a group of Wittgenstein's remarks on the nature of (psychic) subjectivity in relation to reference. In TLP: 5.542, Wittgenstein gives a short interpretation of the sentence "*A* thinks *p*". This sentence is about reference, and at the same time it is about psychology. Wittgenstein suggests that *die Seele ist ein Unding*, that the soul is a nonsense or, as both the Ogden/Ramsey and Pears/McGuinness translations put it, that "there is no such thing as the soul" (TLP: 5.5422). This English translation of *Unding* is not exact; it does not transcribe the very specific weight of *das Unding*, which does not simply mean a non-thing (or: not a thing at all) but a very big one, a huge obstacle and nonsense that is impossible to overcome (very much like a saxonian administrative

---

[5] It is clear that from this point on, the dialogue between the philosophical traditions will be arduous. For in the analytic tradition, we consider a proposition that is incapable of univocally referring to something to be deficient, whereas from a Hegelian (and, I believe, from a Wittgensteinian) point of view, this deficiency appears as a structural moment of speech as such, perfectly accessible to analysis and interpretation (or "investigation").

[6] Stéphane Mallarmé: "Igitur" and "Un coup de dés", in Mallarmé (1945: pp.433–43 and pp.457–77 respectively); Marcel Duchamp presents in his "Box of 1914" an artwork made up of the causal forms of three one-metre-long threads that have fallen to the ground (Duchamp 1975: p.36).

guideline).⁷ The soul is a nonsense because it originates in a bad interpretation of the sentence "*A* thinks *p*". "*A* thinks *p*" suggests that there is something called *A* which undertakes the activity of thinking *p*. Taken in this sense, "*A* thinks *p*" seems to relate to an object called the soul and to its state of thinking *p*. However, Wittgenstein explains that "*A* thinks *p*" has the same form as "*A* says *p*" or even "'*p*' says *p*", so that there is no use assuming the existence of something like a soul. This "bad interpretation", however, contributes to the construction of something very real in human experience and society, an illusion many people are extremely eager to defend, and so much so that sometimes they even try to convince themselves and others of immortality. The soul may be a nonsense, but it is a productive one. Now, we may wonder whether this productivity is just contingent, due to a superficial understanding of the logic or grammar of our language, or whether it is produced by some necessity. In that case, we might conceive something like a structural productivity of thought and language, independently from its possible intrinsic absurdity. This productivity could even allow historical changes, fluctuations and developments. Hegel's *Phenomenology of Spirit* tries to establish a rational history of this structural and performative productivity, including many cases of nonsense such as Gall's project of phrenology. These products of language may be open to reshaping and critique. It would be excessively naive, however, to believe that there is nothing like an *Unding*.

What is a "bad interpretation"? When people say something, we assume that they really mean what they say; we presuppose something like a commitment. This is particularly true in juridical contexts such as contracts. So, if someone says *p*, then this necessarily means that they actually think *p*; otherwise, we could not later object that they did not take into account that *p*. But this does not imply the existence of a soul. The problem concerns the type of reference we make when we say "*A* thinks *p*". Wittgenstein suggests that this proposition encourages the hypostasis of *A*, i. e. it encourages a bad interpretation that gives *A* the status of a being. Here we enter into a very confusing ontological discussion. On the one hand, it is obvious that the analysed sentences cannot support

---

7 I will not enter here into the endless discussions about Wittgenstein's alleged mysticism, nor will I try to minimise, maximise, defend or reject it; but it is worth noting that Wittgenstein is a very careful writer with a very sensitive ear to the sound and semantic richness of the words he uses. A good interpretation of TLP: 5.5421 must be able to explain the exact sense and specific weight of *Unding*. – There is a great deal misuse in the secondary literature concerning the term "mysticism". Many writers believe mysticism to be a sort of meaningless babbling that conceals its lack of meaning beneath a veil of obscurity. In fact, medieval mysticism was based on a very rigorous practice of language capable of producing powerful effects of sense. Cf. Flasch (2006).

the aforementioned hypostasis. On the other, it seems very risky to claim that "*A*" simply does not exist. In fact, we can regard "*A*" as a performative product of speech. Its logical and ontological status is very strange indeed. When we refer to performative products of speech, the type of reference is structurally different from univocal "ontological" reference, for the very simple reason that performative products of speech are not stable, given that they change when we refer to them. This does not, however, imply that they are irrelevant or not real at all. They may be much more real than anything else. They are human reality: institutional, economic, legal reality and so on. Marx's analysis of capital explains how a mere signifier (money) can produce overwhelmingly devastating effects. – The "bad interpretation" consists in the hypostasis of performative speech effects. It makes a good interpretation impossible. Hegel holds that this kind of reference necessarily produces a *Schein* (false appearance), but that it is nevertheless a necessary form of reference with specific applications in certain fields, such as mathematical science.[8] Respectable psychoanalytic psychology does not hypostasise the soul; this point was very powerfully developed by Lacan, who was extremely aware of speech effects and their psychic reality. But the hypostasising "bad interpretation" hints at a very real performative effect of speech. This is something which appears on the margin of Wittgenstein's critical remarks on psychology.

Wittgenstein's remarks on psychology do not delve very deep into the concrete mechanism of the "psyche", but he does show the performative link between speech acts and psychic reality. This link is a fact; the "bad interpretation" arises when we give to this fact an ontological interpretation. It should be noted, incidentally, that the word "ontology" (literally: *Seinslogik*) could be used to designate this kind of hypostasising attitude towards the problem of reference. We may label as ontological (*seinslogisch*) any reference that presupposes absolute autonomy of the correlate with respect to its reflection in a speech act or a proposition, i. e. its absolute independence from it. The logic, products and aporias of this kind of reference are the precise topic of Hegel's logic of Being.[9] Wittgenstein's brief incursion into the field of psychology shows that psychic realities cannot be regarded as "atomic facts", which opens the way to a modern approach to psychology.

---

[8] On the shortcomings of onto-logical reference and Hegel's critique of it, see the classic study Theunissen (1978). Cf. Quante and Moore (2018), especially Pirmin Stekeler-Weithofer's chapter on measure (pp.219–274).
[9] See Haas (2003). There have not yet been any readings of Hegel's philosophy of subjective spirit that take account of his conception of ontology as *Seins-Logik*.

3. I shall now consider some general characteristics of Wittgenstein's theory of reference. I would like to underline here three elements of this theory that are of particular interest in relation to Hegel's treatment of the same question.

(a) First of all, there is Wittgenstein's use of the image paradigm in his explanation of propositions. The two other aspects are intimately linked to this incisive theoretical choice. Wittgenstein interprets thought as a sort of image (TLP: 3). A bit later, this interpretation is extended to the expression of thought, to *der Satz* (a "sentence", "proposition", TLP: 3.1).[10] Wittgenstein does not ignore the radical difference between an image and a proposition: namely that an image as such has no truth value, whereas a proposition does. So he must add, as a second and independent item, that the truth of an image lies in its agreement with reality (TLP: 2.222). Representation and agreement (TLP: 2.221 and 2.222 respectively) are the two aspects which have to be combined in order to be able to use the image as a paradigm, in order in turn to understand propositional reference.

(b) It is very important to Wittgenstein's theory that the image can represent a fact, but that it cannot represent its own form of representation (*Abbildung*) (TLP: 2.172). Here, I will describe this as the *difference between matter and form*. The term "matter" will be used for that which can be the object of representation by an image, whereas the "form" is what the image has to be in order to be able to represent its matter. This use of "matter" and "form" comes close to how Kant used the terms in his theory of reflection ("amphibology"), reinterpreted by Hegel in his logic of essence. Wittgenstein uses this conception of form and matter in his critique of the Fregean judgement stroke (*Urteilsstrich*) in TLP: 4.442: "Ein Satz kann unmöglich von sich selbst aussagen, daß er wahr ist", no sentence can assert of itself that it is true. In fact, every proposition shows through its form that it purports to be true; this makes it superfluous and even absurd to explicitly include this purport in its formulation. If we do, we represent the form of representation, and this makes us hypostasise something that has no reality in itself. Frege's error is not to have recognised that all propositions have this structural purport, but to have symbolised it: "What can be shown, cannot be said." (TLP: 4.1212)

(c) The distinction between matter and form will be used here as the matrix for theorising the phenomenon of logical level shifting. The very general fundamental idea is that whenever we explicitly speak about a form, and thus make it

---

10 The translation of *Satz* as proposition common to both versions is somewhat problematic. A *Satz* is the *expression* of a thought; and we may thus assume that it is the expression of a proposition. The term *Satz* at any rate has a semiotic dimension that is not necessarily included in the term "proposition".

the matter of a proposition, then it will be necessary to introduce a new higher-level form, unless a form can apply to itself. The image paradigm seems not to allow the form of representation to be its explicit matter. It thus leads to a reduction of the logical phenomenon of level shifting in the sense of a shift from matter to form or from one form to another form of a higher level. This motivates Wittgenstein's critique of Russell's paradox (TLP: 3.331–3.333), a refutation that is generally considered insufficient. The refutation is based on the interpretation of "F(fx)" as an image. If "F(fx)" is an image, then F' in "F'(F(fx))" cannot be identified with F, simply because it differs from it in terms of form: F and F' occupy structurally different places in the formula. This difference is *shown* by the formula. Obviously, one may contest the interpretation of the formula as an image; but this is the assumption Wittgenstein tries to articulate in his treatise. And even if Wittgenstein's argument does not hold against the theory of types as a whole, it nevertheless poses the problem of level shifting in an original way worthy of examination. –

The image paradigm seems to concentrate these three aspects in a very efficient way.[11] It also makes it possible to exclude from the outset the forms of self-reference so prominent in German idealism, specifically in its theories of subjectivity. The Hegelian treatment of form in relation to matter, content and essence cannot be explained here. It leads to a very particular conception of the relations of difference and identity between these opposite terms, whereby distinctions are made and then abolished.

This use of the image paradigm may help to define what Wittgenstein actually means by this term in the *Tractatus*. As has been noted, it may have quite different meanings, ranging from purely mathematical to rhetorical uses.[12] As Wittgenstein avoids giving a univocal indication of which meaning he favours, we may suppose that it should be grasped in a more abstract and functional way. I would therefore like to suggest here that the image may be defined precisely by its specific behaviour with respect to form and level shifting.[13] If we undertake our investigation of the image from this point of view, we become aware of a structure that is extremely important to Hegel's theory of the image (and its continuation in Lacanian psychoanalysis): namely, the structural twofoldness of im-

---

11 Cf. Morris (2008: especially pp.131 ff).
12 Cf. Mersch (2006), which offers an extensive bibliography.
13 In his classic study, Erik Stenius (1960) discusses what an image can (and cannot) show through its form. Whereas Stenius develops the idea of structural analogy and isomorphism, I shall focus on another aspect of image theory that seems to be less prominent in the discussion: namely, the question of how an image functions as an *act* of a peculiar nature (an "image act", to cite the well-known formula by Horst Bredekamp (2018)).

ages as opposed to the structural threefoldness of symbols. Unfortunately, this is not exactly in line with the well-known distinctions by Charles Sanders Peirce, who tends to consider icons as a sort of structural "oneness", with structural "twoness" being reserved for indexes.[14] I obviously cannot discuss this problem at length. Still, I would like to suggest here that Wittgenstein's use of the image paradigm is due to a sort of structural deficiency of images (by way of contrast with symbols) that permits him to reduce logical complexity by avoiding forms of self-application and correlative level shifts.

Within Hegel's writings, we find some relevant texts on image theory and its relation to symbolism in the chapters on subjective spirit in the *Encyclopaedia*, especially in E III: §§452–68. This theory, incidentally, underlies his treatment of the different forms of art (symbolic, iconic and functional) described in the Lectures on Aesthetic.[15] For Hegel, the point of images is *substitution*. The image can substitute for its object (to a certain degree) such that the difference between the two is not evident to someone who actually recognises the object or fact represented in the image, although it is always evident to a third-person observer. This sort of substitution is called illusion; it can occur in combination with a form of fascination. As such, it is a very important psychological phenomenon. The same sort of substitution is impossible in a symbol. (Whenever we use a symbol as a substitute for its object, we are using it as an image.) Substitution (and, thus, illusion) plays a very important role in Hegel's theory of subjective spirit, and also in his theory of absolute spirit. Here it shifts from a very deficient sort of sign to the most perfect and "transparent" sign in classical art.

Yet there remain some very serious problems with image theory, especially the place the image occupies relative to symbolism. The problem can be explained by reference to the well-known commonplace on the relation between a score, a gramophone record and a musical thought in TLP: 4.014. Wittgenstein suggests that a score, a gramophone record and a musical thought are images of each other. The problem with this argument is that the score cannot be "translated" into the musical thought without vast musical expertise that can only

---

[14] This terminology resembles that used by Charles Sanders Peirce. A full discussion of the problem would need to make more detailed reference to Peirce's semiotics. I cannot develop the argument here. Stefan Majetschak (2000: pp.39 ff.) has rightly emphasised the semiotic character of Wittgenstein's image theory.

[15] The three forms of art are known as symbolic, classical and romantic. A closer analysis of this theory, however, demonstrates that the classical and romantic forms of art exhibit as firm a semiotic structure as the symbolic form. Cf. Haas (2013) and Hilmer (1997). Classical art is iconic, *sculpture*, whereas romantic art is functional, *music*. The relation between Hegel and Peirce merits closer study.

be obtained by experiencing musical performances.[16] So far, there seems to be a structural asymmetry between images and facts. But what is the difference? Whether something is an image or not depends on the use we make of it; everything can occasionally be used as an image of something else. We can actually use a musical performance as an image of the score, although this would presuppose a highly developed analytical skill as we would have to be able to recognise the relevant unities in the musical continuum in order to write them down in the relatively simple musical notation. If we want to identify such unities, we must be able to use names and to make them correspond to these unities. Their choice must be motivated. They must help structure the musical continuum in such a way as to make the "musical thought" intelligible. We are far beyond a simple representational relation. If we interpret names and the unifying effects of nominal reference as a minimal form and effect of symbolism, then it appears that the image in fact presupposes some symbolic framework. This relation underlies the whole of Hegel's theory of the three forms of art: symbolic, iconic and functional.[17]

Whatever we may say about this symbolic framework, which is necessary for the use of a fact as an image the fact of being an image cannot be a fact in the same sense. There is no criterion entirely independent of convention sufficient to make an image recognisable as such. So if the formal quality of being an image cannot itself be represented by another image, then it must be the object of some other form of reference. This conclusion could motivate a critique of Wittgenstein's extensive use of the image as a logical paradigm. Wittgenstein's very radical and restrictive position must have been adopted in pursuit of a specific objective. If form can only be shown, then it seems impossible to develop a

---

16 In fact, the representational relation between these items is not symmetrical. The score is an analytically reduced notation of a piece of music, which traditionally is considered to exist only as a performance. If you know this art very well, then you can "understand" a score, i.e. know what it means and entails. An average musician may be able to reproduce the notes, but not the thought. So if you want to learn how to read a score, then you must hear real performances, which give vastly more information than a score. But if you have learned music from pieces that were actually performed, then you may be able to read a score in a relevant, competent manner. The case of the tape is a bit more complicated, as it includes properties peculiar to the medium of reproduction. I shall attempt to give an abstract account of what a medium is later in this chapter.

17 Hegel's general idea is that whereas symbolic (Egyptian) architecture is based on the refusal of sense, and thus confronts us with the radical refusal, death, classical Greek architecture gives access to the most transparent signifier possible, the image. Still, the image seems to be in need of this structurally symbolic framing: it must be excluded, isolated from the world. On the relation between symbolism and death in Hegel, see the seminal essay Derrida (1972).

thematic discourse on form; whatever might be said about form would have to be withdrawn again (as per the ladder metaphor). Wittgenstein's concern with images permits him to drop the necessity and even the possibility of a level shift whenever, rather than speaking about some being correlate, we instead try to focus on a logical form (shift from content to form) and make it the explicit object of investigation. In a sense, logical forms are not objects at all. We cannot refer to them as we can to objects. In Hegel's words, reference to a logical form is not onto-logical (*seins-logisch*). But this does not necessarily imply that there cannot be any kind of reference to them. Hegel even develops a typology of reference. In his terminology, reference to a logical form would be *wesens-logisch*.[18]

Given this difficulty, Wittgenstein's image paradigm can respond to another theoretical interest that is not very explicit in the *Tractatus*. If we understand the image as a structural analogy of the fact represented, and conceive the relation between image and fact as symmetrical, then we can understand the image as a reality serving as a *model* for another reality. This implies it may possibly have technical utility in the construction of a machine (e. g. in informatics). The intimate relation between modelling and technique becomes clear very easily when seen through this lens.[19]

We can read Wittgenstein's conception of the image as a means to articulate form and content such that form cannot become the object of explicit expression, but must *show* itself. Still, the concept of the image itself does introduce an explicit conception of form; but it does so in such a way as to force its subsequent withdrawal. This helps Wittgenstein to reduce his logical framework and "scaffolding of the world" to nothing or nearly nothing (TLP: 6). What I would like to suggest here is that the image paradigm serves to abolish all kinds of shifts from content to form. On the one hand, this makes possible Wittgenstein's reductionism and, on the other, leads directly to a very interesting sort of reference (namely to the world "as it is", at the end of TLP: 6.54). The withdrawal of his formal theory is actually the event of reference to the world as it is; this event is its performative effect.

---

[18] Nowadays, Hegel's seemingly old-fashioned terminology very often proves to be an obstacle to thorough comprehension of his ideas. In the *Doctrine of Essence*, Hegel first of all discusses the determinations of reflection (identity, difference, opposition, etc.), which have very little to do with a somewhat mysterious entity called "essence" (or, worse, "Wesen"). In this chapter, Hegel shows that these determinations are not "entities" (i.e. beings) at all. They are nevertheless concepts of irreducible importance to any kind of thinking. Cf. Iber (1990).
[19] Cf. the interesting approach to the relation between image, model and sentence in Morris (2008: especially pp.114–202).

This articulation of the reduction of the level shift between matter and form on the one hand and reference on the other has a logical structure comparable to Hegel's conception of reference as developed in his logic of the determinations of reflection, namely his theory of contradiction. Hegel does not try to justify every kind of contradiction whatsoever, but he tries to show that whenever a proposition refers to something, the Being of that proposition is defined by a structural contradiction: reference is the collapse of the reflection level thanks to the structurally contradictory nature of reflection as such. Reflection puts forward a distinction (between world or Being and thought or reflection, or in Hegel's words between *Sein* and *Gesetztsein*) and then abolishes this distinction through the inherent contradiction of reflection. This (dialectical) process does not entirely collapse into nothing; it is the form of thinking itself, inasmuch as thinking is part of the world and reality, but it is not a possible correlate of onto-logical propositions (i.e. propositions with an onto-logical, *seinslogisch*, reference type).[20] We may note here in passing that there seems to be a correlation between contradiction (or paradox) and level shifting. We try to avoid contradictions by means of level shifts; there would not be any level shifting if there were not a corresponding contradiction or paradox. Wittgenstein appears to want to make a very original use of the image paradigm. Instead of leading to a complex formal theory, his use of the paradigm reduces formal logic to nearly nothing and as a consequence provokes a direct reference to the "world". This experience is considered to be "mystical" by Wittgenstein (TLP: 6.522). From a Hegelian point of view, however, the "mystical" does not prove to be very mystical at all; it comprises the vast area of the performative products of logical acts (acts due to the existence of logical acts, acts linked to the existence of *logos*). As far as reference is concerned, Hegel stresses that simple reference to "something" (*Etwas*) is characterised by "double negation" of this sort (i.e. positing a difference and then withdrawing it). In a passage from the paragraph on the logic of *Etwas*, Hegel explains the minimal logical form of nominal reference to something and what this means for the logical structure of Something (*Etwas*) itself: "Das Factische, was also vorhanden ist, ist das Daseyn überhaupt, Unterschied an ihm, und das Aufheben des Unterschieds." (GW 21: p. 103) Whenever we refer to something (*Etwas*), we have first to establish a difference, i.e. the difference between Being and Positivity (*Sein* and *Gesetztsein*) so that we can use names, propositions and utterances, and then to abolish this self-same distinction again, so that the positivity refers to its correlate. The correlate then presents it-

---

[20] For a more detailed version of this account of Hegel's theory of reference in relation to contradiction, see Haas (2017); see also the older but still elucidating discussion in Wolff (2010).

self in the form of "Etwasheit", i.e. of a being in contrast to Being in general (*als ein Seiendes*, not *als sein Sein*).[21] There is no reference to reality without this double negation.[22] In Hegel's account, *Etwas* turns out to be the stable referent of a name and nothing more; the "*first* negation of negation", as he puts it.

4. Even though the image paradigm serves to withdraw the distinction between matter and form (this fundamental articulation between logical levels), Wittgenstein does not hesitate to introduce some minimal articulations between logical levels. We will now consider these distinctions and their (somewhat paradoxical) logical behaviour. This will aid understanding of some of the most fundamental theoretical peculiarities of German idealism. Wittgenstein distinguishes between names and elementary and complex propositions. These distinctions make it possible to construct a minimal logical form, the "general form of the truth function" (TLP: 6). The way Wittgenstein articulates these levels illustrates the structure of reference and its "contradictory" nature.

Wittgenstein's conception of elementary propositions (*Elementarsätze*) in itself is not original. This conception seems unavoidable in a constructive and axiomatic logic. What is more original is the way Wittgenstein discusses elementary propositions and their constituents, names. Propositions are made up of names. This seems to imply that elementary propositions must be made up of a plurality of names. However, Wittgenstein affirms that the composition and structure of elementary propositions cannot be anticipated, i.e. that their description is not a part of logic (TLP: 5.55). This is perfectly consistent with Wittgenstein's conception of the proposition as an image. There cannot be any anticipation of elementary propositions, as they must be considered independent from one another (otherwise they would be composite and complex[23]). Nonetheless, Wittgenstein is forced to recognise that a proposition is made up of names, and that names refer to their objects (*Gegenstände*) in quite a different way than propositions. A name means an object, the object is its meaning (*Bedeutung*). A proposition, on the contrary, has a sense (*Sinn*). Yet if we want to say what an object is, then we can only give the very formal answer that it is the correlate of a name (TLP: 4.1272 and 2.0232), that it can only be named (TLP: 3.221), that we cannot say what it is (ibid.). Thus, there is no anticipation of the "given". On the surface, this attitude seems to be especially contrary to Kant, but it also runs counter to Hegel. Wittgenstein's refusal to theorise the form of objects and

---

21 The distinction between *Sein* and *Seiendes*, *esse* and *ens* (the so-called *ontological difference*), is "of the utmost importance" in Hegel's logic (GW 21: p.103) but is difficult to translate into English.
22 On the theory of double negation, cf. the classic study Henrich (1976).
23 Cf. TLP: 2.061 and 2.062 with regard to the expression of facts in elementary propositions.

elementary propositions makes them perfectly amorphous and leaves us without any way of telling whether the application of an utterance to a fact by means of elementary propositions and the names composing that utterance is correct or not. For Wittgenstein, this is not a logical problem.[24] Yet if it is not, then we may wonder how complex propositions (which are built up from elementary ones) can have a form.

The problem is more easily explained in relation to Kant, on whom Hegel's own conception relies heavily. Very much like Wittgenstein, Kant refrains from anticipating the given by treating it as the "manifold". Yet in contrast to Wittgenstein, Kant holds that being an empirical object (and a correlate of a judgement) implies certain formal characteristics.[25] In Wittgenstein's terminology, this formulation is necessarily nonsense, because the correlates of the names used in it are logical forms; logical forms have to *show* themselves and must not be expressed explicitly. Kant's own account of transcendental logic uses paradoxes such as that of *a priori* synthesis, which can easily be recognised as a contradiction *in adjecto*. The question here is not whether there is a contradiction or not, but what exactly a contradiction is and whether there may be circumstances in which the paradoxical formulation of a contradiction is a good way to appreciate a logical structure, especially in relation to reference. What Kant points at with his paradoxical formulation of an *a priori* synthesis is the fact that if there is something like an empirical "given", it must have been submitted to a logical synthesis *in advance*, and so for this reason there is no way to accompany or reconstruct this synthesis step by step from the first elements to the complex result. With respect to Kant, the idea of a step-by-step reconstruction is a myth, which relies (as Hegel argues in his *Seinslogik*) on a naive conception of Being and reference.

As Wittgenstein departs from a Fregean/Russellian logical positivism, he is bound to a step-by-step constructive method. But following this method, he reveals its problems and shortcomings. This leads him to a peculiar conception of logical form, level shifts and reference.

Although nothing can be said about elementary propositions and objects, it seems possible to say something about complex propositions. Even here the result is of a disarming simplicity; in a way, the whole theory is encapsulated in

---

24 We should not assign objects the function of "providing us with the conditions of the sense we make", as Eli Friedlander proposes, for the simple reason that this charge does not take into account the fundamentally paradoxical position of objects in relation to propositions. But we can try to describe the paradox and its structure with respect to the object relation and reference (Friedlander 2001: p.163).

25 The definitive account of Kant's first *Critique* is still Baumanns (1997).

the general formula of truth functions, i.e. propositions: $[\bar{p}, \bar{\xi}, N(\bar{\xi})]$ (TLP: 6). This formula is the most general possible propositional variable. It *shows* its logical form. Later, I shall attempt to give an interpretation of this formula and its formal qualities. We will see thereby that they very much resemble the Kantian categories as understood from a Hegelian perspective.

Let us first consider its place in the whole structure. The general formula is actually a symptom. It is what shows itself when we *speak* about what is the case (it is a symptom of the fact of speaking). In order to build this formula, we have to introduce two different and articulated logical levels, the level of names and the level of elementary propositions. The latter are built out of the former. Without the concept of names and elementary propositions, there could not be any complex propositions. But without complex propositions, there would never be a general formula, i.e. a logical form. Names and elementary propositions are presupposed; but they cannot be described in themselves. Wittgenstein's reluctance to give a formal account of elementary propositions is understandable, but somewhat paradoxical. How can one claim that they lack any formal quality and then say that they are made of names? Further, we may wonder how a complex proposition could ever be built from elementary ones, if the latter had no formal qualities that could be anticipated. Names and elementary propositions provide the formal elements which make it possible to give the general formula, i.e. to define in advance the logical form of complex propositions. This means that we must be able to give a definition of the formal qualities of names and elementary propositions (however minimal they may be) with respect to the general formula.

If there are minimal formal qualities we can establish about names and elementary propositions, they will actually be derived from the general formula of complex propositions, so that the preceding and simple forms depend on the subsequent complex ones, the elements on the result. This inversion is paradoxical, but it seems unavoidable.

I would like to suggest here that first Kant and later Hegel developed their theories after becoming aware of this kind of paradox. The circularity is quite recognisable in Kant's idea of *a priori* synthesis and in Hegel's critique of origin (on which more later). Wittgenstein himself makes a similar double gesture in the *Tractatus*. He introduces the formal concept of an image, i.e. the fundamental difference between Being and its representation. The explicit articulation of its formal characteristics, however, leads to the famous gesture of self-abolishment and the correlated reference to the world. The logical forms that can be established on the level of complex propositions are not only the result but also the basis of the whole construction. The movement of construction and reduction seems to be determined from the outset by its result.

The image paradigm helps Wittgenstein present this situation without being obliged to make it explicit; in fact, he has it take place as an event.

5. I will now give an interpretation of the general formula in TLP: 6 from an essentially Kantian perspective.[26] First of all, the application of the general formula presupposes the existence of (elementary) propositions, not objects, so that its material (i.e. the elements it is made up of or applied to) is of the same nature as the result. The resulting proposition is nevertheless supposed to represent reality (*Wirklichkeit*). This situation is obviously paradoxical. Let us formalise it as follows: there is a difference between elementary and complex propositions. The former are the elements of the latter, which have a general form. Propositions built using that general form can represent reality. So do elementary propositions; yet their form cannot be anticipated. Although it cannot be anticipated we can anticipate that they are the only possible material for the formation of complex propositions.

I shall now represent the real with the letter ℜ, the elementary propositions (the form of which is *a priori* unknown) with the letter *p* and the complex propositions (the form of which can be specified *a priori*) with the letter Ξ. Let us specify that *p* can be part of Ξ and that Ξ is an image of ℜ representing the minimal logical "scaffolding" of the world (TLP: 6.124). Still, what cannot be explained is the relation between *p* and ℜ. On the one hand, we do not understand how objects can combine into *Sachverhalte*, given that they are utterly undetermined, names being essentially undefinable (TLP: 3.202–3.203, 3.3221 and 3.261) and objects "colourless" (TLP: 2.0232). On the other hand (and as a consequence), we have no idea of what an elementary proposition could look like. Hence, we obtain the following triangular relation with one side left undetermined:

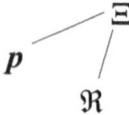

This diagram corresponds closely to the structure of Kant's transcendental argument for *a priori* synthesis. Very much like Wittgenstein, Kant holds that the real in itself is utterly unknown. This is the precise sense of his "manifold".

---

[26] This reference to Kant seems necessary in any thorough study of the relation between Hegel and Wittgenstein. In fact, it is mostly through their relation to Kant that they come into contact with one another.

Kant cannot explain how categories can build some well-structured reality from this manifold, nor does he claim to do so. The immediate relation between the manifold and its immediate concept remains without an explanation throughout the entirety of his critical philosophy, the third *Critique* included.[27] What he can do is show that any event of sense presupposes combination, just as Wittgenstein does in his theory of complex propositions. Kant now turns to a consideration of combination as such and begins his analysis with the formal description of judgements. Then he turns back and suggests that the forms of judgement must serve as a matrix for every kind of combination or connection, especially those we cannot explain but must presuppose (*a priori* synthesis). We may suspect that Kant's table of the forms of judgement contains something similar to Wittgenstein's general formula. Kant states that if the forms of judgement are the most general types of conjunction, it is necessary that every conjunction in reality be consonant with that form. Formulated in Wittgenstein's terms, Kant's idea is that the general form of complex propositions must also apply to elementary propositions: in other words, that there cannot be an essential difference between complex and elementary propositions, or that no proposition can be considered to be entirely elementary.

But if the difference between elementary and complex propositions disappears, the general form of complex propositions will at the same time be the form of elementary propositions, i.e. it will be the form of the objects themselves; and this is the point of Kant's transcendental deduction. The *elementary* application of logical form is necessary even though we cannot show how it actually works: the story of *a priori* synthesis from the manifold up to the final product, the object, cannot be told, because the manifold in itself is unconceivable. What is conceivable must previously have been synthesised. *A priori* synthesis is necessary, but it cannot be traced back to its supposed beginning. We cannot actually follow the steps of the process, we can only grasp it in its result. This is why Kant calls it an *a priori* synthesis, in other words a synthesis that took place *in advance*. The formula is paradoxical insofar as it makes synthesis precede the elements of synthesis. It thus disregards our intuition about how things originate. In fact, it foreshadows the radical critique of origin developed

---

27 This point, I admit, is controversial. I will explain elsewhere why all the interpretations which give an affirmative and constructive answer to the subsumption problem miss the point of the third *Critique* in particular, which should be read as a symptomatology of the reflective faculty of judgement (*Symptomatologie der reflektierenden Urteilskraft*).

by Hegel at the beginning of his *Science of Logic*.[28] Wittgenstein himself formulates the very same paradox in these terms: "Only the proposition has sense; only in the nexus of a proposition does a name have meaning." (TLP: 3.3)[29] The name, despite being the element from which elementary propositions are formed, is here nevertheless asserted to be their result.

Given the paradoxical character of the argument, it appears that it cannot be formulated in an axiomatically constructed formal language. Such a language is based on a progression from the simple to the complex. Hence, it is not compatible with the kind of argument Kant, Hegel and Wittgenstein present us with. The fact that a theory cannot be reformulated in the terms of an axiomatically defined formal language does not necessarily imply that it must be pointless. It only shows that formal and natural languages are not *structurally* equivalent. This difference also appears in their different relation to grammar. The grammar of a formal language coincides with its logic. The grammar of a natural one never does. This non-coincidence is probably not contingent but an essential feature, as Wittgenstein describes in his later writings.

If the form of elementary propositions cannot be anticipated, nor *a fortiori* the form of objects, then we may ask in what sense the general formula and the formal characteristics of complex propositions can be held to describe the "scaffolding of the world" (TLP: 6.124). Wittgenstein indicates in the same passage what this might signify. In Pears and McGuinness's translation, the text reads: "logic is not a field in which *we* express what we wish with the help of signs, but rather one in which the nature of the natural and inevitable signs speaks for itself." – "In der Logik sagt die Natur der naturnotwendigen Zeichen selbst aus". Here we can grasp the performative dimension of the use of logical signs. If the nature of signs can express itself, these signs must themselves be a reality. Obviously, it is a reality with a peculiar ontological status. In fact, the very being of signs is to be understood as a sort of performativity. Its Being is an act on its own. *Logos* is thus not just a means for people eager to exercise their intellect; it is something which implies its own necessities. We can describe the structure of *logos* without any reference to the speakers. What is more, the very idea of a "speaker" (a subject, an "I") seems to be structurally derived from the logical act, as we saw earlier. Wittgenstein here comes very close to Hegel's conception of absolute knowledge. Absolute knowledge is not absolutely certain knowledge, but rather knowledge without a subject, knowledge produced

---

28 Interpreters should not try to veil the paradoxical structure of the transcendental argument. In fact, one strand of the long history of interpretations of this argument is vitiated by the long-running efforts to amend this uncomfortable aspect of Kantianism (and Hegelianism).
29 This translation mixes both versions together.

by the inherent logic and performativity of *logos*. Absolute knowledge occurs whenever *logos* expresses itself by way of form instead of serving just as a means of expression for some contingent subject. Whenever the nature of signs expresses itself (i.e. whenever we observe the performative effects of their use), we have to do with a form of absolute knowledge (i.e. discourse devoid of a subjective standpoint). The very question of certainty in these cases is accidental.

Let us now consider the general formula of TLP: 6 in slightly more detail. It seems to reproduce the first three classes of category and thus express the same *a priori* synthesis as Kant, but excluding modality. I shall try to explain why there is no place for modality here.

In a sense, the general formula defines a machine able to produce any possible (well-formed) complex proposition. Wittgenstein uses the horizontal bar to indicate the successive operation which can produce any complex proposition just by stopping at different points. This device resembles a Turing machine, insofar as its output is determined on the one hand by the rules of a linear and finite sequence of operations to be executed with a finite number of elementary propositions and on the other by the place where it stops after a given number of operations. This place is obviously contingent; it reflects what appears as the empirical aspect of propositions. We may wonder whether Wittgenstein thinks that every meaningful proposition can be formulated in this way without knowing any elementary proposition individually or not. At any rate, the total absence of any example of an elementary proposition in the text and the failure of the secondary literature to convincingly propose one suggests that there is none, and that the whole complexity of the world can be reduced to the complexity of propositions derived from the general formula. This would make elementary propositions superfluous or reduce them to complex ones in a manner similar to Kant's argument. But this hypothesis may go beyond Wittgenstein's intentions.

The following analysis starts from a very abstract consideration of the general formula.

This formula is composed of variables such as p and ξ, of a horizontal bar (which indicates the successive repetition of the same operation in a regulated series of formulae) and of N (the sign for negation). Furthermore, there are some syntactic indicators such as commas and brackets.

First, Wittgenstein's formula is based on two types of propositions: p and ξ, the first indicating the element, the second its combination with one or more other elements. Hence, p has to be inserted into ξ, or ξ applied to p. This insertion/application of one term (in)to the other corresponds to what Kant calls *relation*, the relation between subject and predicate in his conception of the categories and correlative forms of judgement. Wittgenstein's treatment of logical relation is rather reductive, as he goes back to the Sheffer bar (NAND) in order to eliminate the threefold variety of relation present in Kant.

Second, Wittgenstein's formula implies the presence of negation, marked by the letter N in his formula. The different final propositions will be generated by the successive negation of a series of ξ-propositions and the arbitrarily or empirically fixed end of this operation. This aspect of Wittgenstein's general formula ascertains the dimension of *quality* in Kantian terminology.

Third, from the opposition of p and ξ and from the repetition of ξ in the formula, it appears that a term must be identical in the different instances of its use. This identity in a variety of instances is what Kant addresses under the heading of *quantity* in his table of categories. Categorial quantity should not be confused with numbers, but rather concerns the traditional determinations of conceptuality, universality and particularity.[30]

Wittgenstein does not directly address what Kant calls the *modality* of a judgement, its relation to the subject (rather than the object). The elimination of modal logic may be interpreted as another consequence of the image paradigm. This does not mean there is no trace of modal problems in the *Tractatus*; on the contrary, modality may constitute one of its major concerns. In fact, if the movement of constructing and then abolishing a logical form makes the event of reference occur, and thus the event of subjectivity insofar as subjectivity is a performative effect of referential speech, then the *Tractatus* as a whole is nothing but a book about modality (a book enacting the modal dimension of *logos*). But this dimension cannot be made explicit, it has to *show* itself.

The very fact of excluding modality from the explicit logic of the general formula seems to derive ultimately from the image paradigm. It is true that no logical form can be made explicit in an image, but only shown. But it is particularly true of logical modality. We may even define the image as a sign devoid of any modal determination. At the beginning of this chapter, I noted that the image has a peculiar relation between form and content (or form and matter, to use Kant's concepts of reflection as presented in the *Critique of Pure Reason*). The separation of matter and form is a structural correlate to the lack of modal determination in the image.[31]

---

[30] This is the sense of Kant's memorable formulation *durchgängige Identität* in §16 of the *Critique of Pure Reason*, i.e. literally going through, or continuous identity rather than the misleading "thoroughgoing identity" as in the Cambridge edition (translated by Paul Guyer and Allan W. Wood). *Durchgängige Identität* is an identity which remains the same across a variety of states it goes through.

[31] Kant discovered that the concepts of reflection (*Reflexionsbegriffe*) can be constructed in line with the four groups of categories. They later inspired Hegel's theory of the determinations of

Very much like in Kant, Wittgenstein seems to notice that reference is a form of relation not only between the proposition and its correlate, but also between the proposition and a third entity, which we can call the sender or addressee of the message, i.e. what philosophers have traditionally called the subject. This third entity appears to be a product of the very curious logical structure of double negation as described in this chapter. In fact, double negation mediates reference as an event. But what *is* the event of reference? We may remember here the very important Freudian discovery that what occurs in the event of reference is actually consciousness, in other words the openness of a world, as suggested by Wittgenstein in some formulations in the *Tractatus* (e.g. TLP: 5.63). This discovery does not necessarily imply some "superficial" psychology (TLP: 5.5421), and in particular it does not imply any "metaphysical" (i.e. trivially ontological) hypostasis of consciousness.[32]

References

Adorno, Theodor W.: *Drei Studien zu Hegel*, Suhrkamp, 1963.
Baumanns, Peter: *Kant's Philosophie der Erkenntnis*, Königshausen & Neumann, 1997.
Bredekamp, Horst: *Image Acts: A Systematic Approach to Visual Agency*, De Gruyter, 2018.
Chiurazzi, Gaetano (ed.): *The Frontiers of Ethics and Politics of Translation*, Lit Verlag, 2013.
Derrida, Jacques: "Le puits et la pyramide: Introduction à la sémiologie de Hegel", in: *Marges de la philosophie*, Minuit, 1972, pp.79–127.
Duchamp, Marcel: *Duchamp du signe*, Michel Sanouillet (ed.), Flammarion, 1975.
Flasch, Kurt: *Meister Eckhart. Die Geburt der "Deutschen Mystik" aus dem Geist der arabischen Philosophie*, Beck, 2006.
Friedlander, Eli: *Sign of Sense. Reading Wittgenstein's* Tractatus, Harvard University Press, 2001.
Haas, Bruno: *Beiträge zu Hegels Wissenschaft der Logik, der Kunst und des Religiösen*, Duncker und Humblot, 2003.
Haas, Bruno: "Symbol und Symbolische Kunstform bei Hegel", in: Alain Patrick Olivier and Elisabeth Weisser-Lohmann, (eds.): *Kunst – Religion – Politik* (Hegel Forum), Fink, 2013, pp.137–149.
Haas, Bruno: "Urteil", in: Gilbert Gérard and Bernard Mabille (eds.): La *Science de la Logique au Miroir de l'Identité*, Peeters, 2017, pp.195–216.

---

reflection (*Reflexionsbestimmungen*). Kant specifically links the distinction between form and matter to the *modal* dimension of thought. For a recent study on Kant's conception of modality, see Motta (2012). This commentary, however, does not take adequate account of the specific meaning of the concepts of reflection "form" and "matter".

32 Let us recall here Kant's very harsh critique of rational psychology in the *Critique of Pure Reason* (in the chapter on "paralogisms"). This attitude is very prominent in Hegel, who endeavoured to explain subjectivity as the result of performative effects of logical acts in a broad sense.

Henrich, Dieter: "Hegels Grundoperation. Eine Einleitung in die 'Wissenschaft der Logik'", in: Ute Guzzoni, Bernhard Rang, and Ludwig Siep (eds.): *Der Idealismus und seine Gegenwart*, Meiner, 1976, pp.208–230.
Hilmer, Brigitte: *Scheinen des Begriffs. Hegels Logik der Kunst*, Meiner, 1997.
Iber, Christian: *Metaphysik absoluter Relationalität. Eine Studie zu den ersten zwei Kapiteln von Hegels Wesenslogik*, De Gruyter, 1990.
Lacan, Jacques: *La relation d'objet*. Séminaire 4, Seuil, [1957] 1994.
Majetschak, Stefan: "Psychoanalyse der grammatischen Mißdeutungen: über die Beziehung Ludwig Wittgensteins zum Werk Sigmund Freuds", in: Alois Pichler and Herbert Hrachovec (eds.): *Wittgenstein and the Philosophy of Information*, Ontos Verlag, 2008, p.37–59.
Majetschak, Stefan: *Ludwig Wittgensteins Denkweg*, Freiburg, Alber, 2000.
Mallarmé, Stéphane: *Oeuvres complètes*, Henri Mondor and G. Jean-Aubry (eds.), Gallimard, 1945.
Mersch, Dieter: "Wittgensteins Bilddenken", *Deutsche Zeitschrift für Philosophie* 54:6, 2006, pp.925–942.
Morris, Michael: *Wittgenstein and the* Tractatus, Routledge, 2008.
Motta, Gabriele: *Die Postulate des empirischen Denkens überhaupt. Ein kritischer Kommentar*, De Gruyter, 2012.
Quante, Michael and Moore, Nadine (eds.): *Kommentar zu Hegels Wissenschaft der Logik*, Hegel-Studien 67, Meiner, 2018.
Stenius, Erik: *Wittgenstein's Tractatus*, Blackwell & Mott, 1960.
Theunissen, Michael: *Sein und Schein. Die kritische Funktion der Hegelschen Logik*, Suhrkamp, 1978.
Wolff, Michael: *Der Begriff des Widerspruchs. Eine Studie zur Dialektik Kants und Hegels*, Frankfurt University Press, 2010.
Žižek, Slavoj: *Less Than Nothing: Hegel and the Shadow of Dialectical Materialism*, Verso, 2012.

Alexander Berg
Identity in Difference—Wittgenstein's Hegel

Abstract We can say with some certainty that Wittgenstein never read any of Hegel's works, yet he was able to talk about Hegel and even at several points to describe the relation between his own philosophy and that of Hegel. In this chapter, I present two major moments in Wittgenstein's philosophical career where he was explicitly taught about Hegel's philosophy, and attempt to evaluate Wittgenstein's statements about Hegel and what they show about the influence Wittgenstein's knowledge of Hegel may have had on his own philosophy.

In autumn 1948, Wittgenstein is taking a walk in Phoenix Park, Dublin, with his friend and colleague Maurice O'Connor Drury. They are talking about the great historical philosophers and the value of studying them.[1] In this moment of reflection, Wittgenstein thinks about his relation to these philosophers and his own place as a philosopher in the long history of philosophy. His thoughts turn to G. W. F. Hegel, one of the most influential thinkers in that tradition, and he tries to determine the relation between his own philosophical thinking and the philosophy of Hegel. These thoughts culminate in the famous remark:

> Hegel seems to me to be always wanting to say that things which look different are really the same. Whereas my interest is in showing that things which look the same are really different (MDC: p.157).[2]

Considering this famous yet enigmatic remark, I will try to answer two pressing questions. First: how was Wittgenstein able to talk about Hegel? (Did he even had any knowledge about Hegel's philosophy? And if so: how did he get this knowledge, and what exactly did he know?) And second: following on from that, what could be the deeper meaning of Wittgenstein's remark in Phoenix Park?

To answer these questions, I shall investigate two important events in Wittgenstein's philosophical career where he learnt important things about Hegel's philosophy from other major philosophers. Wittgenstein's first contact with

---

[1] "Walking in Phoenix Park one afternoon: Drury: I sometimes regret the amount of time I spent in reading *the great historical philosophers*, at a time when I couldn't understand them. Wittgenstein: I don't regret that you did all that reading" (MDC: p.157).
[2] For more detail cf. Berg (2019).

https://doi.org/10.1515/9783110572780-024

Hegel came right at the beginning of his philosophical studies in Cambridge, through his first philosophy tutor Bertrand Russell. The second contact came years later, when Wittgenstein came back to Cambridge and started to teach philosophy himself, through his colleague and fellow philosophy tutor Charlie D. Broad, who at the time was giving lectures about Hegel's philosophy at the university.

1

To consider the case of Bertrand Russell, we have to go even further back in time to a point before Wittgenstein arrived in Cambridge, namely to the moment in 1890 when the young Bertrand Russell himself arrived there to start his philosophical career.

The young Russell came to Cambridge with some pre-existing philosophical beliefs that he had developed during his private home-schooling. He instantly made friends with John McTaggart Ellis McTaggart, a philosopher already established in Cambridge philosophy, from whom he learnt that the empiricist philosophy Russell had favoured up until that point was now (1890) considered to be "almost laughably old-fashioned" (cf. Monk 1996: p.44). McTaggart—already working on his *Studies in Hegelian Dialectic* (McTaggart 1896)—introduced Russell to his own form of Hegelianism, which stood mainly on Bradleyan shoulders, and by 1894 had completely won him over to his "semi-Hegelian metaphysics"[3].

At that time, Russell even developed the foundations for a complete research programme modelled on Hegel's *Encyclopaedia*. This programme was based on the idea of a "synthesis" of theoretical and practical philosophy. In the literature, it is now called the "Tiergarten programme" because the main idea came to Russell during a walk in the Tiergarten park in Berlin (possibly inspired by Hegel's walks in the same park earlier that century):

> I remember a spring morning when I walked in the Tiergarten, and planned to write a series of books in the philosophy of the sciences, growing gradually more concrete as I passed from mathematics to biology; I thought I would also write a series of books on social and political questions, growing gradually more abstract. At last I would achieve a Hegelian synthesis in an *encyclopaedic work* dealing equally with theory and practice. The scheme was inspired by Hegel [...] (Russell 2009: p.15).

---

[3] "McTaggart had Hegelian answers to the rather crude empiricism which had previously satisfied me. [...] I stood out against his influence with gradually diminishing resistance until just before my Moral Sciences Tripos in 1894, when I went over completely to a semi-Kantian, semi-Hegelian metaphysic" (Russell 1959: p.38).

And in some ways Russell held on to this Tiergarten programme until the end of his life. But there was still one problem with this form of Hegelianism. At that point in time, Russell's Hegelianism mainly came from his discussions with McTaggart about the *Studies in Hegelian Dialectic* and his reading of Bradley's *Appearance and Reality* (Bradley 1893; cf. Hylton 2005; Candlish 2007). It was not until the spring of 1897 that Russell attempted to form his own opinion of Hegel's writings. But he had to read Hegel's *Science of Logic* in German, because the first English translation was only published 15 years later.

For Russell, this reading was deeply surprising. Until then he had thought he was a Hegelian himself, but now he was forced to realise he was not. He could not even understand the content of what he read in Hegel's *Logic*. He attributed this lack of understanding not, as one might expect, to his own possibly imperfect reading of Hegel, but to the quality of Hegel's writing itself.

Years later (1951), he described this surprising experience and concluded that Hegel's philosophy is mere *nonsense:* "I read Hegel's *Greater Logic* [an alternative title for the *Science of Logic*], and thought, as I still do, that all he says about mathematics is muddle-headed *nonsense*" (Russell 2009: p.15, my emphasis). Ironically, at the time Russell said much the same thing about Wittgenstein's later philosophy: "The [later Wittgenstein] remains to me completely unintelligible" (Russell 1959: p.216).[4] And even Wittgenstein himself openly stated that his writings should be seen as a form of *nonsense*, but of course—in contrast to Russell's incomprehension of Hegel—this Wittgensteinian nonsense requires a deeper level of understanding: "My propositions serve as elucidations in the following way: *anyone who understands me* eventually recognizes them as nonsensical [*unsinnig*]" (TLP: 6.54, my emphasis).

As an effect of the surprising experience of finding himself to be a Hegelian who could not understand Hegel, Russell made an effort to find what lay at the roots of the *nonsense* of Hegelian philosophy. His answer to that question is first documented on 6 April 1897 in a private letter to his then-wife Alys that he wrote while reading Hegel's *Science of Logic:* according to the letter, the Hegelian philosophy consists "mainly of puns" (Monk 1996: p.114)[5] in the German language.

Throughout his life Russell held on to this characterisation of Hegel's philosophy as *built on puns*, and it is important to note here that the German transla-

---

4 "The [later work of Wittgenstein] remains to me completely unintelligible. Its positive doctrines seem to me trivial and its negative doctrines unfounded. I have not found in Wittgenstein's *Philosophical Investigations* anything that seemed to me interesting and I do not understand why a whole school finds important wisdom in its pages" (Russell 1959: p.216).
5 Ray Monk was able to study Russell's unpublished letters to his first wife Alys courtesy of the current owner, Camellia Investments in London (Monk 1996: p.613).

tion of *pun* as *Wortspiel* somehow translates back into English as *language-game*. In the following, I will try to develop the argument that Wittgenstein's later description of his own philosophy as *consisting of language-games* ("I shall also call the whole, consisting of language and the actions into which it is woven, the 'language-game'" PI: §7) is in some way rooted in Russell's description of Hegel's philosophy as consisting "mainly of puns"—but without Russell's pejorative assumptions against those "puns" or "language-games."

But back to Russell in 1897. After reading Hegel's *Science of Logic*, Russell was supposedly cured of his early Hegelianism. But it seems he could never fully recover, because Hegel was too important as a background and "jumping-off place" for Russell's new project of developing a new, analytic philosophy. Richard Watson describes the complicated dependence of Russell's new ambitions on his former Hegelianism as follows:

> Russell's Hegel made some obvious errors that the developing philosophy of the day could correct. The shadow Hegel is the rock that logical atomism could take as a jumping-off place [...]. The shadow Hegel's system authenticates the philosophy that casts off from and corrects it (Watson 1993: p.99).

The important role that this early Hegelianism played in the development of analytic philosophy is illustrated by the fact that, one year later, G. E. Moore's paper "The Nature of Judgment" (to this day still widely regarded as one of the founding papers in the analytic philosophy tradition) referred 13 times to the aforementioned British Hegelian Francis H. Bradley and once to Hegel himself.[6]

Other close colleagues of Russell at the University of Cambridge also engaged intensively with Hegel's philosophy: there was of course McTaggart and his *Studies in Hegelian Dialectic*, as well as Alfred North Whitehead, Russell's former tutor and now co-author of the *Principia Mathematica*, who was working in parallel on his deeply Hegelian process philosophy,[7] and several ongoing projects by Hegel scholars who were translating Hegel into English (see below).

---

[6] Moore first discussed the paper on 21 October 1898 at the Cambridge Moral Science Club and on 9 December the same year at the Aristotelian Society, and published it in *Mind* in early 1899 (Moore 1899: pp.176–193).

[7] Whitehead's later major work *Process and Reality* is considered to be based on Hegel's philosophy (cf. Apel 1973). Moreover, according to Whitehead his later work can be understood as a transformation of key tenets of absolute idealism to a "realistic basis": "Finally, though throughout the main body of the work I am in sharp disagreement with Bradley, the final outcome is after all not so greatly different. I am particularly indebted to his chapter on the nature of experience, which appears in his *Essays on Truth and Reality*. [...] Indeed, if this cosmology be

In his autobiographical writings, Russell tells the story of his early Hegelianism and how he turned away from it forever under the influence of Moore.[8] But real life is often more complex, and so even after 1898 Russell made significant contact with Hegel's philosophy on several occasions. For example, in his 1910 work *Commentary on Hegel's Logic* McTaggart expressed his gratitude to Russell for his help and their discussions about Hegel's philosophy (McTaggart 1910: preface). And in 1912, after Henry Stuart Macran published his translation of certain chapters of Hegel's *Science of Logic* (SL 1912), Russell wrote a review of it (Russell [1912], 1992) in which he discussed Hegel's treatment of formal logic. These two events respectively took place shortly before and around the same time that Wittgenstein came to Cambridge and began studying philosophy with Russell.

Consequently, Hegel is very much present in the background at the time when Wittgenstein had the closest contact with his teacher Russell. During this period, he acquired most of his philosophical knowledge through nightlong private lessons in Russell's rooms. The importance of this special educational situation should not be underestimated, given that at the time Wittgenstein had barely any other philosophical influences: his idiosyncratic learning strategy involved reading almost no philosophical books other than Frege's *Grundgesetze der Arithmetik* (1893, 1903) and Russell's *Principles of Mathematics* (1903) and, additionally, attending barely any lectures other than those of Russell and Moore.

In these important private lessons, Russell very likely conveyed to Wittgenstein his particular attitude towards Hegel. This is probable in part because of the extraordinary importance that Russell's "shadow Hegel" had as a jumping-off place for his own philosophy. But also because at precisely this time he was reading Hegel again and discussing Hegel's philosophy (specifically in the form in which it appeared in Macran's new translation of Hegel's *Science of Logic* as well as in Macran's long explanatory introduction to it).

Russell's review of Macran's translation and his manuscripts of lectures from the time are very enlightening because they give hints at what Wittgenstein

---

deemed successful, it becomes natural at this point to ask whether the type of thought involved be not a transformation of some main doctrines of Absolute Idealism onto a realistic basis" (Whitehead 1978: pp.xii–xiii).

8 "In the year 1898 [...] I was at this time beginning to emerge from the bath of German idealism in which I had been plunged by McTaggart and Stout. I was very much assisted in this process by Moore, of whom at that time I saw a great deal. [...] I found occasion to exemplify the new views on logic to which, largely under Moore's guidance, I had been led" (Russell 2009: p.125). For an overview of Moore's influence on Russell, see Griffin (1991).

learnt about Hegel from Russell during this period. As one might expect, in both cases Russell maintains his critical attitude towards Hegel and describes his philosophy as essentially built "upon a pun" in the German language, a joke that Macran "presumably" has forgotten to explain to the readers of his translation:

> Hegel's argument depends upon a *pun*, one could wish for a note to explain the joke; but presumably Mr. Macran thought that the difficulties of Hegel were great enough without the attempt to understand his humour (Russell 1912: pp.739–740; Russell 1992: p.364, my emphasis).

Russell also upheld his critical view of Hegel and the *puns* of Hegelian philosophy in his lectures from the period:

> This is an example of how, for want of care at the start, vast and imposing systems of philosophy are built upon *stupid and trivial confusions*, which, but for the almost incredible fact that they are unintentional, one would be tempted *to characterise as puns* (Russell 1915: p.39, fn.5, my emphasis).[9]

Considering the deep connection between Wittgenstein and his teacher Russell, it is no surprise that at the same time Wittgenstein shared Russell's view about the surprising "mistakes" of some of *the great historical philosophers*. On this point, Wittgenstein's friend David Pinsent (who had just met Wittgenstein at one of the parties in Russell's private rooms) made the following remark on 30 May 1912 about Wittgenstein's surprise at what he had learnt from Russell:

> [Wittgenstein] is reading philosophy up here [in Cambridge], but has only just started systematic reading: and he expresses the most naive *surprise* that all the philosophers he once worshipped in ignorance are after all stupid and dishonest and make disgusting *mistakes!* (Pinsent 1990: pp.4–5, my emphasis).[10]

In his lectures, Russell explained what exactly these *mistakes* of Hegel's philosophy consist in:

> Hegel's argument in this portion of his "Logic" depends throughout upon confusing the "is" of predication, as in "Socrates is mortal", with the "is" of identity, as in "Socrates is the philosopher who drank the hemlock." Owing to this confusion, he thinks that "Socra-

---

9 Russell held this lecture in Boston in March 1914, with the title "Logic as the Essence of Philosophy."
10 Speaking of *philosophical surprises*, after making his remark about Hegel in Phoenix Park, Wittgenstein reflected that "You'd be surprised" might make a good motto for his *Philosophical Investigations*.

tes" and "mortal" must be identical. Seeing that they are different, he does not infer, as others would, that there is a mistake somewhere, but that they exhibit *"identity in difference"* (Russell 1915: p.39, fn.5, my emphasis).

To understand how much the early Wittgenstein was influenced by this explanation, it is worth noting that he took this argument of Russell's against Hegel's *mistaken* logic and made it a prominent argument in his own *Tractatus Logico-Philosophicus* (3.323):

> Thus the word "is" appears as the copula, as the sign of equality, and as the expression of existence; "to exist" as an intransitive verb like "to go"; "identical" as an adjective; we speak of *something* but also of the fact of *something* happening.
>
> (In the proposition "Green is green"—where the first word is a proper name as the last an adjective—these words have not merely different meanings but they are *different symbols*.)

And like Russell, Wittgenstein too sees these mistakes as contributing to the confusions of some of *the great historical philosophers*, concluding: "Thus there easily arise the most fundamental confusions (of which the whole of philosophy is full)." But it is also important to note that, unlike Russell, in the *Tractatus* Wittgenstein already attributes this problem not just to Hegel's peculiar treatment of formal logic and his *puns in the German language*, but to the structure of the *language of everyday life:*

> In the language of everyday life it very often happens that the same word signifies in two different ways—and therefore belongs to two different symbols—or that two words, which signify in different ways, are apparently applied in the same way in the proposition (TLP 3.323).

And because we already know how the later Wittgenstein rehabilitates the language of everyday life for philosophical logic and even calls "the whole, consisting of language and the actions into which it is woven, the 'language-game'" (PI: §7), we can assume that he also rehabilitates Russell's pejorative judgement of these (initially considered mistaken) *puns* of Hegelian logic, i.e., *Sprachspiele* in the German language.

Moreover, in Russell's explanation the *puns* or *language-games* of Hegel's logic arise from the mistaken treatment of the difference between the *is* of identity and the *is* of predication and he believed this confusion needed to be cured using the symbolic system of his own logical atomism. Russell further remarked that Hegel's different way of treating this issue was due to his concept of "identity in difference." This remark is strongly reminiscent of the first half of the comment Wittgenstein later made in Phoenix Park ("Hegel seems to me to be always wanting to say that things which look different are really the same", MDC: p.157). It would appear that in this comment, not just Wittgenstein's characterisation of Hegel's philosophy but also the relation of his own (difference-) philosophy to that of Hegel's (identity-) philosophy were built on a concept of Hegel's as taught by Russell under the heading "identity in difference."

With regard to the concept of language-games in Wittgenstein's later philosophy, the catalyst for changing his mind concerning the "confusions" in the *language of everyday life* or Hegel's "puns" *in the German language* might have arisen during the collaborative process of translating the German *Logisch-philosophische Abhandlung* into the English *Tractatus Logico-Philosophicus*. In 1921, Wittgenstein discussed with Charles Kay Ogden the difficulties involved in translating his German thoughts into English. Like Russell, he referred to the special role that "puns" *play* in the German language:

> I do not know how to translate this. The German "Wir können uns ein Bild von ihm Machen" is a phrase commonly used. I have rendered it by "we can imagine it" because "imagine" comes from "image" and this is something like picture. *In German it is a sort of pun* you see (LO: p.24, my emphasis).

Wittgenstein's discussions with Ogden about how to correctly translate the *Tractatus* show how important he saw language as being for the German original. They also suggest that the structure of the German language plays a critical role with respect to the logical meaning. And it is equally significant that this special role of the German language, with its *games* and *puns*, first becomes obvious in the attempt to translate it into English.

2

I shall now introduce the second important source of Wittgenstein's knowledge about Hegel's philosophy, namely Charlie Dunbar Broad. Broad was about the same age as Wittgenstein, had studied under the same philosophy tutors (Russell, Whitehead and McTaggart) and therefore pursued similar philosophical interests to Wittgenstein. When McTaggart unexpectedly died prematurely in 1925, Broad took responsibility for completing McTaggart's final unfinished work *The Nature of Existence* (McTaggart 1921–1927), dedicated a "full-scale book" to an *examination of McTaggart's philosophy* and taught generations of students in Cambridge about McTaggart's work.[11]

---

11 "In the course of editing McTaggart's posthumous work I came to the decision to devote a

McTaggart's Hegelianism had a further influence on philosophy in Cambridge. It was some of McTaggart's former students who published the first complete English translation of Hegel's *Science of Logic* (SL 1929). This difficult project, which took many years, was completed by W. H. Johnston and L. G. Struthers just in time for Wittgenstein's return to Cambridge. And around the time Wittgenstein was awarded his doctorate for the *Tractatus*, Broad wrote a review of Hegel's newly translated *Science of Logic* (SL 1929) that made reference to the already-familiar characterisation in terms of puns, which at the time seems to have been regarded as common sense in Cambridge:

> The plausibility of some of Hegel's arguments appears to depend largely on *puns in the German language*, and, to this extent, his work must suffer by translation (Broad 1929: p.393, my emphasis).

Regarding Wittgenstein's acquaintance with Broad, the literature often gives the impression that the two avoided each other in Cambridge, if possible "even in print."[12] In his biography, Broad did indeed describe how he felt intimidated by Wittgenstein's philosophical charisma, especially in the lively discussions at the Moral Science Club.[13] But at the same time, Broad also attested to his high regard for Wittgenstein's philosophy. His respect for Wittgenstein's achievement was such that he made an intervention on Wittgenstein's behalf to the commission responsible for appointing a successor to G. E. Moore's chair that could hardly have expressed greater regard: "To refuse the chair to Wittgenstein would be like refusing Einstein a chair of physics" (MDC: p.141). And conversely, in a remark to Drury Wittgenstein praised Broad both as a *very just man* and for his philosophical work: "Broad is a very just man. I have been reading *Five Types of Ethical Theory*. I thought he wrote it very well" (MDC: p.142).

When Wittgenstein began teaching philosophy at Cambridge from 1930 onwards, he and his students explicitly discussed Broad's philosophy and—this is

---

full-scale book to a really careful and thorough estimate of the extraordinarily elaborate and ingenious system which he had excogitated. [...] I thus wrote and delivered the lectures which formed the basis of my book *Examination of McTaggart's Philosophy*. [...] I think it contains about the best work of which I am capable in philosophy" (Broad 1959: pp.58f.; Broad 1933, 1938).

12 "Between Wittgenstein and Broad, contemporaries at Cambridge, there was apparently such incompatibility, both of temperament and thought, that Wittgenstein avoided a meeting even in print" (Hallett 1977: p.762).

13 "I was not prepared to spend hours every week in a thick atmosphere of cigarette-smoke, while Wittgenstein punctually went through his hoops: and the faithful as punctually 'wondered with a foolish look of praise.'" (Broad 1959: p.61) where Hegel comes into play—Broad's reconstruction of Hegelian philosophy. Wittgenstein's fortunately preserved "Comments on Broad" (LWL: pp.72f.) show that Wittgenstein was familiar with the "Elements of Philosophy"[14] lectures that Broad held at that time in Cambridge, and also that he thought Broad's ideas through, commented on them and discussed them with his students.

The notes of Wittgenstein's students taken in his seminars follow the same chronology in terms of content as the lectures that Broad was holding in parallel. Taking together all circumstantial evidence, one could convincingly argue that both Wittgenstein and his students attended Broad's lectures on Hegel's philosophy in Cambridge (cf. Berg 2019: §27). This assumption does at least seem to offer the best explanation for how Wittgenstein was able in his "Comments on Broad" to discuss the content of these lectures so precisely. In any case, Wittgenstein was very familiar with the content of Broad's lectures, and this is important because they covered Hegel's philosophy extensively. Just as in his later remark on Hegel in Phoenix Park, Wittgenstein emphasises in the "Comments on Broad" the deep similarities between his own philosophical practice and the "Hegelian method of examining contradictions, their relations and resolution",[15] combined with an attempt to identify differences:

> the dialectical method [of Hegel's speculative philosophy] is very sound and a way in which we do work. But it should not try to find, from two propositions, a. and b., a further more complex proposition, as Broad's description implied. Its object should be to find out where the ambiguities in our language are (LWL: pp.74f.).

And just as his remark in Phoenix Park, cautiously introduced with the qualifier "Hegel seems to me ...", acknowledges that he is very much aware that he only knows of Hegel's philosophy at second hand, here too Wittgenstein acknowledges that he is only able to judge Hegel's philosophy on the basis of Broad's (possibly imperfect) description of it when he qualifies his cautious judgement with the reservation "as Broad's description implied."

Also of interest to the present investigation of the connection between Wittgenstein's thinking and the philosophy of Hegel, with his "puns in the German

---

[14] The original of the typescript is held in the archives of Wren Library, Cambridge, and has the written title "Elements of Metaphysics." The scholarly literature usually refers to the lectures as "Elements of Philosophy" (Monk 1991: p.322).

[15] Wittgenstein: "Broad said that Speculative Philosophy had two methods. The deductive which started with certain fundamental self-evident propositions and proceeded to deduce further propositions about reality, and the dialectical which he describes as *the Hegelian method of examining contradictions, their relations and resolution*" (LWL: pp.74f., my emphasis).

language", is another remark made by Broad in his lectures, this time (presumably) in the presence of Wittgenstein, in which he again referred explicitly to Hegelian philosophy being based on *language-games:* "[I]n [Hegelian] dialectic we are simply *playing a game*" (Broad C2/5: 34, my emphasis).

With this in mind, it no longer appears to be just a coincidence that on 1 March 1932, shortly after Broad's lecture (in Michaelmas term 1931) and Wittgenstein's "Comments on Broad", Wittgenstein used the term "language-game" for the first time in his private notes (MS 113: p.45r.). This connection between Hegel's philosophy with its *puns*, introduced to Cambridge philosophy by McTaggart and Russell, and Wittgenstein's language-games, an idea which he took up and integrated into his later philosophy, was in a certain sense even recognised at the time. At least, in his biographical reflections Broad himself links together the *puns* of McTaggart's Hegelianism and the *language-games* of the later Wittgenstein school by classing them both as *nugae*,[16] a Latin term in philosophical rhetoric:

> If some of my younger friends and colleagues of the "common language school" [of Wittgenstein] were to twit me with the accusation that it [McTaggart's Hegelianism] consists largely of *difficiles nugae*, I should heartily agree. But I should be inclined to retort that the writings of their school consist largely of *faciles nugae* (Broad 1959: p.60).[17]

3

In summary, Russell and Broad were the main sources of Wittgenstein's knowledge of Hegel. It appears that these two teachers each had a distinct impact on the development of Wittgenstein's philosophy, Russell on the "early-" and Broad on the "later Wittgenstein." Furthermore, it seems that these two different impacts are related in Wittgenstein's remark in Phoenix Park. The first way of interpreting the remark is more ontological, rooted in Wittgenstein's early acquaintance with Russell and his shadow Hegel. The second, more logical interpretation is rooted in Wittgenstein's later acquaintance with Broad's lectures about Hegel and the role that contradictions and language-games play in Hegelian logic.

---

16 Latin for *poetical nonsense*. Translated into German: *poetische (Sprach-) Spielerei* (see the article "nūgae" in Hau 2001: p.345).
17 Broad probably took the term *nugae* from Kant, who insisted on the difference for philosophical purposes between subtle examinations ("Subtilitäten") which are difficult but useful, and difficult examinations which are *difficult but not useful* ("difficiles nugae") (cf. Kant 1800: p.80).

The first interpretation is the Hegelian concept of *identity in difference*, which the young Wittgenstein learnt about from Russell during his early philosophical studies in Cambridge and which in Phoenix Park he transposed onto the relation between Hegel's *philosophy of identity* and his own *philosophy of differences*. [He even considered making differences a motto for the *Philosophical Investigations*, after the dictum in *King Lear* spoken by the Earl of Kent: "I'll teach you differences" (MDC: p.157)].[18]

And with respect to this concept of *identity in difference*, it is noteworthy that in this case, Russell's teaching about Hegel is not actually wrong, and that the concept touches on an essential part of Hegel's philosophy: the idea of *the identity of identity and non-identity*, or as Hegel puts it, "the Absolute itself is *the identity of identity and non-identity*; being opposed and being one are both together in it."[19] Furthermore, this "identity in difference" corresponds to an important point of contention in a contemporary dispute between British Hegelianism and Russell's logical–analytical empiricism, namely the dispute between Bradley's monism and Russell's and Moore's pluralism.

Wittgenstein's first major philosophical work appeared right at the height of this dispute, and occupied an intermediate position (namely, holism) in this conflict of opposites (monism vs. pluralism). It was especially through this concept of *identity in difference* that Wittgenstein became acquainted with an element of Hegel's holism. In Bradley's thought, this element became one-sidedly monistic, and this one-sidedness prompted a countermovement in Russell and Moore with an equally one-sided pluralism. In retrospect, Russell described this one-sidedness of Bradley's idealistic view and his and Moore's *reversion to the opposite extreme* as follows:

> Bradley argued that everything common sense believes in is *mere appearance*; we reverted to the opposite extreme, and thought that everything is real that common sense, uninfluenced by philosophy or theology, supposes real. With a sense of *escaping from prison*, we allowed ourselves to think [...] that there is a *pluralistic* timeless world of Platonic ideas (Russell 2009: pp.15–16, my emphasis)

---

18 *King Lear*, act I, scene 4.
19 "Philosophy must give the separation into subject and object its due. By making both separation and the identity, which is opposed to it, equally absolute, however, philosophy has only posited separation conditionally, in the same way that such an identity—conditioned as it is by the nullification of its opposite—is also only relative. Hence, the Absolute itself is *the identity of identity and non-identity*; being opposed and being one are both together in it" (D: p.156; cf. JS: pp.96, 134, 136, my emphasis).

Hegel himself never shared Bradley's monism. When he says in the *Phenomenology of Spirit* that "the True is the whole", he does not mean—like Bradley—that only the Absolute is real, as is made clear by his subsequent remark: "However, the whole [*das Ganze*] is only the essence completing itself through its own development" (PS 2018: §20). That is, the whole comprises only the complete development of singular facts, through the process of *phenomenology*. Wittgenstein can be understood in a similarly holistic manner when he starts the *Tractatus* with the fundamental claim that the world ought to be understood as the totality (*Gesamtheit*) of all singular facts: "The world is the *totality of facts*" (TLP: 1.1, my emphasis); "The world is determined by the facts, and by these being *all* the facts" (TLP: 1.11, my emphasis).

The ontological interpretation becomes even more manifest if one considers the discourse surrounding the dispute between Bradley's monism and Russell's pluralism, which was raging in the background at the time when Wittgenstein was starting to develop his early philosophical views. This dispute started with Moore's "The Nature of Judgment" and continued with great intensity at Cambridge (and Oxford), until it slowly died down in the late 1920s.[20]

But the transition to Wittgenstein's later philosophy and its language-games seems to have already started around 1917, when Wittgenstein introduced with sentences 6.54 and 7 the idea of a somehow nonsensical reading of the *Tractatus:* a *nonsense* (6.54) if properly understood helps to "see the world aright" (7). This paradoxical conclusion stood in sharp contrast to Russell, who had built his own project of logical symbolism on the need for sharp differences, and explicitly opposed the *nonsense* and *puns* of Hegel's logic, which seem to blur these sharp differences into soft transitions.

So the development of the later Wittgenstein can be regarded as a radicalisation of this view not just that the whole of the logic of language is somehow nonsensical, but also that every single sentence receives its meaning only from

---

20 Broad argued against pluralism in 1904 (Broad 1904: pp.308–335, esp. pp.330f.). The arguments for philosophical pluralism were discussed in 1909 by John Henry Muirhead, Ferdinand Canning Scott Schiller and Alfred Edward Taylor (Muirhead 1909: pp.183–225). In the same year, William James deliberately argued for pluralism, having himself converted from monism to pluralism in 1870 (James 1909). James Ward argued for the (holistic) unity of monism and pluralism in 1911, especially in reference to his reading of Hegel (Ward 1911: pp.138–180). And as late as 1926, John Alexander Smith attempted to renew the discussion between monism and pluralism by pointing to the as-yet unsolved metaphysical problem (Smith 1925/26: pp.1–24). Abraham Edel responded in 1931 by arguing that this problem could not be solved, since there was no way to formulate it in a meaningful way (Edel 1934: pp.561–571).

a language-game that combines difference with unity or sharp distinctions with soft transitions in a paradoxical, contradictory way.

With his notion of language-games, Wittgenstein now claims the opposite to what Russell does when he criticises Hegelian logic for its puns, and so his position is very deeply connected through the complex web of actual philosophical history to Hegel's dialectical logic. Moreover, Wittgenstein also states this openly when he comments on Broad's reconstruction of "the Hegelian method of examining contradictions, their relations and resolution" and refers to the similarities to his own philosophical practice: "the dialectical method [of Hegel] is very sound and a way in which we do work."

One could argue even further that Wittgenstein was not only right about the similarities to Hegel's philosophy when he made his remark in Phoenix Park regarding the connection between identity and difference, but also about the differences between them, except that these differences set in much later than is normally assumed and rest on the basis of a largely shared holistic view.

These later differences consist in the fact that, whereas Hegel wants to understand the relation of identity and non-identity as also being a form of identity, Wittgenstein is more interested in the moment of difference within that identity, that is, the difference between identity and non-identity, or as he himself said: "[the Hegelian method] should not try to find, from two propositions, a. and b., a further more complex proposition [...]. Its object should be to find out where the ambiguities in our language are" (LWL: p.74).

An idea that Hegel might have reformulated to Drury in his own words, if he had been in Wittgenstein's place in Phoenix Park, by referring to his *Doctrine of the Concept* and its distinction between the Concept's three moments, namely *Universality* (Allgemeinheit), *Particularity* (Besonderheit) and *Singularity* (Einzelheit):[21]

> Wittgenstein seems to think that I always want to say that *singular* things only get their meaning from *Universality*. Whereas he himself is interested in showing that we can say this only in *particular* situations.

---

[21] The translations of *Allgemeinheit*, *Besonderheit* and *Einzelheit* are taken from George di Giovanni's translation of the *Science of Logic* (cf. SL 2010: pp.507 f.).

References

Apel, Karl-Otto: *Transformation der Philosophie*, Suhrkamp, 1973, pp.365–366.
Berg, Alexander: *Absolutes Wissen und Grundlose Gewissheit—Wittgensteins Hegel*, forthcoming, 2019.
Bradley, Francis Herbert: *Appearance and Reality. A Metaphysical Essay*, Allen and Unwin, 1893.
Broad, Charlie D.: "On Truth and Practice", *Mind* 13:51, 1904, pp.308–335.
Broad, Charlie D.: "Review of Hegel's Science of Logic (tr. by Johnston, W. H., Struthers, L. G., London 1929)", *Mind* 38, 1929.
Broad, Charlie D.: *Five Types of Ethical Theory*, Routledge, 1930.
Broad, Charlie D.: *An Examination of McTaggart's Philosophy*, Cambridge University Press, Vol. I, 1933, Vol. II, 1938.
Broad, Charlie D.: "Autobiography", in: *The Philosophy of C. D. Broad, Library of Living Philosophers*, P. A. Schilpp (Ed.), Tudor Publishing Company, 1959.
Broad, Charlie D.: *Elements of Philosophy*, unpublished Lecture: Broad C2/5, Archive of Wren Library Trinity College, Cambridge.
Candlish, Stewart: *The Russell/Bradley Dispute and its Significance for Twentieth Century Philosophy*, Palgrave Macmillan, 2007.
Edel, Abraham: "Monism and Pluralism", *Journal of Philosophy* 31:21, 1934, pp.561–571.
Frege, Gottlob: *Grundgesetze der Arithmetik*, Verlag Hermann Pohle, Vol. I., 1893, Vol. II., 1903.
Griffin, Nicholas: *Russell's Idealist Apprenticeship*, Clarendon Press, 1991.
Hallett, Garth: *A Companion to Wittgenstein's "Philosophical Investigations"*, Cornell University Press, 1977.
Hau, Rita (Ed.): *Pons*, Ernst Klett Verlag, 2001.
Hylton, Peter: *Russell, Idealism, and the emergence of Analytic Philosophy*, Clarendon Press, 1990.
James, William: *A Pluralistic Universe. Hibbert Lectures at Manchester College on the Present Situation in Philosophy*, Longmans, Green, 1909.
Kant, Immanuel: *Logik. Ein Handbuch zur Vorlesung*, Gottlob Benjamin Jäsche (Ed.), Friedrich Nicolovius, 1800.
McTaggart, John M. E.: *Studies in the Hegelian Dialectic*, Cambridge University Press, 1896.
McTaggart, John M. E., *A Commentary on Hegel's Logic*, Cambridge University Press, 1910.
McTaggart, John M. E.: *The Nature of Existence*, Cambridge University Press, 1921–1927.
Monk, Ray: *Ludwig Wittgenstein. The Duty of Genius*, Vintage, 1991.
Monk, Ray: *Bertrand Russell. The Spirit of Solitude 1872–1921*, Vintage, 1996.
Moore, George Edward: "Nature of Judgment", *Mind* 5:8, 1899, pp.176–193.
Muirhead, John Henry, Canning, Ferdinand, Schiller, Scott, Taylor, Alfred Edward: "Why Pluralism? A Symposium by J. H. Muirhead, F. C. S. Schiller, and A. E. Taylor", in: *Proceedings of the Aristotelian Society*, 9, 1909, pp.183–225.
Pinsent, David Hume: *A Portrait of Wittgenstein as a Young Man. From the Diary of David Hume Pinsent, 1912–1914*, Georg Henrik von Wright (Ed.), Blackwell, 1990.
Rockmore, Tom: *Hegel, Idealism, and Analytic Philosophy*, Yale University Press, 2005.
Russell, Bertrand: *The Principles of Mathematics*, Cambridge University Press, 1903.

Russell, Bertrand: "Review of Macran's Hegel and the Common Sense", *The Nation*, 11, August 17, 1912, pp.739–740.
Russell, Bertrand: *Our Knowledge of the External World As a Field for Scientific Method in Philosophy*, Open Court, 1915.
Russell, Bertrand: *My Philosophical Development*, Allen and Unwin, 1959.
Russell, Bertrand: *Logical and Philosophical Papers 1909–13*, Routledge, 1992.
Russell, Bertrand: "My Mental Development", in: Robert E. Egner and Lester E. Denonn (Eds.): *The Basic Writings of Bertrand Russell*, Routledge, 2009.
Shakespeare, William: *King Lear. The Oxford Shakespeare*, Stanley Wells (Ed.), Oxford University Press, 2000.
Smith, John Alexander: "The Issue Between Monism and Pluralism", *Proceedings of the Aristotelian Society* 26, 1925.
Ward, James: "Lecture VII. The Pluralism of Hegel and Lecture VIII. The Hegelian Unity", in: *The Realm of Ends or Pluralism and Theism, Gifford Lectures Delivered at the University of St Andrews Between 1907 and 1910*, Cambridge University Press, 1911.
Watson, Richard A.: "Shadow History in Philosophy", *Journal of the History of Philosophy* 31:1, 1993, pp.95–109.
Whitehead, Alfred North: *Process and Reality. An Essay in Cosmology*, David Ray Griffin and Donald W. Sherburne (Eds.), Free Press, 1978.

Part 5 **Wittgensteinian Approaches to Hegel**

Karl-Friedrich Kiesow
Is the System of Personal Pronouns Somewhat Mysterious? Findlay and Weiss as Critics of Hegel and Wittgenstein

> The I, the I is what is deeply mysterious!
> Wittgenstein, NB: p.80
>
> If someone can believe in God with complete
> certainty, why not in Other Minds?
> Wittgenstein, CV: p.73

Abstract Hegel and Wittgenstein have long been regarded as thinkers who are too remote from one another to allow a comparison. They share, however, a common problem: the problem of the limits of a language that has been considered only as a means of communication and a signifying apparatus, with the function of denoting objects and designating facts. I will take as an example the system of (personal) pronouns in order to make a concise interpretation of both thinkers possible. J. N. Findlay and P. Weiss were interested in both Hegel and Wittgenstein, and my discussion will be guided by them. In the case of Weiss, the line of my argumentation is largely hypothetical or a construction of a fictive dialogue, as it were.

Preliminary remarks

If we were to treat the personal pronouns, such as I, You and so forth, as mere *flatus vocis*, they would be the most innocent thing in the world. As everybody knows, however, the logical behaviour of these parts of speech seems to be connected to some deep problems of epistemology and ontology. What is consciousness? Can consciousness be characterised as a substance, and is there a plurality of consciousnesses? Should we prefer instead an adjectival characterisation of consciousness as a unique quality common to certain highly developed beings?

We will find a first precondition for a comparison of Hegel and Wittgenstein in their style of philosophising. The two of them have more in common than earlier generations of interpreters, led astray by their selective loyalty to certain philosophical camps, thought possible. In the preface to his *Phenomenology of Spirit*, Hegel compares the emerging harmony of subject and predicate in a speculative proposition to the conflict between metre and accent in rhythm (PS 1977:

§61). In a similar vein, Wittgenstein describes the hesitancy or wilful retardation of the movement of his thoughts: "Sometimes a sentence can be understood only if it is read at the *right tempo*. My sentences are all supposed to be read *slowly*." (CV: p.57) For both thinkers, philosophy is the art of not drawing conclusions precipitately.

Another precondition for a comparison of Hegel and Wittgenstein and the reconstructions of their views by Findlay and Weiss is a certain contentual affinity between the problems they addressed. I choose as my examples Hegel's theory of acknowledgement, as presented in the *Phenomenology of Spirit*, and Wittgenstein's reflections on other minds, as presented in *Zettel*. The passages under consideration are sufficiently convergent to bring Hegel and Wittgenstein into fruitful contact with one another.

Leopold von Wiese, in an essay that lacks philosophical depth, once coined the term: "the philosophy of personal pronouns" (*"die Philosophie der persönlichen Fürwörter"*). We may ask, therefore, whether there is a philosophy of personal pronouns.

John Niemeyer Findlay: reading Hegel's *Philosophy of Spirit* §184 in the light of Wittgenstein

Let me begin with a few words about J. N. Findlay (1903–1987). Due to the influence of Husserl and Wittgenstein, Findlay was acquainted with semantics and philosophy of language, and is sometimes classed within analytical philosophy, very broadly construed. He was preoccupied with Plato, Plotinus and Hegel, too, and published a book on the latter: *Hegel: A Re-examination* (1958). He praised Hegel for having anticipated some major insights of Wittgenstein, especially in regard to the role of indexical expressions in discourse. Both Hegel and Wittgenstein, he argued, realised that human language consists of universals only; there are no particulars at all. At the same time, he measured Hegel against a theory of meaning attributed to Wittgenstein, and he rejected many of his arguments as verbal sophistry.

Findlay belongs to a small group of thinkers who recognised very early on that Hegel and Wittgenstein held conceptions regarding language and linguistic usage that were not altogether alien to one another. From Hegel, he presents the following quotation: "The battle of reason consists in this, to overcome the rigidity which the Understanding has brought in." And from Wittgenstein: "Philosophy is a battle against the bewitchment of our understanding through the instruments of our speech." (Findlay 1958: p.27) In both cases, it is the instrumental character of the figures of thought and speech or their "finiteness" that is responsible for their misleading philosophical speculation. As we might say, philosophy has to free us from the self-imposed strictures of thinking.

In the first chapters of the *Phenomenology of Spirit*, Hegel investigates the structure of consciousness. He notes the problem of sense-certainty and deception and gives an analysis of indexical expressions such as "here", "there", "now" and "then" and especially of the pronoun "I" that makes it plausible that they are latent universals. A discussion of force and the understanding introduces readers to the study of the social and spiritual world that comes into focus next. In a sense, Hegel has shown that there is no such thing as simple consciousness, since the results of his investigation necessitate a transition to self-consciousness and even collective consciousness:

> What still lies ahead for consciousness is the experience of what Spirit is—this absolute substance which is the unity of the different independent self-consciousnesses which, in their opposition, enjoy perfect freedom and independence: "I" that is "We" and "We" that is "I". It is in self-consciousness, in the Notion of Spirit, that consciousness first finds its turning-point, where it leaves behind it the colourful show of the sensuous here-and-now and the night-like void of the supersensible beyond, and steps out into the spiritual daylight of the present. (PS 1977: §177)

The analysis of mastery and slavery or lordship and bondage, which is actually a description of the act of acknowledgement, has to be seen against the background of the opposed universes of force and the understanding. Forces belong to the universe of mechanical causes whereas the act of acknowledgement arises out of some intrinsic motive. Motives are qualified by their occupying an intermediary position; they mediate between the unintelligibility of the mechanical world and the intelligibility of the spiritual world. But when Hegel speaks of self-consciousness as the "middle term" of two consciousnesses that mark its "extremes", another metaphor comes into play. I take Hegel's allusion to Aristotelian syllogism seriously: the syllogism is a means to transform internal relations into external ones, especially in order to secure the independent reality or truth of the conclusion:

> The middle term is self-consciousness which splits into the extremes; and each extreme is this exchanging of its own determinateness and an absolute transition into the opposite. Although, as consciousness, it does indeed come *out of itself*, yet, though out of itself, it is at the same time kept back within itself, is *for itself*, and the self outside it, is for *it*. It is aware that it at once is, and is not, another consciousness, and equally that this other is *for itself* only when it supersedes itself as being for itself, and is for itself only in the being-for-self of the other. Each is for the other the middle term, through which each me-

diates itself with itself and unites with itself; and each is for itself, and for the other, an immediate being on its own account, which at the same time is such only through this mediation. They *recognize* themselves as *mutually recognizing* one another. (PS 1977: §184)

Findlay makes a wonderful remark comparing this most convoluted passage to the novels of Henry James, "where the characters not only see each other but also see each other seeing each other" (Findlay 1958: p.97). The reciprocity of seeing and being seen, looking on a face that looks back, opens up the opportunity to enrich our categorical analysis with phenomenological content. It underlines the possibility of a reversal of perspectives that makes the transition from the I to the You or from the You to the I intelligible.[1] Hence, interpreting facial expressions may be a paradigm of a hermeneutics of the life-world. Due to the influence of Fichte, however, Hegel prefers to take another step, namely, the step directly from the I to the We, bypassing the You. Moreover, for Findlay this manoeuvre is not only a shift in meaning, but a kind of verbal trickery that he feels obliged to rebute.

The generation of new meanings by means of a series of negations is a standard procedure in Hegel's philosophy, as is the semantic "ascent" from the particular to the universal. In the third edition of the *Encyclopaedia Logic*, Hegel maintains that logic and metaphysics coincide with one another in that they are able to express the essential reality of things. He describes his procedure explicitly as a shaping and re-shaping of meanings. The correlated notions of spirit and man are elevated in a parallel movement of thought: "Nature does not bring its nous into consciousness: it is man who first makes himself double so as to be a universal for a universal." (EL 1830: §24n) In consequence of this, the I receives a new meaning; it becomes a term that is representative of all beings who can say "I" to themselves, i.e., to all thinking beings.

Hegel did not leave behind what we would now call a systematic philosophy of language, but he did incorporate important insights into the nature and function of linguistic discourse into the *Phenomenology of Spirit*, the *Encyclopaedia Logic* and, above all, his writings on aesthetics and philosophy of art. One of the first thinkers, if not the very first, to modify Hegel's scheme of the I that is We and the We that is I was Wilhelm von Humboldt. Systematically oscillating between Kant, Fichte, Schelling and Hegel, he relied on Herder's and Fichte's treatises on language when he placed the You between the first and the third person:

---

[1] It is beyond the scope of my present purposes to extend my discussion to include the early Sartre's conception of the human face and the human look.

> The first thing is naturally the personality of the speaker himself who stands in continuous and direct contact with nature, and cannot possibly fail, even in language, to set over against the latter the expression of his self. But in the I, the Thou is also given automatically, and by a new opposition there arises the third person [...]. (Humboldt [1836] 1999: p.95)

In this passage, Humboldt spells out the You as the "Thou", the divine being. The conjecture that it is only God from whom, or from whose countenance, we derive our original conception of the Other as a personal being suggests a reversal of argumentation: we might say that God is only the Other, although veiled in a sort of religious mythology. Hegel did not take the step from a philosophy of religion or, rather, a phenomenology of religious consciousness to a critique of religion, but some of his followers of the Hegelian Left did. With Ludwig Feuerbach there emerges the principle of dialogue that was then to become prominent in the philosophy of the 20th century. Although I only mention the writings of Martin Buber, there are many examples.

Judged against the standard of a theory of meaning that Findlay erroneously links to Wittgenstein, he denounces the procedures described above for distorting the true meaning of the personal pronoun "I":

> We may admit [...] that Hegel's notion of Spirit does not provide a particularly happy elucidation of the normal meaning of the pronoun "I" [...]. Hegel is wrong in supposing that the word "I" has some covertly universal meaning, that though we may try to use it to refer to our single, momentary selves, the "divine" nature of language frustrates this intention, and forces us to mean something suprapersonal and universal. (Findlay 1958: p.53)

It appears that the Findlay of the year 1958 regards Wittgenstein as a propagator of a theory of ordinary language only. Following his lead, we would have to restate the normal meaning the pronouns have in everyday discourse:

> Obviously, the pronoun "I" usually serves to single out some person who is speaking [...]. Wittgenstein says that the use of the pronoun "I" is like putting one's hand to show who is talking: this is at least its use in dialogue, though its use in soliloquy may raise further complexities. But the mere fact that the pronoun "I" can be used to refer to different persons, and implies no fixed set of properties, does not mean that it stands for something mystically common to various persons and having that sheer indeterminacy of character which Hegel calls the "absolute negativity" of Spirit. (Findlay 1958: pp.53–4)

Findlay overlooks that Wittgenstein's theory of meaning, in all phases of his thinking, is subtler than it first appears. In his early work, Wittgenstein is aware of an impersonal mode of description, a shift from the "I" to the "We", as it were. The implicit universality of the personal pronouns is recognised, in full accordance with Hegel, in the *Philosophical Investigations* §410. In a later publication, Findlay turned away from Wittgenstein's style of philosophising and his theory of meaning (Findlay 1984; *vide* Findlay [1955] 1963). Furthermore, he gave a very sympathetic overview of Hegel's *Phenomenology of Spirit* (Findlay 1977). Following Plato, Plotinus and Hegel, he made the ascent to the Absolute the central theme of his mature works.

Paul Weiss: reading Wittgenstein's *Zettel* §§220-1 in the light of Hegel

In his youth, Weiss apparently aspired to the career of a logician. Due to the influence of Peirce and Whitehead, however, he turned his attention to traditional thinkers such as Aristotle, Aquinas, Locke, Hume, Kant and Hegel and abandoned the study of formal logic in favour of a study of first philosophy, metaphysics and ontology. In two books, *Beyond All Appearances* (1974) and *First Considerations* (1977), he developed an ontology of the person and of interpersonal relations and made the knowledge of other minds a paradigm of epistemology. In the context of this investigation, he corrected his initial neglect of Wittgenstein, as may be seen from his diary *Philosophy in Process*, especially vol. IX. Not unlike Findlay, he identified many parallels between Hegel and Wittgenstein.

In his *Philosophical Investigations*, Wittgenstein wrote: "When philosophizing, it will often prove useful to say to ourselves: Naming something is rather like attaching a name tag to a thing." (PI: §15) One is tempted to conjecture that this passage may reveal a certain prejudice in favour of the grammatical category of nouns, since nouns stand for things and it is only to things that a name tag can be attached. Like Kant before him, Wittgenstein may be accused of having an excessive fondness for thing-like existents that allow for a substantival characterisation of their nature. In contrast, Weiss developed a theory of naming in which the denotative component, or the referential function, of nouns is minimised (Weiss 1977: pp.68–79). For example, JHWH, the "nickname" (Weiss's expression) of God, is only a signal of the pressure that the absolute injunction exerts upon existence.

It is often maintained that the human face is expressive of an inner reality. Like the Hegel of the *Phenomenology of Spirit*, Wittgenstein was doubtful whether there is an isomorphism of body and mind; nonetheless, the theory of representation that he tried to develop in his early work acknowledged the fact that even logical structures such as tautology and contradiction have a sort of physiognomy (NB: pp.12 and 54). Observations such as these may seem peripheral to the young Wittgenstein but they gain considerable weight in his later writings, especially his *Remarks on the Philosophy of Psychology*. Interestingly enough, the interpretation of a sequence of words or of a musical phrase is compared by Wittgenstein to interpreting "facial expressions" (CV: pp.51–2). It may be asked, then, whether these discussions can be extended to the role of personal pronouns in human language.

A characteristic passage from a collection of drafts known as *Zettel* may help us to prepare the ground for our discussion.

> Consciousness in another's face. Look into someone else's face, and see the consciousness in it, and a particular *shade* of consciousness. You see on it, in it, joy, indifference, interest, excitement, torpor and so on. The light in other people's faces.
>
> Do you look into *yourself* in order to recognize the fury in *his* face? It is there as clearly as in your breast.
>
> (And what do we want to say now? That someone else's face stimulates me to imitate it, and that I therefore feel little movements and muscle-contractions in my own face and *mean* the sum of these? Nonsense. Nonsense,—because you are making assumptions instead of simply describing. If your head is haunted by explanations here, you are neglecting to remind yourself of the most important facts.) (Z: §220)
>
> "Consciousness is as clear in his face and behavior, as in myself." (Z: §221)

At first sight, consciousness, conceived as undifferentiated with respect to I, You, He, She, It and the corresponding plural forms, seems to be the basic phenomenon for Wittgenstein. But as soon as we combine the ontological fundamentality of this statement with the epistemological question of how to recognise other minds, consciousness is split into two poles that are connected to one another, and the differentiation hinted at above is laid open to our eyes. A superficial reading of the first paragraph could suggest the assumption that Wittgenstein is tempted to fall back into the untenable position of an isomorphism of body and mind, overarching now even the epistemological *hiatus* that divides the I from the You. The passage in brackets, however, shows that its author is prepared to refuse an illusory solution like this. Moreover, the following paragraph informs us that it was only one of Wittgenstein's voices that spoke to us. Now, let us ask how Weiss might have interpreted a passage such as the one quoted above.

In a book entitled *You, I, and the Others*, Weiss began to combine a realistic ontology of persons and interpersonal relations with the question of how to get knowledge of other minds.[2] On the one hand, there undoubtedly has existed, exists and will exist a plurality of persons, each and every one possessing a status of their own; we may say, therefore, that the fundamental hallmark of this existential situation is discontinuity. On the other hand, each person is capable of probing into her or his own depths and into the depths of every other person. The gap between two persons can be bridged by the me since the me can be approached from both sides, from the I and from the You: "the you is transformed into me-as-known-by another, whereas the me is transformed into I-as-known-by-myself" (Weiss 1980: p.100). Looking into somebody else's face is the phenomenological counterpart of the bridging function of the me.[3]

The startling experience in nearly every human encounter is its exorbitant span over the whole breadth of interpersonal relations, covering both closeness and distance. As Hegel and Wittgenstein saw, our fellow human beings may be near to us or foreign to us, and our knowledge of other minds, as distinct from the knowledge of the inanimate world, accordingly bears a peculiar and significant stress. Knowledge of other minds or, rather, the human encounter in which it is embedded combines continuity and discontinuity, an incessant interplay of otherness and togetherness. If I might be permitted to use a metaphor, I would describe the correlated processes of penetrating into the depths of our psyche and the psyche of another person as asymptotic movements. Weiss, however, was not entirely satisfied with his results: His diary (*Philosophy in Process*, vol. IX) bears witness to his ongoing struggle with the problem.

Weiss believed that epistemology and ontology are interdependent enterprises of the human mind, and this conviction is consequential for his answer to the question of how to acquire knowledge of other minds. I always know more about my fellow human beings than I am able to justify, and my fellow human beings in turn always know more about me than they are able to justify. Philosophy can and must reconstruct the existence of such knowledge in a circular movement of thought: relying on Peirce's theory of abduction, Weiss speaks of adumbration, the art of tracing back a clue to its origin. Whenever two terms are adumbratively related to one another, there is a certain epistemic cohesion, however loose it may be. Where these terms are self-consciousnesses, we may speak of a sort of existential connectivity.

---

[2] Weiss's investigation may be compared to Theunissen (1965) and Ricœur (1990).
[3] In the following section, §222, Wittgenstein notes another important phenomenological fact: although designed to explore the things apart, the observing eye exhibits the psychic depth behind itself.

Weiss attempted to summarise the conclusions of his speculations in a glossary in which, *inter alia*, the personal pronouns are defined. I will confine myself to only one entry:

> *Pronouns, personal:* Grammatically defined as terms which are used in place of nouns, they are, as Peirce observed, primary terms for which nouns are substituted. "You", "I", "me", and other personal pronouns refer in the directest way possible, terminating in and adhering to individuals. Precision would require one to write instead of "I am a man", "*I*, I am a man", where the *I* has the role of an adherent, penetrative term, and the I has the role of a subject in an articulation, itself adumbratively related to the *I*. (Weiss 1986b: p.201)

Weiss took up the Hegelian notion of the I that is We and the We that is I in his work on political philosophy. For Hegel, the history of North America was shaped largely by the facts of physical geography; in his opinion, there was no civil society and no political body in the wilderness of this continent. If we want Hegel's philosophy to stand up to the test of our time, we have to make two modifications. Firstly, the worth and value of the individual person must be acknowledged without qualification (Weiss 1983). Secondly, there is the problem of the representation of a people by their political leaders. The solution to this problem, which has haunted modern philosophy for three or four centuries, calls for a new interpretation of the formula "We, the people" that opens up the Constitution (Weiss 1986a).

In his final writings, Weiss managed to take a position between Hegelianism and linguistic analysis. Generalising Peirce's conception of the pragmatic maxim, he declared that it is the business of the philosopher to study transformations of all sorts (Weiss 1995). Using Hegelian terminology, we may say that personal pronouns, although in some sense lacking conceptual content, are akin to floating universals and that their meaning is open to semantic adaptations and modifications. Weiss explored some of these adaptations and modifications in two books devoted to the study of the life-world (Weiss 2000 and Weiss 2002). But he does not answer the question of how to set limits to the transformation of the meaning of words and phrases.

Wittgenstein once denied that "metaphysical emphasis" should be given to the pronoun I, at least in the epistemic contexts that were of the greatest interest to him (OC: p.63). For Weiss, however, the I maintains its centrality in the system of personal pronouns because of its reflexivity, which is not only an expression of a fortified self-reference—Wittgenstein raising his hand in order to speak—but exhibits a peculiarity of structure that is all its own.[4]

---

4 On this point, *vide* Mohanty (2000: p.125).

As to the complexity and connectivity of self-consciousnesses, let me finish by quoting some lines from "Esthétique du Mal"[5] by Wallace Stevens, a poet whom Weiss greatly admired:

> Is it himself in them that he knows or they
> In him? If it is himself in him, they have
> No secret from him. If it is they in him,
> He has no secret from them.

Concluding remarks

We are now in a position to give a short but, I hope, coherent and conclusive answer to the question of whether there is a "philosophy of personal pronouns". Investigations into the ontology of the person have been a major theme of philosophy since the days of Aristotle; Hegel, however, put this theme on a new footing when he discovered the plasticity of the notions of the self and the I that was unknown to his predecessors. Like Hegel before him, Wittgenstein recognised that the personal pronouns are implicitly universal in meaning and permit, therefore, a shift in meaning according to the context in which they are used. He matches Hegel's insight into the question of how to gain knowledge of other minds.

Findlay is right in his contention that Hegel's speculations on the self and the I distort the meaning that the personal pronouns have in normal linguistic discourse. Relying on a simplified version of Wittgenstein's theory of meaning, however, he missed the point that philosophers are entitled to give parts of speech new meanings according to the objectives of their study. Weiss, in his turn, developed an existential phenomenology in which the meaning of the personal pronouns is adapted to normal linguistic discourse. At the same time, he tried to explore their function in speculative thinking.[6]

---

5 Weiss, however, was convinced that every attempt to probe into the consciousness of a human being results in a reorganisation of its psychic architecture, thereby hiding its deeper layers from the eyes of the observer.
6 Let me thank my colleague J. Mácha for many a fruitful conversation about Hegel and Wittgenstein.

References

Fichte, Johann Gottlieb: "On the Linguistic Capacity and the Origin of Language" (1795), in: J. P. Surber (ed.): *Language and German Idealism. Fichte's Linguistic Philosophy*, Humanities Press, 1996, pp.117–45.
Findlay, John Niemeyer: *Hegel. A Re-Examination*, Routledge, 1958.
Findlay, John Niemeyer: "Review of Wittgenstein's *'Philosophical Investigations'*" (1955), in: *Language, Mind, and Value. Philosophical Essays*, Allen & Unwin, 1963, pp.197–207.
Findlay, John Niemeyer: "Foreword", in: G. W. F. Hegel: *Phenomenology of Spirit*, transl. by A. V. Miller, Oxford University Press, 1977, pp.v–xxx.
Findlay, John Niemeyer: *Wittgenstein: a Critique*, Routledge & Kegan Paul, 1984.
Herder, Johann Gottfried von: "Treatise on the Origin of Language" (1772), in: *Philosophical Writings*, ed. by M. N. Forster, Cambridge University Press, 2002, pp.65–164.
Humboldt, Wilhelm v.: *On Language. On the Diversity of Human Language Construction and its Influence on the Mental Development of the Human Species* (1836), ed. by M. Losonsky, Cambridge University Press, 1999.
Kiesow, Karl-Friedrich: "The Kinship of Poetry and Philosophy. Reflections on W. Stevens and P. Weiss", in: K. Bartczak and J. Mácha (eds.): *Wallace Stevens: Philosophy, Poetry, and Figurative Language*, Peter Lang, 2018.
Mohanty, Jitendra Nath: *The Self and Its Other. Philosophical Essays*, Oxford University Press, 2000.
Ricœur, Paul: *Soi-même comme un autre*, Paris, 1990.
Stevens, Wallace: *The Collected Poems*, A. A. Knopf, 2002.
Surber, Jere Paul: *Language and German Idealism. Fichte's Linguistic Philosophy*, Humanities Press, 1996.
Theunissen, Michael: *Der Andere. Studien zur Sozialontologie der Gegenwart*, De Gruyter, 1965.
Weiss, Paul: *Beyond All Appearances*, Southern Illinois University Press, 1974.
Weiss, Paul: *First Considerations. An Examination of Philosophical Evidence*, Southern Illinois University Press, 1977.
Weiss, Paul: *You, I, and the Others*, Southern Illinois University Press, 1980.
Weiss, Paul: *Privacy*, Southern Illinois University Press, 1983.
Weiss, Paul: *Toward a Perfected State*, State University of New York Press, 1986a.
Weiss, Paul: *Philosophy in Process*, Vol. IX, State University of New York Press, 1986b.
Weiss, Paul: *Being and Other Realities*, Open Court, 1995.
Weiss, Paul: *Emphatics*, Vanderbilt University Press, 2000.
Weiss, Paul: *Surrogates*, Indiana University Press, 2002.
Wiese, Leopold von: *Die Philosophie der persönlichen Fürwörter*, J. C. B. Mohr (Paul Siebeck), 1965.

Jakub Mácha
Particularity as Paradigm: A Wittgensteinian Reading of Hegel's Subjective Logic

Abstract I provide a distinctively Wittgensteinian interpretation of Hegel's Subjective Logic, including the parts on the concept, the judgement and the syllogism. I argue that Wittgenstein implicitly recognised the moments of universality, particularity and individuality; moreover, he was sensitive to Hegel's crucial distinction between abstract and concrete universals. More specifically, for Wittgenstein the moment of particularity has the status of a paradigmatic sample which mediates between a universal concept and its individual instances. Thus, a concrete universal is a universal that includes every individual via its paradigmatic sample. Next, I provide a generic account of the emergence of concrete universals through a series of negations that follows the basic structure of Hegel's judgement—"the individual is the universal"—and the syllogism—"the individual is the universal mediated by the particular". This development is illustrated with examples from Hegel (a plant, Socrates, Caesar, a Stoic sage, Jesus) as well as from Wittgenstein (colour samples, the standard metre, works of art). I take Wittgenstein's argument against private language as implying that we cannot do without paradigms in our epistemic practices. If the conclusion of the section "Subjectivity" in Hegel's *Science of Logic* is that the moment of particularity cannot be ignored or dispensed with, then it would mean that we cannot do without paradigms in our epistemic practices: that is, that private rules are impossible.

Paradigm in Wittgenstein

This essay is about finding parallels, affinities and points of contact between Hegel and Wittgenstein. Let me begin with Wittgenstein or, rather, with my own interpretation of something I have taken from Wittgenstein: namely, what I call paradigmatic thinking, i.e. epistemic activities involving paradigms. Let a paradigm of X be a material object together with the praxis of applying this object in a given situation. I call the object of a paradigm a paradigmatic sample. "Object" is meant very broadly here (e.g. in a Quinean sense as a spatio-temporal hunk of matter). Paradigmatic samples are real material things ranging from clearly defined objects like the metre stick or a colour plate to intricate structures like formalisations of mathematical proofs or works of art. A paradigmatic sample is a model of a situation (what Wittgenstein called "model" in his early notebooks and "image" [*Bild*] in the *Tractatus*). A paradigm is, thus, a model together with a method for its projection or rather comparison. A paradigm of X is a praxis that involves material objects (it is not important whether there is a single object or several); it is a method for deciding whether a given object is X. This is typically done by comparing the paradigmatic sample with the given object. This may be done indirectly, e.g. X may be defined by (with reference to) Y which is in turn defined by reference to a paradigmatic sample.

Wittgenstein wrote on many occasions that colour concepts and standards of measure are introduced by means of paradigmatic samples (the standard sepia and the standard metre). The same is true of numerals, i.e. concepts for numbers. We can give meaning to the numeral 3 using the following definition: "The list ||| means 3." The list ||| serves in this sense as a yardstick. The numeral 3 is a substitution or, rather, an abbreviation for the list |||. I argued in my book *Wittgenstein on Internal and External Relations* (2015) that the same scheme applies in a number of other domains. There are for example paradigmatic mathematical proofs and paradigmatic works of art (Wittgenstein calls them "tremendous"). Furthermore, the standard of length can be introduced and defined by a paradigmatic sample (e.g. the standard metre in Paris) or with the help of other physical constants (e.g. the speed of light) which are ultimately defined by paradigmatic samples (e.g. a beam of light).

Rule-following

Wittgenstein did not claim that this scheme is universal, i.e. that every concept is introduced by a paradigm which refers to a paradigmatic sample. I would like to put forward the claim—which I am aware is controversial—that Wittgenstein's discussion of private language supplies the argument that we cannot do without paradigmatic samples. Wittgenstein pointed out that the idea of a private rule is inconsistent. There has been a long debate about what "private" actually means here. If we take "private" to mean "not referring to any external object" (like naming my sensation S), the desired conclusion would then follow: A private rule-following is a rule-following without the recurrence to any paradigmatic sample.

Of course, this argument is only sketched in broad outline. However, it is enough to allow us to draw a connection to Hegel's logic. If the conclusion of the section "Subjectivity" in Hegel's *Science of Logic* is that every object is the unity of the singular, the particular and the universal, or, more specifically, that the moment of particularity cannot be ignored or dispensed, then it would mean, on my interpretation, that we cannot bypass paradigms in our epistemic practices, i.e. that private rules are impossible. Let us, therefore, examine how Hegel's subjective logic can be employed in support of Wittgenstein's argument against private language.

Paradigms in Hegel's subjective logic

The main claim I want to advance is that a similar structure is to be found in Hegel's subjective logic. In my interpretation, I bring Hegel's notion of the subject closer to Wittgenstein's notion of the linguistic community. Subjective logic, then, becomes the logic of language-games or, more broadly, grammar in Wittgenstein's idiosyncratic sense. For Hegel, the concept [*Begriff*] is not merely the fundamental structure of our thinking, but rather a form that warrants the speculative identity of thought and being. Hegel recognises three basic moments of the concept: universality, particularity and singularity (individuality).[1] Hegel's account of the concept consists of a dialectical movement from universality to particularity and finally to individuality. Hegel also begins his dialectical account of the concept with—it must be stressed—abstract universality. Universality is something that is already available from the logic of essence. Abstract universality is something presupposed. We find an analogous presupposition in Wittgenstein's discussion of the ostensive definition, where he stresses that the place of the defined expression or its role in grammar must be already prepared (PI: §31) in order to carry out an ostensive definition. So, for instance, exclaiming "From now on, this colour shall be called 'sepia'!" and pointing at a colour plate presupposes that we already know what colour is. Colour is a grammatical category in Wittgenstein and an abstract universal in Hegel (E I: §163).

Abstract universality or general conception (*allgemeine Vorstellung*) is characterised by neglecting particular features which would account for specific differences among the subspecies and individuals that fall under the concept in question. What, then, is particularity? The traditional (Leibnizian) view of particularity is that of a subspecies or a subset (cf. Stekeler-Weithofer 1992: p.350). Hegel, however, finds this view too narrow and thus unsatisfactory. Particularity

---

[1] In this essay I will render the German expression "einzeln" and its cognates as "singular" or "individual" depending on the context of the translation. Di Giovanni prefers "singular" (SL 2010: p.lxx), Pinkard "singular" or "singular individual" (PS 2018: p.476), Brinkmann and Dahlstrom "singular" (EL 1830/2010). I do not reserve "individual" exclusively for personal individuality as Di Giovanni does (SL 2010: p.lxx).

is the determinateness (*Bestimmtheit*) of the concept. The determinateness of universality is its difference. It is its outward difference, i.e. the difference between the universal and the particular. The particular is thus a negation of the universal. Hegel says: "the *determinateness* of the particular is *simple* as *principle*, but it is also simple as a moment of the totality, determinateness as against the *other* determinateness." (SL 2010: p.532) Particularity is hence the principle of difference—the difference within the universal concept which is differentiated into subspecies and constituent elements.

Two interpretations of particularity

Understanding Hegel's account of particularity has proven to be anything but straightforward. Hegel probably adopted his conception of particularity from Gottfried Ploucquet, who was active at the time of Hegel's studies in Tübingen. Ploucquet distinguished between "exclusive" and "comprehensive" particularity. An *exclusive* particular A is an instantiation of A. For example, what is meant by the expression "this particular tree" is this tree as opposed to that particular tree over there. This is why this use of particularity is exclusive. Comprehensive particularity, in contrast, does not exclude any singular instance of the term in question. If exclusive particularity is instantiation, then this kind of particularity comes closer to singularity (even "some trees" is understood in a nominalist sense as, say, "this tree, that tree and that tree over there").[2] Then, however, the crucial question remains: how are we to understand comprehensive particularity, that is, the true particularity?

Arguably, this distinction between exclusive and comprehensive particularity aligns with two main contemporary interpretations of particularity. On the first interpretation, the particular is a (comprehensive) perspective on a universal concept. In Žižek's words: "the true particularity is, primarily, the *particular subjective position from which the universal Notion* [concept] *is acceptable to me*" (2012: p.360). A particular is a specific historical appearance of a universal. On the second interpretation, the particular is an undifferentiated example (that

---

[2] See Redding (2014) for a thorough discussion of this issue. He argues that "Ploucquet's 'exclusive' use would correspond to the quasi-naming role of the subject term in its immediacy, but as the properly logical form of the expressed judgement gets redetermined in different functional contexts it gets the properties of Ploucquet's 'comprehensive' sense of particularity." (2014: p.293)

is, an instantiation). This interpretation was advocated by Goethe,[3] and more recently by Winfield.[4,5] The problem with the first (comprehensive) interpretation is that it does not account for the difference within the universal concept. The only difference available is that between different subjective and historical perspectives on the universal concept. The particular is, however, the (first) negation of the universal; it is something that the universal is not (Winfield 2011: p.233). A subjective position on something is not necessarily its negation. The problem with the second interpretation is that an example always exemplifies either too little or too much. Examples are either too imperfect to capture an ideal universality or else, possibly at the same time, exemplify features that do not belong to the universal concept.[6,7] The problem here is that we lack a perspective (Wittgenstein would say a method of projection) on the example that would determine what exactly is being exemplified. Examples thus lack the determinateness of the particular.

We can understand particularity as a process of mediation that goes from universality to singularity (as the development of the predicate in the abstract judgement; see below). In comprehensive particularity, the process, so to speak, has not started yet, whereas exclusive particularity is a result of this process. Comprehensive particularity is too universal, exclusive particularity too singular.

---

[3] "[A] particular [is] considered only as an illustration, as an example of the universal", *Maxims and Reflections*, cited in Žižek (2012: p.97).
[4] "As particular, each instance of the shared quality comprises an undifferentiated example, standing in an identical relation to the quality they hold in common." (Winfield 2006: p.76)
[5] The example view of particularity is supported in the "Sense-certainty" chapter of the *Phenomenology of Spirit*. There, Hegel distinguishes between essence and example. This distinction is further linked to that between immediacy and mediation (PdG: p.83). Cf. Warminski (1986: p.177): "That 'an actual sense-certainty is not only this pure immediacy, but an example *(Beispiel)* of it' means both 'by-play'—particular, inessential and so on—and 'example' as it later appears in the text (and as in its 'normal' usage)."
[6] For Žižek (2012: p.364) this too little and too much marks the difference between the idealist and materialist use of examples.
[7] Exemplifying too much is captured in the German "Bei-spiel", which Hegel links to "beiherspielen" (PdG: p.83). Terry Pinkard renders this verb as "there is a good deal more in play" (PS 2012: ¶92).

Particular as paradigm

My proposal is, so to speak, a synthesis of these two accounts of particularity, with a focus on the actual mediation. I propose to take the particular as the paradigm. Remember that a paradigm is a material object (paradigmatic sample) together with the praxis of its application. A paradigmatic sample of X is (also) an example of X while, at the same time, a paradigmatic sample is different from an example (more about the difference later). What paradigms do share with examples is that a paradigm is different from the universal concept—or more precisely: a paradigm is different from abstract universality. Furthermore, an integral part of a paradigm is the praxis of comparing the paradigmatic sample with other objects or situations. This practical trait provides the particular with its determinateness, with the principle of difference. As paradigm, the particular is a principle. This praxis is always rooted in a specific social and historical context. For Hegel, the particular is also universal and individual. Every paradigm has an individual aspect, which is the paradigmatic sample, and also a universal aspect, which is the universal dimension of the concept.

Individuality is the negation of particularity (or the negation of the negation of universality). The paradigm is a principle, a method (of comparing the paradigmatic sample with other objects). The negation of particularity can be expressed as the determinate determinateness (SL: §1343). For an abstract method (which can be applied on many occasions) is now a concrete application of this method which has a concrete outcome: the individual that belongs to the universal concept.

Wittgenstein was worried that philosophical problems and paradoxes arise when a word or a word-sequence is taken out of its context of use. The context of use means not only a linguistic context (i.e. the surrounding text), but also an extra-linguistic context, i.e. the praxis with the linguistic expression which involves paradigms. The context of use is thus a particularisation of a linguistic expression. This is not surprising. Utilising the points elaborated above, we can attempt a stronger interpretation: neglecting the particular moment, neglecting the context of use, means in fact treating language as something abstract. Ultimately it means failing to consider paradigmatic samples in rule-following practices, which amounts to private rule-following.

We are now in a better position to characterise the two conceptions of universality, abstract and concrete. Abstract universality is devoid of any reference to a paradigmatic sample. As Badiou says in an anti-Hegelian vein: "all true universality is devoid of a center." (2003: p.19) In contrast, concrete universality—in Žižek's words—"bears witness to a scar in some particularity, and remains always linked to this scar" (2012: p.362). This centre, this scar, is a paradigmatic sample.[8]

Judgement

Let us now turn to the next stage of Hegel's development of his subjective logic. The concept in its posited particularity is a judgement. First, I shall discuss judgement in its abstract form: "The individual is the universal" or "The subject is the predicate"; further development of the judgement will be addressed later. The subject is the immediately concrete universal and the predicate is the abstract universal. In the judgement, both sides are being developed, in order to reach a perfect identity which is expressed by the copula "is". The predicate is developed from the abstract universality to the particularity, i.e. to a paradigm. The subject is developed from its immediate individuality into the particularity that is already contained, as such, in the individual, just as a seed already contains the essence of the plant. In the judgement "This rose is red", this individual rose, which contains many particular determinations, e.g. colour, aroma, length, is developed by negation into one of them, the colour. Analogously, the abstract universal "red" is developed, again by negation, into its paradigm. Now, a perfect identity can be achieved when the rose is compared with the paradigmatic sample of red with respect to their colour. The particularised individual is identical with the paradigmatic sample. They can exchange their roles: the particularised individual can become a paradigmatic sample of the original universal (and further, by the negation of the negation, the universal) and the original paradigmatic sample can become, again by negation, a mere instance of the universal. This is the exchange of meanings that happens in the judgement (E I: §196).

On the subject side of the judgement, there is an inverse development from individuality to particularity and then to universality. While the development captured by the succession from universality through particularity to individuality presents a series of presuppositions (particularity presupposes universality and individuality presupposes particularity), the development from individuality through particularity to universality can be taken as a development of an idea and as a real, even historical process in space and time. As we know, the concept

---

[8] Paul Redding suggested to me the term "witness" instead of "scar", which has negative psychoanalytic connotations. A paradigmatic sample is a kind of witness to a judgement. There is an interesting association with Wittgenstein's discussion of the so-called private language argument. A private language would be deprived of this witness.

is for Hegel the fundamental structure of thinking and reality. Hegel provides a great many examples. I have already mentioned the seed that discloses itself into a plant and further into its species. Hegel comments: "the seed discloses itself, something which is to be considered the judgment of the plant." (EL 1830/2010: p.242; E I: §166) The growing of a plant is a real process that, however, does not involve thinking or language. Before proceeding to higher and more complex processes, it has to be noted that if thinking and language are involved in the judgement, the subject, the immediately concrete, is initially an empty name (E I: §169), or as we would say nowadays, a singular term or proper name.[9] What we are looking for is the development from a proper name (individuality) to a paradigm (particularity) and further to a universal term.

Caesar

Hegel discussed Caesar's life and his significance in history on many occasions. Let us now turn to Hegel's *Lectures on the Philosophy of History* (PGh: pp.379–80). Initially, Caesar was the name of an *individual*.[10] He acted in a *particular* way—militarily and politically—that was hostile to the Roman Republic, which was an empty name at that time. After he nominally assumed sovereign power—became dictator for life—the republic was on the verge of collapse. By his assassination, the conspirators hoped to restore the republican regime. But the opposite happened: they precipitated the end of the republic. "Caesar", a familial name, was changed into the title of the Roman emperors.[11] This title then passed into many European languages (English is an exception) as the *universal* concept designating the role of an emperor (e.g. "Kaiser" in German, "czar" in Russian, "císař" in Czech). What we have here is a transition from the individual (Julius Caesar as a person) to the particular (Caesar's military and political way of acting) to the universal (Caesar as a title and a caesar as

---

9 In this connection, Agamben clearly recognises that there are two modes of precedence—presupposition and time precedence: "In the name (in particular in the proper name, and every name is originally a proper name), being is always already presupposed by language to language. As Hegel was to understand perfectly, the precedence that is in question here is not chronological but is an effect of linguistic presupposition." (2015: p.129)

10 This is not strictly accurate. Caesar was in fact a cognomen, a (part of a) family name. What is important, however, is that in a particular context, "Caesar" picks out a single person. This is the typical feature of almost all proper names. They are usually not exclusive (there are many Johns and Smiths). Proper names can, however, refer to a single person in a particular context.

11 This happened in 69 AD with the end of the reign of the Julio-Claudian dynasty.

a property or role). The particular moment can be taken as a paradigm (Hegel writes that Caesar "may be adduced as a paragon [*Muster*] of Roman adaptation of means to ends [*Zweckmäßigkeit*]" (LPH: p.285; PGh: p.379)). Caesar's military and political career is the paradigmatic case of a person who is called an emperor (a caesar with lowercase c) or—in other words—a caesar (with lowercase c) is a person who is such that their political position is similar or comparable to Caesar's (with a capital C). One final remark before we proceed to the next example: as has already been made clear, the passage from individuality to universality is marked by a series of negations. Hegel stresses that the judgement "the individual is universal" expresses "both the perishableness of singular things and their positive subsistence in the concept in general" (SL: §1364). Caesar as an individual had to perish in order to be transformed into a universal concept and to subsist as such (cf. Žižek 2012: p.455). His physical death triggered this transformation. This aspect becomes even more central in the next example.

Jesus

From his early works to his last lectures, Hegel devoted many pages to the life of Jesus and to Christianity. This example is more complex than the previous one, because it is rich in dialectical moments. I would like to begin in the middle with the moment of particularity. In his very early writings from 1793, published as *Notes for a Folk Religion*, Hegel maintained that Jesus is a model [*Muster*] and an ideal of virtue. This is so because Jesus has a supplement of the divine [*Beimischung, Zusatz das Göttlichen*] (FS: p.83). Otherwise, he would be only an *example* of a virtuous man like Socrates. Jesus thus had both a divine and a human nature. Hegel sees this double nature as Christianity's crucial advantage over the abstractness of older religions and ethical conceptions which neglected the moment of particularity.[12] Moreover, Jesus was "a perfect man, [who] endured the lot of all men" (LHP III 1896: p.5; GP II: p.526). Jesus, by the way he lived and died, thus stands for all men. He is the paradigm of a (Christian) man.[13]

---

12 This neglect of the moment of particularity or of the paradigm can be illustrated by the example of Stoicism. The ideal of Stoic virtue, the sage, was an extrapolated, i.e. abstract ideal, not a man of flesh and blood like Jesus. The concrete, paradigmatic sample is absent in Stoicism. Hegel quotes Cicero in this connection: "But who this wise man is or has been the Stoics never say" (LHP II 1894: pp.250–1; GP II: p.269; *Academicae questiones* IV, 47).
13 This indicates that the example conception of particularity is inadequate, to say the least. Jesus is neither an example of a virtuous man nor an example of God.

If we follow the development of the concept of God, then the universality of God the Father is particularised in Jesus, the Son, and finds its final stage in the individuality of the Holy Spirit. The Christian Trinity thus follows the three moments of the development of the concept (cf. Stewart 2011: p.509). The Holy Spirit is for Hegel "*the universal self-consciousness* of a religious community, [... it] is the universal self-consciousness [...], the individual together with the consciousness of the religious community" (PS 2018: ¶763). The Holy Spirit thus demonstrates the moments of both (concrete) universality and individuality. The passage from Jesus Christ to the Holy Spirit can be taken as the passage from particularity to universality—or as the judgement from the individuality of God the Father to the particularity of Jesus Christ and finally to the universality of the Holy Spirit. Now, Jesus is the negation (the first negation) of God the Father, and the Holy Spirit is the negation (the negation of the negation of God the Father) of Jesus. Let us focus on the second negation, i.e. the negation of the negation. This negation of the negation, or the death of death, has two moments: on the one hand, it is the death of the manifested God: "Christ dies; [but] only as dead, is he exalted to Heaven and sits at the right hand of God; only thus is he Spirit. He himself says: 'When I am no longer with you, the Spirit will guide you into all truth.'" (LPH III 1896: p.14; PGh: p.393) The physical death of the particular individual, of Jesus Christ, is necessary for its transition into the universality of the Spirit. This is analogous to the death of Caesar, after which "its spiritual and inward existence was unfolded under Augustus" (PGh: p.385). Hegel clearly recognises this analogy when he opens the section "Christianity" in his *Lectures on the Philosophy of History*. On the other hand, the negation of the negation is the negation of this death; it is the death of death. It is God's preservation; through his resurrection, God rises into life again. Curiously enough, Hegel maintains that Christ's human nature is also preserved; moreover, the death of death is the highest preservation and elevation of his human nature (Rel II: p.291).

Negation and reflexivity

A negation of the particular involves a negation of its individual moment. Caesar or Jesus had to die in order to pass over into the concrete universality. If the particular moment is a paradigm, then its individual moment is a paradigmatic sample. Hegel thus maintained that the paradigmatic sample has to disappear. This position does not seem very plausible. For instance, the standard metre does not need to be destroyed in order to establish the metre as the universal unit of length. Quite the contrary! The standard metre must be preserved, for it must be available to compare with other objects. This praxis constitutes the universal unit. A paradigmatic sample is a prototype which can be copied, but this does not result in the sample being destroyed. How can we thus make sense of Hegel's position?

The paradigmatic sample of X can be used to produce concrete instances of X. These instances make up the concrete universal. We can ask, however, whether the paradigmatic sample of X is an individual part of this concrete universal. Is the paradigmatic sample of X an X? Is the standard metre one metre long? Was Caesar a caesar? Such questions are, however, paradoxical. Wittgenstein says: "There is one thing of which one can state neither that it is 1 metre long, nor that it is not 1 metre long, and that is the standard metre in Paris." (PI: §50) He makes analogous claims about other paradigmatic samples. Hence, we cannot decide whether the paradigmatic sample of X is a part of X. If one cannot say that the standard metre is one metre long then this combination of words has no sense. Such "a combination of words is being excluded from the language, withdrawn from circulation" (PI: §500). This structure of the paradigmatic sample as neither in the universal nor excluded from the universal is the structure of Hegel's sublation. The paradigm is not quite a part of the universal, but it is at the same time preserved in the universal. The paradigm is not an individual moment of the universal, but is its particular moment.

Following Hegel's logic, paradigmatic samples are thus destroyed in the course of the negation of negation. As a material object, it cannot be asked of the sample—deliberately or accidentally—whether it belongs to the universal concept. The sample as such is simply not there any more. We cannot confuse Caesar with a *Kaiser*, for this concept came into existence after Caesar's death and (we can assume) he will never come back to life.[14] The situation is different with Jesus. According to Christian doctrine, he will return on Judgement Day, at the Last Judgement, and resurrect all men (including Julius Caesar). Jesus's second coming thus does not fit into Hegel's dialectics. So it is no surprise that Hegel never paid much attention to the Apocalypse and the Last Judgement in his treatment of Christianity.

---

14 What is left are only historical accounts of Caesar's life. Their epistemic usefulness depends on the following conditions: they must be *true* and we must *understand* the language in which they are formulated. This means that (1) someone (a historian, a witness or Caesar himself) must actually have compared facts about that time with paradigmatic samples and written down the results of these comparisons (truthfulness) and (2) we must have access (albeit indirect through causal chains) to these paradigms (understandability). This is a complex issue that is beyond the scope of the present discussion.

Development of the judgement

Let us return to Hegel's core doctrine of subjective logic. If the judgement is the posited particularity of the concept, then the judgement must be developed beyond its abstract form "the individual is a universal", which abstracts precisely from the particular moment. Hegel developed the judgement into 12 species. Let us examine how they involve the particular moment, i.e. a paradigm.

The first group comprises three judgements of quality. The *positive* judgement has the form "the individual is a particular", as in "the rose is red". Here an individual, this rose, is compared with the paradigmatic sample of red with respect to their colour. A positive judgement consists in their agreement in terms of colour. Of course, the rose also possesses other qualities, that is, it can be compared with other paradigmatic samples. On the other hand, there are more red objects besides this individual rose, that is, other objects are the same colour as the paradigmatic sample of red. The subject and the predicate come into contact at one point or aspect, that is, with respect to their colour. They can be different in other aspects, e.g. in their shapes, sizes, materials, etc.

The first negation of the positive judgement leads to the *negative* judgement. What is negated here is the agreement of the individual subject and the particular predicate, e.g. in "this rose is not red". The individual, this rose, is comparable with the paradigmatic sample of red, but they happen not to agree. This means the rose is a different colour. The individual, the rose, and the particular, the paradigmatic sample of red, belong to the same genus, i.e. objects of (a certain) colour.

The negation of this connection of comparability, of having the same genus, yields the *infinite* judgement. In such a judgement, there is no relation between the individual subject and the particular predicate. The individual subject is not comparable with the paradigmatic sample. Hegel's example is "the spirit is no elephant" (E I: §173). We can also add the example "the number 4 is not red". Hegel adds another example: "a lion is no table" (ibid.). A lion is, in fact, comparable with the paradigmatic table. But lions and tables are of different genera. It is reasonable, however, to keep the method of comparison, i.e. the praxis of comparing the paradigmatic table with other objects, as simple as possible, by restricting the comparison to objects of the closest genus (furniture in this case). Thus, judgements involving what is nowadays called a "category mistake" are, in Hegel's terms, infinite judgements.

Let us move on to the judgement of reflection. Here, the predicate is not "an immediate, abstract quality" (EL 1830/2010: p.248; §174) but instead what we would call a relational property. In the language of paradigms, this means that paradigms involve more paradigmatic samples in these cases. But these other paradigmatic samples are not determined in a judgement of reflection. Hegel's example, "this plant has healing powers", shows this. This sentence does not express what healing powers are meant (which illness, what dosage, any contraindications, etc.). The predicate is, thus, both an abstract universal and something particular. This abstract universal must be fixed by another judgement. The judgement of reflection thus already points towards a higher structure, namely the syllogism.

In the *singular* judgement, the individual subject is equated with the abstract universal predicate. The predicate is also something particular. It is a paradigm relating more paradigmatic samples with the individual in the subject position. This individual, as it were, fills one slot in the paradigmatic praxis, but there are other slots still to be filled.

The *particular* judgement has the same predicate as the singular judgement, but the subject is something particular, as in "some plants have healing powers". The subject can be the same individual as in the singular judgement, but what matters are some of its particular properties determined by a paradigm (of a plant). Any paradigmatic sample has many properties beyond the property it is the paradigm of. For example, the paradigmatic sample of red has a colour (i.e. red), but it also has a shape, a size, a weight, a porosity, a chemical structure, etc., but these properties are not taken into account in its paradigmatic application. In the particular judgement, however, some of these properties do enter the judgement. In "some roses have healing powers", the chemical structure of this or that rose is being compared with the paradigm of healing powers. But in the paradigm of a rose, the chemical structure does not matter (or at least let us assume it does not). In the particular judgement, the particularity of the subject is different from the particularity of the predicate.

This difference is negated in the *universal* judgement. Here, the subject must be something particular, that is a paradigm, and the predicate is again an abstract universal, but also a paradigm involving more paradigmatic samples. But unlike the particular judgement, these two paradigms pick out properties within the same aspect. In the judgement "all predatory animals are dangerous", what makes an animal predatory is the same feature that makes it dangerous (and it remains undetermined how exactly they are dangerous). The universal judgement is a relation between two compatible paradigms with respect to properties they pick out and thus expresses a kind of necessity. This leads to the judgement of necessity.

The judgement of necessity addresses the substance or nature of the subject. Unlike the universal judgement, the predicate is a concrete universal, that is a universal posited in its particularity. In the *categorical* judgement, the subject is something particular (e.g. "gold") or something individual posited in its particularity ("Gaius"). Such a particular is a paradigm, which consists of, as we know, a paradigmatic sample together with a praxis that is its method of application. This paradigm embraces the paradigmatic praxis of the concrete universal predicate. There is a partial identity between these two paradigms, not only between abstract properties they pick out as in the universal judgement. For instance, in "gold is metal", the paradigm of metal is a part of the paradigm of gold (e.g. "gold is a metal that has atomic number 79").

The *hypothetical* judgement expresses a necessary relation between two concrete universals posited in their particularities, that is, between two paradigms: "'If A is, then B is'; or 'The being of A is not its own being but the being of another, of B.'" (SL 2010: p.576) The necessity of this relation comes from its part–whole character (like in the categorical judgement). What is not determined in either the categorical or the hypothetical judgement is the form of the connection between the subject and the predicate.[15] The being of A is *some* or *any* part of the being of B. Being metal is *a* part of the nature of gold.

In the *disjunctive* judgement, this under-determinacy of form is negated. The subject is a concrete universal; the predicate is a disjunctive totality of determinations of this universal. In other words, the particularity of the universal is identical to the disjunctive totality of several particulars. "A is either B or C or D." The paradigm of A is nothing but an application of the paradigms B or C or D (consecutive, in any order). Hegel stresses that these particularities are mutually exclusive and that they exhaust the concrete universal. In the disjunctive judgement, the copula expresses a genuine identity. The judgement emerges, for the first time, as *Ur-teil*, that is, "original or primordial division" of a concept. The disjunctive judgement expresses the identity of the universal and the particular; in other words, it defines the universal as a combination of (mutually exclusive) paradigms.

What is missing in the disjunctive judgement is the moment of individuality. This is remedied in the judgement of concept. In the *assertoric* judgement, the subject is a concrete individual that is related to its general concept, which identifies the individual subject. The predicate expresses this identification. In the judgement "this house is good", an individual house is determined as such, as a house; and it is good as a house (and not as an artwork, for example). We can thus interpret the judgement as "this house is a good house". The asser-

---

[15] The progression from the categorical to the hypothetical judgement lies exactly in this under-determinacy: "Thus, for example, the gold is indeed metal, but silver, copper, iron, and so forth are likewise metals, and being metal as such behaves indifferently to the particular character of its species." (EL 1830/2010: p.251; §177)

toric judgement thus expresses the unity between the individual and its concept (its universal nature mediated by the particular that is expressed in the predicate). The individual is compared with the paradigm of the universal concept and the judgement expresses their fit. This house is compared with the paradigmatic house and their good fit or agreement is expressed in the judgement "this house is good".

The individual in the subject position, this house, is, however, something contingent. A house is designed, built, used, repaired, used again and eventually demolished. These are its moments, which are contrasted with the universal nature of its concept, the house. Hegel calls this the subjectivity of the thing or its negativity.[16] This contingency is expressed in the *problematic* judgement. This house is good, perfect, beautiful, etc. only in a certain stage of its life cycle. This house may or may not agree with its original design (what this house was supposed to be, its ought). This design agrees with the paradigm of the house (otherwise it would not be a design of a house, but of something else, e.g. a car).

In the *apodictic* judgement, the individual subject is given with its particular character (*Beschaffenheit*) and identified with a universal concept. The subject is thus a concept in all three of its moments, individuality, particularity and universality. The predicate expresses their agreement, that is the unity of this concept. In the judgement "this house so and so constituted is good", the individual referred to as "this" agrees with the paradigmatic house "so and so constituted" and for this reason, it is a "good house". The fact that this house agrees with the paradigmatic house in such and such a way is not the object of the judgement, but rather its presupposition. Even the apodictic judgement is true or false within a larger context, which is addressed by Hegel under the heading "syllogism" (*Schluß*).

---

[16] WL II: p.348: "Das Problematische des Subjekts an ihm selbst macht seine *Zufälligkeit* als *Moment* aus, die *Subjektivität* der *Sache*, ihrer objektiven Natur oder ihrem Begriff gegenübergestellt, die bloße *Art und Weise* oder die *Beschaffenheit*." Di Giovanni renders "die Subjektivität der Sache" as "the subjectivity of the fact" and "Beschaffenheit" as "constitution". "The problematic element in the subject itself constitutes its *moment of contingency*, the *subjectivity of the fact it expresses* as contrasted with its objective nature or its concept, its mere *mode and manner* or its *constitution*." (SL 2010: p.584)

Interim conclusion

Let us go back to Hegel's initial definition of the judgement: "The *judgment* is the concept in its particularity as the differentiating *relation* of its moments, which are posited as being for themselves and, at the same time, as identical with themselves, not with one another." (EL 1830/2010: p.240; §166) The judgement is a relation within the concept between two of its moments, e. g. between the individual and the particular in the positive judgement. If we take the particular as a paradigm, we can attempt a bolder interpretation: the particular moment, a paradigm, is involved in every judgement, i. e. in every relation within a concept, and the twelve forms of judgement comprise the complete list of paradigmatic cases of this involvement. Even if we take the judgement in its abstract form, that is, where the individual is the universal, which seemingly does not involve the moment of particularity, its extremes, the subject and the predicate, can be related only through the particular, that is, through a paradigm, and they, in fact, develop into their particular moments—as we have seen in the examples of Caesar and Jesus. The demand of the judgement is thus that the individuality/singularity and the universality must be mediated through the particularity, S—P—U, which is the *Schluß*.

Schluß in general

Hegel famously maintained that everything is a *Schluß*. "Schluß" is usually rendered into English as inference, syllogism or syllogistic inference, which I believe already favours certain interpretations of Hegel's subjective logic. That everything is an inference has become a key claim of "semantic" interpretations of Hegel, and of Brandom's inferentialism in particular. In this paper, I keep the term "Schluß" in the original German in order to preserve the aspect of its meaning relating to completion or realisation (of the concept in objectivity). My aim is to provide an alternative interpretation of subjective logic that does not focus on the notion of inference or on language or semantics in general. On the other hand, I do not want to adopt the traditional full-fledged metaphysical interpretation (mostly because I simply do not address parts of Hegel's system other than his subjective logic). I shall provisionally call my interpretation "epistemic". Let me briefly mention two key passages that fuel my interpretation. Firstly: Hegel's remark in the *Encyclopaedia* that "Everything is a syllogism". Secondly, in the *Science of Logic*, where he writes:

All things are a *syllogism* [Alle Dinge sind der *Schluß*], a universal united through particularity with singularity; surely not a whole made up of *three propositions*. (SL 2010: p.593)

Hegel says explicitly that to be a *Schluß* means that a thing is a unity of a universal through particularity with singularity. A *Schluß* is each thing's unity of the three conceptual moments. An expression of this unity in language as consisting of three propositions is, I claim, an epiphenomenon.[17]

Development of the *Schluß*

The judgement is a unity of two conceptual moments. The *Schluß* is a unity of all three moments: individuality, particularity and universality. That is why Hegel claims that the *Schluß* "is the completely posited concept; it is, therefore, the *rational*" (SL 2010: p.588). The *Schluß* can be expressed in the language of informal logic (which I take to be epiphenomenal) as follows:

$$\frac{\begin{array}{l}\text{A is B.}\\ \text{B is C.}\end{array}}{\text{A is C.}}$$

In its abstract form, the *Schluß* is a connection of term A with term C mediated by term B:

A—B—C

A and C are the extremes and B is the middle term which mediates between them. Let us now look at the development of the *Schluß* and its figures. In the *Schluß* of *existence*, the terms are determined in isolation. The general schema of the first figure is

S—P—U

Singularity is connected with universality through particularity. On my interpretation, this means that a singular object is subsumed under a universal quality by virtue of being compared with a paradigmatic sample. An object is subsumed

---

[17] The same is true of a judgement which applies to things as well. Hegel talks for instance about the judgement of a plant (see above).

under the universal quality "to be one metre long" by virtue of being compared with the standard metre and having the same length. Or an object is subsumed under the universal quality "(to be) sepia" by virtue of being compared with the paradigmatic sample of sepia and having the same colour.

Yet the two connections, S—P and P—U, are supposed to be mediated too. The first figure thus refers to two other figures:

P—S—U
S—U—P

In the second figure, the connection between the particularity and the universality is mediated by the singularity. This means that the paradigm must also be a singular object that is subsumed under the universal quality.[18] In the third figure, the connection between the singularity and the particularity is mediated by the universality. This means that in comparing a singular object with a particular paradigmatic sample, a universal category is presupposed. In our two examples, the categories of length and colour are presupposed when an object is compared with the standard metre or the standard sample of sepia (this point is made by Wittgenstein in his critique of the immediacy of the ostensive definition; cf. my discussion of this idea above).

Let us briefly turn to consider the *mathematical Schluß*, where the moment of particularity is not explicitly mentioned. The abstract form of this *Schluß* is U—U —U. If universal A is equal to universal C and B is equal to universal C, then A is equal to B. The other moments are, however, implicit in this *Schluß*: if two particulars or two singular things are equal to a third one, then they are equal to each other.

Next, I move on to the *Schluß* of *reflection*, where the middle term is posited in its totality. The *Schluß* of reflection is an explicit elaboration of the judgement of reflection, where the singular subject implicitly assumes a genus (SL 2010: p.609) and where the predicate is a relational property involving two paradigmatic samples. In this *Schluß*, this relation is contained in the middle term. More explicitly, the middle term now contains: "(1) *singularity*; (2) but singularity expanded into universality, as an 'all'; (3) the universality that lies at the basis, uniting singularity and abstract universality in itself, *the genus*." (SL 2010: p.609)

---

[18] This is a questionable claim for Wittgenstein (but not for Hegel). The point of §50 of Wittgenstein's *Philosophical Investigations* is that we cannot say that a paradigmatic sample has (or does not have) the quality of which it is the paradigm. We cannot say of the standard metre that it is (or is not) one metre long.

The first figure is the *Schluß* of *allness*, which has the abstract form S—P—U. The middle term is an abstract particularity, i.e. all singulars of a certain kind: "all humans", "all green things", "all regular things"; it is a totality of all concrete things that share a certain property, but that have other properties besides that. The major premise states that these singulars have some other universal property: "mortal", "pleasing", etc. The minor premise states that a singular (e.g. Gaius) belongs to the *alls* picked up in the major premise. The conclusion just states that this singular has the universal property predicated in the major premise ("Gaius is mortal"). This means, however, that the conclusion (S—U) must already be contained in the major premise (P—U). Therefore, the subject and the predicate are connected immediately in the conclusion. The major premise is a universal judgement (e.g. "All humans are mortal"). This judgement involves, as we know, a relation between two compatible paradigms with respect to properties they pick out. But here, unlike in our analysis of the universal judgement, the necessity is not guaranteed by picking out compatible properties, but is mediated by the totality of the middle term. So, for example, we may find out that all regular buildings are beautiful, but we do not define regular things by their being beautiful (we do not compare an individual with the paradigmatic sample of a regular thing with respect to their beauty, but rather with respect to their shapes or other geometrical properties).

The major premise is, in fact, mediated by a totality of singulars. This brings us to the *Schluß* of *induction*, which has the general schema U—S—P. The middle term is the totality of all singulars that have some property in common, which is the one extreme (U). The other extreme (P) is the immediate genus or the subject of the universal judgement. The *Schluß* proceeds as follows: we discover that singulars that are A are also B. We can, so to speak, take the paradigm of B as the necessary condition of being A. For instance, we may find out, by empirical induction, that all animals that are predatory are also dangerous. This may lead us to augment the paradigm of a predatory animal with the property of being dangerous.

In the *Schluß* of *analogy*, S—U—P, the middle term is a concrete universality (U) of a singular thing, or "a singular taken in its universal nature" (SL 2010: p.614). The one extreme is a singular thing (S) and the other is a universal which is also the *nature* of the middle term (P). A singular term is subsumed under a universal that is taken as a singular further subsumed under another particular. The middle term is thus posited as a singular in the one premise and as a universal (of this singular) in the other. But this relation between the singularity and its universal nature must be mediated by a particular, by a paradigm. In Hegel's example, the first premise is "The moon is an earth". "Earth" is here posited as a universal. In the second premise, "The earth is inhabited", "earth" is a singular that is subsumed under the particular "inhabited". Now the relation between the singularity and the universality in the first premise must also be mediated by a particular, by a paradigm. The two mediations are the same. The moon is an earth by virtue of being compared with the paradigmatic earth; and the paradigmatic earth is inhabited by virtue of being compared with the paradigm of being inhabited. Therefore, the moon is inhabited too. Of course, this conclusion holds only if these two paradigms share the same genus (i.e. if being inhabited belongs to the nature of the earth).

The *Schluß* of *necessity* proceeds by further determining the middle term, which is posited as a concrete universal, that is, as a universal in its particularity, as the universal nature of a thing, its genus. The first figure is the *categorical Schluß*, which has the categorical judgement for one or both of its premises (SL 2010: p.618). As we already know, the categorical judgement expresses a relation of subsistence between two paradigms (one is part of the other). The other extreme is a singular whose general nature is captured by the middle term. So, for instance, we may say that "This ring is gold" and "Gold is a metal", which leads to the conclusion that "This ring is metal(lic)". The categorical *Schluß* can have two categorical judgements as its premises. Then it is just a relation of three paradigms, A is B, B is C, ergo A is C. For instance, "Gold is a metal", "Metals are chemical elements", ergo "Gold is a chemical element".

The general scheme of the *hypothetical Schluß* is U—S—P. The one premise is a hypothetical judgement, "If A is, so is B", the other is the being of A. The hypothetical judgement expresses a necessary relation between two concrete universals posited in their particularities, that is, between two paradigms: one is a part of the other. In the hypothetical *Schluß*, this necessary relation is only one extreme mediated by the being of A to the other extreme, the being of B. Hegel concludes that A and B "are two different names for the same basic thing" (SL 2010: p.621). But other things can also be B that are not A (this comes from the underdeterminacy of the hypothetical judgement, where the form of the connection between the subject and the predicate remains indeterminate).

This indeterminacy is sublated in the *disjunctive Schluß*. The major premise is a disjunctive judgement, "A is either B or C or D ...". The subject A is a concrete universal, the predicate is its total determination, i.e. a consecutive application of paradigms. The minor premise "But A is B" / "But A is neither C nor D ..." is a further positive or negative determination of A. The conclusion is the remaining negative or positive determination of A, "Therefore A is neither C nor D ..." / "Therefore A is B". Hegel says that the disjunctive *Schluß* "is in general in the determination of *universality*" (SL 2010: p.623). The universal concept A is further determined as B and neither C nor D. This can be read in two ways: the disjunctive judgement of A, i.e. the complete determination of A is further determined by the minor premise, which may be a result of some experience. One knew that this object is coloured and now comes to know that it is red (and neither blue nor green). Another way of understanding the disjunctive *Schluß* is that it opens up the possibility of combining determinate concepts, i.e. paradigms, into more general concepts. The particular concepts B, C and D—given that they are mutually exclusive and pick out the same general aspect—can be combined into the more general concept A.

Conclusion

Hegel writes at the end of the section "Subjectivity" in the *Science of Logic* that the *Schluß* is the realisation of the concept and that with the *Schluß*, the concept has gained objectivity (SL 2010: p.624). I began the previous section with the crucial claim that each thing is a *Schluß*. I understand Hegel's discussion of the ten forms of the *Schluß* as a kind of proof of this claim, which can now be taken as the claim that what makes up an object is the unity of the singularity and the universality mediated by the particularity. The moment of particularity has a mediating role between the individual and the universal. This is also the role of the paradigm. A paradigm—again taken as a paradigmatic sample together with the method of its application or comparison—is something that defines a universal class and, at the same time, is related to individual elements of this class (via the method of comparison). The general thesis lingering in the background is that we cannot do without paradigms in our epistemic practices. Hegel advanced this thesis by insisting on the moment of particularity. Wittgenstein provided an implicit argument that concepts that are not rooted in our practices with external objects are, in fact, *private* practices and thus epistemically defective.[19]

References

Agamben, Giorgio: *The Use of Bodies: Homo Sacer IV, 2*, Stanford University Press, 2015.
Badiou, Alain: *Saint Paul: the Foundation of Universalism*, Stanford University Press, 2003.
Houlgate, Stephen and Baur, Michael: *A Companion to Hegel*, Blackwell, 2011.

---

[19] I would like to thank Paul Redding for helpful comments and the participants of the conferences Wittgenstein and Hegel: Reevaluation of Difference (Dresden, June 2017) and Themes from Hegel's *Science of Logic* (Istanbul, October 2018) for a stimulating discussion. This work has been supported by the Czech Science Foundation, project no. GA19-16680S.

Mácha, Jakub: *Wittgenstein of Internal and External Relations: Tracing All the Connections*, Bloomsbury, 2015.
Redding, Paul: "The Role of Logic 'Commonly So Called' in Hegel's *Science of Logic*", *British Journal for the History of Philosophy* 22:2, 2014: 281–301.
Stekeler-Weithofer, Pirmin: *Hegels analytische Philosophie. Die Wissenschaft der Logik als kritische Theorie der Bedeutung*, Ferdinand Schöningh, 1992.
Stewart, Jon: "Kierkegaard and Hegel on Faith and Knowledge", in: Houlgate and Baur 2011: pp.501–518.
Warminski, Andrzej: *Readings in Interpretation. Hölderlin, Hegel, Heidegger*, University of Minnesota Press, 1986.
Winfield, Richard Dien: *From Concept to Objectivity: Thinking Through Hegel's Subjective Logic*, Routledge, 2006.
Winfield, Richard Dien: "Hegel's Solution to the Mind-Body Problem", in: Houlgate and Baur 2011: pp.227–242.
Žižek, Slavoj: *Less than Nothing: Hegel and the Shadow of Dialectical Materialism*, Verso, 2012.

Wilhelm Lütterfelds
„In der Sprache" (Wittgenstein) und im „Begriff" (Hegel) „wird alles ausgetragen" – Das Sprachspiel des Idealismus

Abstract Die folgenden Überlegungen möchten bestimmte sprachphilosophische Einsichten des späteren Wittgenstein als einen Sprachidealismus verstehen, der verblüffende Parallelen zum dialektischen Begriffsidealismus Hegels hat. Sie gehen nicht der sprachkritischen Auseinandersetzung Wittgensteins mit dem Idealismus nach, und auch nicht dem Verhältnis von Begriffs-Idealismus und Philosophie der Sprache oder Hegels spekulativem Satz und dessen grammatischer Struktur.

Wittgenstein's Satzwiederholung und Hegels Wahrheitsmaßstab

Ausgangspunkt ist eine zentrale These beider Denker; nämlich einmal Wittgensteins Feststellung, daß man „die Tatsache [...], die einem Satz entspricht (seine Übersetzung ist)", nicht „beschreiben" kann, „ohne eben den Satz zu wiederholen", sodaß dies in der Tat innersprachlich verhandelt wird – Wittgenstein nennt es die „Kantische[] Lösung des Problems der Philosophie", die dann – in der nur möglichen Satzwiederholung – freilich auch die fundamentale „Grenze der Sprache" zeigt[1]; und zum anderen Hegels These, daß die Wahrheitsüberprüfung allen bewußten Wissens um gegenständliches Sein eines Wahrheitsmaßstabes bedarf. Und dieser besteht darin, daß „das auf das Wissen Bezogene", sein propositionaler Gehalt, zugleich das *„Ansichsein"* ist, d. h. das vom Wissen Unterschiedene, das „auch außer" der Beziehung auf das bewußte Wissen existiert, als die *„Wahrheit"* und deren Maßstab, welcher das Bewußtsein quasi begrenzt. Doch

---

[1] VB: S.27. Die „Grenze der Sprache" wird dann nur so durch sprachexterne Tatsachen gezogen, daß dies „von innen", d.h. in der Sprache durch Wiederholung desselben Satzes, der begrenzt, geschieht und dessen Bedeutung dann die Tatsache selbst ist, was noch eine differenzierte Analyse der beiden Satzvorkommnisse erforderlich macht. Dies entspricht Kants Begrenzung der Erfahrung durch die Erfahrung der objektiven Realität der Erscheinung. Vgl. zum Bild einer Begrenzung der Sprache „von innen" (PU: §119).

diese „Unterscheidung" von Wissen und Ansich ist selber wiederum Inhalt des bewußten Wissens, sie „fällt in es" – so, wie die sprachexterne Tatsache als Grenze zugleich in die Sprache fällt, was freilich nur im selbstreflexiven Denken erfaßt wird (PdG: S.75 ff.). Ist aber das Ansich als Wahrheitsmaßstab auch selber Bewußtseinsinhalt, dann besteht die Wahrheitsüberprüfung des bewußten Wissens in einer „Vergleichung" desselben „mit sich selbst", was allerdings nur in der Operation einer – noch zu erläuternden – Selbstwiederholung möglich ist. Einfaches Beispiel im Alltag ist etwa die Wahrheitsüberprüfung einer Wahrnehmung, die dadurch geschieht, daß man nochmal hinschaut.[2]

Eine solche Wiederholung hat freilich bei Wittgenstein eine eigentümliche Struktur. Während nämlich eine Aussage für ihren propositionalen Gehalt zunächst nur behauptet, daß er wahr ist, was verifiziert werden muß, so daß sie in ihrem Wahrheitswert vorerst offen ist, also möglicherweise falsch und ohne Tatsachenentsprechung, während sie also quasi eine wahrheitsoffene Semantik hat, ist die Bedeutung des wiederholten Satzes die entsprechende Tatsache selbst, weshalb Wittgenstein die Tatsache auch als „Übersetzung" des Satzes auffassen kann. Behauptender Satz und Tatsachensatz sind zu unterscheiden – in ihrem Wahrheitswert –, obwohl sie in ihrer Semantik identisch sind, so daß sich die Entsprechungsfrage nicht mehr stellt. Darin, in dieser Wiederholung, liegt (in Hegels Sprechweise) eine „Vergleichung" der Satzsemantik „mit sich selbst".

Diese Differenz der vergleichenden Wiederholung betrifft bei Hegel einerseits das propositionale Wissen um den Gegenstand, wie er *„für ein Bewußtsein"* ist (bzw. den *„Begriff"* betrifft); und andererseits das *„Ansichsein"* des Gegenstandes „außer dieser Beziehung" (das seiende *„Wahre"*), das aber gleichwohl, als Ansichsein, auch *„für"* das Bewußtsein ist.

Deshalb kann Hegels Wahrheitsprüfung – als doppeltes Verfahren – darin bestehen, einmal „zuzusehen, ob der Begriff dem Gegenstande entspricht". Da jedoch auch der bewußtseinsexterne Gegenstand, also das Ansich, begrifflicher Inhalt des Bewußtseins ist, d. h. „in seinem Sein sein Begriff" (PdG: S.54), und da – umgekehrt – bewußtes Wissen ja einen gegenständlichen Gehalt hat, „so besteht die Prüfung [zugleich] darin, daß wir zusehen, ob der Gegenstand seinem Begriffe entspricht" (PdG: S.77). Und genau dies kann nur durch die vergleichende Wiederholung des Begriffs geschehen. Wenn Hegel freilich behauptet, man sehe wohl, „daß beides dasselbe" sei (ebd.), dann übergeht er in dieser seiner Identitätsthese eine fundamentale Differenz. Bei Wittgenstein ist es der Unterschied

---

[2] Genau diese Reflexion auf die Bewußtseins- und Sprachimmanenz der Differenz (!) von Wirklichkeit und sprachgebundenem Wissen, die für Hegel jede Fehlform eines bloß subjektiven, realismus-skeptischen Idealismus (als bloße Alternative zum Realismus) ausschließt, fehlt dem Neuen Realismus völlig. Vgl. Gabriel 2013: S.146 ff.

der beiden Vorkommnisse desselben Satzes, der einmal in einer (möglichen) Entsprechung zu einer Tatsache steht, und zum anderen (in der Wiederholung als Tatsachensatz) diese zu seinem Bedeutungsgehalt hat. Dadurch negiert der Begriff der Tatsache zugleich selbstwidersprüchlich seinen eigenen begrifflichen Gehalt. Die entsprechende Differenz findet sich in Hegels Ansich: „seiend [...] außer" der Beziehung aufs Bewußtsein und – auch dies wiederum – in der Bewußtseinsbeziehung bzw. „*für es*" (PdG: S.76f.).³

Für das Verifikationsverfahren bedeutet die vergleichende Satzwiederholung, daß auch dieses Verfahren „*In der Sprache* [...] ausgetragen" wird (PhGr: §95). Wenn Wittgenstein dann an der Wahrheitskonzeption der Übereinstimmung eines Satzes mit Tatsachen festhält, dann kann er einen Satz nicht deswegen wahr nennen, weil ihm eine Tatsache entspricht. Sondern genau umgekehrt: Ein Satz ist wahr, weil er als Tatsachensatz wiederholbar ist – die hochproblematische Übereinstimmungsmetaphysik wird zu einer grammatischen Bemerkung, die es erst wegen der primären Satzwiederholung möglich macht, von einer Übereinstimmung und Tatsachenentsprechung zu reden, und die „zeigt", was das heißen soll. Die Frage nach der Wirklichkeitsübereinstimmung bewegt sich insofern „schon im Kreise" (ÜG: §§191ff.). Denn die Wahrheit des fraglichen Satzes wird in seiner Wiederholung erst festgestellt und wird doch eben darin bereits vorausgesetzt – wozu sonst seine Wiederholung?

Diese Kreisbewegung macht für Hegel „die Natur der Wissenschaftlichkeit überhaupt" aus. Durch sie werden „Gedanken", die im üblichen Verständnis auf externe Sachverhalts-Objekte bezogen werden, erst zu „Begriffen", indem sie in dieser Kreisbeziehung in „Selbstbewegungen" stehen (PdG: S.37; vgl. S.156).

Wenn Hegel in seiner Identitätsthese diese Kreisbewegung nun idealistisch kurzschließt, ferner zu einer gegenständlichen Selbstentfremdung des Geistes verschärft, worin dieser wiederum zu sich selber zurückkehrt (PdG: S.38f.), so findet sich bei Wittgenstein durchaus eine sprachphilosophische Entsprechung. Seine Feststellung „Die Grammatik ist keiner Wirklichkeit Rechenschaft schuldig. Die grammatischen Regeln bestimmen erst die Bedeutung (konstituieren sie) und sind darum keiner Bedeutung verantwortlich und insofern willkürlich" (PhGr: §133), so liegt darin durchaus ein Sprachidealismus vor, in dem die „Verbindung zwischen ‚Sprache und Wirklichkeit' [...] durch die Worterklärungen gemacht

---

3 Adorno sieht bekanntlich darin die Einsicht Kants, die Hegelkritisch zu lesen ist. Vgl. Adorno 1966: S.174ff – Wenn das Ansich bzw. die Tatsache als Maßstab der Wahrheitsüberprüfung bewußten Wissens zugleich selber Inhalt des Bewußtseins, für dieses, bzw. Begriff ist, dann hat in dieser „dialektische[n] Bewegung" der Maßstab sich selber verändert, und es ist ein „neue[r] Gegenstand" entstanden, ein neues Ansich bzw. Wahres, was Hegel – anti-empiristisch – „Erfahrung" nennt (PdG: S.78).

[werden], – welche zur Sprachlehre gehören", als sprachliche Muster (PhGr: §55), die freilich nicht die Notwendigkeit der Hegelschen Verbindung des Begriffs besitzen. Doch auch Wittgensteins Priorität der Grammatik – d. h., eine Tatsache ist die paradigmatische Bedeutung ihres Ausdrucks in einem Sprachspiel – ist zugleich an ein externes Ansich rückgebunden: „Es ist immer von Gnaden der Natur, wenn man etwas weiß" (ÜG: §505, vgl. §134), also abhängig von sprachvorgängigen Tatsachen, ohne dass diese Paradoxie thematisch wird. Deshalb muß man auch Wittgensteins Unterstellung, man könne durchaus wegen der Rechenschaftslosigkeit der Grammatik „im Sattel [eines Sprachspiels] bleibe[n], wenn die Tatsachen noch so sehr bockten" (ÜG: §616), relativieren: Man bleibt nur, wenn die bockenden Tatsachen sprachspielkommensurabel übersetzt sind, als „alternative Tatsachen".

Apriorische Übereinstimmung von (begrifflicher) Sprache und Welt und deren implizite Falschheit

Wird alles in der Sprache bzw. im Begriff ausgetragen, dann auch die Frage nach der „Übereinstimmung, Harmonie, von Gedanke und Wirklichkeit", also auch nach dem Verhältnis von wahr und falsch. Zwar kann man etwas „fälschlich" als „*rot*" beschreiben, das in Wirklichkeit braun ist (PU: §429). So berechtigt diese feste Unterscheidung zwischen wahren und falschen Sätzen „ohne Gemeinschaft" (PdG: S.40) auch ist, wobei man den falschen Satz in einen wahren überführen kann, indem man seine inhaltliche „Ungleichheit" mit der Wirklichkeit in eine „Gleichheit" mit derselben verwandelt (PdG: S.40 f.) wird. Aber diese „Übereinstimmung" wird durch eine sprachlich a priori bestimmte Wirklichkeit vorgegeben: So kann man „jemandem das Wort ‚rot' im Satz ‚Das ist nicht rot' erklären", indem man „dazu auf etwas Rotes zeig[t]" (PU: §429), also nicht auf etwas sprachlich Bestimmungsloses. Das Falsche wäre dann – so Hegel – „das [gehaltlich] andere, das Negative" zu einer begrifflich bestimmten Sache, „die als Inhalt des Wissens das Wahre ist" (PdG: S.40).

Damit liegt den inhaltsbezogenen Wahrheitswerten von Sprache und Begriff, deren Gehalt realitätskonform sein kann oder auch nicht, was a posteriori zu entscheiden ist, eine apriorische Wahrheits-Harmonie zugrunde. Und diese „liegt" eben auch dann vor, „wenn ich fälschlich sage, etwas sei *rot*", während „es doch [sprachlich] immerhin nicht *rot* ist", sondern etwa (sprachlich) braun (!) (PU: §429).

Umgekehrt, inhaltlich wahre Sätze, die mit der Wirklichkeit, der Substanz, übereinstimmen, sind für Hegel selber auch in bestimmter Weise falsch, d. h. ihr inhaltlich wahrer Gehalt weist in sich eine unterscheidende Ungleichheit, das Negative, auf. Weniger deshalb, weil dieser Gehalt immer nur einige Bestimmungen der Sache treffen kann. Sondern vor allem deshalb, weil gerade auch der wahre substantielle Gehalt des Wissens bzw. Satzes ein „*einfaches* Unterscheiden" und insofern „als Falsches ein Moment der Wahrheit" ist (PdG: S.40f.). Verständlich wird dies, wenn man Hegels idealistische These zugrunde legt, daß alles substantiell Wirkliche, das Inhalt und Bedeutung wahren sprachlichen Wissens ist, bereits an sich „wesentlich Subjekt" ist, „in seinem Sein sein Begriff" (PdG: S.23, 28, 39, 53f.) Dann ist aber das Wahre, die substantielle Wirklichkeit, dasjenige, worin sich eine Bedeutung oder ein Begriff (wie „substantielle Wirklichkeit", „Seiendes", „Tisch", „Person"), auf sich selber bezieht und mit sich selber gleich ist – wie im Sich-Wissen des Subjekts dieses auf sich selber. Doch eben dies ist eine negative Selbstbeziehung, die nur in einer gleichzeitigen Unterscheidung seiner von sich, also von einem Anderen, das sie freilich bereits selber ist, vorliegt: was wiederum ein „*einfaches* Unterscheiden" ist ohne fremde unterschiedene Teile, d.h. ein „Selbst", das zugleich keinen Unterschied hat im Wissen um sich (PdG: S.40).

Das Beispiel: Der Begriff „Hase" nimmt in seinem begrifflichen Gehalt in der deutschen Sprache auf einen Hasen Bezug, und nicht auf irgendeinen Hasen-Teil (Quine; hier gibt es keine Unerforschlichkeit der Referenz), also auch nicht auf irgendein X-Objekt, auf das man ja nicht einmal in einer ostensiven Definition zeigen könnte (vgl. PU: §§6, 28ff.). Ersichtlich ist in dieser Hasen-Referenz letztere (idealistisch) ihr sprachlicher Begriff von sich (Wortwiederholung), und in dessen intensionalem Gehalt ist sie mit sich identisch[4]; also nicht mit etwas Anderem, sondern mit sich (!), womit sie bereits zirkulär a priori identisch ist. Deshalb liegt in der Referenz von „Hase" auf einen Hasen ein Unterschied vor, der nach Hegel keiner ist, ein „einfache[r]" Unterschied oder eine negative Beziehung (nicht auf Anderes, sondern) auf sich, die innerhalb einer apriorischen „Übereinstimmung, Harmonie, von Gedanken [Sprache] und Wirklichkeit" existiert.

---

4 L. Wittgenstein hält den Satz der Identität der Dinge mit sich für „nutzlos"; er suggeriere, als paßten die Dinge in ihre „eigene Form hinein" (PU: §216). Was er freilich übergeht, ist, daß er im Ding ja schon etwas sprach-begrifflich Bestimmtes vor sich hat, für das eine Trennung von Ding und Bestimmung nur möglich ist, wenn Bestimmen „etwas Ähnliches" ist „wie einem Ding ein Namenstäfelchen anheften" (PU: §15). Doch wenn man auf die Innersprachlichkeit dieses Vorgangs reflektiert, stellt sich sehr wohl die Frage nach der Identität des Dinges mit sich in dieser seiner begrifflich-sprachlichen Bestimmung.

Das Aspektmodell der Dingbestimmungen von Wittgenstein statt Hegels Falsches am Wahren

Wenn Hegel diese „Ungleichheit" als Falsches auffaßt, dann handelt es sich dabei nicht um den alternativen, auf die Satzproposition bezogenen Wahrheitswert zum Wahren, der (in beider Einheitsrelation) in der Wahrheitstafel von Wittgensteins Traktat vorkommt. Sondern dieses Falsche ist „ein Moment der Wahrheit", aber kein „Bestandteil". Deshalb besagt Hegels These vom Falschen am Wahren auch nicht den Unsinn einer beliebigen Vertauschbarkeit von wahr und falsch.

Im Hasenbeispiel besteht diese „Ungleichheit [...] als das Negative" im (!) Wahren (PdG: S.41), also nicht: zum Wahren, darin, daß der Inhalt der begrifflichen Bedeutung „Hase" aus unterschiedenen, ungleichen, bestimmten Teilen besteht. In seiner wahren Referenz ist er zusammengesetzt – aber wegen seiner Einfachheit nicht aus Hasen, sondern aus Hasen-Teilen (wie Ohren, Beinen, Rücken etc.). In Wittgensteins Beispiel der platonischen *„Urelemente"* wäre dann Hase ein solches Einfaches, das nicht erklärt, sondern nur benannt werden könnte. Dabei kann die Art und Weise, wie er als zusammengesetzt gilt, ja nach Hinsicht variieren (z. B. Farben, Formen, Moleküle). Wittgenstein erläutert dies am Beispiel des „Sessels", des „Schachbretts" oder des „Gesichtsbildes eines Baumes" (PU: §46f.). Es ist dieses „Negative", diese vielfältige „Unterscheidung und Bestimmung des [einfachen, substantiellen, referentiellen] Inhalts", die Hegel nun „als Falsches" auffaßt, das damit „ein Moment der Wahrheit" ist – also nichts Alternatives dazu (PdG: S.40f.). Denn dann ist die „Ungleichheit [...] als das Negative [...] im Wahren", dem mitsichselber Gleichen, genauer: als das Negative in seinen verschiedenen inhaltlichen Bestimmungen – als solches „noch unmittelbar [im Wahren] vorhanden". Und es liegt eine dialektische *„Einheit"* des Wahren und Falschen vor, die beide ihre Bedeutung nur in und nicht *„außer ihrer Einheit"* haben (PdG: S.41), wie etwa in einer Wahrheitstafel und deren externer Verknüpfung.

Auf dieses Problem, daß etwa „Besen" ebenso auf etwas mit sich Gleiches, Einfaches, in der Wiederholung: auf einen Besen, referiert wie auf einen vielfach unterscheidbaren und bestimmbaren Inhalt (Stiel, Bürste) (PU: §§60ff.) – also auf Falsches (Ungleiches) am Wahren (Gleichen) – , stößt Wittgenstein in der Frage, ob die Aussage über einen in seinen Bestandteilen analysierten Besen (Stiel, Bürste usw.) „besser" verstanden wird als in ihrer „unanalysierte[n] Form"; ob sie nicht semantisch die „fundamentalere" sei – oder ob es sich um „den gleichen Sinn" in „zwei verschiedene[n] Formen desselben Spiels" handelt.

Wittgenstein stellt beide Aussagen, die analysierte und die nichtanalysierte, die nur vom Besen spricht, derart nebeneinander, daß beide einen verschiedenen

„Aspekt der Sache" wiedergeben, wobei der jeweils andere dabei „verlorengeht" (PU: §63). Doch in diesem Aspekt-Modell wird die Frage nach der referentiellen, semantischen Identität der Sache (Besen) in den unterschiedlichen Aspekten gar nicht mehr gestellt und auch nicht die nach der vorausgesetzten Identität „desselben Spiels". Für Hegel handelt es sich dabei um das Hinsichten-Modell des Verstandesdenkens, in dem die Frage: „Aspekt wovon?" offen bleibt – also die Frage nach der referentiell mit sich selber gleichen Sache, die Hegel mit seiner These der Einheit vom Falschen (den analysierten, ungleichen Inhalten) am Wahren (dem referentiell mit sich Gleichen) beantwortet. Diese dialektische Selbstwidersprüchlichkeit findet sich – in Trivialform – im Paradox der Analyse wieder, die entweder falsch ist (weil anderer Gehalt) oder nichtssagend (weil dasselbe). Wittgenstein möchte diese „große Frage, die hinter all diesen Betrachtungen steht", mit seinem Konzept der antiessentialistischen Familienähnlichkeit beantworten (PU: §§65 ff.), in dem es positivistisch „gar nicht Eines" Gemeinsames, Identisches gibt. Aber dies müßte dann nicht bloß für all die vielen Sachen gelten, die verschieden sind, aber mit demselben Wort bezeichnet werden (z. B. „Spiel"), sondern auch für die vielen ungleichen Inhalte einer Sache, auf die mit demselben sprachlichen Begriff Bezug genommen wird: Wenn etwa ein Teil eines Autos (z. B. eine Seitentür) beschädigt wurde und durch ein neues ersetzt wird, wurde darin (Hegel: in diesem Negativen) auch das Auto selbst beschädigt und nicht nur ein Teil von ihm, was seinen (!) Wert schmälert (Unfallauto), was ihn aber wegen der neuen Seitentür gerade vergrößern müsste. Autoverkäufer handeln nach der platonischen Einsicht, daß die seienden Dinge ein nicht zusammengesetztes Einfaches sind, das doch nur als zusammengesetztes in seinen Teilen existiert – als einfaches und (!) zusammengesetztes Ganzes.

Wenn alles in Sprache und Begriff ausgetragen wird und dies auch Folgen hat für eine idealistische Konzeption von wahr und falsch, die neben die auf den propositionalen Satz bezogene Tafel der Wahrheitswerte tritt, so lassen sich die großen Differenzen natürlich auch nicht übersehen, die nahezu jedes philosophische Thema betreffen. So auch die Frage, worin das idealistische Fundament des Wahrheitsverständnisses besteht. Zwar bietet sich Kants Konzept der Anschauungsformen und Kategorien als Möglichkeitsbedingungen wahrer Wirklichkeitserkenntnis an, aber es bleibt in der Differenz von Erscheinung und Ding an sich hängen. Unbefriedigend ist auch der gegenseitige Prioritäten-Zirkel von Realismus-Idealismus in Fichtes früher „Wissenschaftslehre" mit seiner bloß postulierten Lösung eines aufzulösenden Ziels. Hegels metaphysische Identität von Denken und Sein wiederum kann zwar die Einheit des Falschen am Wahren verständlich machen. Aber daß die daseiende Substanz „wesentlich Subjekt" ist „oder der Begriff" und damit die „Trennung" von Wissen und Wahrheit „überwunden" –, dies wird in der „Phänomenologie des Geistes" eben nicht „vollkommen gezeigt", wie Hegel behauptet (PdG: S.39), was die These vom Falschen am Wahren letztlich offen läßt.

Die sprachpragmatische Begründung der apriorischen Harmonie

Wittgenstein vertritt in *Über Gewißheit* auf den ersten Blick eine sprachpragmatische Lösung. Auf dem Hintergrund eines übernommenen Weltbildes, seiner Bezugssysteme und Lebensformen bilden wir in unserem sprachlichen Handeln der alltäglichen Erfahrung wie auch der Wissenschaften ein Verständnis von wahr und falsch aus, für das sich die Frage nach der Wahrheit selber nicht mehr stellt – aber nicht, weil diese nur zirkulär, dogmatisch oder unbeantwortbar ist, sondern weil jenes Wahrheits-Verständnis „eine unwankende Grundlage" all unserer Sprachspiele ist (ÜG: §403). „Die *Wahrheit* gewisser Erfahrungssätze" bedeutet, daß diese „zu unserem Bezugssystem" gehört (ÜG: §83) und „eine[] Norm der Beschreibung" kennzeichnet (ÜG: §167), die von einer inhaltlichen Aussage im Sprachspiel zu unterscheiden ist. Wird deren Wahrheit durch diese „Norm" begründet, dann „ist der Grund nicht *wahr*, noch falsch" (ÜG: §205). Ein solches Sprachspielfundament stellt dann keine „unbegründete" Wahrheitsvoraussetzung dar (ÜG: §111). Es ist vielmehr eine sprachliche „Handlungsweise", auf die der Gedanke der Wahrheits-Begründung, der Vernunft und der Rechtfertigung nicht anwendbar ist, ohne daß sie deswegen unvernünftig oder unbegründet wäre; sie „steht da – wie unser Leben" (ÜG: §559). Für dieses „*Handeln*, welches am Grunde des Sprachspiels liegt" (ÜG: §205), hat „die Begründung ein Ende" (ÜG: §563), und es bleibt nur die Feststellung: „*dieses Sprachspiel wird gespielt*" – jenseits jeder „Erklärung" (PU: §654).

Bei Wittgensteins Position handelt es sich offenbar um eine sprachpragmatische Sprachspielkonzeption, die ein begründungs- und wahrheitsneutrales Fundament hat und in der die Wahrheitswerte nur sprachspielimmanent und auf der Grundlage von dessen Weltbild vorkommen. Sprachspiele selber tragen insofern Züge einer gewissen Irrationalität und einer erklärungsoffenen Faktizität. Die selbstreflexive Frage Hegels nach der Wahrheit dieser Position wird nicht gestellt und auch nicht die nach einem universalistischen Zug des inner- und interkulturellen Sprachspiel-Pluralismus – abgesehen von dessen Konfliktstruktur (vgl. ÜG: §608 ff.).

Hegels Identitätsthese als Paradigmensatz des idealistischen Sprachspiels

Was hat das nun mit einem Sprachidealismus der Sprachspiele zu tun? Dieser gerät in den Blick, wenn man mit Wittgenstein die Frage nach den einfachen Urelementen eines Sprachspiels stellt und darunter dasjenige versteht, „Was es [darin], scheinbar, geben *muß*", also ein notwendiges Sein hat; „denn *wäre* es nicht, so könnte man es auch nicht einmal nennen und also gar nichts von ihm aussagen" (PU: §50).

Sprachspiele hätten dann ein ontologisches Fundament – Seiendes, das substantiell mit Eigenschaften, als Tatsache oder Ereignis existiert und worauf die Sprache benennend und beschreibend Bezug nimmt; was aber nichtidealistisch zu lesen wäre. Wird jedoch der Sprachimmanenz eines solchen Fundaments Rechnung getragen, dann werden die notwendig existierenden, einfachen Urelemente eines Sprachspiels zu etwas, von dem wir sagen müssen: Es „gehört zur Sprache" (PU: §50). Sie sind aber darin nicht etwas „Dargestelltes", dem „eine merkwürdige Eigenschaft", wie notwendiges Sein, zugeschrieben würde. Sondern sie sind in einem Sprachspiel „*Mittel* der Darstellung" bzw. „Instrument[e] der Sprache". Der korrekte Ausdrucksgebrauch ist in einem Sprachspiel nämlich an bestimmte kriterielle Regeln gebunden, denen wiederum ein „Muster", ein „Paradigma" für diesen Gebrauch zugrundeliegt, „womit verglichen wird", ob die Ausdrucksverwendung korrekt ist. Das „Urmeter in Paris" oder Farbmuster sind für Wittgenstein solche paradigmatischen Darstellungsmittel, die ja für jeden korrekten Ausdrucksgebrauch zur Verfügung stehen müssen, etwa auch im Sprachspiel des Messens oder der Farbbeschreibung. Und es ist dann nicht sinnvoll, solchen Ausdrucksmustern die Eigenschaft (etwa analytisch) zuzusprechen oder abzusprechen. Das Muster für blau z. B. ist selber weder blau noch nicht blau – was freilich wegen seiner Vergleichsfunktion in platonische Paradoxien führt.

Der Idealismuskontext entsteht nun dadurch, daß eine solche sprachliche Paradigmentheorie die „Darstellungsweise" eines Sprachspiels betrifft, und sie läßt sich mit Kant als eine sprachliche Bedingung seiner Möglichkeit auffassen, die zugleich eine Möglichkeitsbedingung für die so semantisch bestimmte Wirklichkeit ist, auf die Bezug genommen wird.

Faßt man Hegels Dialektik als ein idealistisches Sprachspiel der Philosophie auf, dann stellt sich für es – in Wittgensteins Denkweise – auch die Frage nach seinen Urelementen; nach dem also, was es neben seinem Denken in mentalem Vokabular geben muß, damit es gespielt werden kann. Dabei kann es sich nur um ein bewußtseins- und begriffsimmanentes Fundament handeln, worin der feste

Dualismus bzw. „Unterschied" von Vorstellung und gegenständlichem an sich Seienden verabschiedet ist (PdG: S.156). Denn dieses Fundament gehört dann zum begrifflichen Denken. Aber nicht derart, daß seine Elemente etwas inhaltlich, thesenhaft Gedachtes und als notwendig Begriffenes wären. Sondern sie sind Mittel oder Instrumente des begreifenden Denkens, und sie kennzeichnen als Muster idealistischen Denkens dessen Art und Weise oder Denkform: sie sind deren Möglichkeitsbedingung.

Das fundamentale Element des Sprachspiels der Dialektik liegt nun in Hegels Feststellung, „das Wahre nicht als *Substanz*, sondern ebensosehr als *Subjekt* aufzufassen und auszudrücken" oder als „Sein, welches in Wahrheit *Subjekt*" ist (PdG: S.23; vgl. S.28, 39, 53) oder „sein Begriff" (ebd. S.54).

Dabei handelt es sich dann nicht – primär – um eine inhaltliche Aussage; etwa mit der (prädikativen) These, daß alles substantiell Seiende trivialerweise begrifflich bestimmt ist, oder (als Identitätsthese), daß es dasselbe wie sein subjektiver Begriff ist; sondern um eine Feststellung der notwendigen instrumentellen Funktion, welche der subjektive Begriff in jenem dialektischen Sprachspiel hat, das die Wirklichkeit des substantiell Seienden darstellt. Sie gibt das paradigmatische Muster dieser Darstellung an: *So* wird dargestellt; nämlich derart, daß alles substantiell Seiende (das Inhalt bzw. Gestalt des Bewußtseins, des Selbstbewußtseins und des Geistes ist) in seiner Darstellung sein subjektiver Begriff ist – oder „selbstisch" (PdG: S.39). Dies ist eine Möglichkeitsbedingung einer solchen Darstellung, also selber nichts begrifflich inhaltlich Dargestelltes – ihre Formulierung betrifft insofern die grammatische Form der Darstellung. Nur in ihr gibt es eine aussagbare Referenz auf die Wirklichkeit, ohne daß von ihr abstrahiert werden könnte.

Was heißt das nun genauer – einen Gegenstand „in *Begriffen*" denken (PdG: S.156)? Das Sprachspiel der „Vorstellungen" kann man zur Präzisierung heranziehen; das bloße begriffliche Subsumtionsmodell (Etwas fällt unter einen allgemeinen Begriff) ist dafür nicht hinreichend. Das „*Seiende*", das im Sprachspiel der „Vorstellungen" bewußt ist, hat darin ein einseitig festes, vom Bewußtsein „unterschiedene[s] Ansichsein", es ist „etwas anderes [...] als das Bewußtsein" (ebd.), ohne Gemeinschaft mit diesem. In Wittgensteins *Traktat* sind das die Tatsachen der Welt mit ihren Sachverhalten und Dingen. Auf sie nehmen wir dann abbildend (vorstellend) in unserem Denken und Sprechen wahr oder falsch Bezug. Bild und Tatsachen sind durch einen Unterschied wie bei zwei verschiedenen Tatsachen getrennt – so ist auch die Vorstellung eine Art psychologische Tatsache (etwa im Kopf). Und was entscheidend ist: Dieser Unterschied ist selber kein Sachverhalt, der Inhalt des gedanklichen und sprachlichen Bildes ist, er wird selber nicht abgebildet.

Genau deswegen ist das Sprachspiel der „Vorstellungen" defizitär. Denn wenn wir z. B. Dinge an einem anderen Ort sehen, als wo wir uns befinden (was a priori der Fall ist), dann ist auch der räumliche Unterschied zwischen ihnen und uns Inhalt unserer Wahrnehmung – oder gesehen (vgl. Kant, *Kritik der reinen Vernunft*, B38).

Es ist dieser Sachverhalt, der das „*Denken* [...] nicht in Vorstellungen [...], sondern in *Begriffen*" kennzeichnet. Denn für das begreifende Denken existiert der „Gegenstand" zwar „in einem [vom subjektiven Denken] unterschiedenen Ansichsein", „welches [jedoch] unmittelbar für das Bewußtsein kein unterschiedenes von ihm ist" – „Ansichsein" ist nämlich ebenso bewußte Bedeutung seines Ausdrucks wie begrifflicher Gehalt; umgekehrt: „ein Begriff [...] ist zugleich ein *Seiendes*" – aber nicht als bloß subjektive Realität, sondern als Begriff des Ansich. Dann fällt aber der „Unterschied" zwischen dem externen Ansich des Gegenstandes und seinem bewußten Begriff bzw. der bewußten Bedeutung desselben als „bestimmter Inhalt" selber ins Bewußtsein und in den Begriff des Gegenstandes – und das heißt: ihn (in dieser Bewegung) begrifflich denken, in dieser „Einheit" der begrifflichen Bewegung (PdG: S.156).

Damit ist das Paradigma der idealistisch-dialektischen Denkform angegeben. Daß das substantielle Sein „wesentlich Subjekt" ist oder „sein Begriff" (PdG: S.28, 54) ist zwar sprachlich eine inhaltliche Identitäts-Aussage des Hegelschen Idealismus. Aber diese Identität von Substanz und Subjekt ist ein instrumentelles Mittel im dialektischen Begreifen des Seienden. Denn dieses gibt es nur als „Bewegung" des Gegenstandes in und zu seinem mit sich identischen Begriff – von seinem begriffsexternen „*Ansichsein*" zu dessen begriffsinternem „*Fürsichsein*"[5], das Hegel freilich noch subjektivistisch zur „Einheit" des freien, weil selbstbezüglichen „Fürsichsein[s]" zuspitzt (PdG: S.156). Damit formulieren jene Sätze eine wesentliche Rolle, die diese Bewegung vom Ansich zur Begriffsidentität im Sprachspiel der Dialektik spielt: In dessen Sprachspiel ist sie das instrumentelle Paradigma, Muster oder auch die Bedingung, nach dem es gespielt werden muß, soll es möglich und korrekt sein. Jene Sätze werden damit zu grammatischen Sätzen, die den korrekten Gebrauch der Begriffe und Ausdrücke (Substanz, Subjekt; Sein, Begriff) in der Einheit ihrer Bewegung im Sprachspiel der Dialektik angeben.

Abschließend ein triviales Beispiel aus dem analytischen Denken: Der Satz „‚Tisch' bedeutet Tisch" ist zwar auch eine sprachliche Bedeutungsangabe. Aber sie ist innersprachlich und soll in Tisch doch gerade den sprachexternen ansich

---

5 Dieser „Bewegung" verdankt sich die Abfolge der „Gestalten" der „Phänomenologie des Geistes", die für Hegel eine dialektische Erfahrung ist (PdG: S.80).

seienden Gegenstand selbst bedeuten. Damit gerät man in eine dialektische Semantik. Entsprechendes gilt für die Feststellung „‚p' ist wahr genau dann, wenn p". Denn es muß sich bei letzterem um ein wahres p handeln, dessen ausgesagte Bedeutung also der außersprachliche Sachverhalt selbst – an sich – ist.

Literatur

Adorno, Theodor W.: *Negative Dialektik*, Suhrkamp, 1966.
Gabriel, Markus: *Warum es die Welt nicht gibt*, Ullstein, 2013.
Wittgenstein, Ludwig: *Über Gewißheit*, Suhrkamp, 1971 (ÜG).
Wittgenstein, Ludwig: *Vermischte Bemerkungen*, Suhrkamp, 1977 (VB).
Wittgenstein, Ludwig: *Philosophische Grammatik*, Suhrkamp, 1989 (PhGr).
Wittgenstein, Ludwig: *Philosophische Untersuchungen*, Suhrkamp, 1989 (PU).

Subject Index

„and so on" 97, 170, 204, 269
a priori *see* analytic/synthetic, philosophy
ability *see* disposition
absolute (*das Absolute*) 64, 66, 142, 145, 146, 151, 182, 196, 221–23, 265, 268–71, 304, 360, 361, 372; *see also* absolute *under* idea
abstraction 9, 31, 34–36, 46, 122, 126, 149, 172, 189, 209, 210, 280, 316
acquaintance 66, 108, 175
action 11, 35, 37, 41–45, 92–98, 101, 193, 201–208, 266, 299
actualism, modal 9, 11; *see also* Findlay, John Niemeyer
actuality (*Wirklichkeit*) 9, 74, 94, 119–139
aesthetics 141–156, 301, 370
agreement/disagreement 11, 13, 89, 97, 98, 103–106, 110, 112, 116, 147, 167, 193, 210, 217, 218, 282–85, 333, 390, 393
algebra 164, 207
ambiguity/synonymy 222, 223, 266, 359, 361
analogy 27, 104, 113, 243, 257, 267, 334, 337, 388
– syllogism of *see* analogy *under* syllogism/inference (*Schluß*)
analysis *see* logical analysis
analytic/synthetic 213, 287, 311–20; *see also* analytic *under* definition, analytic *under* philosophy
anthropology 326; *see also* human being
antinomy, cosmological/second (Kant) 311–321
appearance (*Erscheinung*) 44, 45, 63, 74, 75, 121, 123, 143–146, 181, 222, 281, 304, 361, 382
apperception, transcendental 35, 43, 281, 285, 289
architecture 39, 89, 336
argument 4, 5, 9–11, 62, 63, 66, 74–76, 92, 93, 103–116, 142–157, 190, 192, 200, 208, 213, 245–48, 255, 261, 267, 298, 302, 314, 315, 321, 322, 330, 334, 335, 342, 352–61, 368, 399
– private language 2, 10, 28, 51–56, 103–116, 227, 228, 236–41, 379–81
– transcendental 27, 343–45; *see also* transcendental/transcendentalism
arithmetic 26, 27, 31, 34, 36, 77, 216, 253, 317, 319
art 91, 95, 141–156, 241, 326, 330, 335, 336, 370, 379, 380
aspect 53, 55, 56, 123, 137, 138, 205–11, 262, 266, 267, 277, 284, 327, 328, 333, 334, 343, 345, 390, 391, 394, 399
– conceptual *see* individuality/singularity, particularity, universality
– syncategorematic 320, 321
assertability condition 116
assertion 157, 162, 173, 176, 183, 303, 315
assumption 10, 29, 39, 45, 63, 66, 81, 86, 108, 112, 163, 202, 209, 260, 293–98, 304, 334, 373
atomism, logical *see* logical atomism

beauty 141–57, 397
Bedeutung (meaning/reference) 32, 36, 51, 67, 94, 149, 186, 230, 261, 264–71, 286, 288, 292, 325–347, 343, 376, 401–406, 411; *see also* Frege, reference, *Sinn* (sense/meaning)
behavior 27, 30, 35–39, 81, 106, 111, 207, 210, 263, 268, 269, 334, 339, 367, 373
belief 29, 30, 33, 38, 39, 43, 45, 149, 156, 195, 246, 350
bipolarity 215; *see also* negation
bivalence 26; *see also* bipolarity
brain 193

calculus, differential 317–319; *see also* logical analysis
Categorical Imperative (Kant) 199–204, 207–209
category 29, 37, 64, 65, 89–100, 123, 125, 143, 144, 174–77, 243, 244, 249–57,

260, 267–71, 278, 281, 297, 319, 325, 341–46, 372, 381; *see also* categorical *under* judgment, logical form
causality   29, 33–46, 63, 90, 141, 143, 150–57
certainty   74, 107, 192, 207, 227, 238, 241, 250, 344; *see also* On Certainty *under* Wittgenstein's works
– Sense-certainty   5, 51, 52, 56, 229, 230, 263, 264, 369, 383
chess   99
Christianity   8, 56, 265, 303, 387–89; *see also* faith; religion
clarity/clarification   124, 134, 153, 181, 193, 306
– logical   130, 294, 296–303, 308
colour/colourless   28, 76, 99, 109, 132–35, 147, 161, 168–71, 176, 177, 342, 369, 379–81, 385, 390, 391, 396, 398; *see also* colour *under* concept
common sense   86, 120, 186, 357, 361
complex *see* simple/complex *under* object
computer   91, 93
concept *passim*
– aspects of *see* individuality/singularity, particularity, universality
– colour   380; *see also* color
– Concept (Hegel) 17, 95, 146, 147, 191, 222, 228, 229, 240, 267–82, 291, 305–307, 362, 387
– formal/logical   93, 341; *see also* propositional *under* variable
consciousness   4, 8, 16, 35, 39, 42, 77, 78, 82–86, 89, 90, 99, 185, 191–94, 219–40, 278–81, 347, 367–73, 388; *see also* self-consciousness
consistency/inconsistency   150, 201, 296, 308; *see also* contradiction
constant *see* logical constant
constructivism   59–70
contextualism   5
contingency   29, 32, 38, 39, 44, 83, 183–89, 194, 211, 393
contradiction   99, 144, 148, 176, 178, 184, 186, 189–95, 201–204, 213–25, 243–71, 285–88, 294, 304, 338, 340, 358, 360, 362, 372

convention/conventionalism   91, 154, 163–66, 170, 171, 238, 336
copula   53, 54, 169, 283, 355, 385, 392
correctness   44, 79, 80, 84, 85, 103, 105, 109, 112, 116, 210
criterion/criteria   60, 70, 73, 75, 78, 84, 85, 145, 169–71, 200–202, 224, 238, 267, 336
Critique of Pure Reason   143, 182, 278–82, 311, 346; *see also* Kant, Immanuel
culture   42, 86, 155, 161, 195, 289, 327

decision   29, 30, 141, 157, 235, 247
definition   31, 62, 81, 93, 124, 169, 193, 216, 217, 231, 232, 237, 270, 292, 299, 311, 314, 320, 326, 341, 380, 394
– nominal   282
– ostensive   2, 5, 111, 229, 230, 381, 396, 405
– recursive   26
deixis   51, 208, 263–65; *see also* indexical
deontic   239
description   4, 60, 129, 131, 137, 173, 207, 209, 210, 247, 277, 292, 293, 298, 322, 325, 339, 343, 352, 359, 369, 371
– definite   174–77
designation *see* name, naming
desire   10, 35, 43
– in Hegel   113–15, 235–37, 329
determinacy/determinateness (*Bestimtheit*)   76, 113, 120–23, 134, 137, 172, 175, 176, 222, 245, 278, 281, 369, 382–84
– absolute   260, 267–70, 280
– finite   123, 268–70
dialectics   1, 12, 26, 51, 54, 56, 57, 77, 86, 232, 260, 271, 294, 326, 389; *see also* dialectical *under* method
dialogue   2, 237, 238, 325–27, 371
difference *passim*
– absolute   252, 255
– fundamental   12, 259, 341
– identity and   1, 249, 254, 349–63; *see also* identity
– subject-object   232–39
– subject-subject   237, 241
disposition   11, 35, 43, 46, 77, 319, 321
dogmatism   28, 33

doubt   37, 42, 45, 107, 112, 152, 236
dreaming   67
dualism   33, 37, 45, 143, 292, 410

elucidation   10, 124, 130, 289, 295, 301, 305, 351, 371
emergence   3, 17, 42, 60, 103, 111, 124, 134, 139, 227, 241, 379
emotion   35, 43
empiricism   6, 7, 25–33, 41, 57, 154, 234
– logical   28, 30, 306
enactive   35, 37, 41
energeia   119, 124–27
enlightenment   26
entelecheia   119, 124–27
epistemology   5–7, 10, 11, 27, 32, 52, 59–63, 67, 70, 79–83, 108, 141–156, 175, 177, 227, 228, 234, 239, 241, 291–96, 303, 304, 367, 372–75, 379–81, 394, 399; see also certainty, induction, skepticism
equation   31, 245, 275, 283, 285, 287
erotic   114, 1150
essence   33, 76, 78, 145, 147, 185, 190, 232, 259, 280, 295, 307, 315, 333, 334, 361, 381
– Doctrine of   120, 127, 143, 249, 267, 302, 304
– of language   4, 69, 129, 263
– of the proposition   293–304
– of the world/universe/all being   119, 120, 128–33, 137, 185, 293, 295, 301, 304, 305
eternity   34, 41, 42, 126, 150, 191; see also sub specie aeternitatis
ethics   11, 95, 165, 241, 265, 300, 301, 307; see also and ethics under aesthetics, value, morality
existence   34, 60, 76, 82, 94, 95, 109, 121, 126, 130–36, 152, 186, 202, 262, 271, 280–85, 294, 297, 298, 311–19, 331, 338, 342, 355, 372, 374, 388, 389
– syllogism of see existence under syllogism/ inference (Schluß)
existentialism   2, 54, 187, 374, 376
expectation   29, 30

experience (Erfahrung)   44, 52–55, 61, 66, 90, 107, 109, 134, 136, 168, 188, 223, 224, 270, 278, 294, 323, 351, 401, 408
– perceptual/sensory   5, 6, 168, 173
explanation   40, 42, 97, 126, 153, 190, 306, 333, 342, 355, 356, 358, 373; see also elucidation, justification, ostensive under definition
– causal/mechanical   37, 141, 152, 153, 157
– scientific   39
explication   40, 257

fact (Tatsache)   165, 311, 312, 401–404, 409, 410; see also state of affairs
– atomic (Sachverhalt) 132, 135–37, 165, 166, 311, 312, 320–23, 332, 342, 403, 410–12
– empirical   13, 14, 30, 138, 303
– simple   94, 326
faith   38, 46, 187, 358
fallibilism   236–39
falsehood   137, 215, 217, 224
family resemblance   57, 68, 155, 192, 227
feeling see emotion
finitude   10, 40, 44–46, 83, 252–55, 259, 262–70
fly-bottle   69, 97
football   69
for itself (für sich)   53, 55, 77, 189, 202, 236, 316, 323, 344, 369
form of life   17, 33, 57, 69, 89, 91, 94, 97, 100, 104–106, 110, 181–96, 199, 200, 210, 227, 229, 277, 288, 289, 323, 324
form of representation (Form der Darstellung)   67, 283–85, 333, 334, 410
formalism   26, 32, 40, 201, 245
freedom   35, 43, 55, 73, 96, 97, 100, 146, 148, 191, 280, 307, 369
function   28, 38, 77, 81, 167–69, 224, 225, 313, 319, 372
– truth- see function under truth

game see calculus; language-game
general propositional form (allgemeine Sattform)   4, 244, 292–99, 339, 343
generality see universality
geometry   27, 31–38, 63, 98, 100, 132, 250, 397

Gnosticism 265
God 8, 38–46, 52, 142, 177, 231, 265, 299–302, 307, 315, 371, 372, 388; see also religion
grammar 78, 89–101, 129, 163, 217, 277, 288, 331, 344, 381
ground 12, 13, 25–28, 43, 45, 120–23, 143, 257, 267, 316, 317, 327; see also cause
– common 12, 13, 73, 82, 194
heaven 223, 388
Hegel's works
– Elements of the Philosophy of Right 199
– Lectures on Aesthetics 144, 146
– Lectures on the Philosophy of History 126, 386, 388
– The Difference Between Fichte's and Schelling's System of Philosophy 64–66
– The Encyclopedia of the Philosophical Sciences 124, 137, 138, 196
– The Phenomenology of Spirit 12, 64, 74, 103, 113, 192, 194, 213–225, 228–30, 232, 238, 263–80, 278, 329, 331, 361, 367–72
– The Science of Logic 3, 51, 56, 75, 142–46, 161–66, 181, 191, 192, 206, 213, 214, 220–25, 229, 232, 243, 245, 249–52, 266–71, 275–89, 298, 302, 305, 311, 315, 325, 343, 351–57, 379–99
hermeneutics 26, 57, 370
holism 27, 28, 38, 40, 74, 89, 127, 228, 230, 244, 321, 360–62; see also contextualism
human being 32, 34, 53, 119, 168, 193, 262, 374
humor 354
hypothesis 51–57, 318, 345

I/ego/self 36, 55, 65, 99, 100, 106, 113–16, 174, 240, 299–301, 324, 369–76; see also self-consciousness
idea see also mental image/picture, mental phenomenon, representation
– absolute 95, 191, 229, 232, 244, 279, 279, 294
– fundamental 294
idealism
– absolute 6, 9, 65, 227, 353

– British 2, 61
– German 19, 60, 77, 227, 334, 339
– linguistic 401–12
– objective 65
– subjective 185
– transcendental (Kant) 6, 163, 228
identity 1, 12–19, 123, 131, 194, 205, 221, 227, 240, 243–55, 280, 320, 349–63, 381, 392; see also difference
– and non-identity 360, 362
illusion 52, 60, 61, 89, 96, 321, 331, 335
imagery, ontological 78
imagination 145, 147
immediacy 121, 122, 153, 154, 223, 230, 244, 247, 267, 268, 304, 396
in itself (an sich) 57, 76, 82, 113, 121–28, 143, 182, 185, 191, 202, 207–209, 236, 240, 257, 269, 279, 286, 304, 305, 323, 333, 339, 342, 343, 396, 405, 410, 412; see also thing in itself
indeterminacy 194, 231, 233, 271, 398
indexical 263, 368, 369; see also deixis
individuality/singularity (Einzelheit) 51, 56, 98, 164, 169, 174, 177, 209, 267, 269, 280, 306, 363, 379–95
induction 29, 233, 397
– syllogism of see induction under syllogism/inference (Schluß)
ineffable 296, 298, 305, 313
inference see syllogism/inference (Schluß)
inferentialism 5–9, 167, 168, 394
infinity/infinite 34, 36, 57, 81, 97, 123, 126, 150, 190–94, 203–209, 231–33, 239, 246, 247, 253, 259–71, 316–22
– infinite judgment see under judgment
instruction 204, 205
intentionality/intention 35, 39, 41, 78–80, 98, 104, 109–11, 148, 175, 236, 294
interlocutor 74, 85, 283; see also voice
intuition 34–36, 77, 83, 107, 108, 145, 150, 151, 169, 178, 281, 282, 294, 343
– intellectual 185
– world- 123
isomorphism 78, 230, 285, 334, 372, 373
jigsaw puzzle 95
joke 73, 354

judgement (*Urteil*)
- aesthetic   155, 156, 173
- apodictic   393
- assertoric   392
- categorical   391, 392, 398
- disjunctive   392, 398
- hypothetical   392, 398
- infinite   172, 173, 390
- negative   170–72, 390
- of necessity   168, 173, 174, 253, 391
- of reflection   168, 170, 172, 390, 391, 396
- particular   163, 391
- positive   105, 168–70, 390, 394
- problematic   393
- singular   164, 168, 391
- universal   31, 163, 173, 391, 392, 397

justification   6, 163, 208, 222, 223, 281; see also explanation

kinematics   36, 39

ladder   10, 54, 222, 225, 288, 297, 304–306, 327, 337
language *passim*
- critique of   4
- essence of   4, 129, 263
- natural/ordinary   3, 26, 27, 54, 68, 75, 86, 162, 181, 209, 326, 344, 371; see also ordinary language philosophy
- private *see* private language *under* argument
- sign-   292
language-game   5, 7, 29, 57, 69, 91, 97, 100, 112, 227–29, 241, 260, 262, 271, 277, 288, 352, 356–62, 381, 401–11
law   45, 55, 56, 145, 148, 201, 203, 211, 278, 322
- natural/empirical   29, 92, 136, 137, 233
- of logic   183, 245, 252–55
learning *see* teaching
length   78, 81–84, 176, 256, 380, 385, 388, 396; see also sample
limit/limitation
- limited whole   150, 188, 192, 297; see also *sub specie aeternitatis*
- of knowledge/possible experience   10, 44, 189, 311

- of language   10, 219, 224, 259–72, 293, 311
- of the world   184–88, 196, 299
- of thought/sense   4, 181–83, 188, 191, 195, 196, 302, 306; see also nonsense
linguistics   32
lion   31, 390
logical analysis   25–27, 32, 94, 306
logical atomism   28, 313, 318, 321, 352, 356
logical constant   291–308, 311–13
logical form   26, 51, 161, 168, 172, 176, 185, 246, 248, 256, 257, 315, 324, 327, 329, 337–46
- of facts/propositions   28, 67, 283, 286, 323
- of language/reality/the world   129–37, 183, 259–71
- of the concept *see* individuality/singularity, particularity, universality
logical grammar *see* grammar
logical inference *see* inference
logical necessity *see* logical *under* necessity
logical positivism   25, 28, 340
logical relation *see* logical *under* relation
logical space   97, 100, 133–37, 165, 172, 176, 190
logical syntax   248
logic
- formal   27, 69, 249, 287, 316, 338, 353, 355, 372
- mathematical   27, 165
- objective   75, 252, 280, 302–306
- philosophical   32, 356
- subjective   166, 168, 252, 276, 380–99
- Tractarian   301, 306, 308
- transcendental   289, 301, 326, 340
logos   92, 338, 344, 346

magnetism   109, 110
materialism   25–41
mathematics   31 32, 46, 163, 231, 237, 275, 278, 287, 301, 317–19, 351, 353; see also arithmetic, geometry, set theory
- mathematical syllogism *see* mathematical *under* syllogism/inference (*Schluß*)

meaning *see* Augustinian picture of language, *Bedeutung* (meaning/reference), *Sinn* (sense/meaning)
– as use
meaningless 97, 260, 261, 331; *see also* nonsense, senseless
measure/measuring 33, 36, 73–86, 104, 131, 148, 229, 231, 237–40, 303, 317, 368, 380; *see also* yardstick
mechanism 33, 41, 45, 46, 332
– social 200
mediation (*Vermittlung*) 7, 54, 56, 74, 94, 98, 121, 188, 203, 205, 209, 223, 269, 304, 370, 383, 384, 398
memory 107, 110
mental phenomenon (activity/event/fact/ process/state) 11, 6, 39–42, 93, 193
metaphor 25, 27, 29, 34–46, 77–80, 109, 136, 175, 196, 225, 228, 237, 248, 250, 369, 374; *see also* ladder
metaphysics 9, 25, 28, 29, 37, 43–46, 57, 61, 62, 89–101, 120, 125, 126, 132, 141–44, 161–65, 173, 182, 186, 188, 295–97, 303, 308, 315, 350, 370, 372
method *passim*
– dialectical 359, 362
– projection 275–89; *see also* pictorial/picturing *under* relation
– philosophical 3, 4, 289
– scientific 32, 268, 278
– speculative 275, 276
– zero- 275, 277, 282, 285–89
modality 345, 346
model 26, 38, 40, 51, 57, 81, 94, 153, 169, 181, 208, 232–38, 284, 285, 292, 293, 380, 387; *see also* paradigm
– mathematical 28–32
moment *see* individuality/singularity, particularity, universality
monad 37–43, 177, 317, 323
monism 9, 127, 293, 360, 361
morality/ethical life (*Sittlichkeit*) 11, 55, 199, 200, 211
motive *see* cause vs. reason/motive/ground *under* causation/cause

mystical/mysticism 52, 130, 137, 138, 149, 150, 186, 189, 261, 262, 297–307, 338, 371
mythology/mythos 42, 371

name 41, 42, 65, 73, 162, 166, 169, 177, 312, 321, 323, 329, 343, 372
– proper 175, 335, 386
naturalism 2, 25, 28, 33, 34, 41–43, 94, 235
necessity 9, 35, 83, 100, 145–48, 156, 202, 205, 240, 241, 304, 331, 337, 397; *see also* necessary *under* proposition
– judgment of *see* necessity *under* judgment
– logical 135, 314, 315
– syllogism of *see* necessity *under* syllogism/ inference (*Schluß*)
negation/negativity 56, 96, 239, 260–71, 280, 316, 393; *see also* bipolarity, negative *under* judgment
– absolute 245, 255, 270, 271
– determinate 7, 100
– joint 296, 301, 302, 305
– of the negation 260, 339, 384–89
– self- 225, 261, 297
Neoplatonism 8, 9, 278, 302
nominalism 6, 95, 164, 382
nonsense 2, 10, 12, 150, 172, 182–93, 216, 217, 225, 245, 250, 254, 293, 297, 300, 304, 314, 330, 331, 340, 351, 362, 373; *see also* meaningless, resolute reading
normativity 5, 7, 41, 79, 80, 83, 103, 105, 107, 116, 145, 156, 173
notation 26–30, 93, 254, 256, 298, 336
notion (*Begriff*) *see* concept
number/numeral 28, 36, 170, 204–208, 216, 231, 240, 249–52, 256, 286, 312, 314, 319, 322, 345, 346, 380, 390, 392
– infinite 246, 247

object (*Gegenstand*)
– logical 261, 267–71, 294
– material 33, 37, 379, 380, 384, 389
– simple/complex 4, 17, 97, 134–36, 311–24
ontic 37, 45, 239

Subject Index — **437**

ontology   31, 89–101, 291, 303, 317, 320–23, 332, 372–76
operation   93, 98, 231, 289, 315, 321, 402
– logical   297, 304–306
– N-operation   296–306, 345
ordinary language philosophy   2, 260
other minds   367–76

paradigm   25, 30–37, 55, 56, 84, 109, 110, 167, 205, 370, 372, 379–99, 404, 409–11
– image paradigm   325, 333–46
– paradigmatic sample   379–99
paradox   11, 150, 151, 156, 186, 190, 192, 205, 224, 230, 261, 318, 329, 338–44, 362, 384, 389, 404, 407, 409
– Russell's   314
– sceptical   11, 230, 233–35
particularity (*Besonderheit*)   51, 174, 177, 209, 269, 306, 346, 363, 379–99
perspicuous representation (*übersichtliche Darstellung*)   275, 277
phenomenology   25–27, 41, 361, 371, 376; *see also Phenomenology of Spirit under* Hegel's works
philosophy
– analytic   1–5, 25–46, 60–62, 70, 98, 162, 178
– continental   1, 2, 25, 57, 213
– critical   25, 28, 60, 64–66, 315, 342
– of identity   360
– of language   7, 259, 368, 370
– of nature   89–91, 294
– of religion   371
– political   375; *see also* politics
– systematic   370
– transcendental   4, 37, 52, 323
physicalism   27, 28, 32–39
physics   32, 33, 39, 41, 90, 92, 120, 125, 129, 137, 190, 215, 316, 317, 323, 358
pictorial form (*Form der Abbildung*)   79
picture *see also* picture theory, pictorial/picturing *under* relation
– world-   26, 28, 38, 45, 46
– living   312, 323,
– logical   67, 131, 283

picture theory   56, 78, 79, 275, 276, 282, 283, 289, 292, 293
Platonism   9, 32, 60, 109, 174, 406–409; *see also* Plato
pleasure   41, 168, 195, 291
pluralism   360, 361, 408
poetry   42, 94, 330, 359, 376
politics   55, 91, 95, 101, 316; *see also* political *under* philosophy
possibility
– abstract/formal   126
– of representation *see under* representation
– possible world *see* possible *under* world
– real   126, 217
practice   43, 44, 46, 56, 57, 66, 69, 78–84, 91, 97–100, 105–10, 194, 200, 207–11, 233–38, 351
– epistemic   379, 381, 399
– philosophical   97, 358, 362
pragmatics   54
pragmatism   51, 52, 62
predicate/predication   30–35, 43, 51–53, 154–56, 163–77, 219, 267, 313, 322, 345, 355, 356, 367, 383, 385, 390–98
– particular   390
– universal   52, 53, 173, 391, 392
prejudice   111, 317, 372
presupposition   12, 27, 36, 42, 74, 110, 113, 143, 151, 222–24, 230, 244, 271, 291, 298, 311, 314, 317, 381, 385, 393
principle   26, 32, 37, 39, 40, 45, 52, 64, 65, 76, 96, 112, 123–27, 143, 146, 192, 202–10, 228, 281, 292, 304, 315–24, 371, 382, 384; *see also* axiom, law
– analytic   311–20
– Leibniz's   30, 31
– Lucretius's   34
– synthetic   312
– verification/verifiability   108
privacy   56, 234, 237
private language argument *see* private language *under* argument
probability   29
projection *see* projection *under* method
pronoun, personal   367, 368, 396, 371, 375
proof   45, 142, 148, 270, 315, 380, 399

property, internal/external *see* internal/external *under* relation
proposition/sentence (*Satz*) *passim*
- complex/molecular 322, 329, 339–45, 359, 362,
- elementary/atomic 26, 51, 174, 214, 225, 246–49, 253, 256, 261, 283, 289, 306, 312, 329, 339–42; *see also* logical atomism
- logical 214, 220, 224, 285–88, 314, 338
- mathematical 287
- ordinary/everyday 215–20, 224, 293, 297
- philosophical 293, 301, 307
- pseudo- 254, 288; *see also* nonsense
- speculative 40, 42, 46, 213, 214, 219–25, 367
propositional function *see* propositional *under* function
propositional sign (*Satzzeichen*)
propositional variable *see* propositional *under* variable
pseudo-proposition *see* pseudo *under* proposition
psychoanalysis 327–334; *see also* Freud, Lacan
psychology 86, 152, 153, 326–32, 347; *see also* Remarks on the Philosophy of Psychology *under* Wittgenstein's works
qualia 27, 28, 33, 109, 112
quality 75–81, 94, 144, 155, 172, 229, 233, 239, 240, 245, 294, 336, 341, 351, 367, 390, 395, 396
quantifying 76
quantity 75, 76, 94, 205, 294, 314, 317, 346

rationality/rationalism 7, 52, 54, 120, 123, 233, 315, 408
realism/antirealism 9, 62
- metaphysical 6, 59–62, 67, 69
- vs. idealism 402, 407
reality (*Realität*) 9, 33, 34, 60–70, 78–80, 94, 119–38, 143–47, 176, 185, 188, 191, 206, 215–18, 231, 232, 261, 275, 283–89, 292, 293, 306, 314, 320, 323, 332–44, 351, 369, 370, 372, 385; *see also* actuality (*Wirklichkeit*)
- empirical 125–38

- physical 127, 319
- total 129, 243–47; *see also* world
reason (*Vernunft*) 3–10, 35, 45, 54–56, 61–65, 120–26, 138, 139, 143–49, 154, 167, 173, 178, 227–41, 315, 368; *see also* cause vs. reason/motive/ground *under* causation/cause, Critique of Pure Reason
- pure 61, 185, 187, 194, 294
recognition 37, 40, 45, 46, 55, 84, 99, 100, 103–17, 194, 225, 237; *see also* memory
reductionism/non-reductionism 11, 57, 94, 330, 337
reference 32, 36, 51, 67, 69, 73, 94, 109, 208, 255, 257, 261–71, 325–47, 380, 384; *see also* Bedeutung
- immediate/direct 263–68, 271, 338
- self- 76, 268, 269, 275
reflexivity 77, 83, 116, 240, 375, 388; *see also* self *under* reference
relation
- internal/external 76, 78, 90, 98, 199, 201, 244, 261, 277, 280, 306, 315, 369
- interpersonal 372–74
- logical 134, 144, 189, 305, 315, 345
- pictorial/picturing 79, 283
- representing 283–85
religion 40, 42, 52, 55, 56, 265, 326, 371, 387; *see also* God,
representation (*Vorstellung*) 30, 31, 36, 44, 60–69, 80, 132, 145, 148, 167, 183, 185, 192, 256, 261, 264, 270, 277–85, 299, 312–24, 341, 375; *see also* projection *under* method
- form of 67, 250, 283–85, 333, 334
- theory of 372
- possibility of 277, 282
- perspicuous *see* perspicuous representation
resolute reading of the *Tractatus* 10, 11, 163, 186, 187, 275; *see also* nonsense
rule *see also* grammar; logical syntax
- abstract 202, 206, 210
- general 199–211
- formation 246

- -following   11, 80, 81, 104, 110–16, 156, 193, 199–211, 227–41, 380, 381, 384
ruler *see* measure/measuring, yardstick

sage   379, 387
sample *see* paradigmatic sample *under* paradigm
saying/showing   67, 90, 128–32, 136, 182–87, 195, 287, 289, 298
scaffolding of the world   337, 342, 344
science   25–33, 39, 42, 46, 52–56, 77, 90–94, 120, 145–49, 152, 165, 203, 222, 223, 240, 270, 278, 294, 322, 332, 350; *see also* scientism
– natural   28, 33, 46, 129, 130, 137–39, 149–51, 186, 293, 294, 298; *see also* naturalism
– *Science of Knowledge see Science of Knowledge* (Fichte)
– *Science of Logic see under* Hegel's works
Science of Knowledge   12; *see also* Fichte, Johann Gottlieb
scientism   28–33, 38, 142, 149, 156
self-consciousness   6, 35, 54, 55, 103, 104, 113, 114, 191–95, 222, 228, 232, 235, 280, 281, 329, 369, 374, 376, 388
self-reference *see* self *under* reference
self-reflexivity *see* reflexivity
semantics   32, 79, 106, 162, 167, 368, 394
semiotic   80, 333, 335
sensation   27, 29, 35, 39, 43, 44, 104–108, 111, 112, 145, 147, 238, 380; *see also* private *under* object, private language *under* argument
sense *see Sinn* (sense/meaning)
sense/meaning distinction *see Sinn* (sense/meaning), *Bedeutung* (meaning/reference)
sense-data   33, 80, 108, 109, 175
senseless (*sinnlos*) 182, 215–18, 225; *see also* meaningless, nonsense
sentence *see* proposition, propositional sign
series   65, 81, 106, 143, 147, 166, 168, 172, 186, 204, 262, 345, 370, 379, 385, 387
set theory   27, 31, 32

sign   104–12, 149, 150, 185, 217, 221, 222, 245, 249, 254, 284–88, 305, 315, 335, 344–46, 355
– -language *see* sign *under* language
– propositional/sentence (*Satzzeichen*) *see* propositional sign
simile   27, 81, 83
simple *see* simple/complex *under* object
singularity (*Einzelheit*) *see* individuality
Sinn (sense/meaning)   51–54, 80, 146, 149, 167, 182–94, 215–24, 250, 253, 266, 271, 275, 282–89, 291, 293, 312, 339, 343, 389, 406; *see also Bedeutung* (meaning/reference), Frege
situation (*Sachlage*)   78–80, 135, 250, 283, 384, 321; *see also* state of affairs (*Sachverhalt*)
skepticism   10, 11, 59–70, 86, 151, 155, 228, 230, 233, 234, 239, 240
solipsism   60, 184, 185, 234; *see also* I/ego/self
sortal   27, 30–32, 40, 43, 172
soul   35, 43, 142, 184, 185, 194, 324, 330–32; *see also* I/self, solipsism
space   5, 28, 34, 36, 97, 132, 147, 203, 204, 250, 316; *see also* logical space
– and time   28, 29, 36–44, 95, 236, 288, 299, 319, 321, 385
speech act   326, 332
spirit (*Geist*)   35, 55, 64, 74, 90–100, 119–26, 137, 138, 144–47, 194–96, 219, 222, 223, 234, 241, 278, 288, 289, 369–71, 390, 403, 410
– absolute   8, 146, 195, 228, 335
– subjective   332, 335
– Holy   388
standard of correctness   105
state of affairs (*Sachverhalt*)   26, 28, 30, 34, 79, 80, 133, 135, 150, 154, 157, 165, 166, 182–85, 246–48, 261–68, 283–87, 291, 292, 299, 304, 311, 312, 320–22, 342, 410–12; *see also* fact, situation (*Sachlage*)
stoicism   387
structuralism   2
style   2, 161, 162, 195, 247, 367, 371
sub specie aeternitatis   38, 42, 150–52, 298

subjectivity   37, 53, 55, 56, 95, 104, 146, 174, 181, 185, 191, 196, 234, 238, 307, 329, 330, 334, 346, 379, 393, 399
subject
- and object   64, 65, 144, 231, 239, 360
- and predicate   154–56, 164–69, 219, 245, 367
- individual   55, 329, 390–93
- metaphysical   184, 300, 301
- subject term   168–73, 382
- thinking   33, 45, 183–88, 275
sublation (*Aufhebung*)   126, 127, 143, 148, 188, 237, 239, 257, 260–71, 281, 282, 289, 398
superstition   29, 40, 100
syllogism/inference (*Schluß*)   5–7, 30, 42, 44, 95, 114, 143, 144, 163, 167–73, 190, 233, 244, 253, 305, 379, 391–99
- Aristotelian   164, 169, 369
- categorical   398
- conceptual   30, 42, 44, 46
- disjunctive   398, 399
- mathematical   166, 177, 396
- of allness   397
- of analogy   397
- of existence   395
- of induction   397
- of necessity   398
- of reflection   396
symbol/symbolism   67, 80, 111, 216, 217, 246, 250, 254, 256, 262, 277, 286, 287, 333–36, 355, 356, 362
symptom   325–30, 341
syncategorematic   313, 323, 324; *see also* syncategorematic *under* aspect
synonym *see* ambiguity/synonymy
syntax *see* logical syntax

tautology   43, 176, 249–55, 285–88, 314, 315, 372; *see also* logic
- and contradiction   213–18, 224, 225, 287, 372
teaching/learning   30, 91, 155, 156, 227–41, 350, 353, 354, 358, 360
teleology/teleological   9, 106
theology   8, 29, 38, 45, 56, 265, 315, 361

theory
- picture *see* picture theory
- of meaning   56, 275, 292, 368, 371, 372, 376
- of reference   94, 328, 329, 333, 338
- of representation   372
- semantic/linguistic   161–63, 247
therapy   2, 96, 97, 148, 192, 294; *see also* resolute reading, psychoanalysis
thing in itself   44, 63, 122, 125, 282, 293
thought (*Gedanke*)   67, 120, 312, 323, 403–408
time   28–44, 52, 104–107, 110, 150, 167, 194, 200, 350
- space and *see* and time *under* space
totality   101, 130, 148, 150, 151, 209, 219, 238, 241, 244, 382, 392, 396, 397
- disjunctive   392
- objective/subjective   123
- of propositions   129, 131, 225, 228, 229, 261
- of the world/reality/facts   133, 245, 261, 262, 270, 292, 361
training (*Abrichten*)   207–210
transcendent   31, 42–45, 259, 302, 307
transcendental/transcendentalism   4, 6, 27, 37, 41, 42, 51–54, 143, 228, 232, 234, 241, 265, 275–77, 281–89, 294, 300–306, 323, 326, 329, 340–43; *see also* transcendental *under* argument, transcendental *under* idealism
triangle   203, 292, 295, 304
truth *passim*; *see also* falsehood
- -condition   28, 214–18, 249
- -function   10, 165, 322; *see also* analytic/synthetic, logical *under* inference
- -value   26, 217, 218

unconscious   327
understanding (*Verstand*)   3, 27, 46, 61, 65, 138, 143–47, 172, 192, 262, 280, 281, 295, 298, 368, 369, 407
unity   52, 55, 90, 98, 123, 124, 143, 146, 181, 194, 196, 206, 209, 210, 219, 241, 246–57, 268, 280, 293, 317, 362, 369, 380, 393, 395, 399
- of apperception/consciousness   191, 281

- of identity and difference   249
- of subject and object   65, 144
- of the concept   113, 142
- of thought and being   65

universality (*Allgemeinheit*)   51, 169, 174, 178, 211, 264–71, 306, 346, 363, 371, 379–99
- abstract   172, 381, 384, 385, 396
- concrete   385, 388, 397

universe   40, 42, 119, 120, 123, 185, 240, 369

unspeakable   4, 259–71, 296–301, 307

vagueness   32, 229, 306
value   28, 82, 100, 207, 276, 296, 299, 307, 319, 349, 375; *see also* ethics
- truth- *see* value *under* truth
variable   82, 162, 345
- propositional   256, 296, 341
verification/verificationism   83, 107, 108
Vienna Circle   61, 175
virtue   387
visual field   135, 176
voice   373; *see also* interlocutor

will/willing   183, 186, 190, 275; *see also* intentionality, Schopenhauer

Wittgenstein's works
- *Big Typescript*   219
- *Blue and Brown Books*   4
- *Culture and Value*   152
- *Nachlass*, Wittgenstein's   82
- *On Certainty*   112, 155
- *Philosophical Investigations*   2–5, 62, 68, 74, 103, 104, 108, 110, 111, 151–56, 162, 181, 192, 193, 199, 204, 228–31, 237, 238, 260–66, 276, 283, 288, 321, 323, 360, 371, 372 and *passim*
- *Philosophical Remarks*   129
- *Remarks on the Philosophy of Psychology*   373
- *Tractatus Logico-Philosophicus passim*
- *Zettel*   368, 372, 373

world
- actual/existing   27, 119–28, 135–38, 174, 186, 189, 263
- empirical   120, 128, 134–37, 293
- external   33, 36, 37, 41, 45, 60, 234
- -history   55, 56, 90
- language and   261, 287
- my/microcosm   29, 43, 44, 195, 262; *see also* I/ego/self, solipsism
- objective   43, 146, 181, 184, 195, 238
- -picture (*Weltbild*)   26, 28, 38, 45, 46
- possible   32, 35, 38, 41, 133, 185, 247
- sub specie   150, 297, 298 *see also* sub specie aeternitatis
- -view   33

yardstick (*Maßstab*)   76, 78–84, 148, 380, 401–403; *see also* measure/measuring, paradigm

Author Index

Adorno, Theodor W.   2, 16, 227, 240–41
Anscombe, Elizabeth   165, 169–171, 174–75
Apel, Karl-Otto   54
Aquinas, Thomas   372
Aristotle   31–32, 45, 92, 94–95, 119, 124–25, 163, 166, 174, 196, 297, 316–320, 372, 376
Augustine, of Hippo   68–69, 74, 86, 231
Austin, John L.   26, 326

Badiou, Alain   384
Beiser, Frederick C.   9
Bergson, Henri   318
Berkeley, George   27, 60–61
Bolzano, Bernard   25
Bouwsma, Oets Kolk   89–90
Bowie, Andrew   228, 241
Bradley, Francis Herbert   175, 351–52, 360–61
Brandom, Robert   6–7, 9, 11, 14, 103–105, 113–117, 167–68, 228, 236–37, 239, 241, 325, 394
Broad, Charlie Dunbar   54, 350, 356–359, 362
Brouwer, Luitzen Egbertus Jan   111

Caesar, Gaius Julius   379, 386–389, 394
Candlish, Stewart   111–12, 351
Caravaggio, Michelangelo Merisi da   99
Carnap, Rudolf   25–27, 33
Cassirer, Ernst   26
Chalmers, David   43
Cohen, Rudolf   26
Conant, James   296
Copernicus, Nicolaus   33

Davidson, Donald   2, 98
Dennett, Daniel   107
Descartes, René   13, 27–28, 36–39, 42, 45, 60–61, 63, 92
Diamond, Cora   89–90, 96, 297
Drury, Maurice O'Connor   213, 227, 349, 357, 362

Duchamp, Marcel   330
Dummett, Michael   61

Ebbs, Gary   204, 210

Feuerbach, Ludwig   371
Fichte, Johann Gottlieb   12, 60–61, 64–65, 123, 142–43, 370, 407
Ficker, Ludwig von   302
Findlay, John Niemeyer   3–4, 9, 11, 18, 162, 176–178, 367–372, 376
Floyd, Juliet   217
Frege, Gottlob   25–27, 31–32, 51, 61, 161, 163–64, 167, 171–72, 174, 253, 289, 327, 330, 333, 353

Gellner, Ernest   62
Glock, Hans-Johann   210
God   8, 29, 38–46, 52, 177, 231, 265, 299–302, 307, 315, 367, 371–72, 388
Goethe, Johann Wolfgang von   383
Goldfarb, Warren   105

Habermas, Jürgen   54–55, 116
Heidegger, Martin   2, 25–27, 33, 35, 39, 46, 52, 57, 110, 237
Hempel, Carl Gustav   26
Heraclitus   32, 46
Herder, Johann Gottfried   42, 162, 370
Hobbes, Thomas   25–28, 35, 37, 42, 63, 315–16
Hölderlin, Friedrich   54
Honneth, Axel   55
Horstmann, Rolf-Peter   9
Hotho, Heinrich Gustav   142
Houlgate, Stephen   9, 75, 294
Humboldt, Wilhelm von   370–71
Hume, David   25, 27, 29, 42, 57, 233–235, 372
Husserl, Edmund   26–27, 33, 368
Hylton, Peter   351

James, Henry   370

Jesus, *see also* God   379, 387–389, 394
Johnson, William Ernest   171–72

Kambartel, Friedrich   28
Kant, Immanuel   4, 6–7, 9, 15, 17, 25, 27, 35–36, 42, 44–45, 54, 56–57, 60–66, 68, 70, 90, 93, 113, 121, 141–143, 157, 173, 178, 181–82, 188, 193–94, 199, 201, 227–229, 232–235, 277–78, 280–283, 285, 287, 301, 311, 313–315, 317–18, 321, 323, 326, 333, 339–347, 370, 372, 407, 409, 411
Kenny, Anthony   312, 321
Kepler, Johannes   33
Kierkegaard, Søren   54
Köhler, Dietmar   51
Koreň, Ladislav   7
Kripke, Saul   10–11, 156, 206, 230–31, 233–235
Kusch, Martin   106

La Mettrie, Julien Offray de   39
Lacan, Jacques   328, 332
Lamb, David   4, 11, 213–14, 222, 230
Lear   360
Leibniz, Gottfired   30–31, 34, 36–37, 39–40, 42, 45, 57, 92, 164–166, 174, 177
Lenzen, Wolfgang   164
Levinson, Jerrold   141
Lewis, David   29, 38
Liebmann, Otto   61
Locke, John   25, 27, 35, 42, 63, 372
Lucretius   34
Lyotard, Jean-François   100

Mackie, John   42
Macran, Henry Stuart   353–54
Magee, Bryan   282
Mallarmé, Stéphane   330
Marx, Karl   60, 328, 332
McDowell, John   6–7, 9, 11, 28
McGuinness, Brian   330, 344
McNally, Thomas   107
McTaggart, John Ellis   350–353, 356–57, 359
Mead, George Herbert   116
Mill, John Stuart   26
Monk, Ray   350–51

Moore, George Edward   1–2, 25, 60, 141, 154, 157, 182, 352–53, 357, 360–61
Mothersill, Mary   141

Natorp, Paul   26
Neurath, Otto   27
Newton, Isaac   33, 92, 317
Nietzsche, Friedrich   98
Nordmann, Alfred   217
Nuzzo, Angelica   2, 5

Ogden, Charles Kay   215, 261, 297–98, 330, 356
Ostrow, Matthew   218

Parmenides   32, 59, 62, 65, 67, 70
Pears, David   110, 286–87, 330, 344
Peirce, Charles Sanders   54, 173, 239, 335, 372, 374–75
Pinkard, Terry   8–9, 11, 15, 181
Pinsent, David   354
Pippin, Robert   9
Plato   29, 32, 63, 95, 124–25, 174, 177, 324, 368, 372
Plotinus   368, 372
Ploucquet, Gottfried   164, 166, 174, 177, 382
Poincaré, Henri   318
Poser, Hans   322
Proops, Ian   78

Quante, Michael   294
Quine, Willard Van Orman   2, 27, 35, 42, 62, 94, 405

Read, Rupert   173
Redding, Paul   4–5, 7–9, 11, 15, 161, 165, 168
Reichenbach, Hans   26
Reinhold, Leonard   64–65
Rescher, Nicolas   60
Ricœur, Paul   98
Rockmore, Tom   5–7, 9, 11, 13, 59
Rorty, Richard   5, 62
Rosen, Stanley   222–23
Russell, Bertrand   1–2, 25, 28, 32, 54, 62, 67–68, 89, 108, 161, 163–64, 171–72,

174–75, 229–30, 253, 289, 318–19, 327, 330, 334, 350–356, 359–362
Ryle, Gilbert   26, 323

Schelling, Friedrich Wilhelm Joseph   54, 60, 64–65, 123, 185, 370
Schiller, Friedrich   141, 145
Schlick, Moritz   26
Schopenhauer, Arthur   227
Searle, John   282
Sheffer, Henry M.   346
Siep, Ludwig   9, 55
Skinner, Francis   35
Sluga, Hans   61
Spinoza, Baruch   34, 39, 44, 64
Stekeler-Weithofer, Pirmin   2, 6, 9, 13, 25, 123, 232, 237, 241, 306, 325, 381
Stroud, Barry   110

Taylor, Charles   8, 52, 56, 162–63

Vico, Giambattista   63

Watson, Richard   352
Weiss, Paul   18, 53, 367–68, 372–376
Westphal, Kenneth   9
Whitehead, Alfred North   89, 327, 330, 352, 356, 372
Wiese, Leopold von   368
Williams, Meredith   105
Winfield, Richard Dien   383
Wright, Georg Henrik von   217
Wrisley, George   112

Žižek, Slavoj   9, 382, 384, 387

www.ingramcontent.com/pod-product-compliance
Lightning Source LLC
Chambersburg PA
CBHW031701230426
43668CB00006B/72